JEWISH MARTYRS IN THE PAGAN AND CHRISTIAN WORLDS

This book presents a linear history of Jewish martyrdom, from the Hellenistic period to the high Middle Ages. Following the chronology of sources, the study challenges the general consensus that martyrdom was an original Hellenistic Jewish
idea. Instead, Jews such as Philo and Josephus internalized the idealized Roman
concept of voluntary death and presented it as an old Jewish practice. The centrality of self-sacrifice in Christianity further stimulated the development of rabbinic martyrology and the Talmudic guidelines for passive martyrdom. However,
when forced to choose between death and conversion in medieval Christendom,
European Jews went beyond these guidelines, sacrificing themselves and loved
ones. Through death they attempted not only to prove their religiosity but also to
disprove the religious legitimacy of their Christian persecutors. Although martyrs
and martyrologies intended to show how Judaisim differed from Christianity, they,
in fact, reveal a common mind-set. Although the medieval martyrological option
was played down during the Holocaust, medieval martyrologies still feature in
Ashkenazic prayers of today.

Shmuel Shepkaru is Assistant Professor of Jewish Studies and history at The
University of Oklahoma.

Jewish Martyrs in the Pagan and Christian Worlds

SHMUEL SHEPKARU

The University of Oklahoma

CAMBRIDGE
UNIVERSITY PRESS

CAMBRIDGE UNIVERSITY PRESS
Cambridge, New York, Melbourne, Madrid, Cape Town, Singapore, São Paulo

Cambridge University Press
40 West 20th Street, New York, NY 10011-4211, USA

www.cambridge.org
Information on this title: www.cambridge.org/9780521842815

© Shmuel Shepkaru 2006

First published 2006

Printed in the United States of America

A catalog record for this publication is available from the British Library.

Library of Congress Cataloging in Publication Data

Shepkaru, Shmuel.
Jewish martyrs in the pagan and Christian worlds / Shmuel Shepkaru.
p.   cm.
Includes bibliographical references and index.
ISBN 0-521-84281-6 (hardback)
1. Martyrdom – Judaism – History – To 1500. I. Title.
BM157.S43   2005
296.3'3 – dc22   2005010535

ISBN-13   978-0-521-84281-5 hardback
ISBN-10   0-521-84281-6 hardback

*F*or Shizuka and Leon

"The tyrant dies and his rule is over, the martyr dies and his rule begins."
Sören Kierkegaard

Contents

Preface

This book is the product of many years of labor. A stimulating graduate seminar on medieval European Jewry with Professor Robert Chazan at New York University animated my interest in the, then, insufficiently explored and, still, hotly debated topic of Jewish martyrdom. My seminar paper on the phenomenon of medieval martyrdom evolved and grew into a master's thesis and doctoral dissertation on the history of Jewish martyrdom. Additional teaching, research, publishing of articles, valuable correspondence, and public and academic presentations, further prepared me for the writing of this book.

Until recently, a comprehensive study on this subject was still missing. I hope this book will contribute toward answering that scholarly lacuna, although I have no illusion that such a vast topic can be confined to a single book. Several significant studies focusing mainly on Jewish martyrdom in the Middle Ages appeared after I had finished my dissertation. I was happy to discover that some of these studies were in agreement with several of my early findings. Regrettably, I could not take advantage of Professor Jeremy Cohen's valuable study, *Sanctifying the Name of God: Jewish Martyrs and Jewish Memories of the First Crusade,* because it came out while this book was already in production.

Abundant thanks are in order to known and unknown people. I owe a great deal of gratitude to my adviser, Professor Robert Chazan, who provided perpetual support and guidance. More than just inspiring this study, he himself has become an inspirational model for me. What I have gained personally and professionally from my experience with him goes far beyond the scope of this book. Thanks also are due to another teacher, Professor Lawrence Schiffman, for all I have learned from him while in graduate school. I am deeply grateful to Professor Ivan Marcus of Yale University for his advice and support. After offering to read my dissertation, he made numerous valuable suggestions. He also graciously offered his constructive reactions to my articles. This study benefited enormously from our correspondence. Many thanks to Professor

Joseph Shatzmiller of Duke University for his anonymous (at the time) comments on a different project that proved to be useful in this one as well and for the warm words of encouragement that followed. I am indebted also to the anonymous reviewers of my manuscript for their beneficial comments and critiques. Dr. Beatrice Rehl discussed with me the possibility of submitting this study to Cambridge University Press. Beatrice, Andy Beck, Nicole McClenic, and the rest of the Cambridge editorial team deserve my gratitude for making the production of this book such a pleasant experience.

My research and the resulting publications in recent years were made possible due to the generous support of the Office of the Dean of Arts and Sciences of the University of Oklahoma under Dean Paul Bell. This book could not have appeared in its present length without the support of the University of Oklahoma's College of Arts and Sciences, the Office of the Vice President for Research/Graduate College, the History Department, and the Judaic Studies Program, all of which contributed toward subventing it. Many thanks to the chair of the History Department, Professor Robert Griswold, for doing the "begging" on my behalf. I am especially grateful to the chair of the Judaic Studies Program, Professor Noam Stillman, for first discussing with me the possibility of teaching at the University of Oklahoma, and not least for the true amity that has grown between us. As a true teacher, he has always made himself available to patiently answer numerous questions and provide valuable personal and professional advice.

Words cannot sufficiently express my thanks to and appreciation of my family. My father Leon, of blessed memory, instilled in me the importance of education, the love for history, and Jewish history in particular. My mother Leah has made countless sacrifices for our family. She with my sister Rivka and her family have also made heroic efforts to provide me with the peace of mind that is so necessary in such projects. They have been a source of strength and encouragement. Despite the geographical distance, they all are always so very close.

Aheron, Aheron, Haviv, to my wife Shizuka, I am grateful beyond words for sharing her life with me. Not a single day goes by without me feeling so fortunate to have her as a partner in everything I do. I would not be where I am today without her at my side. As I was submitting this manuscript for publication, came the wonderful news that our son Leon was due to arrive into the world. They both make my life whole, and it is to them that I offer this book.

Introduction

For centuries martyrdom has played a formative role in the Judeo-Christian world. This book investigates how martyrdom came to play this role in Jewish life and how it evolved thereafter. The book attempts to provide a linear history of martyrdom that stretches from the Hellenistic period to the dawn of the modern era, concluding with unavoidable references to the Holocaust. The latter references are preliminary and are intended to be helpful in future investigations.

This study is comparative in nature. It analyzes the conditions that produced Jewish and Christian martyrs in the pagan world and examines both the foreign ideals that the two creeds fed upon, as well as the two groups' own concepts. With an emphasis on Jewish martyrs, I hope to show how those concepts inspired the followers of each faith and how they also influenced each other. Finally, I will explore how and why the theological rivalry between the two groups continued to produce martyrs in the Christian world, until Jews concluded that this highly regarded practice must end.

My investigation, then, is multidimensional. Looking inward, I examine the function of martyrdom within the group: its use as a means to rationalize catastrophes, as a way to restructure Judaism and Jewries after destructions, as a tool for socialization and growth, as a way to legitimize emerging authorities and leaders, and as a didactical tool that instructs how to interact with members of the group and with outsiders. In short, I hope to show how martyrdom functions as one of the group's internal means of survival.

Looking outward, martyrdom is analyzed in relation to its environment. Through martyrological proclamations, symbolic acts, and the acting out of their rivals' customs and convictions, potential and would-be martyrs delivered messages to their adversaries. These polemical messages disclose the ambience that produced resistance unto death. They reveal the existing mentality not only within the Jewish circles but also with the pagan and Christian orbits that circumscribed them. The martyrs' blood demonstrated to all parties involved in the drama the "red lines" that could not be crossed from either side. Going on the offensive, martyrological polemics claim the religious and moral superiority of one group over others. It is not surprising, therefore, to find Jewish martyrdom and martyrologies flourishing in societies that were themselves fascinated by altruism. Thus the history of Jewish martyrdom consists of both tradition and transmutation, perpetuation and innovation. To better trace the evolution of Jewish martyrdom, I will attempt to identify and disentangle these two forces.

Methodologically, two books are of significance for this two-dimensional investigation. In *Rituals of Childhood*, I. G. Marcus has observed that since antiquity Jews "expressed elements of their Jewish religious cultural identity by internalizing and transforming" various foreign customs and rituals "in a polemical, parodic, or neutralized manner." Marcus designated this process of internalizing foreign ideas as "inward acculturation."[1] In the case of Christendom, Marcus has convincingly shown that Jews adapted Christian motifs and fused them with ancient Jewish customs and traditions. As we shall see, the evolution of Jewish martyrdom provides a good case study for Marcus's theory. Here, too, inward acculturation takes place not to assimilate but to exhibit to all, Jews and their rivals, the martyr's socioreligious commitment. Thus, among other issues, I hope to show in the first three chapters that rather than being the contribution of Hellenistic Judaism to western civilization, as the present scholarly consensus argues, the Jewish internalization of the martyrological idea commenced with the Roman occupation of the Jewish kingdom and with the rise of Christianity. It is the Roman and Christian fascination with heroic death that initiated this internalization of the concept that thereafter developed a Jewish life of its own in Judaism.

How these two forces work together is further demonstrated in D. Boyarin's study of the early relationships between rabbinic Judaism and Christianity. Boyarin has shown that innovative ideas traveled between the two religions "like a wave . . . almost in a fashion of a stone thrown into a pond." In the case of martyrdom, Boyarin describes the process as a discourse "that changes and develops over time and undergoes particularly interesting transformation."[2] We shall see that Boyarin's wave theory does not stop at the banks of early rabbinic Judaism and nascent Christianity. Martyrological dialogues between Judaism and Christianity persisted throughout the Middle Ages and beyond. Unlike the early intellectual dialogues, the martyrological discourses between the two creeds become violent from the Middle Ages onward (Chapters 4–9).

These martyrological dialogues appear in a variety of sources. We find them in folkloric tales, historical reports, rabbinic material, and liturgical poetry, to mention only a few. Despite the overall difference in the nature of these sources, their martyrological sections share several characteristics. No martyr has ever written his or her own story, at least not from beginning to end. Yet the stories of martyrdom tend to describe a very personal experience, often in the first person. At best, the narrators may have been an eyewitness to the event in question. But even then, their bias raises the question of historical accuracy. For us, this question becomes more acute when the narrators were not spectators of the scenes described. For the narrators and their audience, the question appears less troublesome, if at all. Insufficient factual information never seemed to stop an author from completing a martyrological story. Nor did the lack of facts affect the enthusiasm of the reader. Imagination and writing skills compensated for the unknown, whereas tradition and familiar literary patterns provided clear archetypes for the audience. In fact, the more remote the narrator seems to be from his heroes, the better they appear. In the end, such literary compensations result in the creation of a very distinctive genre – the martyrology.

At first glance, therefore, historians may question the value of martyrologies. Historians are trained to disjoin fact from fiction, to separate the wheat from the chaff. In the case of martyrologies, however, I believe the "chaff" to be as important as the "wheat." Despite their apparent deficiencies, martyrologies are of great value to our linear study. They may not reveal what their heroes actually said or did even during a *genuine* incident, but they do reflect what the authors and their generations thought about martyrdom and what they expected from themselves in similar situations. When the martyrologist let the martyrs speak for themselves, they are, in fact, speaking for the author and his generation. The interpretation of their flowery language, with its imagery and metaphors, provides significant information on the society that commemorated these heroes. Thus, martyrologies do not only hide a story behind a story. They are telescoping multiple narratives within a story.

These characteristics of the martyrological story are not limited to a place or period. Whether it is the Roman historian Josephus Flavius speaking about his ancestors' tradition of voluntary death, the late antique redactors of the Talmud describing the martyrdoms of first- and second-century rabbis, or twelfth-, thirteenth-, or fourteenth-century reporters, poets, liturgists, and rabbinic commentators mentioning the massacres of eleventh-century Rhineland Jews, all do so through contemporary literary styles and symbols in response to their lifetime experiences. In a flowery style embellished by metaphors and symbols, martyrologists often tend to fuse their own creativity with reality. For these reasons, this study follows the chronology of sources rather than of the events they describe. In my opinion, relying on the chronology of sources provides the best possibility for the study of martyrology in a linear context, even though not all the sources can always be dated accurately.

Finally, a word on who qualified as martyr for this study. Definitions of martyrdom vary from discipline to discipline and from culture to culture. Durkheim the sociologist, for instance, did not differentiate between martyrdom and suicide. Referring to all cases of self-destruction by the modern and impartial term *suicide*, Durkheim suggests the application of the term "to all cases of death resulting directly or indirectly from a positive or a negative act of the victim himself, which he knows will produce this result."[3] For Durkheim, the soldier dying to save his regiment, the martyr dying for his faith, or the mother sacrificing herself for her child, "can be only varieties of a single class." Durkheim identifies several categories of suicide. One of them is the "altruistic suicide," which is motivated by social codes. If this code is religious in nature, Durkheim entitles voluntary death "altruistic obligatory suicide."

Traditional theologians would disagree with Durkheim. The three monotheistic religions strongly oppose all forms of voluntary death that are dubbed suicide but praise their martyrs.[4] Ask representatives of these religions what martyrdom is and you are bound to receive different answers. What compounds the search for definition is that the originally Greek term *martyrdom* lacks a uniform meaning.[5] Narrowing down our search to a Jewish definition does not yield decisive results either. Rabbinic law (*halakhah*) would seem to be a logical starting place for the search.[6] But the Law of the voluminous Talmud can take us only so far. Expressions on voluntary death in Jewish circles had existed long before the rabbis formulated their views on the issue. Moreover, the Talmud does not speak in one voice on this matter. Nor does it provide a clear and single term to describe this act. *Qiddush ha-Shem* ("the sanctification of God's name"), the present Hebrew term for martyrdom, is a medieval fixture. Before this biblical phrase appeared in martyrological texts, rabbis had formulated various expressions to delineate and deal with voluntary death.[7] And although Talmudic rabbis considered only passive voluntary death as an alternative to forced transgression, that is, Jews must let others take their lives rather than take their own (*yehareg ve-al yaavor*), self-slaughter was not an uncommon form of *qiddush ha-Shem* in the Middle Ages, however controversial.

Christians who forced these Jews into such situations generally considered their Jewish counterparts to be irrational or satanic. Even when Jews let their rivals take their lives to prevent torture to their bodies or souls, Christians still ascribed to them such adjectives. About a millennium earlier, Romans employed similar derogatory terms to describe those dying for Christianity.

Derogatory Roman terms, however, never prevented Christians from holding their martyrs in high regard.

It appears, then, that the evaluation of self-destruction is often a matter of self-definition.[8] But although it is true that every society defines its *causa iusta* to legitimize acts of voluntary death, one clarification is in order. Augustine claimed that "It is not the penalty that makes true martyrs, but the cause."[9] Augustine intended to exclude all non-Christians and even the Christians he deemed heretical as martyrs. In essence, the acceptance of Augustine's view would end this study before it could begin. In principle, Augustine raises a valid point. Not all cases of voluntary death belong to a single category. At least historically, the readiness to suffer unto death rather than inflict an injury unto others is the one ingredient that has made martyrdom both controversial and noble. My interest, therefore, primarily lies in the accounts that describe or discuss the voluntary death of the nonviolent believers. These believers may end their own lives or even take their families with them in a most violent way to prevent a violation of their conviction. Yet they achieve this ultimate goal without physically harming their antagonists.

We are about to see that the history of Jewish martyrdom is as complex as it is long. The frequent appearance of martyrs in the pages of history prevents us from discussing all the Jewish and Christian martyrological accounts. For practical reasons, we are bound to address only the most significant descriptions that focus on such nonviolent heroes. We begin, therefore, with the examination of the martyrologies that current scholarship places in the Hellenistic period.

Mythic Martyrs

Religious martyrdom is considered one of the more significant contributions of Hellenistic Judaism to western civilization. Out of the conflict between King Antichos Epiphanes IV and the Jewish people, it is believed, the concept of voluntary death for God unfolded.[1] With few exceptions, this assumption has lasted from the early Christian period to this day, accepted both by Jews and Christians. To mention one example, W. H. C. Frend followed the opinion that from early times "Judaism was itself a religion of martyrdom." In his view, it was the "Jewish psychology of martyrdom" that inspired Christian martyrdom.[2]

An exception to this long-lasting scholarly consensus is G. W. Bowersock's *Martyrdom and Rome*. Focusing on non-Jewish documents, Bowersock viewed martyrdom "alien to both the Greeks and the Jews." In his opinion, "like the very word 'martyr' itself, martyrdom had nothing to do with Judaism or with Palestine. It had everything to do with the Graeco-Roman world, its traditions, its language, and its cultural tastes."[3] According to Bowersock, martyrdom is a Christian concept that developed in the Roman cultural climate. Subsequently, this Christian notion made its way into Judaism. Bowersock's view, however, still remains the exception among scholars.

My approach is compatible with Bowersock's, although with less defined borders with respect to cultural and religious separations. By focusing on the Jewish texts of the Greco-Roman period, I intend to show that voluntary death for religious purposes emerged in the Roman environment in a process that internalized the Roman "noble death" ideal and that was accelerated by the arrival of Christianity. But before turning to the Roman era, it is necessary to show why Jewish martyrdom as an ideal does not belong in the Hellenistic period.

What led early theologians and recent scholars to ascribe the origin of martyrdom to Hellenistic Judaism was their interpretation of the canonical

Daniel and mainly the apocryphal 2 and 4 Maccabees. For Frend, thus, "Without Maccabees and without Daniel a Christian theology of martyrdom would scarcely have been thinkable."[4] The reliance on these sources often ignored the premise that about two centuries set apart 4 Maccabees from the rest. Instead, the views found in Frend's camp focused on the chronology of events alone rather than on the chronology of the narratives that depicted these events. Clumping these diverse sources together may be beneficial for an isolated study of the martyrological literature *per se*. And indeed, such studies have made significant contributions. Such methodology, however, carries trifling value for the study of martyrdom in the context of linear history. The wiggling between the 2 and 4 Maccabees, that is, between texts that are assumed to be of the pre- and post-Christian eras, in search for early Jewish roots, is bound to produce tautological conclusions.[5]

Phenomenal inceptions, conceptions, and their influences, therefore, can be adequately evaluated only in their historical frameworks. The complexity of the Maccabean narratives and the questions they raise, however, compel us first to present these narratives according to their place in scholars' surmised chronological order and their subjective scale of importance before attending to their analysis. Before putting the so-called Maccabean martyrs to the test of history, it is appropriate to turn first to Daniel.

DANIEL

A prevailing scholarly view maintains that the Book of Daniel contains the first Jewish martyrological stories, which provided the foundation and inspiration for the Jewish and Christian doctrines of martyrdom. Thus, for example, J. Rauch identifies Daniel and his three companions – Hananiah/Shadrach, Mishael/Meshack, and Azariah/Abednego – with the "Maccabean martyrs,"[6] whereas R. H. Charles crowned the four biblical heroes the "righteous martyrs of Israel."[7]

What led to this scholarly interpretation of Daniel is the behavioral descriptions of its four heroes during their Babylonian and Persian exile in the sixth century, as well as the allusions to the political condition and social instability during the time of Antiochus Epiphanes.[8] Scholars thus concede that the book, which consists of two different parts, appeared together as a unit during the time of the Maccabean revolt, if not later, as the pseudonymity and *ex eventu* prophecy in the second half of the book suggests.[9] Although the unities of Chapters 1–6 and 7–12 belong to different periods, together they form a literary work that could help rationalize the historical and human crisis of the Jews in cosmic and mythological terms.[10] Because of its limited historical value, which springs from the authors' lack of interest in historiography,[11] the significance of the book lies in the moral and religious advice it echoes, not necessarily in the plain description of its protagonists' demeanor.

Within these descriptions scholars see martyrological elements, if not actual martyrdoms. The first mentioned martyrological element is believed to be the religious nature of the conflict between a powerful oppressor and an unyielding oppressed. For the first time, the Book of Daniel describes religious conflicts between the nation of Israel and foreign kings who attempted to force Jews to transgress the Mosaic law.[12] With Antiochus the book goes further. It describes an endeavor to alter the face of Judaism altogether. According to the book's mystical description, the conflicts stand in sharp contrast to former political confrontations that did not make religion a key issue. Moreover, the first half of the book depicts conflicts between mighty kings and peaceful Jews whose faith in the God of Israel constitutes their only shield.

The second element that is believed to point in the direction of martyrdom is the protagonists' absolute trust in God. In the book, the faithful hero's trust appears stronger than his instinct to life. Faithless life is meaningless. Faith played a pivotal role in protecting the faithful from harm – so pivotal, that it became worthy of dying for when challenged.

These two martyrological elements – religious conflict and trust in God unto death – are believed to appear in the first six chapters. The first story that projects these elements is set in Babylonia, in king Nebuchadnezzar's palace (Chapter 1). Daniel and his three companions, Mishael, Azariah, and Hananiah, refuse to defile themselves by eating "royal food," putting their lives at stake.[13] Ultimately, they survive their ten-day trial. God saves them from starvation in recognition of their devotion.

In Chapter 3, a direct conflict between the king and Daniel's three companions takes place. The famous ordeal by fire that the three undergo stir to the opinion that the story belongs to the martyrological genera.[14] Built on an ancient style entitled, "the Disgrace and Rehabilitation of a Minister," the chapter describes the heroes' religious loyalty and astonishing survival.[15] The king orders his Judaean captives thrown into the fiery furnace unless they agree to worship an effigy of gold. Hananiah, Mishael, and Azariah put their trust in God and refuse to yield.[16] Although thrown into the flames, they remain unharmed because "a man like an angel" saves them.[17]

Based on Daniel's experience in Chapter 6, A. Bentzen has considered the chapter to be a legend of martyrdom.[18] As in the previous episode, the genre of "the Disgrace and Rehabilitation of a Minister" characterizes this chapter as well. King Darius's officials decreed "that whoever shall make a request of any god or man for the next thirty days, other than of you, O king, will be thrown into the lions' den." Daniel continued to worship God. As ordered, the guards threw Daniel into the lions' den, but "God sent his angel and shut the lions' mouths."

In contrast to the human nature of the conflict in the first half of the book, the rest revolves around a direct conflict between mighty kings and God. Against the Maccabeen background of religious enmity and unconditional faith, Chapters 11 and 12 introduce two more elements that will play a significant role in the formulation of Jewish and, especially, Christian martyrdom. This time the conflict is set in Judaea at a time of approaching final cosmic events. King Antiochus Epiphanes' ascent to power, his defilement of the Israelites' Temple, his anti-Jewish decrees, and the breaking out of violence signal the beginning of the end (Daniel 11:21, 29–35). God's final judgment will bring annihilation upon the cosmos and humanity.

This is not discouraging news, however. Catastrophic signs denote a transition to a secondary stage of existence. In this stage, God will reward and resurrect while inflicting eternal punishments on the sinful (Daniel 12:1–3).[19] Such depictions turned the darkness of death from an end into a bright new dawn; the promise of resurrection assured a new, ideal condition of existence for the righteous. For future discussions, it is important to note Collins's observation that the book speaks of resurrection in a communal context.[20]

It is these four elements in the Book of Daniel – religious conflict, trust in God unto death, death as solution and transition, and reward – that led Jewish and Christian traditions to count the heroes of the book among their martyrs, a tradition that has been accepted by modern scholarship as well. The last two chapters have especially influenced the common view that the book speaks of the "righteous martyrs of Israel," who will receive "the blessedness of a resurrection to life," which is "limited to the martyrs" in the Messianic kingdom.[21]

Based on the existence of these elements, the association of the book with martyrdom is indeed a tempting one. But this retrojected connection, influenced by religious interpretations, is without significant merit, not to mention the opinion that the Book of Daniel was designed to launch a tradition of martyrdom during the Maccabean hostility.[22] This association of the book with voluntary death denotes a continuation of religious traditions and nostalgic interpretations by succeeding Jewish and Christian martyrologists who turn to the Hebrew Bible in hope of finding justification for their martyrs' behavior.

No doubt, chapters one and three convey the heroes' readiness to give up their lives for their convictions. Chapter 6, however, misses this fundamental martyrological motif altogether; Daniel's ordeal is without a trial or a confrontation.[23] Without the individuals having the opportunity to make a *choice* between death and life, the basic characteristics of martyrdom are absent. Daniel's tribulation is presented here as an inevitable punishment, brought upon him post factum by conniving and envying rivals for his deeds in the past. Unfortunately for Daniel, even the sympathetic Darius could not revoke the decree once he found out it referred to Daniel's practice.

More significantly, none of the four heroes suffered or died.[24] Obviously, they are not to be blamed for being miraculously rescued by God. But their marvelous survival is precisely the book's central theme: God can marvelously save the righteous from the most precarious situation. Not only does God save the faithful from immediate hardship, He even causes him to prosper in the future. "He saves and rescues and does signs and wonders" (5.28). Even King Darius predicted: "Your God whom you serve constantly, he will save you [Daniel]," from the lions (6.17). He did.

Biblical characteristics put the Book of Daniel on a unique footing. The issue is not whether God will deliver his servant but how ostentatious this salvation will be. Daniel therefore glorifies God's omnipotence, from which only the faithful derives benefits. But the book does not celebrate martyrdom. Daniel and his three companions never declared their willingness to die. On the contrary, when Daniel informs his companions about King Nebuchadnezzar's decision to put to death all the sages of Babylon (2.12), he urges them "to seek mercy from the God of heaven . . . *so that Daniel and his companions should not be put to death* . . . " [2.18, emphasis mine]. Hardly a martyrological desire.

Each of the stories repeatedly conveys what would appear to the unbeliever as a paradoxical configuration: the more one puts himself at risk in the name of God, the better are his chances to survive the most incredible ordeal. As Collins puts it: "The story of the fiery furnace prepares its readers for such an eventuality by assuring them that their God could protect them, and that fidelity to their own exclusive cult was ultimately the best way to advancement."[25] The faithful achieves reward for his ordeal through life rather than through death. As the book demonstrates, the ordeals only advanced the heroes' position *in life*. In Daniel, life harmoniously combines religious adherence and political loyalty to foreign and often sympathetic kings. Conversely, those who are concerned only with their own safety and promotion, at the cost of their convictions, will perish.

The moral of these stories is that God does not forsake those who remain devoted. Daniel and his companions had to express their reliance on God by daily worship. Because they were not required to prove anything beyond that, and because God always saved them, actual martyrdom was unnecessary and, thus, remains out of the picture.

Nor does the second half of the book idealize passiveness. "The people who know their God will stand firm and take action" (11.32), promised the book; namely they will resist militantly.[26] Unlike Daniel and his three companions, the people and their "wise" (*maskilim*) leaders "will fall by sword and flame" (11.33).[27]

The Book of Daniel does not call for voluntary death or even reject active opposition to political and religious oppression. With respect to activism, the case appears to be the opposite.[28] Suffering and death never became the heroes' goal. Rather, they are to be seen as deterministic elements of a divine plan and apocalyptic cycle. What made death a possible bittersweet end was the upcoming cosmic eventuation. The anonymous author, whom some modern scholars describe as a supporter of the Maccabees,[29] suggests that his reader endure the suffering of oppression, until victory is achieved. Oppression, the book promises, will cease and God will reward the righteous in the same remarkable way He delivered Daniel and his companions. Originally, therefore, the Book of Daniel served as "resistance literature,"[30] promising victory through active opposition and divine recognition for the living or the falling.[31]

To be sure, a noncombatant attitude in a conflict, an absolute trust in God, and an expected reward are only the characteristics that come together in future stories of martyrdom, not the phenomenon itself. Martyrological phenomena are missing in the Book of Daniel because it did not intend to promote voluntary death even among those who could not actively participate in the revolt. By concluding its narrative with "happy endings," the book provided support for the revolt and advocated persistence, because the faithful's triumph in life was inevitable. The book's martyrological significance, therefore, does not emerge from the original messages its authors conveyed to their contemporaries. We shall see that Daniel's important contribution to martyrdom stems from the interpretations it received from later Jewish and Christian supporters of the notion.

1 MACCABEES

Unlike Daniel, 1 Maccabees gives little attention to supernatural interventions on behalf of its heroes: Mattathias, the patriarch of the Hasmonean family, and their followers. Written originally in Hebrew, the book describes the emergence of the bellicose and religious Hasmonean dynasty as an opposition to Antiochus's decrees. Believing themselves to have been chosen by Providence to bring deliverance upon Israel (5:62), the book's heroes rely on faith and fighting to rededicate the Temple and defeat the king and his Hellenistic supporters.[32]

Within these descriptions of active resistance, the example of one thousand refugees is believed to introduce "the first martyrs in Jewish history."[33] Attention, however, must be given first to the brief description that precedes the refugees' story. It reveals the punishment that befell those who ignored Antiochus's decrees. His officers

[P]ut to death the women who had circumcised their children, hanging the new born babies around their necks; and they also put to death their families as well as those who had circumcised them. Nevertheless many in Israel were firmly resolved in their hearts not to eat unclean food. (1:60–2)

This statement is often viewed as yet another proof of the prominence of the martyrological idea in Hellenistic Jewish society. M. Hengel probably relies on this statement in his reference to "individual instances of martyrdom."[34] This impressive testimony of determination reveals individual and collective punishments for defying the royal ban on circumcision. Yet the fundamental martyrological characteristic of consciously choosing death over life in the presence of oppressors is missing. Nor does the author seem to be aware of such option. To maintain their creed, the new conditions "forced Israel into all the secret hiding-places of fugitives" (1 Macc. 1:53) rather than into martyrdom. When eventually "found in the cities" (1 Macc. 1:58), swift punishment became their fate. As it appears, they circumcised their children in hiding, hoping to evade the watchful eyes of royal officers and their collaborators, "who were ready to forsake the Law . . . and did evil" (1 Macc. 1:52).

What strengthens the association of Chapter 1 with martyrdom, according to several scholars, is the acknowledgment that some "preferred to die rather than be defiled by food or break the holy covenant; and they did die" (1 Macc. 1:63). This isolated statement was sufficient for Harrington to conclude that, "The martyrs are acknowledged but passed over quickly in 1:62–64,"[35] although how these people perished is not portrayed. Nor do they express their own thoughts and goals. As we shall see, similar choices of death over sacrificing to foreign gods became the basic motif in early Christian Martyrs' Acts, but it would be erroneous to anachronistically approach this verse under the influence of Christian martyrology. Because v. 63 concludes the description of the women who were caught and punished for circumcising their babies, the verse refers to a group of Jews who clandestinely agonized to maintain their religious identity under difficult circumstances. Their silence in the story prevents us from reaching conclusions beyond this basic goal.

In contrast to typical martyrologies, these people received little support for their behavior from the author. More importantly, no benefit is ascribed to their deaths. Despite their loss of life, still "Great wrath came upon Israel"

(1 Macc. 1:64). They did not win God's approval because adhering to Judaism without taking actions to bring their plight to an end was insufficient for the author. He compares those who chose the wait–and–see approach to "a man without honor" (1 Macc. 2:8). In his view, "To sit idly by while it is given into the hand of its enemies" (1 Macc. 2:7). God had to be satisfied in a different manner. Neither on a practical level nor a theological level could such passive behavior earn merit for the righteous or for Israel.

Only after making this point clear does the author turn to the story of the aforementioned one thousand refugees. Their story further advances the benefits of resistance and the disadvantages of conformity. In contrast to the previous general descriptions, actions are preceded by declarations that reveal the escapees' intentions. These refugees withdrew to the wilderness to seek "justice and judgment" after "misfortunes had fallen hard upon them" (1 Macc. 2:29–30). Neither their misfortune nor their rejection of "the command of the king" are delineated. Whatever their crime, it caused sufficient uproar that "[M]any pursued them, overtook them, encamped against them, and organized an attack against them on the Sabbath day." The refugees rejected their rivals' proposal to "come out and obey the command of the king" and live. Their answer, "We will not come forth, nor will we obey the command of the king to profane the Sabbath day," instantly triggered the fatal attack. As promised, they "did not defend themselves nor did they hurl a stone against them, nor block up the hiding place." Saying, "Let all of us die in our innocence," they were all lynched "to the number of a thousand souls."[36]

The refugees' story is immediately followed by a *halakhic*-style debate over a theological dilemma rather than merely a description of an impressive theological phenomenon. As the story continues, Mattathias realized that with such passive patterns of response, even if accepted in the name of religion, the nation would not be able to achieve its religious objectives. Personal benefits are not even mentioned in connection with the act. He is said to have quickly called upon the Jews to cease such passive behavior, for to Mattathias the importance of preserving life exceeded that of observing the Sabbath. Mattathias thus is presented as a revolutionary leader interested in fighting soldiers, not in Jews allowing themselves to be killed. Touched by the disturbing news, the small group of rebels "mourned greatly over them," saying, "If all of us do as our brothers have done, and do not fight against the heathen for our lives and our laws, they will soon destroy us from off the earth." They then made the following decision, "[I]f any man attack us in battle on the Sabbath day, let us oppose him, that we may not all die as our brothers did in the hiding places" (1 Macc. 2:40–41). An overwhelming response followed the decision without delay. Fighting rather than submitting to death marks Mattathias's approach toward the royal policy of assimilation and its Jewish supporters. Based on this story and its version in 2 Maccabees 6.11, it has been suggested that (1) during the early Hellenistic period Jews did not fight either defensive or offensive wars on the Sabbath and (2) that the ideology that permits such warfare started to develop with Mattathias's statement.[37]

His understanding, that there were prohibitions against warfare on the Sabbath, led Klausner to view these refugees as "accidental" martyrs who decided not to fight because of the Sabbath. On any other given day, thus, their reaction to the threat would have differed significantly.[38] Coinciding perceptions are that the refugees refused to fight solely because of the "normative [Jewish] principle" regarding Sabbath combat. Otherwise, on any other day, these victims would have fought or at least protected themselves.[39]

H. Mantel justly discards the view that "Jewish norms" prohibited war on the Sabbath, because there is no solid evidence to suggest that a fixed rule prohibiting war on the Sabbath existed during the Maccabean revolt.[40] The issue of wars on the Sabbath had been discussed earlier, for Jews already served as mercenaries in non-Jewish armies.[41] Thus the rejection of the Sabbath-combat ban, along with the view that the refugees desired to die innocently, persuaded Bar-Kochva to consider these refugees "martyrs (cf. I Macc. I.63) who chose to be passive and refrain from all defensive action, and made no preparations from the outset to fight." In his view, they "would have refrained from doing so on a weekday as well."[42] In other words, these fugitives embraced expiration not because of the timing of their encounter with the enemy, but because of an ideology that amounts to strict pacifism.

The ascription of kindred pacifistic beliefs to the Hasidim led to their being associated with the refugees.[43] However, such identification eliminates further discussion of an existing organized pacifistic ideology that would find expression through voluntary death, for the evidence suggests that the Hasidim believed in, and indeed provided, active opposition against the supporters of Hellenism. Right after Mattathias's denunciation of the refugees' passive response, the rest of the desert fugitives, "a company of the Hasidim" (2.42), are said to have joined the Hasmonean family in their national struggle.

To reconcile the discrepancy between pacifism and belligerence, it has been proposed that the peaceful and apolitical Hasidim turned ardent advocates of active opposition after the traumatic killing in the desert that resulted in the Hasmonean call for an armed struggle.[44] But as Tcherikover has demonstrated, the Hasmonean campaign preceded Antiochus's decrees, let alone their actualization, whereas other desert sects were already engaged in warfare.[45] If indeed the refugees belonged to the Hasidim, pacifism as the reason for their passivity in the conflict must be rejected.[46]

In an attempt to explain the refugees' strict observance and unprecedented behavior, other opinions rejected the identification of the group with the Hasidim. Assuming that the sect of Qumran did not fight on the Sabbath, they associated the thousand refugees with the Essenes and explain their passive behavior on this account.[47] Mantel, however, deems the behavior of the refugees exceptional even by the strict standards of the Qumran sect. The abnormality of this reaction has convinced Mantel not only to disapprove the connection between the groups but also to discredit the reliability of the narrative.[48] Support for his skepticism may be found in 1 Maccabees itself. As if Mattathias's emendation never took place, Jonathan echoes his father's exhortation "to stand up now and fight" for their lives "for today is not like yesterday nor the day before" (1 Macc. 9:43–46).[49] Accordingly, it must be concluded that neither the assumption of an existing ban on Sabbath combat nor pacifistic convictions prevented the refugees from protecting themselves.

If we concur with Mantel's reservation about the story's genuineness, we must search elsewhere for the answer to the question of the refugees' behavior. The refugees' response, "[W]e will not come forth, nor will we obey the command of the king to profane the Sabbath day," appears to revolve around two issues.[50] Not only did they refuse to desecrate the Sabbath by defending themselves, they also denounced the call to come out, which initially the Hellenists did not link to a requirement to transgress. Why they would not then come out the author does not reveal. The author's silence can be linked to his interest in characterizing devotion to the Sabbath as the core of the conflict and not the simple but symbolic act of coming out to join the Hellenists. Obviously, the king would not require Jews to profane the Sabbath by fighting his troops.[51]

As the text stands, the potential violation of the Sabbath by self-defense arose from the refugees' refusal to "come out." It appears that only because they refused to come out did the issue of self-defense arise. There is no indication that the refugees sought death. Hoping not to be discovered or to attract attention to their lack of involvement in the conflict, they prepared for survival in the harsh conditions of the desert rather than for an armed clash. This may be further confirmed by the narrative's opening: that they went down to the desert to "seek justice and vindication." As the allusion to Isaiah 32 attests, the desert dwellers will experience divine justice, which will bring *miraculous victory* and everlasting vindication. Especially, Sabbath observers are promised that they will witness justice and enjoy such a victory.[52] If this is how the many who went down to desert understood their mission, voluntary death was not part of their plan or belief. Echoing the Danielic paradoxical theme of survival against all odds, the author describes the Sabbath observers in the desert as expecting to witness a miracle themselves.

The fusion of the Sabbath and the coming out of the hiding places in the skimpy speech attributed to the refugees helped the author illustrate their unrealistic outlook, which resulted in their demise. At the same time, the author indirectly implies that the refugees were oblivious to the Hasmonean's call for active resistance at Modin *even* when self-defense became the issue. As the absence of reference to Sabbath violation in the refugees' final statement demonstrates (1 Macc. 2:37), their obliviousness to the situation constitutes the author's main concern. Rather than being introduced to discuss martyrdom or a *nonexistent* Sabbath ban, the story is exploited to advance the author's political agenda: victory can be achieved only if all Jews follow the Hasmonean leadership. Although the refugees strictly observed the Sabbath and perished, divine intervention is said to have saved the *combatants* despite their activities on the seventh day.

Through Mattathias's recommendation, the author artfully camouflages his political call by turning the story into a discussion of the significance of preserving life versus that of the Sabbath per se. Undoubtedly, the author would have increased his chances of winning a consensus about the Hasmonean leadership had he related Mattathias's resolution to religious rather than political matters.[53] A laudatory supporter of the family, the author had his reason to include such religious motifs in the family's mundane affairs. As Sievers points out, the story of Mattathias's reaction to the refugees' response and other depictions in 1 Maccabees is as follows:

a skillful presentation of the origin and legitimacy of the dynasty and a defense for some of its central tenets: it claims the right to the high priesthood, asserts complete and zealous dedication to Torah, represents the dynasty's rise to power as resultant from its founder's defense of Torah and leadership of those anxious to defend it, and affirms that changes in observance, at least of the Sabbath, are legitimate when necessitated by the circumstances.[54]

Asserting the Hasmonean religious and political legitimacy was extremely important, given the likelihood that other Jewish groups may have taken up arms before and even against them.[55] Especially did the acknowledgment of Mattathias's legitimacy and his dynasty by the Hasidim play a crucial role here, for in reality the relationship between the two groups often suffered from impediments and disagreements, ending in an open rivalry.

Not only could the Hasmoneans benefit from such "skillful presentations," their Hasidic partners could draw "literary dividends" as well. According to the book, the two groups shared the same passionate dislike of foreign culture, kindled by religious fire. Yet the Hasidic zealous passion for traditionalism surpassed even that of the political Hasmoneans, according them the historical reputation of being adamant spiritual seclusionists with "*rigorous strictness of law.*"[56] According to the pro-Hasmonean account, one thousand souls had to pay the ultimate price before the Hasidim could fully appreciate Mattathias's realistic and practical approach. But as E. Gruen skillfully argues, in reality the Hasidim exhibited more tolerance and, at times, were even ready to compromise their positions in their negotiations with the Seleucid-appointed High Priest Alcimus and the Seleucid general, Bacchides.[57] In the interest of the author's promotion of the Hasmonean dynasty, the account of the refugees has replenished the smokescreen for the Hasidics' and the Hasmoneans' mixing of religious predilection with realpolitik. It also created the rosy impression that all opponents of Hellenism acted as a harmonious group in the conflict.

All in all, the story of the refugees' destruction aspired to deliver messages not related to the concept of voluntary death. The author shows no intention to transform the account into a positive paradigm. According to Mattathias's speech, he put an end to a behavior that, in historical retrospect, could have developed into the phenomenon of voluntary death for God and that four centuries later would be known as *martyrium*. This is not to say that Mathattias prevented the development of the martyrological notion. His contemporaries' unfamiliarity with martyrdom and with the concept that human sacrifice can be beneficial, both to individuals and to the nation, is the main reason for not encountering praises for voluntary death. Promoting martyrdom as an acceptable behavioral pattern, much less as a theological concept, was never the book's intention.

Unlike modern scholars, the account therefore does not regard the refugees as "martyrs" but rather as zealous victims who died unnecessarily.[58] From the author's viewpoint, they belong to the same category as all those who refused to join the war against Hellenism, were "as man without honor" (1 Macc. 2:8) who, despite or rather because of their passive piety, failed to prevent the "great wrath [that] came upon Israel." These descriptions hardly justify the association of the refugees' story with "martyrdom" and "the greatest sacrifice."[59]

Vengeance and salvation was not to be left to God alone. His loyal combatant rebels were expected to achieve these goals (1 Macc. 2:67). Their duty was to fight those who wronged them, because it was "better to die in battle than to look upon the tragedies of our nation and our sanctuary" (1 Macc. 3:59). To offer oneself for the Law meant first and foremost joining the Hasmonean campaign rather than contemplating self-destruction. And through the Law, they were assured, they would achieve vengeance and triumph (1 Macc. 2:64, 67). In this activist manner, many "innocent" followers were asked to heed Mattathias's last words to "give your lives for the covenant of your father" (1 Macc. 2.51). Like the Law, "innocence," the author emphasizes, is what would save the activist from certain destruction (1 Macc. 2:60). At this stage, before they became the language of the martyrs, whom we shall meet throughout this book, such statements had a different connotation. They were made in a style, tantamount to jargon, that emphasizes the rebels' stubborn dynamic resistance in defense of their ancestral practice and polity. Giving up one's life indicates a commitment to the cause rather than an endorsement of self-annihilation.[60] The rhetoric in 1 Maccabees does not glorify passive voluntary death[61] because it believes combative actions and "deeds" earn the Maccabees honor. In the book, therefore, the beneficial function of passive death stems from the efficient utilization of the story as a literary tool that presents passive behavior as *a negative example* to extol the political wisdom and the religious devotion of the heroic Hasmonean family.

To support this political wisdom the author turned to Scripture. According to his theological rationale, God saves rather than destroys the combatant "innocent." With his last breath, Mattathias encouraged his sons to continue their war, reminding them of their ancestors' "deeds." Only through deeds would they survive against all odds. "Daniel because of his innocence was saved from the mouth of the lions" (1 Macc. 2.59–60). Phineas, Elijah, Joshua, and David provided additional examples of loyalty in a matrix of belligerent and zealot leaders. Because of their faith and deeds, like Hananiah, Azariah, and Mishael (1 Macc. 2.49–61), they overcame adversity.[62]

Abraham, too, makes Mattathias's list of role models, because the patriarch was "found faithful in temptation" (1 Macc. 2:52, based on Gen. 22:1). The biblical exemplar provides a significant insight into the role of voluntary death in the book. What makes this example so important is the complete disregard of Isaac's near-sacrifice, which constitutes the real drama of Abraham's test. Had the author associated benefits with the passive acts of the Sabbath observers, Isaac, not Abraham, should have emerged as the role model. It is Isaac's *aqedah* that became one of the greatest rationales behind voluntary death in post-Talmudic literature. At this stage, however, Abraham's strength – namely his absolute trust in God's promise – rather than Isaac's near-sacrifice constitutes the model's admired quality. Everlasting glory is obtained, Mattathias advises his sons, by those who show themselves to "be strong" on behalf of the Law. Evil is to be overcome by fighting for the people and the sanctuary (3.43). With faith, the book promised, none of the rebels "will lack strength" (2.61). 1 Maccabees called for fearless fighters, not meek martyrs.[63]

2 MACCABEES

More than any other work, 2 Maccabees, an epitome of a five-volume history by Jason of Cyrene, is credited with making the notion of voluntary death an integral part of the Jewish experience in the Hellenistic period.[64] M. Hengel styled Jason "the father of the *martyrium*,"[65] who, according to J. Goldstein, describes "many martyrdoms."[66] Amazingly, in the telling of Antiochus IV's religious persecutions and his attempt to enforce Greek culture, only two such stories, in Chapters 6 and 7, could be associated with Hengel's anachronistic term. And although Hengel's qualitative statement is debatable, there can be little doubt about Goldstein's quantitative observation. Van Henten correctly states in regard to Chapters 6 and 7 that "the epitomist no where indicates whether Jews other than the martyrs were subjected to this ordeal" of choosing between eating swine's flesh and death.[67] Others went even further, claiming that the stories of voluntary death never took place and that they merely represent folk tales.[68]

References to the "many martyrdoms" often include the example of *two* women who circumcised their children. Not only quantitatively but qualitatively, there is no justification for including among martyrs these two women who were "publicly paraded around the city with their babies clinging to their breasts," before being cast down from the wall (2 Macc. 6:10).[69] Their brutal end clearly comes as a punishment *after* being caught and "brought up on the charge of having circumcised their children." Thus missing in the story is the women's willingness to die. Rather than demonstrating the women's preference for being executed for the Law, their story was designed to emphasize the Hellenists' determination to execute their new policy.

In addition to circumcision, the new policy included statutes affecting the observance of the Sabbath day, although it is unclear what 1 Maccabees meant by the order "to profane the Sabbaths" (1:45) or 2 Maccabees by "[I]t was impossible to keep the Sabbath" (6:6). Were Jews forced to violate the Sabbath or was it difficult for them to observe the day under the new conditions? It is difficult to determine, consequently, what role the Sabbath played in the story of a group of Jews killed while observing "the seventh day in secret" in a cave, after having been betrayed to Philip (2 Macc. 6:11).

Reading "they were burnt because their religious scruples kept them from defending themselves on account of their reverence for that most sacred day" under the influence of 1 Maccabees 2:32–38, some scholars understood that these Sabbath observers made a martyrological decision to die rather than transgress. The absence of a dialogue, however, makes it impossible to determine if these people were given a choice at all. Did a determined Philip move against these observant Jews on the Sabbath to surprise and destroy them without resistance? Nicanor, for instance, planned to attack Judas and his men on the Sabbath to minimize "personal risk" rather than to test their religious loyalty by trials (2 Macc. 15:1–2).[70] It is also unclear why these Sabbath observers were attacked. Equally ambiguous is whether they refrained from saving themselves from a fire set without warning or if they refused to prevent Philip's attack from the outset. Based on the text, these questions remain unanswerable and the current scholarly association of the story with an early Jewish martyrological doctrine unjustifiable. Perhaps it is this ambiguity that caused early martyrologists and recent scholars to view these heroes as martyrs, or at least associate them with models and inspirations for later martyrdoms. The martyrological components that are missing in these stories of conflict would be provided by the imagination of following martyrologists.

Another reason for this false association may have been the skillful use of these vague descriptions by an author (or authors) as a preparation for the next stories he implanted in the text about a more grandiose and astonishing form of heroism. 2 Maccabees 6:18–31 leaves no room for speculation over the altruism of a scribe named Eleazar.[71] His bravery and proclamations display some basic characteristics of future martyrdoms par excellence. This celebrated sage serves as the Hellenists' best hope for promoting Greek culture. A compulsory (or preferably, voluntary) public submission of a man of his religious and social stature was expected to convince others to compromise their Judaism in favor of paganism. Their plan backfired despite repeated attempts "to force him to open his mouth and eat swine's flesh" sacrificed to gods. Eleazar "welcomed death with glory rather than life with pollution, and of his own free will went to the rack."

The best potential propaganda tool in the Hellenistic arsenal turned into a famous and inspiring example of resistance. "Spitting out the food, he became an example of what men should do who are steadfast enough to forfeit life itself rather than eat what is not right for them to taste, in spite of a natural urge to live" (6:19–20). Forcibly inserting food in Eleazar's mouth would have been a sufficient symbolic victory for the Hellenists, and it could have brought the story to an abrupt conclusion. Conversely, spitting out the meat would have ended any further amicable dialogue between Eleazar and his executioners. But the first contradicting statement – that they failed even to forcibly put the unclean meat in his mouth – kept both Eleazar (if only for a while) and the story alive.[72]

Emphasizing the old scribe's commitment to Judaism, the story furnishes the conflict with one more peaceful solution that would have enabled both sides to compromise gracefully. Friendly officials in charge of the royal sacrifices offered to let Eleazar eat meat prepared by him according to the Mosaic law, if he would only pretend to consume unclean meat and thus ostensibly comply with the king's order. But from childhood the old scribe had earned a distinguished reputation among his people as a just and pious man, and he had no intention of deceiving them now, not even if it required the loss of his life.

Moral as well as religious concerns motivated Eleazar. His reverence for the Law and the fear that he "could not escape, either living or dead, *the vengeance of the Almighty*" motivated him to abandon life gracefully. But pretending to consume unclean meat, when, in fact, it was served properly, carried no religious penalty, not to mention the loss of life. In fact, not even Leviticus 11 includes such drastic actions with the prohibition against forbidden food. What troubled Eleazar incorporates two notions that will become important rabbinic guidelines three centuries later: Rabbi Ishmael's distinction between transgressions in public and in private and *mi-pnei marit ayin*. This is the prima facie concept that if one is believed, even mistakenly, to have transgressed, one's reputation is jeopardized and – worse – the public may be misled.[73]

Eleazar refused to eat the forbidden sacrifice and "suffer this gladly," because of his "*reverence for Him.*" At the same time, he would not collaborate with the officers' plot "lest many of the youth think" that the elderly Eleazar had turned to heathenism. Saving his life through such pretense would lead the youth to "stray through me, and I shall come to a stained and dishonored old age" (6:24–25), even though no actual transgression would occur. By rejecting unclean meat, Eleazar desired to avoid divine punishment, whereas by death he aspired to "have left a *noble example* [to the young] of how to die happily and nobly in behalf of our revered and holy laws" (6:28). With this lesson to the youth, the author concludes that Eleazar has left "in his death *an example of nobility* and a memorial of valor, not only to the young but also to the great majority of his nation" (6:31).

If Eleazar intended to set an example to "the great majority of his nation," his death had little impact on his contemporaries. This appears to be true even in the case of the historically famous, yet anonymous, mother with her seven sons, not only because they constitute the only subsequent instance of passive voluntary death (2 Macc. 7). Surprisingly, the elaborate proclamations of the celebrated seven utterly fail to mention Eleazar by name or make direct references to his inspiring "noble example."[74] Moreover, the seven and Eleazar saw the benefits of death in very different lights.

As in the story of Eleazar, only after his failure to win the sons over by pressured, unexpectedly amiable persuasion mark the dialogue between King Antiochus himself and the seven. Remarkably, the monarch appeared to be interested in having a rational and educational dialogue before watching the brothers eat swine. The straightforward opening answer of the first son, "It is certain that we are ready to die rather than transgress the laws of our fathers" (2 Macc. 7:2), abruptly terminated any elaborate discourse. Instead, the answer initiated the systematic executions of the sons.

The statement of the first son acquaints the reader with the dilemma the family faced. The sons are ready, although not desiring, to die rather than transgress. As in Chapter 6, voluntary death provides a method of avoiding transgressions. But quitting life voluntarily offers more than just the prevention of transgressions in the sons' story. The first son perished hoping that God will have "compassion on *us.*" In other words, the sons expects to earn divine compassion for themselves.[75] Thereafter, each of the following sons masterfully articulated with his last breath what divine compassion meant to him. Compassion is associated with the innovative notion of resurrection, which complements their idea of voluntary death. The protagonists' hope for resurrection runs throughout the macabre narrative.

As the second son proclaimed, torture at the hands of the human king would release the sons from this present life, whereas the King of the Universe would "raise *us* up to everlasting life" (emphasis mine). This was the best solution they could find in their present situation. Mortality terminates tribulations. God is not only the sole author of the present tribulation but also the only power able to turn mortality into immortality if the innocents "have died for His laws."

This deadly solution was accepted without hesitation by the next brother. Hoping to be physically resurrected, he overcame the natural fear of losing his organs. Such determination and optimism struck even the king – but not for long, however. While the fourth son agreed to die in the hope of being raised again by God, the king "will have no resurrection to life." Their acts thus generated a dual bonus: the return of the dead to life and the achievement of vengeance. Although the victims' death is ephemeral, the wicked's punishment is eternal.

The fifth son elaborated on this last issue of vengeance. Binding suffering and vengeance together, he challenged the king to hurt him so that the Almighty will torment the king and his offspring in the future. Rather than condemnation, their ordeal marks a divine correction. Suffering for the purpose of discipline, the narrative affirms, should not be interpreted as God's abandonment of His people.

With the response of the sixth son, the narrator closes his cyclical arguments. A clear-cut distinction between the brothers' sins and the king's is established. In an attempt to rationalize the harsh reality, the sixth son went back to the core of their ordeal. Make no mistake: The king ought not to "vainly deceive" himself by their temporary defeat. After all was said and done, the monarch would be punished "for daring to wage war against God." Suffering was brought upon the family "because of *ourselves*, because *we* sinned against our own God" (7:18) (emphasis mine).

Punishment for "our sins" marks the interpersonal, everlasting relationship between God and his seven sons. No matter what, the bond between them cannot be broken. Thus, the present reality is perceived only as a temporary crisis in which God uses the king as a tool to discipline His people. Before this promise could be fulfilled, however, even the mother's last son had to be added to the already long list of executions.

By now, she could easily have earned her title as the heroine of the book just for watching the systematic torture and execution of her six sons. Unlike them, she was not compelled to choose between life and death or undergo physical suffering, as if the insurmountable agonizing task of watching her sons' lives systematically snatched before her eyes by most gruesome methods was not enough. At this point, it would have been enough only to acquiesce to her loved ones' final desires to become a heroine. Not this mother. How many such gruesome scenes would it take to bring her down? After encouraging each of the six sons, she was ordered to advise the last son to save himself. Her opening statement to her youngest son appeared finally to give Antiochus his first satisfaction. "Have pity on me," she begged her child, do not . . . "be afraid of this executioner." Her expected breakdown turned into a desperate plea for "accepting death." Against her maternal instincts, she went beyond passive acceptance of her children's last wish, begging her remaining son to emulate his brothers and "accept death" (7:29). In return, she anticipated being rewarded by their return to life in the future ("that . . . *I* may receive you back") (emphasis mine). History, meanwhile, awarded her the enduring title of the classic heroine.

She would have elaborated further on these themes of voluntary death and resurrection had the youngest son not interrupted her motivation speech, assuring her that he "will obey the command of the Law." He accepts the family's ordeal as *their* just punishment from their angry God. Repeating the penultimate brother's belief, he is convinced that "We are really suffering for *our own sins*" (7:32). The core of the struggle is temporary and personal. It was a struggle between an anonymous family and a king who was trying to destroy their relationship with God. Although, like the brothers, many are said to have suffered "the wrath of the Almighty which has justly been brought against the whole of our nation," the mother and her sons are the only known family to suffer in this manner. Although they remained resolute in God, they could only pray that He would be merciful to the nation and end the tribulation.

The seven brothers reiterated their belief in God through torture and death. "Through affliction and torment" the king will eventually acknowledge that "He alone is God" (2 Macc. 7:37–38).

The youngest son summarizes the core of the conflict and its future results. Accordingly, it was the struggle of "evil against the *Hebrews*" (emphasis mine), in which the tyrant will not "escape the hands of God." Although they believed they were "really suffering for our own sins," they were still "under God's covenant for everlasting life," whereas the king "will receive just punishment" (2 Macc. 7:1–42).

Based on Chapters 6 and 7, it is understandable why the roots of monotheistic martyrdom are believed to have existed already in the Hellenistic period. Chapter 6 strives to furnish an exemplary behavior to be emulated by others. Chapter 7 creates the immediate, but short-lived, impression that such an example was indeed pursued right after its debut. Chapter 7 also introduces the conventional and supernatural outcome of such altruism: punishment for the enemy of the Hebrews and the expectation of physical *resurrection for the individual.* Except the allusion in verse 37, "I, like my brothers, surrender body and soul for our paternal laws, invoking God speedily to be merciful to our nation," the brothers' purpose in dying did not go beyond personal salvation. At best, they wished to invoke God to be merciful, but did not make the connection between their ordeal and national redemption. Meanwhile, God was still unsatisfied with His nation.

Without diminishing the martyrological characteristics of the brothers' story, it should be noted that the unusual ordeal is theirs to suffer for their own sins. In contrast to some modern scholastic interpretations, the seven brothers do not symbolize the innocent sacrifices who bring salvation unto others. Missing in this personal exchange is the impersonal salvific motif that would have turned the brothers' deaths into vicarious or expiatory sacrifices. As their admission of guilt demonstrates, their actions were not taken on behalf of others nor did they efface the nation's sins. Had the demise of the seven sons been intended to satisfy God, the following chapter would not have insisted that the community had to make "common supplication," beseeching God to "be completely reconciled with His servants" (8:29). However, later martyrologists will see in this nebulous narrative a clear reflection of their own salvific desires.

At this point I will just mention that personal expectations as to the rewards of altruism resurface also in the stories of Razis and of Judas Maccabee's soldiers. The belligerent Razis, otherwise unknown,[76] expressed such wishes in his fight with the Syrian governor of Judaea, Nicanor. Preferring to perish by his own sword rather than by others', he invoked "the Lord of life and spirit to return them [i.e., his organs] to *him* (emphasis mine) again" (2 Macc. 14:46). Resurrection appears to be also Judas Maccabee's hope for his fallen soldiers. Here, resurrection was "a fine reward for those who have fallen into the last sleep in piety" (2 Macc. 12:43–45).[77]

Unlike these two examples, however, the heroes of chapters six and seven emerge as ordinary people, not zealous combatants. They express the thoughts, wishes, and normal feelings of ordinary human beings. Given the prominent role martyrdom has come to play in Judeo-Christian traditions, it is not difficult to view these Maccabean protagonists as authentic, rational individuals who inspired many others to emulate them to attain personal and national salvation. "Let this then be enough about eating of idolatrous sacrifices and inhuman tortures," the author abruptly concludes his story of the seven sons.

DANIEL, FIRST MACCABEES, AND SECOND MACCABEES

Putting these three sources together, the positive attitude toward voluntary death in 2 Maccabees stands out as unique descriptions. More specifically, Chapters 6 and 7 stand out not only in relation to Daniel and 1 Maccabees but also in relation to the rest of 2 Maccabees. In contrast to these two chapters, but in accordance with Daniel and 1 Maccabees, the rest of 2 Maccabees emphasizes the importance of resistance. God can be appeased only by the actions of the activists. Although adhering to passivism did not spare even the pious or cool God's wrath in either First or Second Maccabees, divine intervention miraculously saved the activists. Immediately after the story of the seven sons, the book asserts that God could "be completely reconciled with His servants," through militant victories and the socioreligious programs that the Hasmoneans set for the people. "God wills that He brings about victory for those who are worthy."[78] The distinctiveness of these two chapters in the Maccabean genre has raised legitimate questions as to their authorship and place in the book.[79] They must be investigated further.

To begin with, the ending of Chapter 6 and Chapter 7 as a whole interrupt the fluidity of the book's narrative. They artificially interrupt the description of Philip's activities (2 Macc. 6.11), which is resumed in 8.1 with "But Judas Maccabee and his followers." In addition, the style and structure of Chapters 6 and 7 differ from the rest and led, therefore, to opinions that the two chapters or parts of them were the addition of the epitomist, a redactor, or a "final author."[80]

The interference of these two chapters is not only technical or stylistic in nature but also thematic. Chapters 6 and 7 display a digression from the constant praising of the book's militant hero, Judas Maccabee, and his successful campaigns on behalf of Judaism.[81] Atypically, the chapters focus on the involvement in the revolt of the unknown individuals Eleazar and the anonymous and ordinary family. In contrast to the optimistic nature of the book, which culminates with the purification of the Temple and Nicanor's defeat, the fate of these unidentified commoners, described in a style dubbed *histoire pathétique*, ends in tragedy without a clear benefit for the living.[82]

The attempt to harmonize the stories by the following introduction: "Now, I appeal to those who happen to come upon this book, not to be cast down by these misfortunes, but rather to consider that these were retributions not intended to destroy, but rather only to discipline our people" (2 Macc. 6.12) can hardly settle the thematic differences between what follows in this chapter and the next one and in the rest of the book. If anything, this introduction highlights the artificial fusion and indicates a realization by the epitomist or a redactor that the upcoming stories of voluntary death contradict the book's nature and goals. This exceptional attention to "plebeian folks," in a book that is concerned with famous individuals and that ignores independent popular participation solely to highlight the successful contribution of Judas and his followers,[83] marks another aberrant development.[84]

Heroic passive behavior also contrasts with the activist conduct of the book's main protagonists. Jeremiah appeared in Judas Maccabee's dream to present to him God's golden sword, through which he "will prevail over your enemies" (2 Macc. 15.15–16).[85] As in 1 Maccabees and Daniel 11.32 ("but the people who know their God shall be strong and act"), neither the sword nor righteousness alone would deliver victory. In 2 Maccabees, triumph was to be achieved exclusively by the sword of the righteous whom Judas had urged "to fight nobly even unto death" (13.14). Like Daniel and his three companions, Judas put his faith in God to save him and his soldiers in dire straits (8.2–4, 18–19; 15.21–24).[86] This combination of pragmatism and persuasion is the book's secret weapon, immediately revealed after the story of the seven sons. In sharp contradistinction to the passive behavior of the protagonists in Chapter 7, Chapter 8 has Judas encouraging his troops to "struggle nobly" and rely on God, unlike the enemy, who "rely only on arms and daring deeds" (15.16–18).

In the same spirit, the epitomist describes in his prologue how Judas and his brothers received "heavenly apparitions that appeared to those who magnificently defended the honor of Judaism" and evicted the enemy (2.21). On a similar note he wrote his epilogue.[87] The praising of the heroes' inactive behaviors in Chapters 6 and 7 is particularly striking if the proposal that the author of 2 Maccabees may have belonged to the group of the Hasideans is to be accepted.[88]

Even the hideous suicide of the aforementioned Razis[89] commences with the symbolic display of his waving sword. Chapter 14.37–45 describes the final hour of this "honorable man," surrounded for unspecified reasons by five hundred soldiers and a raging fire, who would not quit life without putting up a fight to destroy the enemy with him.[90] His belligerent behavior is understandable given the implication in 14.38 of his participation in the revolt since its early days, when he was "accused of Judaism."[91] Atypically for a martyr, the "wanted" Razis strove, and was able to avoid execution for the crime, peculiar for the period, of being a Jew. Being accused of Judaism is no where else mentioned as a capital offense during the revolt.[92] No such accusation applied even to the seven sons and Eleazar, who were forced only to eat pork and acknowledge the king's authority.

Nicanor hunted Razis with the sole purpose of humiliating all the Jews who called him "father of the Jews" (14:37). As in Chapter 7, a very personal element characterizes the core of the conflict, from which the hero alone may benefit. Despite his theme that Nicanor desired to inflict "an injury to all the Jews" by killing Razis, the author does not state that his suicide, which should have prevented "injury to all the Jews," actually benefitted the nation.[93]

Razis is described as a desperate, doomed person whose death carried no communal benefits. Moreover, unlike Eleazar and the seven sons, Razis lacked the martyr's extravagance of publically making the ultimate declaration of choosing death over life, for Nicanor planned to make Razis' fate an example of things to come from the outset. In fact, he killed himself to avoid the very public, humiliating torturing that the eight heroes and those who were inspired by them in the future embraced enthusiastically.[94] A dialogue between these two individuals is thus absent in Razis' narrative of self-annihilation.

Razis' method of destruction and the lack of a dialogue are not the only features that separate his story from the famous eight examples of voluntary death. The description itself contains uncommon expressions and notions for the period. Razis' fate is narrated in a fashion typical of the Roman genera of self-destruction in the battlefield. His epithets – "devoted patriot" and "father of the Jews" – recall the Roman exemplary value of *devotio* to the *patria* and the leader. Versions of these Roman epithets for patriotism emerged in Greek from the first century c.e. onward. The honorific is authenticated in texts from the late Imperial and Byzantine periods.[95]

Not only words but also actions evoke Roman notions. Among the *causae moriendi*, self-killing after or during a lost battle counted as an obligatory Roman *virtus* that turned defeat into honor. As statistics show, self-liquidation by the sword became the Romans' (rather than the Greeks') method of choice during the first century c.e.[96] In fact, already in the fourth century b.c. Athens treated self-killers as criminals. According to Aeschines, therefore, "if some-body kills himself, we bury the hand separate from the body."[97] As we shall see, Jews still used similar burial practices for suicides by the first century c.e. The Roman setting in the Hellenistic book thus brings into question the dat-ing of Razis' story. The question of credibility is further accentuated by the absence of a parallel example in 1 or 2 Maccabees.

What this battle scene does have in common with Chapters 6.12–31 or 7 is its impetuous grammatical appearance ("...and returned to prayer..." 14.42) and incompatibility with the circumjacent story about Nicanor's attempt to destroy the Temple.[98] As Goldstein puts it "If our verses [37–46] had been omitted, no one would have missed them."[99] One may wonder, accordingly, whether the story with its relatively late terminology belongs in the Hellenistic text.[100]

Against this opinion, the notion of resurrection in the stories of Razis, Judas' treatment of his falling soldiers, and the story of the seven sons are often viewed as a thematic component of a more elaborated scheme in the book.[101] But this linkage subverts rather than supports the placement of resurrection in the original story. Judas' reaction to the fall of his soldiers who had carried pagan amulets (2 Maccabees 12.42–45) inadvertently invalidates rather than affirms the existence of resurrection in the period. Judas is said to have collected contributions from his solders to redeem the sins of his fallen comrades. "In doing this," the awkwardly constructed sentence explains, "he acted excellently and properly, showing that he took resurrection into consideration." Had the notion of resurrection been common during the crisis or during the writing of the episode, any believer would have found such a statement superfluous. The text here attempts to promote resurrection by praising Judas for considering it.[102]

In Katz's opinion, the narrative "represents an unsuccessful attempt at bringing together the old and the new" parts of the texts. This unsuccessful attempt has led Katz to believe that the hope of resurrection and its associa-tion with reward in verses 43–45 indicate an interpolation, which may have been Christian.[103] If this interpolation could show that already a leader of the caliber of Judas agreed to, or at least was ready to consider, resurrection, the reader may have been inclined to consider this innovative notion as well; not an easy task considering 1 Maccabees' total disregard of the concept.[104] In Daniel's case, the book speaks only of collective resurrection at the end of days. Daniel's resurrection may have symbolized the revival of his afflicted nation. Even if individual resurrection is to be considered, explicit references to martyrs per se are missing.[105] That the belief in physical resurrection for individuals was uncommon is testified to by Eleazar's story itself. It only distinguishes between body and soul without any reference to resurrection.

How can resurrection, then, be explained in 2 Maccabees 7? As in the aforementioned stories of Razis and Judas, the sons' references to resurrection are not free of questionable complications. The second son is the first to mention resurrection in the dialogue with Antiochus. 4 Maccabees, which was written sometime in the first century C.E. and, therefore, will be dealt with more elaborately in the following chapter, omits resurrection in his speech. It is highly unlikely that the concept of resurrection, extremely important both to rabbinic Judaism and Christianity, was removed from first-century 4 Maccabees.[106]

The same applies to the speech of the third and the fourth sons. They mention the notion of resurrection in 2 Maccabees but are silent in 4 Maccabees. Especially does the third son's speech (verse 11) raise some critical queries. They lead Katz to believe that "the original author did not provide the third son with his speech about resurrection." As he indicates, "there is nothing between verses 10 and 12" in the original text.[107] Buttressing such suspicion is Zeitlin's observation that the sages "never referred to bodily resurrection" before the destruction of the Second Temple.[108]

Sons six and seven, the latter also ignoring resurrection, speak of "our sins" (verses 18 and 32). In both cases, however, the placing of these phrases in the original is debatable.[109] It is the coupling of the sons' resurrection with sins that led to the impression of their deaths as expiatory sacrifices for the nation. The text, however, does not support such an interpretation.[110]

Another reason for questioning the authenticity of the stories of voluntary death and resurrection is the absence of the Temple. Eleazar's story is preceded by descriptions of the Temple's condition (6:2); Razis' appalling suicide is immediately followed by a report on Nicanor's defeat and the recently cleansed Temple (2 Macc. 15). After all, the recovery of the Temple by Judas constitutes the authors' raison d'etre.[111] Amazingly, the noncombatant heroes of Chapters 6 and 7, who show prodigious concern for Antiochus's attempt to pollute their bodies – the soul's Temple in Greek philosophy – by forcing them to eat unclean food sacrificed to idols, are silent about the burning issue of the period: the defilement of God's Temple. They speak of their death in no vicarious sense, ignoring any expiatory benefits, whereas nothing is said of the Temple sacrifices. Especially if the Temple sacrifices did cease or were altered during Antiochus's decrees, it would have been perfectly reasonable to present their deaths "in purity" (7:40), as atonements for the nation, or as suitable substitute for the interrupted Temple offerings.[112] Such associations are avoided, however. Neither atonement nor the Temple receives attention in the chapter.

In common with 2 Maccabees 6 and 7, the section about Judas' collecting alms for the sins of his fallen soldiers in hope of their resurrection (14.42–45) completely disregards the Temple. One would expect from Judas, whom the book presents as a champion dedicated to the maintenance of the Temple's integrity, to donate the collected money for "a sin offering" (12.43) to the recently purified Temple (10.1–9). Ironically, even the Seleucid authorities, including Antiochus IV (if 4.37 is to be believed),[113] respected the high priest and recognized the prominence of the Temple (3.2). Yet these pious and effusive Jews evaded the issue of the Sanctuary altogether.[114]

Instead, the protection of the Law serves as the main motivation for their voluntary deaths (6:23, 28; 7:1, 9, 10, 30, 37). Conversely, other sections present the Law as the means through which devoted Jews survived the persecution. As long as they obeyed the Law, they were "invulnerable" to death (2 Macc. 8:36). The function of the Law as protector of life is considerably antithetic to the conclusion of the stories of Eleazar and the seven sons.[115] As we shall see, however, dying for the Law became the aphorism of the *Tannaim* and *Amoraim*, after the destruction of the Temple.[116]

Other references also echo early rabbinic views. Eleazar's distinguishing between transgressions in private and in public has been mentioned. Such parallels are found in P. *Sanhedrin* 3:5, 21 b and B. *Sanhedrin* 74a, where one is not required to submit to death if asked to transgress in private.[117] Additional traces of *halakhic* views exist in the distinction between the prohibition against eating unclean food and the prohibition against eating food sacrificed to idols, which was a far graver sin than eating pork. More misgivings are added by the awkward way in which this issue of idolatry is introduced.[118] Terms and ideas reminiscent of the early rabbinic period are also found in the youngest son's proclamation that "after enduring brief trouble" he and his brothers would be under God's covenant (7.36).[119] One way of dealing with these rabbinic and *halakhic* innuendoes is by considering them products of coming generations, which were to influence the redaction of 2 Maccabees. As we shall see, even early rabbinic sources do not exhibit such Maccabean influence on them. This is especially true in regards to Eleazar, with whom they were completely unfamiliar.[120]

Increasing skepticism regarding the existence of meticulous halakha in the stories of Eleazar and the sons may be also attributed to the author's ignorance of *halakhic* rules, which he demonstrates throughout the rest of the book. In the cases of Nicanor's body hanging in Jerusalem and the Temple, the author's *halakhic* illiteracy amounts to absurdity (2 Macc. 15:30–35). As Bar-Kochva observed, the author had "very little knowledge of the halakha current in Eretz Israel, and especially little in matters of defilement and purity."[121] This is not an observation that redounds to the honor of an author who has made the purification of the Temple his primary concern (2 Macc. 15:18). Not only does the mixture of different-period *halakhot* appear dubious, then, but so, too, does their very inclusion by the *halakhically* illiterate author. On the one hand, then, we find in Chapters 6 and 7 illusions to halakha; on the other hand, we find in other chapters examples of *halakhic* illiteracy.

Attempts to settle this discrepancy attribute the final format of the book to a post-Temple Diaspora redactor. Indeed, the sudden and pointed shift from the Temple to the Law with *Tannaitic* and *Amoraic* characteristics raises the possibility that these stories of voluntary death were added in the first century, or even after the destruction of the Temple, by Diaspora Jews whose form of Judaism assigned more significance to the Law (6.18; 7.6, 30) than to the Temple worship.[122]

The placement of the two stories in first-century Diaspora finds support in the term *Hebraios* in 7.31, referring to Jews' religion, instead of the more common Hellenistic term *Ioudaios*, which points to a geographical region.[123] Although Zeitlin's linguistic observation is not without flaws,[124] his overall distinction between attitudes of Diaspora (Hebrew) and Judaean Jews, more specifically first-century C.E. Antiochian and Judaean Jews, seems to correspond with Chapter 7's characteristics and goals and better equips us to solve the thematic and linguistic difficulties these texts create.[125] In this context, therefore, it is not surprising that the first time the terms *Ioudaios* and *Ioudaismos* carry the more global meaning "Jew" occurs in 2 Maccabees 6:6. Here the term surfaces in the theological and universal sense of "Jew" rather than simply indicating the people of Judaea or Judaeans living in the Diaspora.[126] Such references to Jews as *Ioudaios* became increasingly common after the destruction of the Temple and their gradual dispersion in the ancient world.[127]

The context in which 2 Maccabees 6:6 uses the term *Ioudiaioi* is also significant. The prohibition to "confess that one was a Jew" clearly goes beyond Antiochus's decrees. If the verse is understood literally, such an unprecedented decree has a parallel only in the Roman-Christian confrontation of the first centuries but not regarding Jews. The prohibition against confessing one's religion is reminiscent of the Roman decree against Christianity alone, which produced Christians bearing witness (*martyrein*) for the nascent faith and the renowned confession "*Christianus sum.*"[128] This prohibition can be taken literally only in the context of the conflict between the Roman Empire and emerging Christianity.

This verse, which brings to mind scenes typical of the early Martyrs' Acts, is not the only one to echo notions prevalent in Christian society. Traces of Christianity may be found in the story of the mother and her seven sons as well. What follows the voluntary deaths of the six sons and the hope of resurrection is reminiscent of the Christian belief in the immaculate conception. Although not required to choose between life and death, the mother exhibits exceptional characteristics. Like Mary, she is "worthy of blessed memory" for watching her sons' execution and for being able to bear the pain of losing them. Their resurrection is her consolation. But the manner in which they enter this world is no less impressive than their departure. Her speech, as well as the absence of a father figure throughout the story, attests to the sons' special nature:

> How you ever appeared in my womb, I do not know. It was not I who graced you with breath and life, nor was it I who arranged in order within each of you the combination of elements. It was the creator of the world, who formed the generation of man . . . , and He will give life back to you in mercy, even as you now take no thought for yourselves on account of His laws. (2 Macc. 7.22–23)

These divine attributions go beyond the obvious manifestation of God's power as the only sources for biological life, which otherwise would need no mention by or for the faithful. "How you ever appeared in my womb, I do not know," can be related to her statement in v. 28, which alludes to creation *ex nihilo*. These two complementing statements together with the absence of a father figure in the drama strongly echo Christian doctrinal foundations (Luke 1). While creation *ex nihilo* lacks the support of Greek philosophy, the allusion to a fatherless conception is wholly anomalous for the Jewish believer. It would have been premature for a Jewish writer in the Hellenistic period to insinuate a miraculous creation *ex nihilo* of embryos.[129] With this insinuation the notion of physical and personal resurrection in this world has come full circle. Together they equally represent two exceptional concepts for the Jewish Hellenistic world.[130]

The uncommon stories of Eleazar and the mother with her seven sons, therefore, exhibit a fusion of elements taken from different cultures. Obviously, the Hellenistic culture dominates the scene. Yet allusions to the rabbinic, pagan-Roman, and early Christian cultures can be traced throughout these stories. In contrast to Daniel, 1 Maccabees, and the rest of 2 Maccabees, these two stories depart from these books' belligerent spirit of defiance. Judging by the sources at hand, Eleazar and the seven sons adopted a rare and innovative course of action that had no secular or religious advantages in the view of

Hellenistic Jews. As the permanent focus on fighting and the absence of a fixed martyrological vocabulary, concept, or genre in the analyzed sources reveal, martyrdom, as an ideology or even as an ideal, was not intended during the revolt. Rather than establishing themselves in the Hellenistic period, the infrequent stories of voluntary death and its rewards take us into the orbit of the Roman-Christian world, where dying with honor often became the ultimate glory.

2

∾

Between God and Caesar

If indeed the Maccabean martyrs deserve their present character as heroes of Hellenistic Judaism, Eleazar should, by the early Roman period, have become the "father of all martyrs" and each of the seven sons the "poster child" of martyrdom. As independent Judaea slipped under strict Roman control, new conditions ripened for Eleazar's "noble example" to crop up.

Maccabean independence was crumbling after Pompey's conquest in 63 B.C. Jewish society again found itself divided, with groups of rebels fighting a foreign authority supported by fellow Jews and a Jewish monarch. Pro-Roman culture was believed to have replaced its Hellenistic forebears, and opposition forces ventured to follow in the footsteps of the Maccabean rebels to restore the glory of the past.[1]

Reality, of course, was more complicated. Rebels constituted diverse groups, whereas levels of support for and collaboration with the Romans varied. And then, as in the Hasmonean period, there were the innocents caught between. If under these conditions the vivid memories of the past could bring to life the Maccabean militant, as the commemoration of the great Maccabean victory against the Syrian general Nicanor on 13 Adar demonstrates, it should have also revived the Maccabean martyr.[2] And because the roster of Hellenistic martyrs known by name or fame was limited to eight individuals, Eleazar the scribe and the mother's seven sons should have been the natural choice for inspiring further exemplars or, at least, imaginative writers. Despite the inviting conditions, they did not.

Conditions alone do not always suffice for martyr heroes à la 2 Maccabees to be adopted and become reality. But when proper conditions and prolific stories about voluntary death come together in the Jewish sources of the period, the absence of the Maccabean eight is most enigmatic. This is especially true if indeed important first-century authors such as Philo of Alexandria

34

and Josephus Flavius depended on 2 Maccabees[3] or even if they just became familiar with the book's exceptional heroes through folktales.[4]

H. K. Bond has argued for the existence of literary parallels between Philo and the Maccabean books. She mentions the common style of "pathetic history" and the "verbal similarities" between Philo and the Maccabees. These parallels aroused her speculation that Antichos "served as a model for Philo's description of Gaius."[5] Van Henten finds parallels between the description of the mother in 2 Maccabees 7:21 and Philo's similar phrasing in describing Julia Augusta's character in *The Embassy to Gaius* 320.[6] For Moffatt, the evidence for the use of 2 Maccabees by Philo is clearer than for "Josephus' acquaintance with it."[7] If such parallels exist, why would Philo, and then Josephus, who had mentioned him, borrow style and language from 2 Maccabees without referring to the martyrs? Could it be that Philo and Josephus inspired the language of 2 Maccabees 7? The absence of the Maccabean martyrs in Philo's stories of martyrological nature further refutes the assumption that 2 Maccabees inspired Philo and Josephus. This assumption thus needs to be turned on its head. That is, the two authors' descriptions of conflicts with Rome contributed to the inspiration of the martyrological tales in 2 Maccabees.

This chapter will continue to show why martyrdom is not likely to be an early Hellenistic Jewish product. Instead, I am arguing here that the Roman noble death ideal, which Roman imperialism introduced to the region, was internalized and adorned in biblical grabs by Philo and Josephus. In this manner the two authors championed a Jewish "tradition" of voluntary death. My goal in this chapter is to show that the evolution of Jewish martyrdom and martyrology started as a process of inward acculturation during the Roman occupation of the Jewish kingdom. Philo and Josephus made use of the Roman noble death concept not to acknowledge external influence but to present voluntary death as an original Jewish ideal. Through voluntary death, Philo and Josephus described mostly nonviolent Jews as altruists superior to the belligerent Romans.

PHILO OF ALEXANDRIA

Dying willingly for the Laws featured several times in Philo's scripts. Yet the Maccabean martyrs are nowhere to be found in his extensive work. This is indeed a surprising ignorance on the part of a prolific writer and exegetic, designated by modern historians as the representative of "Hellenistic Judaism."[8] Cyrene in North Africa was Jason's writing place, and the assumption that ascribes the epitomized 2 Maccabees to an Alexandrian Jew only accentuates the dilemma. In fact it was the other Alexandrian, Clement, who first alluded to the Maccabean heroes at the end of the second century c.e.[9]

Philo emerged as an advocate of passive death in the name of religion. He claimed that "Jews would willingly endure to die not once but a thousand times, if it were possible, rather than allow any of the prohibited actions to be committed." Indeed "all men guard their own customs, but this is especially true of the Jewish nation" (*Embassy* 209–210). Considering the conditions under which he lived and worked, we would not expect him thus to muff the opportunity of mentioning the Maccabean heroes. They could have benefitted his descriptions of events whose magnitude and scope pall in comparison to the conditions described in the Maccabean books.[10]

During Emperor Gaius Caligula's regime, Philo and his community experienced first-hand the unprovoked struggle of a peace-loving community against the irrational tyrant Avillius Flaccus.[11] Against Roman policy, Flaccus "ordered the crucifixion of the living [Jews] . . . after maltreating them with the lash in the middle of the theater and torturing them with fire and sword. The first spectacle lasting from dawn till the third or fourth hour consisted of Jews being scourged, hung up, bound to the wheel, brutally mauled and haled for their death march" (*Flaccus* 84–85).[12] Captured women were forced to prove their non-Jewish identity by eating pork publically. Many Jewish women "in fear of punishment tasted the meat . . . and did not have to bear any further dire maltreatment." But the more resolute among them "were delivered to the tormentors to suffer desperate ill-usage, which is the clearest proof of their entire innocence of wrongdoing" (*Flaccus* 96).

Spectacles of torture by fire, the sword, flogging, or tests of their will to refrain from eating pork recall the stories of Eleazar and the seven sons. But Flaccus exceeded even Antichos, who never forced women to eat forbidden food (in 2 Maccabees women were executed for circumcising their male babies). Nor did Antichos crucify his subjects. Philo's passage may also suggest why the eating of pork (and not meat sacrificed to other gods) became so crucial to martyrological narratives. Flaccus attempted to isolate the Jews of Alexandria, whom he could not distinguish from the rest by appearance alone. Circumcision made the identification of males an easy task. Not so with women. Thus eating pork was introduced as, perhaps, the earliest method of "selection," although not always effectively. Many women considered their lives more important than the Law.

As in 2 Maccabees, the tyrant met a violent end. Divine justice brought the execution of the Roman prefect Flaccus for unlawfully putting to death numerous Alexandrian Jews (*Flaccus* 189–191). In an ironic twist of fate, "the will of justice" was performed through the services of the greater tyrant Caligula, who later was to be assassinated himself.

Caligula's assassination could not have come in a better time for his Jewish subjects. Apion of Alexandria accused the Jews of being unfaithful to the emperor. Their rejection of Caligula's divinity was used to prove his point. Outraged by Apion's accusation, Caligula decreed the worship of the emperor as a unifying religion. His decree was without precedent. Although Augustus and Tiberius required the Jews to sacrifice to God for the benefit of the emperor, Caligula demanded the worshiping of the emperor in the Jewish Temple. He dispatched Petronius to Judaea to install Caligula's image in the Temple. Petronius was to execute his orders or those who would object to them.

Philo departed for Rome to persuade the emperor to remove his unjust decrees. Well aware of Caligula's habit of crushing "irresistibly not only those who did not carry out his command but also those who did not do so at once" (*Embassy* 209), he and his delegation expected to pay with their lives for their defiance. "And even if we were allowed to approach him unmolested, what have we to expect but death against which there is no appeal? Well, so be it, we will die and be no more, for the truly glorious of death, met in defense of the laws, might be called life" (*Embassy* 192). These feelings resurfaced while in prison. "We all the time expected nothing else but death" (*Embassy* 366). Like Daniel and his friends, they survived the ordeal because God spared them "not because we clung to life and cringed from death, which we would gladly have chosen" (*Embassy* 369). As he stated elsewhere, no tyrant will deter him, no matter the reason. "I will fear none of the tyrant's menaces, even though he threaten me with death, for death is less evil than dissimulation" (*On Joseph* 68–69). The preservation of Jewish Law justifies not only a glorious death, but also the Roman idea of liberty. "The wise would most gladly choose death rather than slavery" (*Every Good Man Is Free* 135). "The wise," the designated term for philosophers, makes the statement both a personal and a generic reflection.[13]

Meanwhile, in Judea, others are said to have adopted the method of the "wise." Philo makes death the conscious choice of the Jews dealing with Petronius. Their lengthy proclamation is worth quoting in full. It emphasizes the peaceful nature of the people and their will to die in "strange manners" for their laws.

We are unarmed as you see, though some accuse us of having come as enemies in war, yet the parts which nature has assigned to each of us for defense, our hands, we have put away where they can do nothing and present our bodies as an easy target for the missiles of those who wish to kill us. We have brought our wives, our children and our families to you, leaving none at home, and have prostrated ourselves before Gaius in doing so to you, that you and he may either save us all from ruin or send us to perish in utter destruction. O Petronius, both by our nature and our principles we are peaceable, and diligence which parents devote to rearing their children has trained us in this practice from the very first. . . .

After extending a peaceful hand, they uttered how far they were willing to go for their Law.

But if we cannot persuade you [not to install the statue in the Temple], we give up ourselves for destruction that we may not live to see a calamity worse than death. We hear that forces of cavalry and infantry have been prepared against us if we oppose the installation. No one is so mad as to oppose a master when he is a slave. We gladly put our throats at your disposal. Let them slaughter, butcher, carve our flesh without a blow struck or blood drawn by us and do all the deeds that conquerors commit. But what need of an army! ourselves will conduct the sacrifices, priests of a noble order, wives will be brought to the altar by wife-slayers, brothers and sisters by fratricides, boys and girls in the innocence of their years by child-murderers. . . . Then standing in the midst of our kinsfolk after bathing ourselves in their blood, the right bathing for those who would go to Hades clean, we will mingle our blood with theirs by the crowning slaughter of ourselves. When we are dead let the prescript be carried out, not God Himself could blame us who had twofold motive, respectful fear of the emperor and loyalty to the consecrated laws. And this aim will be accomplished if we take our departure in contempt of the life which is no life. (*Embassy* 229–236)

Not only did ordinary Jews express their willingness to die for their religion by taking their own lives, they also uttered their determination to slay their own children and wives, the latter offering assistance in the act. A clear consensus is said to have driven the participants toward abandoning life by taking matter into their own hands. What remains unclear is how the Alexandrian author could provide such a vivid description of the dialogue in Judea from his Roman jail.

Appropriately for that written by a philosopher, symbolism dramatizes the text. The military theater is recast into the serene scene of the Temple. Philo credited his heroes with having played the roles both of sacrificers and of sacrificed. What could have better symbolized a pure sacrifice than that of innocent children? But being sacrificed by Rome's might presented the least difficult moralistic and religious dilemma. As controversial as submission to death may be, it was one thing to allow Roman soldiers to kill Jews for the Law; suicide and homicide evoked entirely different issues.

Symbolism transmuted these potential acts into sacrificial rituals. These Jews thus were transformed into "priests of a noble order," sacrificing themselves and their families en masse on imaginary altars. Because only males served as priests, men expressed their willingness to conduct the ritual "of sacrifice," and their wives would provide assistance before being sacrificed themselves. The infusion of the ordeal with divine ritual doubled the holiness of the actors. Symbolism completed their transmutation not only into pure sacrifices but also into high priests. In this light, their intentions were not seen as illegitimate acts of self-destruction and murder. As "priests" engaged in the "Temple cult," their intention to sacrifice, whether passive or even active, was unquestionable and legitimized in the actors' imaginary world and Philo's literary work. Although Scripture did not address such alternatives, examples could be found in Roman historical narratives about loyal wives joining their husbands in death.[14]

Meanwhile at Rome, the Judean king Agrippa labored to change Caligula's desire to see his image installed in the Temple. He reminded the emperor of Pilate's incident in which his ancestors determined to protect their holy Sanctuary at the cost of their lives.[15] The Temple priests assume the main responsibility for the protection of their place of worship, Agrippa explained. As holy men of peace only one course of action remained available to them. "How many deaths think you would those who have been trained to holiness in these matters willingly endure if they should see the statue imported thither?" Agrippa offered his own answer: "I believe that they would slaughter their whole families, women and children alike, and finally immolate themselves upon the corpses of their kin" (*Embassy* 308).

Agrippa reserves the liberty to "sacrifice" and to "self-sacrifice" to the priests. As for a layperson like himself, he could still entreat the emperor to apply *Roman* solutions and "bid me take myself out of the way forthwith" (*Embassy* 329). Caligula, it is reported, was so impressed by the foreigner's Roman "characteristics of the truly free and noble" (*Embassy* 332) that he reversed his decree. Shortly thereafter, Caligula's reinstatement of his orders to Petronius revived the Jews' promise to shed their own blood. Fortunately for these Jews, and perhaps for the entire empire, Caligula was assassinated. His decrees were never carried out, leaving the protestors' resolution untested.

Blood illustrates another symbolic association of self-inflicted death with Jewish rituals. Through blood, these Jews believed, they would be purified as if they were in the ritual bath in the *mikve*.[16] As the text indicates: "Then standing in the midst of our kinsfolk after bathing ourselves in their blood, the right bathing for those who would go to Hades clean, we will mingle our blood with theirs by the crowning slaughter of ourselves" (*Embassy* 235).

Blood substitutes for the purification ritual, which is a necessary preparatory practice before burial. *In theory*, "sacrifice" turned from being an individual or a priestly act into a popular choice.

Although Philo's imaginary identification of human victims with Temple priests appears logical, it was unprecedented. Given the Jewish fear of blood, his positive and gruesome use of human blood to avert a calamity consti-tuted a daring motif. What appears to have influenced Philo's analogy are the mores and events he witnessed outside Jewish circles. Right after his abhorred tyrant Caligula came to power, the young emperor fell critically ill. As he was considered Rome's best hope, prominent Romans publically offered to sacrifice themselves in the ritualistic games of the gladiators. By spilling their own blood for their "savior" (*Embassy* 22), they wished to reverse Rome's misfortune and secure a peaceful future. Luckily for the benevolent volun-teers, the emperor recovered from his nervous breakdown even without the performance of human sacrifices. But the emperor's good fortune became the altruists' misfortune. Fearing to challenge his good fate, the beloved emperor insisted that they spill their blood for him anyway.[17]

The Embassy to Gaius leaves no doubt as to Philo's familiarity with Caligula's ascent to power and imperial affairs.[18] Caligula's debut made headlines throu-ghout the empire (*Embassy* 15–16). During Caligula's "severe sickness," Philo reveals, Jews showed their concern by sacrificing and pouring the blood of animals on the altar for the emperor's recovery (*Embassy* 356). The focus of the news, no doubt, was the fear of losing the promising young "savior," for the spilling of human blood as an act of *devotion* for the godly emperor was not without precedent.[19] Offers to sacrifice lives for the recovery of an emperor had already been made on Augustus's behalf.[20]

Although written shortly after Philo's time, Tacitus's description of Thrasea's imposed suicide well demonstrates the important role human sac-rifice played in Roman society. Obeying Emperor Nero, he cut his arteries and sprinkled his blood on the ground. With it he made a "libation," asking Heaven to avert the omen.[21] Just as Roman loyalists were ready to shed their blood to ensure the recovery of their godly emperor, so are Philo's Jews said to have been ready to spill theirs for God and His Law. So presented, it was holy blood that was about to be shed, not the *vilis sanguis* (cheap blood) that many were forced to spill to entertain Romans.[22]

Yet, Philo is well aware of his inability to support the unprecedented ritu-alistic nature of his depiction by either specific exemplars or God's Law. The address to Petronius echoes such qualms, "when we are dead let the prescript be carried out; not God himself could blame us who had twofold motive, respectful fear of the emperor and loyalty to the consecrated laws" (*Embassy* 236).[23] With the adoption of Roman costumes came difficult ambiguity. Under the perplexing circumstances, the Jews found themselves between hammer and anvil. "The fear of the emperor and the loyalty to the consecrated laws" made voluntary death an inevitable solution. The dilemma here, however, is not just how to please God and Caesar without insulting the other. These Jews are torn between two powers: a Roman culture that advances self-destruction as the only honorable solution in dire straits, and a Jewish religion that warned its adherents against committing transgressions rather than instructing them how to behave when forced to violate the Law. Symbolism in the text implies that by the first century, the pagan popular concept of self-sacrifice had made its way into Jewish thinking, although not without difficulties.

JOSEPHUS FLAVIUS

It has been suggested that Josephus failed to mention the Maccabean martyrs because he knew only 1 Maccabees. But keeping in mind their early alleged celebrity status, Josephus's unfamiliarity with the Second Book hardly serves as a satisfying solution. Any insistence on Josephus's reliance on 1 Maccabees alone necessitates the conclusion that during his lifetime the reputation of the exalted eight remained within the framework of a forgotten book. Neither solution contributes to the present eminence of the heroes.

Whatever the connection, there can be little doubt about Josephus Flavius's familiarity with Maccabean history and his veneration of the sacrificing of human beings for a cause. An ardent supporter of the "noble" act of voluntary death – although its stronger opponent when his own life hung in the balance[24] – Josephus labored to present voluntary death as an ancient component of Judaism. "It is an instinct with every Jew, from the day of his birth, to regard them [the scriptures] as the decrees of God, to abide by them, and, if need be, cheerfully to die for them. Time and again ere now the sight has been witnessed of prisoners enduring torture and death in every form in the theaters rather than utter a single word against the laws and the allied documents" (*Against Apion* 1:42–43).[25]

The readiness to die gladly for God distinguishes Jews from others. "What Greek would endure as much for the same cause?" None, he replies (*Against Apion* 1:43–44). Not even Roman bravery on the battlefield could equal Jewish traditional heroism.[26] Josephus distinguishes between two types of demise. His type of heroism does not refer "to that easiest of deaths, on the battlefield, but death accompanied by physical torture, which is thought to be the hardest of all" (*Against Apion* 2.232). As a denouncer of the Jewish militant option, the former general could still sympathize with those who restored Jewish dignity through a very different pattern of expiration.

Already the Persian kings and satraps had failed to convince Jews to alter their religious thinking. Claiming to quote Hecataeus, Josephus relates that Jews always elected to face "tortures and death in its most terrible form rather than repudiate the faith of their forefathers" (*Against Apion* 1:191). To be sure, Josephus's description of Persian persecutions lacks the backing of historical facts.[27] Thus it has been maintained that his depiction reflects the religious persecutions of Antiochus IV.[28] "These misfortunes," he writes elsewhere in connection to Daniel's prophecy, "our nation did in fact come to experience under Antiochus Epiphanes" (*Jewish Antiquities* 10:276).[29]

Josephus's narration of persecution under Persian rulers reveals, then, an important characteristic of his history: he describes the past through present lenses and vice versa. In his mind, the struggle with Rome and the desolation of the Temple merely reveal a repetition of Jewish history under Seleucid rule. Read in this light, we may better understand his hyperbolic statement about those "of noble soul" who disregarded Antiochus. "They were whipped, their bodies were mutilated, and while still alive and breathing, they were *crucified* [emphasis mine], while their wives and sons whom they had circumcised in despite the king's wishes were strangled, the children being made to hang from the neck of their *crucified* [emphasis mine] parents" (*Jewish Antiquities* 12:256).

As the stress on crucifixion of Jews indicates, Josephus did not hesitate to introject contemporaneous Roman practices in his presentation of Hellenistic history.[30] His introjections stem from his frequent desire to grant voluntary death a prominent role in Jewish history. One must therefore approach with extreme caution not only his reports on contemporaneous martyrs but also on those of the past. It is not difficult to understand why Antiochus's reputation may have caused Josephus's fertile imagination to hold the monarch responsible for "crucifying" peaceful observant Jews. But how would the execution of innocent and peaceful Jews benefit the Romans, who did not force a policy of religious decrees or assimilation, at least not in Josephus's lifetime?

Aware of his aggrandizement, Josephus explains why the Romans executed nonviolent Jews in a period that did not witness religious persecution. It was not anti-Jewish feelings that motivated the Romans to execute Jews; rather, it was the Romans' curiosity to see Jews volunteering for death in most unusual ways that generated the executions. "To such a death" Jews are exposed by some conquerors "not from hatred of those at their mercy, but from a curiosity to witness the astonishing spectacle. . . . There should be nothing astonishing in our facing death on behalf of our laws with a courage which no other nation can equal" (*Against Apion* 2.233–234). What is astonishing is that the enthusiastic historian of voluntary death remains completely silent about the most celebrated martyrs of 2 Maccabees 6 and 7. What could have been more convincing spectacles than the dramatic dialogues and executions of these chapters' heroes? What would better buttress Josephus's claim that there was an extended tradition of Jews willingly submitting to death for their Law? Would not his assertion, "Even our women-folk and dependants would tell you that piety must be the motive of all our occupations in life" (*Against Apion* 2:181), serve as a perfect introduction to the ordeal of the anonymous mother?

As we are about to see, parallels of 2 Maccabees are traceable in Josephus's works, although Josephus has omitted the only accepted motivation for dying in the Maccabean literature. 1 Maccabees consistently gives importance to the issue of eating unclean food rather than to the controversial dilemma of Sabbath warfare.[31] The fear of eating unclean meat serves as the martyrs' prime motivation in 2 Maccabees. It appears more likely, therefore, that Josephus did not mention the Maccabean martyrs for this simple reason: they were yet to enter either the books of history or oral lore.[32]

The scholarly focus on the Maccabees as the founders of religious martyrdom has neglected Josephus's contribution to misconception – one that has survived to this day. Josephus was not familiar with the Maccabean martyrs, because their stories and fame probably did not exist during his lifetime. The absence of the stories and existence of parallels suggest that Josephus himself may very well have laid down the stories' early foundation.

Several Maccabean literary motifs found in Eleazar's story seem to emerge first in his *Jewish Antiquity* (ca. 93–94 C.E.) and later in *Against Apion* (after 94). In the incident of the golden eagle at the Temple's gate[33] "two doctors with a reputation as profound experts in the laws of their country" take central stage (*Jewish Antiquities* 1:648). There Maccabean names, perhaps not accidentally, were Judas, son of Sepphoraeus, and Matthias, son of Margalus. Like Eleazar, these well-known leaders "enjoyed the highest esteem of the whole nation." There "lectures on the laws were attended by a large *youthful audience....*" Because "it was a noble deed to die for the law of one's country," they "exhorted their disciples" to bring down the golden image despite probable capital punishment. In a speech reminiscent of Eleazar's, the two leaders promised immortality of their souls to the deceased (rather than resurrection).[34]

As in 2 Maccabees, Josephus presents a dialogue of a king, this time Herod, with about forty young men. Like Antiochus, Herod opens the dialogue with probing questions whose answers reveal a familiar motivation behind the youths' disobedience. They would die for the laws of their fathers and overcome fear by the expectation of enjoying "greater felicity" after death (*Jewish War* 1:649).[35] The two leaders and their disciples were burnt alive, whereas others were handed over to Herod's executioners (*Jewish War* 1:655).

Corollaries with Eleazar are evident also in the story of Ezechais. Paraphrasing Hecataeus, *Against Apion* introduces the priest Ezechias in language reminiscent of Eleazar's ordeal in 2 and 4 Maccabees.[36] Among the Jews who migrated with Ptolemy to Alexandria "was Ezechias, a chief priest of the Jews, a man of about sixty-six years of age, highly esteemed by his countrymen, intellectual, and moreover an able speaker and unsurpassed as a man of business." Ezechias's occupation and the references to his age, honor, intellect, and oratorical talent recall the Maccabean introduction of Eleazar. More significant is the telling of the story in relation to Alexandria – the place of serious anti-Jewish violence – and the comment immediately following, which is attributed to Hecataeus. He "mentions our regard for our laws, and how we deliberately choose and hold it a point of honour to endure anything rather than transgress them" (*Against Apion* 1:190). Hecataeus's next paragraph is more explicit and worth repeating. Jews would face "tortures and death in its most terrible form rather than repudiate the faith of their forefathers" (*Against Apion* 1:191). Eleazar would have fit nicely alongside these people.

Josephus's narrative of an anonymous old man who had slain his seven sons recalls the Maccabean story of the mother with her seven sons. According to Josephus, the deaths of the anonymous man and his family took place in the midst of political strife between Herod and his Jewish opponent Antigonus (37–40 B.C.E.). Among the many killed by Herod in the caves of Arbel,

There was one old man shut up within one of the caves with his seven children and his wife: and when they begged him to let them slip through to the enemy, he stood at the entrance and cut down each of his sons as he came out, and afterwards his wife, and hurling their dead bodies over the precipice, threw himself down upon them, thus submitting to death rather than to slavery. (*Jewish Antiquities* 14:429–430; *Jewish War* 1:312–313)

Various Maccabean motifs come to mind. The description of the family as non-combatant refugees rather than active rebels is reminiscent of the thousand refugees in the wilderness when caught in a cave on the Sabbath. In his dialogue with the man, King Herod could easily be associated with both the wicked foreign Hellenistic king[37] and the surrounding assimilated foe of the thousand refugees, now represented by a single man. Like the royal complete amnesty and guarantee of freedom of worship to the rebels who agreed to return to their homes,[38] King Herod's offer to the rebels at Arbel was similar. The nameless father and the number of male children remind us of the anonymous mother and her seven sons. Finally, the man's advanced age may lead to a frail connection with the elderly Eleazar. The association ends here.

Despite his old age and the presence of the family, it is not clear that the man is a refugee; the Sabbath is clearly not an issue. Moreover, Herod is said to have offered the family immunity upon surrender. Perhaps to emphasize the man's will to die, it is told that the majority of the rebels "despaired of their lives . . . surrendered and made their submission." Except for this man's cave, "by such methods all the caves were finally taken." In a moment of mercy, Herod gave him a second chance. "He stretched out his right hand and promised him full immunity." He still declined (*Jewish Antiquities* 18:430).

The presence of a wife and the father's killing, actually murdering, his sons and their mother against their will provide strong contrast. The only voluntary death was his own. His motivation also differed. Rather than dying for the Law or to prevent a transgression, he submitted to death to avoid slavery.[39] The motivation itself is perplexing. Once offered immunity, slavery became a nonissue. Typically, however, contradictions and historical inaccuracies do not disturb Josephus.

History provides an inspiration for Josephus's characters. He enlists Maccabean motifs to support his fascination with voluntary death, yet continues to desert the Maccabean martyrs. Massacres of Jewish residents in Caesarea are rationalized by Maccabean legends of uncompromising Sabbath observance. "The massacre took place on the Sabbath, a day on which from religious scruples Jews abstain even from the most innocent acts. The same day and at the same hour, as it were by the hand of Providence, the inhabitants of Caesarea massacred the Jews who resided in their city; within one hour more than twenty thousand were slaughtered, and Caesarea was completely emptied of Jews" (*Jewish War* 2:457).

Josephus leaves for the reader to make the logical conclusion that Caesarean Jews refused to fight on the Sabbath,[40] although no indication is given that these Jews actually perished because of this practice. The Sabbath tradition cushions the defeat and humiliating expulsion from their city. It is inconceivable that so many Jews unanimously followed the example of the Hellenistic refugees. Equally ridiculous is the implication that Caesarean Jews did not fight on Sabbath days in a period that constantly witnessed wars and that could turn to Mattathias's "Sabbath ordinance" for support.[41] Naturally, these are points that would not serve the apologetic Josephus in this case. They did in the next.

On the recommendation of Hyrcanus II and Aristobulus, Pompey is said to have entered the Temple on the Sabbath to settle their dispute over the succession of the Hasmonean queen Salome Alexandra.[42] Refusing to accept

Pompey's decision in Hyrcanus's favor, Aristobulus and his army fortified themselves in the Temple. With his non-Jewish readers in mind and antirebel feelings in heart, Josephus depicts Pompey as a considerate general who hoped to avoid bloodshed by moving against Aristobulus on the sacred day.[43] Here, the blame for war on this holy day in the holiest place lies squarely on the Jews.[44]

According to Josephus, some rebels refused to flee. Oblivious to events around them,

many of the priests, seeing the enemy advancing sword in hand, calmly continued their sacred ministrations, and were butchered in the act of pouring libations and burning incense: putting the worship of the Deity above their own preservation. Most of the slain perished by the hands of their countrymen of the opposite faction; countless numbers flung themselves over the precipices; some, driven mad by their hopeless plight, set fire to the buildings around the wall and were consumed in the flames. (*Jewish War* 1:150–151)

It would be difficult to draw solid conclusions from this vague description. What is evident are Josephus's attempts to clear his Roman patrons of any wrongdoing[45] while reminding the reader of the brutality of the rebels. It was the latter who would not spare the priests even when in performance of their sacred duty. "Most of the slain perished by the hands of their countrymen of the opposite faction," the account emphasizes. Attention must be paid also to the manner in which the other casualties perished. To parry the enemy's final assault, "Countless numbers flung themselves over the precipices." In preparation for his apologetic account on the traumatic burning of the Temple, he describes the opposition as madmen who did not hesitate to set the Temple on fire to consume their own lives.

Blending blame with blarney, his account of self-killing – which Josephus views as abnormal and abominable when self-serving – holds also benefits. It expresses the astonishing uniqueness of his people, even by the standards of the Roman Stoic world. When referring to the same event in *Antiquities*, Josephus insists

that this is not merely a story to set forth the praises of a fictitious piety, but the truth, is attested by all those who have narrated the exploits of Pompey, among them Strabo and Nicolas and, in addition, Titus Livius, the author of a History of Rome. (*Jewish Antiquities* 14:68)

The fact that Josephus had to persuade his readers that the story was genuine and that Roman historians had taken notice of it, further indicates that martyrological behavior is an unusual Jewish behavior in the second half of the first century C.E. The text also demonstrates its apologetic as well as polemic nature. These Roman foreign historians were mentioned for a reason. From Strabo and Nicolas, Josephus learned about the destructive behavior of the Gazans and Gadarenes.[46]

In the Jewish attack against the Gazans,

> some of them, being left alone, set fire to their houses in order that nothing might remain in them for the enemy to take out as spoil. Others with their own hands made away with their children and wives, this being the means by which they were compelled to deliver them from slavery to their foe. (*Jewish Antiquities* 13:363)

Similarly, when the Gadarenes failed to win Caesar's support in their rebellion against Herod, "they were afraid of being maltreated, and so some of them cut their throats during the night, while others threw themselves down from high places or willfully destroyed themselves by jumping into the river" (*Jewish Antiquities* 15:358–359).[47] These two depictions contradict Josephus's praises of Jewish altruism, which "no other nation can equal" (*Against Apion* 2:232–235). He views the Gadarenes' self-killing "as (self-) condemnation of their rashness and guilt." Escape from slavery provided Josephus with another just cause in his new representation of Jewish tradition.

Religious motifs Josephus could find in Livius (23 B.C.E.–17 C.E.) and Strabo. Livius described with great admiration the suicides of Lucretia and of the famous Chartagen Hannibal, who preferred poison over a humiliating capture.[48] He also presented the sacrifice of Publius Decius Mus in battle against the Latin League as a sacred act of *devotio* with absolving (*piaculum*) powers. Decius satisfied the gods and the League was defeated.[49] Livius similarly described how Marcus Curtius appeased the gods by plunging into a rift that an earthquake had left open in the Forum. Thereafter, both the human and the Forum's faults disappeared.[50]

Strabo wrote (*Kalanos* 15.1.65) about the Indian gymnosophist who chose to exit life by entering fire.[51] As we shall see, Josephus included the "foreign Indian" concept of suicide in the speech of Eleazar, the leader of the rebels at Masada. Jews, Josephus tells his Roman readers and writers, are capable of sacrificing themselves, too.[52]

Apparently Pompey did not bring to the east only Rome's military might to put on display. With conquest come also cultural and ideological influences. Abroad, Romans enjoyed the partial myth of courageous soldiers who out of *fides* and *devotio* would self-destruct rather than face failure.[53] At home, philosophers expounded on the benefits of *voluntaria morte*. Although Greek philosophers such as Socrates made the relinquishing of life the unequivocally rare prerogative of the wise, who receive the gods' approval, Seneca accorded each human the private right to choose death, in the first century C.E. Superior to the gods' wishes was the individual's desire to die free.[54] Freedom rather than wisdom rationalized the *causa moriendi*.

Josephus did not remain apathetic to Roman philosophy and popular ideas. He was well aware of the transition from the individualistic Greek to communal Roman approach toward voluntary death. But instead of contrasting the Greek with the Romans, he substituted Judaism for the latter (*Against Apion* 2:168–169). His singling out of Jews as the only holders of a tradition (also called philosophy) of self-sacrifice, illustrates his attempts to equate Jewish heroism to that of the Roman. Strabo's and Nicolas's attribution of altruism in the name of freedom to Josephus's Gentile neighbors made his efforts to elevate the Jews even more crucial.

Religion per se plays a role in his depiction of the Jewish confrontation with Pontius Pilate (26–36 C.E). It was not a demand to actively transgress that triggered the conflict but rather the Roman procurator's attempt to install Caesar's effigies in Jerusalem. Jewish law prohibited the installation of icons in the city and Pilate's endeavor signaled a change in the status quo. Fatigued by the numerous Jewish petitions, he ordered his soldiers to be "ready to oppress them." When they approached him once more, Pilate commanded his troops to encircle the protesters, and "threatened to punish them at once with death if they did not put an end to their tumult and return to their own places." They refused. "Casting themselves prostrate and baring their throats, [they] declared that they had gladly welcomed death rather than make bold to transgress the wise provisions of the laws." Pilate was so "astonished at the strength of their devotion to the laws" that he ordered "straightway removed the images" from Jerusalem and commanded them to be sent back to Caesarea (*Jewish Antiquities* 18:55–59).[55]

Purporting to know what moved the procurator, Josephus presents the Jewish preparedness to die for the Law as their true backbone. Indeed, the statement ascribed to these unarmed Jews bring us closer to the martyrological phenomenon. But Pilate's first interest in stability, it may be assumed, caused him to change his decision. Voluntary death, therefore, remained unnecessary, making the protestors *potential martyrs*.

Did these Jews really want to die? Can N. Farberow's and E. Shneidman's modern psychological theory of adaptive behavior – namely that suicidal threats signal "a cry for help" – be applied here?[56] In other words, did these individuals gamble with their lives to avert a desperate situation? Obviously, they were not familiar with modern psychological theory, but an important lesson had been learned from the incident. The majority group of pacifist Jews became aware of a daring and paradoxical tactic in their religious struggle. Although active opposition could have led to group suicide, suicidal declarations prevented massive death.

This lesson is immediately made clear by contrasting these passive protestors with a different Jewish group. Members of this group lost their lives while besieging Pilate "with angry clamour" to protest the construction of an aqueduct at the Temple's expenses (*Jewish War* 2:175; *Jewish Antiquities* 18:60–62).[57] The lesson coincided not only with psychological theories but also with the Danielic concept of God's rescuing the peaceful faithful. As the next event indicates, many Jews who had to cope with strict Roman control found the tactic of passive and nonviolent protest valuable.

Some half a century after Philo, Josephus provided his version of the conflict with Petronius.[58] This time the severity of Caligula's decree surpassed Pilate's insensitivity. Caligula ordered Petronius "to set up an image of Gaius in the Temple of God and, if, however, they [the Jews] were obstinate, he was to subdue them by force of arms and so set it up."[59]

To avoid the decree, Jews in Ptolemais and Tiberias employed the same placid tactics that their predecessors had practiced against Pilate. They peacefully protested "with the assurance that for those who are determined to take the risk there is hope even of prevailing; for God will stand by us if we welcome danger for His glory."[60] Daniel and his three friends instantly come to mind. Paradoxically, the option of death was exercised to avoid it.

To the surprise of Petronius and his soldiers in their first encounter:

many tens of thousands of the Jews came to Petronius at Ptolemais with petitions not to use force to make them transgress and violate their ancestral code. "If," they said, "you propose at all costs to bring in and set up the image, slay us first before you carry out these resolutions. For it is not possible for us to survive and to behold actions that are forbidden us by the decision both of our lawgiver and of our forefathers who cast their votes enacting these measures as moral laws. . . . In order to preserve our ancestral code, we shall patiently endure what may be in store for us, with the assurance that for those who are determined to take the risk there is hope even of prevailing; for God will stand by us if we welcome danger for His glory." (*Jewish Antiquities* 18:263–267)

Unprepared for such a large passive reaction, the petulant and perplexed Petronius ignored both Caligula's orders and the protestors by moving to Tiberias. To his regret, he encountered the same response at his next stop. The Tiberians would neither accept the edict nor provide the general with a *casus belli*. "Many tens of thousands" emulated their Ptolemaic kinsmen. Asked if they would "go to war with Caesar . . . regardless of his resources and of your own weakness?" they replied:

"On no account would we fight, but we will die sooner than violate our laws." And falling on their faces and baring their throats, they declared that they were ready to be slain. They continued to make these supplications for forty days. Furthermore, they neglected their fields, and that, too, though it was time to sow the seeds. For they showed a stubborn determination and readiness to die rather than to see the image erected. (*Jewish Antiquities* 18:271)[61]

The sequence of events unfolded in favor of the Tiberians. As in Ptolemais, Petronius's astonishment at their reaction is said to have postponed his actions while he waited for further instructions from Rome. Meanwhile, King Agrippa's diplomacy on behalf of his fellow Jews persuaded Caligula to remove his anti-Jewish policy. Thereafter, reminiscent of Philo's sense of theodicy, Caligula met his violent end for his unjust decrees against pacifist Jews.[62]

Josephus's *Jewish Antiquities* attributes to the Jews only threats that they *will let* the Roman soldiers kill them. In the parallel description in *The Jewish War*, they make similar declarations. Like Philo's heroes, however, they are said to have presented their potential death as sacrifice. Admonishing Petronius that if he insisted on setting up the statues, he must first "*sacrifice* the entire Jewish nation" (*Jewish War* 2:196–197, emphasis mine). What makes this choice of words significant is the context in which it is reported. The presentation of the nation as a sacrifice immediately follows the reminder that Jews "offered sacrifice twice daily for Caesar and the Roman people." This way both God and Caesar received what belonged to them. The Romans could have seen in this description human sacrifices for the emperor; for the Jews the sacrifices would be for God.

It is difficult to tell whether Philo's or Josephus's account is more authentic. But Josephus's portrayal reflects his own misgiving about spilling one's own blood. Self-killing, not to mention killing of others, constituted for him an ungodly, unsocial, and unnatural behavior (*Jewish War* 3:374–378).

The fortunate ending, however, does not diminish the importance of the account to the history of Jewish martyrdom. As with the Sabbath issue, voluntary death furnishes Josephus with a double-edged tool through which he could rationalize defeat and depict the history of his people in a more positive light. Jewish tradition instills courage, not for the sake of warfare, but in preparation for suffering on behalf of the Law (*Against Apion* 2:272, 292). [An audacious comment indeed from the former rebel leader, who refused to turn his own sword against himself, even when his soldiers threatened "to suicide" him with them (*Jewish War* 3:355–360).] In a similar fashion, we are led to believe, Caesarea suffered total collapse with many casualties because the Jews preferred death over Sabbath violation. Temple priests are said to have perished because they put their duties before their lives, not because they were engaged in Temple politics.

On the flip side of the coin, this readiness to die explains the aversion of calamity. Allusions to the Danielic formula of divine intervention ("God will stand by us if we welcome danger for His glory") explain why it was not necessary for these Jews to make good on their promise. It was, however, essential for Josephus the historian.

Voluntary death enabled him to present to his Gentile readers Jews as heroic as their Roman conquerors. In the dialogues with the two generals, the Jews employed the Roman notion of noble death, which both Pilate and Petronius well understood and appreciated. Josephus ascribed to these Jews what Cicero and Seneca had preached in their accounts of the Republican hero Cato. Like him, they would choose the death of freemen. From suicides such as Chaerea and Lupus, Josephus also learned the religious value of the act. Although Lupus lacked both the skill to make a proper exit and courage, for he only "stuck his neck out so gingerly," the public held them both as heroes. Returning a favor, the living "made sacrifices to the dead." These heroes deserved the blessing of the gods because they assassinated Caligula for the common good. They did so knowing the deadly consequences (*Jewish Antiquities* 19:268–272).

Sabinus also earned the sympathy of both people and gods by falling on his sword. He had chosen death in loyalty to his fellow conspirators after "he was not only released by [Emperor] Claudius from the charge [of killing Caligula] but allowed to retain the office which he held." Sabinus, however, preferred the public acknowledgment of a noble hero (*Jewish Antiquities* 19:273). Undoubtedly, Josephus was also familiar with Roman cases of mass suicide such as the example of 64 C.E. Destitute and grief-stricken, Romans preferred to die in their burning city, though they could have escaped.[63] The same motif is at work in his report on the attack on the Jews of Caesarea.

Josephus applies these philosophical and ritualistic ideas to his Jewish heroes. For the sake of presenting Jewish principles in Roman terms he makes even the belligerent Mattathias and his son Judas sound like martyrs dying not only for the Law but also for liberty. "It was better for them to die for their country's laws than to live so ingloriously" (*Jewish Antiquities* 12:267) is his comment on the elegy of the Hasomonean patriarch.[64] To Judas's battle speech he adds the most cherished Roman mores: "Exert yourselves accordingly, bearing in mind that death is the portion even of those who do not fight, and holding firmly to the belief that if you die for such precious causes as *liberty, country, laws* (emphasis mine) and religion, you will gain eternal glory" (*Jewish Antiquities* 12:302–304).[65] In this fashion, Josephus sublimely distorts Judas's speech (1 Macc. 4:35) to convince his Greek readers that, like his Hasmonean ancestors, all Jews "were prepared to die if they could not live as free men" (*Jewish Antiquities* 12:315).[66]

The notion of dying voluntarily held one more advantage for Josephus in addressing his pagan readers. Ignoring the militant Jewish trends reported by him, Josephus fallaciously commented that Jews would patiently submit to any form of defeat. "But when *pressure is put on us* (emphasis mine) to alter our statutes, then we deliberately fight even against tremendous odds" (*Against Apion* 2:272). What might sound here as a bellicose admonition turns into a depiction of his kinsmen's pacifistic nature. They would proudly suffer shame and defeat for all reasons, except for their Law. Even then, they will only react to provocation. But when pressured during the conflicts with Pilate and Petronius, the Jews still acted in a passive manner in accordance with their ancestral tradition. These apologetic statements deliberately contradict his many scenes of rebels as instigators.[67]

Continuing to present the Roman concept of voluntary death as a Jewish tradition, he appends an additional ingredient. Like the Roman philosophers, his compatriots from Ptolemais "cast their votes enacting these measures as moral laws." Adding morality to the dilemma of *mors voluntaria* counterbalances the want of religious support. Despite Josephus's claim that such intentions and acts were merely a duplication of Jewish ancestral behavior, no specific examples are provided. At best, he could transform the nearly sacrificed Isaac of the *aqedah* (Gen. 22) into a willing participant. According to Josephus, Abraham revealed to his twenty-five-year-old son God's horrendous request and urged him to be courageous in death. Words of encouragement proved to be superfluous, for the joyous Isaac ran to the altar to promptly fulfill God's will (*Jewish Antiquities* 1:222–237).[68] Had not the divine request presented merely a test of devotion, Isaac's heroism would have surpassed his father's. Still, even in this light, the two Patriarchs could not become Josephus's desired proof of existing "traditional" martyrological exemplars. Eleazar the scribe and the seven sons are yet to be mentioned.

THE ASSUMPTION OF MOSES

Philo and Josephus were not the only authors to ignore the Maccabean martyrs in their protomartyrologies. The narrative of a certain Taxo in *The Assumption of Moses* (also known as *The Testament of Moses*) displays a certain affinity to Josephus's story and, therefore, to 2 Maccabees 7.[69] The book is another good illustration of a late Hellenistic text that was touched up as late as after the fall of Jerusalem or even during the early second century; its survival in a single Latin translation opens wider the door for speculation.[70] The author, who did not write for historiographic purposes, describes persecutions similar to those of the Hellenistic period and the behavior of Taxo, whom he associates with Mattathias. Taxo's story, however, shows more correlation to Josephus's story about the old man with his seven sons rather than to 2 Maccabees. As in Josephus, Taxo flees with his seven sons to a cave:

There will be a man of the tribe of Levi whose name will be Taxo, who, having seven sons, will speak to them, exhorting them: "Observe my sons, behold a second visitation has come upon the people, and a punishment merciless and far exceeding the first. For what nation or what region or what people of those who are impious toward the Lord, who have done many abominations, have suffered as great calamities as have befallen us? Now therefore my sons, hear me: for observe and know that neither did our fathers nor their forefathers tempt God, so as to transgress his commands. And ye know that this is our strength and thus we will do. Let us fast for the space of three days and on the fourth let us go into a cave which is in the field and let us die rather than transgress the commands of the Lord of Lords, the God of our fathers. For if we do this and die, our blood will be avenged before the Lord. (*The Assumption of Moses*, 9:1–7)

Unlike the anonymous mother and father, Taxo and his seven sons do not come in direct contact with an oppressor. Nevertheless, he finds it necessary to protest an oppressive situation by self-starvation. As his words *observe, behold, hear me*, and *let us fast* may indicate, the narrative expresses a manifesto to the public through his seven sons. Taxo intended to achieve more than avoidance of personal transgression.

Just causes and unjust oppression summon God's intervention to correct the situation. Self-sacrifices, it was hoped, would induce divine retaliation. Vengeance is to be achieved only through the spilling of innocent blood.[71] Attention should be given to the embryonic ritualistic character of the drama. Alluding to self-purification, three-day fasts were to precede the entering of the cave. Through a self-inflicted death, Taxo expected the family's blood to be avenged before God. Given the nonviolent fashion in which death was designed to occur and the uncertainty that it ever took place, the mention of blood in relation to divine vengeance is a significant connection to sacrificial rituals.

Not least significant is Taxo's attempt to present his dangerous solution as an ancient Jewish tradition. The behavior of his "fathers" and "forefathers" in comparable situations entailed his sacrifices. Readiness to renounce life peacefully constituted the strength of his Jewish heritage. Suffering was advanced as a positive feature unique to Judaism. Taxo raised the same question asked by Josephus about the uniqueness of Israel in the same rhetoric fashion. Although not specific to Greeks and Romans, Taxo's question clearly implied that no other nation has required of itself such drastic resolutions. Yet Taxo did not mention by name his forefathers who acted in a like manner.

The Assumption of Moses provides another example of empathetically described voluntary death as the best heroic response to persecution without presenting the Maccabean exemplars.[72] The author's failure to contribute particular examples of such traditional heroes yields the same question previously asked about Philo's and Josephus's knowledge of Eleazar and the seven sons. If it were written in the first century to highlight persecution, its avoidance by the potential voluntary deaths of Taxo's seven sons, and the link between self-destruction and divine retribution, all in the context of Jewish tradition, why does the book ignore the Maccabean examples of the mother with her seven sons?

It is the author's inability to provide specific martyrological paradigms in support of his theological assertions that forces him to identify Taxo with Mattathias. The Maccabean hero, the embodiment of active resistance and militancy in Jewish tradition, and who allegedly went as far as to amend the Sabbath Law in the name of self-defense, undergoes a dramatic transformation to become the strongest advocate of self-sacrifice in the *Assumption*. Mattathias, who is said to have predicted that passivity would lead to the annihilation of his people, now, as Taxo, believes that Israel could be rebuilt by self-destruction. This shift in personality and imagery betokens the rising of a new type of ideal protagonist in the first century, but still without presenting the eight Maccabean heroes.

4 MACCABEES

They surface in 4 Maccabees, which has been dated from the midfirst century C.E. to around the period of the Bar Kokhva revolt (ca. 135).[73] Before discussing this book further, one observation should be made. The way in which the seven sons came to our attention thus far suggests the following sequence: The acclaimed story of the mother and her seven sons presents a mutation of circulating folkloric tales about a man who would *kill* his seven sons, his wife, and himself rather than capitulate. Despite its dreadful implications, the account was intended to earn sympathy and understanding. The milder version, which excluded the presence of a mother (and therefore the natural maternal obstacle to the notion of child sacrifice, as alluded to in Gen. 22) made the act of self-destruction less explicit and less atrocious. The folktale evolved until it assumed its more recognizable form, some time after the destruction of the Temple.

The timing does not appear to be accidental. It was around this period that Plutarch (ca. 46–126) related the story of Cratesicleia, King Cleomenes's wife. She had to watch the executions of her children by King Ptolemy before being executed herself. Like the anonymous mother who would rather die than let the guards touch her (4 Macc 17:1), Cratesicleia's friend, Panteus's wife, "maintained to the end that watchful care of her body" by death.[74] And as in 4 Maccabees, Plutarch presented voluntary death for a common cause as an expression of brotherly love.[75]

As with Josephus, ambiguity marks this love affair with the Roman ideal in 4 Maccabees. Doubts about the legitimacy of voluntary death arise in its version of Eleazar and the seven brothers. Because 4 Maccabees was composed in the Diaspora after the reign of Caligula,[76] the telling of the Hellenistic stories of martyrdom reflects the Jewish attitude toward voluntary death in the first century, if not the second. In this case, the story was written or, at least rewritten, under the impact of Christian martyrology.[77] Although the purpose of 2 Maccabees was to stress the gap between Jews and gentiles, the author of 4 Maccabees utilized his heroes to bridge this gap.[78] Attempts to put Jewish wisdom and Greco-Roman philosophy on a similar footing required 4 Maccabees to justify its martyrs' drastic solution in the terms of their religion.

This requirement is met by the symbols already employed by Philo. 4 Maccabees transforms Eleazar from a scribe (*grammateus* 2 Macc. 6:18) into a "priest by family and an expert in the Law" (*nomikos* 4 Macc. 5:4; 17:9).[79] The justification of Eleazar's choice relies on the association of his decision with the priest's traditional duties. His sacrifice made him a "priest worthy of the priesthood" (4 Macc. 7:6); his following in the footsteps of his ancestor Aaron made his behavior trustworthy. As Aaron "overcame the angel of fire, so did Aaron's scion Eleazar" (4 Macc. 7:11–12).[80] The priestly Patriarch produced the priestly martyrological father.

Eleazar's motivation recalls Philo's second symbol: blood. The newly ordained priest belonged among those who "defend the Law with their own blood" (4 Macc. 7:8). Blood adds more than just a grisly detail to the depiction – "He was flowing with blood" (4 Macc. 6:6) – to perfect the Temple cult imagery. Like Philo's heroes, Eleazar assumed the role of both Temple sacrifice and sacrificer. From the midst of tormenting flames he beseeched God to "Be merciful to Thy people, and let my punishment be sufficient for their sake. Make my blood an expiation for them, and take my life as a ransom for theirs" (4 Macc. 6:28–29).[81] By the alteration of Eleazar's vocation and the addition of sacrificial metaphors, the voluntary spilling of human blood assumes not only expiatory but also vicarious qualities. Also achieved by this metaphor is the subliminal approval of the act through which these divine attributes are actualized. Not only the cause and effect legitimized Eleazar's act, but also his newly assigned role in the drama.

Authorization proved more problematic in 4 Maccabees' version of the seven brothers. Unlike 2 Maccabees, this version has the sons acknowledging Eleazar's exemplary sacrifice. They found death even more fitting for them: "If old men of the Hebrews have died for religion's sake" (4 Macc. 9:6). Eleazar inspired them to become each other's and the nation's *typos* to emulate. Their *typos* of active martyrdom remain more problematic than do the examples of 2 Maccabees.

4 Maccabees skillfully formulates a gradual transition from passive to active patterns of heroism. Although the first four brothers patiently awaited their executions, the fifth "leapt forward, saying, 'I shall not, tyrant, beg off torment for the cause of virtue, but of my own accord have I come forward...?'" (4 Macc. 11:1–3). He did so in the same manner that Isaac offered himself in Josephus. Still, it is the seventh son who eclipsed the rest. After calling upon God to prove merciful to the nation, "he flung himself into the braziers, and so gave up his life" (4 Macc. 12:19).

According to "certain of the guards," the mother did the same. "She flung herself into the fire, so that no one might touch her body" (17:1).[82] Not only does she become the first female martyrological archetype, she completes the transition to activist martyrdom. By so doing, she parallels ideal Roman females such as Mallonia, Arria, Paulina, and Politta, who maintained their integrity by following in the footsteps of the aforementioned Lucretia.[83]

As shown by their declarations, which were similar to those made by Philo's potential martyrs or by Taxo with his seven sons, members of the anonymous family ached to be killed, whereas others killed themselves. They exercised passive, passive-provocative, and active means to martyrdom. Gushing blood dramatized all these types of executions. "Besmeared with blood on all sides was the wheel" of execution (4 Macc. 9:20; also 10:8). Blood signified more than just dramatic effects. It completed the notion of sacrifice on behalf of the nation. "It was through the blood of these righteous ones, and through the expiation of their death, that divine Providence preserved Israel..." (4 Macc. 17:22). Through the blood of Eleazar, the seven brothers, and of the new female martyr that the land was purified and the king defeated. "It was because of them that our nation obtained peace" (4 Macc. 18:4). In contrast to 2 Maccabees 7, which makes the sons the victims of their own sins, these innocent heroes died as a "ransom for the sin of the nation" (4 Macc.

17:20–21).[84] Given the use of blood in our sources, its redemptive function in the first century should not be played down.[85]

As in Philo, such powerful ideas of active self-killing by impeccable individuals entailed moral and religious sanction. The internalization of the Roman "noble death" is accomplished by the presentation of biblical heroes as martyrological archetypes. The brothers did not emulate only each other. They emulated "the Three Youths of Assyria" from Daniel and Isaac, who, according to the book, "endured immolation for religion's sake" (4 Macc. 13:9–12; also 16:21; 18:11). Patriarch Abraham is said to have inspired the mother "whose soul was like Abraham's" (4 Macc. 14:20). She "bethought herself of Abraham's fortitude" (4 Macc. 15:28). Abraham in his zeal "to immolate his son Isaac" encouraged the mother, whereas the biblical son and the Danielic heroes animated her children (4 Macc. 17:20–23).[86] Both Josephus and 4 Maccabees adapt Isaac's role in the *aqedah* to rationalize the acceptance of voluntary death, indicating a search in the first century for theological backing.[87] These parallels, on the one hand, and Josephus's failure to mention the martyrs' story, on the other, make it more likely that Josephus served as a source for such stories and ideas. The movement in the trajectory of theology continues to indicate Josephus's impact on the evolution of martyrdom and martyrology.

The introduction of scriptural heroes and the illusion that Isaac actually suffered immolation is indicative of the attempts to present voluntary death as a legitimate Jewish tradition. But what drives the inclusion of these heroes in the text is the same cause that drives the presentation of the potential martyrs as Temple priests and sacrifices. In other words, these images illustrate the need for legitimizing the Jewish adoption of the Roman idea of human sacrifice. What facilitated the presentation of the seven sons as sacrifices in 4 Maccabees was the mutability of voluntary death in post-Temple Judaism and the crystallization of Diaspora theology.

In this context the number seven may be understood. Seven times did the high priests dip their fingers in the sacrificial blood to sprinkle it on the curtain of the Holy Ark and the altar. The sprinkling of the blood of sin offerings seven times, in the seven month, was intended to absolve the sins of the assembly (Lev. 17:14–30).[88] The cleansing of the congregation by sacrificial blood is reminiscent of Philo's mention of the last "right bathing" in human blood. The number thus complements the first-century imagery of humans as vicarious sacrifices.[89] The presentation of voluntary death as cultic sacrifice, therefore, answered specific contingencies. Jewish sacrificial symbols helped legitimize the absorption of the Roman altruistic ideology.

A closer look at the sacrifices in 4 Maccabees reveals a disconcerting cognizance of the lack of religious approval. The book does not see voluntary death as a *necessary* act in either religious or secular life after all. The author explains why such drastic acts are not imperative. The seven sons could have used the following arguments to avoid their final acts:

Why do we entertain ourselves with these vain resolutions, and make foolhardy venture of fatal disobedience? Shall we not, dear brothers, be afraid of these instruments of torture? Shall we not ponder the threats of torment? Shall we not eschew this vainglory and this death-bringing braggadocio? Let us take pity upon our own youth; let us show compassion to our mother's hoary head. Let us lay it upon our hearts that if we disobey we die. *We shall be pardoned, even by divine justice*, for showing fear of the king under duress. Why do we banish ourselves out of life, that is so sweet, why do we deprive ourselves of the charms of the world? Let us not violate necessity; let us not indulge vainglory at the price of our own torture. *Not even the law itself would willingly condemn us to death for being affrighted by torture.* Why does such love of contention inflame us, why does such fatal obduracy attract us, when it is possible for us to lead an untroubled life if we obey the king? [emphasis mine] (4 Macc. 8:18–26)

Several arguments are made here against voluntary death. Life is "so sweet" that it should not be replaced by premature death. Moreover, the natural human instinct to live takes priority over "vainglory." It is only instinctive to fear torture or death and to desire life. Finally, what may appear in other cultures as glorious and selfless is perceived by the brothers as a selfish act for personal glorification. These are the very same antisuicide arguments Josephus had echoed at Jotapata (*Jewish War* 3:331–91).

The seven sons, we may assume, could have easily overcome these philosophical arguments against death had their history or religion instructed them otherwise. But the Law they are said to have died for provided no answer. On the contrary, their Law required no such sacrifice even when its own integrity was threatened.[90] Had the seven sons decided not to embrace death, they "*shall be pardoned, even by divine justice, for showing fear of the king under duress.*" Obviously, their submission to the monarch's demands would result in violation of the Law, in this case eating pork. But "*[N]ot even the law itself would willingly condemn us to death for being affrighted by torture.*" The son's dilemma echoes Philo's: "not God himself could blame us who had twofold motive, respectful fear of the emperor and loyalty to the consecrated laws" [emphasis mine] (*Embassy* 236). Indeed, by these arguments the author of 4 Maccabees elevates his protagonists to a higher level because their act went beyond the requirements of their religious precepts. At the same time, the sons' arguments indicate an internal conceptual struggle between supporters and critics of voluntary death by the end of the first century.[91]

The arguments voiced by the seven martyrs in support of their acts came from their foreign environment.[92] Martyrdom illustrates the universal victory of the spirit over the flesh. As they demonstrated, "devout reason is sovereign over the emotions" (4 Macc. 13:1). It is this universal wisdom that justified the Maccabean heroes and earns them ubiquitous admiration. Without diminishing the importance of the Law, divine justice would have excused the martyrs had they chosen life.

AFTER DEATH

No wonder such reservations were ignored by the early Christian exegetists, who turned to the Maccabees in search of the universal redemptive qualities of human blood. Modern research has often followed such readings, making the generic association between the so-called Hellenistic Jewish martyrs and celestial reward. Yet the early martyrs owe their divine recompense to modern scholars rather than to God. The idea that Judaism rewarded martyrs projects the long-lasting impact of Christian readings on present research.[93]

Only 2 Maccabees made resurrection the hope of the seven sons. As argued previously, individual revival from death appears prematurely in the Hellenistic texts. Our first-century sources continue to disregard resurrection, thus buttressing Chapter 1's conclusion. Fear of God constitutes the prime motivation for considering the abandonment of life. The dread of transgressing overpowers the fear of death in the proclamations delivered by Taxo, the potential martyrs, and the martyrs of 4 Maccabees. Excluding the vague references in 4 Maccabees that will be addressed shortly, it is clear that no consideration at all was given to the concept of the hereafter. On the contrary, Philo is aware that should he and his delegation to Caligula be executed, they "will die and be no more" (*Embassy* 192).[94] With this nihilistic view in mind, Philo and his group took their chances so they "may not live to see a calamity worse than death."[95]

Josephus makes general references to the question of the afterlife. They constitute various viewpoints, including the rejection of such a notion. He attributes these various opinions to the four sects of his time.[96] We should attribute this diversity of opinions also to Josephus's own partial agenda, which varied in time and according to occasion. Probably his vague familiarity with the different theological trends plays a role as well.[97]

According to Josephus, the Sadducees believed that "As for the persistence of the soul after the death, penalties in the underworld, and rewards, they will have none of them" (*Jewish War* 2:165). He reiterates the same idea in *Jewish Antiquities* 18:16. "The Sadducees hold that the soul perishes along with the body."[98]

The Essenes considered the soul immortal.[99] Also telling is their inclination to "leave everything in the hands of God" (*Jewish Antiquities* 18:18). This implies that the Essenes would not take their own lives. Nevertheless, Josephus speaks highly of their bravery in *Jewish War* 2:150–153. "They make light of danger and triumph over pain . . . death, if it come with honor, they consider better than immortality." How could death be better than immortality? This would suggest that the Essenes glorified death because it prevented transgression.

During the war with the Romans, the Essenes experienced "every variety of test. Racked and twisted, burnt and broken, and made to pass through every instrument of torture, in order to induce them to blaspheme their lawgiver or to eat some forbidden thing. . . . Smiling in their agonies and mildly deriding their tormentors, they cheerfully resigned their souls, confident that they would *receive them back again*" (emphasis mine).[100] For the Alexandrian branch of the Essenes, immortality is not exactly what it appears to be. "Then such is their longing for the deathless and blessed life that thinking that their mortal life already ended they abandon their property" (Philo, *On the Contemplative Life*, 13).[101] Nickelsburg thus rightly speaks with caution of the Essenes' "belief in, or akin to, immortality of the soul."[102]

As presented by Josephus, the expectation of receiving the *soul again* stems from their general conviction in the immortality of the soul. Their acceptance of violent executions plays no role in the fate of the soul. Influenced by "the sons of the Greeks," they viewed reward and punishment after death as the motivation for virtuous conduct and a deterrent in this life (*Jewish War* 2:154–158). Virtue in this life combines the Roman ideal of honor or freedom on the one hand and adherence to Jewish laws on the other. These two principles are further appreciated against the background of Roman sadism that made torture and suffering a prevailing form of entertainment. It is worth mentioning that the instruments of torture, the agony, the requirement to blaspheme or to eat forbidden food, the contemptuous mocking of their persecutors, the struggle of a desert sect, and the expectation to receive their souls back again all recall the literary characteristics of 2 Maccabees 6 and 7.[103] But again, there is no mention of the two stories.

The Pharisees, Josephus continues, "believed that the souls have power to survive death and that there are rewards and punishments under the earth." They believed that "the good souls receive an easy passage to a new life" (*Jewish Antiquities* 18:14). In *Jewish War* 3:374 Josephus reckons that those "who depart this life *in accordance with the law of nature* and repay the loan which they received from God, when He who lent is pleased to reclaim it . . . their souls . . . are allotted the most holy place in heaven, whence, in the revolution of the ages, they return to find in chaste bodies a new habitation" [emphasis mine].[104]

H. J. Thackeray understood these two sets of descriptions to mean a Pharisaic belief in metempsychosis.[105] His opinion may be supported by Josephus's explanation of "new life." "Every soul," he writes about the Pharisees, "is imperishable, but the soul of the good alone passes into another body, while the soul of the wicked suffer eternal punishment" (*Jewish War* 2:163). This sentence corroborates the belief in transmigration. Citing *Against Apion* 2:218, L. Feldman has understood Josephus's descriptions of the Pharisees to reveal their belief in resurrection in the future life.[106] But the connection between the Pharisees and their rabbinic descendents does not justify the introjection of resurrection.[107]

Typically, Josephus's information fluctuates according to circumstances and literary needs. His first statement about rewards and punishment under the world was obviously written with his Greek readers in mind. His second assertion echoes beliefs that resonated within Christian groups about ascending to and descending from heaven. What is crucial to remember, however, is that Josephus made the claim against rewards for voluntary death in his speech at Jotapata, as an attempt to save his own life. As a whole, this speech speaks against any termination of life, regardless of motivation. Attention should be given to the key sentence in the speech, "those who depart this life in accordance with the law of nature." Accordingly, only those who died naturally, when *God decided* to reclaim His gift of life, would be rewarded. Any attempt to return the gift of life prematurely is condemned by God. "Those who have laid mad hands upon themselves" would suffer for their "crime" in the "darker regions of the nether world." Mad hands that "made war" against the self were, therefore, cut off before burial.[108] The descendant of these suicides, too, would not escape divine payment for these suicides (*Jewish War* 3: 374–378).

Regarding the fourth sect, Josephus laconically reveals that they followed the opinions of the Pharisees. But their passion for liberty and for God made them "think little of submitting to death in unusual forms" (*Jewish Antiquities* 18:23). Interestingly, of all the four descriptions it is the latter that alludes to voluntary death in the name of God. Yet, only the description of this sect is bare of reference to the afterlife. This would suggest that the connection between voluntary death and reward was yet to be established.

In his polemical *Against Apion* 2:218–219, Josephus outlines the differences between his and foreign nations. Here too the afterlife comes into play. While the Greeks valued silver and gold and rewarded their heroes with crowns of wild olive or parsley, God's followers were granted "a renewed existence and in the revolution of the ages the gift of a better life."[109] Renewed existence is the fate of "each individual" who lives according to the Law. Keeping in mind that Josephus's message was written with the Gentiles in mind, who may fail to understand the importance of the Jewish precepts, it is not surprising to find the assertion that Jews "willingly meet death" if they "must needs" die for their precepts. The point that should be remembered here is the rewarding of all devotees in a future stage, regardless of the manner in which they reached it. Also important is the affirmation that they submit to death willingly only when death becomes inevitable.

A different conviction yet informs Josephus's story of the two leaders Judas and Matthias, who incited the riots against Herod's golden eagle. The two leaders are said to have encouraged their "disciples" to bring down the images, despite the potential risk to their lives. The Roman and the Jewish principles come into play once again. These two concepts are bound together with the innovative notion of immortality, which would have made Eleazar the scribe a welcome example. "It was a noble deed to die for the law of one's country; for the souls of those who came to such an end attained immortality and an eternally abiding sense of felicity; it was only the ignoble, uninitiated in their philosophy, who clung in their ignorance to life and preferred death on a sickbed to that of a hero" (*Jewish War* 1:650).[110] Although this statement shows the limited acceptance of immortality, it does not articulate what immortality is. It is not resurrection, however.

The famous Sicarii and their leader Eleazar allegedly had discussed the fate of the dead before destroying themselves at Masada.[111] In quoting Eleazar, Josephus mentions the concept of immortality without utopian expectations. Eleazar's speech itself echoes the debate over the validity of the concept of immortality and the more general dilemma as to whether self-annihilation is legitimate and morally acceptable. Several motifs in the famous story need to be stressed. The rebels' rejected Eleazar's first call for mass suicide. Eleazar long deliberates on the issue of immortality to persuade his listeners to accept the notion.[112] He advises them to emulate the "foreign Indian" concept of voluntary self-killing, which argued for the existence of the soul after death. All these elements reflect the infiltration of a postmortem existence into the thinking of certain Jewish circles.

The other dilemma lay in the acceptance of immortality in relation to self-killing.[113] What finally persuaded the besieged at Masada to make their fatal decision was not the notion of reward after death. Love of their freedom in the here-and-now supplied their motivation to depart. Without freedom, life turns meaningless. Death in itself holds no positive advantage: "Yet, even had we from the first been schooled in the opposite doctrine and taught that man's highest blessing is life and that death is a calamity, still the crisis is one that calls upon us to bear it with a stout heart, since it is by God's will and of necessity that we are to die" (*Jewish War* 7:358–388). Clearly, several positive views of death existed in the first century. After all is said and done, the story of the Sicarii at Masada does not revolve around choosing between life and death but rather around choosing a method of death. As in the ideology of their Roman rivals, the positive aspect of death is the rebels' ability to prevent a Roman massacre by their *manus sibi inferre*.[114] In Josephus's view their end was a punishment, not a reward, for the crime of the revolt.[115]

Immortality in the context of militant heroism appears also in Josephus's aforementioned version of Mattathias's speech. Here he equates immortality with memory. Mattathias assures his audience that, "For though our bodies are mortal and subject to death, we can, through the memory of our deeds, attain the heights of immortality" (*Jewish Antiquities* 12:281–282). Clearly Josphus paraphrases First Maccabees' recommendation to "be mindful of the deeds of our fathers … that you may receive great glory and eternal renown."[116] Judas the Hasmonean interpreted immortality similarly. He reminded his solders of the Roman principle that "if you die for such precious causes as *liberty, country, laws* (emphasis mine) and religion, you will gain eternal glory" (*Jewish Antiquities* 12:302–304). Humans come into this world and leave, but only their heroic deeds perpetuate their memory. Daniel served Josephus to establish his assertion. "Since his death, his memory lives on eternally" (*Jewish Antiquities* 10:266).

Memory as immortality concludes Eleazar's oration in 4 Maccabees. Those who die for God are not to be forgotten by Him. Verse 7:19 indicates, "believing that to God they die not." Except for this possibly interpolated phrase, fear of divine punishment constitutes Eleazar's reason for accepting death.[117] Transgression is perceived as being worse than death, and the ability to stand the trial becomes a virtue.

The same objective is said to have motivated the seven brothers. They consistently agreed to die to bring retribution on the king[118] and to avoid their own (4 Macc.13:15). Although 4 Maccabees distinguishes between body and soul, it was the desire to bring retribution on the king that motivated the brothers to sustain torture. Unlike its predecessor, 4 Maccabees makes no mention of resurrection.[119] While in 2 Maccabees 7 the dichotomy is between losing organs and receiving them back, here the distinction is between losing organs and maintaining reason. Reason is the most praised virtue. By suffering, the seven "shall obtain the prize of virtue; and shall be with God" (4 Macc 9:8, 31). Being with God, which scholars have deemed to be a meretricious addendum,[120] should not be misconstrued to mean life with the heavenly God.

The phrase denotes the siding of the heroes with their Creator rather than with the would-be convertor. The third son makes the reason for dying clear: "We ... undergo these sufferings for our teaching and divine virtue" (10:10).

Their mother knows that death will put an end to everything life could offer her through the lost sons. In contrast to 2 Maccabees, she says nothing of receiving them again (2 Macc. 7:29). As with some of Josephus's descriptions, the family's deeds bring immortal fame (4 Macc. 15, 16, especially 16:13).

A few verses may point in the direction of heavenly rewards. But scholars tend to dismiss these verses as late interpolations. Such has been the case with 16:25, "and they too knew well that those who die for the sake of God live with God."[121] More explicit is 17:18: "they have their stand before the throne of God, and live the life of eternal blessedness." But similar textual problems plague the place of the sentence in the text.[122] These verses are in contrast with the general spirit of the book.[123]

More telling is the inscription on their alleged tomb. Unlike the present tradition, the inscription makes no mention of a heavenly resting place. The only benefit ascribed to the "AGED PRIEST, AN OLD WOMAN, AND HER SEVEN SONS" is that they "VINDICATED THEIR RACE, LOOKING TO GOD, AND ENDURING TORMENTS EVEN TO DEATH" (4 Macc. 17:9–10).[124] Also telling is the fact that neither 2 Maccabees nor Philo and Josephus have mentioned the "celebrated" place and the relics that the eight allegedly left. Had such an important and famous cult existed during their lifetime, it would surely not have escaped their pen.

Eusebius, and later Jerome, erroneously ascribed the authorship of 4 Maccabees to Josephus Flavius.[125] Both authors had good reasons to arrive at this conclusion. Anyone who is familiar with Josephus's stories of potential and actual voluntary death could find literary parallels between the writings of the celebrated historian and those of the anonymous authors.[126] 4 Maccabees approximates an extension of these analogues and of Philo's cultic symbolism at the dawn of Christianity.[127] Early Christian theologians could read in Josephus about elderly experts in the Law who submitted to death to inspire their youthful disciples (*Jewish Antiquities* 1:648–649, 655), a father who sacrificed his seven sons when facing an oppressive king (*Jewish War* 1:312–313; *Jewish Antiquities* 14:429–430), and priests sacrificing themselves in the Temple when the oppressors were Roman generals (*Jewish War* 1:150–151). Moreover, the notion of choosing death over the eating of sacrificial meat became extremely appealing to Christians who confessed their fate under similar conditions. Appalled by fellow Christians who agreed to taste the sacrifices to the Roman gods during the persecution at Caesarea, Origen reminds his audience of Eleazar's "noble example" and the salvation it brings.

It took Origen no effort to transform Antiochus into a Roman proconsul and Christianize the Maccabean paradigms.[128]

However, long before Origen discovered Eleazar's example of purity, Philo had already described Jewish women who refused to eat pork as examples of maintaining ethnic identity. Similarly, long before Tertullian (ca. 203) spoke of martyrs "in the baptism of blood," Philo had described his potential martyrs ready to take the "right bathing" in their own blood.[129] Philo's and Josephus's fascination with the Roman virtue of *mors voluntaria*, and their attempts to ascribe to their coreligionists the same Roman values in a Jewish gown, generated the long-lasting impression in later generations that martyrdom and its vicarious power constituted an old component of Judaism.[130] Josephus's inconsistent descriptions of the afterlife in relation to voluntary death further contributed to the misconception that "Jewish martyrdom" generated heavenly rewards. The early Christian theologians quickly turned such ambiguity into basic concepts, which yielded the present misconception about Hellenistic Jewish martyrdom.

Frend correctly observed that Clement (as mentioned, the first Christian to allude to the Maccabean martyrs) established a link between Philo and the early Christian monks, who associated their ascetic ideal with that of the martyrs.[131] By the fourth century, the mother and Eleazar became the *amborum parentum* (two parents) of the *septem fratrum*; They all entered the cult of Christian saints.[132] The current perception that martyrdom and its reward is a Jewish Hellenistic contribution is in debt to early Christians, who, to support their own theological fascination with voluntary death, adopted Philo's, Josephus's, and 4 Maccabees' attempts to equate Jewish altruism with that of their Roman rulers. It should be remembered that except the literary 4 Maccabees, Philo, and Josephus to a lesser extent, mainly speak of potential rather than actual martyrs. Josephus's depictions of actual voluntary death are vague and often imaginative.

The absence of a martyrological theology on the one hand and the infiltration of Roman ideology on the other forced Philo and Josephus to internalize and actualize the idea of the abandonment of life in a ritualistic and traditional context. The new representation of voluntary death as a sacred traditional ritual rationalized the penetrating "noble act" on a "religious" basis. What generated this process during the first century was the need to bridge the gap between a capturing foreign ideal and a Jewish Law that neither rejected nor recognized martyrdom. History left this task to the rabbis we are going to meet in the following chapter.

3

ॐ

"It Is Written in the Law"

Early rabbinic texts presents the greatest challenge to our methodology of linear history. We know that *Tannaitic* and *Amoraic* material take precedence over late midrashic interpretations and commentary and that the *Gemara* is a commentary on the *Mishnah*. Yet it is almost impossible to accurately date the material that comprises this vast literature. Further complication adds the inescapable possibility that many of the rabbinic accounts continued to develop before they saw their final appearance in the edited Jerusalem and Babylonian Talmuds.[1] Equally significant is the recognition that the rabbis did not intend to write histories per se.[2] Although presented in historical settings, not much can be said with accuracy about the historicity of the events that the martyrological accounts describe. Discrepancies and contradictions in a single narrative with different versions from different periods are the more obvious reasons against accepting the information at face value.

We would do better, therefore, to treat these stories as martyrologies rather than histories. These martyrologies are dealt with here as the final product of later Talmudic redactors, who relied also on their memory and imagination to complete their work. Without diminishing the importance of the individual account, it is safer to treat the Talmudic stories of martyrdom as a whole and approach them as the production of late-antique editors. Rather than centering on a specific account to speculate how a second-century rabbi understood his martyrological role, or how his contemporaries viewed his death, I will present here the final martyrological picture that later rabbinic redactors put together. As we shall see, this picture conveys coherent messages that go beyond didacticism, ordinance, or morality, even though rabbinic martyrologies may appear as a pastiche of stories. This means that the proclamations of the martyrs (legendary or authentic) we are about to meet are more likely to reflect the martyrological perceptions of the compilers, not of the legendary heroes whom they described with admiration.

The implication of this approach is that rabbinic martyrologies form the compilers' response to the conditions and realities that shaped their lives. Without knowing these conditions, we are bound to miss the full function of martyrdom in the rabbinic texts. Martyrological messages were not limited to the issue of voluntary death per se, and several nonmartyrological stories shed additional light on this sensitive issue. I believe that only when we understand the socioreligious circumstances in which the compilers lived can we understand their perception of history and explore the meaning and goals of their entire martyrology.[3] After all, when future generations would turn to the Talmud for answers about voluntary death, they would read the individual martyrological accounts as a coherent composite.

REALITY AND MEMORY

Two recollections and a living reality appear to have a great deal of influence on the presentation of rabbinic martyrology in the Talmuds and the midrash. The destruction of the Second Temple in 70 C.E. and the Bar Kokhvah's revolt against the Roman in 135 impacted both the lives of second-century Jews and the rabbinic grasp of history in later centuries.

Rabbinic literature connects the Destruction to the termination of priestly hegemony that, in its version of events, was instantly replaced by that of the rabbinic leaders. Once the central place of worship was demolished, the role of Jerusalem's priesthood vanished and with it its control of Jewish life.[4] In this social and religious vacuum emerged the leadership class of rabbis and their synagogues and academies. As the Talmuds focus on the rabbis, they appear as if they were the only successful Jewish leaders. Rabbinic texts describe the rabbis as prominent and altruistic leaders during Bar Kokhvah's revolt. Reference to the uprising appears in the context of Trajan's and Hadrian's persecution of "Judaism" and the rabbis.[5] As the protectors of their Torah-centered system, the rabbinic story goes, the rabbis refused to comply with the imperial decrees and, therefore, were brutally executed.

In reality, the destruction of the Temple and the direct Roman rule mark the disintegration of the Jewish society, not the beginning of a centralized rabbinic Judaism. With the two revolts against Rome (66 and 132), the situation deteriorated further.[6] By this time, according to S. Schwartz, "Judaism shattered," and it remained in this condition at least until the fourth century.[7] It is during this period that sectarianism flourished in the region. The rabbis represented one of these sects. Like other sectarian leaders, they labored to

develop and preserve a sociotheological system in a fragmented Jewish society. During the Bar Kokhvah rebellion, in fact, the power of the sages of
priestly origin seems to have increased, and the limited political authority of
the rabbi-sages regressed even more.[8] Naturally, the sages of priestly origin
would have supported Bar Kokhvah to restore their position.[9] After all, if Bar
Kokhvah intended to rebuild the Temple, the service of the priesthood would
be indispensable. Furthermore, Schwartz convincingly argues that rabbinic
aspirations were realized only in the seventh century, long after many of the
martyrological accounts had been included in the two Talmuds.

As to the status of Judaism in the Roman empire, Hadrian did not change its
position as a *religio licita*. Neither did he enforce the Roman decrees throughout the Empire.[10] Even the Jewish sources indicate that although Jews were
prevented from performing a number of commandments, they were never
forced to turn from Judaism.[11] Because of the "*antiquitate defenduntur*,"[12] the
privilegia Judaica remained intact even in the hot spot of *Palestina*. Indeed,
this new official name for Judea was indicative of the deterioration of the
relationship with Rome.[13] Despite this deterioration, Jews could still proclaim
Judaeus sum.[14] Under these circumstances, one may wonder how necessary
martyrdom really was.

It is important to bear in mind that the redactors' presentation of *their
history* and of their self-image took shape in a Christian world. Both the
rabbinic and the Christian sects could trace their history back to the same
humble beginning in the pagan world.[15] But although the marginal sect of the
rabbis still struggled for what some modern scholars would call "national"
recognition, Christianity had already emerged as the undisputed victor of the
western world. Whether rightly or not, the Fathers attributed the success of
their church to the Christian martyrs. Their blood, the Fathers repeatedly
argued, carried the *Evangelium* to the four corners of the world.

The real challenge, therefore, was the survival of Judaism in a centralized
Christian world, rather than the coping with the Roman decrees.[16] In the
Christian world, the religious element was to emerge as the main characteristic
of Jewish–gentile conflicts.[17] Under these conditions of cultural confrontation
and social transformation, the rabbis faced a triple mission when looking to
the future. They endeavored to win the hearts and minds of the Jews, restore
and reconstruct the socioreligious system according to their views, and define
the role of the Jew and Judaism in a relatively homogeneous Christian world.
It is these factors that contributed to the rhetoric of martyrdom in the rabbinic
texts of late antiquity.

We will see in this chapter that, in addition to their legal aspect, rabbinic martyrologies were designed to achieve these objectives. This rabbinic

employment of martyrologies resembles the application of this powerful heuristic device by the Christian Fathers. My argument, therefore, is that the rabbinic formulation of martyrdom developed in reaction to the successful Christianization of the world through martyrdom (as the Church Father would argue). To be clear, I am not dismissing the possibility that the Romans executed Jews. They did. Nor am I claiming that rabbinic texts deliberately misrepresented historical events. What I am saying is that late-antique rabbis relied on their memory of the conflict with pagan Rome to assist them in coping with their own reality. Everything the rabbis wrote was designed to promote their views. However, martyrdom as a literary tool differed. Whereas rabbinic maxims were intended to impress the erudite mind, martyrologies played on emotions. Sensational martyrologies could equally touch the hearts of the sophisticated who read them and the simple-minded who heard them. Naturally, before the rabbinic authors could employ stories of self-destruction for self-promotion, they first had to *halakhically* justify the martyrological concept in their theology. For this purpose, they turned to the story of the mother and her seven sons.

"THUS THE LORD MY GOD COMMANDED ME"

She became known as Miriam in early rabbinic literature, but her seven sons remained anonymous. Their story assumed new functions in Talmudic and midrashic versions, becoming one of several depictions of voluntary death for God. As her story traveled through time and space, its first transformation was set in a Roman environment.[18] The family now joined a longer list of Jews whom the Romans had executed. The defiance of the mother and others like her added a new dimension to theology in the vast literature of the rabbis.

The rabbinic variations bypass many of the motifs found in the former Maccabean versions. The rabbinic presentation certainly lacks the philosophical embellishments of 4 Maccabees. There is no emphasis on sadistic tortures or references to atonement or sins. More significant is the vanishing of Eleazar the Scribe. 4 Maccabees failed to achieve in Jewish circles the same success it gained among Church Fathers.[19] The book's early departure from rabbinic awareness may explain the lack of traces of it in the Talmud.[20] Alternatively, it is also possible that lack of traces of 4 Maccabees in the Talmud may explain its departure from Jewish awareness. In either case, the result was the same.

This makes 2 Maccabees a better candidate for inspiration. But there are not many reasons to support this book's direct influence either. For reasons that will be further discussed, the early martyred Eleazar the Scribe would have been a most beneficial addition in the works of the rabbis, who ascribed their origins to the same professional sect of sages.[21] The failure to mention Eleazar may suggest that the rabbinic versions of the mother's story relayed a contemporary oral tradition.[22] In early rabbinic literature, the mother and sons acted without the stimulation that the role model Eleazar is said to have provided in 4 Maccabees.

In the Babylonian Talmud *Gittin* 57b she still maintained her anonymity. The *Amoraic* midrash *Lamentations Rabbah* (*Ekhah Rabbah*) 53 to Lamentations 1:16 named her Miriam, the daughter of Nahtum (the baker),[23] probably a copyist's error of Tanhum (consolation).[24] *Pesiqta Rabbati* 43 of the late ninth to early thirteenth century insists on Miriam bat Tanhum.[25] Because consolation relates to the concluding Psalm 113:9 in the three texts,[26] Tanhum is deliberate and meaningful. Now the mother does not symbolize only defiance. She is the mother of consolations. Mother to mother, her maternal consolations are extended to the many other daughters of Israel who are about to lose their children in resisting religious persecution. Contrary to Antiochus's megalomaniac abuse of one innocent family, the family's new challenge presents a broader feud and bleaker future. The post-Roman *Pesiq. R.* 43 has Miriam bat Tanhum bestowing consolation upon the mothers of Israel who would sacrifice their children, not before Caesar as in *Lamentations Rabbah*,[27] but in the unspecified "days of religious persecutions." There will be many such days to come.

Thus R. Judah's commentary on, "Yea, for thy sake we are killed all the day long, we are counted as sheep for the slaughter," points to the generic "woman" with sons (B. *Gittin* 57b). Her first task was to comfort all the unmentioned bereaved mothers of the four hundred boys and girls (B. *Gittin* 57b). These nameless children drowned themselves in the sea to avoid enslavement in Roman bordellos.[28] Not coincidentally, their story is immediately followed by the affliction of the "woman" of consolation.

But the role of widows goes beyond consolation at the end of ordeals. After Trajan had killed men in a synagogue, he ordered their widows to come out and submit. "And if not I shall do to you what I did to your husbands." They replied: "Then what you did to the men do to the women." Trajan killed them "so their blood mingled with blood of the others" (*Lamentations Rabbah* 1:16). Trajan constituted only one of her many oppressors. Her enemy in the late *Pesiqta* is the ambiguous "They." "They" does not look back to Antiochus's period, but to future threats. It is the "They" that makes her ordeal contemporaneous with any prospective religious conflict. In the other two versions, "Caesar" executes the seven sons of the "woman" or Miriam. Both B. *Gittin*

57b and *Lamentations Rabbah* 1:16 ascribe to Caesar the order to worship other gods.

Caesar's demand was met with various responses, all of which commenced with the statement, "It is written in the Law (*Torah*)."[29] B. *Gittin* includes the sentence in each of the sons' answers. *Lamentations Rabbah* mentions the sons' reliance on the Law eighteen times, with fourteen references in the dialogue with the youngest son alone. "It is written in our Law" follows Caesar's obsessive question "why?" regarding the sons' stubborn disobedience (*Lamentations Rabbah*).

Except for a few instances, both the Talmud and midrash have the sons answer the "why" almost in synonymous fashion. They would not worship other gods for three reasons. Their Law prohibits and admonishes against accepting what Caesar requested from them. The Law instructs the Oneness of God: "I am the Lord thy God" (Exod. 20:2); "Hear, O Israel: the Lord our God, the Lord is one" (Deut. 6:4); "Know this day, and lay it to thy heart, that the Lord, He is God in heaven alone and upon the earth beneath, there is none else" (Deut. 4:39).

The Law demands that "Thou shalt bow down to no other god!" (Exod. 34:14). The answer of the second son further reveals that *God Himself demands* that "Thou shalt have no other gods before Me" (Exod. 20:3).

The "Law" admonishes that "He that sacrifices unto the gods, save unto the Lord only shall be utterly destroyed" (Exod. 22:19) "And the Lord hath avouched thee this day" (Deut. 26:18). Finally, the youngest son explains that he, like his brothers, has "sworn to our God that we shall not exchange Him for another god, as it is written, 'Thou hast avouched the Lord this day to be they God'" (Deut. 26:17).

Their story evidences the sons' absolute obedience to the law of the God of Israel, the only celestial and terrestrial authority. "It is written in the Law," and the biblical structure of the sons' repeated statements compose the theological framework of their story. The Talmudic and midrashic sons show their choice of abandoning life to be rooted in the covenant between God and the Jewish nation.

If biblical verses alone were not transparent enough to anchor voluntary death in theology, the association of the family's ordeal with the story of the *aqedah* transformed the narrative's characteristics from traditional to theological. Rather than revering the past, the new versions incorporated the folktale in the rabbinic theology of the future. "My son," the Talmudic mother instructs her last living son, "go and say to Abraham your father, 'You bound one altar while I have bound seven altars.'" A bolder message to Abraham grows out of her desperation in *Lamentations Rabbah.* "Tell him: 'My mother has said as follows: "Let not your spirit soar with the thought that I have built an altar and I have offered up my son Isaac. Behold our mother has built seven altars and has offered up seven sons, in one day! Yours was a test but mine an actuality!'"

Her actual test does not imply the involvement of sin and punishment, as the Maccabean versions insinuate. Nor do the seven sacrifices indicate a reaction to a rapture between the people and God. Such speculations are eliminated by the biblical example of another potential self-sacrifice. "Why does He not save you from me as He saved Hananiah, Mishael, and Azaria from the hands of Nebuchadnezzar?" asked Caesar of the seventh son. It was because, unlike Caesar, Nebuchadnezzar was a "worthy king," deserving of watching at first hand the greatness of God. Contrary to Antiochus's employment by the divine as an instrument of punishment, Nebuchadnezzar was used "for the purpose of a miracle being accomplished through him as an instrument" (*Lamentations Rabbah*).

With the *aqedah,* the covenant between God and His people was established; with the sacrifice of the sons, the covenant continued. The rabbinic remodeling of the *aqedah* reworked the woman's ordeal into a living covenant between God and Israel. As in the Great Time, when Abraham was in direct communication with God, the mother now could converse with the patriarch through her martyred sons. He of all men should understand.

The rabbinic addition indicates that dying for the Law had become an obligatory act not only in the eyes of spontaneous martyrs but also in the eyes of the rabbis. As *God commanded* Abraham to sacrifice his son, He now requested His people to be ready to lose theirs. Were it not for the mother's last statement ("Yours [Abraham] was a trial"), "I [Abraham] have offered up my son Isaac" leaves the impression of an actual sacrifice in the Bible. Thus especially does *Lamentations Rabbah* employ the *aqedah* to justify theologically the seven martyrdoms. Also of importance is the absence of benefits in the story. It concludes only with the following verse: "A joyful mother of children" (Ps. 113:9). The story of the *aqedah,* which introduced the substitution of animal for human sacrifice, was transformed to approve the choice of passive death theologically. In the new presentation of martyrdom, the original account was changed into a new ritual with "old foundations."[30] The *aqedah* became synonymous with martyrdom, making death for God and His Law obligatory.

Because Abraham was a righteous man of a different generation, he could receive his instructions directly from God. Clear divine commands walked him through his divine trial from beginning to end. No such communication guided the rabbis' generation. In this sense, there is no comparison between Abraham and the mother Miriam. She, as an ordinary human being, had to make seven altars not only to make the biblical hero blush[31] but also to ensure perfection. Ordinary people may elevate themselves to the status of the biblical hero by "following" in his footsteps. And if God took seven sons from one woman in a single day, no one who chooses to walk in Abraham's path should expect it to be just a trial; no one could challenge the legitimacy of her drastic act, at least not according to the Midrash.

By blurring the lines between martyrdom and *aqedah*, the rabbinic versions gave ordinary people an opportunity to become the new biblical heroes of Israel. The fact that Abraham did not sacrifice his son becomes irrelevant. Three essential points emerge from the story: (1) it was God who directly ordered His people to undergo martyrdom/*aqedah*, (2) the prototypal patriarch of the nation accepted the divine call to sacrifice the son he loved, and (3) biblical verses provided the connection between the two notions.

Similar conclusions were deduced from the story of the three biblical heroes in Daniel. They too have emerged in the rabbinic material to justify obligatory death on biblical grounds (*Lamentations Rabbah* 1:16). Regardless of the original message of the book, the Talmud and Midrash employed Daniel to legitimate voluntary death. The Law itself was presented as legitimizing the drastic act because the biblical heroes and the verses quoted by the seven make martyrdom mandatory. To be sure, the seven sons did not quote the Bible to educate a curious foreign ruler about giving up life for God. If *a Jew* were to repeat the *why* attributed to Caesar, the answer would abide: "It is written in the Law."

"WHO ARE THESE [MARTYRS]?"

The powerful consolation that the famed female could offer left a noticeable impression. Her influence is so impressive that it can be detected in nonmartyrological stories as well. She reemerged to consult R. Akiva in his personal tragedy. He lost his son-in-law, Ben Azzai, and his son Simeon, both great scholars of Torah. Many, including Akiva's scholarly rivals, came to pay tribute to the grieving father. They came to comfort but became comforted. Akiva promised them God's reward, for coming to "honor the Torah and to fulfill the commandments" that are required in morning. None of them, however, could relieve Akiva's pain. So the old sage turned to the mother of the seven to find solace. "I should be comforted though I had seven children and had buried them all when my son died" (B. *Moed Katan* 21b; *Semahot* 8:13).[32] Simeon's scholastic greatness increased Akiva's pain as if he had lost seven sons. Like the mother, he finds consolation in the notion that his "seven sons" died while engaging in the Torah.

The mother appears more explicitly in the story of Benjamin the Righteous. One day a "woman" came to him for assistance, as he was the supervisor of the charity in their town:

'Sir, assist me.' He replied, 'I swear, there is not a penny in the charity fund.' She said, 'Sir, if you do not assist me, you are killing a widow and her seven children.' He accordingly assisted her out of his own pocket. Sometime afterwards he became dangerously ill. The angels addressed the Holy One, blessed be He, saying: Sovereign of the Universe, Thou hast said that he who preserves one soul of Israel is considered as if he had preserved the whole world, shall then Benjamin the Righteous who has preserved (*she-hehiah*) a woman and her seven children die at so early an age? Straightway his sentence was torn up. It has been taught that twenty-two years were added to his life. (B. *Baba Bathra* 11a)

As the story develops, the identity of the woman is revealed. This was no ordinary woman. She is the widowed mother of the seven sons. Once her identity was revealed, Benjamin realized that he was about to be guilty of killing the (famous) woman and her seven children. So he made every effort to sustain the family. Past and future are deliberately intermingled here. The sin of not giving charity to the needy is comparable to Caesar's crimes of killing innocent widows with their sons. By the act of giving, Benjamin not only "sustained" but also brought the martyred family back to life. As if looking to the future, by sustaining the family, Benjamin made their future deadly encounter with Caesar possible. Thus in place of vain deaths by starvation, their upcoming deaths earned them everlasting veneration in rabbinic theology.

It is not the habit of the Talmud to make the connection between various notions obvious. But that a connection to martyrdom existed in Benjamin's story is clear from the general context in which it is told. His story follows a discussion about charity and rewards in the world to come. Within this context, we find the closely connected reference to martyrs executed by Romans.

After recovering from a coma, an important question was posed to R. Joseph, the son of R. Joshua. "Who are these [martyrs]?" in the world that he envisioned while sick, asked his father. "Shall I say R. Akiva and his comrades?" asked the son hesitantly. "What is meant," the Talmud comments, "must be the martyrs of Lud" (B. *Baba Bathra* 10b, B. *Pesahim* 50a).

Although they were not forgotten, the spotlight was now shifting from the woman's family to martyred rabbis. Despite the prestige of the mother and her sons, the family ranks second in importance to Akiva and his comrades. The offenses Akiva and his companions are said to have committed against Rome and their suffering differ from those of the family.[33] Instead of disobeying Caesar's direct orders to worship gods, the rabbis are said to have been executed for adamantly ignoring the Roman decrees. In contrast to the Hellenistic persecutions, which the Amoraic version of the mother continued to echo, the Roman edicts never required Jews to sacrifice to gods, nor were Jews required to eat forbidden food.[34]

Instead, rabbinic texts provide postdated and schematic lists of imperial decrees. According to these lists, the Romans outlawed circumcision, gathering for Torah study or teaching, assemblies in synagogues, ordaining new rabbis, reading the Torah in public, reading the Scroll (*Megilla*) of Esther, recitation of the *Shema* prayer ("Hear, O Israel: the Lord our God, the Lord is One," Deut. 6:4), contributions of tithes and offerings, lighting Sabbath and Hanukkah candles, eating *Matzah* on Passover, carrying the palm branch on the Feast of Tabernacles, and the sounding of the ram's horn (*shofar*) on the New Year's Day.[35] B. *Taanit*, for instance, explains as follows: "For once it was decreed that the Jews should not occupy themselves with the study of the Torah nor circumcise their children and that they should desecrate the Sabbath." As "For once" indicates, the historical placement of the decrees is ambiguous.

According to R. Nathan from the important center of Usha, the Jews of the Land of Israel gave up their lives for these commandments: "Why are you being taken out to be killed?" "Because I circumcised my son." "Why are you being taken to be burnt?" "Because I read the Torah." "Why are you being taken out to be crucified?" "Because I ate the unleavened bread." "Why are you being flogged?" "Because I lifted the *lulav*" (*Mekhilta de-Rabbi Ishmael* to Exod. 20:6). The fervent, but nonviolent, resistance to these prohibitions is said to have resulted in a lengthy list of martyred rabbis. However, the Talmud never answered R. Joshua's question regarding the identity of these rabbis. Joshua's question will continue to stand for many generations to come.

To this day, Akiva ben Joseph, Hananiah ben Teradyon, and, to a lesser extent, Judah ben Baba remain the most famous martyred rabbis. The three earn their martyrological fame mainly because the Talmuds detail only their gruesome executions.

Akiva is said to have been executed while proclaiming the *Shema*.[36] B. *Berakhot* 61b reveals that:

When R. Akiva was taken out to be killed it was the time of day for the reading of the *Shema*; and while his flesh was being torn by iron combs,[37] he accepted upon himself the yoke of the Kingdom of Heaven. His students said to him, "Our teacher, so far?" He said to them, "All my life I was distressed by the verse '[And thou shalt love the Lord thy God with all thy heart,] and with all thy soul' (Dut. 6:5 which means 'even if he takes your soul'; I said to myself, 'When will it be possible for me to act that out?' And now that it has become possible, should I not act it out?" He drew out the word "[the Lord is] one" and his soul withdrew on that note. An Echo broke out saying, "You are happy, R. Akiva, for your soul has withdrawn on the note of 'one'."[38]

Akiva's end would eventually be interpreted as the ultimate act of love for God.[39]

A dramatic execution was also the fate of Hananiah ben Teradyon. It came as a punishment for violating three prohibitions. The rabbi learned Torah, taught the Law in public, and publically held the Scroll of the Law in his bosom: "They took him [Hananiah] and wrapped him in the Scroll of the Law and piled up wood around him which they then kindled. And they brought woolen sponges and soaked them in water and placed them on his heart in order that he should not die quickly" (B. *Avodah Zarah* 18a).

Judah ben Baba was spared the calculated sadism that his two coreligionists endured. "The wicked government" is said to have caught the old sage in the act of ordaining students. "It was said that the enemy did not stir from the spot until they had driven three hundred iron spearheads into his body, making it like a sieve" (B. *Sanhedrin* 14a, B. *Avodah Zarah* 8b). The rabbis wished to eulogize their colleague, but the Roman restrictions forbade it. "No funeral orations were delivered over those killed by the Government [i.e., Rome] (*harugei malkhut*)" (B. *Sanhedrin* 11a).

The same tractate reveals the prediction Samuel ha-Qatan (the Little) made shortly before his natural death. He predicted that Simeon and Ishmael would perish by the sword and that their friends would be executed. The identities of Ishmael and Simeon remain inconclusive.[40] As in the vision of R. Joseph, the son of R. Joshua, Simeon's friends who "will be executed" remain nameless in Samuel's prediction, save R. Judah b. Baba.

Despite the anonymity of "Akiva's colleagues" and the "friends" of Simeon and Ishmael, Jewish tradition labored to identify additional Talmudic rabbis as martyrs. Their names emerged especially in midrashic literature, even though their cases are not as explicit. It would have been easier to categorize these cases had the Talmuds provided a standardized term to describe martyrdom. But such technical terminology does not run through the narratives. "Being killed by the State," that is, the Roman Empire, became synonymous with martyrdom in rabbinic awareness. Technically, however, the phrase could be applied also to the activist rebels, who perished in their nationalistic struggle. In fact, in B. *Sanhedrin* 48b the phrase is applied to Jews who were executed by the Jewish state for treason against the king. Only later did the phrase come to indicate the rabbis' passive death in resisting Roman persecutions.

What helped to secure this synonym is the later famous legend about ten rabbis killed by the State [*harugei malkhut*]. It has been translated, erroneously I may add, as "The Legend of the Ten Martyrs."[41] The late *Midrash Elleh Ezkerah*, which will be discussed in the next chapter, combined the names of ten Talmudic rabbis into one unit to describe their executions on a single day.[42] It should be made clear, however, that the midrashic term *Ten Martyrs (Asarah Harugei Malkhut)* or, more accurately the *ten killed by the Government*, is not found in the Talmuds.[43]

The midrashic story of the "Ten Martyrs" is linked to the days of the emperors Trajan and Hadrian (132–135). *Lamentations Rabbah* 2:2 explains that the verse "The Lord has destroyed without mercy all the habitations of Jacob" refers to the following rabbis: Ishmael, Rabban Gamliel, Yeshebab, Judah ben Baba, Huzpit the Announcer, Hananiah ben Teradyon, Akiva, Judah the Baker, Ben Azzai, and Tarfon. But "some drop R. Tarfon and add R. Eleazar b. Harsom." Most of these names emerge in different versions of the legend.[44] Missing in this midrash is both the number ten and the phrase *harugei malkhut*.

As we shall see, it is important to mention three other names. L. Finkelstein replaces Simeon ben Azzai and Tarfon with Lulianus and Pappus, and A. Hyman indicates that *Hekhalot Rabbati*, includes Rabbi Eleazar ben Dama, the nephew of Rabbi Ishmael, among the ten.[45] The lists vary because the identity of the martyrs and the natures of their deaths remains unclear.

Contrary to the cases of Akiva, Teradyon, and Judah ben Baba, and to a lesser extent Simeon and Ishmael, the Talmud does not disclose why or how Judah the Baker, Huzpit, and Yeshebab lost their lives. B. *Hullin* 142a and B. *Kiddushin* 99b only say that Huzpit's tongue was found in the rubbish. A similar fate is related of R. Judah the Baker in Y. *Hagiga* 2, 1, 77b; a dog carried his tongue. Perhaps this description later inspired *Midrash Elleh Ezkerah* to add to the Talmudic version the feeding of Judah ben Baba's body to the dogs.[46] For good reasons, the two *Talmudim* do not apply the legend's phrase *harugei malkhut* in a martyrological sense in their cases. There is no dramatic encounter with Roman authorities, no known martyrological proclamations or climactic endings.

The listing of Rabbi Eleazar ben Dama among the ten martyrs presents a number of difficulties. Eleazar ben Dama died because he "was bitten by a serpent." The description of this proclaimed martyr leaves out any Roman involvement.[47] Nor does the story accord Eleazar a choice between life and death. The question of placement in the list of martyrs applies also to Simeon ben Azzai. In B. *Hagigah* 14b he dies while entering the forbidden *Pardes*, that is, during the dangerous practice of mysticism.

Interestingly, the Talmuds offer other cases of voluntary death that would have been more easily associated with martyrdom, but the midrashic versions chose not to include them. B. *Taanit* 18b, for instance, describes the execution of the two brothers Lulianus and Pappus in Laodicea. The two are also identified by their Hebrew names, Shemaiah and Ahijah.[48] Perhaps for this reason, Finkelstein decided to replace the nonmartyrs Simeon ben Azzai and Tarfon in the legend of *Asarah Harugei Malkhut* with Lulianus and Pappus.[49]

The legend of *Asarah Harugei Malkhut* attempts to resolve the very same question asked by Joshua regarding the martyrs' identity. It does so by artificially combining different individuals into a single narrative. Eventually, legends will come a full circle, adding to the ten rabbis the famous seven. The sons who had comforted their biological mother arose now to condole their mother nation that lost its best. "After these ten righteous men were killed, seven brothers came and eulogized and wept over them profusely, until Caesar heard about it. He called for them and saw their beauty. . . . " Thereafter, he executed the seven one by one.[50]

FROM LEADERS BY BIRTH TO LEADERS BY DEATH

Even the seven brothers, the most qualified martyrs, "admitted" in the rabbinic texts that the rabbinic heroes surpassed all martyrs. Because of the unusual heroism of the rabbis, their deaths resulted in their being venerated. The accounts of rabbis dying voluntarily established a self-image that would serve to justify the leadership they aspired to achieve. Narratives of passive heroism demonstrate how the rabbis served the people in time of great crisis. These narratives describe rabbis as the sole protectors of Judaism who passively defended Jewish identity during the days of destruction. More than anyone else, their martyrologies convey, it was the rabbis who "gave" rather than "took." More specifically, it was "R. Akiva and his companions who gave themselves up" (B. *Sanhedrin* 110b).

Such overpowering images overlook the many others who also perished in the struggle against the Romans. Not only rabbis "were killed by the Government," but only their deaths are said to have retained merit. The vision of the recovering R. Joseph ben R. Joshua captures the rabbis' monopoly on meaningful death. His vision deserves a full citation. R. Joshua asked his son:

'What vision did you have?' He replied, 'I saw a world upside down, the upper below and the lower above.' He said to him: 'You saw a well regulated world.'

[He asked further]: 'In what condition did you see us [rabbis]?' He replied: 'As our esteem is here, so it is there. I also heard them saying, Happy he who comes here in full possession of his learning. I also heard them saying, 'No creature can attain to the place assigned to those killed by the [Roman] Government.' Who are these? Shall I say R. Akiva and his comrades? Had they no other merit but this? Obviously even without this [they would have attained this rank]. What is meant therefore must be the fatalities (*harugei*) of Lud. (B. *Baba Batra* 10b)[51]

Joseph envisions a topsy-turvy world in which those killed by the Romans earn a special status. Because both rebels as well as rabbis expired under Rome, an identity question instantly follows. "Who are these" special individuals? They are Akiva and his rabbinic colleagues who established a Torah center in Lud.[52] To be sure, they do not attain their merit just for being Rome's victims. What makes their deaths meaningful is the reason behind it. Rabbis reached their deaths while in "full possession" of learning. Thus even without their altruism they would have earned the same special position in the "place" that is not described.

On the flip side of the coin, the Roman also executed the rebels. Yet they do not enjoy the rabbis' status because they came to their executions not in "full possession" of learning. Unlike the rabbis, the rebels put their active resistance before the studying of Torah. For both theological and political reasons, these rabbis distanced themselves from the rebels' catastrophic adventure. Politically, they should not be held responsible for the devastating aftermath of the rebellion, even though Akiva and Teradyon were among its open supporters. Theologically, rabbis left the future of human history to be determined by God.

The Palestinian *Midrash Ruth Rabbah* 3, 1 (ca. 500–600) disregarded martyrs altogether in Joshua's vision: "R. Meyasha the grandson of R. Joshua b. Levi was made unconscious by his illness for three days. After three days he regained consciousness. His father said to him: 'Where were you?' He replied: 'In a confused world.' He asked: 'What did you see there? He answered: 'I saw many people who were held in honor here and are in disgrace there.'" Building on this Midrash, the Talmudic text combined the merit of learning with that of death. But the latter act without the first is meaningless. Thus, in contrast to the rebels, it is exclusively the rabbis' giving up of life that counts.

This exclusiveness is made clear by *Midrash Kohelet Rabba* 9, 10 (ed. Romm 24b): "R. Aha longed to see the face of R. Alexander [in a dream]. He appeared to him in his dream and showed him two things: There is no compartment beyond that of the fatalities (*harugei*) of Lud; blessed be He Who removes the shame of Lulianus and Pappus and happy is he who comes here equipped with learning." As seen in B. *Taanit* 18b, Roman authorities are said to have executed the brothers Lulianus and Pappus in Laodicea. Technically, they, too, fall under the category of *harugei malkhut*. Their "shame" in the midrash, therefore, is perplexing. It is reenforced by their own statement. "We have deserved of the Omnipresent that we should die," seems to acknowledge embarrassment in their act. What was so shameful about their deaths? The answer may be found in the encounter between Pappus[53] and Akiva in a Roman jail (B. *Berakot* 61b).

The two had already met once, when Akiva publicly taught Torah. Mockingly Pappus asked: "Akiva, are you not afraid of the Government?" Mockingly, because Akiva hoped to achieve salvation only through studying and teaching Torah (at least according to this story). Given the Roman ban, his activity was certain to bring death upon him. Pappus, in contrast, preferred the militant option of the rebels. Of the two approaches, Pappus deemed his to be the realistic solution for salvation.

The final semisarcastic question was reserved for Akiva when they met again in jail. "Pappus, who brought you here?" asked Akiva. Certainly it was not the study of Torah, Akiva implied. Pappus replied: 'Happy are you, R. Akiva, that you have been seized for busying yourself with the Torah! Alas for Pappus who has been seized for busying himself with idle things!'" Both perished in the same fashion. Yet honor became Akiva's lot for studying Torah. Shame becomes Pappus' fate for relying entirely on the combative solution.[54] Not all *harugei malkhut*, then, belong to an equal class, according to the rabbis.[55] The lack of a martyrological term complicates the distinction between different categories of death. The rabbinic text associates meritorious death only with the altruism of the rabbis of Lud, because they are said to have died for the Torah.[56]

Hananiah ben Teradyon provides another "proof" of rabbinic merit. In a manner reminiscent of Pappus's admonition, Jose ben Kisma demonstrates his belief that Teradyon's stubborn behavior is fatal. He mentions the characteristics of unique leaders, which the rabbis shared.

Brother Hananiah, do you not know that it is Heaven that has ordained this [Roman] nation to reign? For though she laid waste His House, burnt His Temple, *slew His pious ones and caused His best ones to perish* [emphasis mine]; still she is firmly established. Yet, I have heard that you sit and occupy yourself with the Torah, does *publicly gather assemblies and keep a Scroll [of the Law] in your bosom* (B. *Avodah Zarah* 18a).

Hananiah deserved respect, not only because he occupied himself with learning. His greatest contribution was that he taught the Law publicly. Had studying the Law been his only goal, he could have achieved learning in hiding. But, like Akiva, he displayed not merely his personal religiosity but also social responsibility. Eventually, the Romans "found R. Hananiah ben Teradyon . . . bringing together groups of people in public, holding the Scroll in his bosom" (B. *Avoda Zarah* 18a). For teaching Torah publicly, he was executed publicly;[57] for teaching Torah publicly, Hananiah was considered among God's "pious ones and . . . His best ones."

R. Akiva and R. Hananiah afford the most famous examples of heroism in accounts that made the very survival of (rabbinic) Judaism a key issue. The association of R. Judah ben Baba's death with martyrdom was no less effective in achieving the rabbis' goals. Judah ben Baba ordained students despite the decrees: "The wicked Government decreed that whoever performed an ordination should be put to death, and whoever received ordination should be put to death, and the city in which the ordination took place demolished, and the boundaries wherein it had been performed, uprooted" (B. *Sanhedrin* 14a). Judah took precautions not to bring attention to his activity. When discovered, he put his students lives before his. The majority appear to have followed his advice and to have fled, whereas the "enemy did not stir from the spot until they had driven three hundred iron spearheads into his body, making it like a sieve." The spotlight clearly falls on the rabbi. For "With R. Judah ben Baba were in fact some others, but in honor to him, they were not mentioned."

To emphasize Judah's role in the drama, the Roman soldiers do not touch these "others," as one might expect (according to the decree, "whoever received ordination should be put to death"). Instead, the account *sacrifices* the untold story of "some others" to honor R. Judah. Why was the sage honored and the others ignored? Because "were it not for him, the laws of *kenas* would have been forgotten in Israel." His story was not presented as a simple case of forbidden ordination. Without him, we are led to believe, these laws "might have been abolished." Just how significant his role was in preserving the future of Israel indicates the following analogy. R. Judah's role in ordination and the transmission of authority is compared to Moses's appointing Joshua in his stead. The rabbi proved to possess the prodigious leadership qualities and religious authority of his biblical predecessor. What comes to mind is that the rabbis' oral Law (*halakhah*) was given to Moses at Sinai (as the rabbis argued), as well as their destiny to lead the people.

Such stories about second-century sages explain the special characteristics of the emerging leadership of sixth-century rabbis. By putting the interests of society – the preservation of social and religious identity – ahead of their personal gain, the rabbis of the past legitimized the ascendancy of their descendants. In their presentations of the past, a clear-cut distinction existed between the deaths of rabbis and that of rebels. By presenting themselves as direct descendants of these legendary heroes, rabbis of later generations could legitimize their socioreligious aspiration.

The rabbis' concern was not just the positive role the rebels may have enjoyed in the memory of the Jews. Another challenge to the rabbis' attempts to secure their position could have advanced the memory of the priests and the nostalgia for their Temple. As with the rebels, the priests' function had to be rendered obsolete.

Because only the rabbis are said to have displayed leadership in adversity, whereas the previous priestly leadership – consisting of a few aristocratic families and their representatives – remained silent, the authoritative status of this previous ruling class had to be discredited. B. *Taanit* 29a well demonstrates this claim for a shift in authority through what appears to be yet another martyrological story.

When the First Temple was about to be destroyed, bands upon bands of young priests with the keys of the Temple in their hands assembled and mounted the roof of the Temple and exclaimed, "Master of the universe, as we did not have the merit to be faithful treasurers, these keys are handed back into Thy keeping." They then threw the keys up towards heaven. And there emerged the figure of a hand and received the keys from them. Whereupon they jumped and fell into the fire.

This account contains motifs reminiscent of the biblical story of Hananiah, Mishael, and Azariah: fire and divine intervention occurring in the "form of a hand." But unlike in the story of the biblical heroes, God did not save the priests from the fire. The account has the *priests* explain the absence of divine intervention in the house of God. They "did not merit to be faithful treasurers." As the *rabbis* comment on this priestly admission of guilt, the priests lost God's favor for they were "full of controversy." Because He intervened only to receive the keys without saving the priests, their divine authority came to an end. God did not spare the priesthood; nor were the priests worthy of martyrdom.

Just how significant the divine act of taking is, is demonstrated by the story of Hanina ben Dosa. Here, too, the hand of God plays the same role:

Once his wife said to him: "How long shall we go on suffering so much?" He replied: "What shall we do?" – "Pray that something may be given to you!" He prayed, and there emerged the figure of a hand reaching out to him a leg of a golden table. Thereupon he saw in a dream that the pious would one day eat at a three-legged golden table but he would eat at a two-legged table. Her husband said to her: "Are you content that everybody shall eat at a perfect table and we at an imperfect table?" She replied: "What than shall we do?" – "Pray that the leg should be taken away from you!" He prayed and it was taken away. A *Tanna* taught: "*The latter miracle was greater than the former; for there is a tradition that a thing may be given but once; it is never taken away again*" (B. *Taanit* 25a; emphasis mine).

The divine punishment of the priests became the miracle of the rabbis.

The keys of leadership were believed to be given to those whose altruism proved them to be worthy of the leadership of Israel. This divine privilege was allocated exclusively to the rabbis. Through this prerogative they rose to excellence, whereas the priests miserably "fell into the fire." Because the rabbis were divinely given the opportunity to undergo martyrdom, they became God's pristine chosen leaders. When the rabbis gave themselves up and, more importantly, when God accepted their deaths, they proved to be worthy of the new historical role that was awaiting them.

Josephus has provided a similar description of a priestly suicide in reaction to Pompey's invasion of the Second Temple. Perhaps the late rabbinic association of the event with the First Sanctuary is a sincere confusion of an oral tradition. But by placing the break between God and His priest in the First Temple, the rabbis further distance the old guards from God and themselves. To be sure, Talmudic sages did not limit their criticism to the period of the First Temple. Rabbah b. Bar Hana said:

What is the meaning of the passage, "The fear of the Lord prolongs days; but the years of the wicked shall be shortened?" "The fear of the Lord prolongs days" refers to the first Sanctuary, which remained standing for four hundred and ten years and in which there served only eighteen high priests. "But the years of the wicked shall be shortened" refers to the second Sanctuary, which abided for four hundred and twenty years and at which more than three hundred [high] priests served (B. *Yoma* 9a).

Not coincidently, Akiva emerges a strong critic of the priests.[58] Only a martyred rabbi of his status could openly attack the old guardians of God's Temple. Even their direct Aaronic lineage could not maintain their stature. Both Mirian and Aaron, he is said to have argued, had been afflicted with leprosy because they calumniated their brother Moses (B. *Shabbat* 97a). Aaron's "original sin" continued to affect his descendants, the priests, like the infectious disease.

The post-Talmudic *Midrash Mishle* (Proverbs) continues this challenging of the priests' traditional status.[59] According to this midrash, Elijah "the Priest" himself carried Akiva's corpse on his shoulder from jail to his burial cave. Elijah's companion, R. Joshua ha-Garsi, asked in dismay: "*Rabbi!* Did you tell me: 'I am Elijah the Priest.' [But] a priest should not be defiled by the dead."[60] He answered: 'Alas! There is no defilement in *the righteous or their students*'" [emphasis mine]. "Righteous" (*Tzadikim*) clearly refers to rabbis, teachers of students. Elijah, a priest and a rabbi, confirmed the superior purity of the martyred rabbis over that of the priests.

The power of the martyrological accounts springs not from the soiling of the image of the priests.[61] The dramatization of the rabbis' behavior and wisdom was powerful enough to create an image of rabbinic authority. Through the martyrological narratives, the rabbis attempted to assert and justify their role as leaders of the entire "nation" in a time that the Jewish world was carving a niche for itself in a Christian empire. By means of the whole body of martyrological narrative, the shift in leadership, which occurred gradually after the destruction of the Second Temple, from "an assembly of sages" to "rabbis" was presented as an instant event.

The martyrological narratives were designed to lend authority to the leadership of the rabbis as a whole. Such narratives presented the rabbinic group as being composed of unique individuals. In contrast to the priests (and for that matter all the sects that could challenge the rabbis) it was not their descent from Aaron that accounted for their uniqueness;[62] it was the rabbis' personal integrity and ability to conduct the nation in time of crisis. When God tested the righteousness and the right of the rabbis to lead (as He had tested Abraham), devotion to the nation's interest marked their character in the rabbinic texts. Through their martyrologies, the rabbis emerged as perfect popular champions for an aching nation. Because only the rabbis are reported in their own accounts to have undertaken martyrdom for God and the masses, we are to believe that only they emerged from this disastrous crisis victorious. While the rabbinic texts emphasized that the priests received their authority from secular Jewish and spurned Roman rulers,[63] the accounts about second-century martyred rabbis affirmed the assumption of their role through divine authority. As Aaron's "original sin" could affect his priestly successors, the merit of second-century martyred rabbis could be transmitted to their descendants. The priestly concept of born leaders died; the rabbinic concept of dying leaders was conceived.

RESTORING THE SYSTEM

"When Akiva died Judah (the Prince) was born." This statement from B. *Kiddushin* 72b attaches to the idea of earning merit through death the notion of religious preservation. The statement associates Akiva's death with the birth of Judah the Prince, who is considered the compiler of the Mishnah, the corpus of rabbinic Law that was adopted by the Jerusalem and Babylonian schools. In parallel to the creation of a leadership image, therefore, martyrologies presented the rabbis as the sole protectors and restorers of Judaism. With the memory of the destruction of the Temple and the devastating results of the conflicts with Rome in mind, the rabbinic texts of late antiquity emphasize the need for a new socioreligious system to maintain the unity of the Jews throughout the world. To secure the transformation, the importance of the Law and the newly established study centers became a recurrent motif in rabbinic stories about the past heroes. Instead of the Temple that housed the Divine Presence and the priests, the rabbis designed Torah centers to house the divine wisdom and themselves. Both people and place are said to have obtained stature through rabbinic altruism. As the rabbis of late antiquity still labored to establish their roles, there was a desire to promulgate the reputation of their centers.

The same affirmation of newly established centers played its part in the account of R. Judah b. Baba. Roman decrees already implied the recognition of self and space. Both the performer of ordination and "the city in which the ordination took place" were to be destroyed, "the boundaries wherein it had been performed, uprooted." To outsmart this decree and diminish the danger to people and places, it is reported, R. Judah "... went and sat between two great mountains, [that lay] between two large cities; between the Sabbath boundaries of the cities of Usha and Shefaram and there ordained five elders: R. Meir, R. Judah, R. Jose, R. Simeon and R. Eleazar b. Shammua; R. Awia adds also R. Nehemiah" (B. *Avodah Zarah* 8b; B. *Sanhedrin* 13b–14a). If caught, neither Usha nor Shefaram would suffer because the violation took place outside the cities' limits. But the story reflects neither a geographical nor a topographical reality. Usha and Shefaram are not located between two great mountains. It is also unlikely that the Romans based their decree on the Jewish law of Sabbath borders. The dramatic consequences of R. Judah's ordination overpower and suppress these contradictions. The emphasis on the geographical location stresses the significance of these two new Torah centers, which signal perhaps the first institutionalized rabbinate.[64] The story explains why the Roman authority did not destroy Jewish cities, as "it had declared to do," and punish illegal rabbinic activity. What the story does not want the reader to conclude is that these two pivotal centers of studying survived the decrees due to their insignificance in Rome's eyes. Thus B. *Baba Kama* 38a affirms, even the Roman authority understood the significance of Usha as a Torah center and recognized the jurisdiction of its leader, Rabban Gamliel.[65] Other rabbinic sources further tie ben Baba's risky ordination to Usha. The students he ordained by losing his life became the prominent leaders of Usha.[66] They owed their succession and the preservation of *Taqqanot Usha* (the enactments of Usha) to the martyrs.

The geographical discrepancy denotes the first signal that historical accuracy was not the story's aim. It delivered the self-image of rabbinic superiority and the claim for the existence of early authoritative rabbinic study centers.[67] Additional inconsistencies show the narrative's concern with the rabbinic indoctrination over exactness. "The wicked government" did not execute R. Judah ben Baba's five ordained students. Two of the five seem to be out of place. R. Akiva already had ordained R. Simeon and R. Meir and not in time of persecution.[68] Perhaps the double ordination of the two students by two martyred rabbis was intended to double their prestige. Yet far more problematic are the descriptions of Judah ben Baba's death from illness in his bed.[69] All these disparities become irrelevant in the wider goal of establishing a posteriori the authority of righteous leaders and religious loci.

In rabbinic eyes, the sages' centers earned their distinction because the rabbis taught the Law publicly in them, and for them they are reported to have perished. The account against the priesthood legitimacy claims that the priests killed themselves for losing their place in the Temple. With the loss of the Temple, we are to understand that the priests lost their role in the life of the nation. Conversely, the rabbis gave themselves up for the eternal Torah rather than for a place doomed for destruction. The rabbis thus offered a holy system not bound by a sacred place.

When the Romans asked R. Hananiah b. Teradyon, "Why hast thou occupied thyself with the Torah?" he answered, "Thus the Lord my God commanded me" (B. *Avodah Zarah* 17b). This command led eventually to his execution. Seeing her father holding the Torah scroll at the stake, R. Hananiah ben Teradyon's daughter screamed in despair. Although there was no need to cry over him or the Torah, he hoped she was, at least, lamenting the apparent extinction of Torah.

My daughter, if it is for me that you are weeping and for me that you throw yourself on the ground, it is better that a fire made by man should consume me, rather than a fire not made by man. . . . But if it is for the Torah scroll that you are weeping, lo, the Torah is fire, and fire cannot consume fire. Behold, the letters are flying into the air, and only the parchment itself is burning (*Semahot* 8:12).

Teradyon's personal ordeal is insignificant. The burning of Torah forms the real tragedy here. But the tragedy can be measured only in human terms. The truth of the matter is that the Divine Scriptures cannot be destroyed. As to Teradyon, he considered himself fortunate. To be burned for and with the Holy Scroll is a privilege only few experience. It is not the external fire that consumes Teradyon but rather the inner fire of the Torah. All his life he immersed himself in the studying of Torah. Now finally through the fire, he and his object of desire become united. It is only because of the deaths of rabbis like Teradyon, we are led to believe, that the Torah survived such severe "days of destructions." In the words of Resh Lakish, "the words of Torah are firmly held by one who kills himself for it" (B. *Berakhot* 63b). His proof is in the Torah. "This is the Torah, when a man shall die in the tent" (Num. 19:14). Teradyon fulfilled the verse literally.

Jail became Akiva's tent. His pupil, Joshua ha-Garsi, brought his teacher daily enough water for drinking and ritual washing. When the Roman guard reduced the already scanty amount of water, Akiva washed himself regardless of the amount. "It will not suffice for drinking," Joshua worried, "will it suffice for washing your hands?" Akiva's answer followed: "What can we do? when for [neglecting] the words of the Rabbis one deserves death? It is better that I myself should die than that I should transgress against the opinion of my colleagues" (B. *Eruvin* 21b). Akiva provides the paradigm of the observant Jew who will go beyond the initial requirements of the Law to protect the Law. The incident quoted took place in private (before fewer than ten Jews) and did not involve idolatry, incest, or bloodshed. Akiva's piety demonstrated the significance of each commandment and well accords with the opinion of Rabbi Joshua ben Korkha: "R. Akiva and his companions gave themselves up to immolation *for the sake of the Torah*" (B. *Sanhedrin* 110b, emphasis mine).

The second aspect of the story reveals what constitutes this Torah. In the stories of martyrdom, the martyrs die either for God or His Law. In this story, which follows a discussion on the "significance of the Scriptural text," Rabbi Akiva accepted death not to "transgress against the opinion" of his colleagues. The story thus validates the importance of both the written and oral laws of Akiva's associates.

Halakhic validation stems also from R. Eliezer's prediction of Akiva's death. He is said to have predicted that Akiva would die precisely for the reason of placing his *halakhah* regarding *shechitah* (ritual slaughtering of animals) above the Scriptural law. Akiva, Eliezer foretold, "you have refuted me by *shechitah*; by *shechitah* shall be his death" (B. *Pesahim* 69a). At first glance, Eliezer's prediction may sound as a punishment for insolence. But this story about a single *halakhah* also reveals the true reason for Akiva's acceptance of death in the future.

This aspect of the story encouraged commitment by individuals to the new rabbinic system, which could be taught and led only by the rabbis. As B. *Berakhot* 47a–b indicates: "... even if one has learnt Scripture and Mishnah but has not ministered to the disciples of the wise [rabbis], he is an *am ha-aretz*." What do the wise teach the disciple? According to the rabbis' teaching, life without both the written and oral law is an impossible existence for Jews. Rather than encouraging Jews to emulate rabbinic martyrs, what the story attempts to instill is the indispensability of the rabbinic teachings to Jewish life.

Rabbinic authority and restoration of the religious system according to the rabbinic ideal constituted two intertwined goals. R. Akiva, R. Hananiah ben Teradyon, and R. Judah ben Baba quitted life not solely for the Torah but for the "Law." This law is not only the Torah, the Bible; it is also religious and secular law, knowledge of history and the physical universe, Mishnah and exegesis of the Midrash. Thus, for example, R. Joseph praised the decree of King Jannai because through him, "the Merciful One caused Issachar of Kefar Barkai to receive his deserts [his hands were cut off] in this world." R. Ashi explained that God punished Issachar because he "had not studied the Mishnah," and thus he could not make the right decisions.[70]

This is a reflection of a significant distinction from the worldview of the priests – the Sadducees' forebears – who considered only the Temple, their Aaronic descent, and the Bible central to Jews. R. Joshua ben Levi well demonstrates the importance of Torah study over Temple sacrifice. He commentated:

What is the meaning of the [Psalmist's] words, Our feet stood within thy gates, O Jerusalem? [It is this.] What helped us to maintain our firm foothold in war? The gates of Jerusalem – the place where students engaged in the study of Torah! R. Joshua b. Levi said also the following: What is the meaning of the [Psalmist's] words, A song of Ascents unto David. I was rejoiced when they said unto me: 'Let us go unto the house of the Lord'? David, addressing himself to the Holy One, blessed be He, said: Lord of the Universe! I heard men saying, 'When will this old man die and let his son Solomon come and build us the Chosen Shrine and we shall go up there [as pilgrims]?' and I rejoiced at that. Said the Holy One, blessed be He, to him, A day in thy courts is better than a thousand! Better to Me one day spent by you in study of Torah than a thousand sacrifices that your son Solomon will [some day] offer before Me, on the altar! (B. Makkot 10a)

David rejoices in his upcoming death, for God promised that the Temple will be built by his son. Moreover, he shares the impatience of the populace who wants him replaced. But God quickly extinguishes David's altruistic enthusiasm for the Temple. God rejects the king's personal sacrifice, downplaying the importance of the Temple cult and its court oblations. "One day in which you occupy yourself with the Torah" is better for God than a thousand burnt offerings. R. Johanan ben Zakkai made a similar point. Quoting Hosea 6:6, he argued that God "desires mercy, and not sacrifices."[71]

Such stories and comments reminded Talmudic readers that the Temple had lost its place in the life of the Jews while emphasizing the need to replace it with a new centralized form of worship. Late antiquity sages continued to employ the heroes of the past to create images that would serve to secure their own views. Akiva and his colleagues are reported to have lost their lives while occupying themselves with the Torah. They did so not only to honor the historical role of the Torah but also for the future of the Jewish people. According to these late images, leaders advised against rebuilding the Temple as early as the first century. Salvation comes not via the reconstruction of the past but through the construction of the future. Self-occupation with the Law in the fullest sense of the word provides the singular path to fulfillment. In rabbinic eyes, only the rabbis could meet the new high standards of leadership which they established in their teachings and by their deaths.

The interplay between the Law and the martyred rabbis eventually becomes a unity. Rabbis are the Torah; the Torah is the rabbis. And both authorities are said to be empowered by God. Fire had already fused Teradyon and the Scrolls into a single entity. A similar association surfaces at R. Eliezer ben Hyrcanus's deathbed.[72] Just before expiring, Eliezer compares his arms to the "two Scrolls of the Law that are wrapped up" (B. *Sanhedrin* 68a).[73] Although not suffering martyrdom, his last dialogue with his visiting colleagues glimmers with the motif. These colleagues are no other than "R. Akiva and his companions."

The would-be martyrs gathered around his bed to pay their respects. They were careful to keep their distance from the dying sage, for they had previously excommunicated him.[74] His daring interpretation of the Law was more than they could tolerate. On the face of it, they came to see him to fulfill the duty of visiting the sick. But realizing the great intellectual vacuum after his coming death, they also came "to study the Torah." It was too late; Eliezer prepared himself to be wrapped up like the two Scrolls of the Law ((B. *Sotah* 49b). What he had managed to convey so far, he said, was "only as a paint-brush dipping into the vial." What Akiva and his colleagues refused to absorb from the vial of wisdom were his *halakhot*. Eliezer transmitted three hundred *halakhot* only on the subject of *baheret* (leprous symptoms); three hundred, "or three thousand as some say," *halakhot* on the magical planting of cucumbers. Their refusal to learn his *halakhot,* predicted Eliezer, would bring upon Akiva and his friends violent deaths. To Akiva he promised a death "harsher than theirs." Although less favorably, here, too, deaths of *harugei malkhot* are linked to the preservation of the rabbis' oral wisdom.

Eliezer continued with his teaching until he expired on the note of "ritually clean." His last words proved his guiltlessness. So they immediately lifted the ban. The remorseful rabbis were late once again. Eliezer's last lesson was

not to be forgotten, however. Death cleans and convinces. Akiva and his associates would transmit the little knowledge of *halakhot* they had absorbed from
Eliezer. They would do so until the *halakhah* took them along the path of self-
sacrifice. At the end of this path, violent deaths would prove the importance
of all *halakhot* and convince others to accept them.

By the second century C.E., we must recall, these new rabbinic standards
were still without legal authority. As S. Lieberman indicates, the rabbis' written
"*halakhot* and comments" were merely private notes.[75] J. Neusner writes that
the rabbis created a "rabbinic Torah-myth" that rabbinic authority rests on
Mosaic authorship. It asserted for the first time that,

... to live by the Torah of Moses, the whole Torah of Sinai and taught to do so by
men possessing the authentic traditions of Sinai. No one ignored Scripture. But to
those Sadducees who adhered to the view that all Moses had revealed was a Written
Torah, to those remnants of other groups that had had their own written traditions
in addition to the Bible, and above all, to those ordinary folk who knew nothing
other than the Scriptures and local customs, elements of the rabbinic Torah must
have proved alien.... The claim of Mosaic "authorship" for the rabbinic Torah
and its authentication by Moses constituted powerful propaganda.[76]

Martyrologies played an essential role in promoting rabbinic teachings well
after the deaths of their heroes. On the one hand, the deaths of rabbis emphasized the importance of the Law for all Jews. On the other hand, the Law,
which from now on was interpreted according to the rabbis' views, emphasized
their indispensable role. Understanding to the full the meaning of the Torah
without the *halakhot* was said to be impossible, as was the understanding of
the *halakhot* without the rabbis. The Torah, the rabbis, and their *halakhah*
became inseparable in rabbinic texts. The acceptance of the Torah required
the appreciation of the rabbis; the confirmation of the rabbis necessitates the
acknowledgment of their (written and oral) Torah. Rabbinic martyrologies
reinforced the "rabbinic Torah-myth," and the two motifs served to convince
their audience that the righteous rabbis and their sacred system have earned
a unique role in the lives of the Jewish people.

JEWS, JEWISH-CHRISTIANS, GENTILE-CHRISTIANS, AND GENTILES

Emphasis on rabbinic Law denotes also a reaction to the heretical Jewish
movement of *Minut*. Although it is still difficult to determine whether all
the *Minim* were Christians, by the time the rabbis compiled the Talmud, the
association of *Minut* with Christianity was not incomprehensible. The need

to emphasize the Law turned critical, for their Good News infiltrated Jewish circles as well.[77]

The new Israel believed that the incarnated son of God descended from heaven to deliver humanity. Jesus's cosmic event overshadowed previous religious experiences, leading Christianity to minimize the importance of the Torah.[78] Gentile converts welcomed these teachings, which spared them both the complicated restrictions of the Law and circumcision. The Jewish-Christians, also identified as Nazoreans,[79] did not perceive these restrictions as stumbling blocks, thus continuing to observe the Torah, Sabbath, and circumcision.

Different Talmudic sections describe even wider gaps between the Jews and the *Minim* (Jewish-Christians). B. *Sanhedrin* 38b identifies Adam as a *Min* to contrast the theological stands of the *Minim* and the rabbis. Like Adam, *Minim* practiced epispasm;[80] denied God by contradicting His singularity, because of their belief in a divine messenger; and scorned the study of the Torah. These theological positions were held by the rabbis as obvious departures from the covenant with God. Because the *Minim* "rejected the Torah . . . abandoned the ways of the community . . . and sinned and made the masses sin," they now belonged with the pagan unbelievers (B. *Rosh Hashanah* 17a).[81]

The Jewish-Christian theological compromise, and the new Christological interpretations, presented a real menace to *halakhic* Judaism. Any concession could have meant the absorption of Judaism by a growing Christianity. The new *religio* could potentially have caused the disappearance of the old.[82] Unlike the imperial decrees, the *Minim* developed into a grander impediment because they "sinned and made the masses sin." In other words, Judaism was losing souls to *Minut*.

The polemics of rabbinic martyrology appeared antagonistic not only to the Christian call to abandon the Torah. They also distinguished Judaism from the principle of Jesus's divine incarnation. The polemics against the new religion employed the story of the mother with her seven sons. As the Western world witnessed its transformation from paganism to Christianity, the family, *mutatis mutandis*, could be perceived as addressing also their new theological rival.[83] The dialogue between the ruler and the seventh son takes a peculiar turn in *Lamentations Rabbah* 53 to Lamentations 1:16. Suddenly, the discourse revolves around the attributes of God. Now the ruler is eager to learn about the corporeal properties of God. "Does your God have a mouth? . . . does your God have eyes? . . . does your God have ears?" And the questions of physical attributes go on.

Dying for the Law, the seven clarified the theological differences between their religion and its new variations. Even if individuals kept some of the old rituals and acknowledged their Jewish descent, their rejection of the Torah and their belief in divine incarnation banished them from the world of the Jews. The seven thus expressed what they considered the absurdity of the belief in a corporeal divinity. Probably for the same reason, the reminder that God's "messengers are not like the messengers of flesh and blood" precedes a short reference to the *Minim* and their interpretation of the *Shekhinah* (Divine Presence) (B. *Baba Bathra* 25a). In a Christological context, the *Shekhinah* could be construed as the Holy Spirit.[84]

As *Minut* turned into Christianity, the Roman persecution received new meanings in the memory of the rabbis. The importance of reciting the *Shema* was conceived as a reaction to the Christian belief in the coexisting authority of God and Jesus. The seven sons quoted biblical verses to answer Caesar's "why." Of all the verses they quoted, Deuteronomy 6:4 ("Hear, O Israel: the Lord our God, the Lord is one") would eventually develop into the ultimate martyrological cry. In the future, martyrdom will center on this verse, known in short as the proclamation of the *Shema*. It will become the equivalent of the Christian martyrs' proclamation *Christianus sum*.

In part, the *Shema* is believed to have become the final martyrological manifesto because the Romans prohibited its public proclamation. But the early rabbinic versions of the mother and sons still know nothing of such decrees. The verse becomes paramount in the contexts of Christianity.[85] Because the *Minim* accepted only the Ten Commandments, the custom of reciting the Commandments with the *Shema* was abolished. This left only the recitation of the *Shema*, which the *Minim* apparently rejected and for which R. Akiva is said to have died (B. *Berakhot* 12a).

The benediction against the *Minim* (*birkat ha-Minim*) was added to the daily Eighteen Benedictions, not only to prevent their participation in prayers but also to correspond "to the word *One* in the *Shema*" (B. *Berakhot* 28b–29a). Linking the *Shema* and its loud recitation to *birkat ha-Minim* became essential as the rising rival instructed that "There are many ruling powers in Heaven" (B. *Sanhedrin* 38a). To refute such notions, B. *Sanhedrin* 37a explains the creation of only one Man. Man was created alone so that the "*Minim* might not say, 'There are many ruling powers in heaven.'"[86]

The tradition that R. Akiva died while proclaiming the *Shema* became ever important in this new religious atmosphere. In the context of Roman persecutions, however, reciting the *Shema* was not worth dying for. As R. Meir recalled the days of Akiva's confinement in a Roman jail: "One day we were sitting before R. Akiva and reciting the *Shema*, but we did not make it audible to our ears because of the quaesdor [Roman officer] standing at the door" (*Tosefta Berakhot* 2, 13).

The new religious challenges, not the Roman policies toward Jews, reenforced the importance of the *Shema* unto death. An eighth-century *Geniza* fragment buttresses this view. It explains why the *Shema* and the *Ehad hu* ("Our God is One. . . . ") were added to the daily *Kedusha* (the Sanctification) prayer. The reason given is that the Christian-Byzantine empire prohibited the recitation of the *Shema*.[87]

Against the background of *Minut*, the martyrologies are employed to distinguish Judaism from both paganism and Christianity. But eventually both were viewed as a single entity. Rabbinic martyrologies indicated the existence of the only one genuine religion of the sole God and His people Israel. Doctrinal concessions of a single commandment could have led not only to idiolatry but also to the more serious problem of *Minut* (sectarianism).[88]

The caveats that a Jew should be as "careful with a light precept as with a great one," or that one should "also reckon the loss [that may be sustained through the fulfillment] of a precept," could have been read on two levels once Christianity entered the picture.[89] Both Gentiles and *Minim* fit the subject of this caveat. The extra caution with the *mitzvot* became paramount during this theological parting of the ways.[90]

To emphasize the importance of each commandment it was conveyed that "Every precept for which Israel submitted to death at the hour of persecution, for example, idolatry and circumcision, is still held firmly in their minds. Whereas every precept for which Israel did not submit to death at the hour of persecution, for example, tefillin, is still weak in their hands" (B. *Shabbat* 130a; *Sifrei Deut.* 76). This statement, which rabbinic memory often preserved in the context of Roman persecutions, is connected to the unspecific "hour of persecution." Yet it is told from a historical perspective that experienced the spiritual challenges posed by Christianity. Here the responsibility of observing each commandment falls on every individual in any given religious conflict.

THE SERPENT'S BITE AND THE SCORPION'S STING

Unlike the Jewish relationships to paganism,[91] no clear boundaries separated the Jews from the early *Minim*. Thus "No man should have any dealing with *Minim*,[92] nor is it allowed to be healed by them even [in risking] an hour's life" (B. *Avodah Zarah* 27b). To drive this point home, the rabbis enlisted the non-martyrological story of R. Eleazar ben Dama. No wonder that later rabbinic texts downplayed the involuntary nature of Eleazar's death, transforming him into one of the ten martyred rabbis.[93] It should be emphasized, however, that at issue here is the disassociation from the *Minim* rather than the choice of death as a solution.

It once happened to Ben Dama . . . that he was bitten by a serpent and Jacob, a native of Kefar Sekaniah, came to heal him but R. Ishmael did not let him; whereupon Ben Dama said, "My brother R. Ishmael, let him, so I may be healed by him: I will even cite a verse from the Torah that he is to be permitted"; but he did not manage to complete his saying, when his soul departed and he died. Whereupon R. Ishmael exclaimed, "Happy art thou, ben Dama, for thou wert pure in body and thy soul likewise left thee in purity; nor hast thou transgressed the words of thy colleagues, who said, 'He who breaketh through a fence, a serpent shall bite him.'" (Ecclesiastes 10:8; B. *Avodah Zarah* 27b)

Other versions add that Jacob of Kefar Sama came to heal Eleazar ben Dama "in the name of Jesus the son of Pantera."[94] This addition makes the link between the *Minim* and Christianity more likely. A number of *halakhic* difficulties emerge from the story of R. Eleazar's death.[95] On the one hand, he died in purity without sinning. On the other hand, he did perish because of a serpent's bite, which the passage associates with transgression. "He who breaketh through a fence, a serpent shall bite him."

Before addressing this paradox, one matter is certain. The question of whether to allow a sectarian Jew to heal Ben Dama is readily answered. Jews should stay away from Jewish-Christian sects (*ha-Notzrim*),[96] even if such avoidance might cost them their lives.[97] If there is a positive aspect to Ben Dama's death, it is its didactical ordinance against any contact with these heretics. Although a pagan physician is allowed to attempt healing a Jew when death is definite, no Jew is permitted to be cured by *Minim* no matter the situation (B. *Avodah Zarah* 27b). Clearly, the threat from *Minut* surpasses that from paganism. Why is a pagan physician permitted to approach dying Jews, whereas a sectarian Jewish doctor is rejected? I will answer this question forthwith.

First it should be pointed out that in addition to the rejection of dealings with *Minim*, another related consideration is at issue. Ben Dama turned to the Torah for support, whereas Ishmael relied on "the words of thy colleagues." *Tosefta Hullin* makes his colleagues active participants in the dialogue. Ishmael refuses to allow Jacob of Kefar Sama to cure Ben Dama in the name of Jesus ben Pantera. But it is "They" who ruled and said "You are not permitted Ben Dama."[98] Only a timely death prevented Ben Dama from bringing the necessary proof. Unwillingly, therefore, Ben Dama is forced to endure the fate that several of the "They," like Akiva and his colleagues, have met. The fear of transgressing against the opinion of their colleagues (B. *Eruvin* 21b) continues to play the same role in this anti-Jewish-Christian episode. Ben Dama almost broke through the fence that his own colleagues erected to keep the two groups apart. Transgressing the words of the rabbis was as adverse as contacting the *Minim*, for the "bite of the serpent of [which is inflicted upon those transgressing the words of] the Rabbis is such as can never be cured." Thanks to the strike of a physical serpent, and to Ishmael's adamant objection, Ben Dama avoided the far more devastating eternal bite of the spiritual snake.

The bite of the spiritual serpent is linked to the crawling influence of the new sectarian groups. As the story of Ben Dama demonstrates, the rabbis viewed Jewish–*Minim* relations as a matter of life and death. Ben Dama's story taught unequivocally that Jews should not associate with Jewish-Christians. Nor should Jews receive any service or benefit[99] from them even if that meant the *involuntary termination* of life. To be clear, what the story does not try to approve is the active choice of death as an escape from *Minim*.

The threat to Jewish existence doubled with the increased popularity of the new sect. Even an important scholar like the aforementioned R. Eliezer ben Hyrcanus is said to have entered this forbidden realm, resulting in his arrest for *Minut* by the Roman authorities.[100] Interestingly, he escaped punishment by a risky tricky answer to the Roman judge rather than by flatly denouncing Christianity. Only after his conversation with Akiva did he recall (or admit) that the words he had learned from the *Min Jacob* of Kefar Sekaniah indeed pleased him (B. *Avodah Zarah* 16b–17a).[101] In the eyes of the Talmudic compilers, this could have constituted a double offense. Not only did Eliezer make contact with the *Minim*, but their teachings also pleased him. Such close social and religious association with *Minim* perhaps explains Eliezer's excommunication by Akiva and his colleagues. Such cases indeed prove that "The teaching of *Minim* draws, and one [having dealings with them] may be drawn after them" (B. *Avodah Zarah* 27b).[102]

What could have drawn Jews and Gentiles after the *Minim*? The reasons for the success of Christianity go beyond the scope of this book. But some of these reasons became known in a most dramatic fashion by the Christian martyrs.[103] A basic promise that is said to have fired Christian imagination is the reward of eternal celestial life.[104] This goal was believed to be achievable by publicly volunteering for death. Suffice it here to mention Tertullian's conviction that "The sole key to unlock Paradise is your own life's blood." Jesus' emulators are "assuredly, efficacious in the sight of Christ."[105] Self-sacrifice offered an escape from present hardship and the fearful judgment that was believed to await humanity at the end of days.[106] Such teachings challenged the rabbinic belief in both resurrection and in its validation by the Torah (B. *Sanhedrin* 90b–91a).

One, however, need not die a martyr to gain the fruits of the Christian Paradise. Any person on his deathbed was assured a place in the celestial realm had he or she agreed to accept Christianity. For this reason, a *Min*

doctor, who could promise heavenly redemption when remedy failed, was not allowed to attend a dying Jew. A pagan physician, in contrast, was allowed to offer medical treatment to the dying, for he could effect neither physical nor spiritual damage. This ruling defends R. Ishmael's refusal to allow Jacob of Kefar Sama to approach the ailing Ben Dama. It is not a coincidence that Ben Dama's story immediately follows this dictum.

The lifting of the ban against R. Eliezer ben Hyrcanus may be understood in this light as well. Despite Eliezer's brush with *Minut*, his final acknowledgment of the rabbis' rules on purity (and his meticulous concern for the Sabbath, which some of the *Minim* neglected), rather than of the *Minim* promise for the dead, evoked the lifting of the ban. Ben Dama and Eliezer left this world in purity, without making final contacts with or concessions to the *Minim*.

Both Christian and Jewish sources reveal the familiarity of the Jews with the Christian martyrological solution and its salvific nature. Referring to the executions of Egyptian Christians, Eusebius describes how Jews "watched that amazing contest and surrounded the court of justice on all side ... they were the more agitated and rent in their hearts when they heard the heralds of the governor crying out and calling the Egyptians by Hebrew name."[107]

Less sympathetic statements also acknowledge that Jews witnessed the execution of Christians. According to Justin Martyr from Neapolis in Judea and to the Martyrdom of Polycarp, Jews derived enjoyment from observing the executions of Christians.[108] Caesarea turned into the central stage for the execution of defiant martyrs[109] such as Alpheus and Zacchaeus.[110] They and six other Christians hastily presented themselves to gain the heavenly fruits of volunteering for public slaughter.[111]

If indeed Jews witnessed the voluntary martyrdoms of Christians with admiration as Eusebius describes, there can be little doubt that they knew and also appreciated the motivation of these *cultores Dei*. There are good reasons to believe that the same positive impact Christian martyrdom had on the pagans affected also a number of Jews. Expectations of celestial rewards was an integral part of the martyrs' loud proclamations to the public. As Eusebius testifies, many approached these martyrs with personal requests for protection from above. A certain woman, for instance, beseeched these doomed prisoners to remember her "when they come before the Lord."[112]

B. *Avodah Zarah* 28a states that "the *Minim* adopt the attitude of 'let me die with the Philistines.'" Although the statement lacks a term for the act, the comparison of the Christians with Samson in his desire to die with the Philistines (Judg. 16:30) reveals the Jewish familiarity with the different Christian martyrological patterns. The statement indicates intimacy with both passive and voluntary Christian martyrdoms.[113]

Tertullian promised heavenly rewards for those stung by the evil of this world. Only the "baptism of blood," he argued, produces the "*Antidote for the Scorpion's Sting.*"[114] In the case of Ben Dama, it was not a scorpion[115] but a serpent that "did indeed sting him!" (B. *Avodah Zarah* 27b). Here *involuntary* death provides an antidote against the more specific threat of the serpent of *Minut.* At the same time, the story provides an antitoxin to counter the Christian cure for the scorpion's sting. Ben Dama's account belongs to a series of references indirectly opposing the Christian glorification of martyrdom and their expectation of divine recompense. Especially does the Babylonian version show us a rabbinic balancing act between the validity of death and the value of life.[116] This balancing act seemed harder to achieve in light of the popular Christian principle of recompense for martyrs. Similarly, familiarity with the Christian zeal to die a martyr for reward may explain the extrascrupulous ruling that even an "*halakhic* matter may not be quoted in the name of one who *surrenders himself to meet death* for words of the Torah" (B. *Baba Kamma* 61a, emphasis mine).

THE ANTIDOTE: "AND YOU SHALL LIVE BY THEM"

Not the glorification of death nor its redemptive characteristics play a role in Ishmael's arguments in favor of Ben Dama's death. Encouraging news like that of the Christians are missing in the rabbis' dialogue. It is rather the fear of transgression against *the words of the rabbis* that guides Ishmael. The potential bite of the spiritual serpent makes Eleazar's fate imperative. The fear of transgression, then, emerges as motivation behind Ishmael's willingness to hasten Eleazar's inevitable death. Ishmael makes no reference to reward as Jacob was likely to offer Ben Dama.

Despite the positive role Ben Dama's incidental death plays in his story, its final message teaches that Jews "shall live by them" (Lev. 18: 5),[117] that is, the *mitzvot,* and not die for them. This corresponds with the ruling of the house of Nithza. "By a majority vote, it was resolved in the upper chambers of the house of Nithza in Lud that in every [other] law of the Torah, if a man is commanded: 'Transgress and suffer not death' he may transgress and not suffer death, excepting idolatry, incest, and murder (B. *Sanhedrin* 74a). R. Ishmael went further. Relying on Leviticus 18:5, he added "that it [idolatry] may even be openly practiced" to save life. Others permitted it only in private.[118]

The ruling of you "shall live by them" challenged the Christian fascination with voluntary death and its reward. "True life," instructed Paul, may be achieved by self-sacrifice for God (Philippians 1:21). In response to such views that maintained their popularity for centuries, the *halakhic* emphasis on life became more acute. Thus the early first-century Jewish and pagan notions that the Christians had adopted in support of *martyrium* appear less dominant in the rabbinic material of late antiquity. In the previous chapters, potential and a few "actual" martyrs emphasized the importance of their blood, the revenge through blood,[119] the innocent martyr as the nation's atonement and salvation,[120] the assurance of the resurrection of martyrs,[121] the idea of the divine-fatherless-martyred child (as implied already by 2 Maccabees).[122] These fundamental Christian elements have no place in the rabbis' theology.[123] Such elements are ignored in the rabbis' stories to maintain the balance between voluntary death and the value of life. The rabbinic teachings were meant to erect high *halakhic* fences to prevent foreign martyrological concepts from infiltrating Jewish circles.[124]

This balancing act features most explicitly in that most provocative martyr-dom of Hananiah ben Teradyon. The Romans brought woolen sponges and soaked them in water before placing them on his heart so that he should not die quickly (B. *Avodah Zarah* 18a). "Why do you not open your mouth so that the flames will enter into you and put an end to your suffering" asked his students. He replied, "Better that He who gave me my soul should take it, than that I should destroy myself." The paradox of Hananiah's opening his mouth to answer why he would not open his mouth to welcome the destroying fire only stresses the importance of his prolife message.

Hananiah ben Teradyon's last words prove that "life" remains an absolute value. Self-killing cannot be permissible because life in itself is of supreme virtue. This is further supported by the indications that Teradyon's tragic end came as punishment for sin. "The punishment of being burnt came upon him because he pronounced the Name in its full spelling" in public (B. *Avodah Zarah* 17b–18a). In fact, the entire family is said to have suffered very unappealing punishments.

Rabbinic students are reported to have followed the anti-self-killing advice already in Roman times. According to *Bereshit Rabba* 82:8, they rejected the Roman order to kill themselves, because consciously killing oneself was considered unnatural even on behalf of the Law.

Extra caution is taken to avoid the solution of quitting life voluntarily, so popular with the Roman soldiers and later with the Christian martyrs. Even R. Akiva showed no desire to become a martyr. In *Pesahim*, R. Simeon ben Yohai asked the imprisoned Akiva to violate the Roman decree and teach him Torah. Akiva simply replied: "I will not teach you." To R. Simeon's cynical complaints that he would tell his father Yohai about Akiva's refusal, and that Yohai "will deliver thee [Akiva] to the state" (if Akiva would not teach him), Akiva answered, "more than the calf wishes to suck does the cow desire to suckle." R. Akiva's urge to teach Torah was stronger than R. Simeon's eagerness to study, but he did not wish to run the risk of teaching. R. Simeon, conversely, was ready to take the risk and argued that "surely the calf [i.e. the student] is in danger." To this Akiva replied: "If you wish to be strangled, be hanged on a large tree, and when you teach your son, teach him from a corrected scroll" (B. *Pesahim* 112a). Even without teaching, this great teacher still delivered rules about the proper way for teaching Torah. Nevertheless, like the story of Akiva's silent recitation of the *Shema* in jail, this example demonstrates that Akiva sought to avoid death. In fact, Krauss has raised the possibility that *Midrash Mishle* 9:2 speaks of Akiva's death on his prison bed.[125]

The story of Judah ben Baba advances another example of a random execution that indirectly speaks against giving up life. When the Romans caught Judah ben Baba in the act of ordaining five of his students, Judah urged his students to "flee." Because of his old age, he remained behind "like a stone which none [is concerned to] overturn." Namely, he is like a useless item that perhaps the Romans would not bother with. To be sure, Judah ben Baba did not express his willingness to die. Moreover he advised his students to cleave to life.[126] As mentioned, other sections reveal that Judah met a natural death, doing away with his execution altogether.[127]

These martyrs differed from their Christian counterparts. De Ste. Croix has convincingly demonstrated that in early-fourth-century Palestine "very few [Christian martyrs] were sought out: approximately twice as many (if not more) were volunteers or had otherwise attracted the attention of the authorities."[128] Not only did Jewish martyrs abstain from voluntary martyrdom, they are depicted as laboring to avoid dangerous situations that might lead to death. Except Teradyon, imported rabbis are described as trying to avoid their unnatural fates. Without minimizing the hardship under Rome, in reality, there was little need for martyrdom *per se* in the life of the *Tannaim* and *Amoraim*. Excluding the rabbinic material, most of the historical sources indicate that this major conflict with Rome generated mainly warriors, not martyrs. In contrast, rabbinic martyrology delineates an opposite picture in which nonviolent rabbis of various generation feature as heroes almost exclusively.

Contrary to the impression that rabbis resorted to voluntary death, B. *Taanit* 18a appears to offer an alternative solution for dealing with Roman decrees:

For once it was decreed that the Jews should not occupy themselves with the study of the Torah nor circumcise their children and that they should desecrate the Sabbath. What did Judah b. Shammua and his colleagues do? They went and took counsel with a Roman matron with whom all the prominent Romans were wont to associate. She advised them, "Arise and raise an alarm by night." They went and raised the alarm by night thus, "O ye heaven, are we not your brethren? Are we not the Children of one Father? Are we not the children of one mother? Wherein are we different from every other nation and tongue that ye make harsh decrees against us?" Thereupon the decrees were annulled and that day [twenty-ninth Adar] was declared a festive day!

Diplomacy and empathetic appeals put an end to the persecution, making voluntary death unnecessary in this account.[129]

Additional examples on the individual level emphasize the preference for life over glorious death. Teradyon considered R. Eleazar b. Perata happy, for he, unlike Teradyon, would escape execution by the Romans.[130] When put to the test, the same Eleazar proclaimed himself to be a "Master of Weavers" instead of a Master of Torah, that is, a rabbi, to avoid execution (B. *Avodah Zarah* 17b). A progression of miracles helped the rabbi deceive the Roman interrogators. These miracles provide another proof that God desired and approved Eleazar's avoidance of death.

Similarly, R. Meir, who was wanted by the Romans, escaped from them into a harlot house to conceal his Jewish identity. Others say that he "happened just then [when discovered by the Romans] to see food cooked by heathens and he dipped in one finger and then sucked the other" to pass for a gentile (B. *Avodah Zarah* 18b).[131] As with R. Eleazar, the passage approves the avoidance of submission to death by speculating that Elijah miraculously intervened to rescue R. Meir.[132]

The same message is repeated by B. *Taanit* 29a. Contrary to the priests who killed themselves when the Temple was invaded, the condemned R. Gamaliel hid himself while the Romans searched for him in the Temple. To avoid unnecessary executions, the Mishnah also releases Jews from carrying the *tefillin* in time of danger (B. *Eruvin* 96a–b).[133] Similarly, *Bereshit Rabba* 82:8 reveals that rabbinic students changed their distinguishing clothing in such times to avoid arrest. If this was the conduct of towering rabbis and their students, one may wonder how common voluntary death was among the rest.[134]

These examples clearly stand in sharp contrast to the Christian cases of voluntary martyrdom. Although Christianity emphasized the *voluntary* and sacrificial nature of *martyrium*, rabbinic theology stressed both its *obligatory* aspect and restricted practice. Obligatory death could become an option only as the last line of defense against an absolute threat to religious identity. As it was a restricted mandatory act, no attention is given to benefits beyond the utilitarian avoidance of transgression.

Resurrection in the world to come was indeed a central component in rabbinic theology (B. *Sanhedrin* 90b–91b). But rabbinic resurrection should not be confused with the Christian system of martyrological reward. Except for rare cases of gentiles voluntarily dying on behalf of Jews,[135] the Jewish martyrs' place in the world to come hinges on their scholastic aptitude and performance of good deeds instead of altruistic acts.[136]

A good conspectus of this approach is provided by *Baba Bathra* 10b. As a starting point, it asserts, every wise scholar will attain the world to come. R. Joseph the son of R. Joshua, whom we have met, confirmed this view in his trance. The ailing Joseph visualized the martyred rabbis as unique individuals such that "no creature can attain to their place." But "had they no other merit but this [martyrdom]?" the tractate continues. To reconfirm the merit of all Torah scholars regardless of martyrdom, it concluded, "Obviously even without this [act, they would have attained this rank]." Martyrdom was only one aspect of the exclusiveness of these martyred rabbis. They are said to have received their reward on the basis of how they lived their lives, not on the basis of how they ended them. Because of the importance of Torah study in the world to come (B. *Berahkot* 64a, B. *Megillah* 28b), the rabbis' erudite knowledge of their Law was believed to position them above all others.[137]

It is important to recall that in its midrashic version there is no mention of either martyrs or rewards:

R. Meyasha the grandson of R. Joshua b. Levi was made unconscious by his illness for three days. After three days he regained consciousness. His father said to him: "Where were you?" He replied: "In a confused world." He asked: "What did you see there?" He answered: "I saw many *people* [emphasis mine] who were held in honor here and are in disgrace there." (*Rut Rabba*, 3:1)[138]

It is not martyrdom that appears to secure a place in the world to come. Statements regarding the world to come speak clearly only of other factors in determining recompense. "It was repeated in the name of R. Meir: Whoever is permanently settled in the Land of Israel, and speaks Hebrew, and eats his meals in ritual cleanliness, and recites the *Shema* morning and evening, let it be known to him that he is an initiate of the coming world" (Y. *Shekalim* 3, 4 [47c]). And the same R. Resh Lakish, who maintained that the words of Torah were kept only because of those who had died for them, does not associate the act with reward. He too promised "To him who is engaged in the study of Torah in this world, which is likened unto the night, the Holy One, blessed be He, extends the thread of grace in the future world, which is likened unto the day, as it is said: 'By day the Lord, etc.'" (B. *Avodah Zarah* 3b).

One more point is of value. The world to come does not appear to be of a celestial nature. R. Joseph's vision appears to allude to a new corrected social order in a terrestrial world (B. *Pesahim* 50a). According to Sifre Deut. 356.148b, even Moses could not tell what goodness the righteous would receive in the world to come.[139] By the ninth century, works such as Tanhuma and Pirkei de-Rabbi Eliezer still viewed the world to come as posthistoric phase in the eschatological worldly drama.[140] Conversely, Jesus is believed to have already granted Peter a vision of Paradise, the final destiny of the persecuted Christians.[141]

Without referring to Christianity explicitly, the neglect of reward in the above examples contradicts the Christian formula of human sacrifice and divine compensation. Despite the accounts of the rabbis' executions, these stories do not overshadow the importance of life. Dilemmas such as Paul's, whether individuals can personally achieve more through the *imitatio mortis Christi* or life,[142] never surfaced with the same force in the rabbinic texts. Nor do we find parallels to Ambrose's homily *On Death as a Good* (3:7), which advances that "to die [for Christ] is gain." Even in the accounts of the most ardent *harugei malkhut*, life is always preferable. It is a motif that runs throughout their stories, corresponding with *Avot* 4.22's strong opposition against dying voluntarily: "And let not your [evil] inclination assure you that the grave is a place of refuge for you; for without your will you were fashioned, without your will you were born, without your will you live, *without your will you die*" (emphasis mine).

Living as a religious minority in a world that became dominated by the religion of the *Minim*'s descendants, the rabbis recognized that threats to the Judaism that they envisioned would not always be motivated by political or militant agendas alone.[143] Eventually, the triumph of Christianity forced the rabbinic association of the *Minim* with the rest of the idolatrous, becoming now a single coercing force (B. *Berakhot* 12b).[144] Regardless of who might pose the next threats against Jews, such perils were expected to be religious in nature. This awareness is evident in the following commentary.

The Holy One, blessed be He, showed righteousness [mercy] unto Israel by scattering them among the nations. And this is what a certain sectarian [*min*] said to R. Hanina, "We are better than you. Of you it is written, 'For Joab and all Israel remained there six months, until he had cut off every male in Edom' (I Kings 11:16); whereas you have been with us many years, yet we have not done anything to you!". . . . R. Oshaia debated it with him, [and] he said to him, "[The reason is] because you do not know how to act. If you would destroy all, they are not among you. [Should you destroy] those who are among you, then you will be called a murderous kingdom!" (B. *Pesahim* 87b)

By the time the Talmudic redactors immortalized their predecessors in their martyrologies, *Minim* no longer existed as an illegitimate minority among Jews and pagans. As *Minut* substituted the religion of pagan Edom, a designation for Christianity and the Roman Empire,[145] Jews now became the minority in a society ruled by another monotheism. In the above dialogue the *Min* appears to be friendly. Yet intolerance and revenge for the Jewish treatment of *Minim* in the past appears as a possible outcome. Clearly, the text indicates that the Jews are now at the mercy of the *Minim*, that is, Christians, and their "kingdom."

Both "*Minut* and the Government" equally presented an existential threat as they were merging into one. They seduced and destroyed the imprudent like "the two daughters who cry from Gehenna calling to this world: Bring, bring!" them into their realms (B. *Avodah Zarah* 17a). Historically, this practice of seducing others is indicative only of the *Minim* or of the Christian Empire. They, not the pagan Romans, adopted the missionary practice of *compelle intrare* ("compel people to come in," Luke 14:23). "*Minut* and the Government," therefore, may refer to the reality of the rabbis who lived in a centralized Christian Empire. The next religious conflicts could thus come from both the populace and its government. This realization may explain the recommendation attributed to Rabbin, who in the name of R. Johana advocated that "Even without a royal decree," it was permitted to transgress in private; "but in public[146] one must let himself be killed even for a minor precept," such as changing one's shoe strap[147] (B. *Sanhedrin* 74b). Uncertainties and the role religion began to play worldwide made passive death a realistic form of defense.

In this new relationship, death functions to protect the Jewish identity that was being shaped by the rabbis. In defeat and exile, the maintenance of Jewish identity (as envisioned by the rabbis) was established as a meed parallel to the achievement of a *modus vivendi* with the rest of the world.[148] The rabbis of late antiquity had arrived at the conclusion that for a minority concentrated in a non-Jewish environment armed resistance would lead to group suicide, whereas the readiness to die might be the sole means of preserving Jewish life.

This *modus vivendi* abandoned the Zealot prototype for the archetype of the martyr in time of conflict. By late antiquity, the rabbis renounced the model of the biblical fighting Israelite, which inspired both the Maccabees and Bar Kokhvah's followers.[149] Henceforth, peace lovers and harmless martyrs became the exemplars to emulate instead of the Zealots who fought for the restoration of the biblical kingdom and its Temple in the center. Now more than ever, harmonious life had to be achieved in a foreign environment.[150]

Equally important to the establishment of the passive-pacifistic stand was the prevention of non-Jews taking advantage of this peaceful conduct: "If a gentile said to a Jew, 'Cut the grass on the Sabbath for the cattle, and if not I will slay thee,' he must rather *be killed* than cut it; 'Cut it and throw it into the river,' he should rather *be slain* [emphasis mine] than cut it" (B. *Sanhedrin* 74b).

The mention of the Sabbath stresses the religious nature of the gentile's request. Death is recommended here "Because his [the gentile's] intention is to force him to violate his religion." Queen Esther's marriage to the gentile King Ahasuerus, technically a public violation of the Law against marrying a foreigner, is brought to affirm an important distinction.[151] When the demand that one transgress is motivated by personal pleasure, submitting to death is not always required. Not so when demands are motivated by religion. Thus even the seemingly trivial order to change the shoe strap in public from the white of the Jews to the black of the gentiles, was considered a violation of a minor precept if religion were the reason (B. *Sanhedrin* 74a–b). Religion would be a dominant component in the medieval world that the rabbis and their followers were about to enter. These rulings were to have a long-lasting effect on Jewish life. For almost two millennia the martyrological prototype was to dominate Jewish thinking.

CONCLUSION

Not all the above examples refer directly to Christianity. But as the theological threat of the *Minim* compounded the physical peril of the Romans, these selections could not have been written, much less read by following generations, without having the behavior and view of Christian rivals in mind. Christian enthusiasts of *martyrium*, such as Tertullian, Origen,[152] or Eusebius, continued to share the exuberance that Philo, Josephus, and the Maccabean literature had exhibited regarding passive forms of altruism. Compared to the pre-Talmudic accounts of voluntary death, the rabbinic concept of obligatory death shows a considerable diminution.

Although obligatory death is endorsed to maintain identity, there is minimum rabbinic adulation for the act. In fact, attention and admiration is given to those who deceitfully and miraculously avoided executions. When death does occur, punishment often attaches itself to the behavior of these few actors. These are not the innocent sacrifices we have encountered so far.[153] Their martyrologies lack the fundamental *redemptio vicaria* of the Christian formula. The few identified martyred rabbis did not submit their lives to atone for personal sins or divine salvation. Nor is obligatory death said to deliver the martyrs or the nation. Heaven appointed Rome, and it was up to Heaven to destroy it and shape the course of history. The rabbinic association of Rome with Christendom implies that rabbis accepted the conditions in which they lived.

After all was said and done, it was not the blood of martyrs that guaranteed salvation, as the Christian martyrs claimed.[154] The blood of circumcision remains the key for personal and national salvation.[155] Nor were human sacrifices, which Jesus and his followers had introduced to replace the Torah, to bring salvation. Rather, delivery would be acquired through the Torah of the rabbis, which, according to the rabbis, replaced the need for Temple oblations.[156]

An exception that resembles the Christian view is provided by the interpretation ascribed to R. Joshua of the verse, "Gather my saints together unto me; those that have made a covenant with me by sacrifices" (Ps. 50:5). In his opinion, "Gather my saints (hasidai) together unto me – this refers to the righteous of every generation; that have made a covenant with me – to Hananiah, Mishael, and Azariah, who submitted to the fiery furnace; by sacrifice – to R. Akiva and his companions, who gave themselves up to immolation for the sake of the Torah" (B. Sanhedrin 110b). R. Joshua represents a minority. His colleagues ascribed the verse to the generation of the wilderness, which sacrificed animals as burnt and peace offerings (Exod. 24:5). Even in R. Joshua's opinion the benefits do not go beyond the protection of the Torah.

To be sure, the rabbinic martyrology does not assign vicarious and expiatory attributes to its heroes. It is worth repeating the views that God favors one day of studying the Torah over a thousand burnt offerings (B. Makkot 10a) or gemilut hasadim (good deeds) over sacrifices. This opinion would avert attempts to replace the past burnt offerings of the Temple with future human sacrifices. The fact that throughout this period we are still lacking a fixed Hebrew term for martyrdom is indicative of the limited role this notion gained in early rabbinic Judaism. Instead of a noun, a number of phrases, verbs, and adverbs are provided. It is important to note that these various rabbinic terms employ passive verbs, further emphasizing the passive form of the act. When needed, Jews must let others kill them rather than take their own lives. Like the act, its victims also miss a uniform term. As we shall see, the present term for martyrdom, qiddush ha-Shem, and the identification of martyrs as qorbanot (sacrifices) or qedoshim (holy) took off in the post-Talmudic era.[157] Unlike the Christian martyrs,[158] the executed rabbis never reached the status of cultic sainthood.

Despite the restriction on obligatory death, however, the need for it could not be ignored. As the pagan world turned Christian, rabbinic Judaism realized that passive deaths might become the last line of defense against religious oppression. Nevertheless, within the Jewish circle, the rabbis were still moving away from the popularity of voluntary death enjoyed in the pagan world of Philo and Josephus. In addition to the lack of recommendation for such behavior in the Hebrew Bible, the Christian conviction that Jesus's voluntary sacrifice saved the universe and brought about the downfall of Judaism was a good incentive for the rabbis to minimize the importance of martyrdom as a means of survival and salvation. Relative to the Christian world, however, Jewish obligatory death took an opposite vector. For victorious Christianity, voluntary death lost its active position. Augustine labored to make martyrdom the affair of the venerated past.[159] Rabbinic Judaism made obligatory death a facet of its uncertain future. The realization that Jews could not afford another religious defeat set the stage for Jewish behavior in the next possible religious conflict. European Jews were destined to enter such conflicts and put the rabbinic rules (now the rules of Judaism) on martyrdom into practice.

4

❧

Byzantine Burnt Offerings

The absence of the phrase *Asarah Harugei Malkhut* in the Talmud is indicative of its post-Talmudic origin. Unfortunately, a more accurate dating of this phrase and the martyrological story it entitles is yet to be established. Attempts to determine the story's exact place and time of composition are still being made. What has been established with certainty is the legendary characteristic of the narrative.[1]

P. Bloch has already connected the story of the ten with the mystical *Heikhalot Rabbati.*[2] Bloch has proposed that the emergence of the ten in the legend took place in the late sixth or seventh century. In his opinion, the book *Heikhalot Rabbati* is the product of Italian Jewry in response to religious persecutions during these centuries. According to Bloch, out of these mystical mores and the everyday experiences of Italian Jews, the story of *Asarah Harugei Malkhut* was born. Although present research on the *Heikhalot* literature has disputed some of Bloch's conclusions,[3] his instinctive association of the legend with the Italian Jewry of the Byzantine Empire deserves attention. His suggestion provides for us significant leads in the long historical trail of the ten martyrs' legendary trial.

This chapter will show that Byzantine Jewry played a major role in the transmission and transmutation of the martyrological tradition of the past. Byzantine Jewry's greatest contribution to the evolution of Jewish martyrdom, in my opinion, is the reversal of the rabbinic restrictions on voluntary death. By reintroducing the first-century sacrificial symbol, not only did Byzantine Jewry revive the martyrological tradition, it also provided a justification for active forms of self-oblation. As we shall see, the employment of similar symbols by the Christian majority would help us explain these developments.

PERSECUTIONS

At first glance, Bloch's association of the legend of the ten martyrs with per-secutions in Byzantium appears logical. Indeed, the first known systematic attempts to convert Jews in the Middle Ages originated in the Byzantine Em-pire. Its Jewish subjects in the east and in southern Italy became the least fortunate target of these religious campaigns. Although the latter still enjoyed papal protection by the end of the sixth century,[4] their conditions changed after the fall of Byzantine Syria and Palestine into Arab hands. The relative severity of these imperial anti-Jewish enterprises may be attributed to their initiation by emperors. Unlike the crude separation between church and state in Latin Europe, Byzantine emperors acted on behalf of both the Empire and the Church.[5]

In the first half of the seventh century, the Byzantine Emperor Heraclius (610–641) outlawed Judaism and ordered the forcible baptism of all Jewish subjects. How effective these decrees were in reality is difficult to tell. In Palestine Heraclius expelled the Jews from Jerusalem, ordered the disturbance of synagogue services on weekdays, and forbade the recital of the *Shema*.[6] In 630, Heraclius is said to have authorized the massacre of Jews in nearby Jerusalem and in the Galilee.[7]

It should also be stressed that nonofficial aggression against Jews often represented another aspect of the violent and volatile conditions in the em-pire. As with the many other players during this period, Jews may have sided with different internal and external struggling forces.[8] On one occasion, the rebellious party known as the Greens burned an unknown number of Jews in their synagogue for politically supporting a rival group.[9] To be sure, there was no shortage of animosity toward Jews. "They [Jews] are a wicked and most untrustworthy race, trouble-loving and tyrannical, utterly forgetful of friend-ship, jealous and envious," wrote the Heraclean court historian Theophylact Simocatta.[10]

But even two contemporary Hebrew documents, *midrash* "Sefer Zerubavel,"[11] and "The Signs of the Messiah" (*Otot ha-Mashiah*),[12] speak only generally of the suffering of the Jewish nation. They predict that this suffering will come to an end with the death of the anti-Messiah "Armilus," a cryp-togram for Heraclius. The apocalyptic *midrash*, it is worth mentioning, is thematically and linguistically reminiscent of the mystical *Heikhalot Rabbati*. As in the *Heikhalot*, Zerubavel learns from angels about the approaching de-struction of Rome. Auguring this final positive event is Armilus's invasion of "Eretz Israel with *ten kings*" [emphasis mine]. They would murder Messiah ben Yosef and sixteen righteous men in Jerusalem before Israel's redemption.[13]

Armilus performs also in *Otot ha-Mashiah*. He appears in two of the given ten signs that foretell the messianic deliverance of the Jewish people.[14] The only casualties these signs reveal are those who perish in the author's imaginary battle with Armilus. Although these two documents affiliate the number ten with the evils that befell Israel, they seem to support Bloch's assumption of a connection between world historical events and this literary Jewish genre. It is also reasonable to assume that if *midrash* Zerubavel were of Palestinian origin, it would have alluded to, if not mentioned, the massacre of 630.

The significance of the Heracleian policy stems thus from the ideological precedent it created rather than from its results. Heraclius attempted to denounce the legal and canonical *status quo* of the Jews. Previously, force was not considered an acceptable tool in imperial and ecclesiastical legislation in converting Jews.[15] At least in two cases, Heraclius's policy served as an early catalyst for the Hebrew works of Byzantine Jews.

A new series of religious edicts surface a century later. Emperor Leo III (717–741) called for the conversion of all Jews, as well as Christians of the Paulician and the Manichean heresies.[16] These sects rejected the Catholic principle of Trinity that the Holy Spirit proceeds from both the Son and the Father.[17] It is believed that the close connection between these heretics and a militant-messianic Jewish movement brought Leo's rage on all Jews.[18]

The Jewish reaction to these decrees was not martyrdom. Theophanes reports that "the Hebrews ate and partook of the holy gift but, as they had not been baptized of their own free will, washed off their baptism and defiled the faith."[19] Other Jews, we are told, fled to Arab territories.[20] Realizing the failure of his policy, Leo recodified the Byzantine law in 726 without mentioning new sanctions against Jews or Judaism.

Emperor Basil I (867–886) renewed his predecessors' attempts.[21] This time, a number of Jewish writers provide a relatively detailed picture of the events. The important eleventh-century book of genealogies, *The Chronicle of (Megillat) Ahimaatz*, relates Basil's active role in this campaign.[22] He "tried to turn them [the Jews of Byzantium] from the Torah and to convert them to the worthless religion." Basil did so by outlawing the study of Torah in the Jewish communities of his empire.[23] Emphasizing the prominence of the Torah throughout his work, *Ahimaatz* associates Basil's decrees mainly with the prohibition of Torah study. Nevertheless, no specific mention of martyrdom is made in *Ahimaatz's* chronicle, which makes no reference to the story of the ten rabbis.

Basil's biographer, Constantine VII, depicts a more gracious emperor. Instead of coercion, Constantine emphasizes persuasion and the benefits his emperor offered converts. Basil ordered Jews to participate in disputations.

"To those who would join Christ," he promised, "appointment of office ... and to relieve them from the burden of their former taxes, and to make noble and honorable men of obscure ones."[24]

The talented liturgist and mystic Rabbi Amittai ben Shephatiah refers to this policy in his *Yotzer le-Shabbat*. Before I return to his liturgy, suffice it to point out Rabbi Amittai's reminder to his fellow Jews. God miraculously delivered Israel, "... when a wicked man [Emperor Basil I] raised against me in order that I shall forsake the Mosaic Law. He decreed oppression against the sacrificers of burnt offering [i.e., Israel], so [they] would abandon [their religion]."[25] According to *Ahimaatz*, Basil's policy came to an end when he was replaced by his son Leo VI.[26] Constantine authenticates *Ahimaatz's* account. Invectively, though, he writes that "when the king [Basil] no longer lived," most of the Jews "return [to Judaism] like dogs to their vomit."[27] Basil's attempt seems to have failed. Until this failure was realized, however, the Jews dealt with the decrees in a variety of ways. Crypto-observance was one form, but not self-oblation.

The tenth-century Byzantine *The Vision of Daniel* also refers to Basil's persecutions. This anonymous Hebrew work describes how Basil baptized the Jews against their will and then sold them into slavery. Conversion would have prevented their being sold. But the author here responds to the Christian myth of Jewish servitude, which will be discussed below.[28]

Based on the limited information at hand, it appears that Byzantine Jews always found a way to escape conversion. Basil, therefore, never accomplished his mission. To an extent, Basil's policy disturbed Jewish daily life. Adjustments had to be made to cope with the circumstances that ended with Basil's death in 886.

The ensuing relative political ease lasted about sixty years. In 932, at the Church Council of Erfurt, the Patriarch of Jerusalem misinformed the new Byzantine emperor, Romanos, that the Jews of Jerusalem had converted after experiencing a miracle.[29] Inspired by the story, Romanos allegedly did not settle merely for outlawing Judaism and Torah study. His Jewish subjects were ordered to convert. On a broader scale, the anti-Jewish policy fits Romanos's belief that religious unity would grant him God's blessing in his military campaigns.[30]

Jews were not alone in this religious campaign. With their Christian Arian neighbors, they escaped to Khazaria, Western Europe, and Arab lands.[31] Others preferred to ride the oppressive wave in hiding. Our sources imply – as we shall see, with good reasons – that Romanos's decrees did have a significant effect on Byzantine Jewry. Only when Romanos was deposed by his son in 944 did the persecution cease.[32]

Were these anti-Jewish decrees the only catalyst in creating the mystical and martyrological literature, as Bloch proposes? Can the story of *Asarah Harugei Malkhut* be linked to a single event that stands in marked affinity to the legend's depictions?

SIN AND ATONEMENT

Because reports of actual martyrdom appear to be missing, the story of *Asarah Harugei Malkhut* cannot be explained only on the ground of anti-Jewish decrees. The anti-Jewish decrees may have affected this work, but they were not the only factor. A great source of inspiration was provided by the popular hagiographic literature that was circulating in Byzantium. Hagiography adds a significant explanation to the emergence of the story in the literature of Byzantine Jews.[33]

Before turning to hagiographies, let us first examine some of the legend's characteristics and developments. *Sefer Zerubavel* and *Otot ha-Mashiah* suggest a connection between Jewish hardship in Byzantium and the pseudomystical or apocalyptic-messianic literature. A similar link can be traced in the relationship between the story of the ten martyrs and the mystical *Heikhalot Rabbati*. This esoteric work describes the heavenly palaces (*Heikhalot*) and the dangerous technique of ascension. Chapter 4 of this work refers to the six heavenly hymns sung before the Glory of God. The chapter then suddenly ends with a terrestrial event. "A terrible rumor came from the city of Rome to tell that the *four* men, the nobles (*abirei*) of Israel, R. Simon ben Gamliel, R. Ishmael ben Elishah, R. Eliezer ben Dama, and R. Judah ben Baba, and eight thousand scholars of Jerusalem were captured as their [Rome's] ransom."[34] They were captured because Samael, the angelic patron of Rome, was allowed to "eradicate from the nobles of Israel every good portion."

Despite "all these conditions and warnings given to Samael," the next chapter opens, he accepted an unspecified agreement at this point, so "these ten great (*asert adirim*) [individuals] be eliminated."[35] The definite articles before "the four men" and "these conditions and warnings" are confusing because the text reveals this information for the first time. Only subsequently does the text reveal that Samael's obsessed wish to destroy "the nobles of Israel"[36] caused him to accept in return the fall of the empire he was assigned to protect. The obscure and possibly misplaced statement about the great ten, which negates the previous statement about only *four captured* rabbis,[37] does not disclose their names, occupations, or the forms of their demise. Are they rabbis or commoners? Why them?[38]

Later the text reveals that R. Ishmael's colleagues learned about the heavenly decree regarding Rome's destruction. Surprisingly, the news calls for joy and festive celebration, as if the revelation about their fate never emerged.[39] The reason for their mirth is not the prediction of their own death, the demise of "the nobles of Israel." Ishmael's divination says nothing about their above-mentioned upcoming personal affliction.

Without the explicit mention of the numeral ten, its value yet resurfaces in Chapter 14. R. Ishmael assembles the Minor and the Great *Sanhedrin* and nine of his colleagues. Together they compose a group of ten rabbis. Ishmael informs them that "evil Rome" would destroy the "nobles of Israel." The focus of the meeting, however, is the esoteric revelations of the heavenly *Merkavah* (the Chariot). Although many in this assembly will later feature in the legends of the Ten Martyrs, no interjection of martyrdom is made.[40] Nor are these rabbis explicitly associated with the unlucky "nobles of Israel."

In another version, only eight rabbis attend R. Ishmael's assembly. This version further attests the insignificance of the number ten at this stage.[41] Missing from the group in both versions is the would-be preeminent prototypical martyr R. Hananiah ben Teradyon.[42] He is said to have deceived the Romans and their emperor by divine intervention, thus avoiding his Talmudic tragic fate. In Teradyon's "face off" with Lupinus Caesar, the angel Suriel switches the appearances of the two. This ancient form of identity theft causes the emperor's executioners to mistakenly toss their master into the fire, whereas Teradyon temporarily occupies the imperial throne. During six months of roleplay, Teradyon gave six thousand Roman rulers or possibly bishops (*hegmonim*) a dose of their own vicious medicine. One thousand of them were executed each month.[43] The number ten and the individuals it modifies have yet to reach their legendary force.

Asarah Harugei Malkhut is strikingly similar to a tradition popular among the Christians of Byzantium, known in the region as the *Hagioi Deka*, the Ten Saints or the Ten Martyrs.[44] The *Hagioi Deka* describes the systematic execution of ten martyrs by the Roman government in a single day. According to this tradition, upon the publication of Decius's decree in 250, the governor of Crete requested that the ten sacrifice offerings to Jupiter. When they refused, they were severely tortured but endured with joy and love. Instead of giving up, they proclaimed, "We are Christians and would rather die a thousand times." Because of them, Satan was defeated, and their countrymen were delivered from the blindness of idolatry and Christianity prevailed.

From Crete the decapitated saints are said to have been transported to Rome for burial. The Council of Crete in 458 informed Emperor Leo I that until that time the island had been preserved from heresy because of their sacrifices.

The village in which they suffered bore the name Ten Saints and a slab is said to have existed there, showing ten hollow depressions that mark the places where they knelt to receive their fatal strokes. Thereafter, their story spread through the south, where the persecuted Jews and heretics dwelled, and into the mainland.

This traveling of hagiographies fits a growing trend. Before becoming a city of saints' relics and martyrs' shrines, Constantinople lacked apostolic foundation. This deficiency was ameliorated by reversing the east–west direction in which relics had previously traveled and by a blooming local sacred history. From the mid-sixth century, plenty of martyrs joined in this way the only two obscurely known, domestic martyrs, S. Akakios and S. Mokios.[45] The Christianization of Constantinople and numerous other localities, such as Crete, was attributed to the abnegations of martyrs. Imperial indebtedness to martyrs exhibits also the case of the sixty defenders of Gaza, who allegedly were executed in Jerusalem for refusing to betray their Christianity and country.[46]

Byzantium's fate was believed to be at the hands of martyrs. When the Rus threatened Constantinople, for instance, the panicking patriarch Photios pontificated in two sermons in Hagia Sophia. He admonished his people to satisfy God by atoning for their sins. A vast mass of people chanted liturgies for their salvation at the city's holiest relics of saints and martyrs as part of a procession around the city walls. Because of this impressive act with martyrs and relics, it was believed, the city escaped destruction.[47] Certainly the popular tradition that the famous relic protector of Constantinople – the Virgin Mary's Veil – had first belonged to a Jewish woman before being cleverly snatched from her attracted Jewish curiosity toward their neighbors' public rituals.[48]

The *Hagioi Deka* epic and hagiographies explain thus not only the introduction of ten *Harugei Malkhuts* but also its anomalous characteristics.[49] Except for its rabbinic heroes, the legend has little in common with the Talmudic notion of voluntary death. Although the *Book of Jubilees* (34:18–19) had requested the children of Israel to atone by sacrificing a young goat on the Day of Atonement for the sin committed by Jacob's sons in selling Joseph,[50] the *Tannaim* and *Amoraim* abandoned the formula of children's being punished for their fathers' transgressions.[51] The fundamentally Christological principle of martyrs atoning for others is stressed by the Jewish legend and would last in midrashic language for generations to come.[52]

Two important Byzantine authors in particular incorporated such notions in connection to the legend of the Ten Martyrs. Their works may lend Bloch's association of the martyrological legend with Byzantium further support.

Rabbi Amittai ben Shephatiah of Oria (second half of the ninth century) is believed to be a major contributor to the public knowledge of the mystical account of the "Ten Martyrs" and the *Elleh Ezkerah* liturgy.[53] Based on the *Midrash Elleh Ezkerah*, this emotional liturgy for the Day of Atonement narrates how ten learned (*hakhamim*) and pious (*zaddikim*) Jews were chosen by heaven to serve as an atonement for the "original sin" committed by the children of Jacob, who had sold Joseph to Ishmaelite merchants. An important literary mutation takes place here. The reason for the rabbis' execution is not just Samael's compulsive craving to destroy Israel but also the sin of selling Joseph.

On one day, an unspecified Roman emperor viciously executed ten of the most learned leaders of Israel as payment for the children of Israel's original sin of selling one of their own. They offer expiation for their generation, thus preventing a great calamity. Since that day, every generation has to supply ten pious men to keep world Jewry from divine punishment. In the process, human sacrifices turned from being victims to being God's chosen. God's elected were believed to have the power to end persecutions.[54]

For the tenth-century prominent physician and mystic Rabbi Shabbettai Donnolo (913–982), sins triggered his and his community's misfortune.[55] Allusion to the legend of the Ten Martyrs finds mystical expression in his introduction to the commentary on *The Book of Creation, Sefer Hakhmoni*.[56] It venerates and commemorates the destroyed rabbinic leadership of his Oria community.[57] Identifying himself as "Shabbettai Donnolo, son of Rabbi Abraham, commonly known as Donnolo the physician," he adds that,

because of the sins, I was expelled from the city of Oria my birthplace by an army of Ishmaelites ... in the year four thousand and six hundred and eighty five since creation (925).... And ten learned (*hakhamim*), righteous (*zaddikim*) rabbis of blessed memory were slain: Rabbi Hasdyah the son of Rabbi Hananel, may he rest in Paradise, greatly righteous and our kinsman by relation to my grandfather Rabbi Joel, may he rest in Paradise, and Rabbi Amnon and Rabbi Uriel, a righteous rabbi, and Rabbi Menahem and Rabbi Hiyah and Rabbi Zadok and Rabbi Moses and Rabbi David and Rabbi Jeremiah and Rabbi Nuriel, and pious (*hasidim*) elders, the heads of the community, the leaders of the generation, and copious students, and numerous children and women, all of blessed memory and of the world to come, Amen.[58]

What makes this text significant is Shabbettai's mixing of historical facts[59] with elements from the fictitious "Ten Martyrs." Shabbettai reveals the large number of Jewish casualties in this attack that brought the eradication and destruction of Oria. Yet, he identifies by name only ten of the casualties, who happened to be "the leaders of the generation" and "ten learned (*hakhamim*), righteous (*zaddikim*) rabbis."

Mentioning the number ten in this text was no historic coincidence or a literary accident. A careful reading reveals that, although Shabbettai mentioned ten rabbis as perishing in the attack, he managed to insert more than ten rabbis in his list.[60] As a mystic, Shabbettai Donnolo only alluded to an element from the story of the "Ten Martyrs" that was also present in the *Heikhalot* literature. Nevertheless, one can observe the conceptual and phraseological similarities between the two sources. Shabbettai indicated that the tragic end of his community resulted from an unexplained sin. Could it be the "original sin" of the ten sons of Israel? He also referred to the ten dead rabbis in the same terms that appear in the *Heikhalot* sources and in *Elleh Ezkerah*. The ten are the ransom each generation is required to deliver. In both sources the number ten is followed by these expressions: the leaders of the generation, righteous (*zaddikim*), pious (*hasidim*), and learned (*hakhamim*). These adjectives display the rabbis' special characteristics that qualified them for their divine duty.

Another parallel is the role the angel Samael plays in the *Heikhalot* as the patron of the Roman government (*Malkhut Romi*). Samael is the conspirator against the rabbis, eight thousand students, and Israel. Shabbettai concluded this passage from *Hakhmoni* by saying that "he had been ransomed in Otranto . . . in the country which is under the Roman government (*Malkhut Romi*)." *Malkhut Romi* represents the traditional oppressor of Israel and the martyrs in rabbinic literature.[61] For Shabbettai, as for many other Jews of his time, the persecution of the "Roman government" and that of the "Byzantine Empire" were interchangeable. Because heaven demanded that each generation submit ten righteous men, each generation had to relive the Roman oppression.

To be sure, the liturgical formats of *Asarah Harugei Malkhut* and the literature that followed indicate more than just an acculturation of Byzantine symbols. *Asarah Harugei Malkhut* offered a reversed polemical explanation to the Christian accusation of the Jewish historical betrayal.[62] The thought of Israel as having been sold into exile endured prominently in Christendom. The Christian variation explained that because Judas had sold Jesus to be executed for thirty silver pieces (Matt. 26:15; 27:9), Jews were sold into servitude in exile in a reverse value. In an attempt to devalue Judaism, the legend advanced the idea that thirty Jews were sold for one silver piece when brought into exile after Jesus' predicted destruction of the Temple.[63] Judas's betrayal led to Jesus' death as a ransom for "our sins" (1 Cor. 15:3–5). Matthew already had established that the Jews had accepted everlasting punishment for their crime, "His blood be on us and our children." Pilate, says the *Acts of Pilate,* realized that the envious Jews "have punished themselves and their posterity with fearful judgments of their own fault." Centuries later, various versions continued to present the Jews as cursing themselves for their betrayal, crying out "His blood be on us and on our children."[64]

Peter Alfonsi validates the apologetic function I am assigning to the legend of the Ten Martyrs. Reacting to such apologies, this early twelfth-century Jewish convert to Catholicism reiterated the "true" reason for Jewish suffering. Jews had been sold for one coin into exile, where they suffer burning and deadly tortures, only for their original sin of crucifying Jesus.[65] No other sin could better account for Jewish suffering in exile in Christian minds.

In light of these accusations, *Asarah Harugei Malkhut* and other Hebrew works with similar motifs diverted the Christian accusation from the selling of Jesus to that of Joseph. In the process, they employed other symbols that were also popular among their Christian contemporaries. Of significance is the mutual employment of the sacrificial symbol.

Rabbi Amittai ben Shephatiah openly expressed the idea of human sacrifice in his *Yotzer le-Shabbat.* As seen, Amittai refers to his people as "the sacrificers of burnt offering" during Basil's decrees, although no reference to actual victims is made.[66] Similarly, ninth-century Zevadiah Hazzan pleads with God to forgive the people of Israel their sins, because "plenty of pardon sacrifices are to be found" within the Jewish communities.[67] In reality, human sacrifices could be found only in the liturgy and literature of his time, more so in Christian circles and scripts.

Analogous notions of communal survival because of human sacrifice and atonement continued to play a major role in the works of tenth-century Byzantine Jews. For Rabbi Solomon ha-Bavli, the historical importance of the idea of human sacrifice needed no explanation. He believed that "sacrifice brings about the disappearance of afflictions."[68] Therefore, the "Nation of Israel takes upon herself the verdict of self-killing"[69] and "sacrifices burnt offerings."[70] Heavily relying on the notion of the *qorban* throughout his poems, Solomon attributes the lack of sacrifices to the misfortune of Israel. Only by sacrifices can Israel be redeemed.[71] One form of "sacrifice" is performed by daily prayers;[72] the other is the suffering members of Israel,[73] who refuse to accept Christianity. They let the oppressors "crucify them for Your sake" rather than forsake Judaism.[74]

At the end of the tenth century, Rabbi Meshullam ben *Kalonymous* expressed the same idea in his poem for the Day of Atonement, the day in which sacrifice atones for personal sins. Both individuals and Israel benefit from *qorbanot.* On a personal level, Rabbi Meshullam asserted that "a sacrifice (*qorban*) effaces my iniquities";[75] on a national level, God has vowed not to eliminate Israel on the account of the sacrifices.[76]

SEFER YOSIPPON

Qorbanot

Qorbanot feature extensively in the anonymous *Sefer Yosippon*. Its contribution to the history of Jewish martyrdom deserves individual attention. Written in tenth-century southern Italy, this valuable book recaptures the tragic Jewish events of the Greco-Roman period.[77] In the case of *Yosippon*, the influence comes directly from Hegesippus's Latin original book, which the author translated into Hebrew, and from the daily contact he maintained with his Christian neighbors.[78] World events outside the Jewish community also left decisive marks on Yosippon. In his view, sacrifices were needed to correct a present condition reminiscent of that found in legend of the Ten Martyrs and of the disaster in Donnolos's Oria. Placing his own words in the mouth of the biblical Mordechai, the anonymous author comments that "Because of our sins *we have been sold* and because of our inequities we have been exiled."[79] This technique of subliminally interjecting his own opinion and experience via the stories of the past can be noticed throughout the book.[80] The book, therefore, contributes not only to Jewish historiography but also to our understanding of the popular symbolism of Yosippon's period.

A good example is provided by Yosippon's narration of Philo's coping with the Roman decrees. As we shall see, this retelling of Philo, which has yet to receive adequate scholarly attention, will have an enormous impact on medieval Jewish martyrology. The historical Philo makes the installment of Gaius's statue in the Temple and the preservation of the Law the core of the conflict. *Sefer Yosippon* revolves the story around the building of altars for sacrifice to foreign gods. "We shall rather die together than obey him" was the immediate reaction to Gaius's attempt.[81] Thereafter, Philo addresses Apion's allegations in a direct dialogue with Gaius, which the original sources ignore.

Philo said: Indeed we shall build an altar only to God our Lord and we shall not mention the name of foreign gods, except His Name. We shall not sacrifice to other gods, except for Him exclusively. We would first submit our souls to death rather than obey your words.[82] And Gaius became mad and dismissed him with contempt.

A Jewish reaction reminiscent of Patriarch Photios's follows:

So said [Philo] to the Jews who were waiting outside in Gaius' courtyard: Let not your hearts rejoice today, for it is a time of calamity, for Gaius is deeply enraged. But there is a remedy and help in this matter. Let us return to the ancient Temple court, the Temple court of our forebears, to our God our Lord. We shall sanctify (*neqadesh*) a fast and shall call for a mass assembly in the country of our enemy. The Jews sanctified a fast in the country of Rome and called for a three-day assembly. And they cried out to God, the Lord of their forefathers. And God answered their fast and prayers.

Similarly to the Patriarch's way of dealing with the Rus, Philo's advice saves the day (Josephus does not mention a three-day fast). Indeed, the Book of Esther (4:15–16) had already mentioned three days of fasting, which may explain this practice. But the general reaction does echo some of the procedures witnessed by Yosippon in time of danger. As the additions in the story demonstrate, these practices left an impression on Yosippon. The placing of events in "the country of Rome" and "the country of our enemy" – both statements missing in the original – makes the story contemporaneous for the Byzantine reader.[83]

Philo's speech and the gathering of the people in the Temple court display their intention to be sacrificed. Their intentions are said to have paid off on the third day, when Gaius was assassinated. As in Philo and Josephus, the need for sacrifice never materialized because of Gaius's unexpected assassination. But, as we shall see, the falling of the "miraculous" redemption on the third day due to potential sacrifices was no accident.

Yosippon's version of the Maccabean martyrs does not exhibit much more authenticity with regard to sacrifice. Almost naturally, he presents the seven sons and Eleazar as sacrifices. By adding extra lines to the speeches of the protagonists, the author inserts his own opinion on passive self-destruction for religious purposes.[84] Although a direct recommendation to undertake martyrdom is absent, his sympathetic portrayal of the protagonists is transparent.

Eleazar "was killed for God his Lord," begins the Maccabean saga.[85] The sage is a faithful priest who sacrifices his life for the common good. He chooses death so as not to mislead his people by pretending to eat unkosher food. A possible association of Eleazar, "who was tested [by God] and was found faithful," with sacrifices may be provided by the phrase "completed his life" (*ve-shillem nafesho*). This nonmartyrological phrase may present a play on the words "peace-offering" (*shelamim*), which he explicitly mentions elsewhere.[86]

A clearer association of the Maccabean heroes with human sacrifice is revealed in the story of the mother and her seven sons. According to the sixth brother, the family submits itself to death as "the expiatory sacrifice of our nation."[87] This statement, which is missing in 2 and 4 Maccabees (7:18–19; 11:13–27), respectively, further reflects the environmental influence on the anonymous author. This influence is evident also in the mother's speech. She perceives her sons as God's sacrifices and, therefore, expects a family reunion in the future.[88]

Presenting martyrs as God's sacrifices, *Sefer Yosippon* transformed the family from humble into holy. The heroine becomes "the holy mother" (*qedosha*), an adjective missing in 2 Maccabees 7:20.[89] The extra term *holy* surfaces also in the youngest son's speech. The main hero in the drama pleads with his mother not to hinder him further from joining his deceased "holy brothers."[90] Holiness and sacrifice certify the special characteristics of the family, the religious aspect of its performance, and the author's positive presentation.

Holiness led to human sacrifice and vise versa. No great amount of imagination was needed to transform the Jerusalem priesthood into divine offerings. Yosippon's description of the wars in the holy city includes the priests and the many ordinary Jews who volunteered to prevent war. In this description the priests are not consumed by fire but are said to have been killed on their sacrifices. "While the priests were sacrificing their burnt-offerings, they were being killed on their offerings. The corpses of the priests were collapsing on the corpses of the animals, which they were sacrificing . . . and the blood of the enemy mingled with the blood of the holy in the Temple of God."[91] The priest and their sacrifices merge into one.

A correlative description of Pompey's bloody invasion into the Temple (originally, *Jewish War* 1:150–151) makes this analogy explicitly:

As the sacrificing priest was falling, his colleague would come and take the sacrifice out of his hand and [to continue to] sacrifice it. And when the latter was killed, his colleague would come and do what his friend had done. . . . And the bodies of the priests fell on the sacrifices and their blood mingled with the blood of the sacrifices and they died in holiness before the altar of God.[92]

Sacrificers become synonymous with sacrificed.

The identification of casualties as sacrifices proceeds thus naturally in Yosippon's next portrayal of the battle against the Romans in the Temple. To the original proclamations, the author adds his own explanation of the fighters' motivation: "For the sake of our Lord we shall die and for His Temple and sanctuary we shall be considered a burnt offering (*qorban olah*) on this day."[93] The author takes the liberty of including the very same notion in Yohanan's response to Josephus before the fight against the Roman troops in the Temple. Unsympathetic to the rebels for shedding the blood of the priests in the Temple, the author leaves the making of the association to the militants:

"There is no better sacrifice (*zevah*) to be offered in this chamber than our flesh and blood, since for our Lord we shall fight and we shall be considered before Him as the daily burnt offering (*olat ha-Tamid*) and we shall die free in the holy city."[94]

Interestingly, when describing the self-killing of the rebels at Masada, *Sefer Yosippon* suppresses the real nationalistic and militant motive of their action and presents only a clearly religious motive. Yosippon thus describes in this final chapter the suicides at Masada as potential "burnt offerings."[95] In lines appended to Eleazar's original speech, the leader urged his men to sacrifice their families so they would be free to fight unto death. Those killed he considered "burnt offerings that will satisfy God." This notion is repeated in one of the manuscript's two endings. "They gathered their wives, sons, and daughters to slay them to the ground. They will be considered a burnt offering (*qorban olah*) before God, because for His Name they went, not to be killed before the Romans."[96] It was one thing to legitimize the association of Temple sacrifices with those ready to die for God; it was an entirely different issue for a medieval Jewish author to legitimize an association of self-destruction with sacrifices.

Love

This transformation was further advanced by the element of love. To emphasize the unselfish and voluntary aspects of their altruism, *Sefer Yosippon* does not mention the Talmudic ruling on mandatory martyrdom. Instead, self-sacrifice emerges as a pure act of mutual love between God and Israel. God presents Israel with the opportunity to undergo martyrdom out of His love for His people, and Israel undertakes this divine opportunity out of love for Him. Out of love, God bestowed on the brothers "this honor."[97] Love for the nation motivated the rest of the brothers. Moreover, the Maccabean Eleazar rejects Philipus's (rather than Antiochus's) attempt to save him, because of his love of death.[98]

Love, according to *Sefer Yosippon*, also drove the Jewish soldiers to sacrifice themselves in the war against the Romans. In describing the debate between Josephus Flavius and his soldiers in Jotapata, Yosippon interpolates in the soldiers' speech an important rhetorical question. "How can we love our Lord with all our soul and heart if we do not die for His covenant with His servants who are being killed for His name?"[99] The final act illustrates absolute love for God, a love that exceeds the fear of death. Yosippon disregards the soldiers' historical motivation in fighting and dying free for their country. Instead, he presents them as Jews sacrificing themselves out of their absolute love for God.

This literary conjecture echoes R. Akiva's words. Recall B. *Berakhot*, 61 b: "All my days I have been troubled by this verse, 'And thou shalt love the Lord thy God with all thy soul, even if He takes thy soul'. Now that I have the opportunity shall I not fulfill it?"[100] If, indeed, Yosippon relied on Akiva, as Flusser suggested in his note to line 25 there, it is certainly a rare use of Talmudic material by the author. This style, however, was typical for the period as well. The Church of Constantinople demanded that Jews converting to Christianity first denounce Judaism publically and then confess with their "whole heart, and soul, and with a true faith" the acceptance of Christianity.[101] This language was most likely adapted from Matthew 22.37, Luke 10.27, or Mark 12.30.

Certainly, Jewish tradition already connected dying for God, however infrequent, with love.[102] But the overall usage of the idea by Yosippon coincides with his neighbors' Christological understanding of the importance of love vis-à-vis one's enemies. King David gave up his soul for his straying nation, asking God to afflict him and his house instead. Now, Yosippon beseeches the King to awake and arise to straighten up his malevolent people by "holy canticles." 2 Samuel 24:17 is behind Yosippon's turning of the biblical David from a sinner into a medieval saint. This development goes hand in hand with Yosippon's second request from the prophet Elisha (2 Kings 7, 8) to turn the people's hate into love. Straightening up the people is to be achieved not by swords, but by words of prayers that will *blind* the evildoers.[103] Elisha's nonviolent message does not appear in the biblical version. But in Yosippon, the prophet's message resonates with Paul's conversion by a blinding light on the road to Damascus (Acts 9:3–9), and Jesus' words of love (Matt. 26:52–54). In John 15:11–19, Jesus advises his followers to turn the hate directed at them into love for "there is no greater love than this, that a man should lay down his life for his friends."[104]

Recompense

Love for God is not without return in *Sefer Yosippon*. In contrast to many of the Talmudic martyrs, Yosippon's heroes expect to be rewarded for their sacrifices. An exception are the priests in the Temple. They and "many among the Jewish heroes" leaped into the fire because "There is no life after the burning of God's Holy House."[105] This would include life after death. But at Jotapata, Josephus's adamant soldiers bring the notion of reward against their commanders' advice to surrender.

Was it not you who reminded us numerous times that every man who shall die in war for God and for His people and for His Torah shall have a portion in the lot of God. He shall depart to the great light, without seeing the darkening of darkness. . . . Did not you tell us: 'fight to your death in war, because if you die for God's Temple and for His Torah, your death shall be ransom for your souls and you shall leave for the great light. If you have spoken the truth, why does your soul refrain from death, from going after your people who have gone to the great light?'[106]

Promises of heavenly rewards at Jotapata are the development of the Hebrew Yosippon, as they are missing in both Josephus's and Yosippon's Latin sources. The Latin original discusses only the death of the righteous, not of soldiers, who are promised that they will fly back up into the Garden of Eden (*revolare ad superna, ad illam regionem paradisi*).[107] Evidently, the medieval milieu affected the speech of Josephus's soldiers at Jotapata in *Yosippon*.[108] Pontiffs and potentates referred to potential casualties in wars by the terms *holy* or *holy martyrs*.[109]

In the political war over southern Italy and against heretics, popes and secular leaders used martyrdom as a means of massive mobilization, promising the participants a celestial reward if they should die.[110] Popes Leo IV (853) and John VIII (878), who succeeded for a short time in eliminating the schism between East and West, promised indulgence (*indulgentia delictorum*) to Christians who died for the truth of the faith, the salvation of the patria, and the defense of their fellow Christians in their "holy war" against the Muslims. The same style and substance resonates in Yosippon's story of Jotapata.[111]

Pope Leo IV hoped that none of his fellow Christians would be killed:

Yet we want you to know that the kingdom of heaven will be given as a reward to those who shall be slain in this war. For the Omnipotent knows that they lost their lives fighting for the truth of the faith, for the protection of their country, and the defense of Christians. And hence God will grant them the reward which we have mentioned.[112]

The motivation for reward are similar to those listed at Jotapata.

In the same language Pope John VIII wrote to bishops in the realm of Louis II.

You have modestly required to know if those who have recently died in battle, fighting in defense of the holy church of God and for the protection of the Christian religion and of the state, or those who may in the future fall in the same cause, may obtain indulgence for their sins (*indulgentiam delictorum*). We certainly respond that those who, out of love of the Christian religion, shall die in battle fighting courageously against pagans or infidels, shall receive eternal life. For the Lord has said through his prophet, 'In whatever hour a sinner shall be converted, I will remember his sins no longer.'[113]

These notions of the holy dying out of love for God, His religion, and the country to atone for sins to receive everlasting life, dominate also some of Yosippon's war stories. Even the biblical Aaron is painted in the spirit of the papal letters. Aaron is "the holy [one] of God" who stood like a "hero" before the nation and struck the enemy. In an earlier passage, Aaron the "hero" is presented as giving himself up to die for his people.[114]

In the case of Jotapata, the motivation of reward behind the giving up of life fails to persuade both Josephus the general and Yosippon the author. This failure reflects the author's own struggling with the popular Christian use of reward, as is also suggested by the Temple priests' statement, which negates the notion. More persuasive is Eleazar's recompense-argument at Masada. As in Josephus, Masada's story is strikingly similar to that of Jotapata. Here, however, Yosippon elaborates further on the notion of reward. "The great light" relates to eternal life "in the world of justice."[115] Abraham thus did not hesitate to bind Isaac on the altar. King Yeshaiau feared no death for the same reason. He knew that "The great light, which is in *Gan Eden,* was the destiny of Yeshaiau."[116]

If hints of doubts mark the speeches ascribed to the rebels at Jotapata and Masada, Yosippon appears more confident in the afterlife belief in the story of Amittai. To offset his daring additions, the story of Amittai claims a traditional existence of the belief in heavenly recompense after death.[117] But to support his arguments he does not turn to the *Tannaitic* and *Amoraic* material, which does not speak of voluntary death, its recompense, and its actors in these terms. Failing to realize that Amittai and Mattathias are one and the same, he first modestly narrates Mathathias's valedictory address to his five sons: "Be envious of God's zeal, of His Temple's zeal, and his nation's zeal. Fight and do not refrain from death. For if you die in your war, you will be received by your ancestors, and you will be with them, in their lot, because all our ancestors, who envied God's zeal, God gave them honor and grace."[118]

Further elaboration is provided by Amittai's farewell to his four sons. Simon the rebel is about to put the four sons to death before their father's eyes. Amittai, therefore, requests his sons to "go and find us a lasting abode (*malon*)." This was not an unprecedented request according to Yosippon. Amittai knew that a woman had already sent seven sons before her to reserve a place for her. "They prepared an abode for themselves and their mother." Amittai can only hope that he and his sons will come into the dwelling of the seven. "But if we cannot come into their abode, let us be their neighbors, for they died honestly, and we shall die aimlessly."[119]

Here Amittai relies on the story of the mother to justify a future dwelling place. On whom did the author depend in vindicating Amittai's assertion?

The same idea was already expressed by Jesus, according to John, although in reverse order. John's setting corresponds to that of Amittai's. It is the last time Jesus is with all of his apostles. He informs them of Judas's coming betrayal and that he would be with them only a little longer. "There are many dwelling places in my Father's house," he tells them. "I am going there on purpose to prepare a place for you. And if I go and prepare a place for you, I shall come again and receive you to myself, so that where I am you may be also" (John 14:2–3).

Yosippon's contemporaries provided a more immediate channel for cross-fertilization. Monk Cosmas utilized the same language to describe to his brothers his "Awesome and Edifying Vision" of the afterlife. After he became the abbot of his monastery in 933, the mysteries of heaven and hell were revealed to him in a trance. In his journey, he met the deceased who had served with him in the imperial palace, many people from Constantinople, peasants, and some members of his monastery. They were dwelling in the "many mansions that existed in the Lord's house."[120]

No doubt, the messages delivered by Popes Leo and John left a distinct mark on Yosippon's generation. The updated names he adopts for the nations in his political orbit clearly indicate Yosippon's awareness and understanding of ongoing political and religious affairs.[121] The popes' premature calls for what would later take the form of a crusade constituted part of a general Christian endeavor to create a monolithic Christian society in Europe. Throughout the Empire, the endeavor targeted Arian sects and pagan tribes such as the Magyars. The Ottonians' "holy campaign" against the Magyars reached its height in 975. During this time of Christian expansion, Emperor Nikephoros II Phocas (d. 969) aspired to legislate that every soldier dying in the holy war against the infidels would be declared a holy martyr. Church officials rejected the imperial attempt only because they refused to share this powerful tool of mass mobilization and control.[122]

In southern Italy, the attempt to spread Christianity met the opposition of North African Muslim invaders. This was in addition to the resistance of the Normans from the ninth through the eleventh centuries, culminating in the capture of Pope Leo IX by the Norman Robert Guiscard. In parallel to the Christian endeavor in Eastern Europe and Italy, the nobility and the clergy of Western Europe led a fervent holy campaign against the Muslims of Spain.[123]

These developments meant not only the exposure of Byzantine Jewry to the celestial notions but also their experience of religious pressure in one form or another. Additional indicators of the influence of the religious and political ambience on *Sefer Yosippon* can be noticed in what the book does not mention. The author's unfamiliarity with the rabbinic names of the mother of the seven sons, as well as the nonexistence of rabbinic martyrs or their speeches, are an *argumenta e silentio*.[124] Instead, the emphasis lies on humans as sacrifices, personal and national redemption through death, and the "beatification" of the "holy" sacrifices. These are the same motifs that characterize the calls of the popes and the secular leaders.

THE CHRONICLE OF AHIMAATZ

The pathetic result of Leo's declaration of a holy war against the Normans took place in 1053, a year before *Ahimaatz* completed his chronicle of genealogy.[125] At the close of Byzantine sovereignty in southern Italy, *Ahimaatz* still finds the notion of human sacrifice appealing. Not only does he present self-sacrifice as the natural choice for the Jewish people, he also gives the background of this choice. It is the historical context of the religious pressure experienced by his close ancestors, embellished by his own imagination.

The *Chronicle of Ahimaatz* contains two explicit examples of Jews who preferred to endure death over conversion. R. Hananel of Oria entered into a strange bet with the local archbishop concerning the exact appearance of the new moon. Hananel offered conversion, if he lost, against the archbishop's horse. The archbishop challenged Hananel to accept that

if the new moon appear as I [the archbishop] have calculated, you shall do my will and adopt my religion, as my gospel teaches, abandon your faith and the ordinance of your law, and accept my religion . . . If it be as you have calculated, I will do thy will. I will give you my horse, assigned to me at the (ceremonies of) New Year's day, the value of which is 300 pieces of gold. . . . [126]

Being aware of the implications of his defeat, Hananel turned to God to help him and come to his salvation. "So that I shall not suffer punishment; else my death is better than my life. Do not destroy the work of Thy hands [that is Hananel]. . . . "[127] Due to divine intervention, Hananel escaped both conversion and death. This story, which is probably *Ahimaatz's* spin on Basil's compulsory disputations, ends on a positive note. God "delivered His followers from darkness to light."

A Jew named Theophilus demonstrates a similar adherence to Judaism. Although not explicitly designated a sacrifice, his mysterious death on the Day of Atonement makes the *qorban* association evident. R. Bonfil's study of this "squarely hagiographical" work is particularly valuable in this context.

In the case of the character Paltiel, The Day of Atonement "is in the *Scroll of Ahimaatz* a highly convenient framework."[128] Given the prominence of the *qorban* concept in Byzantium, it is not surprising to see this framework repeated in Theophilus's story.

What brought misfortune on Theophilus was not his Jewishness but his sinful life. Theophilus "fell by his sin and was condemned to death by strangulation" for illicit sexual conduct. The governor granted him a second chance. "If you [Theophilus] abandon your religion and truly adopt mine, I will save you from an unnatural death."[129]

At first, Theophilus seemed to accept the governor's condition. Sometime later the governor found Theophilus still "loyal to the religion of the Hebrews." This discovery and the governor's request that Theophilus "truly adopt" Christianity echo the abovementioned crypto-Jewish response to the past imperial persecutions. Eventually, Theophilus turned zealously faithful to his creed. The betrayed governor punished him "with cruelty and with horrible torture"; he "began to strike him, to beat him with fiendish blows; he cut off his hands and his feet, and cast him into prison and confined him there." Theophilus still remained determined. On the holy Day of Atonement, "when the sins of God's people are being absolved," it was found that God had taken him from his prison cell, and he was never found alive or dead. Theophilus redeemed himself of his initial immorality and his former consideration of Christianity to save *himself*.

The occurrence of the miracle on the Day of Atonement turns Theophilus into a symbolic expiation for his own sin. The miracle "proves" his vindication by God on account of his absolute loyalty. *Ahimaatz* chose to leave Theophilus' fate a mystery. Theophilus and Rabbi Hananel never present the act of martyrdom, for God miraculously saved the two.

Theophilus's tale illustrates another Hebrew modification of a foreign fable. *Ahimaatz* makes little effort to conceal this adaptation of a popular Greek folktale about a Christian martyr named Theophilus. Hroswitha de Gandersheim (ca. 925–1002) dedicated her life to the commemoration of the dead and the transmission of their heroic deeds to the public. Among her protagonists was the Christian Theophilus, who was dismissed from his church office by a certain bishop. Seeking to regain his office, Theophilius "turned to a Jewish magician." For a heavy price he could not only reappoint Theophilus, but also elevate him to a bishop's status. The Jewish magician summoned "evil spirits," demanding of Theophilus that he worship the Devil. The Holy Virgin intervened to save Theophilus from the Devil's claws. Thus he was reconciled with the Church by voluntarily submitting to death.[130] This unlikely Christian martyr disappeared without a trace, as was the case with the Jewish Theophilus.

For both the Christian and the Jewish protagonists, mysterious death was the inevitable atonement for their sinful life, as well as the supreme shield against religious temptation.

Mary's intervention illustrates the compassionate attribute in the story of the Christian Theophilus. A similar tone reverberates in its Hebrew counterpart. In an additional departure from the Talmudic views on martyrdom, the attributes of love and mercy replace the attribute of Justice.[131] Although Yosippon may be suspected of a poor Jewish education, no such excuse can explain *Ahimaatz's* switch to the motivation of love.

Like Yosippon, *Ahimaatz* disregards the obligatory aspects of Talmudic martyrdom, and displays his heroes' unconditional adherence to Judaism as an act of love. *Ahimaatz* echoes this by choosing to praise Rabbi Shephatiah in the language with which the Talmud *Berakhot* 61b delineates Akiva. Rabbi Shephatiah "studied the mysteries of heaven and of the Almighty, and served Him all his life with devotion, faithfully loved the Lord and obeyed Him with all his soul and might, and with all his heart professed His unity."[132]

As with his contemporary hagiographers, *Ahimaatz's* language makes Shephatiah look like a martyr. Shephatiah had written about the sacrifices of love in his community, but he himself never became one. *Ahimaatz*, too, considers the Byzantine Jews "descendants of the innocents and holy ones"[133] and of the "pious."[134] We have seen the term *holy* used by the rest of the discussed sources.[135] *Ahimaatz* is no different. Even the late touch-ups of *The Vision of Daniel* still designate martyrs "the pious people of the Almighty," instead of the more known phrase of the present *qiddush ha-Shem*.[136] *Ahimaatz* manifests his familiarity with the phrase *qiddush ha-Shem* by quoting from B. *Baba Kamma*, 113a, "the law of the State has the force of the law."[137] *Qiddush ha-Shem* appears here in Rabbi Akiva's opinion on Jewish–Gentile relations, with no martyrological connotation. Had *qiddush ha-Shem* been the standard reference to martyrdom, B. *Baba Kamma*, 113a, would have served as an appropriate reminder for *Ahimaatz* to employ the phrase as such.[138]

Instead, throughout the Hebrew works just discussed, the *qorban* (sacrifice) symbol dominates the idea of martyrdom. It was perceived that self-fulfillment was, and can be, achieved by self-sacrifice. The readiness to be sacrificed in these works illustrates the highest spiritual experience. By depicting martyrdom in the form of *qorbanot*, the medieval Byzantine Jews expressed their love of God. At least in theory, this spiritual love was stronger than life and greater than death. As an act of love, the idea of the *qorban* demonstrated the personal relationship between God and either the individual or Byzantine Jewry as a whole. By doing so, Byzantine authors reversed the rabbinic attempt to ignore the sacrifice symbol that was so common in the pre-Talmudic writings. Byzantine Jews found justification for their association of humans with sacrifice in the pre-Talmudic Jewish narratives of the Roman period.

LIFE IMITATES LITERATURE

The literature of *qorbanot* promised the survival of Byzantine Jewry under harsh conditions. As seen, this highly charged symbol found expressions in diverse styles. Whether liturgical or mystical, the authors of these works relied on their understanding of the past to rationalize the present and reckon a more favorable future. Such an approach also marks the sacred writings found outside the Jewish circles. As Peter Brown has noticed, "The hagiographer was recording the moments when the seemingly extinct past and the unimaginably distant future had pressed into the present."[139] Or in the language of Delehaye, "The hagiographer, then, shares the ideas of history current in his day. But he writes history with a special, clearly defined object in view, and this is not without influence on the character of his work."[140]

Surprisingly, the rabbinic martyrs of the past play a limited role in the sources under discussion. Even at the close of the tenth century, the legend of the Ten Martyrs was only alluded to in the writings of the prominent Shabbettai Donnolo. His Babylonian contemporary, the luminary Rabbi Sherira Gaon, still cautioned against accepting the legend word for word.[141] His caveat illustrates the growing popularity of the ten rabbis and that the legend was still striving to receive recognition in mainstream Judaism. What seems to be the focus of the Byzantine Hebrew literature is the effect the past still had on their present and future life. Byzantine Jews shared this interpretation of reality with their spiritual mentors from Palestine. This view triggered the Babylonian Geonim's complaint that in the Land of Israel – the spiritual center and guide of Byzantine Jewry[142] – Jews wrongly observed the commandments as if they were still being persecuted. Amittai ben Shephatiah of Oria, other mystical rabbis like him, *Sefer Yosippon,* and the *Chronicle of Ahimaatz* adopted the same approach.

Literature does not always confine itself to the realm of imagery. Given the right condition and wrong interpretation, literary symbols may be taken literally. It appears that it was only a matter of time for this transformation to occur in Byzantium. The first known incident of Jewish martyrdom in the precrusade period is found in the epistle sent by the Jewish community of Bari to the celebrated Hasday ibn Shaprut (915–976) in Cordoba.[143] Unfortunately, a great deal of information relevant to this incident remains obscure. There are good reasons to assume that the epistle was written sometime after 952 in reference to an undated persecution of the recent past.[144] Because the last known persecution in Byzantium took place before Romanos's deposition in 944, it is not too venturesome to assume that the event is related to his persecution.[145] In fact, the author accounted for the gap between the actual date of the persecution and the date of composition, apologizing for the postponement.[146] Around 945, Demetrios of Cyzicus still praised the emperor for converting "numerous Hebrews from their ancestral error, and refuted Athinganoi and Paulicians."[147] If true, this outcome explains the epistle's sense of urgency.

The epistle presents the first reported Jewish case of voluntary death in the Middle Ages. It took place in the community of Otranto. This community of southern Italy experienced oppression for two days. As a result,

... the holy congregation of Otranto has lost three associates for they were compelled by that cursed decree. Their names were Rav Isaiah ... and R. Menahem ... and their disciple Elijah. R. Isaiah with his hands drove a knife into his throat and was slaughtered like a sacrificial lamb in the Temple court. R. Menahem leaped into a pit. Seeing that his sun had darkened, Elijah strangled himself.[148]

In contrast to the Oria victims in Donnolo's report, these three individuals are not accidental casualties who perished in random attacks. Beyond the prohibition against studying the Torah, the exact nature of the persecution remains ambiguous. The Holy Scriptures, it appears, were to be consigned to the flames. Clearly, self-sacrifice was the result of an intended self-designed act. After two days of heroism the persecutions ceased, and on the third day the community was "delivered from darkness to light"[149] on account of the three martyrs. Thus, "even one letter of the Torah was not burned there. Because the sacrifice of His pious men satisfied [Him] like a daily burnt offering." It is unlikely, however, that the authorities found the death of the three so alarming that it decided to annul the decrees. Yosippon had Gaius's "persecutions" ending on the third day because Philo and his delegation were ready to be sacrificed.

Two traditional motifs characterize the narrative. The first is related to the nature of the persecution, the second to reaction to it. The repression resembles Hadrian's ban on Torah study. The response of the martyrs echoes that of the martyrs of the Roman period, however vaguely it approximates the behavior of the Talmudic heroes. Like the early martyrs, the three members from Otranto continued to study Torah, despite the declaration of the death penalty.

More important, however, is the contemporary Byzantine conception of human atonement. This popular liturgical and literary motif became strong enough to materialize into an actual act. Because of the power of this motif, a belief existed that self-sacrifice of human beings can actually satisfy God's wrath and, consequently, deliver Israel from hardship. This theme corresponds to a more general Jewish assertion that the redemption of Israel will occur when the sacrificial ritual in the Temple is renewed. It was not a coincidence, then, that the community is reported to have been delivered on the third day of self-sacrifice. Each martyr is believed to have atoned for one day of persecution.[150] In this respect, the epistle conveys the idea that the martyrs' death not only halted the decree but also caused the community to flourish and become an important center.[151]

To be more specific, R. Isaiah's association with "the sacrificial lamb in the Temple court" brings us back to the stories of the Roman period. Plenty of them could be found in *Sefer Yosippon*. As in the retold stories of Josephus and Philo,[152] Isaiah took upon himself the roles of the Temple priest and the innocent lamb – the holy sacrificer and the innocent sacrifice. The lamb as a Jewish metaphor of the Roman period needs no repetition. But as with the newly adapted martyrological modifier "holy," the presentation of the innocent Isaiah as a lamb may have been especially appealing to an author living in an environment highly charged with Christological symbols. No doubt, the author felt comfortable in utilizing the popular and well-established *qorban* symbol of his time.

Through the *qorban*, R. Isaiah assumed the roles both of the paramount sacrificer and of the purest sacrifice. By these two roles, R. Isaiah "actualized" himself and found the meaning of his life. The cessation of imperial anti-Jewish decrees supplied the proof that eventually God accepted the sacrifices of the rabbi and his two companions. They became God's chosen. R. Isaiah elevated himself to the saintly status of the high priest of the Temple because he was found fit to sacrifice himself as the "sacrificial lamb." As the cessation in the decrees proved, God was listening to martyrs.

The association of the martyrdom of R. Isaiah with the ritual of Temple sacrifice indicates the actual revival of conceptions of voluntary death from the Greco-Roman period. Caught in the myth's boundless time, the community of Otranto became an imaginary contemporary of the Roman persecution and of the Jewish martyrs' heroic epoch. But, unlike the potential martyrs of the Roman period, the author of the story, not the actors themselves, is said to have made the symbolic connection. The concept that was clear and natural to the Jews of the Roman period had to be explained by the medieval author. In this journey between the Greco-Roman and the Byzantine periods, the symbols seem to have skipped the Talmudic station.

Adjoined to the *qorban* concept is the other emblem, holiness. Otranto arises from this incident as the "holy community." As in Yosippon, the two motifs complement each other. On the one hand, only a holy community could produce such pious and loyal members. On the other, no one could question the sacredness of Otranto because of the saintliness of its three heroes.

Despite the dramatic role the three rabbinic associates from Otranto play in the epistle, martyrdom is not its focus. This incident enabled the writer to emphasize the transition of the community from one extreme to another "from days of darkness to days of light." The dispatch's main concern remained the future of Torah centers and the study of mysticism, the celebrated rabbis of the community, and their disciples. These were the reasons for joy and optimism in his Jewish circle.

Contrary to typical martyrological narratives, the incident under consideration lacks pessimism and feeling of despair. A comparison with the Maccabean Eleazar, with the woman with her seven sons, and with the Talmudic martyrs, reveals a somewhat embryonic martyrological account. Unlike future Jewish accounts of defeat, but still in accordance with the general feeling of the time, human sacrifice paid off in Otranto.

As in the hagiographical literature of the period, the existence of martyrs elevated the value of rising communities and their leaders. A closer look at the material at hand reveals their promotion of a particular family nucleus. Among the leadership of the Bari community, the epistle mentions the refugee Rabbi Abraham ben Yehoshaphat, the former leader of the "scattered" Oria community. Also mentioned is the local Rabbi Samuel ben Judah, who prospered in the city.[153] The epistle made clear that Bari became a leading and authoritative study center in its own right after the destruction of Oria. As already mentioned, Oria was the birthplace of the former leadership that perished in the attacks. Survivors like Rabbi Shabbettai Donnolo had found refuge in 925 in the community of Otranto – the community that rose to fame through its three martyrs.

Rabbi *Ahimaatz* further illustrates the links among Oria, Bari, and Otranto. *Ahimaatz* buttresses the notion that the two latter communities became a sanctuary for the Jewish refugees from Oria.[154] The Jews of Oria spread also to other cities in Italy. One of those was Beneventum, which became the new homeland of Rabbi Hananel ben Rabbi Paltiel, the grandson of the martyred Rabbi Hasdaya ben Rabbi Hananel in Donnolo's *Sefer Hakhmoni*.[155] The circle of Byzantine Jews who expressed ideas of mysticism and martyrdom in their writings expanded to places such as Bari, Otranto, Beneventum, and Rome. They carried with them the mystical-martyrological conceptions of their predecessors.

WHY BYZANTINE JEWRY?

Having analyzed the martyrological stories and events in Byzantine Italy, it is possible to reconstruct the social and cultural mobility of the Jews there. At first, the community of Oria dominated Byzantine Jewry in south Italy because of the fame of its talented and learned leaders. It seems that the harsh interior and exterior political developments in south Italy created an unwanted opportunity for Oria's leadership to exhibit its intellectual superiority in action and writing. Eventually, these political events, which had been pounding the community for two centuries, caused its destruction in the middle of the tenth century. Thereafter, hegemony shifted from Oria to Bari and Otranto, which became the new homeland of Oria's refugees and ideology. The story of the three martyrs from Otranto completed the transition of hegemony from Oria to Otranto.

To what extent the members of these communities possessed similar ideas prior to the arrival of the refugees from Oria, we do not know. But even if such ideas did circulate among these communities, the political and military events that affected south Italy, and especially the community of Oria, further increased their martyrological awareness and gave a realistic meaning to the conception of martyrdom. The three "burnt offerings" of Otranto converted popular martyrological symbols and narrations into deeds. The rabbis of Oria, Rabbi Solomon ha-Bavli, and Rabbi Yehiel ben Abraham of Rome could supply the necessary religious legitimacy for this transmutation. Jewish martyrdom in Byzantium, then, was the product and the act of the intellectual elite.

Based on the Bari epistle, Y. Baer argued for a martyrological tendency among Italian Jews.[156] His observation was followed and developed by A. Grossman in a number of places. Grossman has maintained that the roots of Ashkenazic martyrdom go back to tenth-century Italy, which served as a link between the old Palestinian traditions of *qiddush ha-Shem* and that of the newly established Ashkenaz.[157]

As we shall see in the next chapter, Grossman is correct in his important observation, which we can expand to include Byzantine Jewry. Two aspects of the Otranto phenomenon, however, deserve further attention. First, the three martyred associates chose for themselves active and violent deaths. Second, there is no indication in the Bari epistle that the persecutions posed an immediate threat to or placed an immediate demand on the three martyrs. They were not forced to make a choice between life and death. Instead, the letter depicts them as voluntary sacrifices who delivered the community from some unspecified anti-Jewish policy. These two elements – a violent self-inflicted sacrifice and not in the face of a direct threat – appear to contradict the martyrological tradition Italian Jews were allegedly passing on. These martyrs went beyond the *halakhic* requirements. In their violent exits they even exceeded the examples of the four hundred youths (B. *Gittin* 57b) or the exiles from Jerusalem (*Lamentation Rabbah* 1 to 1:16).[158] Their behavior is particularly disturbing, as they appear to be well versed in *halakhah*. All of the Talmudic role models were executed by others.[159]

Such a departure from the *halakhic* norm in Byzantium invites two questions. Why, of all Jewish communities, was Byzantine Jewry the first known to provide a martyrological description in the Middle Ages, and why was martyrdom active? After all, it was not the first time European Jews faced religious persecutions and attempts at forced conversion. In the sixth century Jews in Visigothic Spain and Merovingian France had already experienced religious pressure, forced conversions, and limited expulsions.[160] Absent in these reports is a Jewish martyrological response. It may well be that such earlier anti-Jewish policies did produce voluntary deaths, but not martyrological accounts. Whether for a lack of incidents, recorders, or traditions, one can still not escape the fact that the first known Hebrew martyrological account in medieval Europe was provided by Byzantine Jews and not by other communities that had experienced similar conditions.

INTERNATIONAL DIPLOMACY

One distinctive factor, however, may have contributed to the development of the Byzantine tradition of activism. In Spain the forced conversions were conducted by the newly Catholic Visigothic kings, despite the official opposition of the Third Council of Toledo (589). In France, the mob attacked Jews after the majority of them had rejected proposals to convert, like that of Bishop Avitus of Clermont. As mentioned, in Byzantium the anti-Jewish policies and attempts were orchestrated by the emperors, representing both the Church and the empire. Although the severity of these policies varied, at least in theory, any Jewish means of protection would have been curtailed substantially if the empire initiated the religious decrees against its Jews. In theory, this lack of imperial protection may have opened the door for martyrs. In reality, it took Byzantine Jews a few centuries to actually walk through this door in a unique fashion.

As the above material has already shown, Byzantine Jewry developed its own literature of martyrdom. In the same vein, actual martyrdom suggests that the early Jewish traditions from Eretz Israel do not fully explain the Byzantine phenomenon of self-destructive martyrdom. The acting-out of Byzantine literary symbols became possible not only because of feelings of oppression but also thanks to the development of these symbols in a fertile environment that witnessed living martyrs or that at least presented casualties as such.[161]

Byzantine propaganda presented ninth-century Bulgars qaghans, for example, as persecutors of Christians. A century later, hagiographies turned the persecuted into saints. Even more audacious is the popular beatification of Enravota, the son of the qaghan Omurtage. His political execution by his rival brother became a martyrdom after the conversion of the Bulgarians. His *Martyrion* was produced in time to legitimize the ruling of the Bulgar holy family and to put it on the Byzantine-orthodox flank.[162]

What can be told, then, about the Bari epistle beyond martyrdom? Little attention was given to the epistle's addressee. Flusser has raised the possibility that the letter could have been sent to Hasday ben David of Bagdad, a suggestion Grossman rightly rejected.[163] The three sacrifices represent only one aspect of the epistle. Its real goal was to convince Hasday of the urgency of acting on behalf of the martyrs' Jewry before the Byzantine authorities. The epistle utilized an actual tragedy to exhibit to Hasday the religious devotion of the members of both the Otranto and Bari communities under harsh conditions. To reach these goals, the author employed one of the most powerful and moving literary tools of his period.

It was not Hasday's first encounter with human sacrifice. He happened to be, therefore, a perfect addressee for this matter. He was not only a powerful official but also familiar with descriptions and acts of martyrdom. He certainly was familiar with the "Cordovan martyrs' movement," a piece of information that probably did not escape the epistle's author. The reputation and popularity of this movement reached also Byzantium.

Christian martyrdom reached epidemic proportions in Spain at the turn of the tenth century. The execution of a Christian priest named Perfectus on April 18, 850, and of Isaac on June 3, 851, by the *qadi* of Cordoba turned into what has come to be known as the "Cordovan martyrs' movement."[164] As the list of martyrs grew longer, the would-be martyr Eulogius promised his followers to compose a martyrology that would spread "the news of your struggle, passing through nations and peoples, and will begin to be known to many."[165] Eulogius succeeded in his efforts. Although a council of Spanish bishops denounced martyrdom,[166] cases of Christian martyrs continued to be recorded in Muslim Spain until 983.[167]

These cases demonstrate the increasing popularity of the martyrological notion within European society in a period when stories of miracles and heroism spread like wildfire. A few examples will suffice to demonstrate this popularity. Among the martyrs of Cordoba we find a monk named Georgius from the monastery of St. Sabba, near Jerusalem. Before traveling to Cordoba, Georgius heard the news about the Christian martyrs of Cordoba while on a mission in North Africa.[168] Georgius also asked Eulogius to send his autobiography and records of the Spanish martyrs to his monastery.[169] Other foreign martyrs were the Syrian pilgrim Severus Dei, who made his journey to preach in the Cordovan mosque;[170] the Christian layman Salomon, who arrived from an unspecified foreign country;[171] and a man named Vulfura, who came from France to seek martyrdom in Cordoba.[172]

The more celebrated among the later martyrs are Pelagius, whom the Muslim authorities executed on June 26, 925, and Vulfura and Argentea, who were executed on May 13, 931.[173] The martyrdom of Pelagius became the topic of the popular poem *Passio sancti Pelagii*, composed by the same nun, Hroswitha of Gandersheim, whose story of Theophilus reappeared in *The Chronicle of Ahimaatz*.[174] Also relevant here is the fact that an unknown number of Jews left Spain for south Italy in the ninth and the tenth centuries.[175] It would be logical to assume that these Jewish eyewitnesses to the events in Spain were another important channel for the passing of information from the West to the East.

From contemporary Hebrew sources we learn that information from Muslim Spain frequently flowed to Byzantium and vice versa.[176] In many cases, Jewish travelers played an important role in passing information throughout the world.[177] Diplomatic communication between Emperor Constantine Prophyrogennetos and the Umayyad Caliph in Cordoba, Abd ar-Rahman, could have also included information about events in Spain.

From Cordoba, the Caliph's Jewish advisor, Hasday ibn Shaprut, wrote letters to Byzantium. One such letter he addressed to a king and to a powerful lady, "who can achieve everything and that nothing is impossible for you...when you will it wholeheartedly," to plead on behalf of Byzantine Jewry for religious tolerance.[178] It is plausible that Hasday wrote this epistle in response to the news from Bari and Otranto. Hasday begins his epistle by asking that Byzantine Jews not be compelled to relinquish Judaism. Furthermore, he proposes that one of the "lady's" assistants should be in charge of the affairs of the "remnant of the Jewish community which have remained" in the Empire.[179]

Such flattering words Hasday could have addressed only to Empress Helena (the daughter of the deposed emperor Romanos Lekapenos), who at the time was the acting ruler of the Empire. Unfortunately, the damaged source is not altogether legible. But it is possible to deduce from it that some "...news had reached the king [that is, the Byzantine Emperor] and the ends of the earth."[180] More significant, however, is the fact that Hasday related this news to the "Christian community that dwells...in Cordoba,"[181] and while pointing to his friendly relations with the Christian *dhimmis* of Spain, Hasday alludes to his influential position in the caliphate.[182]

Having written this, Hasday revealed the political goal he had hoped to achieve by his diplomatic epistle. Hasday drew parallels between the "Christian community of Cordoba" and the "Jewish community of yours [Helena]" that cannot practice their faiths freely in Byzantium and him and Helena, who can serve in their countries as the protectors of each other's persecuted coreligionists and "preserve their lives."[183] The parallel was between two oppressed minorities living in perceived hostile societies. Although seemingly different, the members of these communities expressed the same fears and the same readiness to die if asked to forsake their creeds.

Byzantine Jews could see in the Christian behavior in Spain a reaction to a policy that resembled the anti-Jewish approach in the East. Being aware of Hasday's familiarity with the behavior of Spanish Christian martyrs, the Otranto epistle's cry for help aspired to impress Hasday with the behavior of the Jewish martyrs of Otranto, who did not fall short of the Christian martyrs of Cordoba.

The Christian martyrological movement that reached global fame, together with the literary work of the period and the imperial anti-Jewish policies, may explain the popularity of passive altruism and, on occasion, the desire to be sacrificed in Byzantium. It also explains why Hasday became a perfect addressee for the epistle. What is remembered, however, is not the politics beyond the epistle. Historical maneuvers tend to be overlooked in the face of unprecedented heroism as time goes by. But even these events in Muslim Spain cannot fully explain the radical behavior of Isaiah and his two colleagues. We should remember that the three carried the idea of martyrdom a step further than did Spanish martyrs and the Talmudic instructions. They literally took the notion of sacrifice into their own hands. To explain the phenomenon of self-sacrifice, we need to turn to events closer to the martyrs' imperial habitation.

HERETICS AND JEWS

One of the targets in the popes' correspondences that sanctioned martyrdom were the heretics. Heretical sects flourished in Eastern and Southern Europe. By the eighth century, Byzantine Jews could witness the voluntary deaths of the heretical Montanists in reaction to Emperor Leo's decree of forced conversion, crowning their holy heroes with martyrdom. A century later, Emperor Michael I (811–813) decreed the death penalty against the Paulicians, who eventually resorted to violence against the empire.[184] Heretics seem to profit from their diverse forms of resistence.[185]

This Montanistic tradition of voluntary death and self-killing in eastern Europe is said to already have spread in late antiquity. If Eusebius is correct, the phenomenon in Asia Minor and southern Italy denotes an imitation of their leader, Montanus.[186] *The Chronicle of Theophanes* discloses that Emperor Leo the Third (717–741) ordered the baptism of the Montanists and the Jews. As seen, the Jews chose baptism and then resumed Jewish life. The Montanists, in contrast, "settled matters for themselves through an oracle. They set a day on which they went into their heretical church and incinerated themselves."[187] The identical reaction of self-destruction had followed the persecution of their heretical predecessors in the time of Emperor Justinian.[188] Of great significance is the report that the Montanists chose their own date and location of martyrdom. As in the case of the Otranto martyrs, the Montanists "settle matters for themselves." They took the initiative of self-killing without facing an imminent ultimatum.

Despite the efforts to exterminate the heretics, they reappeared in the second half of the ninth century with the same strong convictions.[189] Although they were limited in scope, the ninth century also witnessed the sacrifices of monks in reaction to the persecution of iconoclasm.[190] Evidently, a tradition of self-sacrifice had developed in Byzantium.[191] Leo the Grammarian continued to maintain this tradition in his tenth-century works.[192] The existence of such heretical traditions are mentioned also by Ekkehard of Aura, whose twelfth-century reports on later Jewish events will prove to be of value to us.[193]

Not all heretics resorted to sacrifice. Many preferred to travel north and west in search of more amiable neighborhoods.[194] Both Jews and heretics chose the same roads and destinations for their migrations in reaction to religious pressure. Muslim attacks in southern Italy and internal political-religious rivalry drove Jews and heretics northward and from there into Western Europe. One of the early waves westward consisted of the persecuted iconodule monks, whose coreligionists had had to choose at times between their monastic vows and their lives.[195] These heretical immigrants also brought with them the doctrine of voluntary death, including its active forms. Needless to say, the new locations were not necessarily more hospitable to the heretics. As in the East, the heretic remained a *persona non grata* in the west. Such uninviting conditions would keep the heretical practice of voluntary death alive.

Just before being lost to the Holy Roman Empire, Byzantine Italy witnessed further heretical activity. The eleventh-century historian Raoul Glaber reported that a certain man named Vilgard led this movement in Ravenna. "He was at last discovered to be a heretic and was condemned by Peter, archbishop of that city." Peter's involvement places the incident between 921 and 970.[196] His attempts had little impact on the popularity of heretical movements. "Many throughout Italy at this time were found to be tainted with this perverse doctrine, and they too perished, by the sword or by fire.

At this very same time more emerged from Sardinia, an island that generally abounds in heresy; they managed to corrupt some of the people of Spain, but they too were exterminated by the orthodox (*et ipsi a uiris catholicis exterminati sunt*)."[197] The discovery of these new sects in Italy corroborates the previous reports that many oppressed heretics left the east in search of new homes in the west.

From the behavior of these immigrants in their fresh residences we may further learn of the traditions they had left behind in the east. For now, suffice it to mention the heretic Leutard. Sometime before the end of the millennium, many followed the "empty sermons" of this *Satane legatus*. Leutard's movement is said to have come to an end when he was defeated in a dispute. "As for Leutard, when he saw that he was defeated and deprived of the support of the common people, he sought death by throwing himself into a pit."[198] Coincidently, in Otranto "Rabbi Menahem leaped into a pit."

To be sure, heretics posed a greater ideological threat to the unity of the Church than did the Jews. For this reason heretics were treated more severely. This probably explains the two groups' different reactions following the imposition of imperial policies of forced conversion. While the authorities overlooked the return of converted Jews who "accepted baptism and then washed them off,"[199] it did not permit the heretics to do the same. Overzealous heretics, therefore, were more likely to resort to mass suicide as their last line of religious defense.

In addition to the mutual fate of forced conversion, Jews and Montanists, or Byzantine heretics in general, are said to have lived in close proximity, sharing friendly relationships. As we shall see, they will continue to live as neighbors in their new communities in the West. What this relationship demonstrates is, at least, the exposure of some Byzantine Jews to the heretics' extreme martyrological behavior and ideologies. In fact, the messianic tendencies of the Montanists are said to have influenced a similar movement among Byzantine Jews.[200] In turn, the Montanists were believed to "have been (those who) have separated from the Hebrew religion and community."[201] This closeness may have led some of the imperial decrees to confuse the Montanists with Jews or at least with their messianic faction. It was in reaction to this messianic movement influenced by heretics that the Gaon Natronai issued a *responsum* for the treatment and readmittance into the community of Jewish sectarians.[202] Based on such messianic and theological parallels, Leo the Grammarian concluded that some Jews were "also known as Montanists."[203]

Glaber reported that the heretics who infiltrated Italy and France, "would rather have suffered a cruel death than allow themselves any return to the saving faith of Christ the Lord." In Glaber's eyes, they were "Like the pagans, they worshiped idols, and *like the Jews they made vain sacrifices (ac cum Iudeis inepta sacrificia litare nitebantur)*."[204] Because Glaber speaks of the desire of the heretics to die, it is more than likely that "vain sacrifices" refers to humans. Conjoining Jews and heretics as the enemy of the faithful believer, an old allegation pointed to the old Jewish friendly relations with the latter.[205] The behavior of the three friends from Otranto, who may have been inspired by their heretical neighbors, would have made this confusion even stronger.

At least in the incident at Otranto, confusion was not limited to the authorities. Bewilderment regarding the role of martyrdom led the three colleagues to their desperate acts. More than being the prey of an immediate peril, the two rabbis and their student became the victims of their period's literary genera, propaganda, and environmental behavioral norms and mores. Otranto's martyrs directed the notion of sacrifice in a novel trajectory.

BETWEEN *QORBANOT* AND *QIDDUSH HA-SHEM*

An effort to correct this failure to separate suicide from sacrifice – a failure that took its toll on the three martyrs from Otranto – is reflected in the anonymous *Book of Legal Decisions (Sefer ha-Miqtsoot).*[206] Its reference to martyrdom is more than likely to be the work of an authoritative early eleventh-century Byzantine rabbi.[207] In an attempt to stop the influx of foreign ideas, the author turns to Talmudic terminology to define who is a Jewish martyr.

He who is slain for the sanctification of the name or the profession of the unity of the Name of the Blessed One, whether in a period of general persecution or any other time;[208] for instance if Gentiles ordered him,[209] "Worship the idol, or else we kill you!"[210] but he resisted to death and was slain [by the sword],[211] crucified or burned[212] for the sanctification of the Name, such a person [requires even more exceptional treatment]. Because he had sanctified the Name with his body and soul,[213] all of Israel are obliged to tear their garments for him, to mourn and eulogize him in their synagogues and houses of learning. His wife must never remarry for the honor of Heaven and his honor.[214]

As in the Talmud, martyrdom is a religious obligation, "whether in a period of general persecution or any other time." In a legal rather than metaphorical jargon, the author reminds the reader that dying for the sanctification of the Name should be a passive act. Instead of utilizing the standard Byzantine symbol of "*qorbanot,*" the document speaks of "*qiddush ha-Shem.*" This attempt to relinquish the symbols of the sacrificed and the sacrificer as atonement for the nation indicates an attempt to return to the Talmudic obligatory death only when needed to avoid an immediate threat.

New roles are also assigned to the community vis-à-vis martyrs. The fact that the author had to explain who a martyr is or how the community should treat its martyrs and their families indicates the inexperience of the Jewish community in such cases. This clarification is another step in the direction of distinguishing the sanctification of the Divine Name from suicide. "For suicide no rites whatsoever should be observed," according to the post-Talmudic tractate *Semahot* 2:1. But the requirement of an even more special treatment coincides with the period's veneration of saints. Despite the restrictions, these instructions to the community signal that martyrs became *fait accompli* in European Jewry. By the mid-eleventh century, because of anti-Jewish activity, the leaders of Byzantine Jewry realized that the time had come for them to consider the practical aspects of martyrdom. In parallel to the restrictions on *qiddush ha-Shem*, rabbis appear to prepare their Jewry for situations that might require the very same act.

It is plausible, then, that *Sefer ha-Miqtsoot*, which instructs the Jewish community how it should treat martyrs and their families, was written in reaction to the self-killings in Otranto and in the general context of the phenomenon of self-sacrifice for the common good.[215] To be sure, the restrictions on *qiddush ha-Shem* did not betoken a complete rejection of the idea. The intellectual struggles with the phenomenon reflect its late-tenth-century transformation from potential to actual martyrdom – not a smooth transformation, by any means. Rabbinic leadership had to stimulate this transmutation by bestowing on the act an explicit religious legitimacy. At the same time, the leadership felt obligated to keep the martyrological seeds sown at Oria, Bari, and Otranto by the intellectual elite within the boundaries of the *halakhic* code.

5

∾

Zarfat

"For out of Bari shall go forth the law, and the word of the Lord from Otranto." This phraseology of Isaiah 2:3 ("for out of Zion shall go forth the law, and the word of the Lord from Jerusalem") by the French Tosafist, R. Jacob ben Meir (or Rabbenu Tam), epitomizes the formidable influence Byzantine-Italian Jewry had on the Jews of Latin Europe.[1] Jacob's comparison bestows on these Italian communities almost a divine authority. It is only logical to presume that Bari's "law" and Otranto's "word" included also their martyrological views and literature.[2] Put differently, the *halakhic* guidelines found in *Sefer ha-Miqtsoot*, the martyrological spirit expressed in Otranto and in Byzantine Jewish literature, appear to have burgeoned in the rising Jewish communities of northwestern Europe.

Franco-German Jews constitute these communities, which usually bear the title *Ashkenaz* in Jewish historiography. But early eleventh-century French Jewry deserves to be treated in its own right.[3] French Jews, we shall soon see, played an indispensable role in the evolution of *qiddush ha-Shem* already at the beginning of the eleventh century, if not earlier. The *Ashkenazim*, the Jews of the Rhineland region, will join this evolution more than half a century later. Growing scholarly focus on the dramatic massacres of the First Crusade has overshadowed the importance of events in early-eleventh-century France.[4] This scholarly direction was set by Abraham Habermann, as he titled his collected documents on these communities, *Sefer Gezerot Ashkenaz ve-Zarfat* (The Book of the Persecutions in Germany and France). Contributing to this thinking are the thirteenth-century Ashkenazic myths that established direct links between prominent Italian families and German Jewry.[5] The early Italian immigrations into France, and only then into Germany, obviously did not serve such myths. These myths aggrandized Ashkenazic prestige by engrafting genealogy of the mystical Italian Jews, who had maintained strong contacts with the authoritative Palestinian and Babylonian centers.

In the context of Jewish martyrdom, the impact of Byzantine Jews was felt first in France before expressing itself in the communities of the Rhine River in 1096. My intention is to show, moreover, that the conceptions of martyrdom that arrived in the German vicinity had already undergone a Judeo-Franco reshaping. French Jews made martyrdom a collective act, performed by ordinary men and women. *Zarfat ve-Ashkenaz* would be a more telling title for the course of this investigation, in my opinion. As we shall see, four factors encouraged this change: (1) a coordinated effort by the royal authorities to create a unified Catholic kingdom; (2) the Jewry's strict socioreligious standards; (3) the martyrological reaction of heretical groups to the royal decrees; and (4) the general atmosphere of admiration for martyrs.

"THE LAW AND THE WORD"

Shortly after premiering in Italy, *Sefer Yosippon* became a hallmark of the poetry of French rabbis. The Maccabees, their reaction to religious oppression, their victory, and the martyrdom of the seven brothers and of Eleazar served as important themes in the liturgy of Joseph bar Solomon of Carcassonne.[6] In the style of Byzantine Jewish liturgists, the rabbi venerated the altruistic behavior of his heroes.[7] Rashi's (Rabbi Solomon ben Isaac) exegesis of Ezekiel 21:18 bears the influence of Rabbi Joseph bar Solomon's liturgy for *Hanukah*.[8] Rashi's commentary shows familiarity with *Sefer Yosippon*. His reference to Daniel 11:2 specifically mentions the book.[9] More than any other eleventh-century French or Ashkenazic scholar, argues A. Grossman, R. *Shemaiah* of France used *Sefer Yosippon* extensively.[10] Such luminaries disclosed a particular interest in the book's presentation of events regarding the Second Temple. As we have seen, copious martyrological statements enhance this presentation. Another Italian book that featured in France was *Sefer Hakhmoni* by Shabbettai Donnolo. As with *Sefer Yosippon*, Rashi mentioned the book in his works. His student, R. Joseph Kara (d. ca. 1080) continued to rely on the book in his academy at Troyes.[11]

Byzantine poets such as Rabbi Solomon ha-Bavli served as a direct linkage with the communities of west Christendom. The celebrated Kalonymides of Italy formed one of the transmission channels for Solomon's ideas and writing style.[12] A case in point is provided by the epistle of Rabbi Meshullam ben Kalonymous to the sages of Lothar (Lotharingia, Lorraine).[13] A more specific proof is presented in his epistle to the French rabbi, Shimon ben Isaac (ca. 950–1020),[14] who eventually settled in Mainz.[15] Shimon's liturgies (*piyyutim*) follow in the path of Solomon ha-Bavli.[16] His *Reshut le-Hatan*,[17] *Selihah*,[18] and *Kerovah le-Rosh ha-Shanah*[19] deliver Solomon ha-Bavli's *qorban* symbol.

In the Rhineland, Rabbi Gershom, the Light of the Exile (950 or 965–1028 or 1040),[20] used *Sefer Yosippon* in his study center. The book also inspired Gershom in his liturgical composition for *Hanukkah*.[21] Grossman has considered the possibility that R. Gershom's roots originated in France. A fifteenth-century tradition traces his origin to Anacona, Italy.[22] The latter proposal appears unlikely, but it shows the direction in which the Italian "law" and "word" blew.

By the time these French luminaries lived, violence against Jews had erupted in different places. It would be, therefore, difficult to assess whether their works reflect only a continuation of a literary genre *à la mode Byzantine-Italian* or also poetic expression of their living conditions. French Jews may have turned to such literature in search of intellectual support during times of crisis. An early Hebrew letter from the community of Le Mans, or Limoges, describes such times in France in the year 992.[23]

TIME OF CRISIS

A converted Jew derogatorily named Sehoq (i.e., a mockery) ben Esther "from the land of France" unjustly incriminated Jews for plotting to kill the local count by practicing magic.[24] In a region that practiced the *colaphus Judaeorum*, the public punching of a Jewish representative on every Easter in Toulouse to avenge Jesus' crucifixion, Sehoq's allegations were not a hard sell.[25] Sehoq advised the Christians to take advantage of the incident to avenge the crucifixion in a less symbolic fashion. Similar recommendations were made every Palm Sunday by the bishop of Béziers until 1161.[26] This violent rationale was use to disguise, if not generate, many of the deadliest attacks to come against European Jews. Both the anonymous count and the populace are said to have taken the opportunity to requite this historic crime. Letters quickly followed, calling for the "elimination of the Jews from the surface of the earth."

Voluntary conversion could have deflected the near calamity promptly. Conversion had worked in Sehoq's favor. As in the story of Theophilius's initial escape from punishment through conversion, Sehoq's corrupt and criminal conduct went unpunished. He called for forced baptism, the destruction of communities, and the burning of Jews, "from the young to the elderly, infants and women."[27] Such statements may be hyperbolic. But they are a testimony to the mounting religious pressure against French Jews. Compulsory disputations and forced baptism of Jewish children were not unheard of in northern France.[28] But the author appears to have preferred to blame Sehoq alone rather than implicate the generally friendly secular authorities.

The Jewish response to an offer made by a local count to settle matters in trial by duel deserves attention. If a Jew had overcome the count, his devastating orders would have been overturned. The Jews declined the offer, because "The Jewish religion differs from the laws of the Gentiles and does not permit fighting nowadays."[29] Nor did the local custom allow Jews to bear defensive arms,[30] a fact that would have made a duel even a more anomalous spectacle. In accordance with medieval tradition, a substantial bribe was offered instead. The count's refusal left the Jews no choice.

At that day . . . all the congregation announced: God has decided to terminate the remnant of His people among the nations of the earth. Now, [they said] let every wise and intelligent man gather. Pour out your hearts before Him in fasting, crying, and mourning. Perhaps the Lord God will pardon the remnant of His portion, without destroying them in His anger and wrath from among the nations. For great wrath has come out from our Lord God because of our sins.Who knows, perhaps the Lord God will subside His great wrath and we will not expire. . . . Let us gather at the house of the Lord and call upon all the congregation, from small to great, to gather there in the synagogue. On the morrow, the entire congregation gathered at dawn at the house of the Lord, declaring a fast. They dressed themselves in sackcloth, put ashes upon their heads, and fasted together, men and children, elderly and young. For the fear of the Lord had fallen upon them, and the calamity weighed heavily.[31]

The Purim motif (The Book of Esther) is transparent in the story.[32] But the account also echoes the behavior of the pacifist protestors and Philo's party of the Roman period. Josephus Flavius and Philo reported how the Jews nonviolently refused to permit the installation of Caligula's statue in the Temple. They also rejected Petronius's alternative suggestion to fight his troops. Instead, men, women, and children halted their daily activities to gather and pray, "ready to be slain."[33] The refusal to fight the count and the call to gather in the synagogue instead to fast and atone for "our sins" in hope of salvation is reminiscent of Philo's conduct in *Sefer Yosippon*. There the early leader advised the people to congregate in the Temple, fast, and hope for God's intervention.[34] Overall, the Jewish reaction in 992 coincides with *Yosippon's* subliminal recommendation in his rendition of Josephus's speeches to bank on passivity rather than on violent resistance.[35] Similar approval is expressed in the Talmud. Of the two styles, the former characterizes the Hebrew letter, perhaps for further dramatic effect.

Regrettably, the outcome of the conflict remains unknown in this incomplete document. The parallels to the Book of Esther as well as the letter's introduction suggest a happy ending.[36] The peaceful conclusion demonstrates another affinity to Philo's story. In both cases, the refusal of combat and the readiness to depart paid off. Nevertheless, it should not be forgotten that the Bari letter also ended on a positive note despite, or more accurately because of, the sacrifices of the three colleagues. It is impossible, therefore, to speculate on the full impact of Sehoq's allegations.

The implication of this positive outcome goes beyond the goals of literary dramatization. The letter was written as a guideline for successfully dealing with the authorities and to teach an appropriate Jewish conduct in the future.[37] The community turned the letter into "a record (*sefer*) of the salvation by God, who acted for those who maintained His covenant and observed His commandments." It continued to recommend a nonviolent defense of the commandments. Because God's covenant with Abraham, Isaac, and Jacob (Lev. 26:42),[38] the "holy people" survived this ordeal.[39] The letter does not elaborate on this covenant. But the centrality of Isaac's near sacrifice could not have been ignored when speaking in such terms.

Within less than two decades, the calls for communal prayers resonated again in France. This time public summons were ordered in response to an official royal policy of forced conversion. An anonymous Hebrew account places this campaign in the kingdom of King Robert of France between the years 1007 and 1012.[40] Clearly, the document is greatly embellished by motifs found in the Book of Esther. But the overall picture of official intolerance toward non-Catholics is almost unblemished. Latin sources authenticate the atmosphere and deeds depicted by the Hebrew account.[41] Before turning to the martyrological reaction, let us first consider the conditions that generated it.

The Orléans community appears to have been the first to suffer. Allegedly, the Fatimid Caliph Al-Hakim decided to demolish the Holy Sepulcher in Jerusalem in 1009 on the recommendation of the Jews. The fact that synagogues and Jews also came under attack in Jerusalem held no significance in the eyes of the European accusers.[42] Raoul Glaber reports that these events culminated, but did not end, in the expulsion of the Jews from Orléans and other cities.[43] An unknown number remained only because they had accepted baptism. Glaber is quick to point out that they did so "through fear of death, out of love of this present life rather than aspiration after eternal joy." These converts, however, "soon shamelessly returned to their former state."[44] Five years later they returned to the city in small numbers only to live in fear.[45] The duration of time Glaber gives for the persecutions corresponds with the period given by the Hebrew account.

Adémar of Chabannes states in his chronicle that in 1010, Bishop Alduin of Limoges offered the Jews the alternatives of conversion or expulsion.

Local preachers were called to assist in religious disputations.[46] Most of the Jews at Limoges responded as did their coreligionists from Orléans. They left the city for a new destination, but not before three or four converted to Christianity.

A question sent to R. Joseph Tov Ellem (Bonfils) mentions an allegation against the Jews of Sens.[47] They were accused of destroying a Christian holy image.[48] A heavy fine satisfied the authorities, but did little to relieve the pressure in the long run. The community is said to have suffered a sharp decline in numbers, which may have resulted from an increasing pressure to convert.

Based on Rashi's exegesis of Isaiah 53:9, it seems that his community of Troyes was targeted as well.[49] Having been a witness to the First Crusade, Rashi's exegesis may reflect also this traumatic event. But his exegesis and the Hebrew account share a denominator uncharacteristic of the First Crusade reports. Rashi and the anonymous Hebrew report ascribe the initiation of the attacks to the French secular authorities. Rashi mentions "a ruler," whereas the anonymous account implicates King Robert.

A ruler seems to be the instigator of the persecution of the Jews of Mainz. The *Annales Quedinburgenses* recounts that "an expulsion of the Jews was enacted by the king in Mainz."[50] The delineation in this Latin source is supported by an undated and stereotyped lament of R. Gershom of Mainz.[51] Referring to the citizens of Mainz, R. Gershom writes: "They required us to stop praying to the Lord, Our Deliverer . . . instead to receive as our deity a scorned being, to prostrate down to an effigy and before it to make obeisance."[52] Most of the Jews of Mainz refused to accept Christianity. They were, therefore, "expelled in all directions . . . weary, hopeless and desolate."[53] Around 1066, Bishop Eberhard forced the Jews of Trier to choose between expulsion or baptism. His sudden death, ascribed to Jewish magic, is said to have averted the ultimatum.[54] In numerous poems Rabbi Gershom echoes attempts to forcefully convert Jews in northern Europe.[55] Although these case take us beyond the boundaries of this chapter, they demonstrate the contribution of the nobility to the general atmosphere of religious pressure.

The same impression arises time and again from the poems of Gershom's contemporary, Rabbi Shimon ben Isaac.[56] In addition to his poetic support of the community, the rabbi's fame and political recognition among Christian authorities enabled him to act "on behalf of his brethren and to halt the persecutions."[57] Unfortunately for these Jews, such skillful lobbyists would be in high demand throughout the century.

European monarchy is implicated also by a Norman historian. William Godell briefly reports that the persecutions reached Normandy in the year

1009. "In this year Henry the Emperor and King Robert forcefully baptized many Jews by means of fear."[58]

Further information amplifies the anonymous Hebrew account:

It came to pass in the year 1007 that the wicked kingdom of Robert,[59] the king of France, decreed conversion upon Israel. And the Gentiles of the nations shrewdly plotted to kill and destroy all the Jews throughout the country. Then the king and the queen counseled his ministers and governors throughout his kingdom's boundaries.

The conspirators demanded the annihilation of the Jews so "there will be no reminiscence of the name of Israel."[60] The king and the ministers agreed with this scheme, but offered the Jews a way out:

Then the king had called upon the Jews of his kingdom, and they came before him. The king said: I demand you to come before me to reveal your opinions and conceal nothing. I have counseled my ministers and servants and I desire one nation, whereupon [if you convert] you will be distinguished rulers. Thus return to our doctrine since it is more genuine than yours. If you shall refuse to obey, I shall kill you by sword. Now take consultation as to my request.

It is important to note that the Hebrew source blames the king, the queen, and ministers for the persecution. If indeed Jewish dignitaries "came before" the king, the couple launched this campaign against the Jews in Orléans. "There were great many of that race" in this royal city, says Raoul Glaber.[61]

MARTYRDOM

Time was given to the Jews to consider Robert's ultimatum. "After taking counsel, they refused to abandon the Torah of Moses and to exchange the awe of God." Putting their trust in God, they dispatched a delegation to the king. The author ascribes to them a blunt reply: "Our lord, we shall not heed you in this regard. We shall not deny it [the Torah]. Treat us as you wish. Then they stretched out their throats for the sword [to be slain] for the sanctity of His name and His great unity."[62]

The king and his magnates were not impressed. His threats were implemented at once. "The enemy assembled and slew the pious of the Most High. Their blood was shed as water and Israel was put under the sword."

A more detailed description follows:

At that time precious women gathered joining hands, and said: let us go to the river and drown ourselves, and we shall not desecrate the Name of Heaven, since our holiness [the Torah] is trampled and our delight is on fire, better death than life.

Some had fled. The father did not preserve his son's soul, nor the son his father's, so as not to profane the Venerable Name. The elders who could not flee were dragged in the mud by their legs for they refused to heed them.

One man of the people of Israel, Shneor by name, was one of the most pious and clever men in the country. He was assaulted by the uncircumcised who wanted to convert him. Looking at them in disgust he scorned their idols, blaspheming their statues. Hearing this they cut him with their swords and trampled him with their horses' hoofs.[63]

Looking back at past narratives, a few motifs come to mind. Although some of the themes here do not bear full linguistic parallels to *Sefer Yosippon*, thematic corollaries to Philo's story do exist. In parallel to the book's description of Philo and his delegation to Gaius, French Jews send their envoy before King Robert. In both stories the Jews reject the rulers' proposal to obey even under threat to their lives. A similar statement to "We shall not heed you in this regard" was also echoed by *Sefer Yosippon*.[64] The exact expression "They refused to heed," appears in both *Yosippon*'s description of Gaius and our account. The lack of this exact phrase in the Book of Esther disqualifies the biblical book as the source of this expression.[65]

Similarly to the actors of the Roman period, their medieval descendants leave their fate in the rulers' hands. In both stories the Jews "stretched out their throats for the sword." The recounted slogan of Philo and his contemporaries that death was better than life reemerged in the speech ascribed to the French Jewish women. Finally, the medieval account delineates the shedding of blood like water. This metaphor exists in *Sefer Yosippon*, but its common use makes it difficult to determine the relation between the two accounts.[66]

If a direct reliance on *Sefer Yosippon* is faint in the Hebrew account, the impact of the stories contained in the book on French theologians is explicit. Josephus and Philo were a popular source material for the ninth-century Agobard and Amulo of Lyon. In their intense polemical disputes with Jews, they also transmitted Josephus's and Philo's accounts.[67] Although the content of Jewish–Christian disputes is not always available to us, the tone and techniques set by the two clergymen continued to be practiced. In 1010, Aludin, the bishop of Limoges, encouraged such disputes in his hometown.[68]

With respect to future developments, a few facts are worth remembering. Women rise first to take matters into their own hands by destroying themselves.[69] Drowning in a river became their method of choice. B. *Gittin* 57 and *Midrash Lamentations Rabbah* 1:16 also depict enslaved young women as being the first to choose self-destruction by drowning. Their example is said to have inspired the self-drowning of captive males. But there is no need to assume that the medieval account duplicates a stereotypical literary portrayal. Medieval women in general were known to self-inflict death to maintain their dignity, whereas males were expected to be more active in their own protection. Josephus of *Sefer Yosippon* equates self-killing in time of crisis with standard feeble female behavior.[70] Does the description in the French account reflect thus a reality or a literary womanish characterization? As we shall soon see, reality is very much a part of this description.

Males are also depicted as submitting passively or taking their own lives. Shneor provides an example of passive submission. In contrast to the women, Shneor did not take his own life. But his provocative posture almost made him the author of his own death. His portrayal as "one of the most pious and clever men in the country" amounts to an endorsement of his provocative conduct.

The elderly fell prey because they were too weak to flee, yet firm enough to stand torturous ordeals. Other males faced a more horrific dilemma. "The father did not preserve his son's soul, nor the son his father's, so as not to profane the Venerable Name." This statement is not entirely clear. Does it mean that fathers and sons did not intervene to prevent loved ones from being massacred by their assailants? Did fathers and sons refrain from averting the self-killings of loved ones? Or did fathers and sons destroy each other?

Compounding these questions is the extension of the *aqedah* symbol in the liturgy of the period. Building on Solomon ha-Bavli's concept of self-sacrifice (*qorban*) and of his undeveloped idea of the *aqedah*, Shimon bar Isaac makes an extensive use of the *aqedah* in his *Reshut le-Hatan, Selihah,* and *Kerovah le-Rosh ha-Shanah*.[71] Shimon presents God blessing Abraham on account of his readiness to sacrifice his son Isaac. Because of the *aqedah*, God redeems Israel from sins and eventually brings about salvation.[72] Thus, "this day will be appointed before You as an opportunity for deeds for the sacrificer (*oqed*) and the sacrificed (*neeqad*)."[73] Obviously, by "*oqed*" Shimon refers to a Jewish sacrificer.

Similarly, Shimon views Israel as "the holy nation ... that has been selected to be His portion [of sacrifice]."[74] His *piyyut* indicates that "for Your sake we are being killed."[75] From Rabbi Shimon's point of view, these killings were not in vain, because he perceived them as "atoning sacrifices [*qorbanot*]."[76] As we shall soon see, Franco-German literature extensively employed the *aqedah* metaphor to describe the voluntary immolation of coreligionists. Whether Shimon's *aqedah* refers to such killings (1007–1012) or just metaphorically describes the mood of his generation remains unknown. But the poetry of the period and the language of the anonymous account may point in the direction of the possibility.

Our Latin sources supply some clarifications. According to Raoul Glaber, after the Jews of Orléans were indicted in the destruction of the Holy Sepulcher

they were expelled from their country and cities; some were slaughtered by the sword, others drowned in rivers, and many found other deaths, some of them even killed themselves in diverse manners.... They exempted those who wished to convert to the grace of baptism and renounce all Jewish ways and customs.[77]

Although Glaber is known to exaggerate, his report cannot be disregarded. The slaughtering of Jews by the sword (*alii gladiis trucidati*) and the (self-?) drowning in rivers (*alii fluminibus necati*) coincide with the Hebrew report. References to diverse manners of killing (*mortium generibus*), and the self-killing (*nonnulli etiam sese diversa cede interemerunt*), clarify a bit the reference to fathers and sons. Based on the two reports it appears that fathers and sons, at least, did not prevent each other from taking their own lives.

Additional corroboration is offered by Adémar de Chabannes. He helps us identify another city where this conduct took place in the year 1010:

Alduin the bishop of Limoges forced the Jews of this city by issuing a decree which gave them [the Jews] the choice of accepting baptism or exile. At the same time, he ordered the learned Catholics to enter into disputes with the Jews in order to bring them out of their creed. Three or four Jews became Christians, the rest, men, women and children, quickly left for other cities. Some of the Jews who refused to accept baptism slew themselves.[78]

Here, too, Jews are said to have killed themselves to avert baptism.

Of significance is the ultimatum issued to the Jews. By and large, the choice given was between conversion or expulsion. Occasionally, however, death formed the only alternative to baptism. Unlike the events in Byzantium, clear-cut ultimatums were made in France. The choice of baptism or death comes across forcefully in the Latin reports. As with the Hebrew documents from Byzantium, the Hebrew account still speaks in terms of "rejecting the Torah of Moses" and accepting "ours." Baptism in itself is not spelled out even once. Self-killing is presented as an act of *qiddush ha-Shem* that intends to prevent *hillul ha-Shem* (the desecration of the Divine Name). Christian demands appear in Jewish terms. The presentation is one-sided, failing or refusing to understand the Christological significance of accepting their neighbors' creed.

Attention must be given also to the phrases describing the victims and their deeds. As in *Yosippon*'s version of the mother and seven sons, Shneor receives the epitaph holy. Others, "the pious of the most High," exposed their necks to die "for the sanctity of His name and His great unity." Unlike in *Sefer Yosippon*, missing in the account is the Byzantine symbol of the *qorban*. Dying for the sanctification of the Divine Name replaces here the *qorban* metaphor. The *halakhic* material fully approves only passive self-destruction as martyrdom. Active self-destruction was not the choice of Talmudic rabbis, which may amount to the sin of committing suicide. Regardless of their method of choice, French victims were considered martyrs because they perished "for the sanctity of His name and unity."

For future discussion, it is important to note that there is no reference to reward in these terms. The only positive outcome here is reminiscent of the Bari letter. The deaths of the innocent resulted in the prosperity and expansion of the community. Absent in both documents is a sense of defeat. The medieval account contains two sections. The first section dealt with the massacres *per se*, whereas the second turned death into the birth of the prosperous French Jewry. This transformation was achieved by the rising family of R. Jacob ben Yequtiel. In the author's view, the establishment of Flanders Jewish community and the close relationships among French Jews were the outcome of the crisis.

First, of course, the persecutions had to be halted. R. Jacob son of R. Yequtiel from the city of Radom (Rouen)[79] appealed to the Pope (John XVIII, 1003–1009) for this reason.[80] Before the pope, he spoke on behalf of all the Jewish communities of northern Europe. As a result, a papal legate (the Bishop of Piperno) was sent throughout northern Europe to notify the authorities that neither Jews nor Judaism should be harmed.[81] As with the letter about events in 992, important lessons in dealing with the authorities were provided here.

Similarly to the Bari epistle, the account relates that French Jewry extended its geographical boundaries further north, increasing its prestige in the Latin West. We are to ascribe this positive result to martyrs – a stereotypical pattern in foundation myths.[82] According to the psychoanalyst R. Girard, there exists in new societies a mythical link between birth and sacrifice that is necessary to the process of group formation. The members of the new society believe that sacrifices effect their coming into being as a discrete group.[83] In times both of contention and contentment, the birth and expansion of French Jewry would be associated with the deaths of the martyrs, even though other factors contributed to this expansion in reality.

Girard's observation seems to be the case in the anonymous account of the events of 1007–1012. Suddenly the anonymous author asserts that:

Thereafter [after the persecution], Baldwin the governor of Flanders, wrote to that leader [R. Jacob bar Yequtiel] inviting him to his domain. Thus, he assembled

thirty Jews who were his favorite associates and went there [to Flanders]. The
governor welcomed him and his two sons, Isaac and Judah, with great reverence.
They stayed with the governor for three months until he [R. Jacob bar Yequtiel]
passed away... he was brought to the city of Reims for burial....[84]

It is not a coincidence that the second section of the source employs the
bloody events to portray the beginning of Flanders community. R. Jacob
bar Yequtiel became the leader of the new community of Flanders and the
representative of the Jewish communities of Northern Europe. He proved to
be an effective and loyal leader. Jacob's activism could have cost him his and
his family's lives were it not for a miraculous intervention. In the spirit of
altruism, a personal sacrifice was required from R. Jacob, too. He had to leave
his son behind with the bishop of Rouen as a pawn to ensure his return from
Rome, risking the loss of his son to Christianity.[85]

By the juxtaposition of Jacob's conduct and the sacrifices, events in northern
Europe were transformed into a "foundation myth" with hagioraphical characteristics. It tells its legendary version of how some Jewish communities in
France came into existence.[86] Places like Arras, Rouen, Normandy, Flanders,
and Reims are mentioned thus as integral components of this cohesive
society.[87] Such a creation of social mythology, states J. Arlow, is a step toward
the formation of a society and is unconsciously utilized as an instrument of
socialization among the members of the group.[88] Given the fact that numerous medieval villages and towns associated their foundation with local saints
and martyrs, there is nothing surprising in the coexistence of martyrs and
budding new communities in our narrative.

Women assumed a leading role in this process of group formation. They
are the first to be mentioned as taking matters into their own hands. High
standards of belonging to this community were set thus by these women.
Women became more than the classical role model. Heroine-martyrs were
transformed into the "early collective conscience" of the group, a known dynamic in a young and troubled society in the process of crystallization,[89]
as early-eleventh-century French Jewry was.[90] Females would be remembered as the first to have taken their own lives. Through the new representations of heroism, the nature of the "group" was beginning to take
shape.

Little is known about Jacob's family after its expansion into northern
Europe. The martyrs' deeds and their ordeal, however, did not fade away.
Violence and voluntary death would gradually become embedded in the fresh
heritage of the forming Jewry.[91] Henceforth, the martyrological option is likely
to be considered in similar conflicts. Because of the legacy of birth through

voluntary death, guilt for not acting in the same manner and obligation to the martyrs' memory would be an essential element in Jewish behavior. Common hardship would be likely to strengthen these ties because of the centrality of martyrdom in the emerging Judeo-Franco history. Northern French Jewry contributed to the crystallization and characterization of other small and new Jewish communities in Europe, which, all together, formed the nascent Northern European Jewry, known today as Ashkenaz.[92]

Overall, French Jewry passed a martyrological milestone. Otranto martyrs made self-killing the limited response of selected leaders. French Jews turned this extraordinary act into the option of ordinary people. The protection of the community was not left to its professional leaders only. Maintaining religious identity at all cost became now the responsibility of every individual. For the first time on European soil, collective Jewish martyrdom is taking place – in France.

WHY FRANCE?

Several interrelated factors actuated this shift to communal and equal-gender sharing of martyrological responsibilities. As the 1007 narrative reveals, the early settlements in northern France consisted of a small number of settlers.[93] Key to the survival of these young settlements in the volatile and violent region were the conformity of each individual[94] and the conformist conduct of each community. Internal communal discipline taught each man and woman mutual responsibility for the common good. Individual surrender to communal necessities constituted a prerequisite for joining the group.

Rashi's eleventh-century ordinance decreed "under threat of excommunication, upon every *man and woman* living here (in Troyes) that they be forbidden to remove themselves from the yoke of communal responsibility" [emphasis mine].[95] Economic issues constitute the concerns of this ruling. But its spirit and expectations translated into deeds in time of external threats. Rashi's rationale behind such rulings was that "nothing can resist the will of the community."[96]

Pressure on the individual community assured conduct conducive to sustaining the Jewry as a whole. Although the individual community enjoyed considerable autonomy in economic matters, religious and security issues entailed upon French Jewry uniform conduct. Thus when Jews from Rheims were taken captive, the responsum of Joseph Tov Ellem reveals how their coreligionists from Troyes risked their own lives to negotiate with the captors. Additionally, they imposed a special tax on themselves and on the communities of Sens, Auxerre, and Chalon-sur-Saone to ransom the captives.[97]

Particularly telling is the use of language in this responsum. Troyes Jews are described as "handing over their souls for" the captives, a phrase repeatedly used to convey martyrological sufferings. A greater sacrifice was made by the community of Sens. It had been already in great political and economic distress, for one of its members broke a local Christian image. Despite their dire situation and their protest that Troyes lacked the authority to levy the tax on Sens, the latter voluntarily participated in paying the ransom.

In justifying their harsh demand on the impoverished community of Sens, Troyes relied on the Talmudic example of the two travelers who had enough water to sustain only one person.[98] The Talmudic sage ben Patora believed that it was better for the two to share the insufficient amount of water and perish together than for one to survive at the other's expense. This way, at least, they would die together without having to witness the other's dying. Conversely, Akiva ruled that one is not obligated to share the water, because one's life takes precedence over others'. Troyes accepted ben Patora's view, even though Akiva's opnion was preferable, according to the Talmud.

Following the Talmudic opinion, R. Joseph Tov Ellem rebuked Troyes for its decision. But the action taken by the communities of Troyes and, especially, Sens illustrate how the commitment of northern French Jewry went beyond the letter of the law. The consensus was that individuals and communities must sacrifice themselves in whatever form for the others. Troyes's siding with ben Patora's opinion indicates an all-for-one-and-one-for-all outlook. It also mirrors a fatalistic viewpoint – all or nothing. Only a strong sense of a mutual fate, adamant commitment, and effective social control could ensure the obedience of individuals and communities for the common good.[99] The small size of the Jewry as a whole, and of the individual communities that formed it, made social control by consensus relatively easy to exercise.[100] In the eleventh century, these features of commitment and altruistic behavior reached new levels.

An eleventh-century responsum of the Geonim of the family of R. Yehiel of Rome illustrates this new level of altruism. Here the spirit of self-sacrifice for the rest comes even at the cost of committing a personal sin. An eleventh-century Jew, runs the responsum,

once stood near a cistern of wine. Non-Jews came and purposely put their hands into the wine in order to render it 'forbidden.' The Jew, however, filled a goblet with that wine, drank it in their presence, and said to them: 'We are not troubled by your violent acts.'[101]

Halakhically, the wine is rendered forbidden once touched by non-Jews. Because the only purpose of drinking the wine was to end further aggression against fellow Jews, the act was deemed commendable. Communal appreciation of benevolence could thus lead to individual sacrifice of life. It did, according to another version of the story in the book of Eliezer b. Joel ha-Levi (end of the twelfth century). A clear connection between such altruism and the ultimate sacrifice is evident.

The cistern of a Jew was full of wine. Whereupon a violent non-Jew came and stuck his hand in the wine, in order to vex the Jew. Nearby stood a very pious, elderly Jew, one who eventually was martyred for his faith, and this man took some of the wine and drank it in front of the violent non-Jew. *His purpose was to stop the latter from doing the same to other Jews* [emphasis mine].[102]

The owner of the wine would have been in violation of the *halakhic* code had he drunk the wine in protest, for he would be the prime beneficiary of his act. The old man, in contrast, achieved no personal benefit from his act. By the seeming sin he had committed, he did not let non-Jews intimidate the community and disturb the religiously important wine manufacturing. In this way, Jews could deter such acts without yielding to violence, yet at the cost of committing a religious transgression. This legitimization of *halakhic* violations that resulted from the moral-religious understanding of the hour turned the man into pious and the wine into "permissible." Moreover, this version of the responsum turned the man into a martyr hero. Agus alluded to his martyrdom as having taken place in the First Crusade. But as this responsum reads, he may have been killed after his "in your face" act by the "violent non-Jew." The historicity behind the man's story of martyrdom is of little value here. What is significant in these two variant responsa is the exemplars they presented.

What triggered such drastic behavior and communal standards were the conditions outside Jewry.[103] Individual and communal religious commitment to the end resulted from the scope of the royal campaign. As in Italy, heretics and Jews found themselves under the suspicions of the French authorities. Only this time, the Jewish and the heretical "threats" to Catholicism were taken equally seriously. Comprehensive royal and ecclesiastical measures against the individual unbeliever and the community as a whole were more likely to yield drastic consequences. At issue now were not just religious restrictions, as was the case in Byzantium, but also eternal baptism. Heretics faced a more acrimonious condition, as overzealous crowds often preferred to see them burning rather than baptized. This violent mood spilled over onto the heretics' Jewish neighbors. At the council of Erfurt in 932, Pietro Candiano II, the doge of Venice, backed by Marin, the patriarch of Grado, recommended the expulsion of Jews who refused baptism. Even educated ecclesiastical officials, such as Archbishop Frederick of Mainz, were ready to consider forced baptism as a legitimate tool for dealing with Jews around 937. Obviously, the rejection of this idea by Pope Leo VII (936–939) was not reiterated enough by the turn of the millennium.[104]

Jews and heretics crossed paths once again under the watchful eye of the cross. From Orléans the royal couple is said to have initiated their drive against the two persuasions.[105] Immediately following the story about the Jewish conspiracy against the Sepulcher, Raoul tells how heresy was brought to Gaul from Italy. The heretics and their *female leader* were discovered in Orléans but had existed there before in hiding.[106] Adémar reports that many Manichaeans appeared in Toulouse. Theodatus, their leader, served as a cantor of the canons of Orléans. Heretics spread to Cambrai and Arras as well. Their country of origin was Italy.[107]

Adémar additionally reveals that Robert himself ordered the persecution of heretics.[108] Paul, a monk from Chartres, specifies that "the king [Robert] and Queen Constance had come to Orléans with a company of bishops"[109] to lead a final campaign against the heretical movement. These are the same royal actors that feature in the Hebrew account. Orléans was perceived as a hornets' nest of Jews and anti-Catholic Christian sects alike.[110] The destinies of Jews and heretics, some among both of Italian descent, met again under these circumstances of intolerance.

The doctrinal charges leveled against the heretics applied also to the Jews in these Latin accounts. Both rejected baptism and Jesus' divine attributes. They both sought religious autonomy, rejecting (especially the heretics) ecclesiastic authority. Both therefore were seen as the devil's agents. Such dangerous accusations deserved the close attention of royal supervision.[111] The identification of the king and queen as the authors of the persecution of both heretics and Jews in the independent Latin and Hebrew sources further demonstrates the reliability of these reports.

The timing of these violent eruptions was not a coincidence either. Millennial movements intensified Christian feelings of insecurity and intolerance. European society witnessed the growing popularity of the Christian millenarian movement that preached about "*termino mundi*" in anticipation of the second coming of Christ in the year 1000. An imperative condition for this to take place was the elimination of heretics and especially the conversion of the Jews. Their refusal to accept Christianity was perceived as a (if not *the*) reason for the delay of universal salvation. The violence that followed the year 1000 demonstrates Christian disappointment in their obstinate Jewish neighbors. For some, including Raoul Glaber, this Jewish stubbornness not only prevented the cosmic salvation but also stirred a divine wrath at the "end of days."[112]

Natural disasters contributed to the notion of the "end of days." Floods, epidemics, famine, and the eclipse of 1010 charged the Europeans with religious poignancy and panic.[113] Often, the masses and their leaders held Jews responsible for these disasters. When an earthquake terrified the Europeans on Good Friday in 1020 or 1017, Jews were blamed for causing the catastrophe by desecrating a holy image. It was believed that only after Pope Benedict VIII gathered the usual suspects and condemned to death the "guilty Jews" did the cataclysm cease.[114] A random earthquake could extend the list of martyrs. At least in this case, natural disasters were seen as a divine punishment for the Jewish hindering of Christ's second coming.[115]

M. Barkum, who studied the connection between disasters and millenarian movements, states that people stricken by disasters

operate with diminished mental efficiency and can no longer 'perceive reality'. Panic is rare; rather individuals attempt to interpret the unfamiliar in terms of the familiar and, when that fails, lapse into behavior patterns that are non-rational and reflexive.[116]

The natural disasters and the patterns of human behavior seen between 992 and 1022 correspond with Barkum's observation. From the Christians' point of view, their actions were preventive and protective. Raoul Glaber viewed the turning of the millennium as a danger period for the faithful. "This can be shown in the religions of many people and their provinces, and it was nowhere more manifest than amongst the priests and the Levites of the Jews."[117] Although a metaphor, the statement reveals Glaber's biased impression of the Jews.[118] The general atmosphere of phobia and piety led to "nonrational and reflexive" patterns of behavior on the part of Catholics. The aggression toward the non-Catholic Christian sects and the Jews of France illustrates one aspect of this socioreligious dynamic; the reaction of the victimized parties illustrates another. This point bring us to the second factor contributing to the process of individualizing martyrdom. This second factor comprises the reaction this violent approach triggered outside Jewish circles.

Most of the Jews found expulsion a reasonable alternative to baptism. Some, however, responded in the tradition of self-sacrifice that had arrived from Italy. Communal self-killing signified a novel Jewish phase in France, but not an aberrant practice for the period. A few examples illustrate the heretics' enthusiasm for self-killing. Of course, these antiheretic accounts by the Catholics must be read cautiously.

Adémar of Chabannes reports that in Orléans "ten persons proved to be Manichaeans...were sentenced to flames, among them Lisoius," the canon of the Cathedrals of the Holy Cross in Orléans. Indeed an alarming case, for Lisoius had enjoyed a close friendship with King Robert.[119] These "distrustful" heretics are depicted as gladly going to their death to stress their diabolic belief in Satanic supernatural powers: "Unconcerned, they showed no fear of the fire, predicted that they would emerge unscathed from the flames, and laughed as they were bound on the pyre. They were promptly reduced to ashes.... "[120] According to Paul Chartres, heresy broke out throughout the Gallic land. Catholic attempts to correct the situation gave heretics opportunities to become martyrs: "They had been taken out beyond the walls of the city [probably of Orléans] to a little hut where a great fire was kindled, they were burned, except for one cleric and one nun.... The cleric and the nun, by divine will, recovered their senses."[121]

These were not spontaneous acts. Bishop Aibert of Milan (1018–1045) is said to have confronted "a strange heresy which had recently taken roots in the citadel above the place called Monforte."[122] Aibert's concern was that "those most wicked persons, who had come into Italy from some unknown part of the world, daily, albeit secretly, like good priests were implanting false principles.... " To know more about this new doctrine, Aibert interrogated the sect's leader, Gerard. Facing Aibert, Gerard "stood with eager countenance ready to answer all questions, his mind fully prepared for suffering, happy if he were to end his life in the severest torture."[123] From the outset, Gerard revealed that none of them ended their lives without torment. When asked to elaborate, Gerard continued, "if we expire through torments inflicted upon us by the wicked, we rejoice; but if nature at any time brings us near death, *the one nearest us kills us in some way before we yield up our soul*" [emphasis mine]. Eventually, "some came to the Cross of the Lord," but others "covering their faces with their hands, leaped into the flames."[124]

Both the charges against and the responses of the Jews correspond to the situation and behavior of the heretics. In both camps women assumed similar active roles. As in the Hebrew report, Raoul Glaber ascribed to heretical women leading roles. Ironically, what the Catholics viewed as heroic and holy for themselves became the ultimate acts of devil worship when practiced by heretics and Jews. "Irrational" womanish behavior only substantiated the association with Satanism. Gregory of Tours (538–593/4) had already irrationally linked "irrational" Jewish conduct against French Christians to the instigation of the devil (*diabulo instigante*).[125] About 1066, a similar allegation to that made by Sehoq of Jews killing Christians by practicing magic surfaced in Trier. Jews were believed to have caused the death of Archbishop Eberhard by drowning his image to prevent his decree to expel the Jews of his city.[126] The alleged heretical fascination with death as a diabolic worship finds expression in the belief that heretics carried with them the ashes of their martyred children.[127]

Perhaps none of the Latin authors provides a better example of clustering together Jewish and heretical behaviors than Paul of Chartres. He believed that heretics tossed their eight-day-old children into the fire to purify their souls. Thereafter, "in the manner of the old pagans...ashes were collected and preserved with as great veneration as Christian reverence is wont to guard the body of Christ."[128] Pejorative accusations of child sacrifice against heretics and rival persuasions are not unprecedented. Paul's charges certainly could have stemmed from the misunderstood Jewish practice of circumcision on the eighth day, causing further confusion in the Christian mind between the two groups.[129] The Jewish ritual of male circumcision on the eighth day was to give rise to similar anti-Jewish allegations of children killing a few decades later. A vicious cycle was set in motion. The reasons for forcing conversion and their deadly reactions fed on each other.

To be sure, the production and veneration of martyrs were not limited only to heretics. Human sacrifices were both an essential element of a spreading doctrine and a sought-after act. In a letter to a fellow bishop, Gerard I, the bishop of Arras-Cambri (1013–1048), complained about groups of heretics who had claimed that "only the apostles and martyrs should be venerated."[130] Gerard did not object to revering the apostles and martyrs. His concern was the heretics' rejection of Catholic authority. Gerard and other Catholic authors of the period made many positive references to the issue of martyrdom and to past and contemporary martyrs.[131] Adémar, for example, included the Patriarch of Jerusalem in the category of martyrs and with him two Christian German boys who died in Egypt in 1010.[132] Helgald speaks in his *Vitae Roberti Regis* of the value of martyrs, reminding his readers of Christ's words, "Martyrs, you did not shame me on earth, therefore I shall not shame you above heaven."[133] This statement was not only a repetition of Christ's words; it could also have been an incentive to join Christ's celestial army of martyrs.

According to Raoul Glaber, this old promise did inspire the believer. Catholic martyrs, he made sure, differed from other casualties. In terms reminiscent of the language used by Pope Leo IV and John VIII, Raoul martyred Christians falling in their religious wars. "Many religious in the Christian armies were killed; they had longed to fight for love of their brothers, not for any vain glory of renown and pomp." To ensure that these fighters did not die purposelessly, monk Wulferius's vision is introduced. His church was suddenly filled with men dressed in white robes and wearing purple stoles. They followed a man carrying a cross in his hands. After celebrating mass on the altar of St. Maurice the Martyr, they revealed to Wulferius their identity. "We are all men of Christian professions, but while we were fighting for the defense of our country and the Christian people against the Saracens, the sword severed us from this earthly flesh. Because of this divine Providence is now taking us all into the lot of the blessed."[134]

Both the need to eradicate the unfaithful and the promise of celestial reward to the casualties of the church's various endeavors signal the harbingers of the upcoming violent attempts to create a monolithic Christian society.[135] The first arrow of the First Crusade was perhaps fired in this campaign. Equally indicative of matters to come was the Jewish reaction. Both Christian insecurity and Jewish behavior of the early eleventh century herald the violent end of this century.

6

∾

Ve Ashkenaz: Traditional Manifestations

One of the more notorious chapters in the history of Jewish martyrdom was written during the First Crusade. Three well-studied Hebrew accounts captured the crusaders' massacres of Ashkenazic (German) Jews in the spring and summer of 1096 or of *TATNU* in Jewish historiography. Written in the first half of the twelfth century, these unique narratives are known today as: *The Chronicle of Rabbi Solomon bar Simson, The Chronicle of Rabbi Eliezer bar Nathan,* and *The Mainz Anonymous.*[1] It is these accounts that have made medieval *qiddush ha-Shem* almost synonymous with Ashkenazic Jewry as they focus on the tragic events that unfolded along the Rhine River. In this chapter I continue to argue that French Jewry developed a martyrological legacy that not only preceded but also influenced the Ashkenazic tradition of martyrdom. Furthermore, although the Ashkenazic authors present their heroes as unprecedented martyrs, they build their claim on old symbols. These symbols will demonstrate a continuity with past Jewish literature and a hermeneutic relationship that existed between different martyrological literatures.

THE FRENCH CONNECTION

Scarce references to France are made in these reports. They do so mainly to indicate the origins of the crusaders. A short reference to French Jewry reveals that it sent letters to the Rhineland Jews, forewarning them of the great approaching upheaval. Based on this information, the letters, which are lost, exhort Rhenish Jews to prepare for the worst, for a great danger was spreading throughout France. Ashkenazic Jews were advised to take the coming menace seriously. From the response Mainz Jewry is reported to have sent back, French Jewry appears greatly distressed. They "were seized by trembling, anguish, and terror." Mainz Jews became "greatly fearful" for their French brethren.

"But we," they replied, "have less reason to fear for ourselves." What exactly occurred in France is unclear in these reports. Based on the reply from Mainz, "we did not hear that a decree had been issued and that a sword was to afflict us mortally," it is plausible that French Jews had mentioned some physical harm at the hands of crusaders.[2]

Indeed, the near-contemporaneous Abbott Guibert of Nogent confirms that the crusaders' swords afflicted the Jews of Rouen:

At Rouen on a certain day, the people who had undertaken to go on that expedition under the badge of the Cross began to complain to one another, "After traversing great distances, we desire to attack the enemies of God in the East, although the Jews, of all races the worst foe of God, are before our eyes. That's doing our work backward." Saying this and seizing their weapons, they herded the Jews into a certain place of worship, rounding them up by either force or guile, and without distinction of sex or age put them to the sword. Those who accepted Christianity, however, escaped the impending slaughter."[3]

Baptism appeared to be the only escape from the sword; death the only deliverance from baptism.

Rouen was not an isolated case. Richard of Poitiers adds that after Rouen the "crusaders continued to hold large massacres of Jews almost throughout Gaul."[4] Richard's report is usually taken with a grain of salt, but a kernel of truth cannot be dismissed out of hand. Other contemporaries, such as Hugh of Flavigny, Sigebert of Gembloux, and the late twelfth-century *Historiae Regum Francorum*, make similar claims.[5]

Solid support for massacres in France is furnished by a Genizah document. According to a letter from Midi, violence erupted also in the Provençal village of Monieux. In a manner similar to the attack at Rouen, Jews were killed in their synagogue and their children kidnapped to be raised as Christians, and their property was plundered.[6] It is not difficult to imagine that these Jews could have saved themselves had they agreed to be baptized. Although the conflict in France had, relatively, not gotten out of hand, the attacks and the Jewish reaction it triggered preceded the events in the Rhineland.

French crusaders had begun the attacks in Rouen with what would become the crusaders' rationale for assaulting the Ashkenazic Jews;[7] there was no point in doing battle with the remote Muslims of the east while those whom they held responsible for the killing of Jesus would continue to live unpunished at home. The eleventh-century convert to Judaism, Obadyah the Norman, ascribes to the French crusaders similar antagonistic views of Jews. Declared the enemy of Christians and Christianity, Jews could not have been trusted to stay behind with the crusaders' unprotected wives.[8] Although Obadyah's crusaders view the Jews as the first public enemy of the French, Guibert's crusaders considered Jews to be God's worst enemy of all races.

Given the circulating anti-Jewish abstractions of the eleventh century, such radical perceptions at the close of the century are not surprising. Nor should we be astounded by the Jewish reaction at Rouen and Monieux during the First Crusade. In addition to the previously discussed high standards of belonging to the Jewish communities of northern Europe, there is the fact that voluntary death had already taken place between 1007 and 1012 in the very same city, as mentioned by Guibert. Moreover, as was the case in the past, French Jews lived in an environment highly fascinated by sacrifices. Guibert echoed concerns and complaints about the problem of popular canonization of saints and martyrs and the worship of their relics. As Guibert indicates, almost every town and district adopted saints or martyrs and erected shrines to preserve the alleged martyrs' relics, despite the Church's opposition to the swelling trend.[9] Once again, the behavior of French Jews coincided with the trends that swirled around them.

In fact, not only northern French and Provençal Jews took their cues from their predecessors from Rouen. On at least one occasion, Ashkenazic behavior is reported to have been directly influenced by the martyrological tradition of French Jewry. When crusaders converged on the German town of Xanten, the dismayed community is said to have received guidance from an unnamed French rabbi. His exact place of origin remains unknown. It is worth mentioning, however, that relatively Rouen is not geographically far from Xanten:

There was a pious man named "the Rabbi from France," who told everyone: "Thus we do it in our place." He dug a pit and declaimed the ritual slaughter blessing, slaughtered himself, and thus died before God. All the others called out, "Hear, O Israel," etc., in a great voice.[10]

Little is told about the ritual of self-slaughtering of the "Rabbi from France." But it is rather explicit that a tradition of self-killing existed in France ("Thus we do it in our place") prior to the attacks of 1096 in the Rhineland. The slaughtering in a pit recalls *Sefer Yosippon*'s report of the slaughtering of the women and children at Masada and the three martyrs of Otranto. Masada's defenders are said to have "gathered their wives, sons, and daughters to slay them to the ground. They put them in the pits and threw dust over them."[11] At Otranto, R. Menahem martyred himself in a pit.[12] While the local Jews at Xanten appear stunned as to how to react properly to the ultimatum of death or conversion, the anonymous rabbi is already equipped with a routine martyrological response and practice. His example was quickly followed.

The anonymous rabbi's is not the only example that recalls past French conduct. Both the Hebrew and Latin reports of the early eleventh century describe French Jewish men and women as having taken their own lives. Reminiscent of the behavior of the French women we have met is that of some Ashkenazic women who are also reported to have drowned themselves to avoid baptism. Women "went to the bridge and threw themselves into the water out of fear of the eternal King." Echoing B. *Gittin* 57b, the chronicle ascribed to Solomon bar Simson connects Ps. 68:23, "I will retrieve from Bashan, I will retrieve from the depths of the sea," to these women "and others like them" who died by drowning.[13] Both the self-killing by the French rabbi in Xanten and the drowning of Ashkenazic women have their precedents in the early eleventh century.

What is innovative in the Ashkenazic narrations is the detailed description of the women's drowning and of the rabbi's self-slaughtering in ritualistic terms, accompanied by biblical and midrashic embellishments. As we shall soon see, the French rabbi's story provides just a modest example of this trend. At first glance, therefore, it is surprising that these detailed Hebrew narratives of the First Crusade would not report the incident at Rouen. How could the Ashkenazic sources ignore such a dramatic event in neighboring France? Is their silence because of a lack of information or of interest?

These questions reveal only the tip of a larger and more problematic issue that will be discussed as the chapter progresses. What was the purpose of the three Hebrew accounts? Do they accurately reflect the historical events of 1096? Or were they the literary products of imaginative twelfth-century religious minds that were ignited by *actual* events and destruction? Were these twelfth-century sources designed to speak to subsequent generations? If so, what are the messages they convey?[14]

Among the obvious goals of the Hebrew narratives lies the praising of the Rhenish Jews for their unique heroism and their special relation with the divine. Boastful statements thus claim that since the Second Temple, humankind has not seen such heroism. Since the destruction of the Second Temple, "there were none like them in Israel and after them there will be no more. For they sanctified and proclaimed the unity of [God's] Name with all their heart and with all their soul and with all their might."[15] Several statements went even further back. "Now come the entire people of the world and see, has there been such a sanctification of the Name since the time of Adam?"[16] Put differently, the generation of 1096 performed unprecedented heroic deeds.

Mention of the events at Rouen would obviously attenuate the Ashkenazic claim for martyrological originality. Introducing the French roots of the crusaders did not jeopardize the Ashkenazic authors' goal, because it had no bearing on the impression they labored to create. According to this impression, the Jewish tragedy originated in and snowballed from Germany throughout Europe. More important to these authors was the presentation of Ashkenaz as setting the tone for the rest of European Jewry. Crusaders gathered first in France, but for our authors, Jewish heroism began in Germany. All that remained for other communities was to emulate the admirable Ashkenazic exemplar. In the same way that the authors glossed over the massacre of the Palestinian Jews, they skipped the events in France.[17]

For that matter, the French Jewry did not show much interest in the events along the Rhine River.[18] The silence was not because of a French counterban on information but rather to the different levels of impact these events had on different communities. These communities differed in the amount of interest they took in the events. Except for Worms, the experiences of 1096 received little to no attention even in twelfth- and thirteenth-century Ashkenazic liturgy and mourning customs.[19] Only later did these events receive more attention in various works. Not much information on massacres in France, then, should be expected to surface in these early-twelfth-century Ashkenazic accounts. Nor should we expect Ashkenazic authors to credit French Jews for embracing such responses before their Rhenish protagonists did. They did acknowledge, however, the crusade's French genesis.

SETTING THE ASHKENAZIC STAGE

It originated at Clermont on November 1095 with the call of Pope Urban II for a sacred war. To inspire his audience to fight the Muslim, Urban turned to past and more recent role models.[20] He reminded his listeners of the deeds of the Maccabees, Jesus, and his Apostles. Biblical, apocryphal, and martyrological heroes spearheaded his propaganda. The pope's goal in presenting old and more recent heroes was transparent. "Let the deeds of your humble ancestors move you and incite your minds to manly achievements; the glory and greatness of King Charles the Great, and of his son Louis, and of your other kings. . . . recall the valor of your progenitors."[21] Other significant role models were Abraham the Patriarch, Job, Daniel with his three companions, and Christian martyrs and saints. They all presented altruistic paradigms of devotion to God. The use of these *exempla* would prove a crucial method of recruitment and of justification for killing and self-sacrifice in all the Latin accounts of the First Crusade.

In the hope of achieving the desired crusading conduct, these ancient archetypes underwent considerable imaginary transformation. Pacifistic martyred paragons of the past now composed the new *Militas Christi*, miraculously led by Jesus himself to do ardent battle alongside crusaders against the "enemy of God." Europeans could now join the soldier-saints of Jesus' army. This imaginary amalgamation of role models and their new images fueled crusading propaganda for the next two centuries.

Utilizing historic paragons as propaganda was not Urban's invention. Gerald of Avranches, the chaplain of Earl Hugh of Chester, had preceded Urban by a few decades. To control and correct his lord's followers, reports Orderic Vitalis, Gerald "offered up the sacrifice of the Mass" every day:

He did his best to convert the men of the [earl's] court to a better way of life by *showing them the examples of their progenitor.* He rightly condemned the worldly wantonness that he saw in many, and deplored the great negligence that most of them showed for the worship of God. To great barons, ordinary knights and noble boys he gave salutary counsel; and recollected tales of combats of holy knights *from the Old Testament and from modern Christian stories for them to imitate.* He told them vivid stories of the conflict of Demetrius and George, of Theodor and Sebastian, of Duke Maurice and his companions, who won through martyrdom the crown in heaven (*per martirium coronari meruerunt in coelis*).[22]

Despite Urban's usage of a commonplace method to transmute crusaders into past heroes, a sense of pioneering a new brand of pious protagonists emerges from the Latin accounts. These Christian duplicators of classic martyrs and saints were expected to exhibit the same exceptional heroism and homage. According to Latin crusading reports, they did. The same question asked by the Jewish narrators surfaces in their Latin counterparts. With dismay and admiration they rhetorically asked: "Who has ever heard of such things?"[23] Although presented as emulators of Christian *exempla*, crusaders also appeared as a new breed of Christian warrior. Past and recent martyrological role models, combined with promises of celestial rewards, were intended to inspire. After Clermont, they overwhelmingly did – both Christians and Jews.

BETWEEN TRADITION AND INNOVATION

The same mechanism that characterizes the Latin accounts can be noted in their Hebrew contemporaries. Two forces are thus at work in the Hebrew accounts. On the one hand, Jewish behavior in 1096 is presented as innovative; on the other, as traditional. To be sure, this distinction between traditional and contemporary medieval symbols is merely methodological. Both old and new sets of symbols are incorporated by the Jewish authors, who present them in biblical, liturgical, Talmudic, and midrashic jargons. This fusion makes the distinction between traditional Jewish and contemporary Christian symbols difficult to detect.

In parallel to the claims of innovative, altruistic behavior, the Ashkenazic martyrs are antithetically described as following in the footsteps of past heroes. At the same time, the Hebrew narratives attempt to match the sense of heroism and ethnocentrism that Pope Urban II employed in his historic call for the First Crusade at Clermont. In the same style that characterizes many of the Latin reports of Urban's sermon to the "race" of Christians or Franks, the Jewish authors preserved for posterity the events of 1096.

The response of the "rabbi from France" constitutes one of several old and new Asheknazic reactions to crusaders' violence.[24] They varied from negotiation to conversion; from self-defense to self-sacrifice; from taking flight to taking the lives of loved ones. Martyrological reactions in 1096 are most perplexing to comprehend. The graphic descriptions of Jews stoically awaiting the crusaders only to be killed are chilling enough. Stories of men and women taking the lives of their own children before quitting their own make the martyrological phenomenon even more gruesome and insoluble. To the participants in the drama of 1096, these modes of reaction appeared not only legitimate but also laudable, at least in the way they are reported by the narrators. Despite the actors' familiarity with the *halakhic* emphasis on the passivity of martyrdom, activist forms of *qiddush ha-Shem* were both embraced and praised.

Thus consonant with the tendency to depict Ashkenazic Jews as unique and innovative altruists is the need to show them as walking in the footsteps of their ancient role models. In a manner strikingly similar to the style and scheme of the Latin reports, a cluster of classic role models recurs in our three narratives from start to end. In this way, the need for *qiddush ha-Shem* could gain justification more effortlessly. The question of who exactly benefitted from the deployment of these classic paradigmatic heroes is not entirely clear. Did the actors of 1096 use these archetypal protagonists in their speeches to justify their own acts and motivate others? Or did the authors find these aged exemplars useful to rationalize their actors' radical deeds as these writers delivered messages to their generation? Perhaps both actors and authors referred to their models for the same purpose: presenting innovative forms of martyrdom as an imitation of their old heroes.

Daniel with his three companions, Abraham and Isaac, and Temple priests are among the medieval Jewish role models. They emerged in Ashkenaz prior to 1096. The *aqedah* appeared already in Shimon bar Isaac's poems. Written no later than the first quarter of the eleventh century, his poems were widespread and had a considerable impact on Ashkenazic Jews.[25] Like Rabbi Shimon,

Rabbi Gershom of Mainz extended the *qorban* image[26] to include the concept of the *aqedah*. Both scholars turned to the *aqedah* to assert God's unconditional protection of Israel.[27] Gershom entreated God to remember Abraham's *aqedah*, to notice the self-sacrifices of "young men in their Temples," and of children and mothers. "All day long they are being slaughtered for Your sake." On account of such sacrifices, Rabbi Gershom expected God to deliver Israel from their oppressor.[28] These examples may suggest that the generation of 1096 was already familiar with some of these exemplars.

If past heroes did inspire the generation of 1096, a different question comes to mind. How did nonmartyrological figures inspire voluntary death? Moreover, how could they and, even more, past passive martyrs lead Ashkenazic Jews to take their own and others' lives in a seemingly clear violation of the *halakhic* rule?[29] Generally, our texts settle this question in a threefold process, which can also be noticed in crusading texts. First, the past hero to be emulated is presented. Next, the emulator's self is fused with that of the mythical figure to present them as equals, even though the emulators exceed the acts of the heroes they follow. Then, the original story is adjusted to harmonize it with the new extravagant act. Let us first explore the use of traditional heroes and motifs. We shall meet some of these protagonists a number of times because their stories function on different levels. One of the functions of these heroes is to rationalize the harsh events.

CATASTROPHE

The justification of the Jewish reactions necessitated, first, the rationalization of the harsh conditions that induced them. Put differently, an Ashkenazic need arose to explain why this self-perceived righteous community was so severely punished. This need was answered by associating the event with a Jewish historic sin. This rationale explains particular failures like that of Kalonymous bar Meshullam and his followers to defend Mainz's gates. "Because of the sins, the enemy overwhelmed them and seized the gate."[30] Although acknowledgments of sins do exist, these sins are set in the larger context of human history. "We have sinned," admit the sources, but what immediately follows is God's relinquishing His Temple in Shilo.[31] Obviously, the reason for suffering in 1096 goes way back.

A clue to what this grave sin might have been is provided by the following passage. "And their Father did not answer them. He blocked their prayer and concealed himself off with a cloud, so their prayer might not pass through.... For a decree had been enacted before him 'in the day when I visit'" (Exod. 32:34). Exodus 32:34 alludes to the sin of the Golden Calf.[32] All future Jewish suffering, therefore, will contain an element of punishment for this sin.

Indeed, a later Ashkenazic report explicitly blames this historic sin for the events along the Rhine River. The bishop of "Halle"gave up his attempts to rescue Jews when he realized that they must have committed a sin. "A grave sin must exist among you that dooms you all," argued the bishop. The rabbis did not know of any general sin among them, "neither hidden or apparent, except the sin of the [golden] Calf.... This is the *Kolbo* sin in the language of Ashkenaz, as it is written 'in the day that I visit'" (Exod. 32:34). Thereafter, the bishop agreed that at least "some of you must be destroyed."[33]

The three Hebrew narratives are not as explicit as this text. Why would they acknowledge guilt associated with the behavior of their remote Israelite ancestors, but not elaborate? Could this sin alone justify the punishment and, more significantly, the mass martyrdom of 1096? And if the Calf represented the apparent sin, what then constituted the hidden transgression? It seems that even a graver sin was unjustly attached by association to the righteous generation of 1096.

This dilemma of theodicy had already emerged in the legend of the ten righteous martyrs and could, therefore, suggest an answer for the events of 1096. Indeed, our texts frequently refer to Akiva and "his companions," namely the Ten Martyrs, as the exemplar of the generation. Yet surprisingly, *The Mainz Anonymous* and the *Solomon bar Simson Chronicle* make no direct mention of the legend. Instead, only several motifs of these legends surface obscurely in these two sources. Their force should not be ignored, however.

As in the legend, the three narratives first established the innocence of their heroes by ascribing their suffering to a divine plot. In the legend of the Ten Martyrs, Samael [or Satan] the minister of "evil Rome" contrived this plot, knowing too well that it would bring God's vengeance on the people he was safeguarding. The *Solomon bar Simson Chronicle* associated Samael's role with the pope. "Satan, the pope of evil Rome, also came" to participate in the events that had been decreed by heaven. He "came and mingled with the nations."[34]

More disturbing was the fatalistic belief that nothing, save conversion, could be done to avert the calamity. In the famous legend of the Ten, a similar fatalistic motif required the sacrifice of the rabbinic elite to expiate the historic sin of selling Joseph and to secure the future of the people. In 1096, the entire generation was viewed as the elite of the nation. Therefore, no other generation had been worthier. This view allegedly caused the Ashkenazic Jews to accept their role cheerfully. Like their ten predecessors, they appear ready to honor the consequences of this sin, despite being innocent. In accordance with the mystical concept of the punishment of the elect, the first signs of upheaval manifested themselves before 1096. "A year prior to the coming of 'the day of the Lord,' before the persecution struck, most of the rabbis in all of the communities died, and the notable of Israel also perished, to fulfill what is written: 'Prior to the evil the righteous is taken away'" (Isaiah 57:1).[35] The early and mysterious deaths of these rabbis further reinforced the legendary view that the best of Israel must pay first for the sins of the past.[36]

A year later, the heavenly decree continued to manifest itself in Speyer, where eleven Jews lost their lives on the Sabbath. Immediately after revealing the issuing of the divine edict against this selected generation, the chronicle continues with the seemingly superfluous information that "That year, Passover fell on Thursday" (*ba-hamishi be-Shabbat*). On the same day of *hamishi be-Shabbat*, claims *Heikhalot Rabbati*, came the dreadful news from the evil city of Rome about the need to destroy the Ten Martyrs. A different midrashic version adds that the executioner showed up with a sword in his hand while the ten were in the midst of studying the laws of Passover.[37]

Additional clues for the usage of the midrashic legend are provided by the story of Samuel ben Gedaliah and his friend Yehiel ben Samuel. Samuel requested to be slaughtered first "so I shall not see the death of my friend." In *Midrash Elleh Ezkerah*, R. Ishmael requested that he be allowed to die before R. Shimon, "so I shall not see the death of my friend."[38]

For the *Mainz Anonymous*, the events at Speyer fulfilled the verse "And at my sanctuary (*miqdashi*) shall you begin" (Ezekiel 9:6). In its biblical context, the verse is predicting God's severe punishment of his sinful nation. The verse thus serves the first half of the medieval equation for the attack against the Jews – the belief in a historic sin. A homiletic reading of the verse provided the second component of this formula. B. *Shabbat* 55a suggested altering "my sanctuary" to "my sanctified ones" (*mequdashay*) to imply that God begins the persecution of his people with the righteous. Combining these two exegeses, the anonymous author shows that the persecution of 1096 began in Speyer (God's sanctuary) with the sacrificing of the best. More generally, by putting all these mystical insinuations together the obvious emerges. Ashkenazic Jewry suffered because God had chosen the generation of 1096 to atone for past sins and to save the nation. Conversely, the crusaders and their pope from "evil Rome" are doomed to fail, for they are just a pawn in a larger divine scheme. At the end, those who rise to destroy the innocent will be destroyed themselves.[39] Bits of information from the mystical tradition are interjected into the narratives of 1096.

Establishing the involvement of a heavenly decree and the wickedness of the crusaders did not require a great deal of effort from the Jewish authors. More difficult was explaining the severity of the calamity, which no person could undo. In the eyes of the narrators, the total destruction was disproportionate and unfathomable. No one could explain "how the sin of the innumerable people was so heavy and how the souls of the saintly communities were so destructive, as if shedding blood."[40] Admission of guilt first requires an accusation of crime. The question is whose bloodshed could trigger such a collective calamity.

The post-Talmudic tractate *Mourning* (or *Semahot*) already ascribed the same dilemma to R. Ishmael, before his execution by the Romans. Conversing with his colleague R. Shimon, Ishmael is puzzled by their coming execution. In his opinion, such an execution befits those who shed blood, not innocent people.[41] The two, we recall, are among the ten innocent rabbis chosen to atone for the ancient sin of the children of Israel. It should also be remembered that the dialogue between Samuel and Yehiel repeated Ishmael's request to be executed before R. Shimon. By implication, the selling of Joseph by his brothers corresponds in its severity to murdering. In fact, "shedding blood" (Gen. 37:22) was the brothers' first intention.

In the medieval text, the self-imposed question of a historic bloodsheding is immediately answered, although the context differs. While the Jews grappled with this issue of murder and punishment, the question was answered effortlessly by the crusaders.

You are the descendants of those who killed our deity and crucified him. And he also said: 'A day will come and my children will avenge my blood.' We are his children and its is our responsibility to avenge him upon you, for you are the ones who rebelled and offended against him. Your God was never satisfied with you even though he had intended to do good for you, for you did evil before him. For this he forgot you and did not desire you anymore, for you have been a stiff-necked nation. And he divorced himself from you and has shone [his light] upon us and has taken us as his portion.[42]

Coinciding with Guibert's report of the crusaders' reason for the massacre at Rouen, the three Hebrew accounts cite revenge for the spilling of Jesus' blood as the crusaders' self-proclaimed motivation for the massacres. Duke Godfrey of Bouillon is also reported to have been motivated by the same reason. He avowed not to leave for the east before "avenging the blood of the crucified one by shedding the blood of Israel."[43] Interestingly, in the abundant dialogues between Jews and crusaders, the historic accusation was never denied. Yet, there was no justification in the mind of the Ashkenazic Jews for the violence. Whoever shed Jesus' blood, it was not they; if a sin did occur, it was not theirs.

Why then would the *Mainz Anonymous* and the *Solomon bar Simson Chronicle* esoterically use mystical motifs from the legend of the Ten Martyrs, but fail to mention it by name? An integral part of the *Asara Harugei Malkhut* legend is the association of the death of the ten chosen rabbis with the ancient sin of selling Joseph. Given the Christological interpretation of the Jewish condition in 1096 as their punishment for selling Jesus, the plain use of the legend may have appeared much too close for comfort to the *Mainz Anonymous* and the *Solomon bar Simson Chronicle*. In other words, the selling of Joseph could reinforce the Christian belief that Jews, as repeated offenders, sold also Jesus to be killed. This would be especially true if the legend still had not broken out of the mystical Ashkenazic circles. The two texts seem apologetically to replace the Christian view of the Jewish sin with that of the Golden Calf. Thus the reality in Ashkenaz is explained as a punishment for worshiping the Golden Calf. Sinning against the God of the Israelites, rather than against Jesus (as the Christians claimed), accommodated a safer refutation of the Christian accusation. Not a sin against Jesus caused God to select the crusaders as His army and abandon Rhenish Jews on "the day that I visit."[44]

Less concerned about the similarity between the betrayals of Joseph and Jesus is Eliezer bar Nathan. "In the day that I visit" surfaces also in Eliezer's account to foreshadow the explicit association of Speyer community with the Ten Martyrs. Although the other two narratives number the victims at eleven, Eliezer speaks of "ten holy souls" from Speyer sanctifying the Name of God. Reminiscent of Shabbettai Donnolo's technique, Eliezer quickly follows the loss of the ten with the self-slaughtering of a certain woman, bringing the number up to eleven.

Eliezer is more specific in his eulogy, still without mentioning Joseph's betrayal. Speyer becomes the "special community which sanctified the Name [of God] like the 'Ten Martyrs' of the state (*Harugei Malkhut*)."[45] Remarkably, Ashkenazic women could also penetrate the circle of Talmudic pride. Perhaps these women should be indebted to their female French predecessors who had set the stage for female Jewish martyrs at the beginning of the century. Men and women now expiated for the historic sin. Eliezer's explicit references to *Harugei Malkhu* explain why a catastrophe befell German Jews, refuting along the way Christian polemics. Similarly to the Christian theological arguments, the need for human sacrifices was rationalized on a cosmic scale. Leaders and congregations thus "sanctified the Name of the King of all kings, the Holy One blessed be He, like Akiva and his companions who stood the test like Hananiah, Mishael, and Azariah."[46]

Certainly, the shedding of blood seems a less likely motif in association with the Golden Calf sin. And, by ascribing the unfolding event to a sin, the authors rationalize their harsh reality. But by the same mechanism, they could also rebut the crusaders' mantra that God had abandoned the Jews because of their ancient sin of shedding the blood of their messiah. "Where is [God's] promise [to you] now? How could you be saved?" asked the crusaders in 1096.[47] By employing motifs from the legend of the Ten Martyrs, the Ashkenazic narrators turned the crusaders' theological argument on its head. God's promise was still valid because the catastrophe itself proved His commitment. Although the Golden Calf indicated a sin and the reason for the punishment of the elect in the present, the Ten Martyrs justified both the divine verdict and the need for the human sacrifices of 1096.

TEMPLE PRIESTS

Sacrifices bring to mind Temple court images. Unlike the symbol of the Ten Martyrs, Temple images were not limited to heroes executed by the enemy. In Xanten, where we have met the "rabbi from France," a leader of the community assumed the role of the high priest in the Temple; the community, the role of the burnt offering; and the table around which they gathered became the altar.

Then the pious and the faithful one – the higher priest than his brethren (*ha-Kohen ha-gadol*, Leviticus 21:10) – said to the congregation seated around the table: "Let us recite the grace to the living God, our father in heaven. For the table substitutes now for the altar. Now, because the enemy is coming upon us, let us rise up and ascend to the house of the Lord and do immediately the will of our Creator to slaughter on the Sabbath sons, daughters, and brothers, so that He bequeath upon us this day a blessing. Let no man spare himself or his friend. And the last one to remain shall slaughter himself by the throat with a knife, or thrust his sword into his stomach.... We ourselves shall offer the sacrifice of God 'as a whole burnt offering' (I Sam. 7:9) to the Most High offered on the altar of the Lord."[48]

God Himself demands the sacrifices. Presented as the fulfilment of God's command, self-killing and sacrificing others arose no controversy. On the contrary, such acts aimed at evoking God's blessing. So "They themselves became like the daily offering of the morning."[49]

Temple metaphors abound in the three Hebrew narratives.[50] They were used to justify the taking of others lives' as innovative martyrdoms. Linguistically and thematically, however, such descriptions are reminiscent of several accounts found in *Sefer Yosippon*. Suffice it to recall the defenders of the Temple and Masada. The former appeared ready to die to "be considered a burnt offering on this day."[51] Their assumption was that "There is no better sacrifice (*zevah*) to be offered in this chamber than our flesh and blood, since for our Lord we shall fight and we shall be considered before Him as the daily burnt offering and we shall die free in the holy city."[52] Even more affinity is shown by *Sefer Yosippon*'s presentation of the suicides of men, women, and children at Masada. "They gathered their wives, sons, and daughters to slay them to the ground. They will be considered a burnt offering before God, because for His Name they went, not to be killed before the Romans."[53] The *qorban* symbol, it should be recalled, also characterizes the self-killings of the rabbis from Otranto.

Nevertheless, additional metaphors and terms continue to show affinity to *Sefer Yosippon*. Frequently, a preparatory stage of three days of fasting and mourning preceded Ashkenazic martyrdoms. As mentioned, the practice of a three-day fast, which appears in the Book of Esther, became a part of *Sefer Yosippon*'s narrations involving human sacrifice. Thereafter, the practice continued among early eleventh-century French Jews.[54]

Ashkenazic martyrs are described as "handing over their souls to God," among other phrases. *Sefer Yosippon* made use of the phrase abundantly, although not always to indicate voluntary death. Aspects of the heavenly reward concept, which will be discussed shortly, are formulated in the language of the martyrs of *Sefer Yosippon*. Ashkenazic victims are believed to exchange a world of darkness for a world of light, whereas their oppressors descend to the darkness of the abyss.[55]

Still, the story of Xanten was not devoid of contemporary stimulus. The audience's reaction to the ardent speech of the anonymous leader who is transformed into "the higher priest than his brethren" is reminiscent in concept and language of the well-known reaction to the sermon of a more famous Christian priest. Urban, the priest higher than his brothers, presented the crusade as God's will. His audience reacted to the historic call with the same slogan "God wills it" (*deus uult*), which became their battle cry. "They all with one accord said they would follow in the footsteps of Christ."[56] As in the reports of Urban's address at Clermont, "They [the Jews at Xanten] all replied loudly, with one mouth and one heart: 'Amen, so be it and so is His will.'"[57] Acting out the famous scene at Clermont, it was the priestly authority in the rabbi that approved all types of sacrifices at Xanten.

PATRIARCHS

In conjunction with Temple imagery, the *aqedah* image dominated the Hebrew narratives of the First Crusade.[58] These metaphors, writes Marcus, "represent an acting out of the central self-image in Ashkenaz of the holy people as

Temple, according to which German Jews in 1096 acted both as Temple priests and as sacrifices."[59] A few examples will adequately establish this point and demonstrate how it took shape.

Rabbi Kalonymous the *parnas* and his group underwent manifold martyrdom while fortified in the village of Rudesheim. "They all arose together and blessed their *aqedah* and justified the judgment[60] in one voice and singleheartedly accepted upon themselves the fear of [God]."[61] Rabbi Kalonymous is reported to have sacrificed his son Joseph in such a manner.

As in the biblical story, the Ashkenazic *aqedot* took place in the presence of God. Words ascribed to the besieged Jews at Mainz address God directly.

They cried out loudly: "Behold and see our Lord, what we do for the sanctification of Your holy Name without exchanging You with the crucified one . . . The precious children of Zion, the children of Mainz, were tested ten times, like our ancestor Abraham and like Hananiah, Mishael, and Azariah. They sacrificed [*aqedu*] their children as Abraham had sacrificed [*aqad*] his son Isaac."[62]

The *aqedah* aimed at reminding God of His commitment to Abraham. "The children of Mainz" reaffirmed their commitment to God, hoping to witness His intervention in return. It also reminded twelfth-century Ashkenazic Jews of their commitment to Him.

The replication of the medieval version of the *aqedah* was almost perfect in the case of Rabbi Meshullam bar Isaac. No great deal of imagination is required to discern a reworking of the *aqedah*. Meshullam sacrificed the elderly couple's only son, Isaac, whom God gave to the couple in their old age. Meshullam is reported to have addressed to the Jews around him.

He called out loudly to all those standing there and to Zipporah his wife: "Listen to me both small and great, this son was given to me by God. My wife Zipporah bore him in her old age and his name is Isaac. . . . " He then bound his son Isaac and he took in his hand the knife in order to slaughter his son and made the benediction of slaughtering. The lad answered amen. He then slaughtered the lad.[63]

Both Isaac and Abraham feature in the story. Like Abraham, who "took in his hand the knife" with the intent to slay his son (Gen. 22:10), Meshullam "took in his hand the knife" and actually slew the medieval Isaac.

Numerous Jews are reported to have transformed themselves into the actors of the original *aqedah*. Every new Abraham and every fresh Isaac encouraged the rest to "emulate" their ancestral father and son to allay God's wrath. If a potential sacrifice satisfied God once, surely multiple actual *aqedot* would appease Him now. As God promised His commitment to Abraham after the *aqedah*, He was expected to bring the killing to an end in 1096. The ritualistic reenactment of the *aqedah* was intended to end the persecution and redeem both victims and survivors. It was hoped that "the blood of his pious ones may serve us as a merit and atonement for our succeeding generations and for the sons of our sons forever, like the binding of our ancestor Isaac, when our father Abraham bound him on the altar."[64]

Following Shimon bar Isaac and Gershom of Mainz, the narratives of 1096 added to the Byzantine *qorban* symbol the critical image of Abraham's trial. Its symbolism fits the *halakhic* deviation that was evolving. Similar to the new dualistic interpretation of the passive/active *qorban* symbol, the *aqedah* psychologically rationalized and religiously legitimized both self-sacrifice and the immolation of others. In the same ritualistic manner in which Abraham was supposed to take the life of his son Isaac, their descendants are described as taking the lives of their medieval "Isaacs."

This preexisting symbol could have inspired Jews in 1096. The concept of the *aqedah* could supply legitimacy to the sacrifices of coreligionists in the name of God. On a literary level, the *aqedah* could help the narrators rationalize the radical behavior of their heroes. Abraham and Isaac served as exemplars for those who sacrificed their relatives to avert forced conversion. This new Ashkenazic representation of the *aqedah* – as an actual sacrifice of Isaac by Abraham – assisted the narrators of the three Hebrew chronicles to make sense not only of the act but also its numbers.

The *aqedah* held the additional function of rebutting Christian polemics. In his study of Jewish acculturation in medieval Europe, Marcus refers also to the example of martyrdom in Christendom. He writes:

In resisting the powerful culture that surrounded them, the Jews of Ashkenaz polemically denied the central root metaphor of the sacrificed Jesus but at the same time internalized the process of generating new polemical rituals drawn from ancient themes and images that placed Israel, not Jesus, as the locus of the sacred and even of sacrificial martyrdom.[65]

This is precisely the process we have witnessed so far and that we will continue to observe with other examples. By making Abraham an actual sacrificer and Isaac a genuine offering, Ashkenazic Jews created a parallel to the central Christian theme of the period, Christ's sacrifice for the salvation of humanity. Faithful Christians were called at Clermont to sacrifice themselves for the sake of their Father, as had the divine son. Many took up the cross, viewing this potential outcome as the apogee of their sacred journey. By turning Isaac into an actual sacrifice, Rhineland Jews followed in the steps of their sacrificed son, Isaac. Through these parallels the Jews perceived themselves and their patriarchs to be equal in enthusiasm and altruism to the Christians and their founders. Crusaders could no longer claim that only their first son surrendered himself to his Father to justify their sacrifices. Jesus' cosmological drama inspired the crusaders to be sacrificed like God. New representations of the *aqedah* could arouse Ashkenazic Jews to sacrifice themselves for God. As Isaac was "immolated" by Abraham, so were the medieval Isaacs sacrificed by the medieval Abrahams. Myth and reality fed on each other.

MATRIARCHS

Daniel with his three companions, Temple priests and sacrifices, R. Akiva and "the pillars of the universe," the Ten Martyrs, and Abraham and Isaac provided male role models. The maidens who drowned themselves to escape Roman captivity (B. *Gittin.* 57b) and "the saintly woman with her seven sons" served as female exemplars. If the medieval heroine were to strictly follow these paradigms, her role would be limited to encouraging loved ones to face the executioner and submit passively. The "woman," and by that the myth indicates every Jewish woman in her position, could only passively watch her seven sons undergoing death. Neither Antiochus nor God had previously required a woman's martyrdom. More female behavioral patterns, however, are reported in 1096.

The first pattern of behavior duplicated the behavior of the mother of the seven sons as presented in the original story. These women were expected first and foremost to encourage the males to undertake martyrdom or to assist them in performing the *aqedot* and *qorbanot*. Women of this category "sacrificed" their own martyrdom to assure the proper ritualistic performance of their male companions. Supporting functions were demonstrated only by women who excited the males to perform their ritualistic duties. The encouragements of the women provided incentive to the men, which well suited the medieval narratives.

There was also a Torah scroll in the chamber. The crusaders came into the chamber, found it and tore it to pieces. When the holy and pure women, the daughters of kings, saw that the Torah had been torn, they called out loudly to their husbands: "Behold, behold the holy Torah, for the enemies are tearing it." The women said unanimously: "Woe, holy Torah, 'perfect in beauty' (Lam. 2:15), 'the delight of our eyes' (II Kings 20:6; Ezek. 24:16, 21, 25). We used to bow down to it in the synagogue and our little children used to kiss it, and we used to honor it. How has it fallen now into the hands of those uncircumcised and impure." When the men heard the words of the holy women, they became extremely zealous for God our Lord and for his sacred and beloved Torah.[66]

When the "holy" women "saw" the condition of the Torah, "they called out loudly"; these phrases recall *Sefer Yosippon's* heroine. The book focused on one "holy mother." When she "saw" her seven sons dead, "she raised up her voice and called. . . ."[67] Ashkenazic women, however, surpassed the intensity of this one mother. Their duty to inflame the situation was both essential and substantial. Even the crusaders are reported to have told one another in Trier: "All this the women do who instigate their husbands, invigorating their hands to rebel against the Crucified one."[68]

Women actively strove to assist the men in performing ritualistic sacrifices of children. In this case, the women's specific role was to hold back the crusaders to provide the men with enough time for their sacrifice. The besieged women at Mainz "threw coins and silver out the windows at the enemy, so that they be busy with gathering the money, in order to hinder them slightly until they finish the slaughtering of their sons and daughters." Similarly, indicates the *Mainz Anonymous*, "pious women threw the money outside, in order to hinder them [the crusaders] a bit, until their children were slaughtered."[69] Time was crucial, for the killing had to be performed in a manner identical to the ancient slaying ritual of burnt offerings in the Temple and to the *halakhic* practice of animal slaughter. While men reenacted the sacrificial ritual in the fullest detail, women granted the essential time for it to take place.

Occasionally, women gained time by serving as cannon fodder, paying with their lives to impede the attackers. Thus they enabled the male to fulfill his obligation of sacrificing the children. Women of this group appear to have acted mainly with the intent of temporarily distracting the crusaders. Although they welcomed death with ecstasy, they did not act with the intent of being killed. It is important to note that these women acted when being besieged by the crusaders along with the rest of their family. "The pious women threw stones out the windows against the enemy, and the enemy threw stones against them. They received the stones until their flesh and faces became shredded."[70] This supporting role demonstrates the fusion of the female self with both the original Jewish heroine and the heroine of early medieval times, who, according to *Pesikta Rabbati*, had been executed with her seven sons by a ruler.

This fusion led Rhenish women toward a third pattern of behavior. The women of this group intentionally let the crusaders slay them to escape baptism:

The saintly ones were brought before the courtyard of the church and they implored them to immerse themselves in their sullied water. When they [the women] arrived at the church, they did not wish to enter the shrine of idolatry and they stuck their feet, against their will, at the threshold. They did not wish to enter the shrine of idolatry and to smell the fragrances of [?] abomination. When the crusaders saw that they did not wish to be baptized and that they increasingly trusted with all their heart in the living God, then the enemy jumped on them and struck them with axes and blows. There the pure ones were killed for the sanctification of the Name.[71]

To this group of women we may add the martyrdom of Guta and Scholaster. The two "stretched forth their necks and were struck by the crusaders without mercy." A woman named *Mina* also belongs to this category. Other women "likewise abundantly sanctified the Name publicly."[72] These examples correspond with the pattern that had been set by the Hellenistic mother, who let her children be killed, and the mother of *Pesikta Rabbati*, who let the oppressor kill her, too.

Other Ashkenazic women took a more active role. Two methods of female self-killing can be observed. The majority of women in this group are reported to have preferred a nonviolent method of self-destruction. Others did not hesitate to undergo a violent death. Rivers served as a popular instrument of nonviolent female martyrdom. Their voluntary death corresponds to the Talmudic example of the four hundred girls and boys. They drowned themselves so that they would avoid the imposed performance of immoral sex. The Talmud concludes this episode with the verse from Psalm 68:23, "The Lord said: 'I will retrieve you from Bashan, I will retrieve you from the depths of the sea.'" The same verse is ascribed to Rhenish women who "went to the bridge and threw themselves into the water out of fear of the eternal King," and of "two young girls from Cologne." Psalm 68:23 refers to these women "and others like them" who died by drowning.[73] A more recent exemplar from their own culture also existed. In France, drowning had constituted the women's method already in the years 1007–1012. As mentioned, *Sefer Yosippon* acquainted women with the idea of self-killing in time of crisis as being standard female behavior.

Although traditional references and historical narratives may have inspired an active, nonviolent female martyrdom, violent female martyrdom was without precedent. Like their French female predecessors of the early eleventh century, women reacted faster than men in Germany. A certain woman was among the first to undertake violent martyrdom in Speyer: "She was an important and pious woman who slaughtered herself for the sanctification of the

Name. She was the first among those who slaughtered themselves and those who were slaughtered in all the communities."[74] The report immediately continues with the events at Worms. There "Mothers and babes were dashed together" (Hos. 10:14). This biblical verse further cements the association of Ashkenazic women with the mother and the seven sons.

More daring are the depictions of women sacrificing their own children. The mayor of Moers kept Jews in isolation to prevent them from killing one another. Yental and Rebecca, and a "young beautiful lass," were held together when one of them gave birth to a baby boy:

When the women saw that the enemy rose against them, they slaughtered the beautiful lass; she was ten years old. They also took the young infant, who was born that week, and swaddled him in his cradle, for they were overcome with feeling toward him. [Then] they let go of him from the tower in which they stayed.[75]

Women taking others' lives present a further deviation from the prototypic mother. Despite this anomaly, the three chronicles continued to present such acts as equivalent to the legendary mother's deed.

Although she killed her own children, a woman named Rachel was made a parallel to the anonymous mother. Rachel, her children, and her female friends were kept in isolation. As the crusaders were breaking into their room, Rachel said to her female companions:

I have four children. Do not have mercy on them as well, lest these uncircumcised come and seize them and they live in their erroneous faith. Also by them you shall sanctify the holy Name. One of her female friends came and took the knife to slaughter her son. When she saw the knife, she cried loudly and bitterly. She beat her face, crying and saying: "Where is Your benevolence, O Lord?" She took Isaac her small son, he was very lovely, and slaughtered him. . . . She took the two daughters, Bella and Matrona, and sacrificed them to the Lord God of Hosts, who commanded us not to forsake his pure awe and to remain loyal to him. When the pious one finished sacrificing her three children before our Creator, she raised her voice and called out to her son Aaron: "Aaron, where are you? I shall not have mercy or pity on you either." She pulled him by the legs from under the cabinet, where he had hidden, and sacrificed him before the sublime and exalted God.[76]

When the crusaders brook into the room, they found Rachel holding the lifeless bodies of her children. Appalled by the gory scene, they "killed her upon them (her children)." Still the text claims, "she died for them [her four children] as did that saintly woman with her seven sons." With regard to Rachel it is said: "'Mothers and babes were dashed together'" (Hos. 10:14).

Now, "The mother of the children is happy" (Ps. 113:9; B. *Gittin* 57b; Lam. Rabbah 53 to1:16).[77]

The failure of the text to identify the mythical mother by her midrashic name suggests that it did not follow the early rabbinic versions of the story. The anonymity of the paradigmatic mother is maintained just as it was in *Sefer Yosippon.* Further proof of the book's impact is afforded by the linguistic parallels. Like the mother in *Yosippon* (1:75), Rachel was killed upon her children. She thus "handed over her soul" until her "spirit departed."[78] The parallels end here.

Unlike the mythical mother, Rachel is the mother of four, two of whom are girls. Rachel, not her offspring, is the focus of the story. The strongest literary deviation is presented by Rachel's killing of her children. In the case of the young Aaron, she sacrifices him against his will. Nevertheless, she is compared to the anonymous mother, "She [died] with her four children as did the saintly woman with her seven sons."Rachel clearly exceeded her role model. We have already noted a similar transformation in the story of Abraham and Isaac. They too evolved from potential to actual sacrificers and sacrifices.

In fact, Rachel's story is not far apart from the new representation of the *aqedah.* Abraham, we recall, took the knife to slaughter his son. One of Rachel's friends offered first her assistance in performing the horrible act. So she "took the knife to slaughter her (Rachel's) son," before it eventually ended up in Rachel's hands. More generally, the women of Mainz are described as stretching out their necks for each other to be sacrificed.[79]

Not only Ashkenazic men, therefore, could personify their Abraham as the actual sacrificer. Women like Rachel were also transformed into the patriarch's equal.[80] By the same token, were young medieval girls molded into the Ashkenaic view of biblical Isaac. The women of Mainz are said to have performed both roles. Rachel's daughters, Bella and Matrona, prepared the slaughtering knife themselves so their mother could sacrifice them. *Aqedot* in the Rhineland became gender-blind.

The sparse examples of women taking others' lives suggest that such responses were not the expected norm. Moreover, the casting of women into the role of Abraham only by insinuation reveals the authors' discomfort in making such associations. The term *aqedah* is usually attached to men to depict them as sacrificers. Indeed, references to women exiting life violently, and to women taking other lives, do exist. But these references are general and sketchy, with only a few detailed descriptions.

Two concrete examples of women taking others' lives exist in the narratives. The only relatively detailed example of a woman slaughtering herself is the woman from Speyer. Her only common ground with the mythical woman is her anonymity. The *Mainz Anonymous* leaves out this woman from Speyer altogether. Attention must be given to the absence of males in these examples of women sacrificers. Rachel's husband enters the picture much too late, only to see his deceased children. He appears to have been elsewhere fighting the crusaders. According to Eliezer bar Nathan, Yental, Rebecca, and the young lass were kept in isolation because the burghers "put them under guard, each one separately, until the morrow, so that they would not kill themselves, for they heard that others had killed themselves."[81] Necessity shifted to the besieged women the responsibility of saving the children from forced conversion by simulating the sacrificial ritual. Under this condition, the same maternal instinct that often impels women to sacrifice their own lives for the sake of their children drove these women to sacrifice the *halakhic* code and the traditional female martyrological role.

These two examples of women killing their youngsters constitute an exception that proves the rule in the Hebrew accounts. This rule appointed males to be the sacrificers of women, children, and themselves. Sacrificing was presented by Abraham and Temple priests as the male religious duty. Women had to make themselves available in assisting their husbands to perform this duty. These examples demonstrate the tension that was created by the simultaneous representation of martyrs as traditional and innovative figures. On the one hand, the authors assure the readers that these women emulated their ancestors; on the other, they repeated the rhetorical question: "Behold, has such a thing ever happened before?"[82]

By presenting women as original and daring martyrs, the authors could praise them as exceptional. For the same reason, even the crusaders are said to have noticed the women's role in motivating men to fulfill their ritualistic duties. This observation spurred the authors to include the "new Ashkenazic women" in their attempt to hold up the entire generation as distinctive and superrighteous. As the images of the Ten Martyrs, the Temple priests, and the *aqedot* were incorporated to rebut Christian polemics, so was the equality between Ashkenazic men and women.

Christian women had already proven that gender distinction and traditional restriction did not apply to them.[83] To Albert of Aix's dismay "adulterers, murderers, thieves, robbers and deceivers, all the multitude of Christians, *among them even women*," took the cross.[84] Regarding the massacre of the Jews, he added, "Count Emico, Clarebold, Thomas [the mob's leaders], and all that intolerable company of *men and women* continued on their way to Jerusalem overloaded with the Jews' booty."[85] The response of Christian women to Pope Urban's call constituted an integral component of the "miracle" that was taking place in Europe. Even women who did not partake in the crusade enjoyed papal support in deciding whether their spouses should join the crusade. Young married men, urged Urban, needed to receive the consent of their wives before participating in the crusade.[86]

Once fighting against the Turks took place, Christian women actively participated in battle. Similar to the Hebrew reports of Jewish women offering support from the windows, "Christian women" are said to have encouraged the crusaders from the windows in the walls.[87] At Nicaea, women assisted the crusaders constantly with logistics. They were also "courageously yelling encouragement" to the crusaders who fought and defended them. These were not isolated cases. "Christian women" watching the battles encouraged the crusaders and applauded their victories as was their "customary way" (*sicut mos erat illorim*).[88]

The Hebrew reports are well aware of the participation of Christian women in the crusade and in their contribution to the Jewish disaster in particular. "Every man and woman" undertook the pilgrimage until they exceeded the locusts on the land.[89] Christian women did more than just take up the cross, however. They ignited and guided some of the attacks on the Jews. "A gentile woman" is stated to have sparked the attack at Mainz. She arrived with her goose "that she had raised since it was a gosling," screaming at all passersby: "Behold this goose understands by itself that I intend to go on the crusade and wishes to go with me." As a result, "the crusaders and the burghers and common folk gathered against us . . . with swords to destroy us."[90] In Trier, we are led to believe, Jewish women initiated the aggressive response.

Christian women assumed an active role in the attacks on the Jews and in the crusade in general. It was noticeable enough to draw the attention of the Hebrew chroniclers. The participation of women in the holy pilgrimage required the Jewish authors to keep the balance between Christian and Jewish heroism in the narratives. Jewish females assumed thus the function of devaluing Christian female zeal. Only by the heroism and ardor of Jewish women could the Hebrew narrative appropriately devalue the same claims about Christian women. Christians like Albert of Aix viewed Jewish women differently. Horrified, he wrote: "mothers slashed the throats of suckling children with knives and stabbed others. They preferred that they perish by their own hands rather than be killed by the weapons of the uncircumcised."[91]

Albert reported about these killings, but failed to see their ritualistic and social aspects. Jewish women desired first and foremost to fulfill an inner social and religious need. The Jewish versus Christian race for piety stimulated the Jewish authors to depict their heroines in a similar way.

The three narratives of 1096 do not openly present the Jewish craving for heroism as a counterresponse to Christian aspirations of the time, much less as being inspired by Christian zeal. Both Jewish men and women are presented as an incomparable breed of martyrs that the world had not seen before. This violent form of polemics aimed at parrying the theological challenges presented by the crusade and crusaders. In the examples presented thus far, this polemical goal was achieved by Jewish symbols. Even though undergoing significant mutations, these traditional symbols spoke plainly and directly to their Jewish audience. The next set of symbols still spoke to Jews, but they were taken mainly from the authors' twelfth-century environment, and so the crusaders could appreciate them as well.

7

∾

Ve Ashkenaz: Manifestations of a Milieu

In parallel to the use of traditional Jewish symbols, a number of twelfth-century popular concepts filtered into the Hebrew narratives. They represent the fusion of old and new images. Three of these motifs are discussed here: (I) the concept of absolute love and devotion, (II) the ideology of chivalry, and (III) the belief in celestial reward for the martyr. Twelfth-century Jews and Christians made extensive use of these concepts, reflecting the nature of their shared milieu.[1] While the Jewish symbols turned the Rhenish heroes into emulators of past protagonists, the examples in this section also depict the Ashkenazic martyrs as *defending* themselves as Jewish crusaders. It is the presentation of these modified symbols that could have lent support to the authors' claims of unprecedented heroism in 1096.

Although the use of these concepts in a martyrological context was an adaptation of contemporary Christian ideals, such use reveals the internal function martyrdom had within Franco-German Jewry. Together with their old symbols, the martyrs and the narrators utilized these concepts mainly to deliver messages to their fellow Jews, who would judge the martyrs' behavior by the ideals of the period in addition to the ancient principles of their religion.[2] At the same time, these messages addressed the polemical arguments that Christians were making during and after the attacks. Contemporary symbols in the martyrological proclamations made these counterpolemics comprehensible to the Christians as well.

"THEY LOVED YOU UNTO DEATH"

As I argued earlier, love in the context of martyrdom does not abound in Talmudic and midrashic literature. *Midrash Elleh Ezkerah* ignores this theme. Its only use of love appears in R. Yeshabav's nonmartyrological recommendation to love justice and peace.[3] A later version of *Asarah Harugei Malkhut* makes only one reference to love. That is, the angels proclaimed that already the first generations had loved God, even in hardship, and that Akiva and his friends received upon them the kingdom of heaven with love.[4] More frequent references to love in terms reminiscent of the papal bulls appeared in *Sefer Yosippon*.

It is no surprise, of course, to find martyrs in the Hebrew chronicles pronouncing the *Shema*, "with all their heart, soul, and might" (Deuteronomy 6:5), such as Akiva. The eleven hundred casualties from Mainz appear as martyrs who sanctified God's name "with all their heart and soul." In the anonymous account the biblical phrase is quoted word for word.[5]

Another biblical expression of love is provided by Song of Songs 1:3, erroneously attributed in our texts to King David. "Therefore do the maidens (*alamot*) love you, they love you unto death," was given martyrological significance.[6] Our texts follow the midrashic play on the word *maidens* to mean "love unto death" (*ad mavet*). But in these texts the old concepts of love resumed new meanings.[7]

Although the medieval heroes appear as "old-fashion" martyrs, love of God becomes their motivation. Therefore, they are said to have "accepted out of love the divine judgment." More hyperbolically, "out of love and affection they accepted upon themselves seven deaths." They were therefore held as God "lovers [who] are as the rising sun in might" (Judg. 5:31). Collectively, the communities are said to have "sanctified the sacred Name with love and affection."[8] In fact, the reason for the entire ordeal was presented as an opportunity "To announce to all and in the retinue of high [heaven] their affection" for God.[9]

More than being a manifestation of adoration of the divine, love of God appears as the reason for voluntary death. The martyr Shemaryah is quoted as saying, "All I accept upon myself out of love." His proclamation recalls Akiva's final hour (B. *Berakhot* 61b). But the verse is in fact the only resemblance to Akiva, who was executed by others. Shemaryah took the life of his family to prevent their forced conversion. After he survived his own suicide attempt, the crusaders buried him alive with his family.[10] The chroniclers do not seem disturbed by the chasm separating Shemaryah's actions from Akiva's passive death. On the contrary, more Ashkenazic martyrs are said to have made use of the sage's words to compare their self-sacrifices and others' to his.

Such was the function of the *Shema* in the story of the forced convert Isaac bar David the *parnas*. The *Shema* here endures one of its several unconventional applications. Isaac had slaughtered his two children in a synagogue, set his mother's house on fire with her inside (against her will, we may add), and eventually, set the synagogue ablaze on himself. All this took place after the crusaders had already left town and the danger had dissipated. Although Akiva refused only to bypass the opportunity of loving God with all his heart, Isaac is described as fulfilling God's command to cleave to Him "with all our hearts and souls."[11]

These biblical verses and metaphors did more than embellish the Ashkenazic text: they helped rationalize all patterns of voluntary death. Thus also the self-killings and the killing of coreligionists in "*Ilana*" are defined as acts of love commended by God. There Jews "roused themselves to perform their Creator's command and loved Him unto death."[12] The reference to martyrs in the third person clearly indicates the authors', not the actors', attempt to rationalize such radical acts as resulting from an imperative love desired by God and that had been performed already by Akiva. The *Mainz Anonymous* indiscriminately concludes that all martyrs and communities acted like Akiva and his companions.[13]

This comparison did not stem only from a contingency to rationalize radical forms of voluntary death that the Talmud never recommended. It derived also from a pressure to present events in contemporary Christian terms. We should recall that only a few decades earlier, such terms still had not enhanced the story of the French Jewish martyrs. Christian martyrological prescriptions for loving God penetrated the Ashkenazic delineations of *qiddush ha-Shem* in the twelfth century. Augustine's strongest desire to "see and love, love and praise [God]"[14] was regenerated by early papal calls and during the crusade in particular. In the last two decades of the eleventh century, Anselm of Canterbury urged every person to strive for God "by loving and desiring it with all his heart, all his soul, and all his mind."[15]

Quoting these symbolic verses was typical of the twelfth century. The First Crusade chronicler, Peter Tudebode, expressed the notion of love by this biblical verse. Knight Bohemond's comrades asked him not to punish William Carpenter for defecting from the battlefield. Only because of love did he agree. But he could trust William not to defect again only if he would swear "with all his heart and mind" (*toto corde et mente*).[16]

For God's love, the crusader Rainald is reported to have "undertaken martyrdom" (*pro cuius amore martyrium suscepit*). "Those knights of Christ," are said to have suffered cremation for the God whom they loved.[17] According to Fulcher of Chartres, the crusaders suffered many different painful deaths, "all for the love of God." Love of God remained one of the crusaders' strongest motivations for martyrdom. So strong, in Fulcher's opinion, that love alone would have driven crusaders to volunteer for martyrdom. If the enemy's sword had failed, he still believed, "Many of us would not have refused martyrdom for the love of Christ."[18] Love of God remained the crusaders' motivation for dying, even when it was not voluntary. In fact, love became a synonymous term for martyrdom. Cyclically, this love of God was the gift of God. Only those implanted with divine love could offer their love in return. In a view similar to that found in the *aqedot* of the Hebrew accounts, Christians deemed the challenges of the crusade as "trials" (*temptationem*) of their love (*diligeremus*) for God.[19]

In addition to loving God, brotherly love formed an equally important reason for giving up life.[20] Because Jesus had shed his blood for Christians, repeated Urban, it was "charity to risk your life for your brothers."[21] As part of the campaign to free all Christians, Urban deemed it significant that the "almighty God aroused in your hearts a love of your brothers."[22] The two loves, or in other words, dying for God and humans, remained indistinguishable throughout the expedition. Crusaders were said to have risked their lives "out of their love of God and their neighbor."[23] Dying for these two reasons was important enough for Urban to grant remission of sins in return. "No one must doubt that if he dies on this expedition for the love of God and his brothers his sins will surely be forgiven. . . . " Not only love of Jesus, but also "love of your brothers" could bring heavenly and earthly rewards.[24]

The cultural impact on the Hebrew texts is demonstrated most forcefully by the appendage of brotherly love to the martyrological love of God. Love in the Hebrew texts meant a desire to die for God and, not least significant, for coreligionists. Dying for brethren veritably qualified as *qiddush ha-Shem* in 1096. Ashkenazic brotherly love meant the readiness to perish for the other and for the community's important symbols. Moreover, brotherly love implied the willingness not only to expire but also to inspire. In our texts, martyrs exhibited their loyalty to God and, not least important, to their group. To die a martyr meant to belong.

Such social factors played a role in the story of Jacob bar Sullam, who "did not come from a notable family and whose mother was not from Israel [i.e., not Jewish]." Jacob is reported to have "called out in a loud voice to all those standing around him: 'Until now you have scorned me. Behold what I shall do now.'" He took a knife and slaughtered himself. Through martyrdom, Jacob proved his loyalty to Judaism and, by proving it, he gained the recognition of his new brothers and the author's admiration.[25]

Dying voluntarily also confirmed the Jewish identity of a certain new convert from Xanten. He asked Rabbi Moses the *Cohen*: "What will be my fate if I slaughter myself for the unity of his great Name?" The rabbi assured him, "you shall sit with us in our circle . . . and with other saintly true converts in their circle . . . You shall be with our ancestor Abraham who was the first of the converts." The convert slaughtered himself without hesitation to be with his brothers in life and death. Martyrdom reconfirmed the convert's Jewishness.[26]

In these two examples, social forces did not drive fully integrated individuals to martyrdom but rather individuals whose commitment to the group's ideology was doubted by the group. Martyrdom gave Jacob bar Sullam and the convert from Xanten the opportunity to put to rest the group's doubts and, as we learn from the convert from Xanten, the martyrs' own doubts. By dying voluntarily, Jacob bar Sullam and the convert could gain the group's final and absolute acceptance as their equals in society.[27]

The report about Rabbi Yequtiel bar Meshullam and his son-in-law demonstrates not only the wish of two individuals to die together but also their wish to die with their brothers, who had been previously killed, and lie next to their bodies. After fleeing from Mainz, the two decided to return to their town to realize their death wish.

Rabbi Yequtiel bar Meshullam and his son-in-law were killed there on the

road between Mainz and Rudesheim when they returned to the place where Rabbi Kalonymous, his brother, the *parnas*, had been killed [with his followers], for they intended to return to the city, Mainz, *in order that the enemy would kill and bury them there in the cemetery with their brethren* the pious, the upright, and innocent.[28]

Brotherly love is said to have impelled the two to seek death and to expire with and for their fallen comrades.

Love is said to have compelled Rabbi Samuel bar Gedaliah, "the bridegroom," and Yehiel bar Samuel toward their joint martyrdom. These two were

"cherished in life," for *they loved each other* exceedingly; "they were never parted in death" (II Sam. 1:23). When they decided to throw themselves into the water, they kissed one another and held one another and embraced one another by the shoulders and wept to one another.[29]

Somehow they survived their *salto mortale* from a tower into the Rhine River. They continued to float there alive until the rest of the community arrived. Yehiel's father found his dying son in the water. In an act of mercy killing, the father took the life of his dying son. When Samuel heard the father's intentions to destroy his friend Yehiel, he begged to be killed first, "so I shall not see the death of my friend." Thus they were slaughtered together. Echoing King David's elegy on King Saul and his son Jonathan, the two friends are said to have fulfilled the verse: "They were never parted in death" (II Sam. 1:23).

As seen, the desire to die to avoid witnessing the death of colleagues is reminiscent of R. Ishmael's request in *Midrash Elleh Ezkerah*. But the criteria and conditions of the milieu invigorated this principle of brotherly love unto death. Even the borrowing from David's elegy on the first king and his son could hardly disguise this cultural tendency. The biblical dirge may have indirectly legitimized the drowning and slaughtering of the two friends. Yet in the cultural context of the period, the final hour of the two was meant to look more like that of the praised crusaders who died in battle for each other. As Saul died together with Jonathan in the battlefield, the rabbi and his friend died in their battle with the crusaders in the same manner European nobility had been animated to do. The special relationship between Samuel bar Gedaliah and Yehiel bar Samuel signifies more than just a relationship of two friends. Like Saul and Jonathan, the relationship paralleled a blood bond between father and son, between two heroic combatants. It is this praised bond of the period that encouraged each to undertake death for the other.

The desire to join coreligionists in death was the highlight of heroism in Europe. It was considered noble and meritorious to die honorably with and for others. A good illustration is furnished by "the very noble knight" Guy. After hearing the false report that the Turks had killed all the besieged crusaders with their leader Bohemond at Antioch, Guy delivered an elegy that well captured this principle. While the Hebrew story about Samuel bar Gedaliah and Yehiel bar Samuel used David's dirge to express brotherly love, David's elegy on his son Absalom (II Sam. 19:1) adorns Guy's lamentation over his beloved Bohemond:

Woe's me, sorrowful as I am! I have not even been found worthy, to my grief, to see your most excellent countenance, although there is nothing that I desire more. *Who will give me a chance to die for you*, my sweeter friend and lord? Why did I not die at once when I came out of my mother's womb? *Why have I lived to see this accursed day?* Why did I not drown in the sea, or fall off my horse and break my neck so that I might have died at once? *O that I had been so lucky as to suffer martyrdom with you, that I might behold your glorious death!* [30]

Guy's dirge may look like an emotional breakdown. As Tancred's dramatic elegy on the death of his overlord, whom he disliked, demonstrates, it was proper knightly conduct to lament so dramatically over fallen comrades. [31] The entire picture of besieged crusaders, their massacre by a cruel enemy, the survival of some, and the survivors' wish to join the casualties in an unnecessary martyrdom is duplicated by our Hebrew texts. Death not only for the love of God but also for the love of brothers was considered noble. Both theological and social reasons (if we can really distinguish between these two factors in the Middle Ages) are said to have driven Jews and crusaders toward voluntary martyrdom. Unlike the crusaders, Jews found themselves in this contest for heroism unwillingly. Once trapped in this violence, the same brotherly love that is said to have convinced many Europeans to embark on their heroic journey accounted for many instances of *qiddush ha-Shem* in our texts.

"THE VALOROUS WHO REPEL ATTACKS"

"Love of God" and "love of brethren" coalesced in the well-known medieval ideal of chivalry. The twelfth-century English philosopher John of Salisbury explained the function of orderly knighthood. The knight's duty was "to protect the Church, to fight against treachery, to reverence the priesthood, to fend off injustice from the poor, to make peace in your own province, to shed blood for your brethren, and, if needs must, to lay down your life."[32] Basically, John consolidated the missions assigned to the nobility in various papal calls for sacred campaigns against the enemies of the church. At the turn of the eleventh century, then, the chivalrous ideal, which combined paradoxical elements of cruelty and love, peace and bloodshed, the celestial and the terrestrial, became popular, international, and completely Christian. In the name of love of God and brethren, the knights exhibited their valor on the battlefield when enlisted by the Church. The knight's heroism became the celebrated motif of the troubadours and the topic of various medieval myths. European interest in chivalrous heroism increased especially during the crusades.[33]

The strong possibility of dying as a soldier of Christ was turned from an impediment into an inducement. "With the authority of the prophets" Urban urged his audience to " 'Gird thy sword upon thy thigh, O mighty one . . . ' *for it is better for you to die in battle* [emphasis mine] than to behold the sorrows of your race and your holy places."[34] Urban stimulated more than just the "the minds of knights." The image of the knight also stimulated the minds of the masses, who then desired to join this elite brotherhood and be transformed into the "knights of Christ."

If fighting to the death was considered the most noble and religious act, escaping from the battlefield became the most sacrilegious act crusaders could have committed. Fleeing was considered disgraceful and evil. William Carpenter became the "most shameful and wicked" person in all the provinces of Gaul because he had attempted flight from battle. His treason earned him the dubious title "vilest man on earth." By this "disgraceful" and "vile" act, William and alike betrayed more than just the cause. They betrayed the "army of Christ" (*milites Christi*).[35]

Even those returning from battle unsuccessfully were remonstrated against as the "vilest and saddest of Christians." Abandoning the camp went beyond a betrayal of military comradery. Failure in combat alone could be qualified as treason against the leader of the sacred campaign, Jesus himself.[36] Thus when the chance of survival seemed grim, "the knights of the true God" (*milites igiture veri Dei*) were urged to remember how their ancestors had made war and charged as "the most valorous Christian athletes" (*fortissimus Christi athleta*), a phrase traditionally applied to Christian martyrs. The inevitable message of these examples coincides with Urban's advice that it was better to die in battle than to survive in defeat.

In a letter to the Monks of Vallombrosa, Urban calls the participation of the knights in the crusade the "right kind of sacrifice" (*recta oblatio*). Those staying behind were advised to follow the model of the altruistic knight. They should devote their lives to the protection and support of their communities as did the knights. "If the knights of other provinces have decided with one mind to go to the aid of the Asian Church and to liberate their brothers from the tyranny of the Saracens, so ought you with one mind and with our encouragement work with greater endurance to help the church so near you resist the invasions of the Saracens."[37]

Left behind with the Christians were the Jews. Ashkenazic Jews did not remain apathetic to this trend. Nor could they be ignorant of the knights' important ceremonial tournaments. When one reads the three Hebrew chronicles of the First Crusade, the heroism at the core of these sources becomes self-explanatory. Equally praised were those who fought back. Yet, the chances of overcoming the attackers were scanty from the outset. In fact, the term "fighting" may be misleading. Given the discouraging conditions that suddenly surrounded the Jews, fighting the masses would have been illogical. After all, even the professional armies of the bishops and mayors were occasionally overwhelmed by the crusaders.[38] The initial solution seemed to lie in avoiding confrontation rather than in trying to overcome the enemy by force.

From the Jews' point of view, the crusaders could deprive them of their lives, but they could not take the spiritual victory from the martyrs. Unlike the temporary victory of the crusaders, who succeeded in driving some of the Jews into the bosom of Christianity until Emperor Henry IV permitted the converts to return to their original faith,[39] the Jewish martyrological victory was irreversible and eternal. As a number of descriptions claim, the Jews awaited the crusaders because they desired a heroic ending. Jewish martyrs felt compelled not to desert the conflict. Fleeing would be impious and ignominious. This attitude fitted in not only with the martyrs' religious world but also with the spirit of the period. This spirit venerated the chivalrous ideal of fighting to the death and of committing suicide when victory appeared to be out of reach.[40]

The "passive" martyrological pattern consists of two subgroups. Jews who were declared martyrs although they tried to avoid death form one subgroup; Jews who awaited the crusaders only to be killed by them form the other. It is the latter that gives testimony to the influence of the medieval chivalrous ideal on Rhineland Jews. Our interest here lies with the martyrs who "did not wish to flee." Once again, the chivalrous virtue contains the component of love. At Mainz, Jews seeking shelter at the bishop's palace are described in such terms:

They clothed themselves in their fine prayer shawls and had seated themselves in the courtyard to rapidly do the will of their Creator. *They did not wish to flee into the rooms in order to live transient life* [emphasis mine], for out of love they accepted upon themselves the heavenly judgment. The enemy cast stones and arrows at them, but they were not anxious to flee. "They struck all those whom they found there, with blows of sword, death, and annihilation." (Esth. 9:5)[41]

Others who witnessed the slaughter of their brethren were inspired to sacrifice their lives as well. This honorable demise is immediately followed by the depiction of women who sacrificed their children. Terms and metaphors helped create images of chivalrous combat that included men and women. "The men of Israel drew out their weapons in the innermost courtyard of the bishop." Women "gird their loins" with strength to make sure that they and their children would perish before the crusaders could reach them.[42] The "battle" here does not appear to be with crusaders. It is a struggle between these women's maternal affection and their will to perform the sacrifices.

The prelude to the description of the events at Mainz speaks in broad, but clear, military terms. Echoing David's dirge over the death of King Saul and his son Jonathan in battle, the introduction in Mainz alludes to the tragic end of this encounter. Because they were "pleasant in their lives and in their death they did not part" (II Sam. 1:23), these Rhenish casualties desired to stay together to the bitter end. They were like "the valorous who repel attacks" (Isa. 28:6) in a battlefield of no withdrawal. Through Isaiah 28:6, Jews appear as crusaders doing battle. At the same time, the verse distinguishes Jews from the Christians they imitated, for the verse speaks of the righteous's just wars.[43]

In the *Mainz Anonymous*'s version, events at Mainz mirror a typical medieval battle. A "tremendous multitude" of crusaders approached the besieged city's gate with banners. The Jews, then, "donned their armor and girt on their weapons of war, great and small, with Rabbi Kalonymous bar Meshullam at their head."[44] As in the Latin reports, a motivating speech is addressed to the warriors just before the battle. Next, "They all approached the gate to do battle with the crusaders and the burghers and they fought one against the other."

Kalonymous and his group failed to protect the gate because of sins. The same reason accounted for the crusaders' military fiascos in the Latin reports.[45]

Surely, Jews took protective measures and were perhaps legally permitted to carry weapons in self-defense.[46] But the combative terminology inflates, if not distorts, the picture of events at Mainz. No concrete information of a real battle is reported and, surprisingly, no casualties are reported on either side. What offsets the "shameful" withdrawal from the gate at Mainz is the final, self-inflicted martyrdom. It restored Jewish honor in both the survivors' and their neighbors' eyes.

Several individual cases of chivalrous conduct are also provided. To die honorably was the task of Isaac bar *Elyakim* of Cologne. According to Eliezer bar Nathan, the crusaders captured Isaac because he refused to escape from his house. The *Solomon ben Simson Chronicle* turns this story – tragic but otherwise banal for this violent episode – into a more admirable event. Accordingly, Isaac was caught after leaving his house. He was then taken to a nearby church to be baptized.

He spat before them and before their shrine and cursed and rebuked them. They killed him there for the sanctification of the Name, for *he did not wish to flee because of the custom of honor* [emphasis mine] and because he was happy to accept the judgment of heaven.[47]

The incident is transmuted into a chivalrous duel. The author is well aware of the knightly "custom of honor," which explains Isaac's refusal to flee. Isaac thus is presented as following his religious code in a manner that coincided with the chivalrous criterion of *honoris causa*. By the standards of the period, fleeing from battle would have been both sacrilegious and atrocious.

A customary overture, similar to the general introduction to the events at Mainz, precedes the more detailed example of doing battle at Worms. Villagers and burghers joined the crusaders in their attempt to eliminate the Jews who had found shelter at the bishop's palace: "They [the crusaders] laid siege on them [the Jews], and they fought with them. There transpired a very great battle, those against the others, until they [the crusaders] captured the chambers in which the children of the sacred covenant were." Realizing that "they were surrounded by war" and that "they were not able to fight against them," the Jews accepted the "decree of the King of Kings" and slaughtered themselves. Surprisingly, no actual casualties of battle are reported on either side in this great war.[48] Instead, Jews are reported once again to have destroyed themselves and their families.

Almost all lay dead when the crusaders wished to baptize the survivor Rabbi Simhah the *Cohen*. "In his wisdom," a hint that things are not really what they appear to be, he consented to be baptized before the bishop. In the presence of the bishop and his nephew, Rabbi Simhah vented his true intentions.

He took out his knife and "*gnashed his teeth*" [emphasis mine] (Ps. 37:12; Job 16:9) against the prince, the bishop's relative, as does the lion over its prey (Isa. 31:4). He ran toward him [the prince] and stabbed the knife in his stomach, and he fell and died. From there he turned away and stabbed two more until the knife broke in his hand. They all fled to and fro. When they saw that the knife had broken, they attacked him and killed him.[49]

This time actual fighting is detailed, however nominal. For once, a Jew put the crusaders on the run. The story is reminiscent of Eusebius's martyrs. Like Simhah, these martyrs turned the table on their executioners. They

gnashed their teeth [emphasis mine] and made signs with their faces and stretched out their hands, and gestured with their bodies.... before anyone could seize them they rushed up to the tribunal saying that they were Christians, so that the governor and his council were affrighted. And those who were on trial appeared most courageous in prospect of their suffering, while their judges trembled. And they went exultingly from the tribunal rejoicing in their testimony, God himself having caused them to triumph gloriously.[50]

How exactly Eusebius's nonviolent martyrs came to the attention of the *Mainz Anonymous* cannot be determined. It is possible that they reached the *Anonymous* via crusading preaching that turned Eusebius's heroes into modified combative role models.[51] A similar modification characterizes the Hebrew account and was easily achieved by the two biblical verses that embellish the report. Both verses allude to sacred military confrontations. Psalms 37 describes the attempts of the impious to capture God's land. By swords and bows the impious "gnashes his teeth" in an attempt to massacre the pious (*yishrei derekh*), literally those who take the "straight path" (Ps. 37:14). But God foils the evil plan and protects His righteous.

For the medieval author and his readers, the implication was crystal clear. Crusaders captured the Holy Land by swords and bows, massacring European Jews on their way. As in the past, God will eventually destroy the crusaders (*ha-toim*) – literally those going astray, but also the homophone "the erroneous ones" – and protect those staying the "straight path" (*yishrei derekh*). By association, Psalms and the reverse application of 37:12 turn the reality of 1096 on its head. Ashkenazic Jews become the pilgrims of a "straight path," on which the righteous combatant Simhah "gnashed his teeth" (a biblical metaphor originally applied to evildoers) against the evil crusaders, who were on the wrong path.

An analogous metamorphosis is achieved with Isaiah 31:4. It speaks of the "army of God" that will swoop from heaven to protect Zion. Descriptions of the heavenly army of God descending to do battle on behalf of crusaders abound in the Latin reports.[52] In the reality of the twelfth century, the verse could allude only metaphorically to a Jewish "military" victory. A sense of utter defeat, as opposed to the triumph of the crusaders, left the author no other choice.

As a literary tool, Isaiah sets Simhah's story in a battle atmosphere suitable to the period. Isaiah, too, assisted the narrator to reverse the roles and self-images of the players in this drama. Simhah represents a concrete example of the knightly Jewish hero, who refused to capitulate and single-handedly took three lives. The death of a prince, a high-ranking knight in other words, was Simhah's first victory. The prince and his fellow Christians dramatize the defeat of cowardly villains, as "They all fled to and fro" in panic. Moreover, they were able to overcome Simhah only when they realized that his knife had accidentally broken. It is hard to imagine, however, that the armed crusaders encircling Simhah would wait for his knife to break to strike him.

This description of Jews and Christians engaged in great battles is antithetical to their medieval images. An indication of this unique role reversal arises from the author's conclusion. "There the young man [Simhah], who sanctified the [Divine] Name, was killed. He did what *the rest of the community did not do* [emphasis mine], that he killed three uncircumcised with his knife." This conclusion contradicts the general tenor of the story and sheds light on the proportions of the great battle depicted in the opening statement. As we observed above, then, the "great battle" itself claimed no combative casualties after all, except for Simhah.

A more modest and realistic picture is painted by Eliezer bar Nathan. He says nothing about Simhah's request to be taken to the bishop. It was the crusaders who took him to the church. There, Simhah managed to kill only a "knight," the bishop's nephew, in a surprise attack, before "they immediately cut his body into pieces." Regarding Simhah and his like, Eliezer quotes Judges 5:31, "They that love Him shall be as the sun when it goes forth in its might."[53] This was Eliezer's way of alluding to the knightly qualities of a victorious Jew, who gave up his life as an act of love for God. Judges 5:31 concludes Deborah's and Barack's victory poem after the defeat of Sisera against all odds. The verse mocks God's enemies and praises His heroes. The presentation of love of God as Simhah's motivation for fighting sits well with the medieval knightly idea.

The *Solomon bar Simson Chronicle* omits the entire story. Thus we are presented with two different stories of Simhah's heroism – and no story at all. Discrepancies, of course, are not unheard of in such confusing circumstances.

It is more than likely, however, that we may attribute such discrepancies to the interest of the two authors (especially the *Mainz Anonymous*) in creating images of heroic Jewish knights in grand battle scenes. What started as a seemingly Jewish defeat in a great combat at the bishop's palace ended in "an impressive victory" of honorable self-sacrifice.

The above descriptions create a picture of medieval Jewish fighters, always ready for combat, rigged with armor and weapons. More accurately, our accounts employed temporary metaphors to depict the Jews of 1096 not only as passive sacrifices but also as heroes fighting the enemy. So understood, these depictions restored Jewish honor both in the context of the old Jewish and the more current Christian traditions.

The Jewish narrators aspired to illustrate the unique martyrological qualities of their protagonists. But these depictions of fighting Jews include attributes that were characteristic of the period. In trying to emphasize the uniqueness of this particular Jewish behavior, the metaphors described acts that were praised by the Europeans. Unlike knights, however, Jews were not equipped with galloping horses, shining armor, lances, and swords. They girded themselves with the weapon of spirit, whereas creative authors girded themselves with the quill to build their heroes on the chivalrous models of their time.

In describing the spiritual battle between Jews and crusaders, the Jewish narrators could not acknowledge external influences openly. Writing, however, for different purposes and in a distinct style, the Ashkenazic author of the twelfth-century *Sefer Hasidim* felt comfortable in drawing a comparison between the Christian chivalrous and Jewish approaches to the challenges of daily life. The chivalrous characteristics shaped the standard thinking of the Ashkenazic Pietists (*Hasidei Ashkenaz*), the descendents of the 1096 martyrs. The force of this concept is shown by its influence on the Pietists' everyday "inward decision making."[54]

If heavy misfortune befalls a man let him think of the knights who go to war and do not flee before the sword for they are ashamed to flee, and so as not to expose themselves to shame they let themselves be killed or wounded . . . Thus let him speak with the Scripture: 'Though he slay me, yet will I trust in Him, and I will serve him without hope of reward.'[55]

Sefer Hasidim explicitly reflects on the two poles of the knightly honor code. As in the examples of 1096, Pietists are reminded of the honor associated with the knightly altruism and the shame that follows a failure to exhibit it. To be a Pietist was as difficult as death, but to abandon "death" was to succumb to shame.[56] Precisely the fact that martyrological language is used to describe everyday nonmartyrological challenges reveals the influence of this mentality on Ashkenazic Jews.

Other indications for the prevalence of this mentality in Ashkenaz are furnished by the medieval annotations (*Tosafot*) of Franco-German rabbis. This legal material confirms that it was the custom of Ashkenazic Jews to emulate the knights' tournaments at joyous events. Young men performed before the bridegroom make-believe knightly fights in which they were permitted to tear each other's clothes or slightly injure the rival's horse.[57] Similar make-believe depictions of great battles were applied to the *real* Jewish casualties of 1096.

Jewish law obliged the faithful to cleave to their religion unto death in certain cases, but it was the standards of an elite Christian order that made the faithful's flight from challenges an unbearable plight. Crusaders envisioned death as a better solution than defeat. Rhenish Jews attempted to prove themselves equal in spirit and service to their zealous Christian neighbors who agreed to lay down their lives to achieve their physical and spiritual goals.

"A GOLDEN THRONE UNDER THE TREE OF LIFE"

While the application of the crusaders' chivalric ethic to Jewish martyrs meant that they could be presented as crusaders, the employment of an innovative system of celestial recompense also allowed Jewish martyrs to be rewarded like crusaders. Our earlier Jewish sources provided no significant details about martyrs' heavenly rewards.[58] Vague references to *olam ha-ba* or *Gan Eden* refer at times to terrestrial messianic events and even to the garden's geographic locations. Yet, no celestial world of martyrs is detailed in these descriptions. *Sefer Yosippon* indeed employed the metaphor of light and darkness to indicate a better possible existence, but its contemporary, the letter from Bari, has no rewards for its three martyrs. Let us also recall that just about half a century prior to the First Crusade, the "1007–1012" report assigned no celestial benefits to the French martyrs.[59]

In contrast to this comparison with the early martyrological accounts, a comparison between the Ashkenazic accounts and their contemporary twelfth-century Latin sources reveals a great affinity. Pope Urban's speech promised *indulgentia* and celestial rewards to crusaders. Europeans left for the Holy Land with Urban's promise of remission of sins to "whoever shall offer himself to Him as a living sacrifice." By sacrificing, promised Urban, they would receive "an hundred-fold [more than on earth] . . . and everlasting life . . . in the kingdom of heaven."[60] Baldric of Dol's version has Urban urging those who would "sacrifice" themselves to "be sure that to have died on the way is of equal value, if Christ shall find you in His army. God pays with the same shilling, whether at the first or eleventh hour." Whether occurring on the road to Jerusalem or on the battlefield, "celestial Jerusalem" became the final destination of the dead.[61]

As the crusade progressed, so did the number of casualties. They all were believed to continue living in a very well-defined heaven. "We ought not at all consider them [the casualties] as dead," admonished Emperor Alexius, "but as living and transported to eternal and incorruptible life" (*sed ut vivos et in vitam aeternam atque incorruptibilem transmigratos*).[62] Based on Luke 16:22, the martyrs' resting place was also known as Abraham's bosom.[63] Adhémar, Bishop of Le Puy, "who by God's will fell mortally ill and by God's nod, resting in peace, fell asleep in the Lord, namely in the *bosom of Abraham*, Isaac, and Jacob (*in Abrahe videlicet sinu et Isaac et Iacob, in sancti Petri a Vinculis Sollempnitate*). His most happy soul rejoiced with the angels."[64]

Abraham's bosom became also the destination of the captured crusader Rainald Porchet. Forced by Emir Yaghi Siyan to choose between Islam and death, "Rainald with clasped hands prostrated himself in prayer toward the east, humbly he beseeched God to come to his aid and that his soul be received with dignity in the bosom of Abraham" (*suamque animam in sinu Abrahe dignanter suscipiat*). His wish is said to have been granted. "The angels immediately received his soul with joy and singing of Psalms in the sight of God."[65]

Life in heaven was lavish. But three inducements are said to have motivated crusaders to strive for Paradise.[66] Martyrdom guaranteed the reunion with relatives, friends, and brothers in arms. It also earned crusaders an exclusive place in the divine ranking with saints and with past heroes in whose footsteps they followed. Among them we find Abraham the Patriarch, whom we just met, Saint George and Saint Michael, and the Maccabees, who were seen as the perfect combatant martyrs. The strongest motivation, however, remains the old Christian offer to be next to (or in) God and enjoy the vision of Him. Anselm of Canterbury already had promised that in heaven God's lover "*shall then see [the Supreme Beatitude] face to face* [emphasis mine]."[67] Crusaders similarly beseeched God that He might make all Christians, all bishops, clerks, and monks "who are leading devout lives, and all the laity – to *sit down at the right hand of God* (*ut ille vos ad dexteram Dei considere faciat*) [emphasis mine]."[68] The "*visio Dei*" (or beatific vision) constituted the crusaders' ultimate compensation.

Jews, too, are said to have overcome the natural fear of death by heeding the promise of everlasting life. Remarkably analogous to Emperor Alexius's exhortation is a contemporary Hebrew poem cautioning that "We ought not question [the destiny of] the dead (*redumim*), for they have been destined and bonded for everlasting life."[69] Life in the Jewish heaven was as lavish as in its Christian equivalent. Golden thrones awaited martyrs in heavenly palaces. On each head a golden crown with precious stones and pearls was placed;[70] golden necklaces adorned their necks.[71] In the heavenly palace each newcomer was dressed in the eight vestments of clouds of glory, "crowned with two crowns, one of precious stones and pearls and one of fine gold."[72]

Martyrdom offered life in a heavenly world full of all the riches of this world, "a world full of bounty."[73] Biblical verses embellish this popular medieval connection between voluntary death and martyrological compensation: "'How abundant is the good that You have in store for those who fear You, that You do for *those who take refuge in You* [emphasis mine]' (Ps. 31.20). They shall forever exult. 'Light is sown for the righteous, radiance for the upright'" (Ps. 97.11).[74]

Although the Hebrew sources speak collectively of the generation of 1096 as the generation that "had been chosen to be His portion,"[75] they emphasize their protagonists' personal heavenly rewards. "Everyone who has been killed and slaughtered for the sanctification of His Name" enjoyed these heavenly bounties:[76] rabbis and congregants, men and women, boys and girls, slaves and maidens. Yet what is said to have motivated Ashkenazic Jews to die are the very same three inducements that appear also in the Latin accounts.

Securing a place with deceased friends and family in heaven appears to be of great importance to the martyrs. Coinciding with the concept of brotherly love, this desire further explains the importance of collective killing and self-killing. It also explains why individuals like Rabbi Yequtiel bar Meshullam and his son-in-law returned to Mainz only to be killed next to their slaughtered brothers, who had already been "whole with God."[77] Being with friends in Paradise provided another reason for Rabbi Samuel bar Gedaliah and his friend Yehiel bar Samuel to perish together. The verse, "they were never parted in death," takes on a new meaning. These two, who "loved each other exceedingly" in life, would continue to be together in heaven. For the convert Isaac the son of David, the slaughtering of his children and himself became more than his atonement. He hoped that "Maybe He will do according to His benevolence and *I shall still join my comrades and come with them to their circle, to the great light* [emphasis mine]."[78]

Isaac's atonement earned him much more. In the author's view: "His soul is hidden in the portion of the saintly in *Gan Eden*."[79] Being with the saintly is presented as yet another motive for voluntary death. Among the saintly could be found biblical, Maccabean, Talmudic, midrashic, and more recent martyrs who had inspired voluntary death in 1096. If, by emulating reworked past heroes, Rhenish Jews could become like them, then through death they could dwell with them. The Jews of Mainz are said to have known that "Blessed is everyone who is killed and slaughtered and dies for the unity of His name. He is destined for the world to come and will sit in the circle of the righteous, R. Akiva and his companions, 'the pillars of the universe,' who were killed for His Name."[80] Others are said to have joined the three biblical models Hananiah, Mishael, and Azaria.[81] More generally, R. Shmuel and Yehiel desired to die together because it was "Better for us to die here for His Exalted Name and *we shall stroll with the saintly ones* in *Gan Eden* ... [emphasis mine]."[82]

Abraham the Patriarch plays an essential role in the martyrs' exits from life as well as in their existence in the afterlife. Abraham's *aqedah* is said to have both inspired child sacrifices and insured the martyrs a place next to him in heaven. As in the Latin accounts, however, Abraham assumed additional roles. Abraham is not only a celestial inhabitant, but also the heavenly habitation. In the story of R. Meshullam ben R. Isaac of Worms and his wife Zipporah, Abraham's bosom serves as the final heavenly resting place of their sacrificed son, Isaac. God Himself "will take him as his portion and place him (*va-yoshivo*) *in the bosom of Abraham*."[83] The phrase "in the bosom of Abraham" appears to blend in almost naturally with biblical motifs. As the focus is on the *aqedah*, no details are provided to explain the meaning of Abraham's bosom.

In the following story, Abraham's bosom denotes the martyrs' immediate reward in heaven in the same manner as it appeared in the Latin accounts. After watching the mass self-killing of three hundred Cologne Jews, the young Sarit attempted to escape the horrifying scene. Her fiance's father, Judah ben R. Abraham, would not let her fear stand in the way of her religious loyalty. Despite her initial reluctance to join the mass sacrifice, her place in heaven was unquestionable. Reenacting in fact the *aqedah* story (the binding of Isaac), her father-in-law,

[S]eized her and held her outside the window and kissed her on the mouth and raised his voice in weeping along with the lass. ... The pious Judah said to her: "My daughter, *come and lie in the bosom of Abraham* our ancestor, for in one moment you shall acquire your future and shall enter the circle [*mehitzah*] of the saintly and pious." He took her and placed her *in the bosom of his son Abraham* [emphasis mine], her betrothed, and cut her with his sharp sword into two pieces. Thereafter he slaughtered his son as well.[84]

The *aqedah* is not the primary theme in Sarit's story. Central to the story is the phrase "in the bosom of Abraham" as a metaphor for martyrs' salvation. Sarit was assured this heavenly reward, despite her refusal to be sacrificed. She was destined to be with the saintly in their gathering place, Abraham's bosom.

Particularly does Sarit's narrative echo the Christological interpretations of the phrase. Christian martyrology often describes martyrs as the virgin bridegrooms or brides, martyrdoms as weddings, and the heavenly reward as a union with the spouse Jesus or the father. The liturgy for Catholic celebration of the Feast of the Assumption provides one of numerous such examples:

The Virgin Mary is taken up into the bridal chamber of heaven, where the King of Kings sits on his starry throne. O Virgin most prudent, whither goest thou, bright as the morn? all beautiful and sweet art thou, O daughter of Zion, fair as the moon, elect as the sun.[85]

In addition to liturgy, medieval art frequently presented the popular theme of Abraham with souls on his lap, this being the final intimate bond of the soul with the Divine.[86]

Sarit's story combines these elements of eroticism with the image of Abraham's bosom. She is described as the beautiful virgin bride. Because the crusaders would not let her wed her fiancé, Abraham, his father dubbed her coming sacrifice "the wedding of my daughter-in-law." Next, he invited her to "*come and lie in the bosom of Abraham.*" (It is no coincidence that in R. Meshullam's story Isaac is *seated* in Abraham's bosom.) Sarit's father-in-law, continues the account, placed her (*va-yashkivah*) in the bosom of her fiancé, Abraham, and sacrificed them both. Sarit's eternal union, therefore, starts on earth with Abraham of the flesh and is immediately consummated with the heavenly Abraham of the spirit.

Sarit is merely one of many such references to brides, bridegrooms, and weddings. By this symbol, a tragic event was turned into happiness. The analogy of bridegrooms and brides illustrated the martyr's commitment and loyalty to God and God's people, and the allusion to sexuality represented the generation and regeneration of Jewish life. Thus Samuel the *bridegroom* and his friend Yehiel lamented, "Woe for our youth, for we have not been deemed worthy to see seed go forth from us," before trying to take their own lives. But they were comforted by their coming heavenly compensation.[87] Sexuality and regeneration was an important aspect of the narratives, for it contradicted the crusaders' goal of discontinuing Jewish tradition. Obviously, the martyrs intended to avoid transgression by death. But as paradoxical as it might sound, death affirmed the continuation of life under the canopy of religion.

Seeing and sitting next to God constituted the ultimate martyrological reward. Even *Hikhalot Rabbati* was not ready for such a daring notion when speaking of the Ten Martyrs. Accordingly, "Everyone who watches Him is immediately torn and everyone who gazes at Him is immediately poured out like a jar."[88] In parallel to the Latin reports, the martyrs of 1096 were seated on God's right side. "They shall be of that *section*, preferable to Him more than the other. They are destined to *stand and sit in the shadow of the Holy One*, blessed be He, *standing on His right* [emphasis mine], as is said: 'From His right [hand] a fiery law' (Deut. 33.2)."[89]

Perhaps the best illustration of the three heavenly rewards as motivations for voluntary death is provided by the aforementioned event at Xanten. Enjoying the divine vision constitutes the optimal fulfillment in the imagery of this account. The congregation assembled for their last Sabbath meal. Then the priest leader said to the congregation: "Let us recite the grace to the living God, to our Father in heaven, for the table is set before us instead of the altar." Christian and Jewish symbols are at work here. I already mentioned the association of the "priest higher than his brothers" and his speech with the highest priest, Urban, and his sermon at Clermont. The meal becomes the would-be martyrs' last supper, the table is transformed into an imaginary altar and the Grace after Meals into their sacrificial benediction; the Xanten community turns into the morning burnt offering.

Whether expressed by the anonymous leader or added by the narrator to embellish an actual event, it was done with the Talmudic tractate B. *Berakhot* 5b in mind. It reveals that "Not everyone has the merit of two tables," symbolizing this world and the world to come. But "Whoever says the benediction [in the Grace after Meals] over a full cup of wine will be granted a boundless inheritance and will be worthy to inherit two worlds, this world and the world to come" (B. *Berakhot* 51a). This ritual, together with the coming sacrifices, assured the congregants a place in heaven. As Urban authorized celestial rewards, it is, once again, the priestly authority in the rabbi that confirms the celestial benefits of their immolations.

The difference between Xanten's narrative and *Berakhot*, however, is critical. The Talmud alludes to a world to come lived on earth; the passage below refers to the heavenly Gan Eden.[90] The association of voluntary death with the burnt offering points to the heavenly direction the martyrs of Xanten are about to take.

We shall exist in a world that is entirely light, in Gan Eden, in the *shining speculum*, and *we shall see him eye to eye* (*ayin be ayin*, Isaiah 52:8), *in his actual glory and greatness....* We shall be *seated there among 'the pillars of the universe'* and shall *dine in the company of the saintly* in Gan Eden. We shall be *in the company of R. Akiva and associates.* We shall *sit on a golden throne*, under the Tree of Life, and *each one of us shall point at Him with his finger and say: 'Behold this is our God Whom we hoped for.* Let us cheer and gladden in His salvation'[Isa. 25.9; *Taanit* 31a]. *There we shall observe our Sabbaths* [emphasis mine], for here, in this world of darkness, we cannot rest and observe it properly.[91]

Thereafter, continues the account,

They themselves became like the daily offering of the morning. . . . *They all came happy and rejoicing before the exalted and sublime God.* With regard to such as them it is said: '*Like a groom coming forth from the chamber,* like a hero eager to run his course.' [Ps. 19.6] So did they rejoice to run and enter into the *innermost chamber of Gan Eden.* Pertaining to them the prophet prophesied: '*No eye has seen [O] God except you who acts for him who waits for Him.*' [Isa. 64.3; *Ber.* 34b][92] [emphasis mine]

"We shall see Him eye to eye" is another addition of the twelfth-century Jewish author. It is strikingly reminiscent of Anselm's jargon and his promise of seeing God face to face. Isaiah 64.3 intensifies this notion in Jewish and Christian works. In *The Life of Marie d'Oignies* (1177–1213), the very same verse is used to indicate that the vision of God is reserved for the suffering Christian believer.[93] In the Hebrew text, "No eye has seen [O] God except you who acts for him who waits for Him," stresses the point that the martyrs' ultimate reward is their direct vision of the divine. In the medieval syntax this verse could easily be read, "No eye has seen God, except you . . . ," that is, the martyrs. This reconstruction of Isaiah meant that only martyrs could enjoy such a reward. On a polemical level, this reading also assured that only Jewish martyrs – not Christian casualties, as Crusade thinking maintained – enjoyed this unique vision of God.

The language is the language of the Bible, Talmud, and midrash. The images, however, are taken from the twelfth-century medieval world. The salvation of the martyr and the triumph of the messiah, which follow the last supper motif,[94] a "pontiff's" motivation speech, both terrestrial and celestial hierarchies, and seeing God face to face had also marked the Latin narratives of the period.

In contrast to the previous depictions of martyrdom, the narratives of the martyrs of 1096 offer a rich corpus of symbols of heavenly reward. This eruption of martyrological symbolism and the remolding of the concept of reward must be seen, then, against the background of the First Crusade and the flourishing of the concept of heavenly reward in Christian circles.[95]

The concept of reward has a paramount function in the Christian propaganda of the period, promising the faithful every desired object of this world and beyond. The Hebrew narratives could not content themselves with an inferior reward. The concept of extraordinary reward was picked up simultaneously by Jews and Christians. It enabled both sides to enlist their zealous recruits for the ongoing spiritual battle for their truths. Equally significant, a celestial afterlife enabled Christians and Jews to rationalize massive loss of life.

The importance of heavenly recompense in the First Crusade's propaganda made the concept correlatively important for Jews, for it offered eternal existence to the martyrs and a bearable life to the survivors. Christian attempts to colonize and monopolize a martyrs' heaven stimulated the same trend among Rhenish Jews. Paradise's gates, therefore, were opened for *all* Jews by the three Ashkenazic accounts. With the help of biblical verses, these accounts introduced a novel heavenly world that had its parallels in Christian thinking. The martyrs' heaven became a major attribute of Ashkenazic writing and belief.

POLEMICS

Whether old or new, the previously discussed symbols were not without a polemical dimension. Although this cluster of symbols spoke to both Jews and Christians, until now we focused mainly on their messages to the former. New female and male martyrs were presented to the Jewish reader as chivalrous crusaders, and the new heavenly compensations were intended to praise and justify Jewish acts and encourage the reader of the Hebrew reports.

The following symbols were used to address crusaders in their own theological language.[96] Dialogues and metaphors were proposed to make the crusaders feel sordid and sour about their own conduct and their unsuccessful campaign of conversion. Moreover, through dogmatic Christian symbols, the Jews intended to frustrate and insult their rivals. Symbolic public acts and proclamations targeted Christian dogmatic principles. Dogmatic differences were challenged not only to exhibit strong Jewish convictions but also to display a holy Jewish resistance. Like Christian martyrdom, the polemical nature of the Jewish response required that the acts be witnessed and heard by all.

The principle of the Trinity was among the main targets of the Jewish martyrological counterattack. "Hear, O Israel! The Lord is our God, the Lord is one" (Deut. 6:4) was one such tool in a series of rebuttals. This proclamation assumed a special meaning in 1096. With this final proclamation of one living deity, the principle of the Trinity was refuted. In conjunction with the *Shema* the divinity of the dead Christ was also scorned. His human corporeality and transientness could not be compared to their living, illimitable, and immaterial God.

The theological differences are demonstrated by David the *Gabbai*. He is said to have called out loudly to his attackers: "I believe in the God who lives forever, who resides in the highest heaven." David expected to be with His God in heaven, whereas his audience would be in hell with their "deity, who was crucified."[97] Moses the *Cohen*'s address to the Jews at Xanten as the "children of the living God" made this point clear. He reenforced the point by "proclaiming loudly and in unison: 'Hear O Israel! The Lord is our God, the Lord is one.'" The same proclamation reverberated in Mainz, Worms, and other localities.[98]

That Christians understood the polemical nature of the *Shema* against the Trinity is clear, for instance, from Peter of Blois. His twelfth-century *Contra Perfidiam Judaeorum* specifically addresses such Jewish polemics.[99] He writes: "the trinity in one God and unity in three beings excites scandal and horror in the Jews." To show their disbelief in the trinity they proclaim: "'Hear, O Israel, the Lord is our God, the Lord is one.'" And as the Jews admonished their Christians neighbors in their proclamations, Peter forewarned that "Anyone who fails to believe in the eternal generation of the Son from the Father and the temporal generation from the mother incurs the sentence of prophetic curse."

A more direct dialogue regarding the characteristics of the true God appears in the story of Shemaryah. After surviving his own attempted suicide, he was buried alive with his deceased wife and children for a day to rethink baptism. The following day, the villagers dug him out to hear his response. Shemaryah refuted the Christian axiom of Jesus' live return from the grave, mocking their belief in a hanged man. Several times Shemaryah refused to acknowledge the Christian dogma, which, of course, must have included Jesus' resurrection from the grave. Instead, he proclaimed: "I shall not deny a living God for a dead, rotting corpse."[100] Women are said to have addressed the same question to crusaders. "In whom do you place your trust? In a decaying corpse."[101]

Baptismal water also came under verbal attack. Abraham bar Asher was vigorously asked to "defile himself" with baptism. Despite the physical threats, Abraham placed his trust in the "Living God" instead of in "the evil waters."[102] The Hebrew chronicles repeatedly convey the crusaders' intention to baptize the Jews in "sullied" waters. Xanten Jews, for instance, reacted with voluntary death to the "'seething water' that came upon them." In Mainz, the mortally injured refused to be "defiled" and revived by the baptismal water, despite their great thirst and suffering.[103] Natronai ben Isaac combined these two elements in his response to an attempt to "defile him in their evil water." Instead, he slaughtered himself "for the unity of the unique and holy Name."[104]

Reverse reenactments of baptism became another way to refute Christianity. In every suicide, the method of killing is a function of the available tools. Rivers and lakes, however, served as more than a drowning place; they became a public stage for the ritualistic sacrifices to spite baptism before the crusaders. Regarding this mechanism in the more general context of medieval polemics, Marcus writes:

they [Jews] managed to act out and reconstitute those combinations of Jewish and Christian traditions to fashion a parody and counterritual as a social polemic against the truth claims and values of the majority culture ... They [Jews] assimilated reworked aspects of Christian culture, in the form of a social polemical denial, into their Judaism.[105]

Several examples demonstrate the mechanism described by Marcus. A number of Jews had foreseen the crusaders' attempts to baptize them and had averted the danger by escaping to the lakes near an unidentified town. To be sure, these Jews did not seek a hiding place, but a specific public platform.

Toward evening they sanctified the Name there exceedingly. Bridegrooms and beautiful brides, old men and old women, young men and young women stretched forth their necks and slaughtered one another and gave their souls for the sanctification of the Name in the lakes which surrounded the town.[106]

Jews fled to the lakes not simply to slaughter themselves. Any other place would have been suitable for self-annihilation. Their first intention was to sacrifice themselves ritualistically in the water. It was important for this group of people to sacrifice themselves in the lakes and before the crusaders' eyes. Others chose a less violent death; they "ascended the tower and threw themselves into the Rhine River that was around the town and drowned themselves in the river."

That ritualized killing in water was by design is suggested also by the story of Rabbi Samuel ben Yehiel. He and his only son "*fled* into the water." Only then and there, did the son "stretch out his neck to his father for slaughter as they stood in the waters." As the statement "Behold, all ye mortals" implies, Samuel's act was not addressed merely to Jews.[107]

In the previously discussed version, Samuel's son, Yehiel, died with his friend Samuel bar Gedaliah. They were slaughtered together in the water after having survived their plunge from a tower. In the dialogue attributed to the two friends lies an explanation as to why water provided the proper arena for their final hour. The two deemed it "Better to die here [in the water] for his great Name ... than that these uncircumcised and unclean capture us and sully us against our will with their evil waters."[108] A sharp symmetry between the "evil waters" of baptism and the pure lake water is kept. Only after avoiding the "evil waters" and washing themselves in the lake could they ascend clean and sacred to heaven. In reality, the crusaders ascribed the same purity to the same bodies of water, and it is the same thought that drove both groups to these meeting places.

The rest of the community approached the lakes later on. A grim sight of floating bodies was revealed to them and they, with Yehiel's father, Samuel, began to identify the dead. When finding his living son among the dead, Samuel immediately decided to help his son realize his death wish in the water, although it seems that the danger had already passed. The graphic depiction includes words and actions.

"Yehiel my son, my son, stretch forth your neck before your father and I shall offer you up as a sacrifice before the Lord, the life of my son. I shall make the blessing of slaughtering and you shall respond amen." So did Rabbi Samuel the pious and slaughtered his son with his sword in the water.[109]

The story does not end with Yehiel's death. Samuel bar Gedaliah urged Menachem, the beadle of the Cologne synagogue, to slay him, too, in the water. Menachem agreed. Next came the turn of Yehiel's father, Samuel, to die in the same fashion. Eventually, Menachem fell on the sword in the water. Rabbi Solomon bar Simson concludes his description of the event by emphasizing "... in this way these pious ones sanctified the holy Name of the zealous and avenging [God] in the water." Many others, according to Solomon's report, perished in the same manner.[110]

Apart from its symbolic refutation of baptism, this gory scene of multiple mutual and self-killings in water made perfect sense theologically and polemically, precisely because it was taken from the medieval Latin world. Orderic Vitalis, who narrated how the chaplain of Earl Hugh of Chester presented martyrs as exemplars, provides a correlative scene in the battle between the Franks and the Normans: "Soldiers clutching each other as they fell, killed themselves and their companions with their own weapons; others, mortally wounded or battered, fell into the sea to drown."[111] Such behavior on the battlefield was praised as martyrdom. Drowning is also given theological significance by the crusader Fulcher of Chartres. He applied this view to the crusaders' drowning catastrophe at Brindisi. Some of the four hundred bodies that floated in the port of Brindisi after their ship had capsized were found with crosses imprinted on their backs. "By such a miracle, those dead had already by God's mercy obtained the peace of everlasting life. . . ."[112]

The Hebrew texts, then, put to work various medieval socioreligious standards in a Jewish context. In so doing, they justified the Jewish behavior and simultaneously rebutted the very same socioreligious ideas that contributed to the martyrs' extinction. If Jews could not avoid conversion, they would at least die heroically. By falling on their swords in the water, they not only protected their identity but also symbolically thrust a sword in the hearts of the religion of those who attempted to convert them.

Not all escaped forced conversion, however. Others were "baptized against their will."[113] Forced baptism was reversed by voluntary immersion unto death. Isaac the Levite was "defiled" after being tortured into insensibility. Regaining his consciousness, "he returned to his house in Cologne, stayed there a short while, and then went to the Rhine River and drowned himself." Clearly this acting-out by reverse baptism, which was intended to deny the very same Christian rite, was not spontaneous. Nor was it without merit. "It is of him and the likes of him that it is said: 'I will bring back from Bashan, I will bring them back from the depths of the sea' (Ps. 68:23)."[114]

Psalm 68:23 brings back to the surface the Jewish connotation of the immersion in water. First, by dying in water the bodies underwent the obligatory ritual of purification before burial. Apart from the allusions to recompense and purification, the verse approves here the return of forced converts to Judaism. Bringing Isaac back from the depths of the sea meant first and foremost his rescue from Christianity and reconciliation with Judaism. Jews fought baptismal water with water.

Both Jews and converted Jews chose water as their final forum, so to speak, for one more reason. Returning to water denotes returning or cleaving to Judaism. Water had long symbolized Torah and Torah study as a source of learning and life.[115] Dying in water, therefore, meant cleaving to the Torah and to everlasting life. One author applied the symbolism of yearning to die for the Torah and God as one craves water to all types of voluntary death. "These pious ones yearned to sanctify the awesome and honorable Name joyfully and good-heartedly and as a man going to the banquet, and [they yearned] to sanctify [the Name] as the heart pants after the water brooks."[116]

The symbols associated with qiddush ha-Shem were not random. Nor did they address only Jews. Actions and words were addressed to the watching crusaders. From the Gesta Treverorum's statement that Jews were "stabbing their children in their stomach in order to transmit them into the bosom of Abraham" (in sinum Habrahae transmittere), we know that Christians paid attention to the Jewish proclamations and actions.[117] From the point of view of the actors involved in the drama of 1096, a spiritual war was in progress. For the crusaders, a victory meant the conversion of the Jews. For the defenseless Jews, victory was achieved by refusing to do the crusaders' will. This, however, was not enough. By acting in a manner opposite to that which was expected from Jews, they brought Christological principles under attack. The crusaders offered the Jews life by the water of baptism; the Jews preferred instead death by the waters of the Rhine or, metaphorically, eternal life in the Torah. From the martyrs' standpoint, the method of self-killing was as significant as the killing itself, for through these provocative rituals statements were delivered.

The crusaders' growing frustration, which one can sense time and again in the Latin and Hebrew chronicles, indicates the effectiveness of the martyrological strategy. Polemics thus added a new dimension to Jewish martyrdom. Polemics contributed to a development of a new martyrology that, like Christian martyrology and hagiography, presented martyrs as voluntarily dying in public spectacles to deliver taunting proclamations, with the new assurance that it would earn them a place next to the Divine.

These social martyrological polemics made clear to both sides how far apart they had grown. Crusaders brought Jews unwillingly to the Rhine River intending that they should become one people.[118] Rivers and lakes became their meeting place. But instead of uniting the groups, waters became a physical and spiritual platform for departure, both from each other and for heaven. A river broadened by martyrs' blood separated the two groups forevermore.[119]

8

∾

Singing in the Fire

In the Hebrew chronicles of 1096, *qiddush ha-shem* appears as an indispensable and dominant characteristic of German Jewry.[1] Contributing to this impression was the long scholarly interest in Ashkenazic martyrdom, which
tended to minimize, if not to ignore, the chronicles' reference to forced
conversion.[2] As the authors and scholars focused on the different forms of
self-destruction, long-lasting effects on both European Jews and Christians
were attributed to these destructive reactions. Let us first examine the impact
of the Jewish behavior on the immediate Christian environment.

CHRISTIAN PERSPECTIVE

In a most controversial and instrumental study, I. J. Yuval has suggested
that the phenomenon of Rhenish Jews taking the lives of their own children
created a negative Jewish image in Christian eyes, which led to the infamous
blood libels of the Middle Ages. If Jews could take the lives of their own children, some Christians would believe, they would not hesitate to take the lives
of their children to fulfill what Christians saw as religious Jewish rites. Indeed,
Yuval's argument looks logical.[3] But as Yuval himself warns, the Jewish behavior alone cannot fully explain the connection he has made. Clearly, the
Ashkenazic self-inflicted violent reactions to baptism did not help the Jewish
image in already prejudiced Christian eyes. But given the direction in which
anti-Jewish and antiheretical feelings were taking during the eleventh and especially the twelfth centuries,[4] I believe that libels were bound to arise anyway
in relation to the "other." It is essential, therefore, to examine these negative
images in Christendom in a general context prior to 1096. Equally important is
to inquire how common was the phenomenon of Jews sacrificing their own
in the twelfth century.

As seen, accusations of heretics sacrificing their own children to Satan had already been made in Orléans in 1022. In the twelfth century, Guibert of Nogent leveled the very same accusations of orgies and child sacrifices against the heretics of Soissons.[5] It should come as no surprise to find the local Jews being artificially linked to these heretics and their alleged perversity. Count Jean of Soissons (ca. 1082) is said to have "practiced the perfidy of the Jews and heretics," saying blasphemies that even "the Jews did not dare to do." Jean's mother exceeded her son's immorality – once again, with the assistance of a certain Jew. "With the help of a certain Jew she had poisoned her own brother through greed for his county." The Jew was burned "because of that," whereas the murderous mother was stricken by paralysis and for a while "lived the life of a pig."[6] It was only a matter of time until the violence against the heretics caught up with eleventh-century French Jews. And it was only a matter of time for Jews to be moved from "supporting" to "leading" roles in these calumnious plots, regardless, of course, of their actual conduct.

By 1096 Jews were also seen as poisoners of wells. But the allegation that Jews scalded a Christian body to pollute a well with the boiled water had surfaced as a pretext for the massacre at Worms before Jews had a chance to put their martyrdoms on display.[7] Yet there was nothing in Jewish behavior able to be misconstrued in any way to create these imputations. It was also suggested that the Jewish practice of scalding vessels on the Passover eve contributed later on to the image of Jews scalding Christians and polluting waters.[8] But rather than reflecting Jewish behavioral contributions to anti-Jewish images, such accusations project Christians' fears of their own actual and imaginary practices and behaviors. After all, it was the Christians who dug out the "rotten body" to support their plot against the community of Worms. They were successful only because the general fear of polluted waters had existed in Christian minds beforehand.

The poisoning of water was only one of the fears that predated the First Crusade. Already Raoul Glaber had described how the great famine at the turn of the millennium drove good Christian women to lose "all maternal love" and kill their babies in the same way Christian sons killed their fathers.[9] Graphic stories of Catholic mothers killing their own incestuous children, sons murdering their parents, or women applying magic to kill their husbands also circulated in the Latin West. Very often such stories of religious *moralis* narratives ended on a positive note. Realizing they were doing the devil's work, these murderers become meritorious through repentance and loyalty to the church.[10]

The First Crusade, especially, offered the Europeans an opportunity to repent. Had not Pope Urban called on faithful Christians, "the children of

Israel,"[11] to sacrifice themselves for their Father, as Jesus died to satisfy his? Was it not Mary who gave up her son for the salvation of humankind, thus encouraging the Europeans to do the same for her? Did not Christian men and women promise the pope "with one accord ... to follow in the footsteps of Christ," namely to literally sacrifice themselves and all that stood in their way for him if needed?[12] Through Christian lenses, such abnegations were seen as the zenith of religiosity. In a Jewish context, Christian society viewed such devotion as diabolical. These two sides of the same coin were viewed differently by the factions involved. The resurgence in stories of parents and children sacrificing themselves and others in the twelfth century should not surprise us, then.[13]

Similar projections of unconscious fears because of a Christian practice are reflected in the accusations of body scalding and poisoning water. Saints' bodies were boiled in water to remove the flesh before transport of the skeleton for burial in a different locale, where it would become the saint's shrine. Thomas Aquinas's body provides one of the more famous examples.[14] A less known example is provided by Bede's *Ecclesiastical History of the English People*. Seven years after her burial, the brothers resolved to raise the bones of the abbess Æthelburh and translate them to another church. They found her body untouched by decay. "They washed it again, clothed it in other garments and translated it to the church of St. Stephen the Martyr."[15] One can only imagine the awe and horror created by such scenes of holiness.

Such stories were not confined to churches and monasteries. Popular stories about Christina the Astonishing (ca. 1150–1224), for instance, claimed to have her jumping "into cauldrons of boiling water and standing there immersed either up to the breast or the waist depending on the size of the cauldron." Christina performed these miracles after she had returned from the dead to show the power of God and convert the unbelievers – including Jews.[16] And poisoning wells and cities by catapulting dead bodies over the walls of besieged enemy cities was the crusaders' favorite method of biological warfare.

Finally, Gregory of Tours accused a Jewish father of killing his own son to prevent his voluntary conversion. The child is said to have survived his ordeal in the fiery furnace because of Mary's miraculous intervention.[17] By the ninth century, Amalarius of Metz's *De Ecclesiastis Officiis* presented the killing of children as an evil Jewish practice that had been introduced by King Herod (Matt. 2) in an attempt to prevent Jesus' birth.[18] Obviously, these early negative depictions of Jews, not to mention heretics, killing their own were unrelated to the massacres of 1096. Eventually, contemptuous Christian views of both themselves and heretics, with their rational and irrational insecurities, were attached to the growing anti-Jewish feelings. The distinction between the various groups made no difference to the frenzied rioters. As Baldric of Dol put it, the crusaders "hated all passers-by alike, whether Jews, heretics or Saracens, for they regarded them all as the enemy of God."[19]

The more immediate impact of the 1096 events on the Christian majority was different, in my opinion. The violent interaction resulted in a greater Christian mistrust of Jews.[20] Unknown numbers of Jews promised to convert, but reneged on their commitment by destroying themselves and their families. Others who did convert redeemed themselves by the same ultimate method.[21] Many others did convert, yet returned to Judaism when the opportunity arose. That was the case, for instance, with the Jewish community of Trier.[22] Even clergymen overlooked on some occasions the Church's traditional policy and permitted forced converts to relapse to their original faith shortly after conversion.[23] The Jews of Prague, who had suffered forced conversion at the hands of Volkmar in 1096, were allowed to return to Judaism after receiving the permission of the bishop of Prague, Hermann.[24] Pope Clement III's complaint against the reversion to Judaism clearly indicates that Hermann was not the only one to act in this manner.[25]

For its part, the Jewish community welcomed back forced converts immediately after the bloodshed of 1096 and expressed sympathy and understanding for the less fortunate converts who could not return to their former communities and creed.[26] The moral support of the community and the flexible religious rulings of its leadership in regard to forced converts demonstrated that forced conversion should not always be conceived as a dead end, and they allowed, to some extent, leeway in similar cases to come. A number of Tosafists walked in the path that had been paved by Rabbi Gershom, the Light of the Exile, and Rashi[27] and accepted the return of forced, and even voluntary, converts.[28]

Those who remained Christian were probably remembered as former Jews, in the same way the aforementioned martyrs Jacob bar Sullam was remembered as one who "did not come from a notable family and whose mother was not from Israel [i.e., not Jewish]" or the new convert from Xanten. Involvement of force in the conversion of the new Christians was likely to arouse suspicion as to their true motivation. Baptism by force and backsliding of converts would only intensify the old Christian image of the stiff-necked, untrustworthy, and hopeless Jew.[29]

Nor could the Christian masses trust their own political and religious leaders in the matter of Jewish forced converts. Although Jews had not yet been seen as *servi camerae*, the violence against Jews might well have damaged the order and authority of the secular power in the eyes of the public. Dealing successfully with the mob became not only a Jewish problem but also the authorities'. Their commitment, especially that of Henry IV, Henry V, and Conrad III of Germany, where such efforts seemed to be needed the most, proved to be valuable and encouraging.[30] Henry IV and William II permitted the forced converts of the First Crusade to return to Judaism and recover their wealth.[31] Despite the canon law, several such leaders often permitted and even organized the backsliding of Jewish converts. Such policies would not be appreciated by the religious masses. As we shall soon see, this popular mistrust would have devastating effects on the Christian treatment of Jews in the long run,[32] significantly curtailing the key martyrological element of being able to choose between conversion or death. It is difficult, however, to detect this new development because the Hebrew accounts continued to employ the martyrological style of their Ashkenazic predecessors.

SHADES OF 1096

A clear test for assessing the impact of 1096 on future Jewish generations came sooner than expected. "Not even fifty years, the number of years of Jubilee, have passed since our blood was shed in witness to the Oneness of Your Revered Name on the day of the great slaughter," lamented Ephraim of Bonn.[33] His *Sefer Zekhirah* recalled the events of the Second Crusade as they were experienced by the thirteen-year-old Ephraim, who at the time was hiding with his family at the fortress of Wolkenburg. In additional accounts he related other tragic events that occurred in the second half of the twelfth century.[34]

A year after the fall of Christian Edessa in the east in 1144, Pope Eugenius's *Quantum praedecessores* bull called on the French nobility and King Louis VII to come to its defense. Attempts to exclude the lower classes from what would be known as the Second Crusade failed, however, and dark, menacing clouds gathered over European Jewry once again. In the language of the Hebrew First Crusade Chronicles, Ephraim reported, "Satan came to Ashdod to pillage Israel and Judah," once again.[35]

A major reason for alarm was the 1096 style of preaching of a Cistercian monk named Ralph – or Rudolf – in Ephraim's play on the Hebrew word *persecutor*. Repeating the calls of the First Crusade, he urged his listeners to do away with the Jews before encountering the Muslims. "At every place he arrived he spoke evil of the Jews ... saying: 'Avenge the Crucified One upon his enemies who stand before you; then go to fight against the Ishmaelites.'"[36]

Bishop Otto of Freising reported that Rudolf preached "in Cologne, Mainz, Worms, Speyer, Strasbourg and other places." As a result, "many Jews were slaughtered" in France and Germany. Rudolf's venomous preaching came as a surprise to Otto, for Rudolf was a learned priest who should have been familiar with the nonviolent Jewish policy of the Church.[37] Rudolf's venture came to an end when the archbishop of Mainz appealed to Bernard of Clairvaux. Bernard traveled to the Rhineland to contain Rudolf and address the populace.[38]

Overall, the Second Crusade demonstrates a successful example of ecclesiastical protection of Jews and of the control of violent mobs. Bernard of Clairvaux and Peter of Cluny succeeded in their efforts to suppress anti-Jewish feelings both in Germany and France. Bernard's words, "It is good for you to go against the Ishmaelites, but whoever touches a Jew to take his life, is as one who harms Jesus himself," could not have been more explicit.[39] Similarly, Bernard argued in France "not to persecute the Jews, not to kill them, and not to expel them," because the Church says, "Do not kill them, lest my people be forgetful."[40] Peter of Cluny expressed the same basic ideology, believing that Jews "should not be killed but rather punished for their crime."[41]

Ephraim of Bonn spoke in praise of Bernard. "When they heard [Bernard's words] many ceased oppressing and killing us." Were it not for Bernard, continued Ephraim, "no remnant and survivor would have remained of Israel."[42] Naturally, the absence of large-scale attacks on Jews reduced the need for performing the act of martyrdom. Words, however, were not enough. They were backed up with actions. When the Wolkenburg community suffered two casualties, the bishop swiftly reacted and "the eyes of the murderer were gouged out."[43] A deterring eye-opener, indeed. Bernard's preaching did not put an end to anti-Jewish feelings, but his moving sermons did prevent organized violence in the style of the First Crusade.[44] Who were, then, the unfortunate slaughtered Jews and how did they die?

Otto claimed that "the seed [Rudolf's call] struck a strong root in many German and French towns and cities" but described only German Jews who sought refuge from rioting mobs.[45] Ephraim referred to attacks against German and French communities. Both Otto and Ephraim did not mention attacks on English communities during the Second Crusade.[46]

Sefer Zechirah describes violent incidents mainly against German Jewry. Using the language of the First Crusade, Ephraim drew a picture of limited, spontaneous assaults by a few attackers. These assaults usually took place on roads between major centers. Such was the case of Simon of Trier, at Cologne. Exiting the city, he "encountered worthless persons ... who entreated him to profane himself and deny the living God" Simon "chose death out of love for God," and was decapitated. A choice is implied in the case of Gutala. After having been "caught" at the Main River town of Aschaffenburg, she is said to have rejected baptism in the "bitter (*marim*) water" until she *was drowned.*[47] This unclear account seems to indicate that she was forcibly baptized in the river, perhaps the Main River, as the play on the word *marim* may indicate.[48] If indeed forced baptism was the intention of her captors, her death makes little sense, unless it was only their initial intention, as the noticeable lack of choice in the brief account may suggest.

To the category of incidental attacks on individuals we may add a few more names. Unlike Simon, however, these individuals were deprived of the martyrological privilege of choosing their fate. Isaac bar Joel the Levite and Judah of Mainz were ambushed by a certain crusader while making wine at the harvest season outside the city. He struck them and went off.[49] A few crusaders attacked Rabbi Samuel bar Isaac "on the road between Mainz and Worms." In words similar to the chivalrous metaphors applied to the 1096 martyrs, he is characterized as "a valorous and pleasant man," for he succeeded in injuring three of his attackers.[50]

Others in this category of random violence were killed because of their own poor judgment. Riding out the storm in a shelter appears to have been a successful Jewish method of defense. To do otherwise proved to be a grave mistake. "In their youthful impetuousness," the brothers Abraham and Samuel decided to leave their shelter. "A wicked man" (*rasha*) struck and killed them, and went his way."[51] Conversion or religion does not come up in this encounter. This *rasha* (rather than crusader) is described as "an impudent Gentile who did not respect the elder and had no compassion for the adolescent." He immediately struck the brothers, without making any demands. Later on, the archbishop severely punished the murderer, after he was identified by the Jews. This information further attests the irrelevance of the ongoing crusade to the brothers' misfortune. These descriptions are of unplanned attacks on victims of opportunity in unpopulated places. Moreover, most victims appear not to have had the martyrological opportunity to choose between death and baptism. The victims of this group seem to have suffered an immediate end for being Jewish rather than an attempt to convert them.

At first glance, conversion does appear to play a role in the story of Rabbi Alexander bar Moses, Abraham bar Samuel, and Kalonymous bar Mordecai. Like the brothers Abraham and Samuel, the three fatally miscalculated the conditions. They were safe with their family in the fortress of Stahleck but decided to leave to take care of financial matters. A number of crusaders (*ha-toim*) urged the three to convert: "They refused, for they deeply loved their Creator even unto death. Kalonymous spat on the image of the crucified one in front of their eyes, and they slew him there. The others hid under the beds, but were severed and cut off."[52] Anti-Jewish feelings appear to have motivated the slaughter. But the three were also killed because they left the castle "to look into their debts and other matters." Financial benefits may have been an incentive to kill the already socially vulnerable Jews. The financial motive behind the attacks was clear to the Würzburg annalist. One of the severest critics of the crusade, the annalist believed that many crusaders pretended to act piously to cloak their true interest: gaining profits from their violence.[53] If financial gain constituted the attackers' motivation, baptism could not offer an escape for these Jews. Nor could we always assume that baptism was a sincere proposal. As we shall see, the masking of vengeance with virtue was to be a growing trend.

Although the advice to ride out the storm in shelters is clear, the incident itself appears a bit murky. Kalonymous was killed on the spot, whereas the others are suddenly reported to have "hid under the beds." How the jump in scenery occurred is not explained. Certainly, the spitting motif and the killing under beds appeared early in the First Crusade chronicles. Like the martyrs of 1096, these martyrs, too, are said to have died because they "loved their Creator unto death." Was Ephraim applying here more than just stylistic motifs found in the First Crusade chronicles to depict an incident of his own time? Answers may be provided by the following stories.

Continuing to focus on the tragic error of leaving shelter, Ephraim tells the story of a Jewess from Speyer named Mina. She "suffered for the sanctification of her Creator" after going out of the city.[54] Of importance here is that there is not only no ultimatum as to death or conversion, but there is a complete absence of any attempt to forcibly convert Mina. *The Mainz Anonymous* had already told the story of a Mistress called Mina, also from Speyer. She, too, found refuge in a house "outside the city." The anonymous account provides Mina's detailed dialogue with the crusaders, who persuaded her to convert. Conversely, Ephraim laconically reported that "they sized her and cut off her ears and the thumbs of her hands." The option of choosing her fate is not given to Ephraim's Mina.

It is, of course, entirely possible that the stories refer to two different women named Mina. Such a coincidence appears less likely in the case of Isaac ben Elyakim. In February 1147, the "evildoers" attacked Würzburg. There, "a saintly person named R. Isaac, son of our Rabbi Elyakim . . . was slain over his book, and there were twenty others with him."[55] The *Solomon bar Simson Chronicle* had also reported on a pious man named Isaac ben Elyakim. He was brought to a church, where he "spat before them and before their shrine and cursed and rebuked them. They killed him there for the sanctification of the Name."[56] As in the previous comparison, the difference between these two stories is that no choice is reported to have been given to Isaac and his group. It is plausible that Ephraim, who based his Second Crusade account on hearsay and on his recollection, mistakenly included First Crusade names in his First

Crusade-style martyrology. It is interesting to note that Isaac ben Elyakim is the only martyr who is mentioned by name here. The reader, therefore, might tend to associate these reports with large massacres and the slogan "death or conversion." But this association needs to be examined more carefully in each case.

Isaac ben Elyakim represents one of the twenty-two lives lost at Würzburg.[57] The description thus differs from the rest as it represents the sole instance of a collective attack on a Rhineland community during the Second Crusade. Unlike those in other locales, Würzburg Jews made the costly decision not to escape to a nearby fortress. This fatal miscalculation drew the poor and the crusaders, who had falsely accused the Jews of killing a Christian man and dumping the body in the river. He was turned into a Christian martyr who allegedly continued to perform miracles from the water. In the Christian mind, these miracles provided undisputable proof of Jewish foul play.

The violence came to an end after the rest fled to the fortress of Stuhlbach.[58] The First Crusade served as a reason in its own right to massacre the Jews who rejected baptism, whereas in the Second Crusade a "reason" had to be found or, more correctly, fabricated. Fabrications were needed to legitimize large-scale attacks on the Jewish communities. The "finding" of the holy body, which was now performing miracles in the river, provided the "religious" *casus belli* for the attack. By its nature, the false accusation could be satisfied only by the punishment of the Jews. "So the errant one [crusaders] and all the poor fraction of the people, who rejoice for no reason, rose and struck them." Conversion could play an insignificant role, as the reported attempt to forcibly convert R. Shimon bar Isaac's sister testifies. She survived by playing dead.

What were, then, the characteristics of Jewish martyrdom in twelfth-century Germany? Clearly, Ephraim reported the developments of the Second Crusade in the style of his Ashkenazic predecessor. Yet a sense of better protection for the Jews is conveyed this time around. Most of the attacks appear to have been random outside the cities. Other attacks commenced with rumors of Jews murdering Christians. Many of the casualties might have been prevented had the victims shown more prudence. Despite the given background of the Second Crusade and the language of the First Crusade chronicles, the motive for victimization only infrequently appears to be related to crusading or to a desire to convert these Jews. Telling, therefore, is the fact that only rarely is a choice between death and baptism said to have been given.

Even more significant is the fact that none of these martyrs took their own lives or the lives of others. Based on the language and metaphors of our documents and, especially, the poetry of the period, however, these two factors may be forgotten. Following the First Crusade style and symbols of the *aqedah* and *qorbanot*, these twelfth-century documents aspire to match the heroic behavior and the magnitude of the First Crusade. This use of language occurred despite the crucial differences in the attackers' motivation and the attacks' unavoidable results. The culmination of the process is the development of the phrase *qiddush ha-Shem*. Although Shimon bar Isaac's sister survived her brush with coerced baptism, Ephraim describes her as "sanctifying the [Divine] Name."[59] Rejecting Christianity alone qualified as martyrdom. Such a philological cultivation necessitates a more careful reading of the post-1096 Hebrew accounts.

This literary tendency to present events against a First Crusade-like background with all its nuances of forced baptism and resistance continues to exhibit itself in the account of the incident at Neusse in 1186. An "insane" man brought a disaster on his community after slaughtering a young Christian woman in public. The "uncircumcised" reacted instantly to this insanity, looting and massacring their Jewish neighbors. Others were brought outside the city to be broken on the wheels. The mother of the "insane" was seized and buried alive, without a chance to convert. Yet the attack is made reminiscent of the First Crusade by a detailed description of her as the archetypical "mother who sanctified and professed the unity of the [divine] Name." Martyrological designations are also given to several rabbis mentioned by name, despite what appears to be their involuntary deaths. The ultimate act of associating these victims with the martyrs of 1096 is shown by their burial in Xanten, "at the graves of the righteous who were buried there during the persecutions of *Tatnu*."[60]

Analogous to the opening by Eliezer bar Nathan and the chronicle ascribed to Solomon bar Simson is Ephraim's report that "in the year 1196, in [the month of] Tamus, in the cycle of *Ranue*, the year in which we expected salvation and consolation turned instead to mourning," because many crusaders left to do battle with the Muslim. This fact, however, had little to do with the murders of R. Solomon and fifteen other Jews. Solomon, the Duke's administrator, imprisoned a certain thief for stealing from him. The arrest turned into a riot that claimed the sixteen lives. Not even conversion, which is not reported to have been offered anyway, could have saved Solomon and his coreligionists.[61]

Ephraim also paints an incident at Speyer in 1196 with the brush of the First Crusade. This time, the finding of a murdered Christian corpse triggered the looting and violence that claimed the lives of R. Asher ha-Levi and of the eight souls that were with him. Duke Otto's firm imperial policy quickly brought the turbulence to an end, forcing the attackers to compensate the Jews for the damages. Once again, conversion was not at issue, and the numbers of those *killed* are relatively minimal. Nevertheless, Ephraim inserts a line reminiscent of the First Crusade narratives. Without elaborating, he adds, "In that year many of the Speyer community took their own lives." Ephraim's laconic statement does not agree well with his constant reports of a small number of Jews being killed randomly or with his reports of firm imperial handling of the attackers.[62]

The assertion that some Jews were randomly attacked for being Jewish, with no intent to convert them, demonstrates the accurate report of Elazar bar Judah of Worms. Statements such as "this is the day that we (the crusaders) shall kill all the Jews," or "we decreed fasting and mourning," bring to mind the violence of 1096. However, the twelfth-century reality differed. Both the Jews and the authorities are said to have successfully "advanced a cure before a blow was landed," thus preventing numerous casualties.[63]

This does not mean that prevention always prevailed, as Elazar could personally testify. Two crusaders burst into his house, killing his wife Dulza and their two daughters. Dulza, it should be mentioned, was struck as she was screaming for help to save her family. Elazar, his son Jacob, and a student survived their severe injuries. Later on, the murderer was caught and executed. The killing of Jews for the sake of killing dominates Elazar's touching report. Neither a demand to convert nor self-killing is part of the swift encounter.[64] This first-hand report, I believe, is indicative of the violence, its motivation, and Jewish behavior in twelfth-century Germany. Avoiding conversion and martyrdom became equal goals.

Following the assaults on the German communities, Ephraim mentions larger attacks on the communities of Ham, Sully, and Carentan.[65] Quite significant is Ephraim's use of the First Crusade authors' style to report incidents that he clearly knew little about. Ephraim first briefly states that "also in Ham about one hundred and fifty souls were slaughtered . . . also in Sully many were slaughtered . . . [and] also in Carentan countless people were slaughtered." According to Ephraim, these Jews "were killed." Not so dry is his eulogy to the "martyrs of Ham." It praises the victims in the style and symbols of the First Crusade: "[Ham's] saints have been given over to slaughter. . . . Their share is with the righteous. None may enter into their realm. How great is their merit, for they have bound their immolates and prepared their sacrifices, like Isaac, their father."[66] The sketchiness of Ephraim's report hinders us from drawing solid conclusions regarding the behavior of the casualties. What can be said with more certainty is that the literary style of the First Crusade Hebrew narratives continues to dominate Ephraim's eulogy. Perhaps these narratives also influenced his brief reference to Carentan. In a manner reminiscent of descriptions of the Ashkenazic battles with the first crusaders in the courtyard of the Mainz bishop, Epraim reports of two "valiant brothers" who fought to save themselves and their brethren. "They also wounded and slew their enemies. Their opponents could not overcome them, until they [the enemy] came upon them from the rear into the courtyard and slaughtered all of them."[67]

Based on a careful reading of *Sefer Zakhirah*, it appears that martyrdom was scarce and spontaneous. Ephraim's identified martyrs perished at the hands of their attackers. Self-killing or the killing of coreligionist appears to be absent. But Ephraim's liturgical talent, which adopted the literary style of his Ashkenazic predecessors, presents his reports as an extension of the *aqedot* and *qorbanot* witnessed in 1096. *Aqedot* for Ephraim does not necessarily mean shedding the sacrificial blood of beloved ones. Yet, Ephraim concludes *Sefer Zekhirah* in a way analogous to that of Eliezer bar Nathan. Each martyr, writes Ephraim, "possesses eight vestments like a High Priest, and two crowns. Their glory [of the martyrs] surpasses that of the High Priest, for the High Priest sprinkled the blood of sacrifices, whereas [the martyrs] sprinkled their own blood and the blood of their beloved children. *They bound aqedot, built altars, and prepared sacrifices.*"[68] Martyrdom, Ephraim writes, benefitted the victims themselves, the survivors, and the rest of the community. In the twelfth century, the concept of divine punishment and collective atonement continued to constitute a frequent theme in what had become almost a traditional medieval Jewish style of writing in Hebrew literature, although the realities of the First and Second Crusades differed substantially.

POLEMICS

So presented, Ephraim transforms his heroes from arbitrary casualties of "hate crimes" to voluntary martyrs. Ephraim's tendency to equate his martyrs' heroism with those of the First Crusade did not emerge only from his adoption of an existing liturgical and literary fashion. As with his Ashkenazic precursors, polemics also played a role in his narrative. Ephraim acknowledges the existence of martyrological concepts and behavior among Christians as well. Their martyrological concept was too powerful to be completely overlooked.

Peter the Venerable, the abbot of Cluny, for example, explained in a letter to King Louis VII that a true Christian king "sacrifices to God his kingdom, wealth, and even life" and assured him that none would stay in the way of those who chose to "toil themselves, fight, die, and live for their savior."[69] Bernard of Clairvaux too made use of the martyrological notion in crusading sermons, viewing the crusade as a divine test and a means of salvation. Bernard promised the participants "divine glory" and a war they "can fight without danger to your souls; a cause in which to conquer is glorious and for which to die is gain."[70] Bernard's words fell on attentive ears. Even the skeptical Würzburg annalist could still find among the crusaders a few lovers of God who were prepared "to shed their blood for the holy of holies."[71]

The Hebrew chronicles of the First Crusade, one may recall, presented the martyrological concept as a uniquely Jewish characteristic, distinguishing between righteous martyrs and ruthless murderers. Unlike his Ashkenazic predecessors, Ephraim was openly conscious of the prevalent sharing of martyrological ideas.

May the blood of our pious ones that was shed like water ferment His purple garment (*purpurin*), as His son Rabbi Meir declared: "When a man is grieved, what does the Divine Presence say? 'My head is heavy upon me, my arm is heavy upon me.' If God suffers such distress for the [shed] blood of the wicked,[72] how much more is His mercy aroused for the shed blood of the righteous?" For Israel has been compared to the dove, as it is written: "Thine eyes are [as] doves" (Song of Songs 1:15). What is [special of] this dove? Whereas all other birds quiver when being slaughtered, the dove does not, but rather stretches out its neck, so none offers his soul for the Blessed Holy One except Israel, as it is written, "For Thy sake are we killed all the day."[73]

The news from the East about Christian casualties, defeat, and heroism, on the one hand,[74] and the scarce numbers of Jewish martyrs, on the other, drove Ephraim to draw the analogy of the dove. Ephraim clarifies the contrast between Christian and Jewish deaths. Jewish victims should always be seen as martyrs, whether they survived their ordeal or not, whereas non-Jews were simply slain. And those responsible for the shedding of Jewish blood would suffer divine vengeance. Judaism therefore takes precedence over other religions because Israel willingly and honorably undertakes death for the divine, whereas other nations stumble upon their death only to perish in humiliation without cause or reward.

Paradoxically, to demonstrate this difference between Jewish martyrs and Christian casualties, Ephraim borrowed images from his Christian environment. The dove already symbolized the martyrdom of Polycarp (d. 155 or 156), whom we shall meet again soon. After his martyrdom, a dove is said to have flown out of his open wound.[75] In *The Life of Marie d'Oignies* (1177–1213), "the Holy Son of the Virgin manifested Himself in the form of a dove."[76] Shedding blood on purple garments to bring divine vengeance represents another martyrological image of the period. Hrotsvit of Gandersheim's hero, Pelagius, is said to have been dressed in "purple garments" before his martyrdom.[77] Of course, the dove, the color purple, and the punishment of the martyrs' offenders existed also in Jewish imagery. But the martyrological transformation these images underwent in the medieval Hebrew texts attests to the environmental influence on them.[78]

To be sure, Ephraim's analogy was not a call for martyrdom. Nor was it an attempt to rationalize a large-scale catastrophe. During the Second Crusade there was no need for extensive rationalization of numbers or behaviors as was the case in the aftermath of 1096. By the analogy, Ephraim focuses on polemics without diminishing praise for Jewish heroism. In the First Crusade, Jews and Christians expressed their religious ideas by dramatic actions; in the Second Crusade, the arguments between Jews and Christians were, by and large, limited to words.[79]

FRANCE

France was relatively more tranquil than Germany in the first half of the twelfth century. French authorities served as an effective protector of Jews from mob violence. Only sparse references to France and England during the Second Crusade are made in *Sefer Zekhirah*. Two descriptions of anti-Jewish violence compose the French segment of the book. They continue to portray randomness and depict the victims as targets of opportunity. Rabbi Peter "was slain while marching in the funeral procession of a certain *parnas*." Here again an arbitrary attack occurred on the road[80] for the purpose of killing rather than converting.[81]

At Ramerupt, a few French crusaders did attempt to convert the celebrated *Tosafist* Rabbi Jacob Tam, the teacher of the above-mentioned Peter:[82] "They took him out to a field. They disputed with him about his religion and *plotted to kill him.* They inflicted five wounds upon his head, saying: 'You are the greatest of Israel. We shall therefore take vengeance upon you for the Crucified One and wound you the way you inflicted five wounds on our god.'"[83] The crusaders' motive and Jacob Tam's reaction remind us of the martyrological events of 1096. The reenactment of Jesus' stigmata, once again by Christians rather than Jews,[84] added a religious flavor to the attack. Fortunately for R. Tam, an "important nobleman" happened to pass by. R. Tam "called to him and offered him a bribe of a horse worth five *zekukim*." The attackers handed him over to the nobleman after he had promised to continue their conversion attempts. If he failed, he would return Jacob to them to finish their task. More interested in making a profit than a new Christian, the nobleman set Jacob Tam free upon receiving the promised horse.

Although the Jewish leadership of 1096 is frequently said to have provoked or, at least, welcomed martyrdom, Jacob Tam cleaved to life without conversion. Undoubtedly, the behavior of a leader of the stature of R. Jacob Tam made him an exemplar to emulate almost automatically, for he was a model of piety and conduct to twelfth-century European Jewry. Does the behavior of Jacob Tam and the relatively scarce number of martyrs suggest, therefore, a change in the attitude toward life and death under duress in the Second Crusade? Was the Ashkenazic fascination with voluntary death in twelfth-century Europe dwindling? Did the attitude of the French Jews differ from that of their German coreligionists?[85] Although R. Tam is said to have formulated the unprecedented *halakhic* decision that accepted even self-destruction as a form of *qiddush ha-Shem*, life without conversion took precedence over voluntary martyrdom. The stipulations he is said to have established played a significant role after French Jewry had experienced one of its two devastating executions.

These executions swung the martyrological pendulum back to France because of the involvement of the authorities in the persecution of Jews. Unlike in Germany, the only two reported cases of collective execution are unrelated to the crusades or the mob. In these two horrifying incidents, the aristocratic protector of the Jews became their ardent persecutor.

On May 26, 1171, "the oppressing government" of Blois headed the trial and burning of its Jewish community.[86] An accidental encounter between a Jewish leather merchant named Isaac ben Eleazar and a French nobleman's boy-servant triggered this tragic event. The imaginative and frightened young servant believed one of Isaac's skins to be the body of a Christian boy. Upon returning to his master, he reported the "murdering" of a Christian child in the Loire's water.[87] This news was music to the ears of the master, who already held a grouch against the Jews of Blois. Accusations against the entire community came instantly, for resentment toward the Jewish residents had been simmering since the torrid affair of Count Theobald of Blois with the Jewess Pulcellina had become known.[88]

"As was the legal practice of the Gentiles," a trial by water was ordered. It was supposed to provide the prosecutors with the necessary "proof" to indict the entire community. To the prosecutors' satisfaction, the young witness to the alleged murder floated when dropped in a tank of water.[89] There was no doubt in their minds now that the servant was telling the truth. Given the preexisting resentment, the fate of thirty-one or -two Jews was sealed long before the trial.[90] Perhaps for this reason, the persecutors refused to accept the reasonable ransom of one hundred pounds plus the annulment of a one-hundred-eighty-pound debt to let the Jewish community live.[91]

Following the advice of a certain priest, Theobald refused the ransom. The Blois incident appears to show that there was more interest in eliminating rather than converting the accused.[92] Yet the various Hebrew sources at hand dramatically delineate the refusal of the Jews to accept the priest's proposal:[93]

The oppressing government ordered to bring [the Jews] and put them in a wooden house. They surrounded the house with thorn bushes and piles of branches. When they brought them out they told them: "Save your souls! Abandon your faith and turn to us." They tortured, struck, and tormented them, hoping in vain that they might exchange their honor [creed]. They [the Jews] refused and told each other: "Be strong in the faith of God." The oppressor ordered to take the two high priests, the pious Rabbi Yehiel bar Rabbi David the Priest and the righteous Rabbi Yequtiel bar Judah the Priest, and bind them to a post inside the house of fire, for they both were brave men, the students of our rabbi Samuel and our rabbi Jacob [Tam]. And also Rabbi Judah bar Aaron's hands were bound there. They set the branches on fire, and it burned the bindings on their hands and they got loose.[94]

Three Jews miraculously came out from the burning house unhurt. Normally surviving such an ordeal by fire would prove the innocence of the accused – a point that the three were arguing.[95] But the oppressors ignored their own "defective rules" because they were determined to execute. Several times the trio were returned to the flames. Still the fire did not affect these supernatural beings. Only by putting them to the sword could their bodies be thrown into the blazing house. Their resistance to the flame remained the same. "Neither they nor the others were consumed by the fire, thirty-one souls, only their souls burned, but their bodies remained." All this time, they were singing in "a pleasant voice" in the fire. Eventually, even the dismayed "uncircumcised" could not avoid the conclusion that these are "holy [people]."

The assertion that the Jews were continually returned to the fire was aimed at emphasizing their heroism and the voluntary nature of the deaths of these victims. The motif of three heroes in the fire recalls Daniel's three companions in the fiery furnace. Despite the correlation to Daniel, Ephraim continues to respond to Christian polemics with this motif. Martyrs miraculously enduring torture have dominated Christian hagiography to illustrate their ultimate victory. St. Lawrence, who called from the grill, "I am done on this side, you can turn me over now," is one of the more tragicomic examples.[96] Polycarp's Passion had introduced this hagiographical motif. He was bound with cords and set on fire. Although the flames "surrounded the martyr's body as with a wall," the fire could not consume him. He was therefore assailed by the sword, until a dove flew out of his wound. His blood gushed out in such a quantity that it put out the flames. Even the hostile crowd eventually marveled at the scene.[97]

Emphasizing such miraculous characteristics continued to be a preoccupation of eleventh- and twelfth-century martyrologists and hagiographers. Miracles turned sceptics into believers, believers into martyrs, and martyrs into saints. As Peter Damian (d. 1072) explained:

> The marvelous lives of the holy men offer richer fruit for the listener than do their visible miracles. The former prompt imitation, while the latter elicit only admiration. The miracles teach how these men were saints (*Miracula docent quodmodo illis sancti furent*); their lives teach us how even now men can become saints.[98]

To be certain, turning Jews into Christian believers formed one goal of these stories. In the case of Christina the Astonishing, God gave her the ability to creep "into fiery ovens where bread was baking" and come out intact. In other versions the Roman Judge Julanus ordered Saint Christina to be thrown into a fiery furnace. She walked in it for five days, "*singing with the angels*, and was unharmed."[99] The purpose of giving her such abilities was to return to faith not only Christians but also "the very large group" of Jews in town.[100] By the eleventh and twelfth centuries, the hagiographies of the past were increasingly translated into Old High German and the vernacular French.[101] With this literary renaissance, not only the miraculous Christian martyrs of the past came to life but also the negative portrayals of the Jews who often were said to have been involved in their executions. Oral transmission in the form of ecclesiastical preaching as well as vernacular literature familiarized the medieval European with these stories. No doubt these narratives, which also addressed Jews, reached in one form or another Ephraim of Bonn and his peers.

Apart from reflecting the influence of this literary renaissance, the miracle at Blois countered the current Christian declarations that their dead martyrs continued to perform miracles as a sign of Christian superiority. Ephraim had already argued that only Jews should be seen as martyrs, comparing them to the dove, the same symbol that betokened Polycarp's marvelous martyrdom. Now Ephraim added to his First Crusade-style martyrology the hagiographical motif of miracles. By performing miracles, Ephraim and his generation could refute both the Christian sense of divine election and their argument that God had abandoned Israel.

In addition to polemics, miracles enabled Christians to accuse Jews of murdering Christian martyrs. As mentioned, Ephraim himself reported that a miracle combined with a murder triggered the tragedy at Würzburg. A defective Christian legal practice erroneously found Blois Jews guilty, while creating a spurious Christian saint. A Christian trial by fire acquitted the innocent Jews, creating supernatural Jewish saints.

Representations of sainthood appear repetitively in the miracle at Blois. Similarly to the First Crusade Hebrew reports, it emphasizes the novelty of the Blois martyrs. Because God "had set the fire in our Temple, such most holy saints (*qodsei qodashim*) have not been sacrificed." "Satan also came among them" in the form of the anonymous priest to cause the destruction of these saints, as the *Solomon bar Simson Chronicle* had claimed in 1096.[102] As in the three Ashkenazic accounts, Temple symbolism abounds. *Qodsei qodashim* turns the martyrs into Temple sacrifices of the highest sanctity. The play on the word burnt ones (*serufim*) turns these "thirty one angels of the [Divine] Name" into the "*Serafim* who stand above Him."[103] In good hagiographical fashion, the miracles that vindicated these martyrs lead their adversaries to the realization that they had executed saints, not sinners.

To intensify the supernatural motif of overpowering the flames, the Hebrew reports have their saints singing in "in one voice" in the midst of the flames. To increase the reports' credibility, this information is said to have been retrieved from the Jews' Christian neighbors.

The Gentiles came and told us, asking us: 'What is that song of yours, which was so delightful. For we have not heard such a pleasant melody. At the beginning the sound was low, and at the completion they raised their voice in a great sound and uttered together "*Alenu le-shabeah*," and the fire raged.[104]

Singing in the fire had already accompanied the martyrdom of the convert Isaac ben David in 1096. In the burning synagogue, he was able to "Pray to God from the flames in a loud and pleasant voice."[105] Isaac's body succumbed to the flames, however, and his prayer remains unidentified. At Blois, the Christian witnesses reportedly heard the prayer *Alenu le-shabeah* (we should praise [God]), which accentuates the differences between Judaism and other creeds. Moreover, the keynote of the *Alenu* is the proclamation of God as King of Israel and the Universe. It concludes with Zechariah 14:9: "On that day the Lord shall be One and His Name shall be One." The *Alenu* here contains the same polemical charge against the Trinity that the martyrs of 1096 are said to have proclaimed through the *Shema*. Not accidentally, therefore, the ancient *Alenu* prayer was included in a subsequent effort to present the Jewish martyrs as superior to their Christian counterparts in a fashion that the latter could have understood. Around 1300, the martyrs' prayer of *Alenu le-shabeah* became the conclusion of the daily service in Ashkenaz.[106]

The singing of prayers should not have come as a surprise to these alleged witnesses. Angels were believed to have sung *Te Deum Laudamus* over twelfth-century Christian martyrs. It was especially sang in celebration of saints' miracles.[107] Certainly, the fact that the *Te Deum* was associated with Christian martyrs who were allegedly murdered by Jews brought this martyrological motif to the attention of the Jews.[108] By such miracles Christians justified the persecution of Jews; by the same miracles Jews parried this justification. Through miracles Christians expected Jews to convert; through miracles Jews hoped to justify their resistance. So eventually, "all the uncircumcised testify that their [Jews'] bodies did not burn. Only their antagonists said that their bodies were consumed. It appears that only because of their enmity they said these things."[109] Blois martyrs thus surpassed their Ashkenazic predecessors, for they qualified also as saints, in the Christian sense of the word.[110]

Nine years later, Philip Augustus ascended the French throne. If his early education was any indication, French Jews did not have a friend in the royal palace. Rigord writes in the biography of his king what young Philip "heard many times" growing up:

The Jews who dwelt in Paris were wont every year on Easter day, or during the sacred week of our Lord's Passion, to go down secretly into underground vaults and kill a Christian as a sort of sacrifice in contempt of the Christian religion. For a long time they had persisted in this wickedness, inspired by the devil, and in Philip's father's time many of them had been seized and burned with fire. St. Richard, whose body rests in the church of the Holy-Innocents-in-the-Fields in Paris, was thus put to death and crucified by the Jews, and through martyrdom went in blessedness to God; wherefore many miracles have been wrought by the hand of God through the prayers and intercessions of St. Richard, to the glory of God, as we have heard.[111]

It is not surprising, therefore, that more costly than the drama of Blois was the incident at Bray-Sur-Seine or Brie-Comte-Robert during Philip's reign.[112] Ephraim's short report describes Philip Augustus[113] himself as conducting the massacre of more than eighty Jews. It came as retaliation for Jewish lobbying for the capital punishment of one of his murderous dependents.[114] Philip thus "ordered to burn the Jews." A choice between conversion or death is not said to have been offered, although Ephraim does write that "they did not wish to sully themselves and deny God's oneness." As in the tragedy at Blois, the Jews faced swift execution.[115] Only the youngsters under thirteen years of age were not hurt, but no elaboration on their fate is given. Not unusually for this period, many of the children who could not escape to their relatives often found themselves raised in Christian houses or monasteries. Philip's primary aim appears to have been the public exhibition of his firm authority rather than the conversion of the Jews.[116]

Toward the close of the twelfth century, it seems, the choice between conversion or death was critically diminishing. Jews who wanted to be saved had to ask for conversion. However, given the growing Christian suspicion of Jews and the belief in the irreversible devilishness of Jewish nature, it is plausible that the populace questioned the benefit of conversion. Understandably, it was in Ephraim's interest to ascribe a choice to his heroes in his First Crusade-style accounts. Thus he concludes his Blois report: "About thirty-two holy souls sacrificed themselves as an oblation sacrifice (*qorban minhah*) to their Creator."[117] In his poetry, Ephraim went even further. He and his brother Hillel continued to describe *qiddush ha-Shem* in their effulgent poetry as sacrifices and *aqedot*. Contrary to the passive deaths in his report of Blois and Bray/Brei, Ephraim's *piyyut* delineates families, fathers, and sons sacrificing burnt offerings, and mothers raced to offer their children as *olot*. At the same time, Ephraim's poem concludes with the more likely desire of the antagonist to destroy.[118] Also worth mentioning is Ephraim's and Hillel's emphasis on the extreme torturing of Jews. Despite this abuse and inevitable death, none of these martyrs destroyed themselves.

As before 1096, these events made French Jewry the authority in matters of *qiddush ha-Shem*. In the aftermath of Blois and Bray/Brei, it was clear that the martyrological impact of 1096 had reversed its direction, now flowing from France to Germany. This change of directions is also reflected in the legal discussions of the period.

HALAKHIC ASPECTS

It is against this background that we need to consider the *halakhic*-oriented material and decisions in this century. The following illustrations exemplify the Jewish martyrological dilemma in the twelfth century. Let us first turn to the Ashkenazic *Sefer Hasidim*.

Cautious opinions regarding the issue of *qiddush ha-Shem* surface in *Sefer Hasidim*.[119] It seems that the book considers also nonmartyrological patterns of Jewish behavior in times of duress.[120] The book permits women to dress as nuns to obviate random attacks while traveling. In time of actual persecution, the book goes further. It allows widows to escape to monasteries and eat their forbidden food rather than being forcibly wed to a Christian, with no opportunity to escape and return to Judaism in the future.[121] Although not recommending such a course of action, *Sefer Hasidim* reveals that some males even presented themselves as priests, shaved their heads, and learned to recite prayers to deceive their attackers and avoid the test of martyrdom.[122] Based on the Hebrew sources of the First Crusade, it is hard to believe that such behavior would have been acceptable to or even considered by the martyrs of 1096.

The potential drawback of such an approach was that it would undermine Jewish resistance in the future. It is a point made by the following example. When persecutions took place,

the Jewish community had said: "What shall we do?" The rabbi declared: "Watch me and do the same!" He took a cross and carried it so that the Christians would not kill him, and they forcefully converted him along with the other Jewish residents of his town. For this reason, his [the rabbi's] sons converted. Therefore, one should pray that he would not cause a fault which would bring others to sin, and that all the sinners [that is, converts] would return to God's wish.[123]

Two different results ensued from the rabbi's behavior. He and his community escaped the immediate threat. His sons, on the other hand, fell victim to his own scheme. They would not have converted if their father had undergone martyrdom. It was the responsibility of those who recommended conversion, therefore, to ensure the return of each convert to Judaism.[124] The final recommendation, that "one should pray that he would not cause a fault which would bring others to sin, and that all the sinners [that is, converts] would return to God's wish," seems to endorse this tactic if it is carefully employed.

Sefer Hasidim also reveals a favorable attitude toward martyrdom. This time, the emphasis is on the necessity of choosing death.

Once it occurred during the period of forced conversion that the bishop said to the [Jewish] community in his town: "Send a Jew to that certain town, for it has a bishop and Jews. You see what that Jewish community will do and you do likewise. What that bishop will do to the [Jewish] community in his town I shall do to you." They sent a good Jew and he saw that the Jews were forcibly converted. When he returned, they asked him what he had seen. He said: "They *were killed* for the unity of the Divine Name," for if he had told them [what they actually did], they would have done likewise. Hence, he said this, so that they would *be killed* for the sanctification of the Divine Name and would have a place in the world to come.[125]

This endorsement of *qiddush ha-Shem*, in fact, reveals the prominence of the temporary conversion tactic. Moreover, "a place in the world to come" had to be included as an incentive for quitting life. These examples mention only death by the enemy as a possible form of martyrdom.[126]

The stories well demonstrate the complexity of the situation faced by European Jewry. They depict a Jewry torn between the options of insincere conversion and martyrdom, when being attacked. What was needed was the invisible golden passage that would allow twelfth-century Jews to tread safely on the road between physical and spiritual extinctions. This balancing act is attempted in the following example.

An incident took place concerning a bishop who decreed in Mainz that the Jews should *either be killed or converted.* He sent for the crusaders and said: "Be extremely careful that you not touch the money of the Jews, but only their persons. Anyone who does not convert *should be killed,*" but the matter was told to the Jews. Immediately upon hearing this, the Jews closed up their homes and threw into the streets all their silver and gold and clothing. While the crusaders were occupied with plundering, many of the Jews fled through the courtyards to the homes of the burghers and were saved. The bishop heard and sent for the crusaders. He then commanded them: "Do not harm the Jews." The crusaders returned and said: "Why did you permit harming the Jews initially, and now you forbid it?" He said to them: "Initially [I permitted it because,] so long as they had money, it would have been painful for them to lose large sums of money along with their lives and therefore they would have converted under duress. Now that the money is gone and they are already fearful for their lives, they will be killed before they transgress their law. Moreover, if you had not plundered but had immediately *begun killing,* you would have found them all – old and young men and young women. Since some of these would have converted under duress, others would have as well. Now, while you were occupied with plunder, the young men and the wealthy and the young women have fled. Only the old men and the old women and the very best remain. *These will certainly allow themselves to be killed.*[127]

Neither conversion nor martyrdom befell the Jews in this anecdotal story. Parts of it recall the throwing of goods through windows by Ashkenazic women so the men would have time to slaughter their children. Here, in contrast, the act was intended to save life by diverting the crusaders' attention from coerced conversion and killing. It should be noted that the passage considers only death by the enemy.

Surprisingly, little can be extracted from *Sefer Hasidim* about the events of 1096.[128] *Sefer Hasidim* skips the abundant exemplars of its Ashkenazic predecessors and turns to the classical examples for martyrological guidance. "'Even if He takes one's soul'" (B. *Berakhot* 61 b), advised the book, "one should not rebel against Him who kills and gives life. For if you lose your life for Him, He will save (lit. revive) you. But who will save you from His hands." This section can be read on two levels, for the faithful person is offered a win–win situation. By being ready to endure martyrdom, he will be rewarded postmortem. Exactly the same message surfaced in the papal calls for crusades, which reiterated Jesus' message to his followers. But the passage also focuses on the same paradoxical intimation found in Daniel. God accordingly miraculously saves those who do not flinch from the test, as when "Abraham wanted to take Isaac's life."[129]

Other references to voluntary death in *Sefer Hasidim* center on the *Talmudic* lessons of the remote past to give practical guidance. Thus if a student and an ordinary Jew are caught by the "enemy" to kill one of them, the ordinary man should volunteer to *be killed*.[130] Similarly, if the "Gentiles say: 'Give us one of you to be killed or we will kill all of you,' let them be killed and not surrender one soul from Israel," unless the wanted Jew is provocative and violent toward the Gentiles. He then should be turned over so as not to put others at risk.[131]

Given the background of crusades, these examples should come as no surprise. As in Ephraim's account, *Sefer Hasidim* advises on proper behaviors during random attacks "on the road," when the choice is between conversion and being put to death. Such decisions, in any case, should be the last line of defense. Prevention is deemed more useful, as the book instructs how men and women should prepare themselves for traveling. It recommends that emergency plans should be made in advance to avoid tragic results and minimize sacrilegious conduct.[132] With respect to martyrdom, *Sefer Hasidim* offers no innovations. By and large, the book follows the traditional guidelines.[133] Self-reliance appears to be the key issue for *Sefer Hasidim*, as it puts little trust in Christian promises because, when Jews turned to them for protection, "they killed them anyway."[134]

Altogether, these stories reflect the complexity of the post-1096 reality. This reality presented the Jews with the potential option of returning to Judaism. The secular authority, some semisovereign bishops, and the Jewish leadership made the reversion to Judaism legally possible.[135] At the same time, forced conversion meant first and foremost continuation of life under a new religion. The sympathetic treatment of converts thus became a two-edged sword. On the one hand, the community felt the pain of the forced converts and allowed their return when possible; on the other hand, this policy threatened to soften the spiritual strength of the community and Jewish resistance to conversion.[136]

How indicative are *Sefer Hasidim*'s examples of the behavior of the entire German Jewry is hard to tell.[137] It is also difficult to know how these stories were interpreted by contemporaries. The examples seem to coincide with Ephraim and Elazar in emphasizing the importance of preventive measures.

Somewhat different is the legalistic view expressed by the Tosafists of France.[138] Their discussions revolve around the need for active martyrdom. Whereas the given Ashkenazic examples dealt with destruction at the hands of non-Jews, a ruling *ascribed* to Jacob Tam addressed the question of self-inflicted martyrdom.[139] Like *Sefer Hasidim*, this towering Tosafist is said to have relied on Talmudic illustration instead of the precedents of his immediate

Franco-German ancestors.[140] Had 1096 constituted the martyrological norm, there would not have been a need to debate self-killing or to turn to the remote past for support. According to this ruling, in cases of unbearable torture that could lead to conversion, "it is a *mitzvah* to harm oneself, as in the case found in B. *Gittin* (57b) with regard to the youngsters who were taken captive for immoral purposes and threw themselves into the sea."[141]

To be sure, the Tosafists did not speak in one voice. "One may under no circumstances harm himself," argued opposing *tosafistic* voices.[142] The Tosafist and the would-be martyr, Rabbi Elhanan (d. 1184 or 1189),[143] explicitly disagreed with Jacob Tam's reliance on *Gittin*, although he, too, recommended self-destruction to avert conversion. "Although from that episode (in B. *Gittin* 57b) there is no convincing proof... for they [the youths] were taken captive for immoral purposes... nonetheless it is reasonable (*sevara*) that such behavior is permissible and a *mitzvah*."[144] According to the sixteenth-century R. Solomon Luria, Elhanan's father and R. Tam's nephew, Ri of Dampierre (R. Isaac ben Samuel), opposed self-destruction.[145] This was also the opinion of R. Joseph Bekhor Shor. In his opinion, one cannot shed "even his own blood."[146]

The absence of an elaborate legal discussion over the option of taking others' lives as a form of *qiddush ha-Shem* is telling. Rather than make hasty decisions on the spur of the moment, the following story from *Daat Zekenim* urges Jews to apply the long-term perspective in decision making during a potential "time of duress," because anti-Jewish threats did not always become reality:

There is a story about a rabbi who slaughtered many infants during a period of persecution, because he feared that they [the persecutors] would convert them. There was another rabbi with him who was extremely angry with him and called him a murderer. Still he [the first rabbi] did not hesitate. And the [second] rabbi said: "If I am correct, that rabbi will be killed in an unusual way." Thus it was. The idolaters caught him; they stripped off his skin, separating it from the flesh. Subsequently the persecution ceased. If he had not slaughtered those infants, they would have been saved.[147]

The inability to predict how threats are going to evolve turned even a rabbi into a murderer, according to a fellow rabbi. This *tosafistic* source, then, rejected both self-destruction and the sacrifice of children.

From Jacob Tam's following ruling on the death of forcibly converted infants we may deduce that he held a similar view in regards to children. Contrary to those who permitted Jews to mourn over young forced converts for not having the physical and the intellectual ability to resist conversion, Jacob Tam not only disapproved of mourning but also urged Jews to rejoice in an infant's death, for he would not become a non-Jewish adult.[148] Nevertheless, no decision is made about taking the lives of children to prevent their forced conversion.[149] Judging by the infrequent deliberations over taking one's own life, this alternative appears to have been less reflective of twelfth-century reality. Unlike *Sefer Hasidim*, which more discernibly affixed Talmudic examples and dicta to contemporary problems, these Tosafists made no connection to concrete cases or conditions in their intellectual discussions. Nevertheless, one may sense a stricter approach in the Tosafists' rulings, which hints at the rapid deterioration of the Jewish condition in France.[150]

This deterioration made the Tosafists the authority on martyrdom. About fifty years after the First Crusade, the major events of martyrdom occurred in France and, therefore, the major decisions and guidelines in this matter came from French rabbis. From France, their contribution branched out to England, the new arena of Jewish martyrdom.[151] Jacob Tam is said to have dispatched letters to the "Island of the Sea," informing English Jewry about the events at Blois. A series of mourning rituals were declared in these letters, including a day of fasting on the 20th of Sivan to commemorate the thirty-one or -two souls.[152] According to D. Wachtel, such a fast was not observed until after the Chmielnitzki massacre of Polish Jews in 1648–1649.[153] By ascribing the commemoration decrees to Jacob Tam, these commemoration rituals could gain authority. Perhaps in the same way, later Tosafists lent authority to their decisions about self-killing and the killing of children to project a "martyrocentric self-image."[154]

ENGLAND

English Jewry escaped the Second Crusade unharmed thanks to monarchial protection. Ephraim of Bonn ascribes the lack of Jewish casualties in England during most of the twelfth century to a king (Stephen?) "who determined in his heart to protect them [i.e. the Jews] and save their lives and "property.""[155] But English Jewry's good fortune came to an end toward the close of the twelfth century. English Jews suffered bloody massacres because of a lack of royal intervention. Ironically, the first-known outbreak of violence unfolded at the threshold of their protector's palace at Westminster in 1189.[156]

During the coronation of King Richard I, a Jewish delegation attempted to enter the palace to present endowments to the new king. Fearing Jewish magic, the guard refused to admit the Jews into the palace. The rejection quickly turned into a riot. Scores of rioters drove the Jewish delegation out of the royal court, beating and trampling to death those too slow to escape. Benedict, the representative of the York Jewish community, got away with his life only because the mob baptized him (apparently against his will) at the Church of the Innocent. Both the king and the archbishop of Canterbury later on let Benedict resume his first religion without punishment so he could be again "the Devil's man." He died a short time later – a Christian to the Jews and Jew to the Christians.[157]

Claiming they were following the king's orders and God's will, the growing mob rapidly moved into London's Jewish neighborhood. Burning Jewish houses lit London's sky at sunset. Limited choices were given to London's Jews. They "were either roasted in their own houses or, if they came out of them, were received with swords."[158] An invitation to join the majority religion does not seem to have preceded the killing by the bloodthirsty mob. Important to note is that among the thirty-something slain was the new emigré from the Continent, Rabbi Jacob of Orléans.[159] In contrast to Blois and Bray/Brie, not all the slain met death passively. "Some of them slaughtered themselves and their children," says Ephraim without elaborating.[160]

From London the violence spread to Lynn, Norwich, Stanford, York, and St. Edmunds. At Lynn, narrates William of Newbury, the violence began in retaliation for a Jewish attempt to harm a former coreligionist who had converted to Christianity and taken refuge in the local church. Foreign sailors arriving at the port of Lynn reportedly were the main perpetrators of the massacre, from which the community never recovered.[161] On February 6, 1190, a new mob "butchered all the Jews who were found in their own houses at Norwich." Those who had taken refuge in a nearby castle survived.[162] Survivors thus owed their good fortune to fortified shelters rather than to baptism.

Stanford Jewry endured a similar fate on the following day, "and many were killed in that place [i.e. the market place]."[163] William of Newbury again blames the attack on "a number of youths from different provinces." This time, only "some of the Jews were slain, but the rest escaped with some difficulty by retreating to the castle."[164] William ascribes the attacks in Lynn and Stanford to foreign elements. In London, Lynn, and Stanford, the mob raced to destroy their victims. Baptism is not reported to have been an option for survival. Only those fortunate enough to find refuge in fortresses are said to have escaped with their lives.

York witnessed the culmination of the ongoing rampage. A large number of Jews took refuge in a royal castle. Because of a lack of official protection, the castle became a trap rather than a shelter. According to Ralph of Diceto, "nearly five hundred were put to death" at York. Like the early Ashkenazic martyrs, they are reported to have "attacked one another with mutual wounds, for they preferred to be struck down by their own people rather than to perish at the hands of the uncircumcised."[165] In 1096, self-destruction generally followed the crusaders' call to convert. Ralph's report does not seem to indicate such an initial offer. Nor is forced conversion an option. Ralph laments, therefore, "It cannot be believed that so sad and fatal a death of the Jews can have pleased prudent men, since that saying of David often comes to our ears, 'Do not slay them.'"[166] From the outset, the alternatives appear to be self-killing or being killed "at the hands of the uncircumcised." Yorkshire Jews, then, had less control over their lives than their German predecessors.

William of Newbury affirms this conclusion more decisively. A native York-shireman himself, William provides the fullest contemporary account of this incident. A well-organized attack was underway. "The leaders of this daring plan were some of the nobles indebted to the impious usurers [i.e. the Jews] in large sums." First, the rioters "burst into the house of the aforementioned Benedict." They killed his widow and children and looted the house. There-after, they set the house on fire. As a result, the Jews and their well-to-do leader, Joce, asked for the intervention of the Warden of the royal castle. Large sums of money were transferred to him for what turned out to be inadequate protection. For a few days the violence abated, until the attackers "returned with greater confidence and boldness and many [others who] joined them." Joce's impressive house became their first target. Luckily, he had already found refuge with his family in the castle of York. No longer content with booty only, the mob moved on to eliminate the Jews of York for good. Monetary gain ranked high in the mob's priorities. Moneylenders to whom the assailants and their leader, Richard Malebysse, were heavily indebted therefore became primary targets.

Meanwhile, most of the community joined Joce in the castle. A few, who were late in finding refuge at the castle, received, at this stage, the unusual "option of sacred baptism or the extreme penalty." The reaction of these unfortunate Jews resembles, once again, the behavior of the martyrs of 1096. Among them was also "The Holy Rabbi Elijah of Aborak (York): "Thereupon some were baptized and feignedly joined Christianity to escape death. But those who refused to accept the sacrament of life, even as a matter of pretense, were butchered without mercy."[167]

Witnessing from the castle's towers the killing of their fellow Jews, the be-sieged became increasingly anxious, whereas their attackers became exceed-ingly impassioned. The Warden requested the sheriff to intervene.[168] Sheriff John Marshall arrived with his troops, ready to retake the fortress by storm. By that time, the circle of conspirators had grown wider. "And there were not lacking many clergymen, among whom a certain hermit seemed more vehement than the rest."[169] Survival looked increasingly dismal. The situation deteriorated further after a rock fell on the attackers' fiercest leaders, killing the anonymous Premonstratensian priest.[170] Now even conversion would not deliver the Jews from their fate.[171] A solution to the situation was suggested by "a most famous scholar of the Law." This rabbi revealed that it was God who "orders us to die now for the Law." His rationale was twofold. First, "A most glorious death" was preferable to "dishonest life." As he continues, "For many of our people in different times of tribulation are known to have done the same, preferring a form of choice most honorable for us."[172]

Not all agreed with the rabbi. "Very many of them therefore withdrew, preferring rather to try the clemency of their enemies than perish in this way with their friends." In light of the situation, the rabbi delivered his final speech. "Let those whom this good and pious plan pleases not, seat themselves apart from this holy assembly, for to us this life on earth is now thought nothing of through our love of the law of our fathers."[173]

And while the fire was blazing,

they prepared their throats to be sacrificed. At the order of that inveterate [author] of wicked days that those men whose courage was most steady should take the life of their wives and pledges, the famous Joce cut the throat of Anna, his dear wife, with a sharp knife, and did not spare his own sons.[174] And when this had been done by the other men, that wretched elder cut Joce's throat so that he might be more honored than the rest. All of them were thus slain together with the author of their error.[175]

If William's presentation recalls Josephus Flavius's story of Masada, it is because of his familiarity with the classic story.[176] Predisposed to give credence to this Jewish "madness," William deliberately transformed the York castle into a medieval Masada: "Indeed that fury of rational beings against themselves seems stupendous, nay irrational. But he who reads the history of Josephus about the Jewish war knows well enough from the ancient superstition of the Jews that madness has lasted down to our days if perchance any sad occasion arises."[177] Naturally, this association calls to question the authenticity of William's report. As with Josephus in the case of Masada, William could not record so vividly the dialogues of the would-be martyrs behind the walls. Contrary to Ralph's report, William adds fire to the scene. He blames the Jews for setting the castle on fire to prevent the attackers from collecting their booty. William's addition of the fire recalls Josephus's description of the priests' fiery death in the Temple. Moreover, it is hard to believe that the Jews who had survived the fire and rejected death threw down from the walls the dead bodies of their companions "as an ocular proof of so great sacrifice," calling out, "Behold the bodies of wretched men who were guilty of their own death with wicked fury." Most likely, the story of Masada had already shaped William's biased view, which he saw as now being supported by the Jews themselves. Overall, this important account allows us to gain an additional glance at the Jewish martyrological world as it was seen by a Christian reporter.

William's report, however, should not be dismissed entirely. The rabbi's speech and the reaction it created are all too familiar from other medieval Hebrew and Latin reports to be dismissed as fictitious. As had been the case in the former attacks on medieval Jewry, the elder leaders took control of the situation and addressed their speech to the "holy assembly," a phrase repeatedly used by medieval Jewish authors. Their motivation to die – "love of the law of our fathers" – is another repeated motif in Jewish martyrology.

It is not likely that William can be suspected of inflating the heroism of those "slain together with the author of their error." The order of self-killing, the roles of Joce and the "rabbi," the phrase "sharp knife" (the special knife used for Jewish slaughtering of animals), and the presentation of the killings as ritualistic sacrifice, which William failed to fully comprehend, recalls also the reality of the First Crusade. These classic and contemporary parallels could not have emerged only from a shared literary style. Contemporary Jewish views must be ascribed to William's contact with Jewish survivors.

William's account of what happened outside the walls and the dialogues of the surrendering Jews with their antagonists can especially be given more credibility. These deeds and dialogues bring us to the rabbi's second reason for recommending self-destruction. This rabbi is aware that "if we fall into the hands of the enemy we shall die at their will and amidst their jeers." Because God demanded their lives back, it was better to return them "with our own hands."[178] The rabbi's recommendation emerged from his understanding that the situation was hopeless. He thus followed the Tosafists' view on martyrdom in time of unfolding crisis.

In perspective, that rabbi read the conditions accurately. From the outset, the Premonstratensian hermit, who led the attack, was "frequently repeating with a loud voice that Christ's enemies ought to be crushed." Thus he labored "to persuade others that the work on which he was engaged was a religious one."[179] He completed his "work" with those Jews who survived the fire in the castle and "preferred to try Christian clemency" all along. As Josephus claimed to have survived his ordeal at Jotapata because of God's intervention, so these survivors argued that,

God has preserved us both from the madness of our brethren and the danger of the fire so that at last we may be at one with you in religion. For our trouble giving us sense, we recognise the Christian truth and desire its charity being prepared to be laved by the sacred baptism, as you are accustomed to demand and, giving up our ancient rites, to be united to the Christian church. Receive us as brothers instead of enemies, and let us live with you in the faith and peace of Christ."[180]

In stark contrast to the events of 1096, now these Jews beg to be converted. More astonishing is the reaction to their request. Although the besiegers had promised clemency to the Jews if they would accept baptism, "as soon as they [the Jews] came out [of the castle], they seized them as enemies, and though *they [the Jews] demanded* [emphasis mine] the baptism of Christ, those cruel butchers destroyed them."[181] This plot signaled an alarming trend. It buttresses my previous suggestion that Christian mistrust of Jewish converts and backsliders contributed to the development of this trend. Converting Jews was not on the agenda of these rioters:

If there was no deceit in their demand for sacred baptism, their own blood baptised [*sic*] them.... But whether they demanded the sacred laver deceitfully or not, the execrable cruelty of those butchers is without excuse... they were influenced more by pang of malice than the zeal for justice... *they despised men seeking Christian grace* [emphasis mine] ... they deceived the wretches with lies so that they come forth to the sacrifice.[182]

Forced conversion, however, was only one component of this developing tenor. After looting Jewish property, the crowd destroyed the debt records that were kept in the local cathedral.[183]

How many died voluntarily and how many died despite their will to convert cannot be determined. Ephraim of Bonn does not make such distinctions in his report. For him, all the Jews died as martyrs at York. He made no attempt to rationalize the behavior of the Jews at York, as self-killing for the name of God was self-explanatory to him. From Ephraim's brief report, the Yorkisher "scholar of the Law" can be identified as Rabbi Yom Tov of Joigny.[184] Despite its sketchiness and inaccuracy, Ephraim's report corroborates William's description. Ephraim focuses only on the behavior of "about one hundred and fifty holy souls," who died in "the house of worship" (rather in the castle). Only in the case of "a city which had only Jewish converts" does Ephraim mention a choice between death or conversion. Perhaps here the attackers distinguished between Jews and former Christians and gave a second chance to the latter.

Ephraim adds, without mentioning the story of the Jews who did try in vain to convert to save their lives, a few more important details to William's report. Ephraim reveals that Rabbi Yom Tov of Joigny "slaughtered about sixty souls." Following Rabbi Yom Tov's example, "others slaughtered too. There were even men who ordered [others?] to sacrifice their only son ... and there were some who were burnt for the sanctification of the Name." According to Ephraim, the acts of killing did not end at York. Jews of other locales in England met their deaths because they refused to be baptized. Many who did not perish by their own hands were slaughtered by "our enemies."

Ralph of Diceto adds that large organized massacres came to an end in England on March 18th, when fifty-seven Jews were slaughtered at St. Edmunds. Still, the Jews were far from being safe. "Wherever the Jews were found," continues Ralph of Diceto, "they were massacred by the hands of the Crusaders, unless protected by the town authorities."[185] Once more, according to Ralph of Diceto, relief from violence came to the Jews of England from the authorities and not via the option of conversion. In Ralph's description, the option of conversion is missing, creating the impression that even baptism could not have saved the Jews. This appears to be the situation of English Jewry by the turn of the twelfth century and, by and large, of all Ashkenazic Jewry. We therefore must carefully balance the negative Christian reports of Jews "traditionally and irrationally" obsessed with self-destruction and the positive Jewish reports that made active martyrdom their key motif. They did this, as we have seen, to magnify their heroes, on the one hand, and in response to the increasing interest in destroying the Jews rather than giving them a chance to decide their own fate, on the other.

THE MARTYRS

Unfortunately, not all the names of twelfth-century martyrs have come down to us through memorial books (*Memorbuchen*) and other historical records. Understandably, the reports on the martyrs focus on the leaders of the groups and the most dramatic acts in the crises. Ephraim of Bonn's Blois report spotlighted the three saints: Rabbi Yehiel bar David the Cohen, Rabbi Yequtiel bar Judah the Cohen, and Rabbi Judah bar Aaron. Ephraim's brother, Rabbi Hillel bar Jacob of Bonn, adds in a eulogy for the martyrs of Blois the names of Judah, Isaac, Moses, the brothers Baruch and Samuel, Menahem and Judah, who all followed the example of the traditional martyrs, "Hananiah and his companions and Rabbi Akiva and his companions."[186]

Ephraim's short report on the death of the eighty Jews at Bray/Brie failed to mention the names of the victims. Gross suggested that Isaac, the father of the known Parisian financiers Elie and Dieudonne, was one of the victims at Bray/Brie. A Hebrew legal document of the thirteenth century designates Elie and Dieudonne as the sons of "the holy Rabbi Isaac." The term *holy*, may indicate Isaac's involvement in a martyrological test.[187]

Among the casualties of London, only Rabbi Jacob of Orléans is mentioned by name. The list of the martyrs of York includes Rabbi Elijah of York, the leader of the group that the mob managed to catch and slaughter outside the walls of the castle. The known martyrs of York Castle are Rabbi Yom Tov of Joigny and Joce, the spiritual and secular leaders of England's Jewry; Joce's wife, Anna, is mentioned only by William of Newbury.[188] Other York martyrs appear in the eulogy of Rabbi Joseph of Chartres. The best known in the eulogy is again Rabbi Yom Tov.

Excluding several individuals and Anna,[189] the rest of the victims share more than a tragic fate. They were all the students of Rabbi Jacob Tam or, at least, students of his school. As mentioned already, Jacob Tam is said to have led the school that permitted self-killing. It is not surprising, therefore, that the leaders of the martyrs at the close of the century were the French students of Jacob Tam. The leading martyrs at Blois – Yehiel, Yequtiel, and Judah – were, according to Ephraim, "the students of Rabbi Samuel [bar Meir (Rashbam)] and Rabbi Jacob [Tam].[190]

Rabbi Jacob of Orléans, often called Rabbi Tam of Orléans and "our holy Rabbi Jacob,"[191] was one of Jacob Tam's famous students before emigrating to "the Island" (i.e., England). So was Rabbi Yom Tov of Joigny,[192] who, like the leadership of Orléans, had taken an active role in the negotiations with the French authorities in the aftermath of Blois before settling in London.[193] The incident at Blois had a personal impact on Rabbi Yom Tov, which finds expression in his eulogy to the memory of Blois's martyrs.[194]

The close mentor–student relationship between Rabbi Jacob Tam and Rabbi Yom Tov may supply a better motivation for the active role of the latter in the self-killing at York than the explanation offered by William of Newbury. According to William, "that wretched elder [that is, Rabbi Yom Tov] cut Joce's throat so that he might be more honored than the rest."[195] Various medieval Hebrew reports present self-killing as the most honorable act, but the duty of "sacrificing" often fell on the shoulders of the outstanding male leader of the community, the person who led the community to the final act.

All this demonstrates the importance of Rabbi Jacob Tam and his school in the lives of European Jews and the impact his views had on his students and thus on their followers.[196] The impact of the Tosafists on English Jewry was strong enough to be recognized even by William of Newbury. Although not aware of the connection between Jacob Tam and his celebrated student, William writes about Rabbi Yom Tov, "[he] had come from parts beyond the sea to teach the English Jews. He was honored by all and was obeyed by all as if he had been one of the prophets."[197]

Jacob Tam and his Tosafist students, therefore, played an essential role in the spreading of qiddush ha-Shem. The dramatic reports on the attacks on German Jewry in 1096, and their costly results, may have created the impression that it was German Jewry that mostly accounted for the Ashkenazic ideology of martyrdom. Both the Hebrew and the Latin sources at hand, however, indicate that, while German Jewry experienced relative peace during the later crusades, the French and English Jewry paid the heaviest toll during the Second and Third Crusades. In fact, the Ashkenazic martyrdom of 1096 was sandwiched between the martyrological events at France. Twelfth-century reality steered the French Jewry into acting as the leader of the European Jewry, especially of the young English community. French Tosafists became both the important commentators on *qiddush ha-Shem* and the leading martyrs of the period. In sum, the Franco-German tradition of martyrdom, which commenced in northern France at the beginning of the eleventh century and matured in the Rhineland in 1096, had come full circle at the close of the twelfth century.

9

∞

Fire from Heaven

Throughout the thirteenth century, crusaders continued to come and go through European Jewish communities. But crusaders were not the only instigators of organized anti-Jewish attacks. As a result, the number of martyrs steadily increased in the memorial books (*Memorbuch*) and eulogies of European Jewry.[1] These Hebrew sources concerned themselves mainly with the names of the martyrs and only occasionally with their methods of dying. Metaphors of priestly sacrifices and *aqedot* remained prominent in these documents. Less emphasis was given to the events themselves and the reasons for their outbreak. The picture these authors depict, therefore, is not always clear. As we shall see next, this caveat is worth remembering when dealing with our thirteenth- and fourteenth-century sources. These centuries, I shall argue, witnessed the growing tendency to eliminate rather than convert Jews, for popular Christian opinions viewed the "unredeemable" Jew as a tangible threat to Christianity and Christians. In some instances, the latter justified their attacks on the grounds that medieval Judaism had become heretical. Yet despite these developments, the twelfth-century Ashkenazic martyrological genre continued to characterize our sources. They depict all Jewish casualties as willingly dying to avoid conversion. Moreover, the traditional use of metaphors may give the inaccurate impression that numerous Jews took the lives of fellow Jews before destroying themselves.

IMAGERY AND REALITY

Elazar bar Judah dedicated a eulogy to the martyrs of Erfurt in 1221. Elazar's poem provides limited and general information. Noticeable is the slaughter of his martyrs by unspecified antagonists. These martyrs were "devoured," "cut," "hanged," "burned," "the innocent killed and burned," and "the holy ones dragged and put to death." Their adversary "maliciously killed" young men and women. R. Shem Tov Ha-Levi is the only martyr identified in the poem. "He came and was slaughtered."[2] Additional names are furnished by a poem ascribed to Rabbi Solomon bar Abraham. Employing the miracle motif, it has Moses' son and daughter "running in the fire together." Two unnamed "holy" sisters jumped into the fire without fear.[3] They are identified as Madrona and Rachel in the later *Memorbuchen*.[4] Among the names it mentions is R. Shem Tov ha-Levi. Contrary to the two poems, in the *Memorbuchen* he is said to have slaughtered himself in the synagogue. It also includes a young Joseph who jumped into the fire.[5]

The memorial books affirm two more attacks in 1235 in Fulda and Wolfshenim, Germany.[6] Once again, the attacks and the blood libels followed sermons against heresy.[7] Eight lives were lost in the violence. They were all tortured on the wheel and eventually burned. The poems describing the incident emphasize that the "motive" behind the assault was the fabricated allegation that the Jews had disposed of a cadaver. The "discovery of a corpse" called for the intervention of the inquisition, designated in the poems by the Hebrew term *hovlim*.[8] Because the inquisitorial proceeding could not single out the individual responsible for the alleged crime, eight prominent leaders were chosen to pay for the murder.[9] The serious nature of the allegation triggered a decisive punishment, which probably ruled out even voluntary conversion as a means of escape from death on the wheel, at the stake, or by decapitation.[10]

These inflicted slaughters did not prevent R. Yehiel bar Jacob from presenting some of the executions as *aqedot*. Inspired by his name, Yehiel ha-Cohen is presented as "bringing near the offering." The poem, in any event, does not mention the persecutors' offering Christianity as an alternative to death. It should be remembered that inquisitory confessions were not always designed to prevent punishment.[11]

A larger tragedy took place in Frankfurt am Main six years later.[12] A Jewish family frantically tried to stop one of its members from converting voluntarily to Christianity.[13] Almost the entire community perished in the ensuing retaliation for this bold act. Over one hundred sixty members perished. No self-killings are described in the poem on this event. Only twenty-four Jews are reported to have saved themselves by conversion. It is not clear if these survivors requested baptism to be saved (as was the case in York) or if they constituted the only members of the community who accepted from the outset an offer to exchange their creed for their lives. An answer regarding such situations can be found in the next incident.

Frederic II's crusade in 1228–1229 and, especially, the preparation for the crusade of Theobald of Champagne in 1236 served as pretexts for anti-Jewish violence. Pope Gregory IX repeated unsuccessfully the all-too-familiar papal appeals for a controlled and professional crusade. A large popular army gathered unexpectedly in Europe nonetheless. The political fracture between the pope and the emperor only deepened the fall of the Jews between these two opposing thrones.[14] Masses quickly took advantage of the political split, inflicting substantial damage upon the Jewish communities of western France. Pope Gregory responded to "tearful and pitiful complaints from the Jews of the Kingdom of France" in a number of letters to the bishops of France. The letters retell the events:

They (the attackers) try to wipe them almost completely off the face of the earth. In an unheard of and unprecedented outburst of cruelty, they have slaughtered in this mad hostility, two thousand and five hundred of them; old and young, as well as pregnant women. Some were mortally wounded and others trampled like mud under the feet of horses. They burned their books, for greater shame and disgrace, they exposed the bodies of those thus killed, for food to the birds of heaven, and their flesh to the beasts of the earth. After foully and shamefully treating those who remained alive after this massacre, they carried off their goods and consumed them. And in order that they may be able to hide such an inhuman crime under the cover of virtue, and in some way justify their unholy cause, they represent themselves as having done the above, and they threaten to do worse, on the ground that they (the Jews) refuse to be baptized.[15]

Contemporary Hebrew sources remain uncharacteristically silent about this large-scale catastrophe. Solomon ibn Verga's sixteenth-century *Shevet Yehudah* is the only known source to describe the slaughter of more than three thousand Jews and the conversion of over five hundred. Regrettably, Solomon does not support the information with a source.[16] Moreover, this Spanish exile viewed the events in Ashkenaz through the lenses of his own experience; Namely, Solomon tended to apply the Spanish ultimatum of conversion to the Ashkenazic incidents he described from afar after their occurrence. Gregory's letters are thus the key sources that explicitly reveal this growing aspect to the anti-Jewish animus: killing for the sake of killing. At this rate and under such "impious designs," feared Gregory, no "remnant of them [Jews]," would survive to serve as "the proof for the Christian faith" at the "end of days."

Of course, destroying Jews was not always the rioters' only goal. Conversion was not a thing of the past. Europe is a large continent and the rioters were not a monolithic group. But a different trend was unfolding. Blind hatred and greed played a major, and occasionally the only, role in the violence of the thirteenth century. Baptism was not always the only preferred Christian option for Jews. Forcible conversion of the survivors after massacres had already taken place served as a method of hiding "such an inhuman crime under the cover of virtue," in Gregory's words. Massacres were developing into a vehicle for revenge and for punishment of the supposed incurably malicious Jewish nature – a nature that would not let them truly convert. Past experience with relapses could only have reinforced this growing impression. The by-product of this distrust was an opportunity to benefit financially from the killing of Jews; the higher these feelings of hate ran, the more did Jewish property become legitimate spoil in the eyes of the public. Greed as a symptom of distrust also marked the second half of the thirteenth century. It is a point well made by R. Isaac ben Moses of Vienna. His mid-thirteenth-century *opus magnum, Or Zarua*, clearly states what was the rioters' intent. "When they rob, they also kill."[17]

Spoil and slaughter also characterize the attack at Bourges in 1251. A popular crusade led by the "Master of Hungary" pillaged and massacred for the sake of killing. This extreme motivation seems to have driven these unruly bands more than did the old apocalyptic-millennial wish to convert Jews before fighting the Muslims.[18] Here again, it seems, the populace had given up on the idea of converting the Jews.[19]

This was clearly the intention in the case of R. Abraham the Convert. He was killed while disputing with his former Christian coreligionists. Still, two different poets could not resist the association of R. Abraham's fate with the *aqedah*. Although Abraham was burned at the stake for shattering crucifixes in a heated dispute, the two poems represent via literary allusion Abraham and the many Jews who died in the ensuing riots as offering their souls themselves before God.[20] Both the medieval and biblical Abrahams were converts, both shattered idols, and both offered *aqedot*. One offered his son but was stopped; the other offered himself and was praised. It is the literary style that created the association of the medieval Abraham with the *aqedah*, which usually was reserved to actual sacrifices of others in 1096.

To mention all the local attacks of the thirteenth century would be solemnly tedious and repetitive. Attention, however, must be given to the information regarding the martyrdoms at Pforzheim toward the end of the century in Germany. An Oxford Hebrew manuscript reveals that the Jews there were slaughtered and put on wheels. R. Yakar ha-Levi, the son of R. Samuel, is the main person mentioned. In the *Memorbuch*, R. Samuel bar Yakar ha-Levi and two other colleagues are said to have slain themselves at Pforzheim. Strangely, the three are reported to have been put on the wheels thereafter. A eulogy by R. Abraham bar Baruch claims, to the contrary, that R. Samuel ha-Levi and his son R. Yakar were killed in the violence.[21] To settle the discrepancy, Habermann hypothesized that there might have been two men by the name Yakar bar Samuel or two assaults. I would attribute the discrepancy to the use of different literary styles and metaphors. It is this use of metaphors that may have created the impression of active self-killing. Almost an identical incongruity, we should recall, marks Elazar's poem and the *Memorbuch* in the case of R. Shem Tov ha-Levi. We should proceed carefully, therefore, without letting literary metaphor cloud our view of the events.

Worth mentioning is also the violence that broke out at Troyes in April 1288 and at Champagne two years later.[22] These incidents further demonstrate the curtailing of the Jewish opportunity to choose between death and life in the cases fabricated to produce this result. This trend could have been noticed already in 1273. A convert known as "Paul the *Hovel*" (the Franciscan) attempted to equate Judaism with the heretical movements of his time.[23] Such an equation questioned the theological legitimacy of Judaism to exist. A short Hebrew polemical work captured this dangerous equation of Judaism with the heretical Bougres, that is, the Cathars:

In the year 5033 (1272–3), the unbeliever Paul came and gathered all the rabbis. Thus he said to them before the bishop of Paris and the heads of the monks who were there: "Listen to me, O house of Jacob and all the clans of the house of Israel. You shall be convinced to repent and to abandon your faith in the face of the compelling claims that I shall reveal to you. I shall not rest till I am avenged of you, and *I shall demand your blood. Indeed, I wish to prove that you are faithless, a people of 'Bougres,' fit to be burned.* I shall inform you of the charges; on each you should be judged guilty of a capital crime. Now send for your greatest sages and answer me without delay. For thus have I been commanded by the king, *to bring you to your deserved end...*" [emphasis mine].[24]

As we have seen in the previous chapters, violence against the heretics often spilled over onto the Jewish neighborhoods.[25] The Catholic campaigns against the Albigensian heresy had the same devastating potential to harm the Jews in the thirteenth century. Paul's goal was clear to the Hebrew reporter. Paul "came from Spain to destroy totally the remnant of Israel... throughout all the territories of the King of France. He sought to wipe out and obliterate even children and women...." Fortunately for the Jews, it seems that Paul failed to convince the royal and ecclesiastical authorities that the Jews "were faithless." Such an indictment would have made the Jews heretics "fit to be burned." Despite Paul's failure, his attempt reveals the growing antipathy toward the

Jews.[26] At the same time, the increase in voluntary converts to Christianity reveals that the ecclesiastical pressure was not without success.[27] Such threats to Jewish survival would only increase the high praises for martyrdom in the Jewish reports.[28]

Against this background, the official trials and burnings in Troyes are not surprising. During the celebration of Easter – often a time of dangerous schemes plotted against the Jews in the high Middle Ages – a corpse was dumped at the house of the well-to-do Isaac Chatelain. Isaac was not a religious leader nor did the allegation include a blood libel. Still, the planted evidence called for the investigation of the inquisition, which found the Jews of Troyes guilty. These serious accusations could have produced only one conclusion: the Jews of Troyes had to pay collectively for the alleged crime. Because the authorities could not find the criminals, it found satisfaction by executing thirteen leaders from the community. R. Meir bar Eliav correctly sensed that from the outset "the wicked conspired to destroy the chosen." Although "they spoke peaceably with him [Isaac], they craftily prepared his snare."[29]

Baptism does not come into play as a possible salvation, because of the martyrs' own alleged malice and doomed nature. No wonder, therefore, that the three poems describing the fate of the Troyes community nowhere mention conversion as an alternative to death. This is in contrast to eleventh- and twelfth-century Hebrew sources that repeatedly tried to magnify the martyrs' heroism by emphasizing the choice they had between Judaism and Christianity, between life and death. Instead, R. Jacob bar Judah employs Ephraim's motif (and that in Polycarp's story) of the holy martyrs as "doves that fly to their cotes" (*arubot*, Isa. 60:8). Genesis 7:11 uses *arubot* as the openings of heaven. Thus the poem's general idea is that the martyrs fly straight back to God, after they "well chanted together their song" in the fire.[30]

Two years after the events at Troyes, anti-Jewish allegations had expanded to Paris and further jeopardized the community as a whole. At the French capital, the allegation clearly took on a religious dimension during Easter. Jews were accused of reenacting the crucifixion by torturing the host wafer. By desecrating the *sacrosanctum Christi* corpus, it was believed, Jews could again gain access to Jesus' body to repeat his torturing. Shortly after, even Pope Boniface VIII and King Philip IV acknowledged what the common people of Troyes had already argued vigorously. What was seen as the pathological nature of the Jews was believed to compel them to destroy not only innocent Christians but also Christianity. Such perverted views reenforced the skepticism that Jews would ever accept Christian salvation. Even the baptismal water could not wash away the anti-Jewish mythology in the minds of the

populace and monarchs. As the expulsion of 1306 demonstrates, France followed England in giving up on its Jews. By the end of the thirteenth century,
France exhibited "a profound desire that [the Jews] would just go away for
good."[31]

COMMUNITY AND COMMEMORATION

R. Solomon Simhah ha-Sofer's poem about the events in Troyes marks another significant development. He considered not only the victims as holy
martyrs but also "the entire holy community," although the inevitable death
included only the thirteen Jews. Solomon repeats this line nine times, after
each stanza. Correlating with the *Memorbuchen*, Solomon's poem portends
a shift to a shared sense of martyrdom that encompassed also Jews who did
not die as martyrs.[32] This transition to a collective application of martyrdom
that includes all dead of every household further explains the innovations in
Ashkenazic liturgy. The Christian accusation that all Jews had to pay collectively for the killing of Christ[33] could only intensify this sense of collective
martyrdom. Thirteenth-century liturgy commemorated not only the martyrs
of 1096 and those who followed, but all types of family deaths. Abundant
evidence for this transformation is exhibited by the embracing of the commemoration *Yahrzeit*, the *Qaddish* mourners' prayer, *Av ha-Rahamim* (Father
of Mercy), and *un'thanne tokef*, for the New Year and the Day of Atonement,
that emerged during this period.[34]

As noted, the Orléans epistle and Ephraim of Bonn's report on the singing
of *Alenu le-shabeah* at Blois provided an early illustration for this transformation from a martyrological incident to a collective Ashkenazic prayer. This
transformation of the prayer from the individual to the collective intensified
in the second half of the twelfth century.[35] *Mahzor Vitry*, the French collection
of prayers and liturgy, offers the first use of *Alenu* as a daily prayer.[36] From
France the *Alenu* reached England.[37] Ephraim appears also to be the first to
report the inclusion of a prayer dedicated to martyrs in the Sabbath liturgy.[38]
It beseeches God to remember not only "the pious and righteous and pure"
but also "the sacred communities that sacrificed themselves for the sanctification of the Divine Name." God was entreated to remember individuals and
communities "beneficently along with the other pious of history."[39]

After the *Alenu*, the Mourner's *Qaddish* is recited in the Ashkenazic tradition. Initially, the *Qaddish* served as the doxology recited at close of a teacher's
discourse before dismissing his students with the hope of redemption. *Qaddish*
had yet to be associated with mourning rites.[40] But its references to eschatology, the sanctification of the name of God, the coming of God's kingdom, and

resurrection made the *Qaddish* very alluring to the Franco-German Jewish survivors of the numerous massacres. Events gradually turned this general doxology into a collective mourning practice. In turn, it has become the orphan son's duty to recite it for a year to secure the dead a place in Paradise. The notion of heavenly reward for the martyrs that intensely characterizes the Hebrew documents of the First Crusade,[41] gradually made its way into standard Ashkenazic mourning rites for all.

To be sure, the transition was not smooth. R. Elazar of Worms addressed this issue of prayers for the dead cautiously. His Spanish near-contemporary, R. Abraham b. Hiyya (d. 1136), rejected the idea altogether. "They busy themselves with vain hopes," he commented, "... that the actions and prayers of their sons would benefit them after death." A similar view was held even by the Ashkenazi Elyakim ben Joseph (d. 1150 in Mainz).[42] According to R. Isaac ben Moses of Vienna's *Or Zarua* (1220), the *Qaddish* was not restricted to a particular individual in France, whereas orphans bore the responsibility for its recitation at the end of the service in Bohemia and in the Rhineland.[43]

But the polemical need to counter and eclipse the Christian views of their own martyrs, and the miracles they were believed to have performed, made the association of the *Alenu*, the *Qaddish*, *Av ha-Rahamim*, and later the *Yahrzeit*, which begins with the word *yizkor* ("may He remember"), with the Franco-German casualties irresistible.[44] Two centuries after Isaac ben Moses of Vienna, R. Jacob of Möllin was the first to mention the *Yahrzeit* as the anniversary commemoration of parents' death by reciting the *Qaddish*. What had started as a commemoration for martyrs now became a standard practice. The term *Yahrzeit*, it has been observed, derives from the usage of the Catholic church, as does the term *Memorbucher* ("the books of martyrs"), which resembles the Christian term for the martyrs' books, *Libri memorialis*.[45] From a specific martyrological incident, these practices have developed into the collective Ashkenazic mourning and commemoration rituals for all forms of demise. *Av ha-Rahamim*, therefore, beseeches God to remember not only the "innocent ones" but also "The holy congregations, who laid down their lives for the sanctification of the divine Name."

A good additional illustration of this transition from the individual martyr to the collective practice is provided by the meditation *un'thanne tokef*. Tradition ascribes this meditation to Kalonymous ben Meshullam, who learned it in a dream from the martyr R. Amnon of Mainz.[46] Although legendary in nature, the story is indicative of the evolution of prayers in Ashkenaz. In a variant of the Christian and Jewish stories of Theophilius, who refused to capitulate and eventually mysteriously vanished, the mutilated and dying Amnon is said to have recited this meditation in the synagogue before he perished. It is precisely the martyrological death of Amnon that gave this prayer its liturgical importance in the Ashkenazic ritual.

It is not only the dead in Paradise who benefit from these rituals and commemorations but also the living. Through the tributes to martyrs, it was hoped that God would avenge the blood of the innocent.[47] As the distinction between different deaths evaporated, the benefit from the dead became more inclusive as well. The *Qaddish* and even the response "Amen" at the end of the recitation were believed to influence divine decrees and the collective well-being of the nation.[48] This process of the codification of rites was lengthy and influenced by the events of the twelfth and thirteenth centuries.

Given the general developments of the period, this expansion of martyrological terminology and associated practices into the communal standard liturgy is not at all surprising. Similar developments are traceable in the majority Christian society. I have already argued that the singing miracle of the *Alenu* at Blois countered similar miracles ascribed to Christian martyrs singing the *Te Deum*. Martyrs' miracles were meant "to be seen" not only by adherents but also by nonbelievers, which would have brought these polemical miracles to the attention of the Jews.

For Augustine, such miracles by saints and martyrs attested Jesus' resurrection and were also seen as an important tool for the conversion of Jews.[49] Pope Honorius III noted in regard to William of York (ca. 1227) that the function of saints is to "confound Jews and heretics, to shame pagans, and lead sinners to repentance."[50] Moreover, miracles affirmed the martyrs' power and their ability to punish offenders through "divine vengeance."[51] As many of the Latin narratives of the First Crusade indicate, the benefit from praising the martyrs was mutual.[52] The living prayed for the rewarding of their fallen comrades in heaven, whereas the latter were expected to protect and ensure the success of the mission by defeating the enemy from above.

Because of these supernatural abilities ascribed to martyrs, their shrines, relics, and commemoration demanded special treatment. At first, Christian practice reserved all honors to martyred saints alone. Special vigils and prayers for martyrs ensured the reception of their souls in Paradise. Their graves became the focal point of the community. The desire to be close to martyrs and for burial *ad sanctos* contributed to the development of cemeteries around martyrs' tombs. And the aspiration to be remembered as the martyrs were, to receive their heavenly rewards, eventually turned the rituals of commemoration for the martyrs into general Christian rituals of death. As F. S. Paxton has put it: "the cult of the martyrs was a central factor in the development of the Roman Christian funeral ritual."[53] In the thirteenth century, a dramatic increase in the celebration of the Requiem Mass for the dead is noticeable in the Latin West. The increase was accompanied by a similar creative boom in Mass Books and literary productions having to do with death.[54]

A similar process, then, marks the Ashkenazic ritualization of death. In terms of the rites alone, the death of an Ashkenazic individual became a martyr's death. In this respect, too, the process was not unique to Ashkenazic Jews.[55] "It became sufficient [for a Christian] to have died a violent death to be regarded as a martyr, so long as a cult developed."[56] In the case of Jews being killed by Christians, the religious differences only intensified this sense of dying a martyr.

A fundamental distinction, however, separates Jewish martyrdom from its Christian counterpart. Christian martyrdom signifies the defeat of death and the triumph of Christianity. In contrast, Jewish martyrdom in *Ashkenaz* revolves around catastrophes and despair. The shift in collective mourning practice manifests the unfolding deterioration and vulnerability that the entire community shared. The yearning for revenge and redemption *for the community* in the mourning rituals reveals its acute distress.

HALAKHIC DISCUSSIONS

It is against this background of increasing violence for the sake of eradicating Jews that R. Isaac ben Joseph of Corbeil (d. 1280) wrote *Amudei Golah* (The Pillars of Exile), also known as *Sefer Mitvot Qatan* or *Qasar* (*SMQ*). The halakhic language of his book was more reserved than the metaphors of the poems about the events of his time. What concerned this great Tosafist from the school of Evreux was whether the opinion of R. Akiva or R. Ishmael should be followed in regard to voluntary death.[57] Isaac agreed with R. Ishmael that certain commandments may be violated in private to save one's life. "But according to the quality of righteousness, one should not transgress" these commandments even in private. Isaac brings the examples of King Saul and the opinion of R. Judah the Pietist to support his siding with Akiva. It should be noted that Isaac presents Saul as being killed (by his armor-bearer). Rather than killing himself, Saul "handed over himself for death."[58]

Isaac's reference to Judah the Pietist recalls an incident of Judah's students, whom he warned against traveling to a wedding, for they would be surely killed by robbers. Confident in their ability to perform magic by mentioning the Divine Name, they disobeyed their master. They are said to have survived their encounter with the robbers because of their supernatural capabilities. When they told Judah what had taken place, he predicted that they had just lost their share in the world to come. Their predicament could be reversed only by their submitting themselves to the robbers to be destroyed, which they did.

For Judah the Pietist the vain use of the Divine Name was at issue. Even the Ten Martyrs did not dare to use such powers to prevent God's decree against them. For Isaac of Corbeil, the example took on a different meaning. It meant that passive martyrdom was not restricted to R. Ishmael's opinion. In fact, Isaac appears to go even beyond R. Akiva's view, for Judah's students created their own doom. In any case, Isaac considers only passive martyrdom. But despite his harsh approach, he concludes that if the "Gentile's purpose is to entertain himself [by forcing transgression]," one may still transgress in private. Only if the purpose is to convert, one "should *let himself be killed*, and not transgress." At the end, Isaac still speaks in the Talmudic terms of submitting passively.

Isaac's books enjoyed a wide circulation. His *SMQ* turned into a popular *halakhic* guide book. The book reached also *Ashkenaz* and was endorsed by the celebrated Rabbi Meir ben Baruch of Rothenburg (ca. 1215–1293).[59] As a student of the academies of France and a major leader of Franco-German Jewry, Meir's endorsement came naturally. Meir, too, lamented these thirteenth-century events in several poems.[60] More significant is one of his famous *responsa* that addressed a man who had considered repentance for his preemptive slaughtering of his wife and four children during a bloodbath in Koblenz.[61] The man himself was saved by Christians who prevented him from taking his own life. The issue of this *responsum* went beyond Isaac's endorsement of R. Akiva. At issue here was self-destruction and the sacrifice of family members.

Meir justified self-sacrifice on the same grounds that Rabbenu Tam and his school had permitted self-destruction earlier. "One is permitted to harm himself," argued Meir, like the four hundred youths in *Gittin* 57b. From the same Talmudic reference, Meir also added the example of the mother of the seven sons, who "fell from the roof and died," to support his decision. His echoing of Jacob Tam is understandable. Meir of Rothenburg himself indicated in a different *responsum* that, while studying at his father's school in Worms, he "heard from his father and teacher, may he live, that he [his father, Rabbi Baruch bar Meir] had received from his teachers in the name of our rabbi [Jacob] Tam."[62] This statement was intended to make clear that what Meir received from his teachers was the teaching of Jacob Tam. Meir was Ashkenazic by birth, but of Jacob Tam's school by training. Unlike Jacob Tam, however, Meir viewed self-inflicted martyrdom to be an option rather than a *mitzvah*.

As for taking the lives of others, he writes, "I am not sure what to decide here." Such matter "requires consideration and proof." His best evidence is offered by the martyrs of 1096. Then, "Many great ones slaughtered their sons and daughters, including our rabbi Kalonymous." Meir thus answers that no repentance is required from the mourning man. Approving repentance would indirectly amount to "slandering" the "*early hasidim*" of 1096.[63] *Halakhically*, R. Meir is thus hesitant to authorize the slaughtering of children but quick to absolve those who had done so. The *Ashkenazic* precedent left this towering Tosafist limited choices. But it fell short of a ringing endorsement, as might be the impression from some of the Hebrew poems.

Two points are significant here. Meir's *responsum* is generally seen as a testament to the popularity of Jewish self-sacrifice and the sacrifice of others. Had that been the situation, it is rather surprising that almost two centuries after the First Crusade, Jews still questioned whether such acts were permissible, and rabbis still struggled legally with the issue. Given the permanence of the sacrificial metaphors from 1096, which were still in place in thirteenth-century poems and in anti-Jewish slanderous propaganda, one might not expect such a question to resurface. However, the fact that rabbis still debated these two aspects of active martyrdom by the late thirteenth century is understandable in light of the limited number of such cases. This is especially true when we remember that these rabbis would not have taken the metaphors at face value. Generally, even the more extreme debates tended to approve self-sacrifice but ignored the question of slaying coreligionists.[64]

Second, Meir appears to be grappling with his own example of King David killing the Amelekite boy for slaying King Saul (II Sam. 1:16) as a justification for taking the life of others. *Halakhically*, Meir does not find his example a convincing precedent for the sacrifice of others. His best proof, and this is no less surprising, is the behavior of his early *Ashkenazic* ancestors. Could he not have found more recent and more specific examples of Jews slaying their own from his own time? The psychological weight of the early *Hasidim* is understandable, but could Meir have referred to more recent convincing examples, it is likely that he would have done so to ease his own dilemma.

To be clear, I am not excluding the existence of the taking of others' lives as *qiddush ha-Shem*. What I am arguing is that both the question to R. Meir and his *responsum* reflect the infrequency of active voluntary death and the sacrificing of others. In a strange way, both the Jewish liturgies that continued to employ First Crusade metaphors (especially the *aqedah* and the Temple cult) to show off the religiosity of their heroes – even when active martyrdom was not the case – and the blood libels that intended to demonize Jews helped create an impression that has lasted to this day of massive active *qiddush ha-Shem*. In my opinion, such images represent what was, toward the end of the thirteenth century, the exception rather than the norm. Active martyrdom became less necessary, as impatient rioters showed more interest in simply eliminating their "unredeemable" Jewish neighbors.

AT THE CLOSE OF THE CENTURY

The same dynamic marked the end of the thirteenth century as well. Rothenburg, Nurenberg, Würzburg, and "more than hundred [nearby] communities[65] came under attack. In the Hebrew month of Ab of the year 1298, about seven years after the fall of the Latin Kingdom in the East, a nobleman by the name of Rindfleisch led riots against German Jews. The riots were triggered by the old allegation of profanation of the host. By this time, events unfolded in a routine pattern throughout almost the whole of Bavaria. "The lies that they accused me of," writes R. Joshua bar Menahem in the name of the victims, and the "snare and net they [the rioters] set"[66] resulted in the execution of Jews by fire "without a trial," according to the poem of R. Moses bar Elazar.[67] Here too, it appears, the purpose was not to offer the Jews Christianity as an alternative to death but rather to find the supposedly guilty criminals and punish them. According to the Bohemian chronicler, Abbot Peter of Zittau, even Christians questioned the reasons for killing Jews. Love of money (pro amore pecuniam) rather than Christian piety is mentioned as the attackers' motivation. Not that Peter cared. He had no doubt that God was satisfied with "King Rindfleisch's" massacres of the Jews.[68] The First Crusade's slogan of conversion or death is missing in these poems and the Latin report. Instead, the recurrent motif is the violence unleashed by the organized mob, whether before or after an investigation and its conclusions. Also absent in these riots is the assistance of Christian neighbors, as occasionally was the case during the First Crusade.

According to the memorial books, more than one hundred thousand Jews perished as martyrs in the devastating attacks against one hundred forty-six communities.[69] Judging by the numbers of victims in these geographically widespread massacres, it is understandable why scholars have viewed the Rindfleisch violence as a turning point in regard to the physical security of Jews.[70] It is little wonder that the medieval Jews saw themselves as potential martyrs and all victims as martyrs in this violent atmosphere of "snares and lies."

The Hebrew poems following the Rindfleisch massacres continued to describe the victims of these events as martyrs. These poems employed the same style, terms, and symbols as the earlier medieval sources. Joshua's poem described fathers and mothers preparing the altars for the sacrifice of their own flesh and blood. "Fathers kindled the fire and the sons gathered the wood." In this light, the anonymous mother with her seven sons underwent a similar transformation. Her children were taken forcibly from her while "she burned like a blaze." Despite the repetition of metaphors and of old-style sacrifices, Joshua still pondered, like his First Crusade ancestors, whether "such a thing has happened since the two destructions [of the Temples]."[71]

Metaphors aside, what dominates the poem is the burning of the "holy communities." They all went up in smoke when the "Christians came with their fire." Joshua correctly observed that the "times have changed." The conditions that produced the execution of the Jews appear to differ from the circumstances of the crusading period. The typical late medieval death at the stake made a perfect metaphor for the older *aqedah* symbol.[72] But descriptions of active martyrdom slowly disappeared from thirteenth-century writings, probably because of a lack of will and because of lack of time for negotiations between the would-be martyrs and the eager inquisitors and mob. Given the negative image of Jews, it is also reasonable that this mob's interest in converting Jewish children also decreased. Moses bar Elazar reveals in his dirge that "our big and small, our wives and children, our elders and youths, our sons and daughters" were all burned. With the same sense of dismay echoed by the First Crusade chronicles and by R. Joshua, Moses wondered "if such a thing ever happened to any nation."[73] At least with regard to the conditions that led to the sacrifices, Moses was correct. Now, the mob assigned to all Jews one destructive fate. This policy eliminated the fear that Jewish children would be forcefully converted after the death of their parents, consequently diminishing the need to sacrifice the children.

Although the stake had been prepared before the victims received a chance to defend themselves and express their wishes, the metaphors in R. Joshua's eulogy gave the martyrs "control" over their fate. Although at Blois the adversary set the fire from below, for these martyrs "God's fire fell down from heaven" (Job 1:16)[74] to kindle "on Your altar . . . all the offered sacrifices."[75] Following Ephraim of Bonn, the martyrs entered the fire "like a groom [lit. an eighteen-year-old] enters the *huppah* [the canopy] with drums, and harps."[76] God's fire from heaven served also as polemics. It countered Christian claims that God rejected

the Jews like the hateful Cain, the pagans like the worshipers of Baal, and you [God] do not light a fire on their offerings. Yet you do desire the hosts of the Christian people, just like the offerings of Abel; you approve of its sacrifice, like the holocaust of Elijah, and thus with a fire sent from heaven do you irradiate the grave in which your son, offered as a sacrifice on our behalf, lay at rest.[77]

There was little Jews could do to put out these fires. At least, through the metaphor of heavenly fire, they could put to rest such theological arguments. Here again, the symbols that feature in Jewish and Christian accounts are employed to stress the differences between the two groups.

Together with Ephraim's symbol of the dove, the heavenly fire marked another clear-cut distinction between Jewish and Christian casualties. Moses bar Elazar incorporated Ephraim's dove, which became now a burnt offering. In the eyes of R. Joshua and his generation, there was no difference between the crusaders' Jewish victims – the martyrs who generally were killed for choosing Judaism over Christianity – and the martyrs of the postcrusading period.

Although Ashkenazic *qiddush ha-Shem* matured against the conditions of the crusading period, Ashkenazic Jewry kept alive its tradition of voluntary death in the postcrusading era as if European Jewry were still living under the crusader's sword. Indeed, the new conditions brought with them new ecclesiastical pressures and calamities, which often caused the killing of Jews without their having even the chance of choosing between their faith and Christianity.[78] But in the hearts of the writers, who maintained the tragic stories in the Ashkenazic collective memory, there was no doubt what would have been the answer of these victims had they been able to choose their own fate.[79] For these reasons, all Jews were viewed as potential martyrs, including the previously mentioned thirteenth-century victims who, like their Franco-German predecessors, had chosen death over Christianity. Thus vows Menahem bar Tamar in the language of the Ten Martyrs liturgy, "these I shall remember (*Elleh Ezkerah*), the community of Würzburg" or the "holy community of Rothenburg" with the other hundred communities that were "burned and murdered."[80] The use of the Ten Martyrs liturgy elevates the status of all victims and places them in the circle of Akiva and his nine martyred companions.

Because the 1096 ultimatum of conversion or death was gradually eroding, how to react to this ultimatum became less relevant. At issue now was how to deal, physically and emotionally, with what seemed to be an inescapable death. Hence, Meir of Rothenburg reassured his readers: "when a man insists on sanctifying the Name [of God] and on handing over his soul for the sanctification of the Name, all that is done to him: stoning, burning, live burial, hanging, do not pain him ... and many hand themselves over *to be burnt and killed* [emphasis mine] for the sanctification of the blessed Name and they do not scream."[81]

Given the nature of the popular attacks on Jews, Meir of Rothenburg offered, *prima facie*, solace and a way of dealing with the torture and death that even baptism could no longer always avert. Declaring the oneness of God, we may recall, served the martyrs of 1096 as a polemical protest against the notion of trinity and the crusaders' invitations to share Christianity during the "persuasion process." In the thirteenth century, R. Meir offered the same statement to overcome the pain of torture. "As one recites the Unique Name at the onset [of the torture] he is assured of enduring the test," both of physical pain and divine love. Ephraim of Bonn and the letter from Orléans had introduced the motif of martyrs miraculously defeating physical pain in Blois. The motif comforted the community and countered Christian hagiography. Meir of Rothenburg ascribed to the method benefits in the face of suffering. His self-proclaimed student, Rabbi Peretz of Corbeil, expressed similar thoughts on the issue of overcoming torture.[82] R. Meir's technique would become especially valuable in the fourteenth century.

BY MAN AND MALADY

Southern France witnessed large-scale massacres during the so-called Shepherd's Crusade of the 1320's. Jews and lepers were accused of poisoning wells in southern France and Spain.[83] A dove, the popular martyrological symbol of the period, is said to have inspired and guided the rioters' young leader in Spain.[84] These popular riots bear all the characteristics of the thirteenth-century anti-Jewish allegations and had very little to do with the masses' goals of the First Crusade.[85] Guillaume de Nangis reports that in southern France Jews were accused of hiring lepers to poison the wells in 1322. Persecutions and further expulsions followed in a ritualistic manner.[86] According to an anonymous Jewish mystic, the *Pastorelli* slew about eight thousand men. On pretext of having poisoned the waters, "they slew most holy ones in France."[87]

The charges in southern France herald the devastation brought by the Black Death. European Jews fell victim in great numbers not only to this cataclysmic pandemic but also to the hysterical and irrational actions of Christian crowds.[88] It is not surprising, therefore, that the first massacres took place in southern France in the spring of 1348.[89] Apart from being targets for the accusations of well poisoning, Jews furnished these hysterical crowds with a far more tangible "reason" for the plague than the initial belief in the *Pest Jungfrau* that flew from city to city in a blue flame. Spurious trials like the one at Chilon, in September 1348, and the "confessions" extorted from Jews confirmed the Christian suspicions of a worldwide Jewish conspiracy to poison Europe's water. "In the month of November [1348] began the persecution of the Jews," wrote Henry of Diessenhoven. Jews were burnt at Solothurn, Zofingen, and Stuttgart. A month later, Landsberg, Burrn, Memmingen, and

Lindau burned their Jewish residents. Ulm and Speyer joined in the torching of Jews the following January. Gotha, Eisenach, Dresden, Cologne, Worms, Baden, and Erfurt are only some of the towns that followed suit.[90]

With the launching of the Flagellants' movement, many Europeans were convinced they would have a better chance to survive the plague if they destroyed the Jews. Executions of Jews were expected not only to stop the poisoning but also to appease God's wrath. Ecclesiastical appeals to the populace's logic failed. "As a result of this theory of infected water and air as the source of the plague," reports the Carmelite friar, Jean de Venette,

the Jews were suddenly and violently charged with infecting wells and water and corrupting the air. The whole world rose up against them cruelly on this account. In Germany and other parts of the world where Jews lived, they were massacred and slaughtered by Christians, and many thousands were burned everywhere, indiscriminately. The unshaken, if fatuous, constancy of the men and their wives was remarkable. For mothers hurled their children first into the fire that they might not be baptized and then leaped in after them to burn with their husbands and children.[91]

Children still appear to have had the option of conversion in this incident. But even Jean is not sure that the sparing of children would be the case. Their parents' insistence on seeing them burned first may have derived from the knowledge that the adults' fates had been sealed. In this way, parents could, at least, spoil attempts to convert the children after the demise of their parents.

That seems to have been the case at Strasbourg. On St. Valentine's Day, Strasbourg burned its Jews on a wooden platform in the Jewish cemetery. "Many small [Jewish] children were taken out of the fire and baptized against the will of their fathers and mothers." Strasbourg still seems to have shown some interest in converting the "innocent" Jews. "Those who wanted to baptize themselves were spared." At the same time, the report claims that "the money [of the Jews] was indeed the thing that killed the Jews." If monetary benefit motivated the burning, one may wonder how interested the crowds were in baptism. After the burning, "the [city] council took the cash that the Jews possessed and divided it among the working-men proportionately . . . wealth was divided among the artisans, some gave their share to the Cathedral or the Church on the advice of their confessors."[92]

What sealed the fate of the Jews, however, was the seriousness of the allegations against them. Jean Le Bel's *Chronique* reports that Jews were believed to poison wells "in order to poison all Christendom and to have the lordship over all the world."[93] Therefore, "great and small were so enraged against them [the Jews] that they were all burned and put to death by lords and judges of the places along the route of the Flagellants." Jean describes the Jewish reaction vividly.

They all went to their death dancing and singing joyously as though they were going to a wedding, and they would not be converted, nor would fathers nor mothers permit their children to be baptised [*sic*] ... saying that they had found in the books of the prophets that as soon as the sect of the Flagellants had overrun the world, that all Jewry would be destroyed by fire, and that the souls of those who remained firm in their faith would go to paradise. Wherefore as soon as they saw the fire, men and women leaped into it, always singing and carrying their little infants with them for fear that they might become Christians.

It is difficult to determine what Jean meant by "they would not be converted." His statement may indicate a Jewish refusal to convert or the Flagellants' rejection of the baptismal option. Jacob von Königshofen's report of the so-called confession of the Jewish Agimet of Geneva clearly states what the populace had in mind and what the investigation was expected to yield. Prince Amadeus of Savoy ordered the arrest of all Jews after the public demanded "that they [the Jews] die, that they are able to be found guilty and, therefore, that they should be punished."[94] If in the twelfth-century inquisitorial pressure was designed to extort confession followed by conversion, the fourteenth-century public expected the inquisition to find the Jews guilty to destroy them.

   The motifs of the twelfth and thirteenth centuries continued to resurface in the documents of the fourteenth century. These martyrs actualized the miraculous singing imagery of Blois while employing Meir of Rothenburg's technique to overcome pain. They were accorded further comfort from the expectation of reaching paradise. During the Black Death, Paradise was on the minds of both Jews and Christians as their only escape from their hellish experience. Jean's description and metaphors recall the language of the Jewish martyrologists. The correlation does not stem from Jean's having read Hebrew martyrology. He described the death of the Jews as going to a wedding in the same way that Christians described the death of their martyrs.[95]

   Because of these wholesale massacres that occurred throughout Europe, it would be unrealistic to speak of a monolithic treatment of Jews. Mock trials preceded the attacks in some cases, whereas in others the massacres came without warning.[96] Conversion was still offered in several places – at times perhaps sincerely and in other times *pro forma*. Pope Clement VI's bull sounded a familiar complaint. It shows which of the two possibilities was more likely. Most of the Flagellants, he wrote, "beneath an appearance of piety, set their hands to cruel and impious work, shedding the blood of Jews, whom Christian piety accepted and sustains."[97]

Such masquerades of piety were not limited to these "Brethren of the Cross." Indicative of the general mood and the many sinister conspiracies is the letter of Landgrave Frederic of Thuringia to the Council of the City of Nordhausen in May 1349. Frederic proudly announced that he had burnt his Jews for the honor of God, advocating that the Council follow suit. Even Emperor Charles IV offered the Archbishop of Trier the property of the Jews in Alsace "who have already been killed or may still be killed." To the Margrave of Brandenburg, Charles offered the choice of the three best Jewish houses in Nuremberg, "when there is next a massacre of the Jews there."[98] As these communications disclose, Jews were doomed well before the massacres had taken shape. Two thousand Jews were massacred in Strasbourg several weeks before the first reports of the infection.[99] Just the news that the Flagellants were coming to Brussels was sufficient to trigger the massacre of six hundred Jews there.[100]

In Mainz, the Jews refused to exit life without resistance, taking the lives of two hundred Christians in the process. The twelve thousand Jews who lost their lives in the Christian retaliation did not stand a chance even to convert.[101] In the Hansa towns those who had escaped the flames were sealed in houses and left to starve or suffocate to death.[102] It is not difficult to understand why some reporters claimed that the Jews had set fire to their houses and "cremated themselves."[103] In a cynical way, this accusation gave these victims, in subsequent Jewish writings, the required martyrological element of control over their fate. Although unsympathetic reports held the Jews responsible for the deadly fires, which spread beyond the Jewish quarters, such rumors further helped Jewish martyrologists depict their heroes as having died of their own volition by the fire from heaven.

COMMENTARY AND COMMEMORATION

Under such circumstances, R. Moses of Zurich added his commentary on the *SMQ*. Despite this evolving backdrop, Moses continued his legal discussion over the forms of voluntary death in the traditional spirit of the Talmud and the language of the 1096 accounts. He claimed to relay the opinion of the early-thirteenth-century R. Eliezer bar Joel ha-Levi, known by the acronym Ravyah.[104] Without providing any specifics, he absolved "those holy ones who slaughtered themselves and their offspring," for they doubted whether they could withstand their test.[105] Comparing these "holy ones" to the three Danielic "martyrs" and the four hundred youths from B. *Gittin* 57b, Moses is confident that the more recent "holy ones" received their place in the world to come, despite their activism.

Based on these examples, the slaughter of children was permitted during the period of persecution. The sacrifice of children was justifiable in Moses' opinion, for children are too young to "distinguish between good and evil." "For we fear that [if they live] they will dwell among the Gentiles [and become non-Jews] when they grow up. It is better that they would die innocent and not die guilty."[106] Clearly, Moses provided an intellectual discussion about past events "at the time of the persecution," and addressed the possible Jewish reactions of that time. According to our non-Jewish accounts, however, children perished together with their parents in the flames. More often than not, these flames were set by the non-Jews.

A reality different from Moses's account is seen in the eyewitness-based report on events at Strasbourg. It recapitulates the desire to both burn the Jewish inhabitants and eliminate them for good. "So finally the Bishop and the lords and the Imperial Cities agreed to do away with the Jews. The result was that they were burnt in many cities, and wherever they were expelled they were caught by the peasants and stabbed to death or drowned."[107]

It is entirely conceivable that some Jews joined in the spreading of the fire as an act of desperation. Such actions should not be seen in Jewish martyrological terms alone. In their despair, many Christians gave up on life, actively destroying their own families to avoid suffering.[108] It fits a universal pattern in such devastating circumstances. As Mollaret wrote:

Psychologists and sociologists know that man reacts to violent pain by flight, by violence or by sublimation. The plague stirred up these three reactions. Flight took the form of a stampede towards altars and processions; doctors and quacks; workers of miracles and visionaries. Violence found its outlet in the massacre of the Jews or those believed to have spread the plague, in the hysteria of the Flagellants, often in suicide. Sublimation was the works of the artists.[109]

Jewish self-destruction was therefore not necessarily motivated by the same desire to escape forced baptism or to avert the baptism of Jewish orphans seen in the First Crusade. What motivated these widespread massacres was not the desire to convert Jews or even to punish them for what their assailants considered to be their historical sin. At issue was the belief that the unredeemable Jewish nature drove these Jews to destroy Christian society.

Artistic works further demonstrated the desire to physically eliminate Judaism. A. Foa points to Paolo Uccello's fifteenth-century polyptych to correctly argue that all Jews became targets for destruction rather than conversion. A sign of the time was the dropping of the legal "dying age" for Jews from thirteen to seven. It meant that children, also, were seen as active participants in the Jewish plot against Christianity.[110] Not that age mattered. One of

Uccello's panels depicts how "the Jews – children included – end up at the stake," after a Jewish moneylender had profaned the host with his family.[111] The devastation of the Black Death substantiated the irrational fear that Jews were gaining the upper hand in their conspiracy against the Christian majority. It is this distorted perception of events that viewed the massacre of all Jews as a necessary act of self-defense.

The Black Death affected also how Jews commemorated the events. Whether because of the pogroms or the pestilence, the complete destruction of so many communities further crystallized the sense of a shared collective martyrdom. R. Solomon Simhah ha-Sofer entitled the entire Troyes community "holy" after it lost thirteen of its members in 1288. During the Black Death, seeing the devastation as being of communal proportions was not an imaginative stretch. Martyrological terminology and liturgy were adjusted according to the new reality.

Jews were not unique in representing the casualties of the Black Death in such a manner. Christian casualties are also described in a pseudomartyrological jargon. They are portrayed as glorious martyrs, although there was nothing gorgeous about falling victim to the plague. "Man died the more willingly," we are told, because of the papal collective absolution from penalty. "However suddenly men died, almost all awaited death joyfully," reported Jean de Venette.[112] Reading only a few lines from the available sources would suffice to convince one that death in these years was nothing but joyous. Others who died while attending the sick reached the status of saints. They now "rest in peace with Christ, as we may piously believe."[113] At Clermont, Pope Urban had promised *indulgentia* to the martyrs of the First Crusade. Now, the "Pope gave plenary remission of all sins *to all* [emphasis mine] receiving absolution at the point of death."[114]

Humans often react universally to major catastrophes. Muslim theologians also provided eloquent rationalizations of the high praise paid during the Black Death:

The martyrs and those who died in their beds argue with Our Lord about those who were killed by the plague. The martyrs say, our brothers died as we died. The deceased, on their beds, say, our brothers died on their beds as we died. Our Lord said: "Consider their wounds, which resemble the wounds of the slaughtered, and they are among them." And behold, their wounds had been similar; so they joined the martyrs.[115]

If that was the approach toward the victims claimed by the Black Death, Jews were doubly persuaded to crown their brethren and their decimated communities with holy martyrdom. "In Mainz they fasted [to commemorate] the persecution of 1349 every year on the eighth of Ellul. Once it fell on the eve of

the Sabbath so they fasted and said *Selihot* [penitential prayers] in the morning. And in the evening, during the *Minhah* [prayer] they mention the souls of
the holy ones [*ha-qeddoshim*] – the slain – after they had read *vayekhal* and the
aftarah, and delivered homilies – May He Who blessed the congregation – *Av
ha-Rahamim*."[116] In the tradition of *Ashkenaz*, no distinction is made between
the different casualties during the Black Death. They were all considered martyrs. When names were not provided, the memorial books of the time listed
the communities and "their students and dwellers." God was beseeched to
"remember all the souls of those killed and burned and all the communities
and their dwellers with the souls of Abraham, Isaac, Jacob, Sara, Rebecca,
Rachel, and Leah, for they labored for the communities and caused the cancellation of the persecutions. . . . "[117] Often, the magnitude of the devastations
forced the survivors to commemorate the names of places, instead of people.[118]

The process of collective commemoration and the building of death rituals
came to a close in *Ashkenaz* after the Black Death. Known as the "plague
of rites," this process ensured that the young *Ashkenazic* liturgical traditions
would not be forgotten in the devastation caused by the plague of God.[119] The
many martyrs it created only intensified this need to commemorate. Now
all the *Ashkenazic* martyrs, starting with those of 1096, were commemorated
together, and their names recited.[120] By reciting *Av ha-Rhamim* and other
dirges on the "Black Sabbath" before the Ninth of the month of Av – the
date that designates the destruction of the two Temples in Jerusalem and
the month in which the Jews of 1096 were attacked – Ashkenazic liturgists
compared their tragedies to that of the Destructions.[121] For the Ashkenazic
Jewry, the commemoration of their sacred martyrs became as important as
remembering the sanctity of the Temples.

By 1351, the number of Jews left in northern Europe to become martyrs per
se, had decreased dramatically. What King Edward I of England started in 1290,
and Philip IV of France in 1306,[122] was now completed in the rest of Ashkenaz
by man and malady. Together, nature and the dark side of human nature
wiped out sixty large and one hundred fifty smaller communities in three
hundred fifty massacres.[123] Those fortunate enough to survive fled eastward.
Their old Ashkenazic legacy endured and continued to develop in their new
Polish and Lithuanian communities. What brought them there and the many
"holy" martyrs whom they left behind will never be forgotten.

SPAIN

While the Ashkenazic tradition was rebuilding itself in the east, its martyrological thinking could be traced also in the west. Spanish Jewry was relatively
less affected by riots during the Black Death, although the plague was equally

devastating to all the Iberian inhabitants. Spain thus provides a good illustration of effective government protection. Governmental protection had its limits, however. More than three hundred Jews were slaughtered in Tarragon. Thanks to decisive actions by King Pedro IV of Aragon, the numbers of casualties remained relatively small.[124]

Violent Spanish anti-Semitism caught up with the rest of western Europe toward the end of the century. Anti-Jewish preaching alone was enough to stir the violence this time around. A letter by the towering leader Hasdai Crescas reported a series of massacres. In June 4, 1391, rioters set fire to the gates of the city of Seville "and killed many of its [Jewish] people." Most changed their religion; some women and children were sold to the Muslims. Many, continued Hasdai, "died for the sanctification of the Name, and many desecrated the holy covenant."[125] By grouping together these two contrasting behaviors, Hasdai probably intended to emphasize the martyrological nature of the former casualties. His description, however, makes it clear that "most of them converted."

In Gerona, maintained Hasdai, "in one place the rabbis publicly sanctified the Holy Name."[126] Few converted, whereas most found refuge in the homes of their Christian neighbors. Gerona's councillors placed the blame for the massacre on the peasants. Washing their hands further, the *jurados* of Gerona, who provoked the riots, blamed the Jews for the killing. Many of the women and children, the *jurados* claimed, had been slaughtered by the Jews themselves. It was in the interest of the *jurados* to shift the blame for the deaths and put it squarely on the "self-killer" Jew. Hasdai's letter gives no such indication. How many chose to die as martyrs is hard to tell, as the prevalent term *qiddush ha-Shem* had become associated with all Jewish casualties in our sources. Even more difficult to know is how many engaged in active martyrdom, if any. The choice at Gerona of baptism or expulsion gave its Jewish habitants some leeway.[127] It was in Hasdai's interest to depict the "rabbis of the community" as martyrs, as it was in the interest of the rioters to depict the entire community as dangerous self-killers.

At Barcelona, "God cast his anger like fire" on Saturday.[128] Popular rioters, known as the "little people," started with the slaughter of about one hundred Jews. Thereafter, this *populus minutus* turned against another one hundred fifty Jews who had fortified themselves in the "New Fortress." According to Hasdai,

they fought the Jews that were in the fortress with bows and catapults and beat and struck them there in the tower. Many sanctified the Holy Name, among them my only son, a bridegroom, an innocent lamb; him have I offered up as a burnt offering. I shall vindicate God's judgment against me, and I shall be comforted with his good portion and pleasant fate. Many of them slaughtered themselves; some threw themselves from the tower . . . and some went out [of the tower] and sanctified the Name in the street. All the rest converted.

Hasdai's description recalls the incidents of the First Crusade. Particularly does the sacrifice of his *only son*, "a bridegroom, an innocent lamb," echo the Ashkenazic language and biblical symbols (Abraham's only son). Without details, the passive and active martyrological patterns seen in the First Crusade are alluded to. Hasdai's archetypal depiction may create the impression that he himself sacrificed his son. It also paints Hasdai as a supporter of martyrdom.[129]

To be sure, Hasdai could only write about the event using the Ashkenazic metaphor of the Temple priest and the *aqedah*. At the time of the riots, Hasdai was at Saragossa. All he could do was to write a letter, endorsed by the queen, to Barcelonean officials to spare his family. His letter arrived too late. What is evident in his report is the use of the Ashkenazic metaphors and style. No wonder, therefore, that Hasdai viewed these martyrs in a way similar to that of the Talmud (B. *Baba Batra* 10b) and the Ashkenazic reports. For Hasdai, the casualties were martyrs. They constitute an exceptional group, for no creature could come into their presence.[130]

Martyrdom continued to occur in Spain into the early fifteenth century, according to Solomon ibn Verga. "Many sanctified the [Divine] Name and were burned" reports his *Shevet Yehudah*.[131] However, the increased use of martyrological phrases and the impression *qiddush ha-Shem* left on these generations require of us a more careful reading. R. Joseph Yaabets, for instance, used the phrase in a nonmartyrological sense to describe Hasdai Crescas's greatness. "God's Name was sanctified" by Hasdai, according to Yaabets, for through him "many of the great men of the kingdom were inwardly Judaized."[132] For Yaabets, the "sacrifice" of Hasdai's son and his communal services earned him a place among the martyrs. Hasdai himself described the approximately two hundred fifty Jewish casualties of the riots at Valencia or the three hundred fatalities at Majorca as "dying for the sanctification of the Name," without providing further information.[133] Although the sources at hand are not always detailed enough to determined the exact nature of many of these martyrdoms, it is clear that voluntary death was practiced in Spain.[134] Moreover, it is clear that our authors made an extensive use of the Ashkenazic martyrological style in their reports.

WHY NOW?

What is significant about Spain is not the nature of the allegation or the violence it triggered. By now, the negative image of the Jew had spread like the plague itself throughout the Latin West. More puzzling is the Jewish martyrological reaction. To be more specific, the question that arises is why martyrdom came into play during these years in Spain and not earlier. Maimonides is believed to have established an antimartyrdom culture in Muslim Spain and northern Africa. His *Epistle on Conversion* distinguished between the conditions of the Jews in Christendom and Islam. He perceived Christians as idolators but not the "Ishmaelites."[135]

Maimonides' advice appears to have been followed almost throughout the Muslim conquest of Spain.[136] An exception is revealed in a letter by Solomon Cohen. He reports that Jews were rounded up at the city of Saglamasah to be converted in 1148. One hundred fifty Jews resisted and "were killed for the unity of the [Divine] Name," whereas the majority converted.[137] In relative terms, this was the exception. As seen, a significant change in the approach of Spanish Jews to voluntary death can be noticed both in their writings and behavior from the middle of the fourteenth century.

Obviously, the martyrological phenomenon in Spain cannot be ascribed to one factor, just as its relative absence in the previous years cannot be attributed only to the study of philosophy.[138] Hasdai Crescas's son is said to have rejected baptism, although his father did not exclude the study of philosophy from his curriculum.[139] In addition to the deterioration in conditions, what led to the consideration of *qiddush ha-Shem* could be attributable to the settling of Franco-German Tosafists and rabbis in the Iberian Peninsula. From the early fourteenth century, their growing influence on Spanish Jews is noticeable. R. Peretz ha-Cohen, who settled in Barcelona, and R. Dan, the Ashkenazi, were among these important emigrés.[140]

The French expulsion of 1306 brought to Majorca R. Aaron ha-Cohen of Lunel. His *Orhot hayyim* recounted the Talmudic opinion that in time of duress one can submit to death. But he also referred to R. Ishmael's opinion that death is not always mandatory. In case of torture, he referred to the opinions of R. Meir of Rothenburg and R. Isaac ben Joseph of Corbeil[141] that a person may "Submit himself for death and kill himself if he sees that he cannot stand the test."[142] Without mentioning the rabbis' names, Aaron explained that such opinions were based on the examples of King Saul, R. Judah the Pietist, and the three heroes from Daniel. From these examples some scholars deduced that the slaughtering of children was permissible in time of duress, whereas others still prohibited this practice.

Aaron's opposition to any active martyrdom is evident.[143] Hananiah, Mishael, and Azariah, reminded Aaron, submitted themselves, "but they did not injure themselves." "And Saul ben Kish acted against the opinions of the sages." Next, Aaron mentioned the story from *Daat Zekenim* about the rabbi who was considered a "murderer" by another rabbi, for he had slaughtered children. And finally, Maimonides' rulings are mentioned to emphasize the passive nature of martyrdom. Moreover, Aaron seems to accept Maimonides' opinion that the best solution in time of persecution is to escape and avoid the martyrological test altogether. A person who fails to do so, "loses his place in the world to come, and descends to the lowest level of Hell."[144] Clearly, the person who goes to hell is the one who converts rather than leave. Aaron ha-Cohen of Lunel followed Maimonides' latter advice.

R. Asher ben Yehiel (Rosh) provided an especially critical link between the Tosafists and Spain.[145] Born in Cologne and educated in the Tosafist school, R. Asher was invited to hold the key leadership position at Toledo. He brought with him not only exceptional erudition but also personal experiences. Of the more significant occurrences that left powerful memories in R. Asher's mind were the arrest of his teacher, R. Meir of Rothenburg, and the devastations of 1298 in Germany and France.[146] R. Asher's decisions reflect the impact of his French teachers and of Rabbenu Tam's rulings.[147] In fact, R. Asher's goal was to compose a *halakhic* work for his new community that would capture the Franco-German contribution from Rabbenu Gershom to his own day.[148]

Just how influential R. Asher was is demonstrated by his ability to leave his two sons, Judah and Jacob, in leadership positions after his death in 1328.[149] But this rabbinic dynasty was short lived. R. Judah, the Rosh's grandson, is reported to have led his family and students to martyrdom at Toledo in 1391. Employing the familiar metaphors of the First Crusade, Hasdai's letter briefly described the events in this "holy city from which the Torah and the word of the Lord came forth."[150] His letter basically singled out R. Asher's family and its school as the only martyrs. "In Toledo," it said, "a priest and a prophet were killed in the Temple of God." Toledo's rabbis, "the chosen and pleasing seed, the seed of R. Asher, sanctified the Name publicly with their children and students." Except for the family and its close followers, "also there many converted."[151] In Hasdai's eyes, the presence of the family in Toledo turned the city into God's Temple, and its Ashkenazic leaders into priests and prophets. It was only fitting for Hasdai to describe their demise in Ashkenazic terms. Unlike in Ashkenaz, however, the emphasis in Spain remained on the martyrdom of rabbis and their close students.

Another illustration of the Franco-German influence is exhibited by the Hebrew literature of Spain. Profet Duran, a student of Hasdai Crescas, chose the methodology of martyrological events for his work *Zikharon ha-Shemadot* (The Record of Persecutions).[152] After the Iberian expulsion, Spanish Jews carried their version of the Tosafists' legacy to their new destinations.

Tosafistic influence is more explicitly expressed in the later works of Spanish exiles. A good illustration is the fifteenth-century work, *Megillat Amraphel*, by

Rabbi Abraham ben Eliezer ha-Levi, the Spanish Kabbalist who left his home country for Palestine:[153]

This is a tradition among the sages: If someone determines in his heart to sacrifice himself for the honor of His great Name, come what may and transpire what may, such a man will not feel the pain of wounds, which torment only those who have not determined this with all their hearts. Now if one leads such a person forth, in order to subject him to pain and torment of terrible torture, as was the case with the holy martyrs, those great young men, the sons of saintly Hannah... if such a man concentrates and put between his eyes the awesome and great Name, and determines in his heart to sanctify Him, and his eyes will incline toward the Holy One of Israel, and he can focus his entire mind and thought on Him... then he can rest assured in his heart that he will withstand the test. . . . He will not feel any pain, blows or torments, nor tremble with the fear of death. . . . These things should be made known to His people Israel, for the generation is one of religious persecution, and no Israelite should go in ignorance of this principle. . . .

Abraham elaborates here on the technique R. Meir of Rothenburg had offered for overcoming torture and the fear of death. This method, Abraham writes, "is a tradition among the sages... [and] has been already practiced." This tradition of the "sages and the martyrs," as Abraham repeats once more, was the creation of Rabbi Meir of Rothenburg, according to G. Scholem.[154]

I have already mentioned that Rabbi Peretz of Corbeil referred to this technique of his teacher and colleague, R. Meir of Rothenburg. According to R. Menham ben Aaron ben Zerah, the holy, he and his colleagues turned to R. Peretz's works "every day and night," at Alcolea, Spain, between the difficult years of 1350 and 1368.[155] R. Peretz thus provided another channel for the teaching of the Tosafists in Spain.

Based on R. Peretz's example and R. Moses Galante's commentary to Ecclesiastes 8:5 ("One who obeys the command will not experience evil") Scholem's opinion can be taken a step further. In his sixteenth-century *Kehillat Yaacov*, Galante wrote that other Tosafists, too, toiled to offer a spiritual technique for overcoming physical pain. Moshe Galante explained, "the meaning of this [verse] is similar to what the Tosafists have adduced... following the tradition of the [French] sages: 'Those who are burnt and killed for the sanctification of His Name do not experience this torment but die [painlessly] by [divine] kiss.'"[156]

Two relevant points emerge from Galante's interpretation. First, the Tosafists' need to offer the Jews a method of facing inescapable pain resurfaces. In the same spirit, Galant contemporary, R. Solomon Luria, spoke against suicide, but permitted one to set his house on fire. In this way, one could still avoid forced baptism and still be considered a passive martyr.[157] Second, the statement affirms the steady transmission of the Tosafists' view of *qiddush ha-Shem* to historical periods and geographic places outside the boundaries of Franco-German Jewry. This tradition constitutes the collective work of the Tosafists, who were drawing on living examples of torture and unavoidable death. Rabbi Meir of Rothenburg held a leading role in forming the new face of this tradition. As the Jewish immigrants established themselves in more hospitable countries after the expulsions from *Ashkenaz* and *Sephard*, the Tosafists' practical advice became less necessary. Nevertheless, the Tosafists' martyrological legacy continued to live in the collective Jewish memory.

10

ॐ

Shifting Paradigms

Ashkenazic and Sepharadic exiles carried their martyrologies, hagiographies, and the liturgies that commemorated their medieval heroes to their new localities. With the migration from west to east and the transition from the Middle Ages into the modern period, there emerged also alterations in the use of the martyrological idea. Martyrological symbols and metaphors continued to be extensively utilized in different aspects of Jewish life and lore. Based on the medieval perception that all Jews lived as potential martyrs in the "hour of persecution," life in exile was compared to a form of martyrdom.

"Many cremations for the sanctification of your Name were there, and many times they chose suffocation for their souls. They sacrificed their sons and daughters not to defile Your Name." This is how R. Joseph ibn Yihyya of the exile generation described the life of the many *forced converts (ha-anusim)*.[1] Even Rabbi Abraham ben Eliezer ha-Levi's *Megillat Amraphel*, which instructed readers how to mentally prepare for actual martyrdom, described life in exile as a virtual voluntary death. Every man who "decides in his heart to submit himself to Him by his body and soul, and also his wife and his children, in order to love Him with all his heart and all his soul and all his might," promised the rabbi, "goes to the light of life with the righteous and the *hasidim* and the holy ones."[2] Both the decision and the act remain "in his heart."

The very same images and metaphors that abound in medieval martyrology *symbolized* the daily struggle of these tormented exiles and their sons and daughters. Forced conversion and life in the new exile were symbolically addressed as *qiddush ha-Shem*. Similarly, the complicated life of subsequent generations was compared to child sacrifices. God, the *anusim* believed, knew that in their hearts they remained loyal. The torment caused by their submission to a life of suffering became their sacrifice. Good intention alone could count as martyrdom. One, therefore, should practice Judaism "as if he died" (*keillu met*).[3]

Qiddush ha-Shem thus came to characterize the spiritual practices of the devoted in his quest for union with the Divine. Love of God unto death symbolized the submission of the individual to his Creator. Spiritual self-denial was meant to release the soul to lead the self to perfection. While the medieval martyrs achieved perfection through death, virtual sacrificers of the self could attain spiritual perfection in life; whereas medieval martyrs gained divine union in heaven, meditation and practice could duplicate a similar state for the seeker of God on earth. Simulated death stimulated this desire for unification with the Divine.[4]

On a different level yet, it was only natural to employ the medieval martyrological style in reports of actual massacres. Polish Jews resorted to their Ashkenazic literature to describe the butchering of their communities by Chmielnicki and his Cossacks in 1648–49. Nathan Nata Hanover, "the son of the martyred Rabbi Moses Hanover Ashkenazi," captured the events in his *Yeven Metsulah* (*The Deep Mire*). His introduction opens with a familiar medieval demand. "The 'Greeks' [i.e., Orthodox Christians], in their typical manner, offered the following ultimatum to the Jews: He that wishes to remain alive must change his faith and publicly renounce Israel and his God."[5]

The Jewish reaction is described in an archetypical style as well. "The Jews, however, heeded not their words, but stretched out their necks to be slaughtered for the sanctification of His Holy Name." As in the description of events in 1096, all are said to react in this manner: "land's leading scholars as well as the men, women and children; the whole community." The destruction was also rationalized in familiar terms. Corresponding with the central theme in the legend of *Asarah Harugei Malkhut* are Nathan's esoteric calculations proving that the tragedy of the innocent congregations had been predetermined.

On the twentieth of Sivan, the massacre began at the "holy community of Nemirow." In 1171, Blois burned its Jews on the twentieth of Sivan. Polish Jewry adopted this date to unite the anniversary of the two tragedies. All victims, the six thousand of them, became the new Ashkenazic martyrs. Following in the footsteps of their medieval predecessors, women and young girls "drowned in the waters." In another incident, "a beautiful girl" jumped from a bridge into the water and was drowned for the sanctification of the Name." Rabbi Jechiel Michael, the head of the academy of Nemirow, and his followers are presented in a style reminiscent of the Xanten incident in 1096. "On the Sabbath before the catastrophe (*ha-gezerah*) he preached and admonished the people that if the enemy should come (God forbid) they should not change their faith, but rather be martyred for the sanctification of His Name. This the holy people did."

Yeven Metsulah, however, reveals some of the previously noted developments of the later medieval period. Chmielnicki and his Cossacks attacked Polish Jews without always offering conversion. Thus, upon hearing about the coming danger, the "holy communities" did not know whether the enemy would "bring upon us an implacable extermination or would force us to change our creed, God forbid."[6] Nor did the victims share their predecessors' enthusiasm for *qiddush ha-Shem*. Women who jumped into the water did not do so to deliver antibaptism polemics. They jumped into the moat surrounding their refuge "that the uncircumcised should not defile them." Many of these women "were able to swim ... believing they would escape the slaughter ... but the Ukrainians killed them in the water."

Also Rabbi Jechiel Michael "jumped into the water believing that he would save himself by swimming." And when a Ukrainian wanted to slay him, "the scholar implored him not to kill him." He agreed upon receiving "silver and gold." Two days later, the rabbi and his mother were clubbed to death by a Ukrainian shoemaker. This is not to say that choices were never given and that actual cases of voluntary death did not exist.[7] But J. Katz's correct observation that socioeconomic reasons, rather than religious alone, motivated the attackers could only intensify the determination to do away with the Jews.[8]

This determination manifested itself during a series of libels in the late eighteenth century. The towering hasidic rabbi Israel *Baal* Shem Tov (the Besht) refers to these libels briefly in his letter, "The Ascension of the Soul."[9] Modeled after the legend of the Ten Martyrs, the letter replaces Ishmael with the Besht in the dialogue with Samael. In the chambers of heaven, he asked Samael why Jews who had converted during the pogroms were still murdered. Their deaths, he answered, were meant to inspire others to die "for the Name of Heaven." His answer was intended to urge others to perform *qiddush ha-Shem*, because the antagonists were determined to kill Jews even though they had converted. At least by undergoing martyrdom they would die loyally and with dignity. Although it is reported that in future libels all Jews stood the test, the letter is another testimony that conversion did not always satisfy the attackers.[10]

Victims of following pogroms in Russia were still compared to the medieval martyrs. In the case of a certain cantor and his family, the comparison seems reasonable. Their martyrdom in 1768 Ukraine followed the stabbing of a Jewish woman by a "treacherous" non-Jew for no apparent reason. A female witness immediately called on others not to betray the living God. "Let us all instead sanctify His Name, thereby making us worthy to enter the world-to-come." Upon seeing this, the cantor (*hazan*) "ran to the ritual bath to immerse himself, and he wrapped himself in his prayer shawl and [put on] phylacteries and recited the Confession before the death in a loud and crying voice." Without explaining the shift from one scene to another, "he then *took the knife* from the treacherous one and slaughtered his [own] wife and children; and thereafter, himself."[11] Opening the incident with a female martyr, the initial call for martyrdom by a woman, the desire to die for the living God, the world-to-come, the ritualistic preparation for death, and the taking of the knife (Gen. 22) dominated the 1096 chronicles. These modern-era pogroms are beyond the scope of this study. But the many reports of such violence, which often seemed to deprive the victims of a choice,[12] fashioned the "medievalization of [modern] Jewish [martyrological] literary consciousness."[13]

With respect to the concept of *qiddush ha-Shem*, a significant change commenced during the Nazi Holocaust.[14] The six millions who died *al qiddush ha-Shem* were murdered without the choice that was granted in the Middle Ages. All these new martyrs could do in their final hour was to recite the *Shema* Akiva had immortalized by his martyrdom. Following Maimonides' ruling that all Jews who are killed only for being Jewish should be considered martyrs, all the Holocaust victims become martyrs.[15] Like the mystics of the early modern era, suffering alone qualified one for *qiddush ha-Shem*.

Toward the end of the Middle Ages, Jews increasingly experienced massacres without being offered a real chance to determine their own faith. This was especially true when Jews were blamed for spreading the deadly pestilence of Europe. In Nazi ideology, self-determination became the first victim. Before taking life, the death factories systematically removed this fundamental human property from those the Nazis considered to be pestilence itself. Even the desire to exhaust life by running into the camps' electric fences had to be approved by the camp guards.[16] Such approvals were rare. Self-destruction as an act of self-determination was forbidden.[17] As E. Fackenheim puts it, "Hitler murdered Jewish martyrdom itself."[18] *Qiddush ha-Shem* became thus a sacred end, not a choice.

From the time of the potential Jewish martyrs of Philo and Josephus, throughout the Middle Ages, martyrdom functioned as a means of communication in violent dialogues. Voluntary death as threat or act provided, in effect, a form of communication between Jews and their rivals, between Jews and God. For the potential martyrs, martyrological proclamations in the ears of Roman generals indicated a cry for help. In the medieval period, apart from its inner function, *qiddush ha-Shem* delivered polemical messages against the attacker. The martyrs' meanings were crystal clear, for their martyrological language and acts "spoke" in terms that the attackers too were well versed. *Qiddush ha-Shem* showed not only how Judaism and Christianity differed from one another but also how much they had in common. Indeed, their basic belief in God made one group kill for Him in order to become "one nation" and the other to die for Him to remain His only nation. Martyrdom in the Middle Ages was an answer to oppressors who aimed to turn Jews into Christians. Even when the oppressors' goal was the killing of Jews, they still used conversion as an excuse for the massacres. Nazism was different. It was not interested in a dialogue with Judaism or Jews. What need, therefore, was there for this age-old deadly means of communication if even the right to a dialogue could not be provided? What need was there for voluntary death, if life itself was a capital crime?

Torture, humiliation, and systematic slaughter made this ominous prospect clear to the living dead in the ghettoes.[19] The fundamental change in attitude vis-à-vis Jews triggered a fundamental adjustment in the Jewish attitude toward martyrdom. For centuries Jews believed they had survived death thanks to those who volunteered to die for life. They chose death for a "living God," for the life of their religion, for the life of their coreligionists, and, since the twelfth century, for the afterlife. This logic flourished especially after the crusaders gathered in great numbers "as the sand of the sea" to convert or destroy Jews. In the ghettoes, an instinct urged the prisoners to fulfill God's promise that "the children of Israel shall be as the sand of the sea, which cannot be measured nor numbered" (Hos. 2:1). Only "a resisting life" could revive the living dead and ensure the survival of Judaism.[20] In the hellish places that glorified mass murder, there was no place for martyrdom. Dying voluntarily for *qiddush ha-Shem* was now considered *hillul ha-Shem* (desecration of the Name). Not coincidentally, the term *qiddush ha-hayim* (the sanctification of life) surfaced in the Nazi death camps.[21] Enduring life, not death, became the ultimate test of loyalty to God and the human race.[22]

An "imperative to sanctify not death but life," was justified on scholarly grounds. For R. Ephraim Oshry of ghetto Kovno (in Lithuania), what was once considered the ultimate expression of love of God would now signify loss of trust in Him. "In former times," explained R. Yizhak Nissenbaum of the Warsaw ghetto, "when the enemy demanded the soul of the Jew, Jews sacrificed their bodies 'for the sanctification of God's Name'; now, however, the oppressor wants the body of the Jew, it is therefore one's duty to protect it, to guard one's life."[23] A similar view held R. Menahem Zembah. Calling on the Jews of the Warsaw ghetto to rebel, the rabbi explained, "*qiddush ha-Shem* nowadays is not like *qiddush has-Shem* of the past."[24] For the Berliner rabbi,

Leo Baeck, both the coerced death and the cleaving to life became holy. This survivor of Theresienstadt wrote, "To live, as to die, became a divine service."[25]

For others, sanctifying God through life came as an instinct. In the words of an Auschwitz survivor: "I felt under orders to live."[26] And to live meant more than to exist. It meant to be human in an inhuman place. A new aphorism resonated in the death camps: "Now to die is not bravery. Bravery now is to live."[27] Even children adhered to this principle, according to the poem of Eva Pitzkova of Theresienstadt. "Not to die, to live we are commanded. To live, to live, in the name of God."[28]

Fackenheim provides a logical explanation of this instinct to live. "When every effort is made to reduce dying to a banality, life does not need to be sanctified. It already *is* holy."[29] Divinity and human dignity, therefore, needed to be sanctified through life, not death.

Because of the sanctification of God's Name by death in the Middle Ages and by life in the Nazi ghetto, European Jewry survived its numerous ordeals. The Holocaust was the culmination of a long interplay between persecutors and the persecuted, between sacrificers and the sanctified.[30] The unprecedented magnitude of the Holocaust triggered theological, moral, and philosophical dilemmas, followed by various reactions. After centuries of contribution to European civilization, many of the living dead arose out of the ashes and left for new destinations. For Baeck, rebuilding Jewish life and reconciliation with Christendom became a high priority. Elazar of Worms was his role model. In a time that *qiddush ha-Shem* and *martyrium* were viewed as the highest sacrifice, Elazar still cleaved to life. Although the crusaders brutally killed his wife, Dulza, and his two daughters and injured his son and student, Elazar did not write "one word of hatred against his enemies," writes Baeck.[31]

After surviving Auschwitz and Buchenwald, Elie Wiesel made America his new country. His view on the role of martyrdom is expressed through Moshe (Moses), the hero of his novel *The Oath*:

It has been going on for centuries, for centuries players on both sides have played the same roles – and rather than speak, God listens; rather than intervene and decide, He waits and judges only later. We do everything we can to attract His attention, to amuse or please Him. For centuries now we have given ourselves to Him by allowing ourselves to be led to the slaughterhouse. We think that we are pleasing Him by becoming the illustrations of our own tales of martyrdom. There is always one storyteller, one survivor, one witness to revive the murderous past if not the victims.[32]

Realizing that the glorification of martyrdom inspired for too long, Moshe prohibits the telling of the martyrological story. Martyrdom, in his opinion, failed to impress both man and God. Wiesel's Moses realizes that not even human sacrifice would cause God to intervene directly. The Holocaust produced enough suffering, enough martyrs, and not because of "our sins," as Jewish martyrologies so often have claimed. Moshe's desire to prohibit the retelling of the martyrological story remains unfulfilled, however. Commemorating centuries of violence and valor has made the story of the powerless too powerful to be vanquished. As martyrs are destined to die, martyrologies are designed to live; martyrs to stand the test of death, martyrologies the test of time. They have.

Notes

INTRODUCTION

1. I. G. Marcus, *Rituals of Childhood: Jewish Acculturation in Medieval Europe* (Yale, 1996), 11–12.
2. D. Boyarin, *Dying for God: Martyrdom and the Making of Christianity and Judaism* (Stanford, 1999), 1–21, especially 9.
3. E. Durkheim; *Suicide. A Study in Sociology,* tr. J. A. Spaulding and G. Simpson, sixth ed. (New York, 1966), 43–44.
4. The rabbinic objection to suicide is based on the interpretation of Genesis 9:5, "And surely your blood of your lives will I require; at the hand of every beast will I require it; and at the hand of man, even at the hand of every man's brother, will I require the life of man." See *Baba Kamma* 91 b. According to the posttalmudic tractate appended to *Nezikin, Semahot* 2:3, a suicide (*meabed atzmo lada'at*) is one who intentionally and consciously (*b'da'at*) kills himself:

    Not one who climbs to the top of a tree or to the top of a roof, and falls to his death. Rather, it is one who says, "Behold, I am going to climb to the top of the tree, or to the top of the roof, and then throw myself down to my death," and thereupon others see him climb to the top of the tree, or the top of the roof, and fall to his death.

    To emphasize the transgression, a person who proclaims his or her suicidal intentions is denied Jewish burial rights. In contrast, continues the text (*Semahot* 2:3), "If a person is found strangled from a tree, or slain impaled upon a sword, he is presumed to have taken his life unwittingly. Under these circumstances no rights whatsoever may be denied to the deceased." To underline the point of rational and intentional death, the text of *Halakhot Gedolot* regards the suicide as one who declares: "I am going to climb to the roof in order (*al menat*) to fall." *Halakhot Gedolot, Hilkhot Avel,* 445, J. Hildesheimer's edition (Jerusalem, 1972). Rabbi Tarfon added that no rights whatsoever should be denied a minor who commits suicide, since a minor cannot make a rational judgment (*Semahot* 2:5). When a death is regarded as suicide, tractate *Semahot* concludes, "No rites whatsoever should be observed." The tractate states, in the name of R. Akiva, "Leave it [the body] to its oblivion, neither bless him nor curse him." In addition, the tractate declares, "There may be no rending of clothes, no baring of shoulders, no eulogizing for him, but people should line up for him and the mourner's blessing should be recited over him, out of respect for the living." Finally, it concludes: "The general rule is: the public should participate in whatsoever is done out of respect for the living. It should not participate in whatsoever is done out of respect for the dead." See M. Higger, ed., *Semahot* (New York, 1931) and D. Zlotnick's edition, *Semahot: Tractate "Morning,"* Yale Judaic Studies, no. 17 (New Haven, 1966). The translations here are by Zlotnick.

In the same spirit as in *Semahot*, to restrain the will to self-destruction, *Yoma* 85b instructs with respect to the commandments: "live through them, but do not die through them" (Lev. 18:5). As we will see below, this coincides with the opinion of R. Akiva and R. Ishmael (San. 74a and A. Z. 24b). *Bereshit Rabbah* 82:8 tells that when a Roman officer had commanded two of R. Joshua's students to kill themselves for the Law, they replied that it would be unnatural for a person to commit suicide, "*le-abed atzmo mi-daat.*" See also H. H. Cohen, "Suicide in Jewish Law," in *Encyclopaedia Judaica* (1972), vol. 15; S. Goldstein, *Suicide in Rabbinic Literature* (New Jersey, 1989).

5. Before assuming its present meaning, the term *martyr* was part of the legal lexicon of the Greek court, strictly indicating a witness. The phenomenon of martyrdom preceded the late interpretation of the word. The first time the Greek word *witness* appeared in its martyrological sense was after the martyrdom of Polycarp, "who put an end to the persecution by his own martyrdom," in about 150 c.e.; *Martyrdom of Polycarp* 2. The narrator of Polycarp's martyrdom goes on to indicate that "Blessed indeed and noble are all the martyrdoms that took place in accordance with God's will." In the Gospels the Greek word *witness* refers to those who witnessed Jesus' suffering and resurrection. In the New Testament the expression *witness* had not yet obtained its current meaning. See H. Chadwick in *Oxford History of Christianity*, ed. J. McManner (Oxford, 1990), 41. Even when the term *witness* referred to Jesus in the New Testament, G. W. Bowersock argues, Jesus was not described as a martyr in the present sense of the word but rather as "a witness who was slain." *Martyrdom and Rome* (Cambridge, 1995), 15.

6. The Bible briefly mentions six events of self-destruction: the death of Abimelech (Judg. 9:53–54), Samson's death at Gaza (Judg. 16:28–30), King Saul and his armor-bearer (I Sam. 31:3–5), Achitophel (II Sam. 17:23), and Zimri (I Kings 16:18). See David Daube, "The Linguistics of Suicide," *Philosophy and Public Affairs* 1 no. 4 (1972), 437–487; H. J. Rose, "Suicide," in *Encyclopaedia of Religion and Ethics*, ed. J. Hastings (New York, 1925), 12:24–26; L. D. Hankoff, "Judaic Origins of the Suicide Prohibition," in Hankoff and Einsidler, eds., *Suicide: Theory and Clinical Aspects* (Littleton, 1979), 6; and F. Rosner, "Suicide in Biblical, Talmudic and Rabbinic Writings," *Tradition: A Journal of Orthodox Thought*, 11 no. 3 (1970–1971), 25–40. In the Bible, these cases are neither "suicide" nor "martyrdom." They are reports of individuals punished by God.

7. E. Gruenwald, "*Qiddush ha-Shem*: An Examination of a Term" (Hebrew), *Molad* 24 (1968), 476–484; A. Holtz, "Kiddush and Hillul Hashem," in *Faith and Reason: Essays in Judaism*, eds. R. Gordis and R. B. Waxman (New York, 1973), 79–86; S. Safrai, "*Qiddush ha-Shem* in the Teachings of the Tannaim" (Hebrew), *Zion* 44 (1979), 28–42.

8. In some cultures, ending life voluntarily might be an accepted, normal social behavior. For example, the burning of widows with their husbands' bodies, known as the Sutti,

in India, and the self-killing, or Seppuku, in Japan. L. I. Dublin, *To Be or Not To Be: A Study of Suicide* (New York, 1933), 154–158, 166–167.

9. *"Martyres veros non facit poena sed causa."* Augustine, *Epistolae,* no. 89:2, *PL,* 28:310.

CHAPTER 1: MYTHIC MARTYRS

1. Different reasons for the persecutions have been suggested. E. R. Bevan, *The House of Seleucus*(London, 1902), 2:153; J. Klausner, *The History of the Second Temple*(Hebrew), second ed. 5 vols. (Jerusalem, 1950), 2:177–181; V. Tcherikover, "Antiochus' Decrees and their Problems" (Hebrew), in *Eshkolot* 1 (1954), 109; idem, *Hellenistic Civilisation and the Jews,* fifth printing, trans. by S. Applebaum (New York, 1979), 175–203; D. J. Harrington, *The Maccabean Revolt: Anatomy of a Biblical Revolution* (Wilmington, 1971), 32; F. Miller, "The Background to the Maccabean Revolution: Reflections on Martin Hengel's 'Judaism and Hellenism,'" *Journal of Jewish Studies* 29 (1978), 1–21; E. J. Bickerman, *The God of the Maccabees,* tr. by Horest R. Moehrning (Leiden, 1979), 84–85; J. J. Collins, *Daniel, First Maccabees, Second Maccabees, Old Testament Message,* vol. 15 (Wilmington, 1981), 11–144; S. L. Derfler, *The Hasmonean Revolt: Rebellion or Revolution* (Lewiston, Lampeter, Queenston, 1990), 5:49–57, 59–70; P. Schäfer, *The History of the Jews in Antiquity: The Jews of Palestine from Alexander the Great to the Arab Conquest* (Luxembourg, 1995), 35–56.

2. W. H. C. Frend, *Martyrdom and Persecution in the Early Church: A Study of a Conflict from the Maccabees to Donatus* (Garden City, 1967), 31, 50, and the rest of his chapter two. According to A. Rophe, the Jewish Bible contains the martyrological seeds. *The Prophetical Stories* (Hebrew) (Jerusalem, 1982), 166–177. Several similar views are discussed below.

3. Bowersock, *Martyrdom and Rome,* 7–8, 28.

4. *Martyrdom and Persecution,* 65.

5. A. J. Droge and J. D. Tabor, *A Noble Death: Suicide and Martyrdom among Christians and Jews in Antiquity* (San Francisco, 1992), 75: "Taking these accounts in the Apocrypha together we observe a number of common elements." T. Rajak, *The Jewish Dialogue with Greek and Rome: Studies in Cultural and Social Interaction* (Leiden, Boston, Köln, 2001), 104–105.

6. J. Rauch, identifies the heroes of the book with the "Maccabean martyrs." "Apocalypse in the Bible," in *Journal of Jewish Lore and Philosophy,* ed. D. Neumark (1919), 1:189.

7. R. H. Charles, *Eschatology: The Doctrine of a Future Life in Israel, Judaism and Christianity* (New York, 1970), 126. See also H. A. Fischel, "Martyr and Prophet," *Jewish Quarterly Review* 37 (1946–1947), 383–384; N. W. Porteous, *Daniel: A Commentary* (Philadelphia, 1965), 55; and as U. Kellermann already suggests by his article's title, "Das Danielbuch und die Märtyretheologie der Auferstehung," in J. W. Van Henten, ed. *Die Enstehung der Jüdischen Martyrologie* (Leiden, 1989), 51–75; cf. J. J. Collins, "Apocalyptic Eschatology as the Transcendence of Death," *Catholic Biblical Quarterly* 36 (1974), 21–43; idem, *Daniel* (Minneapolis, 1993), 61, 192–193; J. W. Van Henten, *The Maccabean Martyrs as Saviours of the Jewish People: A Study of 2 and 4 Maccabees* (Leiden, New York, Köln, 1997), 8–9.

8. J. W. Van Henten, "Antiochus IV as a Typhonic Figure in Daniel 7," *The Book of Daniel in the Light of New Findings*, ed. A. S. Van Der Woude (Leuven, 1993), 223–243; U. Rappaport, "Comments on the Period of Antiochus' Decrees with Relation to the Book of Daniel" (Hebrew), in *The Seleucid Period in the Land of Israel*, ed. B. Bar Kochva (Tel Aviv, 1980), 65–83. For a more traditional view, *Daniel*, translation and commentary, by H. Goldwurm, with an overview by Nosson Scherman (New York, 1979).

9. Collins, *Daniel*, 60; and more generally, W. E. Heaton, *The Book of Daniel and the Qumran Community* (London, 1956). F. F. Bruce, "The Book of Daniel and the Qumran Community," *Neotestamentica et Semitica: Studies in Honor of Matthew Black*, eds. E. E. Ellis and M. Wilcox (Edinburgh, 1969), 221–235; L. F. Hartman and A. A. DiLella, *The Book of Daniel* (Doubleday, 1978), 44–45; G. W. E. Nickelsburg, *Jewish Literature between the Bible and the Mishnah* (Philadelphia, 1981).

10. On the different languages of the books, see F. Zimmerman, "The Aramaic Origin of Daniel 8–12," *Journal of Biblical Literature* 57 (1938), 255–272.

11. Collins, *Daniel*, 145–146. More generally, see M. Delcor, *Le Livre de Daniel* (Paris, 1971).

12. As also argued by Van Henten, *The Maccabean Martyrs*, 8–13, for example.

13. According to R. H. Charles, they rejected the food not only because it consisted of unclean animals, but also because the food had been submitted to idols. *A Critical and Exegetical Commentary on the Book of Daniel* (Oxford, 1929), 19.

14. N. W. Porteous, *Daniel*, 55.

15. J. J. Collins, "The Court-Tales of Daniel and the Development of Apocalyptic," *Journal of Biblical Commentary* 94 (1975), 218–234; L. M. Wills, *The Jew in the Court of the Foreign King: Ancient Jewish Court Legends* (Harvard Dissertations in Religion 26; Minneapolis, 1990).

16. The dialogue between the three and the king is analyzed by J. W. Wesselius, "Language and Style in Biblical Aramaic: Observations on the Unity of Daniel II–VI," *Vetus Testamentum* 38 (1988), 194–208.

17. For the phrase, see Collins, *Daniel*, 190.

18. A. Bentzen, "Daniel 6: Ein Versuch zur Vorgeschichte der Märtyrerlegende," in *Festschrift A. Bertholet*, eds. W. Baumgartner, O. Eissfeldt, K. Elliger, and L. Rust, (Tübingen, 1950), 58–64. See also Kellermann's treatment of Chapters 3 and 6. "Das Danielbuch," 54–57.

19. On the contribution of Chapters 11 and 12 to future martyrdom, Kellermann, "Das Danielbuch," 51–54.

20. Collins, *Daniel*, 60.

21. Charles, *Eschatology*, 141, 211.

22. Droge and Tabor, *A Noble Death*, 71.

23. Collins, *Daniel*, 272.

24. R. Doran makes the same observation, "The Martyr: A Synoptic View of the Mother and her Seven Sons," *Ideal Figures in Ancient Judaism: Profiles and Paradigms*, eds. G. W. E. Nickelsburg and J. J. Collins; Society of Biblical Literature Septuagint and Cognate Studies 12 (Chico, 1980), 189–221, especially, 189.

25. Collins, *Daniel*, 194.

26. V. Tcherikover, *Hellenistic Civilisation and the Jews*, 477 n. 37; A. Lacocque, *The Book of Daniel* (Atlanta, 1979), 230; J. Efron, *Studies on the Hasmonean Period* (Leiden, New York, 1987), 37.

27. Cf. Collins, *Daniel*, 385; Rajak, *The Jewish Dialogue*, pp. 105–106. Rajak's conclusion stems from, what seems to me, a misleading translation of Daniel 11: 33–34.

28. J. Efron, "Holy War and Redemption in the Period of the Hasmoneans" (Hebrew), in *Milhemet Kodesh u-Martirologiah*, (Jerusalem, 1967), 7–34.

29. J. Kampen, *The Hasideans and the Origin of Pharisaism* (Atlanta, 1988), 23, 29; cf. Collins, *Daniel*, 66.

30. J. Sievers, *The Hasmoneans and Their Supporters: From Mattathias to the Death of John Hyrcanus I* (Atlanta, 1990), 24.

31. J. Levinger, "Daniel in the Lions' Den: A Model of National Literature of Struggle," *Beth Mikra* 70 (1977), 329–333; 394–395.

32. The scholarly literature on 1 Maccabees is extensive and addresses various aspects. For general remarks and summary, see W. O. E. Oesterley and G. H. Box, "I Maccabees, Sirach," in *The Apocrypha and Pseudepigrapha of the Old Testament*, vol. 1, ed. R. H. Charles (Oxford, 1913), 59–124; F.-M. Abel, *Les Livres des Maccabées* (Paris, 1949), i–ix; R. H. Pfeifer, *History of New Testament Times with an Introduction to the Apocrypha* (New York, 1941), 461–524; J. C. Dancy, *A Commentary on I Maccabees* (Oxford, 1954), 1–22. M. Stern, "The Books of the Maccabees," (Hebrew) in *Biblical Encyclopaedia*, vol. 5 (Jerusalem, 1958), cols. 286–303; J. A. Goldstein, *I Maccabees: A New Translation with Introduction and Commentary* (AB 41; Garden City, 1976); L. Rost, *Judaism Outside the Hebrew Canon: An Introduction to the Documents*, tr. by D. E. Green (Nashville, 1976), 75–80; Collins, *Daniel, First Maccabees, Second Maccabees*; B. Bar-Kochva, *Judas Maccabaeus: The Jewish Struggle against the Seleucids* (Cambridge, New York, 1989), 151–170.

33. According to S. Zeitlin's commentary in *The First Book of the Maccabees*, tr. S. Tedesche (New York, 1950), 19.

34. M. Hengel, *Judaism and Hellenism: Studies in their Encounter in Palestine during the Early Hellenistic Period*, tr. by J. Bowden (Philadelphia, 1974), 1:292.

35. D. J. Harrington, *The Maccabean Revolt: Anatomy of a Biblical Revolution* (Wilmington, 1988), 63.

36. According to Josephus Flavius, "they burned them as they were in the caves, without resistance. . . . " But not all of them perished in the attack, "many of those that escaped joined themselves to Mattathia . . . who taught them to fight, even on the Sabbath day." *Jewish Antiquities*, xii. vi. 2. In *The Loeb Classical Library*, 9 vols, Ed. A. Wikgren, (Cambridge, 1926–1965).

37. G. F. Moore, *Judaism in the First Centuries of the Christian Era: The Age of the Tannaim* (Cambridge, 1930), 2:63; J. N. Epstein, *Introduction to Tannaitic Literature: Babylonian Talmud and Yerushalmi* (Hebrew) (Jerusalem, 1957), 278; M. D. Herr, "The Question of *Halakhot* of War on the Sabbath in the Second Temple and the Talmudic Periods" (Hebrew), *Tarbitz* 30 (1961), 242–256, 341–356; A. Oppenheimer, "Oral Law in the Books of Maccabees," *Immanuel* 6 (1976), 34–42; R. Goldenberg, "The Jewish Sabbath in the Roman World up to the Time of Constantine the Great," in *Aufstieg und Niedergang der römischen Welt*, II, vol. 19.1 (Berlin, 1979), 414–447. Tcherikover, *Hellenistic Civilization*, 197.

38. Klausner, *History of the Second Temple*, 3:17–18. He also has noted the word "testify" in 1 Maccabees 2:37, "heaven and earth testify."

39. E. Weiner and A. Weiner, *Martyr's Conviction: A Sociological Analysis* (Atlanta, 1990), 37.

40. H. Mantel, *The Men of the Great Synagogue* (Hebrew) (Tel Aviv, 1983), 102–107. Mantel's view on fighting on the Sabbath finds support in Kampen's book, *The Hasideans*, 78–80. On the issue of fighting on the Sabbath, see also L. H. Schiffman, *Law, Custom, and Messianism in the Dead Sea Sect* (Hebrew ed.) (Jerusalem, 1993), 130–131.

41. B. Bar-Kochva, *The Battles of the Hasmoneans: The Times of Judas Maccabaeus* (Jerusalem, 1980), 331–342. See also J. M. G. Barclay's comments regarding the Ptolemaic army, *Jews in the Mediterranean Diaspora: From Alexander to Trajan (323 B. C. E.–117 C. E.)* (Edinburgh, 1996), 441.

42. Bar-Kochva, *Judas Maccabaeus*, 482.

43. L. Finkelstein, *The Pharisees: The Sociological Background of their Faith* (Philadelphia, 1962), 2:592; followed by Hengel, *Judaism and Hellenism*, 178; Tcherikover, *Hellenistic Civilization*, 197.

44. Finkelstein, *The Pharisees*, 1:156.

45. *Hellenistic Civilization*, 198; cf. Hengel, *Judaism and Hellenism*, 287.

46. According to L. L. Grabbe, not much is known about the group, but what can be said with certainty is that they were not pacifist. *Judaic Religion in the Second Temple Period* (London and New York, 2000), 184–185.

47. K. Schubert, *The Dead Sea Community: Its Origin and Teachings* (New York, 1959), 32–35. Although for different reasons, a similar connection is made also by Harrington, *The Maccabean Revolt*, 66; Hengel, *Judaism and Hellenism*, 1:175–180 and especially 178, and 2:116 n. 456; Sievers, *The Hasmoneans*, 26; Mantel, *The Men of the Great Synagogue*, 104; Goldstein, *I Maccabees*, 5–6. P. Davies, "Hasidim in the Maccabean Period," *Journal of Jewish Studies* 28–29 (1977), 127–140, tries to show that the very existence of the Hasidic sect is an assumption which the texts "do not justify." J. Kampen also links the refugees to the Essenes' ancestors or the Pharisees. Kampen, *The Hasideans and the Origin of Pharisaism*, 23, 29, 73–76, 81, 121, 148, 209–222. Kampen's attempt "goes beyond the evidence," according to L. L. Grabbe, *Judaic Religion in the Second Temple Period* (London and New York, 2000), 185. See also S. Safrai, "The Pharisees and the Hasidim," *Sidic* 10 (1977), 12–16; idem, "The Hasidim and the Men of Deeds" (Hebrew), *Zion* 50 (1985), 133–154; Bar-Kochva, *Judas Maccabaeus*, 484, 493. Of course, there is always the possibility that the desert runaways did not constitute a homogeneous group. A. I. Baumgarten, *The Flourishing of Jewish Sects in the Maccabean Era: An Interpretation* (Leiden, New York, Köln, 1997), 18–33 and bibliography there, 198–199.

48. Mantel, *The Men of the Great Synagogue*, 102–107. His skepticism can be further justified if we accept Zeitlin's opinion that 1 Maccabees was compiled after the destruction of the Temple, *The First Book of Maccabees*, 29–32. Mantel's view on fighting on the Sabbath finds support in Kampen, *The Hasideans*, 78–80. See also Sievers's argument: "There is no indication that the strict Sabbath observers belonged to it [the group of the Hasidim]," *The Hasmoneans*, 39. On the issue of fighting on the Sabbath, see also Schiffman, *Law, Custom, and Messianism*, 130–131.

49. 2 Maccabees makes the contradiction even stronger. Jews refrained from combat on the Sabbath "as it was by that time appropriate and necessary for them to do" (2 Macc. 8:26–28, 12:38–39). Zeitlin points out that v. 39 is missing in some Manuscripts, *The Second Book of Maccabees*, 39. In these two cases, though, the campaigns were offensive and therefore controlled by the rebels. According to other stories, even the Hellenistic Jews in Nicanor's army are said to have refused to attack Judas and his men on the Sabbath day (2 Macc. 15:1–5). As J. A. Goldstein speculates, 2 Maccabees' efforts to present Judas as a strict Sabbath observer is contradicted by its own description of Judas's arrival at Jerusalem to celebrate Pentecost (2 Macc. 12:31–3). *2 Maccabees: A New Translation with Introduction and Commentary* (AB 41a; Garden City, 1983).

50. The problems with the structure of this sentence are discussed by Goldstein, *1 Maccabees*, 236.

51. According to Charles, just the coming out of the cave with their possessions would have been considered a violation.

52. Goldstein, *I Maccabees*, 235–236.

53. Judging by the second half of the Book of Daniel, the Hasmoneans, whom he calls "a little help," were very much in need of such consensus. Baumgarten, *The Flourishing of Jewish Sects*, 169.

54. Sievers, *The Hasmoneans*, 36.

55. L. L. Grabbe, *Judaism from Cyrus to Hadrian* (Minneapolis, 1992), 2 vols. [with continuing pagination], 285; idem, *Judaic Religion*, 79.

56. As Hengel has put it, *Judaism and Hellenism*, 178; italics in the original.

57. E. S. Gruen, *Heritage and Hellenism: The Reinvention of Jewish Tradition* (Berkeley, Los Angeles, London, 1998), 8; Grabbe, *Judaic Religion*, 184.

58. Doran is a rare and welcome exception. These are "examples of unjust aggression in the context of war." "The Martyr," 189.

59. Hengel, *Judaism and Hellenism*, 1:292.

60. Similar interpretation applies to the bellicose Hasidim (*Hasidaioi*), "mighty men of Israel who willingly offered themselves for the Law, every one of them" (2.42). Such statements indicate their dedication and loyalty to Judaism, but do not refer to passive and submissive patterns of religious adherence in facing the decrees. Indeed, numerous loyalists to the Law did perish in their combative struggle against the religious persecutions, as is the case with every war. Yet this unfortunate outcome of the war was not the desire of its participants.

61. Goldstein, *I Maccabees*, 12.

62. According to Zeitlin, 1 Maccabees is a compilation of two parts. Mattathias's mentioning of Daniel and his three companions is an interpolation. *The First Book of the Maccabees*, 32 and 87 n. 60.

63. According to P. Schäfer, "The backbone of the Hasmonean state was the *military*" (italics in the original). *The History of the Jews in Antiquity*, 65.

64. Droge and Tabor, *Noble Death*, 73; Harrington, *The Maccabean Revolt*, 47.

65. *Judaism and Hellenism*, 1:98.

66. Goldstein, *I Maccabees*, 30.

67. *The Maccabean Martyrs*, 97.

68. Tcherikover, *Hellenistic Civilization*, 200; idem, "Antiochia in Jerusalem" (Hebrew), *Tarbiz* 20 (1949), 61–67; idem, "Antiochus' Decrees and Their Problems" (Hebrew),

Eshcholot, 1 (1954), 86–109; Y. Baer, "The Persecution of the Monotheistic Religion by Antiochus Epiphanes" (Hebrew), *Zion* 38 (1971), 32–47; Derfler, *The Hasmonean Revolt,* 64; Sievers, *The Hasmoneans,* 24.

69. Droge and Tabor, *Noble Death,* 73; Harrington, *The Maccabean Revolt,* 46. 1 Maccabees 1:60 does not mention numbers.

70. The same is true about Bacchides' attack against Jonathan and his men. 1 Macc. 9:43–45.

71. But a Sadducee, according to F.-M. Abel and J. Starcky, *Les livres de Maccabées* (Paris, 1961), 20.

72. This contradiction did not escape C. Habicht, "*2 Makkabäerbuch,*" Jüdische Schriften aus hellenistisch-röischer Zeit, vol. 1 *Historische und legendarische Erzählugen,* Gütersloh (1976b), 231; P. Katz, "Eleazar's Martyrdom in 2 Maccabees: The Latin Evidence for a Point of the Story," *Studia Patristica* 4 (Berlin, 1961), part 2, ed. F. L. Cross, pp. 118–124; idem, "The Text of 2 Maccabees Reconsidered," *Zeitschrift für die neutestamentliche Wissenschaft,* 51 (1960), 14; but see also Abel, *Les livres,* 367; R. Hanhart, "Zun Text des 2. und 3. Makkabäerbuches: Probleme der Überlieferung, der Auslegung und der Ausgabe," *Nachrichten von der Akademie der Wissenschaften in Göttingen; Philologisch-Historische Klasse* (Göttingen, 1961), 474–478; Rajak, *The Jewish Dialogue,* 127 n. 76. For the different Latin versions of 2 Maccabees, I consulted *Les Anciennes Traductions Latines Des Machabées* [Anecdota Maredsolana, vol. 4], ed. D. de Bruyne and B. Sodar (Abbaye de Maredsous, 1932).

73. See discussion in Chapter 3.

74. A fact that some ascribe to the stories' independent sources. Doran, "The Martyrs," 191; Van Henten, *The Maccabean Martyrs,* 96. As will be discussed below, Eleazar's absence in Chapter 7 and the possibility of several sources are not trivial matters. Doran points out an attempt by a "final author" to link the two stories. "The Martyrs," 191.

75. According to Bowersock, "us" in the *Martyrdom of Pionios* refers to an individual and not to groups. *Martyrdom and Rome,* 29, 35. Both in our case and in the *Martyrdom of Pionios,* "us" refers to an individual who is persuaded to eat forbidden food.

76. On this unique name, see Goldstein, *2 Maccabees,* 491–492; Van Henten, *The Maccabean Martyrs,* 116.

77. As in the stories of Eleazar and the seven sons, 1 Maccabees does not mention Razis.

78. 2 Maccabees 8:27–29, "God wills," 15:21; Goldstein, *I Maccabees,* 79.

79. Not in van Henten's view, *The Maccabean Martyrs,* 25.

80. See Habicht's notes on 7.1. Rost, *Judaism Outside the Hebrew Canon,* 82–83; Doran notes that certain words are unique to Chapters 6 and 7, appearing nowhere else. He believes them to be the work of a "final author." "The Martyrs," 190–191. According to Katz, 7:1 "was not necessary for Jewish readers." "The Text of 2 Maccabees," 19. The problem that the statements about resurrection create in the text constitute probable support for such a position. Katz, "Text," 14; Habicht, "2 Makkabäerbuch," 234; cf. R. Doran, *Temple Propaganda: The Purpose and Character of 2 Maccabees* (Washington, 1981), 12, 22; followed by Van Henten, *The Maccabean Martyrs,* 174–175 and notes there. This important issue of resurrection is discussed below.

81. J. Geiger characterizes the book as militant history. "The History of Judas Maccabaeus: One Aspect of Hellenistic Historiography" (Hebrew), *Zion* 49 (1984),

1–8; Van Henten considers Chapters 3–15 "a history of liberation and restoration of the Jewish temple-state." *The Maccabean Martyrs*, 51.

82. Abel, *Les Livres*, 26; Pfeifer, *History of New Testament Times*, 518; M. Hadas, *Hellenistic Culture: Fusion and Diffusion* (New York, 1959), 126–127; R. Doran, "2 Maccabees and 'Tragic History,'" *Hebrew Union College Annual* 50 (1979), 110–114; on "tragic" and "pathetic" features in the book, Bar-Kochva, *Judas Maccabaeus*, 172–179, especially, 175.

83. Tcherikover, *Hellenistic Civilization*, 190–191.

84. For example, "the day of Mordechai" demonstrates that the book's interest revolves around famous and historic personalities. Zeitlin, *The Second Book of Maccabees*, 23; Habicht, 173; Bar-Kochva, *Judas Maccabaeus*, 372–373.

85. In my opinion, Goldstein fails to prove a connection between Daniel and the story. *II Maccabees*, 292–294.

86. I am not suggesting here a conscious correlation between the two sources but rather a common attitude to reality.

87. A. Momigliano, *Prime linee de storia della tradizione Maccabaica* (Turino, 1931; second ed. Amsterdam, 1968), 98–101.

88. Van Henten, *The Maccabean Martyrs*, 296. Recall 1 Maccabees: the Hasideans were the first to accept Mattathias's rejection of the refugees' passive behavior and join his militant campaign.

89. Rather than martyrdom, as its treatment together with 2 Maccabees 7 and 4 Maccabees 5, 7, 17 in *Noble Death*, 74, may imply, or as Harrington defines Razis' death, as "a kind of martyrdom." *The Maccabean Revolt*, 53; cf. J. R. Bartlett, *The First and Second Books of the Maccabees* (Cambridge, 1973), 334: "patriotic suicide." Goldstein settles for "suicidal martyrdom." *II Maccabees*, 491. Doran correctly distinguishes between the deaths of Eleazar and the seven sons and that of Razis. He appropriately calls it suicide. "The Martyrs," 189.

90. This he futilely attempted when "he bravely ran up on the wall and manfully hurled himself headlong into the crowds." 2 Macc., 14.43.

91. Abel, *livres*, 467; Van Henten, 93–94, and n. 21 there.

92. 2 Maccabees 6:6 indicates that the people could not "confess themselves to be Jews." According to S. J. D. Cohen's interpretation, this means that "they could not declare themselves to be practitioners of the ancestral laws, the laws of God (6:1)." "Ioudaios: 'Judaean' and 'Jews' in Susanna, First Maccabees, and Second Maccabees," *Geschichte-Tradition-Reflexion: Festschrift für Martin Hengel Zum 70. Geburtstag*, eds. H. Cancik, H. Lichtenberger, and P. Schäfer (Tüsbingen, 1996), 1:211–219, especially 217; idem, *The Beginnings of Jewishness: Boundaries, Varieties, Uncertainties* (Berkeley, Los Angeles, London, 1999), especially 69–106; Goldstein offers a connection between the verse and the ritualistic recitation of the *Shema*, *II Maccabees*, 276; As will be discussed in Chapter 3, cases of martyrdom in the rabbinic period were related to the *Shema* declaration. D. Boyarin tends to accept Goldstein's proposal, which leads him to consider the idea that the roots of martyrdom and the term *martyrein* "go deeper than late antiquity." *Dying For God: Martyrdom and the Making of Christianity and Judaism* (Stanford, 1999), 188. In my opinion, this dating of the *Shema* in connection to martyrdom is another case of retrojection. As A. I. Baumgarten demonstrated, the declaration of the *Shema* was *not* practiced during

Antiochus IV's persecutions. In his opinion, the ritual of the *Shema* was an invention of the first or even the second Hasmonean generation, "sometime between Ben Sira and 100 BCE." "Invented Traditions of the Maccabean Era," *Geschichte-Tradition-Reflexion*, 1:197–210, especially, 207–209. If indeed "confess themselves to be Jews," refers to the *Shema* and martyrdom as Goldstein and Boyarin argue, Baumgarten's assertion supports my argument that the story was added later, long after Antiochus's persecutions constituted an issue.

93. Against the interpretation of Van Henten, p. 150. The text does not support Van Henten's assumption that Judas defeated Nicanor because of Razis' sacrifice. *The Maccabean Martyrs*, 150.

94. These are the essential differences between Razis and the *voluntary death* of Eleazar and the seven, and not just Razis' self-killing, as Van Henten suggests; *The Maccabean Martyrs*, 31.

95. L. Robert, "Epigrammes d'Aphrodisias," *Hellenica* 4 (1984): 127–135; followed by Van Henten, *The Maccabean Martyrs*, 207.

96. Y. Grisé, *Le Suicide Dans La Rome Antique* (Paris, 1982), especially 31–57, 93–113; Bar-Kochva, *Judas Maccabaeus*, 336; as A. J. L. Van Hooff puts it, "the replacement of the Greek rope by the Roman sword," *From Autothanasia to Suicide: Self-Killing in Classical Antiquity* (London and New York, 1990), 13, 47–54 and Appendixes A and B.

97. Quoted in Van Hooff, *From Authanasia to Suicide*, 162.

98. Verse 14.35 ends with the priests' prayer in reaction to Nicanor's threat to level the Temple to the ground if they did not deliver Judas Maccabee to him. The story is resumed in 15.1 with Nicanor chasing Judas in the region of Samaria.

99. Goldstein, *II Maccabees*, 491.

100. Perhaps this is the reason 1 Maccabees and Josephus do not mention the story.

101. Van Henten, *The Maccabean Martyrs*, 25, 31, 36.

102. Zeitlin believes it to be the epitomist's later contribution, *The Second Book of Maccabees*, 24. See also Harrington, *The Maccabean Revolt*, 47. Goldstein accepts it as an interpolation by a skeptic to deny resurrection; *II Maccabees*, 451. I believe it was a supporter of resurrection who corrupted the text. About critical problems in the text that may indicate a late addition, see again Katz, "Text," 20–21; Abel, *Les livres*, 445–446; Habicht, "2 Makkabäerbuch," 266; Van Henten, *The Maccabean Martyrs*, 182 n. 256.

103. Although the possibility that they are late pre-Christian is not ruled out. Katz, "The Text of 2 Maccabees," 20–21. According to Bar-Kochva, "the prayer and offering for the resurrection of the dead (II Macc. 12.43–44) has no analogue or root in Jewish tradition." *Judas Maccabaeus*, 372.

104. Goldstein believes he finds allusions to Daniel in both 1 and 2 Maccabees, especially when such statements in the text suffer from "inelegant" awkwardness or redundance. *II Maccabees*, 55, 305–306. If so, the author's reliance on Jeremiah rather than on Daniel is very strange. One would expect the author to mention Daniel explicitly to legitimize the support for resurrection instead of leaving the matter for the reader to speculate on. Keeping in mind that 1 and 2 Maccabees' statements are straightforward, Goldstein's explanation that "Jason dealt with the difficulties of Dan. 11:25–39 by making his narrative vague and by applying key words to show that the seer's prophecies were at least partly fulfilled," 64–65, is very unconvincing. As will be

discussed below, 4 Maccabees 18.11–13 has no problems with an explicit mentioning of the Danielic heroes. Obviously, Goldstein's analysis must reject Daniel's prophecies as *ex eventu*.

105. Bartlett, *The First and Second Books of the Maccabees*, 272 n. 9; Van Henten, *The Maccabean Martyrs*, 173 n. 205.

106. Zeitlin, *The Second Book of Maccabees*, 51; Katz, "The Text of 2 Maccabees," 20.

107. Katz, "The Text of Second Maccabees," 19 and 14 for problems with syntax regarding verses 7:22–23.

108. Zeitlin, *The Second Book of Maccabees*, 84. See also Van Henten, *The Maccabean Martyrs*, 173–174, especially nn. 206, 212. Although Zeitlin's argument is from silence, it fits well in the larger picture that incorporates elements from different periods, cultures, and views.

109. Katz, "The Text of 2 Maccabees," 20.

110. See also M. De Jonge, "Jesus' death for others and the death of the Maccabean martyrs," in *Text and Testimony: Essays on New Testament and Apocryphal Literature in Honour of A. F. J. Klijn*, eds. T. Baarda, A. Hilhorst, G. P. Luttikhuizen, and A. S. van der Woude (Kampen, 1988), 142–151, especially 147–151.

111. Habicht, 176, 186–187, rightly referring to 2 Macc. 5.19; Abel, *Les livres*, xliv, cf. Van Henten, *The Maccabean Martyrs*, 190; Goldstein, *II Maccabees*, 24–26. This is especially true if Doran's characterization of the book as propaganda for the Jerusalem Temple is correct. *Temple Propaganda*.

112. This should be the case especially if 2 Maccabees were indeed written in Jerusalem by someone who belonged to the elite of the Temple, and if "The centrality of the Temple in 2 Maccabees might point to a priestly origin of the book," as Van Henten presumes. *The Maccabean Martyrs*, 53, 55, and n. 113, 244, or p. 296: "The Jerusalem Temple is of central importance in the history of chs. 3–15."

113. M. Zambelli, "La composizione del secondo libro di Maccabei e la nuova cronologia di Antioco IV Epifane," *Miscellanea greca e romana* (Studi pubblicati dall'Istituto italiano per la storia antica 16, Rome, 1965), 195–299.

114. Van Henten's attempt to establish a connection between the martyrdoms and Judas's victory is only a matter of interpretation. *The Maccabean Martyrs*, 36. None of the martyrs themselves allude to such a connection.

115. This Law is obviously different from the "royal laws" that are mentioned for example in 2 Maccabees 4:11.

116. In the same spirit, Augustine wrote a few centuries later that these Maccabean heroes became martyrs for the Law (*"pro canonicis habet propter quorundam martyrum...."*). Augustine, *De civ. dei*, 18:36. The suggestion that this reference to the Law is the product of a Torah-centered stream that already existed at an earlier time is unlikely. If that were the case, we should have seen more similar reference in the rest of the book. See discussion below.

117. To be discussed in Chapter 3. Eleazar's epithet "the scribe" (*grammateus*) corresponds with the late Second Commonwealth era Hebrew title "*sofer*" and appears in the Christian Bible. Zeitlin, *The Second Book of Maccabees*, 155; Goldstein, *II Maccabees*, 286.

118. "As an afterthought," in Goldstein's words; *II Maccabees*, 283.

119. As Goldstein, among other, points out, the syntax of the quotation has puzzled both ancient and modern scholars; *II Maccabees*, 316.

120. For now, see Zeitlin, 2 *Maccabees*, pp. 82–83. His argument that the rabbis knew Eleazar's story but did not use it because of political reasons is far-fetched.

121. Bar-Kochva, *Judas Maccabaeus*, 489, 371–372.

122. For different reasons, G. W. Bowersock also considers the prospect that the stories in 2 Macc. 6 and 7 may be dated later than 70 A.D. *Martyrdom and Rome*, 11.

123. Zeitlin, *The Second Book of the Maccabees*, 21; idem, "The Names Hebrew, Jew and Israel: A Historical Study," *Jewish Quarterly Review* 43 (1952–1953), 369–379; P. W. van der Horst, *Ancient Jewish Epitaphs: An Introductory Survey of a Millenium of Jewish Funerary Epigraphy (300 BCE–700 CE)* (Kampen, 1991), 87–88.

124. Van Henten, *The Maccabean Martyrs*, 195, points to Lysias' statement after failing to capture Bet Zur: "the Hebrews were invincible, because the mighty God fought on their side" (2 Macc. 11.13). In my opinion, if the author were a Diaspora Jew, he would still prefer the more inclusive term "God of the Hebrews" to indicate His protection of all Jews, even when narrating a case that took place in the region of Judaea. See again Cohen, "Ioudaios;" Y. Amir, "The Term *IOUDAISMOS*, A Study in Jewish-Hellenistic Self-Identification," *Immanuel* 14 (1982), 34–41; J. D. G. Dunn, "Two Covenants or One? The Interdependence of Jewish and Christian Identity," *Geschichte–Tradition–Reflexion*, 3:107–113.

125. Of course a relationship between Diaspora Jews and the Temple already existed before the Maccabean revolt. As suggested by U. Kellermann, *Auferstanden in den Himmel: 2 Makkabäer 7 und die Auferstehung der Märtyrer* (SBS 95; Stuttgart, 1979), 38–40, 54–59. He suggests Antioch as the place of composition and that Jason had incorporated it into his text; followed by J. Goldstein, *II Maccabees*, 298, 303. But a pre-Maccabean setting would not have the element of religious persecution that would make voluntary death an option. Zeitlin suggests Gaius Caligula's anti-Jewish decrees in the early forties A.D. as the background and inspiration for the abridged Maccabean stories. Zeitlin, *The Second Book of Maccabees*, 27–30. Caligula's decrees will be discussed below. Bowersock, too, places the stories of Eleazar and the mother with her seven sons in the early Christian era. *Martyrdom and Rome*, 12–13; Habicht attributes Chapter 7 to a late redactor of the epitome, 171, 174, 233.

126. Cohen, "*Ioudaios*," 215–220; Y. Amir, "The Term *IOUDAISMOS*; Cf. Boyarin, *Dying For God*, 188. Concurring with Boyarin that the verse should not be accepted at face value, I believe it makes more sense to understand the verse in the context of the early Christian Martyrs' Acts, when confessing Christianity became a capital offence. See again Dunn, "Two Covenants or One?"

127. Other terms, such as those for Jewish holidays, are also taken from the pagan world. The author is either unfamiliar with the Jewish customs in Eretz Israel or addresses Diaspora readers in their terms. Examples are the terms that are used to describe the Feast of Tabernacles; the "three species" after the purification of the Temple; and the species of plants, which do not correspond in number or kind to those listed in Lev. 23:40 or Nehemiah 8:15. Bar-Kochva, *Judas Maccabaeus*, 372.

128. See discussions by Goldstein, *II Maccabees*, 275–276; Van Henten, *The Maccabean Martyrs*, 90; Boyarin, *Dying for God*, n. 11, 187–191. As we shall see in Chapter 3, Judaism was not outlawed even at the height of the Roman–Jewish conflict, which produced the martyrdoms of famous rabbis.

129. It is difficult to agree with Goldstein's association of Ecclesiastes 11:5 with the mother's question. Ecclesiastes wonders how the fetus develops in the womb, whereas the mother ponders how her sons appeared in her womb. The difference goes beyond "technical philosophical terminology." *2 Maccabees*, 309, 313–314. Rost admits that *ex nihilo* exhibits "important points of contact with the New Testament," but the connection does not raise his suspicions. *Judaism Outside the Hebrew Canon*, 84. Rajak claims that 2 Maccabees 7:22–23 was designed to depersonalize the mother's role "not only as a Jewish martyr but also as woman." *The Jewish Dialogue*, 118.

130. As with the sons' statements of resurrection, the mother's proclamation suffers from awkwardness as well as textual corruption and emendations. Cf. Goldstein, *2 Maccabees*, 312–313.

CHAPTER 2: BETWEEN GOD AND CAESAR

1. W. R. Farmer, *Maccabees, Zealots, and Josephus: An Inquiry into Jewish Nationalism in the Greco-Roman Period* (New York, 1956), 158; cf S. Hoenig, "Maccabbees, Zealots, and Josephus – Second Commonwealth Parallelism," *Jewish Quarterly Review* 49 (1958/1959), 75–80; the influence of the "Maccabean revolt had aroused not only strong religious but also political forces – the two can hardly be separated in ancient Judaism," according to Hengel, *Judaism and Hellenism*, 307, 308.

2. According to Farmer, Nicanor's Day was celebrated by the first century C.E. *Maccabees, Zealots, and Josephus*, 149.

3. Zeitlin, *The Second Book of the Maccabees*, 76–77; J. R. Bartlett, *Jews in the Hellenistic World: Josephus, Aristeas, The Sibylline Oracles, Eupolemus* (Cambridge, New York, 1985), 179; Goldstein, *I Maccabees*, 56–57; idem, *II Maccabees*, 26–27; especially 302. The state of mind of the seven Maccabean sons is "expressed with the same determination and éclat after Masada," according to V. Nikiprowetzky, "Josephus and the Revolutionary Parties," in *Josephus, the Bible, and History*, eds. L. H. Feldman and G. Hata (Detroit, 1989), 219. I could find no such parallels in the narratives. Also, the use of the term *martyrs* is too loose, in my opinion. More generally, I. M. Gafni rejects a link between Josephus and 2 Maccabees. "Josephus and I Maccabees," in *Josephus, the Bible, and History*, 130 n. 39. See also Bartlett, *Jews in the Hellenistic World*, 178.

4. Tcherikover, *Hellenistic Civilization*, 200; idem, "Antiochia in Jerusalem," 61–67; idem, "The Antiochus' Decrees and Their Problems," 86–109; Y. Baer, "The Persecution of the Monotheistic Religion by Antiochus Epiphanes" (Hebrew), *Zion* 38 (1971), 32–47; Derfler, *The Hasmonean*, 64; Sievers, *The Hasmoneans*, 24. According to W. R. Farmer, the memory of the Hasmoneans continued to inspire in the Second Temple period. They provided "influential prototypes." *Maccabees, Zealots, and Josephus* (New York, 1956), 158.

5. H. K. Bond, *Pontius Pilate in History and Interpretation* (Cambridge, 1998), 29–31. Bond attributes the similarities to cultural influences. W. H. Bronwnlee, "Maccabees, Books of," *Anchor Bible Dictionary*, ed. D. N. Freedman (New York, London 1992), 3:201–215.

6. Van Henten, *The Maccabean Martyrs*, 234. The author also points to the parallels between the four Roman virtues found in 4 Maccabees and Philo, 277 n. 32. Other parallels in 280–282, 284.

7. In Charles, *The Apocrypha and Pseudepigrapha of the Old Testament*, 1:131.

8. Grabbe, *Judaic Religion*, 90, with bibliography.

9. Stromateis, 1.21; 5.14.97. Zeitlin, *The Second Book of Maccabees*, 26; Bowersock, *Martyrdom and Rome*, 10.

10. *The Embassy to Gaius* in *The Loeb Classical Library*. The magnitude of the events led Klausner to consider the events, "the first anti-Semitic pogrom in Jewish history." *The History of the Second Temple*, 4:274–275.

11. On the demand to worship the emperor, R. Borgen, "Emperor Worship and Persecution in Philo's *In Flaccum* and *De Legatione ad Gaium* and the Revelation of John," in *Geschichte–Tradition–Reflexion*, 3:493–509.

12. *The Loeb Classical Library* (Massachusetts, London, 1941), tr. F. H. Colson.

13. The quotes from *On Joseph* and *Every Good Man Is Free* are from *The Loeb Classical Library*.

14. See Plutarch, *Agis and Cleomenes*, 38, *The Loeb Classical Library*, vol. 10, tr. B. Perrin (London and New York, 1916); other examples in Van Hooff, *From Autothanasia to Suicide*, 50.

15. Philo's description of Pilate is standard for his enemies. Nevertheless, Pilate appears milder in Philo than in Josephus. Bond, *Pontius Pilate*, 32, 33.

16. Grabbe, *Judaism from Cyrus to Hadrian*, 507–511.

17. Van Hooff, *From Autothanasia to Suicide*, 56; additional explanations of Caligula's demand in A. A. Barrett, *Caligula: The Corruption of Power* (New Haven, London, 1989), 74–75.

18. *The Embassy to Gaius*, , 14–21, 30–31.

19. Van Hooff, *From Autothanasia to Suicide*, 56–57.

20. Dio Cassius, *Roman History*, 59.8.3, 53.20.2–4. *The Loeb Classical Library*. According to Cassius, this was a Spanish practice. Barrett, *Caligula*, 73. Dio Cassius also relates Antinos's self-sacrifice. To save his friend Hadrian, he drowned himself in the Nile. 69:11.

21. Tacitus, *The Annals* 16:35, in *The Loeb Classical Library*.

22. Tacitus, *The Annals* 14:44.

23. As mentioned, the seven sons echo the same dilemma in 4 Maccabees.

24. His *apologia pro vita (sua)* in Jotapata will be discussed below.

25. In *The Loeb Classical Library*, tr. by H. St. J. Thackeray (London, 1926).

26. On the meaning of ethnic terms in Josephus, see T. Rajak, "Greeks and Barbarians in Josephus," *Hellenism in the Land of Israel*, eds. J. J. Collins and G. E. Sterling (Indiana, 2001), 246–262.

27. B. Bar-Kochva, *Pseudo-Hecataeus on the Jews: Legitimizing the Jewish Diaspora* (Berkeley, Los Angeles, London, 1996), 91–97; Gruen, *Heritage and Hellenism*, 201.

28. Discussion and bibliography by B. Bar-Kochva, *Pseudo-Hecataeus*, 91–97.

29. *The Loeb Classical Library* (London, 1937), tr. by R. Marcus.

30. The mention of mass crucifixion by Philo is perhaps what inspired Josephus to include this practice in his description of Antichos's persecutions. Josephus narrates Philo's dealings with Rome in *Jewish Antiquities* 18.259–260.

31. Recall 1 Maccabees 1:62–63, "Nevertheless, many in Israel were firmly resolved in their hearts not to eat unclean food. They preferred to die rather than be defiled by food or break the holy covenant, and they did die." In contrast, their dying for the Sabbath is refuted in Chapter 2. A point well observed by Rajak, *The Jewish Dialogue*, 127. For possible use of 2 Maccabees, see Bar-Kochva, *Judas Maccabaeus*, 190, although he believes 1 Maccabees to be Josephus's main source. *Judas Maccabaeus*, 158, 192.

32. Goldstein's argument that Josephus, as a descendent of the Hasmoneans, only drew upon the stories of the martyrs, without mentioning them because of their anti-Hasmonean nature, is very unconvincing. *II Maccabees*, 303. Goldstein himself admits that "Josephus knew how fallible they [the Hasmoneans] proved to be." *I Maccabees*, 56. For additional, unconvincing attempts (in my opinion) by Goldstein to connect Josephus and 2 Maccabees, *II Maccabees*, 284, 285, 299, 302. At the same time, however, Goldstein claims that Josephus did not know Razis' story, 493.

33. Based on the existence of very limited terminology Van Henten believes 2 Maccabees to have influenced Josephus. But Josephus's failure to mention the Maccabean martyrs is ignored. *The Maccabean Martyrs*, 89–91.

34. A point to which I will return later.

35. *The Loeb Classical Library* (London, 1976), tr. H. St. J. Thackeray.

36. As Thackeray comments on the text, "the name Ezechias is not mentioned elsewhere," 238 n. a. Bar-Kochva provides a useful discussion on this unknown person. *Pesudo-Hecataeus, "On the Jews,"* 82–91.

37. For different reasons, A. Kasher makes a similar analogy in "The Causes and the Circumstantial Background of the Jewish War Against Rome" (Hebrew), *Ha-Mered Ha-Gadol*, 21, 42–43.

38. Gruen, *Heritage and Hellenism*, 9–10.

39. Josephus's report on Simon of Scythopolis falls into a different category. Simon's self-killing and killing of his father, mother, wife, and children are a negative case. Simon preferred that they and he die "as cursed wretches" by his own hands rather than by the enemy's. In Simon's view, he was "justly punished" for his previous "crimes." *Jewish War* 2:469–476. Josephus displays a more positive attitude when narrating the strange suicide of Phasael. Here, however, we must note that Phasael "was marked for slaughter" and, therefore, only the method of death was his choice. *Jewish Antiquities* 14:365–369.

40. On Sabbath combat in Josephus, see Bar-Kochva, *Judas Maccabaeus*, 474–481.

41. Josephus does not leave only logical conclusions for the reader to make, he also leaves out Mattathias's approval of Sabbath combat (1 Macc. 2:41). A. A. Bell, Jr., "Josephus and Pseudo-Hegesippus," in *Josephus, Judaism, and Christianity*, eds. L. H. Feldman and G. Hata (Detroit, 1987), 355.

42. J. Sievers, "The Role of Women in the Hasmonean Dynasty," in *Josephus, the Bible, and History*, 135–139.

43. Josephus, *Jewish Antiquities* 14:58–68; *Jewish War*, 1:145–146; Strabo, *Geography*, tr. by H. L. Jones (London, New York, 1917–1933), 16:2.40; A. Kasher, "The Causes and the Circumstantial Background of the Jewish War against Rome," 13.

44. On a Sabbath, Josephus reports, the zealots slaughtered the Roman garrison at Masada. Josephus, *Jewish War*, 2:456.

45. Josephus's sympathetic view of Rome in *The Jewish War* is discussed by M. Stern, "Josephus and the Roman Empire as Reflected in The Jewish War," *Josephus, Judaism, and Christianity*, 71–80.

46. Bar-Kochva, *Pseudo-Hecataeus*, 293–295.

47. *The Loeb Classical Library* (London, 1980), tr. R. Marcus. The text is somewhat obscure. But because the Gadarenes accused Herod "of violence and pillage and the overthrowing of *temples* (emphasis added)," it seems to me that the Gadarenes mentioned here were the non-Jewish residents of Gadara who objected to Herod's territorial and political expansion.

48. *Roman History*, 1 :56–57; 39:51, *The Loeb Classical Library*.

49. Livy, 8.6.6–8.11.1 ; 8.9.9–10; 10.28.18. H. S. Versnel, "Self-Sacrifice, Compensation and the Anonymous Gods," *Le sacrifice dans l'antiquité*, eds. O. Reverdin and B. Grange (Genève, 1981), 135–194; on atonement, 159–163; on Roman *devotio*, H. S. Versnel, "Two Types of Roman Devotio," *Mnemosyne* 29 (1976), 365–410.

50. Livy, 7:5.

51. On the tradition of the *Kalanus* and Judaism, Bar-Kochva, *Pseudo-Hecataeus*, 96. Other examples of Romans killing themselves are provided by Dio Cassius, *Roman History*, 51 :35; 56:17.

52. On Josephus's Greek and Roman sources, see Rajak, *The Jewish Dialogue*, 83–84.

53. As attested by Pliny the Elder, *Natural History*, 8.7, 18, *The Loeb Classical History*; Livy, 37.42.5; additional references are provided by Bar-Kochva, *Judas Maccabaes*, 336. And see again, Grisé, *Le Suicide Dans La Rome Antique* and Van Hooff, *From Autothanasia to Suicide.*

54. Droge and Tabor, *Noble Death*, 34–35; Van Hooff, *From Autothanasia to Suicide*, 17.

55. *The Loeb Classical Library* (London, 1981), tr. by L. H. Feldman. The version in *Jewish War* concludes with the same assertion: the readiness of the Jews to die rather than transgress the Law astonished the governor who "gave the orders for the immediate removal of the standards from Jerusalem" (*Jewish War* 2.174).

56. The behavior of the "potential martyr" appears to coincide with the psychological theory of adaptive behavior. The adaptive behavior theory, known also as "the cry for help theory," asserts that a "suicide" does not necessarily wish to die. Rather, he or she uses the act as a means of obtaining attention from others. N. L. Farberow and E. Shneidman, eds., *The Cry for Help* (New York, 1961), 11–13, 52–53. E. Shneidman states that "individuals who are intent on killing themselves still wish very much to be rescued or to have their death prevented." E. Shneidman, "Preventing Suicide," in *American Journal of Nursing*, 65, no. 5 :10–15 (1965), 10. In this regard, suicide is viewed as a desire to change things for the better, a way of communication and literally "a cry for help." N. Farberow and E. Shneidman state that the "cry for help" is a method of expressing feelings of suffering and distress. The suicides, however, really believe they wish to die. Unfortunately, statistics show that when suicides "gamble with their lives," the results are often tangible and quite fatal. Gene and David Lester, *Suicide: The Gamble with Death* (New Jersey, 1971), 1–6.

57. Bond makes a similar point. *Pontius Pilate*, 52–69.

58. Josephus mentions Philo with his delegation and his advice to them to "be of good courage," *Jewish Antiquities* 18:259–260. A comparison between the two accounts is provided by E. M. Smallwood, "Philo and Josephus as Historians of the Same Events,"

Josephus, Judaism, and Christianity, 114–129. Smallwood tends to find Philo's account more credible.

59. *Jewish Antiquity*, 18:55–62; *Against Apion*, 2:41; Kasher, "The Causes and the Circumstantial Background of the Jewish War gainst Rome," 58–66.

60. *Jewish Antiquity*, 18:267. This statement echoes the approach taken by the heroes of the Book of Daniel, who welcomed the king's challenges with the conviction that God would deliver them from death because of their acceptance of these challenges. Daniel, 3:12–28; 6:3–22.

61. The parallel version in *Jewish War* 2:196–197 will be discussed below.

62. Rajak believes that Josephus "might have had Philo in mind in some of his emphatic assertions." *The Jewish Dialogue*, 124.

63. Van Hooff, *From Autothanasia to Suicide*, 57.

64. And again in *Jewish Antiquities*, 12:281–282.

65. For Josephus's presentation of 1 Maccabees here see Gafni, "Josephus and I Maccabees," 121–122. According to Gafni, by paraphrasing 1 Maccabees, Josephus attempted to present the Hasmoneans in a positive light for his Greek readers, 127.

66. Out of context, Jonathan also emerges as a "martyr." After being asked to replace his brother Judas, who "had died on behalf of the liberty of them all," Jonathan agreed and promised that he was "ready to die for them" (*Jewish Antiquities* 13:5–6). Love of liberty also characterizes the Galilaean sect. Its members have "a passion for liberty" thus "they think little of submitting to death in unusual forms . . . if only they may avoid calling any man master" *Jewish Antiquities* 18:23.

67. According to P. Bilde's interpretation of Josephus, the Jews prepared to fight Caligula's decree rather than submit peacefully. "The Roman Emperor Gaius Caligula's Attempt to Erect His Statue in the Temple in Jerusalem," *Studia Theologica* 32 (1978), 79. Gafni dismisses the reading as erroneous. *Josephus and I Maccabees*, 129 n. 37. S. G. F. Brandon claims that Josephus deliberately omitted Petronius's warning to Caligula that the Jews threatened to fight back. *Jesus and the Zealots: A Study of the Political Factor in Primitive Christianity* (Manchester, 1967), 87–88. Feldman differs in *Loeb Classical Library, Josephus*, 9:175. Another example that demonstrates the apologetic nature of Josephus's work is provided by the account of the House of Adiabene, as demonstrated by L. Schiffman, "The Conversion of the Royal House of Adiabene in Josephus and Rabbinic Sources," *Josephus, Judaism, and Christianity*, 293–312, especially, 308.

68. More attention to G. Vermes's important analysis of the *aqedah* will follow. *Scripture and Tradition in Judaism: Haggadic Studies* (Leiden, 1983), 197–198.

69. Charles also notices similarities, *The Assumption of Moses* (1987), 58. Summary in G. W. E. Nickelsburg, *Resurrection, Immortality, and Eternal Life in Intertestamental Judaism* (Cambridge, 1972), 97; for the relationship between the two sources, 99–102; 106–109. Nickelsburg's thesis missed Josephus's story of the father and the seven sons.

70. Baron, *A Social and Religious History*, 2:59; G. W. E. Nickelsburg, *Studies on the Testament of Moses* (Cambridge, 1973); idem, *Resurrection, Immortality, and Eternal Life*, 43–44; Rost, *Judaism Outside the Hebrew Canon*, 146–149; J. J. Collins, *The Apocalyptic Vision of the Book of Daniel* (Atlanta, 1977); J. Charlesworth, ed., *The Old Testament Pseudepigrapha*, 2 vols. (Garden City, 1983–1985), 1:918–926; J. Tromp, *The Assumption of Moses: A Critical Edition with Commentary* (Leiden, 1993).

71. See also J. Licht, "Taxo or the Apocalyptic Doctrine of Vengeance," *Journal of Jewish Studies* 12, 3 and 4 (1961), 95–105.

72. Cf. Van Henten, *The Maccabean Martyrs*, 212; Rajak, *The Jewish Dialogue*, 106. See also Nickelsburg, *Resurrection, Immortality, and Eternal Life*, 97–102.

73. Van Henten, *The Maccabean Martyrs*, 73–81.

74. Plutarch, *Agis and Cleomenes*, 38:6.

75. This important parallel is carefully studied by H.-J. Klauck, "Brotherly Love in Plutarch and 4 Maccabees," *Greeks, Romans, and Christians: Essays in Honor of A. J. Malherbe*, eds. D. L. Balch, E. Ferguson, and W. A. Meeks (Minneapolis, 1990), 144–156. The article also argues that 4 Maccabees was written by the end of the first century, if not later.

76. E. Bickerman, "The Date of Fourth Maccabees," in *Louis Ginzberg Jubilee Volume* (New York, 1945), 105–112; also in *Studies in Jewish and Christian History* (Leiden, 1976), 1:276–281; Nickelsburg, *Jewish Literature*, 226–227.

77. R. A. Coles, *Reports of Proceedings in Papyri* (Bruxelles, 1966), especially 26–27, shows that the introductions to the interrogation, the actual dialogue between the interrogator and the accused, and the conclusion bear the characteristics of Roman protocols. These elements are found in the early Martyrs' Acts. They also mark 2 Maccabees 6 and 7. This is another indication that these two narratives carry a Roman writing style. Coles's conclusions are further supported by L. Robert, *Le Martyre de Pionios, Prêtre de Smyrne*, eds. G. W. Bowersock and C. P. Jones (Washington, DC, 1994), 105–111. See also Bowersock, *Martyrdom and Rome*, 37–39, regarding the Martyrs' Acts.

78. J. Gutman, "The Mother and Her Seven Sons in the Aggadah and the Second and Fourth Books of the Hasmoneans" (Hebrew), in *Commentationes Iudaico-Hellenisticae in memoriam Iohannis Lewy*, eds. M. Schwabe and J. Gutman (Jerusalem, 1949), 33–34.

79. Other important figures were also turned into priests. Bar-Kochva, *Pseudo-Hecataeus*, 90.

80. A. O'Hagan correctly observed that the book employs cultic terms, without referring to the Temple. He links Eleazar's blood and burnt offering to Isaac. "The Martyr in the Fourth Book of Maccabees," *Studii Biblici Franciscani Liber Annuus* 24 (1974), 94–120.

81. In his commentary on the *Testaments of the Twelve Patriarchs* (London, 1908), R. H. Charles claims that "the idea of vicarious suffering and propitiation was not unfamiliar to pre- Christian Judaism, and especially with regard to the martyrs under Antiochus Epiphanes." M. De Jonge rejects this early possibility. "Test. Benjamin 3:8 and the Picture of Joseph as 'A Good and Holy Man,'" *Die Entstehung Der Jüdischen Martyrologie*, ed. J. W. Van Henten (Leiden, New York, Köln, 1989), 204–214. More generally, L. Batnitzky, "On the Suffering of God's Chosen: Christian Views in Jewish Terms," in *Christianity in Jewish Terms*, eds. T. Frymer-Kensky et al. (Colorado and Oxford, 2000), 203–220; R. Gibbs, "Suspicions of Suffering," *Christianity in Jewish Terms*, 221–229.

82. On the mother in 2 and 4 Maccabees, see R. D. Young, "The 'Woman with the Soul of Abraham': Traditions about the Mother of the Maccabean Martyrs," *'Women Like This': New Perspectives on Jewish Women in the Greco-Roman World*, ed. A.-J. Levine (Atlanta, 1991), 67–81.

83. Van Hooff, *From Autothanasia to Suicide*, 50–51. As a Christian model, Tertullian, *Ad Martyras*, in *The Writings of Tertullian* (Ante-Nicene Christian Library) (Edinburgh, 1870), 3:4.
84. Rajak prefers "a sort of substitute" instead of "ransom." *The Jewish Dialogue*, 110–111, especially n. 38.
85. Cf. Rajak, *The Jewish Dialogue*, 109.
86. L. H. Feldman disagrees with R. J. Daly's views that Christian writers had become familiar with the theology of the *aqedah* through Philo and Pseudo-Philo. Daly, "The Soteriological Significance of the Sacrifice of Isaac," *Catholic Biblical Quarterly* 39 (1977), n. 35. In Feldman's view Christian theologians read the biblical story itself. "Josephus's *Jewish Antiquities* and Pseudo-Philo's Biblical Antiquities," 78 n. 37 in *Josephus, the Bible, and History*. 4 Maccabees may be suggested as another source.
87. On their contribution to the *Targumim* see again Vermes, *Scripture and Tradition*, 192–218.
88. First Maccabees 1:36–37 speaks of the defilement of the Temple by Antiochus' officers:

    They shed innocent blood around the altar,
    And polluted the sanctuary.

    As long as the Temple stood, the reader could be outraged by the spilling of innocent blood on the altar. When the Temple ceased to exist or was out of reach, such images could be replaced by an imaginary altar and human sacrifices. Again, in contrast to 2 Maccabees 6 and 7, 1 Maccabees emphasizes the sanctuary. D. S. Williams, *The Structure of 1 Maccabees* (Washington, 1999), 19–20.
89. Van Henten suggests a different connection: "the number seven may emphasize symbolically the solidarity of the brothers (cf. 2 Macc. 7:2, 36–37) or the blessed fertility of their mother." *The Maccabean Martyrs*, 103, 287. 4 Maccabees associates the brothers' harmonious behavior with the seven days of creation; 14:7–8.
90. The requirement from the Maccabean martyrs to eat pork sacrificed on behalf of the king, is identical to the Roman demand of the Christians to eat meat sacrificed for the emperors. Eating sacrificial meat indicated their apostatizing from Christianity and the acknowledgment of the emperor's authority. On the trials of Christians see G. E. M. De Ste Croix, "Why Were the Early Christians Persecuted?" in *Studies in Ancient Society: Past and Present Series*, ed. M. I. Finley (London and Boston, 1974). These were Antiochus's two demands from the seven sons: first, accept his authority verbally and, second, demonstrate their loyalty by eating the sacrifices on his behalf. But Jews were always spared this religious procedure. Why would then the author of the Maccabees include a Roman practice in a Hellenistic story? For the same reason Josephus included mass crucifixions of Hellenistic Jews who, he claimed, died for their religion. Writing from afar, both authors relied on their imagination rather than on fact. By including practices of their own times in past stories, they could hope to convince their readers that their "history" happened exactly as told.
91. The elevation of the mother from an unexplained death (2 Macc. 7:22) to an "unexplained heroic status" in 4 Maccabees mirrors, as do the rest of our sources, the increasing popularity of the notion of voluntary death during this period.
92. See again Klauck, "Brotherly Love in Plutarch and 4 Maccabees."

93. M. De Jonge, "Jesus' Role in the Final Breakthrough of God's Kingdom," *Geshichte–Tradition–Reflexion*, 3:265–286, especially 270.

94. Philo echoes here Epicurus's view: "when we are, death is not come, and, when death is come, we are not. It is nothing, then, either to the living or to the dead, for with the living it is not and the dead exist no longer." Droge and Tabor, *Noble Death*, 47 n. 42.

95. Philo referred to the platonic idea of immortality in philosophical terms, which appears to be different from the later understandings of these terms. See Moore, *Judaism*, 2:295. In any event, although Philo employed this platonic idea, he does not mention it in his reports on the potential martyrs. With respect to Lev. 18:5, "He shall live by them," Philo does not interpret the verse as a confirmation of immortality and eternal reward. Rather, life lived in accordance with Torah is the true and eternal life, while the wicked are doomed. *Embassy*, 229–236.

96. On Josephus, Philo, and these sects see Baumgarten, *The Flourishing of Jewish Sects in the Maccabean Era*, 58–62.

97. E. P. Sanders, *Judaism: Practice and Belief 63 BCE–66 CE* (London and Philadelphia, 1992), 379. In general, the resurrection concept is not completely clear. L. Finkelstein, *Mavo le-Masekhtot Avot ve-Avot de-Rabbi Natan* (New York, 1950), 222–233. On the relationship between the "world to come" and the resurrection of the dead see Moore, *Judaism*, 2:378–385, 387, 392–395. The notion of "future existence" seems to represent, in its early stages, a new order in the terrestrial realm that would be attained only by the believer, whereas the evildoer would be destroyed. L. H. Schiffman, "At the Crossroads: Tannaitic Perspectives on the Jewish-Christian Schism," in *Jewish and Christian Self-Definition*, ed. E. P. Sanders, 2 vols. (Philadelphia, 1980), 2:115–156, especially, 140–144. On the Pharisees' and Sadducees' messianic understanding and the problems they present to the modern study, see Schiffman, *The Eschatological Community of the Dead Sea Scrolls* (Atlanta, 1989), 1–9. Then, the human and mortal Messiah would restore Judean independence and destroy the Roman power, leading the people to a new utopian age of glory, peace, solace, and pure holiness. S. Sandmel, *Judaism and Christian Beginnings* (New York, 1978), 200–208, and especially, 208. L. H. Schiffman, *Law, Custom, and Messianism in the Dead Sea Sect*, 268–311; Moore, *Judaism*, 2:323–376. As Schiffman points out, a clear ideological combination of the restorative and the utopian trends is evident for the first time in the Qumran documents, which set the foundations for the Jewish messianic ideology, with its special dialectic characteristics. Also, Schiffman, *Eschatological Community*, 3–8; idem, "Jewish Sectarianism in Second Temple Times," in *Great Schisms in Jewish History*, ed. R. Jospe and S. M. Wagner (New York, 1981), 1–46. On the Pharisees' messianic hopes, see also Finkelstein, *The Pharisees*, 503–507.

98. L. L. Grabbe, "Sadducees and Pharisees," *Judaism in Late Antiquity: Part 3. Where We Stand: Issues and Debates in Ancient Judaism*, eds. A. J. Avery-Peck and J. Neusner (Leiden and Brill, 1999), 1:35–62.

99. More generally on Josephus and the Essenes, Rajak, *The Jewish Dialogue*, 219–224; on their cult and belief, M. A. Larson, *The Essene Heritage* (New York, 1967).

100. Bartlett suggests that Josephus "may here have had in mind also the martyrdom stories of 2 Macc. 6:18:31; 7:1–42." *Jews in the Hellenistic World*, 179. If indeed

Josephus had had these stories in mind, it is very unlikely that he would have ignored them throughout his works.

101. *The Loeb Classical Library* (Cambridge and London, 1941), tr. F. H. Colson.

102. *Resurrection, Immortality, and Eternal Life*, 169. In this context, W. D. Davies' article is of value. According to Davies, the term *angelos* (angel) in Josephus refers to priest or prophet as the leaders of the community. His interpretation makes heavenly rewards less likely. "A Note on Josephus, Antiquities 15:136," in *Harvard Theological Review* 47/3 (1954), 135–140.

103. Although in 2 Maccabees 7 the seven sons and the mother expected to receive their bodies back again. The dichotomy between body and soul is made by Eleazar.

104. M. Smith masterfully explains the variations in Josephus's attitude toward the Pharisees and the Sadducees in *The Jewish War* and *Jewish Antiquity*. "Palestinian Judaism in the First Century," *Israel: Its Role in Civilization*, ed. M. Davis (New York, 1956), 75–81. These changes of heart may also contribute to the variations in his depictions of their theological beliefs. Eschatology in Josephus is discussed by L. L. Grabbe, "Eschatology in Philo and Josephus," in *Judaism in Late Antiquity: Part 4, Death, Life-after-Death, Resurrection and the World-to-Come in the Judaism of Antiquity*, eds. A. J. Avery-Peck and J. Neusner (Leiden and Brill, 2000), 163–185.

105. A. Dihle, "C. Judaism: I. Hellenistic Judaism," in *Theological Dictionary of the New Testament*, eds. G. Kittel and G. Fridrich (Eerdmans, 1974), 9:632–635.

106. Feldman's commentary on *Jewish Antiquities* 18:14–15; followed by Rajak, *The Jewish Dialogue*, 124–125.

107. In this context, J. Neusner's admonition not to accept the Pharisees as the "normative" sect of pre-A.D. 70 Palestinian Judaism is of value. According to Neusner, the Pharisees believed in "the immortality of the soul." "Josephus' Pharisees: A Complete Repertoire," *Josephus, Judaism, and Christianity*, 274–292. According to Grabbe, "Josephus gives no evidence of belief in resurrection," *Judaic Religion*, 263.

108. Recall the fourth-century B.C. Athenian practice, mentioned in Chapter 1. See again Van Hooff, *From Autothanasia to Suicide*, 162.

109. Josephus depicts positively even the act of the mother who consumed her child when suffering famine during the siege of Jerusalem. Such an act was unheard of among "the Greeks and Barbarians" (*Jewish War* 6:199). This depiction of a mother overcoming her maternal instinct is another missed opportunity to introduce the mother and her seven sons.

110. Also *Jewish War* 1:653 "after our death, we shall enjoy greater felicity."

111. V. Nikiprowetzky, "La mort d'Eleazar fils de Jaïre et les courants apologétiques dans le *De bello judaico* de Flavius Josèphe," *Hommages à André Dupont-Sommer*, eds. A. Caquot and M. Philonenko (Paris, 1971), 461–490; L. H. Feldman, *Josephus and Modern Scholarship (1937–1980)* (Berlin, 1984), 772–789.

112. M. Luz, "Eleazar's Second Speech on Masada and Its Literary Precedents," *Rheinisches Museum für Philologie* NF 126 (1983), 25–43.

113. A dilemma that continues today, S. Hoenig, "The Sicarii in Masada–Glory or Infamy?" *Tradition* 11 (1970), 5–30; S. Spero, "In Defense of the Defenders of Masada," *Tradition* 11 (1970), 31–43.

114. According to D. J. Ladouceur, suicide forms the punishment of the Sicarii for crimes against their own countrymen. "Josephus and Masada," in *Josephus, Judaism, and Christianity*, 95–113. Rewards would be inappropriate in this case.

115. Droge and Tabor, *A Noble Death*, 95.
116. 2 Macc. 2:49–68. And "As for you my children, be strong and courageous in behalf of the law, for through it you will be glorified."
117. In any case, this verse, which echoes the Christian Bible, has been regarded as an interpolation. See Hadas's commentary on the verse and his references to the Christian Bible.
118. As the seven sons told the king: "In recompense for this, justice will keep you in store for intense and eternal fire and torment; and these shall never release you throughout time" (4 Macc. 12:12).
119. For example the fourth son stated: "you take away my organ of speech" but the king could not take his reason; 10:18–19.
120. According to Hadas, "be with God" is found only in the S manuscript and is probably not a genuine addition.
121. According to Hadas, they will live like angels. The verse, however, is loosely connected to the rest of the text. Freudenthal rejected the verse, and the possibility of a Christian gloss cannot be dismissed. Hadas, *The Third and Fourth Books of Maccabees*, 231.
122. See Hadas's unsuccessful attempt to settle these problems in his commentary on this verse; 18:23: "ranged in the choir of their fathers," does not indicate immortality. It recalls the biblical notion of being gathered to one's forefathers, Judges 2:10, repeated in Judith 16:32 and Acts 13:36. No need to confuse 18:17–19 with resurrection. See, for example, 1 Maccabees 69, Mattathias "Then he blessed them and was gathered to his fathers. According to A. DuPont-Sommer, *Le Quatrième Livre des Machabées: Introd., traduction et notes* (Paris, 1939), 18:17–19 shows an illogic order. See also Hadas's commentary.
123. Young's interpretation of "placed firmly with them in heaven" is worth quoting. "Like Abraham, her children are numbered among the stars (clearly a modification of the biblical text, in which Abraham's descendants will be as numerous as the stars)." "Woman with the Soul of Abraham," 80. The statement indicates a metaphor rather a conviction of heavenly rewards.
124. M. Schatkin discusses their burial place in "The Maccabean Martyrs," *Vigilae Christianae* 28 (1974), 97–113. M. Hengel, *Jews, Greeks and Barbarian: Aspects of the Hellenization of Judaism in the Pre-Christian Period* (Philadelphia, 1980), 108–109. On the importance of Antioch, A. Grabar, *Martyrium: Recherches sur le culte de reliques et l'art chrétien antique* (London, 1972), 1:21–227.
125. *Eccles. Hist.* 3.10.6. On Eusebius's usage of Josephus to support his Christological interpretations and the long-lasting effects of such misuse, see S. Zeitlin, *Josephus on Jesus: With Particular Reference to the Slavonic Josephus and the Hebrew Josippon* (Philadelphia, 1931), especially 61–70. The parallels between 4 Maccabees and Paul's account of Jesus' death are discussed by D. Seeley, *The Noble Death: Graeco-Roman Martyrology and Paul's Concept of Salvation* [Journal for the Study of the New Testament, Supplement Series 28] (Sheffield, 1990), 92–112.
126. On Josephus's influence on the intellectual history of the early church, H. Schreckenberg, "The Works of Josephus and the Early Christian Church," *Josephus, Judaism, and Christianity*, 315–324; Hadas, *The Third and Fourth Books of Maccabees*, 114.
127. Eusebius refers to Philo's speech before the Roman senate in *The Ecclesiastical History*, 2:18.8. in *Loeb Classical Library*. On the "potential martyrs" and Pilate, *The*

Ecclesiastical History, 2:6–7. Reference to Josephus, *The Ecclesiastical History*, 3:5. On Blandian as "a noble mother," *The Ecclesiastical History*, 5:1.54.

128. *Exhortation on Martyrdom* 45–46, 22–27, 30. 4 Maccabees and martyrological literature are addressed by H. Musurillo, *The Acts of the Pagan Martyrs: Acta Alexandrinorum* (Oxford, 2000), 236–242; The influence of pagan martyrs does not escape Musurillo's significant study, 243–255.

129. Tertullian, *Antidote for the Scorpion's Sting* 6, in *The Writings of Tertullian* (Ante-Nicene Christian Library) Vol. 3 (Edinburgh, 1870).

130. Origen, for example, incorporated Josephus's description of the fall of Jerusalem in his theology of Jesus' crucifixion. Origen's "theology of history" continued to demonstrate itself in Augustine' *De civitate Dei*. W. Mizugaki, "Origen and Josephus," *Josephus, Judaism, and Christianity*, 325–337. Relying on Origen, Eusebius states that Josephus confirmed that the calamity of the Jews began with the time of Pilate and the crime against the "Savior." *History of the Church*, 2.6.3. See Z. Baras, "The Testimonium and Martyrdom of James," in *Josephus, Judaism, and Christianity*, 338–348.

131. Frend, *Martyrdom and Persecution*, 356. H. Najman's comments in "The Writings and Reception of Philo of Alexandria" are significant. She writes: "Apparently lost to later Jewish exegetes and philosophers, Philo was appropriated so completely by some Christians that he was regarded as a Christian. Only centuries later, during the Reformation, was it recalled that Philo Christianus had in fact been Philo Judaeus," 100. Or, "Not Jews, but Christians church fathers such as Clement of Alexandria (ca. 150–220) and Origen (184–253) were thus the direct inheritors of the legacy of Philo and Hellenistic Judaism. Philo offered these recent converts to Christianity a way of incorporating their philosophical training into their appreciation of Scripture. These interpreters made great use of Philo and were ultimately responsible for the preservation of Philo's writings," 102. In *Christianity in Jewish Terms*.

132. M. Simon "Les saints d'Israel dans la dévotion de l'Eglise ancienne," in *Recherche d'Histoire Judéo-Chrétienne* (Paris, 1962), 158. Eleazar becomes their biological father based on the erroneous understanding of Gregory of Nazianzus' homily in *Machabaeorum Laudem*, where he is described as their spiritual father. Schatkin, *The Maccabean Martyrs*, 111. More generally on the development of martyrs' cults and relics, Grabar, *Martyrium*, 1:400–581.

CHAPTER 3: "IT IS WRITTEN IN THE LAW"

1. See R. Goldenberg, "Talmud," in *Judaism: A People and Its History. Religion, History, and Culture: Selections from the Encyclopaedia of Religion*, ed. R. M. Seltzer (New York, London, 1989), 102.

2. S. Lieberman argues that the Jerusalem Talmud my provide a more accurate historical picture about events in the Land of Israel than its Babylonian counterpart, "*The Martyrs of Caesarea*," *Annuaire de l'institut de philologie et d'histoire orientales et slaves* 7 (1939–1944), 395.

3. Despite the geographical distance between Babylon and *Ertz Israel*, the two centers were communicating with each other. Both centers were reacting to the interior and exterior religious and historical developments of the time. And both centers

expressed their reactions in their texts. See Boyarin, *Dying for God*, 147 n. 86; I. Gafni, "Babylonian Rabbinic Culture," 238–239. In *Cultures of the Jews: A New History*, ed. D. Biale (New York, 2002).

4. For the early active role of the priesthood in the revolt see, Josephus, *Wars*, 2, 17, 1–5.

5. S. Lieberman, "Persecution of the Jewish Religion" (Hebrew), in *Salo W. Baron Jubilee Volume*, Hebrew vol. ed. S. Lieberman (New York, 1974), 213–244; M. D. Herr, "Persecutions and Martyrdom in Hadrian's Days" (Hebrew), in *Milhemet Kodesh u-Martirologiah* (Jerusalem, 1967), 76–83; idem, "Persecutions and Martyrdom in Hadrian's Days," *Studies and History*, eds. D. Asheri and I. Shatzman, *Scripta Hierosolymitana*, 23 (Jerusalem, 1972), 85–125. Further discussion to follow.

6. M. Mor, *The Bar-Kochba Revolt: Its Extent and Effect* (Hebrew) (Jerusalem, 1991), 218–223; J. Efron, "Bar-Kokhva in the Light of the Palestinian and Babylonian Talmudic Traditions" (Hebrew), in *The Bar-Kokhva Revolt*, eds. A. Oppenheimer and U. Rappaport (Jerusalem, 1984); G. Hasan-Rokem, *Web of Life: Folklore and Midrash in Rabbinic Literature*, tr. by B. Stein (Stanford, 2000), 164–166.

7. S. Schwartz, *Imperialism And Jewish Society, 200 B.C.E. To 640 C.E.* (Princeton and Oxford, 2001), 15. See also D. Ben-Haim Trifon, "Some Aspects of Internal Politics Connected with the Bar Kokhvah Revolt" (Hebrew), in *The Bar-Kokhva Revolt*, 13–26. During the period of R. Gamliel II, the nation suffered from internal political and spiritual divisions.

8. D. Ben-Haim Trifon, "Some Aspects of Internal Politics Connected with the Bar-Kokhva Revolt," 17. According to Trifon, by the first half of the second century, the rabbis still lacked a strong central leadership, 20–21.

9. H. Mantel, "The Bar Kokhvah Revolt," 280.

10. Dio Cassius, *Roman History*, 69, 13, 2; 14, 1. Schäfer, *The History of the Jews in Antiquity*, 158–160.

11. Herr, "Persecutions and Martyrdom" (Hebrew), 81–82. The Roman policy was not aimed against the Jewish religion but rather against the Jewish rebels who were seeking the independence of Judea from Roman rule. Even after the uprising, Judaism continued to be a legal religion in the empire, despite the growing resentment against the Jews. Lieberman, "On Persecution of the Jewish Religion," 213–244; Herr, "Persecutions and Martyrdom" (Hebrew), 76–83; E. M. Smallwood, *The Jews under Roman Rule: From Pompey to Diocletian* (Leiden, 1976), 430–434, 463–476; P. Schäfer, "The Causes of the Bar Kokhba Revolt," in *Studies in Aggadah, Targum and Jewish Liturgy in Memory of Joseph Hinemann*, eds. J. J. Petuchowski and E. Fleischer (Jerusalem, 1981), 74–94; idem, *The History of the Jews in the Antiquity*, 145–158. For some Jews such religious compromises may have meant stop being Jewish.

12. "Have the recommendation of being ancient," Tacitus, *Hist.* 5:5.

13. Tacitus, *Hist.*, 5:13. About Tacitus' account, see E. M. Smallwood, "Some Comments on Tacitus' *Annales* XII," *Latomus* 18 (1959), 560–567.

14. Even the decrees against the Christians were not as severe as their documents describe. According to G. E. M. de Ste. Croix, only the Fourth Edict of the early fourth century ordered all the imperial subjects to sacrifice to gods, on pain of death. But there is no conclusive proof that the edict was invoked. G. E. M. de Ste. Croix, "Aspects of the 'Great' Persecutions," in *Harvard Theological Review* 47 (1954), 77, 79, 92, 98–100,

especially 104: "The so-called Great Persecution has been exaggerated in Christian tradition.... Other persecutions of Christianity were sporadic and short-lived..."

15. Eusebius, *The History of the Church*, 2.1. See also, Y. Baer, *Studies and Essays in the History of the Jewish People* (Hebrew) (Jerusalem, 1985), Chapter 11, 254–302; Schiffman, *Who Was a Jew?*, 51–78.

16. The threat did not have to be physical. According to Schwartz, the legal position of the Jews declined in the fourth century. *Imperialism and Jewish Society*, 186. J. Cohen has argued that the early Christian emperors were sympathetic to the Jews. "Roman Imperial Policy toward the Jews from Constantine until the End of the Palestinian Patriarchate (ca. 429)," *Byzantine Studies* 3 (1976), 1–29.

17. F. Blanchetière, "The Threefold Christian anti-Judaism," *Tolerance and Intolerance in Early Judaism and Christianity*, eds. G. N. Stanton and G. G. Strounsa (Cambridge, 1998), 185–210, especially 192.

18. Doran, "The Martyrs," 189–205. See also, A. Agus, *The Binding of Isaac and Messiah* (Albany, 1988), Chapter 1.

19. S. Shepkaru, "From after Death to Afterlife: Martyrdom and Its Recompence," *Association for Jewish Studies Review* vol. 24.1 (1999), 17–18.

20. G. Stemberger, "The Maccabees in Rabbinic Traditions," *The Scriptures and The Scrolls: Studies in Honour of A. S. Van Der Woude on the Occasion of His 65th Birthday*, eds. F. G. Martinez, A. Hilhorst, and C. J. Labuschagne (Leiden, New York, Köln, 1992), 193–203.

21. Recall that 4 Maccabees emphasizes Eleazar's priestly origin.

22. Doran offers different reasons for oral transmissions. "The Martyrs," 198–199.

23. *Lamentations Rabbah*, ed. S. Buber (Vilna, 1899), 84–85; *Seder Eliyahu Rabbah*, Chapter 28, ed. M. Friedmann (Meir Ish-Shalom) (Vienna, 1904), 151–153.

24. G. D. Cohen ascribes the name Nahtom to a copyist's error. "The Story of Hannah and Her Seven Sons in Hebrew Literature" in *Mordecai M. Kaplan Jubilee Volume*, Hebrew section, ed. M. Davis (New York 1953), 117, especially n. 45. J. Neusner calls her "Miriam, daughter of Tanhum," *Israel After Calamity: The Book of Lamentations* (Pennsylvania, 1995), 62.

25. *Pesiqta Rabbati*, Chapter 43, ed. M. Friedmann (Vienna, 1880), 180b. Other versions are *Midrash Zutta*, ed. Buber (Berlin 1894), 69, and *Yalkut Shimoni* (no. 1029) to Lamentations 2:17. See again Cohen, "The Story of Hannah and Her Seven Sons," 109–122, and Z. M. Rabinowitz, *Ginzei Midrash* (Hebrew) (Tel Aviv, 1976), 143 and n. 58.

26. Doran, "The Martyrs," 197.

27. Neusner's translation of Lamentations has "ruler." *Israel After Calamity*, 62.

28. *Midrash Lamentations Rabbah* 1:16 opens with a similar story. Vespasian sent three ships full of men and women "of the nobility of Jerusalem" to brothels in Rome. The women and men jumped into the sea to maintain their morality.

29. Or, "It is written in our Law (*be-Toratenu*)."

30. On the *aqedah* story (Genesis 22:1–19) and its interpretation in Jewish sources, see S. Spiegel, "From the Legends of the *Aqedah*" (Hebrew), *Sefer ha-Yovel le A. Marx* (New York, 1950), 476–477. Spiegel's essay was translated into English by J. Goldin: *The Last Trial: On the Legends and Lore of the Command to Abraham to Offer Isaac as a Sacrifice: The Akedah* (New York, 1993). The evolution of the story is discussed by

J. D. Levenson, *The Death and the Resurrection of the Beloved Son* (New Haven and London, 1993), 111–124, 173–199. On the meaning of sacred narrations or "foundation myths," M. Eliade, *Images and Symbols*, tr. by P. Mairet (New York, 1969), 115, 167; M. Eliade, *Myth and Reality*, tr. by W. R. Trask (New York, 1968), 5. For a general view on symbolism, see A. Brelich, "Symbol of a Symbol" in *Myth and Symbols*, eds. J. M. Kitagawa and C. H. Long (Chicago and London), 1969, 195–208.

31. As Spiegel suggests, *The Last Trial*, 16.

32. L. Finkelstein, *Akiva: Scholar, Saint and Martyr* (London, 1990), 246–247.

33. Batnitzky, "On the Suffering of God's Chosen: Christian Views in Jewish Terms," 206–208.

34. If local governors did require some Jews to offer libation, as Lieberman suggests, "The Martyrs of Caesarea," 431, they went beyond the official Roman policy.

35. Herr, "Persecutions and Martyrdom" (Hebrew), 79–81; Lieberman, "On Persecution of the Jewish Religion," 213–215; L. Finkelstein, "The Ten Martyrs," in *Essays and Studies in Memory of Linda R. Miller*, ed. I. Davidson (New York, 1938), 41–42.

36. A. Oppenheimer considers the possibility that Akiva was executed for reciting the *Shema*. His interpretation relies on Y. *Berakhot* 9, 14:b: "The time of the reading of the *Shema* came. He [Akiva] began to read the *Shema* and smiled." A. Oppenheimer, "The Sanctity of Life and Martyrdom in the Wake of Bar Kokhba's Rebellion" (Hebrew), in *Sanctity of Life and Martyrdom*, ed. I. M. Gafni and A. Ravitzky (Jerusalem, 1992), 90–91, especially, ns. 24, 25. Oppenheimer also indicates that some of the statements attributed to Akiva may have been a late interpolation. 90 n. 22. Finkelstein, *Akiba*, 276–277.

37. Also, B. *Gittin* 57b reports on this practice.

38. Other versions in Y. *Sotah* 5, 20c; Y. *Berakhot* 9, 14b.

39. See *Mishnah Berakhot* 9:5; *Sifre on Deuteronomy*, ed. S. Horovitz and L. Finkelstein (New York, 1969), 55; B. *Pesahim* 25a; *Mekhilta de-Rabbi Ishmael*, eds. H. S. Horowitz and D. A. Rabin (Jerusalem, 1970), 127. Discussions in Boyarin, *Intertextuality and the Reading of Midrash* (Bloomington and Indianapolis, 1990), 122–126; idem, *Dying for God*, 105–111; M. Fishbane, *The Kiss of God: Spiritual and Mystical Death in Judaism* (Seattle and London, 1994), 66–71.

40. See also Tosefta *Sotah* 13. The post-Talmudic *Semahot* 8 identifies Simeon with Simeon ben Gamliel the First, the father of Gamliel of Jabneh. He, however, lived *before* the destruction of the Temple, whereas Samuel died almost half a century after the event. The other Simeon, the Son of Gamliel II, lived after the time of the persecutions and died in a natural death. Simeon, the son of R. Hanina, affords another possibility. He lived to witness the destruction of the Temple (B. *Menahot* 100b). Ishmael is identified with Ishmael ben Elishah, the high priest. This would mean that he, too, lived *before* the destruction of the Temple. But B. *Shabbat* 12b indicates that Ishmael lived after the destruction of the Temple. "When the Temple is rebuilt, I [R. Ishmael ben Elisha] will bring a fat sin-offering" B. *Shabbat* 12b; also B. *Baba Bathrah* 62a. The two thus could not have been contemporaries. Further discussion in S. Zeitlin, "The Legend of the Ten Martyrs and Its Apocalyptic Origins," *Jewish Quarterly Review* 36 (1945–1946), 2–3, especially n. 13a. Cf. S. Krauss, "Ten Martyrs" (*Asarah Harugei Malkhut*) in *ha-Shilloach* 44 (1925), 19–20, 107–108.

41. The different variations with their different titles are presented by G. Reeg, *Die Geschichte von den Zehn Märtyren: Synoptische Edition mit Übersetzung und*

Einleitung (Tübingen, 1985), especially 2–3; M. Hirschler also published a midrash with an introduction. "Midrash *Asarah Harugei Malkhut*" (Hebrew), *Sinai* 71 (1974), 218–228.

42. *Midrash Elleh Ezkerah, Bet ha-Midrash*, 6 vols., ed. A. Jellinek (Jerusalem, 1967), 2:64–72; 6:19–30; 6:31–35.

43. Zeitlin, "The Legend of the Ten Martyrs and Its Apocalyptic Origins," 1–16; E. E. Urbach, *The Sages*, 2 vols., tr. by I. Abrahams (Jerusalem, 1975) 1:521–523. A strong believer in the authenticity of the story of the Ten Martyrs was S. Krauss. See his efforts to support his thesis in *ha-Shilloach* 44 (1925), 10–22, 106–117, 221–233.

44. Neusner's translation is missing R. Judah ha-Nahtom (the baker), Israel *after Calamity*, 80, but, he is found in Zeitlin's "The Legend of the Ten Martyrs," 1 n. 2. *Midrash Psalms* has: Simeon ben Gamliel, Ishmael ben Elishah, Yeshebab the Writer, Huzpit, R. Jose, Judah ben Baba, Judah the Baker, Simeon ben Azzai, Hananiah ben Teradyon and R. Akiva. Siddur R. Saadia refers in a poem to a somewhat different list of ten martyrs.

45. Finkelstein, "The Ten Martyrs," 29 n. 1. And see *Taanit* 18a where it reads, "Nevertheless [Turyanus] killed them immediately." One Eleazar ben Dams, *Hekhalot Rabbati, Bet ha-Midrash*, ed J. Jellinek, 3, chapter 4, 86. A. Hyman, *The History of the Tannaim and the Amoraim* (Hebrew), 3 vols. (Jerusalem, 1964), 1:161. H. L. Schiffman, *Who Was a Jew?* (New Jersey, 1985), 100, n. 3. Further discussion to be followed in the next chapter.

46. *Bet ha-Midrash*, ed J. Jellinek, 2:69.

47. B. *Avodah Zarah* 27b; Y. *Avodah Zarah* 2:2 (40d–41a); Y. *Shabbat* 14:4 (14d–15a); also in T. *Hullin* 2:22–23.

48. See n. 8 in B. *Taanit* 18b in the Soncino Talmud.

49. Finkelstein, "The Ten Martyrs," 29 n. 1.

50. Quoted by Cohen in "The Story of Hannah and Her Seven Sons," 110 n. 6 (my translation).

51. Also in B. *Pesahim* 50a.

52. Rashi erroneously identifies Laodicea with Lud. Laodicea is a city in the district of Lyyda in Asia Minor. For Laodicea as a city in Asia Minor, see B. *Baba Metzia* 84a. Rashi's erroneous designation led him to identify the brothers Lulianus and Pappus, who were executed in Laodicea (B. *Taanit* 18b), as the martyrs of Lud (see the notes below). The English translation of the version in *Pesahim* 50a follows Rashi. It has Lydda [Lydia] for the original Lud. Rashi's interpretation will change the message of B. *Baba Batra* 10b. It gives the wrong impression that B. *Baba Batra* 10b distinguished between two types of martyrs, scholars and nonscholars, in the vision. As we shall see in the medieval part of this study, Rashi's interpretation is not surprising. He lived in eleventh-century Christendom in a culture that often praised all kinds of casualties as martyrs who were believed to be rewarded in heaven. This may also explain his erroneous association of the world that was envisioned with *Gan Eden*. But the identity of the martyrs and the exact nature of the topsy-turvy world remain unclear.

53. Here identified as Pappus ben Judah. It is not unusual to find the same figure in several stories, with conflicting information.

54. *Bereshit Rabbah* (ca. 400–500), 64:7 reports that in the time of R. Joshua ben Hananiah the "Government" ordered the rebuilding of the Temple. Lulianus and Pappus "set

up tables from Acre unto Antioch" to assist those returning from exile to celebrate the event. The Samaritans, however, convinced the authorities to abrogate the plan. As a result, the community gathered into the valley of Rimmon and "wished to rebel against the government." *Midrash Bereshit Rabbah*, chapter 64, eds. J. Theodor and C. Albeck (Jerusalem, 1965); *Ekhah Rabbah* (*Lamentations Rabba*) 2:2, ed. S. Buber (Vilna, 1899); Y. *Taanit* 4, 1, 69a; B. *Sanhedrin* 97b. See also Y. *Taanit* 2, 13, 66a; *Megillah* 1, 6, 70c; *Mekilta of R. Simeon* 21, 13, *Semahot* 8, 15. Reference also in Eusebius, *History of the Church from Christ to Constantine*, tr. by G. A. Williamson (New York, 1965), 4:6; 1–4. Ben Shalom believes that "Hadrian's decision to build Aelia Capitolina served as a catalyst which hastened processes which in any case would have brought about a confrontation with Rome." I. Ben Shalom, "Events and Ideology of the Yavneh Period as Indirect Causes of the Bar-Kokhva Revolt" (Hebrew), in *The Bar-Kokhva Revolt*, 11.

According to Farmer, for Bar-Kokhva and his men, the rebellion was a natural continuation of the Maccabees' struggle for independence. *Maccabees, Zealots, and Josephus*, 25–26, 175, 185; Ben Shalom argues that although the Romans were able to put an end to the revolt of 66, they never succeeded in extinguishing the ideology that triggered it. "Events and Ideology," 1–3. A. Kasher argues that messianic expectations existed already before 66. *Ha-Mered Ha-Gadol*, 87–90; Klausner, *The History of the Second Temple*, 4:162–165; E. Schürer, *The History of the Jewish People in the Age of Jesus Christ* (175 B.C.–A.D. 135), 3 vols., eds. G. Vermes and F. Millar (Edinburgh, 1973–1987), 2:489.

This reversal in Roman policy is said to have ignited the Bar Kokhva revolt. Dio Cassius claims that the emperor's plan to turn Jerusalem into a pagan city, Aelia Capitolina, triggered the great revolt. Dio Cassius, *Roman History*, tr. by E. Cary (London, New York, 1914–1927), 69, 11–15. Some scholars do not accept Dio's account. Cf. B. Isaac, "The Revolt of Bar-Kokhva as Described by Cassius Dio and Other Revolts Against the Romans in Greek and Latin Literature," in *The Bar-Kokhva Revolt*, 1. See also H. Graetz, *History of the Jews*, 6 vols. (Philadelphia, 1891–1899), 2:403–404; G. Allon, *The History of the Jews in the Land of Israel in the Time of the Mishnah and Talmud*, 2 vols. (Tel Aviv, 1966), 2:9–11. According to A. M. Rabello's philological examination, the prohibition of circumcision that preceded the revolt and the construction of Aelia Capitolina in Jerusalem were the causes of the revolt. "The Edicts on Circumcision as a Factor in the Bar-Kokhva Revolt," in *The Bar-Kokhva Revolt*, 27–46; especially 46. On Roman legislation against circumcision, see Smallwood, *The Jews Under Roman Rule*, 429–431, 464–473.

Others have suggested that Hadrian's persecutions were a reaction to the Jewish rebellion. H. Mantel, "*Ha-Meni'im le-Merd Bar-Kokhva*," in *Milhemet Kodesh u-Martirologiah*, 35–57. See also S. Lieberman, The "Martyrs of Caesarea," 395–446; and in *JQR*, 36 (1945–1946), 239–253. According to Mantel, it had already commenced in the year 119 and the decrees gradually followed. H. Mantel, "The Bar-Kokhva Revolt," *Jewish Quarterly Review* 58 (1967–1968), 277. Archaeological findings show that preparations for the war were made a long time before the revolt. A. Kloner, "Hideout-Complexes from the Period of Bar-Kokhva in the Judean Plain," in *The Bar-Kokhva Revolt*, 153–171.

55. The inability of Lulianus and Pappus to repeat the miracle of the three Danielic heroes may convey the same message. When asked by Trajan to repeat the miracle of

Hananiah, Mishael, and Azariah to save their lives, the brothers Lulianus and Pappus echoed the same sentiments.

> We have deserved of the Omnipresent that we should die, and if you will not kill us, the Omnipresent has many other agents of death. The Omnipresent has in His world many bears and lions who can attack us and kill us. The only reason why the Holy One, blessed be He, has handed us over into your hand is that at some future time He may exact punishment of you for our blood. (B. *Taanit* 18b)

The identification of Trajan is discussed by E. Schürer, *The History of the Jewish People*, 1:660 n. 62, who identifies him with Trajan's general, Lusius Quietus.

56. B. *Berakhot* 61b connects Akiva's reward to his death for the Torah. But even there, the reward is not automatic.

57. On the importance to die publically, B. Chilton and J. Neusner, *Comparing Spiritualities: Formative Christianity and Judaism on Finding Life and Meeting Death* (Harrisburg, 2000), 92–112.

58. Finkelstein, *Akiba*, 291–292.

59. *Midrash Mishle*, 9:2, ed. S. Buber (Jerusalem, 1964–1965), 62.

60. Priests (Cohens) are not permitted to come in contact with the dead.

61. Mishnah *Horayot*, 3,8 makes a direct disparagement of the High Priest: "A learned bastard takes precedence over an ignorant High Priest."

62. B. *Taanit* 18a; Urbach, *The Sages*, 91.

63. Josephus, *Ant.*, 20, 1, 3; 20, 6, 2; 17, 8–12; 17, 13, 1; *Wars*, 2, 1, 1; and see E. M. Smallwood, "High Priest and Politics in Roman Palestine," in *Ha-Mered Ha-Gadol*, 231–250.

64. A. Guttmann, *Rabbinic Judaism in the Making: A Chapter in the History of the Halakha from Ezra to Judah* I (Detroit, 1979), 230–233.

65. See also, Y. *Baba Kama* 4, 3, 4b. It was, of course, in the Roman interest to support the moderate Gamliel. On the improvement in relationships, Schäfer, *The History of the Jews in Antiquity*, 163–164.

66. Y. *Hagigah* 3, 78d; *Song of Songs Rabbah*, 2, 16; B. *Berakhot* 63b. See also Oppenheimer, "The Sanctity of Life and Martyrdom," 92–93.

67. According to the Babylonian Talmud, a self-sufficient community existed even before the destruction of the First Temple. Gafni, "Babylonian Rabbinic Culture," 225.

68. Y. *Sanhedrin* 1, 19a; B. *Sanhedrin* 14a.

69. Tosefta, *Baba Kama* 8, 13; Y. *Sotah* 9, 24a, B. *Baba Kama* 80a and *Temurah* 15b. See again, Oppenheimer, "Sanctity of Life and Martyrdom," 92–93.

70. B. *Pesahim* 57b.

71. *Avot de-Rabbi Nathan*, 1, 21. Ed. S. Schechter (Vienna, 1887); J. Goldin, *The Fathers According to Rabbi Nathan* (New Haven, 1995).

72. Agus also discusses this story. *The Binding of Isaac*, 210–216.

73. Also B. *Sotah* 49b: "With the death of R. Eliezer the Scroll of the Law was hidden away" and B. *Sanhedrin* 101a.

74. The reason for his excommunication is still debatable. A. Guttmann sees in Eliezer's practice of magic to overcome his colleagues' opinion the reason for the ban. "The Significance of Miracles for Talmudic Judaism," *Hebrew Union College Annual* 20 (1974), 383, 386. Following Guttmann, and relying on B. *Baba Metsia* 59a, Boyarin makes the intriguing argument that the reason for the excommunication was Eliezer's close contact with Christians. Eliezer, Boyarin writes, "had more than some sympathy

for Jesus and his followers and their Torah. . . ." *Dying for God*, 28 and 29–33. Others disagree. See Agus, *The Binding of Isaac*, 212. He relies on Y. *Moed Katan* 3, 1, 81 c, d and his interpretation of B. *Baba Metsia* 59b; Y. D. Gilat, R. *Eliezer Ben Hyrcanus: A Scholar Outcast* (Ramat Gan, 1984), 483–485.

75. S. Lieberman, "The Publication of the Mishnah," *Hellenism in Jewish Palestine: Studies in the Literary Transmission, Belief, and Manners of Palestine in the I Century B.C.E.–IV Century C.E.* (New York, 1950), 83–89.

76. J. Neusner, "The Rabbinic Traditions about the Pharisees before A.D. 70: The Problem of Oral Transmission," *Journal of Jewish Studies* 21–23 (1971), 17. See also J. Neusner, "From Exegesis to Fable in Rabbinic Traditions About the Pharisees," *Journal of Jewish Studies* 24–25 (1974), 263–269. A more general study on the issue of the rabbinic system can be found in J. Neusner, *Ancient Israel after Catastrophe* (Charlottesville, 1983), especially 18–49, 77–80.

77. R. Kimelman questions the association of *Minim* with Christianity. "Birkat Ha-Minim and the Lack of Evidence for an Anti-Christian Jewish Prayer in Late Antiquity." In *Jewish and Christian Self-Definition*, eds. E. P. Sanders et al. (Philadelphia, 1980), 2:226–44; 391–403. But see Boyarin, *Dying for God*, 152 n. 21, 159 n. 59 and the bibliography cited, which apply the term *Minim* to all Christians. Additionally, see Schiffman, *Who Was a Jew?*, 67, 75; J. Neusner, *From Politics to Piety: The Emergence of Pharisaic Judaism* (New York, 1979), 95–96; idem, *The Incarnation of God: The Character of Divinity in Formative Judaism* (Philadelphia, 1988), 194–196.

78. *The Letter to the Christians at Rome* 5:20–21; 7:1–6; and especially 10:4, where it reads: "For Christ means the end of the struggle for righteousness by the law for everyone who believes in him." See also H. Maccoby, *The Mythmaker: Paul and the Invention of Christianity* (San Francisco, 1987), 3–18; L. Gaston, *Paul and the Torah* (Vancouver, 1987), 15–20; P. E. Sanders, *Paul, the Law, and the Jewish People* (Philadelphia, 1983), 50–55; F. Thielman, *From Plight to Solution: A Jewish Framework for Understanding Paul's View of the Law in Galatians and Romans* (Leiden, 1989), 1–27. On different approaches to the Law, see D. Novak, "*Mitsvah*," 115–126; S. Hauerwas, "Christian Ethics in Jewish Terms: A Response to David Novak," 135–140, and E. N. Dorff, "Another Jewish View of Ethics, Christian and Jewish," 127–134, all in *Christianity in Jewish Terms*.

79. M. C. De Boer, "The Nazoreans: Living at the Boundary of Judaism and Christianity," *Tolerance and Intolerance*, 239–262; R. A. Pritz, *Nazarene Jewish Christianity: From the End of the New Testament Period until Its Disappearance in the Fourth Century* (Jerusalem, 1992), 53. E. Laupot discusses the validity of this term in Tacitus' annals. "Tacitus' Fragment 2: The Anti-Roman Movement of the *Christiani* and the Nazoreans," *Vigiliae Christianae* 54:3 (2000), 233–247.

80. Removing the mark of circumcision.

81. The fierce Christian attacks against the rabbinic homilies, exegesis, and *midrash* constituted specific challenges to the rabbis' views. C. Merchavia, *The Church Versus Talmudic and Midrashic Literature [500–1248]* (Jerusalem, 1970), 3–12.

82. Schiffman, *Who Was a Jew?*, 77–78. On Paul and the Pharisees, see J. A. Ziesler, "Luke and the Pharisees," in Neusner's book, *From Politics to Piety*, 161–172.

83. The story of Zekhariah's death in the Temple (*Lamentations Rabbah*, poem 23, 2:2, 4:3; Y. *Taanit* 4, 5; B. *Gittin* 57a–b; *Pesikta de-Rav Kahana*) has been analyzed in the context of the first-century Jewish–Christian dialogue. S. H. Blank, "The Death of

Zechariah in Rabbinic Literature," *Hebrew Union College Annual* 12–13 (1937–1938), 327–346, especially 337–338; J.-D. Dubois, "La mort de Zacharie: mémoire juive et mémoire chrétienne," *Revue des études Augustinennes* 40 (1994), 23–38, especially 37; Hasan-Rokem, *Web of Life*, 169–171.

84. Of course, the approaches of the two religions to God's anthropomorphic image are not always so distinguishable. E. R. Wolfson, "Judaism and Incarnation: The Imaginal Body of God," 239–254; R. Rsahkover, "The Christian Doctrine of the Incarnation," 254–261; S. A. Ross, "Embodiment and Incarnation: A Response to Elliot Wolfson," 262–268; D. R. Blumenthal, "*Tselem*: Toward an Anthropopathic Theology of Image," 337–347; all articles in *Christianity in Jewish Terms*.

85. See also Boyarin's similar reading, *Dying for God*, 121–122.

86. *Genesis Rabbah* refers to this theological deviation more explicitly. The *Minim* asked R. Simlai, "How many gods created the Universe," supporting their argument by Gen. 1:26 "Let us make man in our image, after our likeness." Alluding to the trinity, they asked: "What is that which is written, 'The Lord, the God of gods, the Lord, the God of gods, He knows (Josh. 22:22)?'" The three biblical references to God (*El, Elohim, and YHVH*), explained R. Simlai, "are a Divine name, just as a person refers to a king as Basileum, Caesar, and Augustus," but not references to a split divinity.

87. A. Z. Idelsohn, *Jewish Liturgy and Its Development* (New York, 1932), 97.

88. According to M. Simon, Jews applied the term *Minim* to all Christians. *Versu Israel: A Study of the Relations between Christians and Jews in the Roman Empire (135–425)*, tr. by H. McKeating (Oxford, 1986), 183.

89. *Avot*, Chapter 2, Mishnah 1.

90. P. S. Alexander, "'The Parting of the Ways' from the Perspective of Rabbinic Judaism," *Jews and Christians: The Parting of the Ways A.D. 70 to 135*, ed. J. D. G. Dunn (Tübingen, 1993), 1–25. According to Lieberman, by the beginning of the fourth century "Christianity was no longer the creed of Jewish heretics, for it had long became the faith of the Gentiles." "The Martyrs of Caesarea," 409. A fuller discussion with important bibliography is provided by Boyarin, *Dying for God*, 1–21. Boyarin argues for a later date, in some places as late as the sixth century. The negative influence that the *Minim* had on the Jews is demonstrated by the story of the woman who came before R. Hisda. She considered her incestuous relationship "the lightest sin." Her immoral behavior was explained on the ground that "she had also adopted *Minut*" (B. *Avodah Zarah* 17a).

91. M. Halbertal, "Coexisting with the Enemy: Jews and Pagans in the Mishnah," *Tolerance and Intolerance*, 159–172.

92. Not even to refute them. Only skilled rabbis like Idith could do so (B. *Sanhederin* 38b).

93. *Bet ha-Midrash*, 6:20.

94. T. Hull, ed. Zuckermandel, 2, 22–23; Y. *Avodah Zarah* 2, 2, 4; Y. *Shabbat* 14:4, J (Neusner's translation). See also, D. Schwartz, "What Should He Answer? And He Should Live by Them" (Hebrew), in *Sanctity of Life and Martyrdom*, 73–76, especially ns. 10, 11, 12. On the name, see R. T. Herford, *Christianity in Talmud and Midrash* (New York, 1978), 39; and Boyarin's discussion, *Dying For God*, 154–155 n. 27.

95. Discussed by D. Schwartz, *Sanctity of Life and Martyrdom*, 69–83.

96. M. C. De Boer, "The Nazoreans," 247–252.

97. Schiffman, *Who Was a Jew?*, 69–73.

98. Schwartz corrects "He said to him," 74. Boyarin keeps "They," 34.

99. Again, Schiffman, *Who Was a Jew?*, 71–73.

100. See again Boyarin's stimulating analysis, *Dying For God*, 26–41.

101. MS. M has "one [of the disciples of Jesus the Nazarene] Jacob of Kefar Sekaniah." And see again, T. Hullin 2:24, ed. Zuckermandel. On the identification of Kefar Sekaniah, see R. A. Pritz, *Nazarene Jewish Christianity*, 120. Whether this Jacob is the same as Jacob of Sama, see R. Kalmin, "Christians and Heretics in Rabbinic Literature of Late Antiquity," *Harvard Theological Review* 87, no. 2 (April 1994), 169; cf. Boyarin, *Dying for God*, 159 n. 59.

102. Other examples of close relationships with *Minim* are R. Abbahu and R. Safra (B. *Avodah Zarah* 4a) and R. Judah Nesia (B. *Avodah Zarah* 6b).

103. W. H. C. Frend attributes the failure of the Roman persecution to the determination of the martyrs. Although Frend tends to exaggerate their importance, he makes valid arguments. "The Failure of the Persecutions in the Roman Empire," *Studies in Ancient Society*, ed. M. I. Finley, Past and Present Series (London and Boston, 1974), 263–287. Cf. R. L. Fox, *Pagans and Christians* (New York, 1989), especially 419–492.

104. A. J. Mason. *The Historic Martyrs of the Primitive Church* (Longmans, 1905); C. Rowland, *Radical Christianity: A Reading of Recovery* (New York, 1931); G. W. E. Nickelsburg and M. E. Stone, *Faith and Piety in Early Judaism* (Philadelphia, 1983), 150–153; Fox, *Pagans and Christians*, 445; D. Riddle argues that the belief in celestial rewards in the presence of the angels and God played an important role in controlling the Christians. *The Martyrs: A Study in Social Control* (Chicago, 1931), 36, 56, 59, 82, 86.

105. Tertullian, "To Scapula," in *Apologetical Works*, in *The Fathers of the Church* (New York, 1950), 10:130; "in the sight of Christ," Tertullian, "On Purity," tr. William P. Le Saint, in *Ancient Christian Writers: The Works of the Fathers in Translation* (London, 1959), 125. Seeing the "Son of Man" is mentioned in Matt. 24:30, 25:31.

106. As Frend points out, not all Christians supported martyrdom. In fact, he believes that the difference of opinion on the issue led to schisms within the Church. *Martyrdom and Persecution in the Early Church*, 360–361, 288.

107. Eusebius, *Martyrs of Palestine*, 8:1. See also Lieberman, "The Martyrs of Caesarea," 410, where he speculates that Jews witnessed the execution of Agapius of Gaza at the Stadium of Caesarea. The quote is from Lieberman.

108. J. M. Lieu, "Accusations of Jewish Persecution in Early Christian Sources, with Particular Reference to Justin Martyr and the Martyrdom of Polycarp," *Tolerance and Intolerance*, 279–295.

109. According to de Ste. Croix, "Aspects of the 'Great' Persecution," 101.

110. Eusebius, *Martyrs of Palestine*, 1:5; Romanus is another example, although his execution took place in Antioch. *Ibid.*, 2:2.

111. *The Martyrs of Palestine*, 1:5; 3:2–4.

112. *The Martyrs of Palestine*, 7:1.

113. G. E. M. de Ste. Croix noted this behavioral distinction among Christians. "Why Were Early Christians Persecuted?" *Studies in Ancient Society*, 210–249, especially 234–237. Regarding the Roman–Christian relationship, see A. N. Sherwin-Whit's response to de Ste. Croix, "Why Were the Early Christians Persecuted? An Amendment," *Studies in Ancient Society*, 250–255, followed by de Ste. Croix, "Why Were the Early Christians Persecuted? A Rejoinder," 256–262; also de Ste. Croix, "Aspects

of the 'Great' Persecution," 83, especially 101 where he divides martyrs into three groups.

114. The source is discussed by T. Barnes, "Tertullian's *Scoriace*," *Journal of Theological Studies*, n.s., 20, no. 1 (April, 1969), 105–132.

115. According to Y. Baer's analysis of *De Idolotaria*, the opinions of the Mishna and Baraitot influenced this work by Tertullian. "Israel, the Christian Church, and the Roman Empire from the Time of Septimius Severus to the Edict of Toleration of A.D. 313," *Studies in History*, ed. A. Fuks and I. Halpern. Scripta Hierosolymitana 7, 79–147, especially, 88–93 (Jerusalem, 1961); Similar argument is made by G. G. Stroumsa, "Tertullian and the Limits of Tolerance," *Tolerance and Intolerance*, 173–184; cf. J. B. Rives, *Religion and Authority in Roman Carthage from Augustus to Constantine* (Oxford, 1995), 220–221.

116. Schwartz, "What Should He Answer?", 82–83.

117. Schwartz's interpretation differs. *Sanctity of Life and Martyrdom*, 76–81. On the association of sin and martyrdom, see Urbach, *The Sages*, 389–391 especially ns. 68, 70; idem, "Ascesis and Suffering in Talmudic and Midrashic Sources," in *Y. F. Baer Jubilee Volume*, ed. S. W. Baron (Jerusalem, 1960), 48–68, especially, 59, 61, and 67 ns. 98, 99.

118. See also Y. *Sanhedrin* 3, 21 b; B. *Avodah Zarah* 27b; B. *Pesahim* 25a–b, 26a. On the two different views, I. Gruenwald, "Intolerance and Martyrdom: from Socrates to Rabbi 'Aqiva," *Tolerance and Intolerance*, 7–29, especially 24–26.

119. See again the martyrdom of the seven sons in 4 Macc. chapters 8–12; Philo, *The Embassy to Gaius*, 32:229–236, and *The Assumption of Moses*, 9:1–7: "For if we do this and die, our blood will be avenged before the Lord." See again, Licht, "Taxo or the Apocalyptic Doctrine of Vengeance," 95–105.

120. The Maccabean martyrs hoped "to stay the wrath of the Almighty which was justly brought against the whole of our nation." The martyrs also hoped that because of their martyrdom God will "be merciful to our nation." 2 Macc. 7:37–38.

121. "... the King of the Universe will raise us up to everlasting life because we have died for His laws." 2 Macc. 7; 4 Macc. chapters 8–12.

122. 2 Macc. 7:22.

123. Riddle discusses the importance of the Christian martyrs' blood and the glorification of death. *The Martyrs*, 58, 61.

124. According to D. Flusser, the Jewish concept of martyrdom influenced Christianity. "Jewish Origin of Christianity" (Hebrew), in *Y. Baer Jubilee Volume* (Jerusalem, 1960), 75–98; and his article, "Jewish Sources of Christian Martyrdom and their influence on its Fundamental Concepts" (Hebrew), in *Milhemet Kodesh u-Martirologiah*, 61–71.

125. Krauss, "The Ten Killed by the Government," 110.

126. B. *Sanhedrin* 14a; B. *Avodah Zarah* 8b, 27b; Y. *Avodah Zarah* 2:2, 4, I; *Shabbat*, 14:4, J. See also, Krauss, "Ten Martyrs," 111–112; Oppenheimer, "Sanctity of Life and Martyrdom," 92–93.

127. Tosefta, *Baba Kama* 8, 13; Y. *Sotah* 9, 24a, B. *Baba Kama* 80a and *Temurah* 15b.

128. De Ste. Croix, "Aspects of the 'Great' Persecution," 103.

129. Lieberman suggests that the Roman fears of the rebels led to the decrees, which were issued as preventive measures. In his view, the decrees against the *mitzvot* were issued for military reasons. Lieberman, "Persecution of the Jewish Religion,"

213–215. Following this suggestion, Mantel states that the decrees were intended to prevent rebel assemblies for political and military purposes. For example, Jews could not blow the *shofar* because many times attacks against the Romans started with the sounding of the *shofar*. Y. *Rosh ha-Shanah*, 4, 59c. The Romans were already "sensitive to every movement of the Jews that could mean an attack or an act of revolt." Mantel, "*Ha-Meni'im le-Merd Bar-Kokhva,*" in *Milhemet Kodesh u-Martirologiah*, 40. See also A. Oppenheimer, "The Sanctity of Life and Martyrdom," 95 n. 44. Eusebius blamed the rebels for the decrees and saw in the renaming of Jerusalem, Aelia Capitolina, a punishment of the defeated rebels. Eusebius, *The History of the Church*, 4:2, 3, 6.

130. Happy art thou [R. Eleazar ben Perata], who hast been arrested on five charges, but wilt be rescued; woe is me [Teradyon] who, though having been arrested on one charge [studying Torah], will not be rescued (B. *Avodah Zarah* 17b).

131. Jews would not eat food prepared by idolaters.

132. The avoidance of martyrdom by the "trickster" is discussed by Boyarin, *Dying for God*, 55–57, 69–74, 81.

133. Rashi associates "danger" with violent robbers. In the context of rabbinic martyrology, the association of the word with the alleged Roman decree reflects the attitude toward the issue of voluntary death.

134. A question already raised by Herr in "Persecutions and Martyrdom" (English), 112. "If the Sages conducted themselves in this manner [of avoiding martyrdom], how much more was this behaviour prevalent among ordinary people?"

135. The Roman officer who committed suicide rather than arrest R. Gamaliel is said to have been motivated by the desire to have a place in the world to come (B. *Taanit* 29a). This bizarre case permits the officer to take his own life, an act which even the martyrs rejected (see again Teradyon's case). The story also leads us to believe that the Romans stopped the decree against the rabbis only because the officer killed himself. This story may have been inspired by Christian examples of Roman soldiers dying as martyrs to attain heaven. For other examples see, B. *Avodah Zarah* 10b; 18a.

136. For a fuller discussion see Shepkaru, "From After Death to Afterlife," 18–28. Cf. S. Safrai, *Be Shilhe ha-Bayit ha-Sheni uvi-Tekufat ha-Mishnah* (Jerusalem, 1983), 103; Urbach, *The Sages*, 307–308. See also, D. Flusser on the Torah and reward, "He Has Planted It [i.e., the law] as Eternal Life in Our Midst" (in Hebrew), *Tarbiz* 58 (1988–1989), 47–153; Schiffman, "At the Crossroads," 141.

137. Again, in B. *Berakhot* 61b, Akiva does not submit to death to be rewarded. Only after the intervention of the ministering angels on his behalf, does "A *bat kol* went forth and proclaimed, Happy art thou, R. Akiba, that thou art destined for the life of the world to come." No description of the world to come is provided.

138. Lieberman, "The Martyrs of Caesarea," 437–438.

139. From *Sifre Deut.* 34.74b, "when thou walkest it [i.e., the Torah] shall talk with you," we understand that the world to come connotes physical resurrection. B. *Berakhot* 17a promised the righteous that they would "sit enthroned, crowns on their heads and enjoy the luster of the *Shekhinah* (the presence of God)," but this does not necessarily mean in heaven. Compare to Matthew 22.30. The Christian mystics that are examined in this book also believed that God's presence can be experienced in this life.

140. *Tanhuma, Reeh*, 4; *Pirkei de-Rabbi Eliezer*, chap. 24 on Deut. 32.39. But hints of a somewhat different world to come appear in *Tanhuma, Vayikra* 8.

141. R. Bauckham, "Jews and Jewish Christians," 232.

142. Paul's dilemma is discussed by Droge and Tabor, *A Noble Death*, 119–126.

143. Among the high Roman officials and the families of emperors were also openly practicing Christians, even before it became the Empire's official religion. Frend, "The Failure of the Persecutions in the Roman Empire," 276.

144. Another reaction to the *Minim* is R. Sheshet's style of praying. This blind rabbi "held that the *Shekhinah* is in all places, because [when desiring to pray] he used to say to his attendant: 'Set me facing any way except the east.' And this was not because the *Shekhinah* is not there, but because the *Minim* prescribe turning to the east" B. *Baba Bathra* 25a.

145. G. D. Cohen, "Esau as Symbol in Early Medieval Thought," *Jewish Medieval and Renaissance Studies*, ed. A. Altmann (Cambridge, 1967), 19–48.

146. Ten Jews was considered the minimum for publicity.

147. This is against R. Dimi, who taught that in times of royal decree "one must let himself be killed (*yehareg*) rather than transgress even a minor precept" (B. *Sanhedrin* 74a).

148. See again Halbertal, "Coexisting with the Enemy: Jews and Pagans in the Mishnah," *Tolerance and Intolerance*, 159–172.

149. This is not to say that the transformation was absolute and immediate. For example, a conflict in the Diaspora broke out in 115–117 C.E. Nor am I saying that there was a rabbinic influence over the Diaspora rebellion.

150. B. *Berakhot* 61b; *Sanhedrin* 12a; *Avodah Zarah* 18a. This is not to say, of course, that the rabbis abandoned the will to reestablish their Jewish homeland.

151. She married the gentile king Ahasuerus publicly.

152. Droge and Tabor, *A Noble Death*, 144–152.

153. Urbach, *The Sages*, 312, 390. See also the story of Haninah ben Dosah in Ber. 33a. Urbach, *The Sages*, 91. On the issues of reward and punishment, see also, 239–241; on the absence of the notion of salvation through death, see 587–594.

154. "Understand that the blood of that circumcision has been made useless, and we have believed the blood that brings salvation . . . Jesus Christ circumcises all those who will. . . . Come, let us go in the light of the Lord, for he has set his people free, even the house of Jacob." Justin Martyr, *The Dialogue with Trypho*, 24, 3. tr. by W. A. Lukyn (London, New York, 1930). See G. N. Stanton's comment, "Justin Martyr's Dialogue with Trypho: Group Boundaries, 'Proselytes' and 'God-Fearers,'" *Tolerance and Intolerance*, 263–278, especially 270.

155. Blanchetière is correct to distinguish between the celestial redemption of the Christians and the concept of "liberation" in Judaism. "The threefold Christian Anti-Judaism," 197.

156. Hasan-Rokem makes a similar observation regarding proem 24 in *Lamentations Rabbah*. She writes: "Despite the testimony of the patriarchs [before God] about their own sacrifices and efforts, particularly in their role as parents, the emotional intensity of their words cannot alter the divine decree. . . . Love, in its most human and tender variation, rather than the zealous love of God expressed in the willingness to sacrifice a son, bears the power of redemption." *Web of Life*, 127–128.

157. R. Judah I was called *qadosh* already in his lifetime. As A. Guttmann points out, the term has to do "with Judah's saintly way of life, with his stature as a man of

deep religiosity and high morality." *Rabbinic Judaism in the Making*, 254 and ns. 234–236. In B. *Baba Kamma* 113a, R. Akiva uses the phrase *qiddush ha-Shem* in a nonmartyrological sense. I. Gruenwald discusses this issue in *Qiddush ha-Shem*, An Examination of a Term" (Hebrew), *Molad* 1 (1968), 476–484.

158. Riddle, *The Martyrs*, 93–98. Recall the woman who asked the would-be Christian martyrs of Caesarea to remember her when they came before the Lord. Eusebius, *Martyrs of Palestine*, 7:1.

159. Droge and Tabor, *A Noble Death*, 167–183. The transition from actual to spiritual forms of martyrdom is treated by E. Malone, *The Monk and the Martyr* (Washington, DC, 1950).

CHAPTER 4: BYZANTINE BURNT OFFERINGS

1. Zeitlin, "The Legend of the Ten Martyrs." As mentioned, Kruss approaches the legend differently. "The Ten Martyrs Killed by the Government" (*Asarah Harugei Malhut*).

2. P. Bloch, "Rom und die Mystiker der Merkaba," *Festschrift zum siebzigsten Geburtstage Jakob Guttmanns*, ed. M. Philippson (Leipzig, 1915), 113–124, especially 114–120; implied also by E. E. Urbach, "The Tradition of Mysticism in the Period of the Tanni'm" (in Hebrew), *Studies in Mysticism and Religion Presented to Gershom G. Scholem on His Seventieth Birthday*, ed. R. J. Z. Werblowsky et al. (Jerusalem, 1967), 1–28, especially 20–28; J. Dan, "The Importance and Meaning of the Story of the Ten Martyrs" (Hebrew), in *Studies in Literature Presented to Simon Halkin*, ed. E. Fleischer (Jerusalem, 1973), 15–22; idem "*Pirqe Hekhalot Rabbati* and the Story of the Ten Martyrs" (in Hebrew), *Eshel Be'er Sheva* 2 (1980), 63–80; idem, *The Hebrew Story in the Middle Ages* (Hebrew) (Jerusalem, 1974), 62–68; idem, *Jewish Mysticism: Late Antiquity* (Northvale and Jerusalem, 1998), 1:47–48, 90–93, 189–203; M. Oron, "Parallel Versions of the Story of the Ten Martyrs and of the Book of *Heikhalot Rabbati*" (Hebrew), *Eshel Be'er Sheva* 2 (1980), 81–95. Dan's view follows Scholem's brief statement on the evolution of the story of the "Ten Martyrs" in the latter's book *Major Trends in Jewish Mysticism* (New York, 1961), 51, 360, n. 39. On the *Merkabah* mysticism in general, see G. Scholem, *Jewish Gnosticism, Merkabah Mysticism and Talmudic Tradition* (New York, 1960), and *Major Trends*, 41–79, M. Idel, *Kabbalah: New Perspectives* (New Haven and London, 1988), 88–95.

3. J. Dan gives a useful survey in *The Ancient Jewish Mysticism* (Tel Aviv, 1993), 7–24, 29; idem, *Jewish Mysticism: Late Antiquity*, 40–49. See also E. E. Urbach, *The Sages: Their Concepts and Beliefs* (Jerusalem 1979), 1:212–213, and the abovementioned works by Scholem and Dan.

4. In *Patrologiae cursus completus, series Latina* (*PL* below), 77:566, ed. J. P. Migne (Paris, 1844–1855).

5. More generally on Byzantium in Italy, see M. Whittow, *The Making of Byzantium, 600–1025* (Los Angeles, 1996), 298–309.

6. J. Mann, "Changes in the Divine Service of the Synagogue due to Religious Persecutions," *Hebrew Union College Annual* 4 (1927), 252–259.

7. W. Kaegi, *Byzantium and the Early Islamic Conquests* (Cambridge, 1992), 117.

8. The *midrash* "The Image of Solomon's Throne," in *Bet ha-Midrash*, 2:83–85, has been associated with these events and the rebellious activity in the hippodrome

at Constantinople. A. Sharf, *Jews and other Minorities in Byzantium* (Jerusalem, 1995), 100.

9. Sharf, *Jews and Other Minorities*, 99.

10. Translated by M. and M. Whitby, *The History of Theophlyact Simocatta* (Oxford, 1986), 142. Anti-Jewish feelings also dominate the polemics of the period. Kaegi, *Byzantium and the Early Islamic Conquests*, 220–227.

11. *Bet ha-Midrash*, 2:54–57. I. Levi, "L'Apocalypse de Zerubabel," *Revue de études Juives* 68 (1914), 131–150.

12. *Bet ha-Midrash* 2:58–63.

13. *Bet ha-Midrash*, 2:56, 57. Heraclius's march through the Holy Land and Jerusalem after defeating the Persians is documented. Sharf, *Jews and Other Minorities*, 101.

14. *Bet ha-Midrash*, 2:60–62.

15. J. Starr, *The Jews in the Byzantine Empire* (New York, 1939), 1; A. Linder, *Roman Imperial Legislation of the Jews* (Jerusalem, 1983), 53. For persecutions and Jewish reactions during the third and fourth centuries, see S. Lieberman, "Palestine in the Third and Fourth Century," In *Jewish Quarterly Review* 36 (1945–1946), 329–370, and *Jewish Quarterly Review* 37 (1946–1947), 239–253; Urbach, "Ascesis and Suffering in the Torah of the Sages" (Hebrew), in *Yitzahk Baer Jubilee Volume* (1961), 48–68; A. Sharf, *Byzantine Jewry: From Justinian to the Fourth Crusade* (New York, 1971), 12; 15; idem, *Jews and Other Minorities*, 96–108; idem, "Heraclius and Mahomet," *Past & Present*, 9 (1956), 1–16; S. Bowman, *The Jews of Byzantium 1204–1453*, (Alabama, 1985), 6.

16. G. Ostrogorsky, *History of the Byzantine State*, tr. by J. M. Hussey (New Brunswick, 1969), 161. According to Ostrogorsky, an atypical case of imperial coercion; Sharf, *Jews and other Minorities*, 61–64; 109–118.

17. R. Jenkins, *Byzantium: The Imperial Centuries A.D. 610–1071* (New York, 1966), 61–68; 82–84.

18. Sharf, *Jews and Other Minorities*, 116.

19. *The Chronicle of Theophanes*, tr. by H. Turtledove (Philadelphia, 1982), *Annus Mundi* 6214, 93. Starr, *The Jews in the Byzantine Empire*, 91, n. 11.

20. Starr, *The Jews in the Byzantine Empire*, 91, n. 11.

21. B. S. Bachrach, *Early Medieval Jewish Policy in Western Europe* (Minneapolis, 1977), 124–129.

22. Bibliography in R. Bonfil, "Tra due mondi, Prospettive di ricerca sulla storia culturale degli Ebrei dell Italia meridionale nell alto Medioevo,' *Italia Judaica. Atti del I Convegno internazionale, Bari 18–22 maggio 1981* (Rome, 1983), 135–158; idem, "Myth, Rhetoric, History? A Study in the Chronicle of Ahimaatz" (Hebrew) in *Culture and Society in Medieval Jewry: Studies Dedicated to the Memory of Haim Hillel Ben-Sasson*, ed. M. Ben-Sasson, R. Bonfil, and J. R. Hacker (Jerusalem, 1989), 99–135. On the uniqueness of this source, E. Yassif, "Folktales in Megillat Ahimaatz," *Mekharim Yerushalayyim be-sifruth ivrit* 4 (1984), 18–42; idem, "The Hebrew Narrative Anthology in the Middle Ages," *Prooftexts* 17 (1997), 153–175, especially, 156, where he designates the source as "chronological anthology."

23. *The Chronicle of Ahimaatz*, ed. B. Klar (Jerusalem, 1944). The quotations are from the second edition (Jerusalem, 1974), 17; cited by Starr, *The Jews in the Byzantine Empire*, 127–128, n. 63. An English translation of the *Chronicle* by M. Salzman (New York, 1924; reprint, 1966), is available.

24. Starr, *The Jews in the Byzantine Empire*, n. 69.

25. *The Chronicle of Ahimaatz,* 70:20–22.

26. *The Chronicle of Ahimaatz,* 20.

27. Starr, *The Jews in the Byzantine Empire,* n. 69, n. 70.

28. The *Vision of Daniel,* ed. L. Ginzberg in *Ginze Schechter* (New York, 1927), 1:317–323; Starr, *The Jews in the Byzantine Empire,* 134–135 n. 71, 152 n. 93. Ginzberg tries to find a factual basis for the selling of the baptized Jews. *Ginze Schechter,* 1:315. It should be stated that this apocalyptic work underwent an update in the thirteenth century. S. Krauss, "*Un nouveau texte pour l'histoire judeo-byzantin,*" *Revue des études juives* 87 (1929), 1–7; Baron, *A Social and Religious History of the Jews,* 3:317 n. 12; Sharf, *Jews and other Minorities in Byzantium,* 119–135; Sharf, *Byzantine Jewry: From Justinian to the Fourth Crusade,* 88. See also the introduction in *Ginze Schechter,* 1:313–317.

29. Baron, *A Social and Religious History,* 3:182.

30. Whittow, *The Making of Byzantium,* 291.

31. More generally on the Jewish relations between Italy and North Africa during this period, M. Ben-Sasson, "Italy and Ifriqua from the 9th to the 11th Century," *Les Relations intercommunautaires juives en Méditerranée occidentale XIIIe–XXe siècles,* ed. Miège, J. L. (Paris, 1984), 34–50.

32. Baron, *A Social and Religious History,* 3:183.

33. For a definition and the function of hagiographical works, see H. Delehaye's classic work, *The Legends of the Saints,* tr. by D. Attwater (New York, 1962), especially, 49–68.

34. *Bet ha-Midrash,* 3:86–87, ed. Jellinek.

35. *Bet ha-Midrash,* 3:87.

36. *Bet ha-Midrash,* 3:93.

37. J. Dan was aware of these contradicting numbers. In his opinion, the reference to the ten is not an addition to the original text. He concludes that these texts and the story of the ten martyrs are of early origin. Dan, "The Importance and Meaning of the Story of the Ten Martyrs," 15–22.

38. Another version, "The Addition to *Heikhalot Rabbati* Chapters 4 and 5," is shorter and more organized. This version, too, speaks of the capturing of the four rabbis, followed by Samael's being given permission to destroy "ten nobles" or "these great ten." *Bet ha-Midrash,* 5:167.

39. *Bet ha-Midrash,* 3:87. But see Hirscheler, "Midrash Asarah Harugei Malkhut," 221.

40. *Bet ha-Misrash,* 3:93.

41. *Bet ha-Midrash,* 5:169.

42. To be discussed in the next chapter.

43. *Bet ha-Midrash,* 3:88

44. J. P. Migne, *Patrologiae cursus completus, Series Graeco-latina* (Paris, 1857) (*PG* below) 116:565–573; *Butler's Lives of the Saints,* eds. A. Butler, S. J. Thurston, and D. Attwater (New York, 1968), 599.

45. C. Mango, "Constantinople, ville sainte," *Critique,* 48 (1992), 625–633; Whittow, *The Making of Byzantium,* 127.

46. H. Delehaye, "Passio sanctorum sexaginta martyrum," *Analecta Bollandiana* 28 (1904), 289–307; Kaegi, *Byzantium and the Early Islamic Conquests,* 95–96, 109.

47. Whittow, *The Making of Byzantium,* 239.

48. On the power of the Veil, C. Mango, *Byzantium: The Empire of New Rome* (New York, 1980), 155–156.

49. *Avot de-Rabbi Nathan* chapter 1, 33, ed. S. Schechter (Vienna, 1887; New York, 1967), speaks of Abraham's ten trials. The legend of the ten martyrs, however, makes no thematic or linguistic allusions to this *midrash.*

50. Similar notions are found in other extracanonical books, such as *II Baruch, Pseudo-Jonathan to Genesis, the Testament of God,* and the *Testament of the Twelve Patriarchs.* Zeitlin, "The Legend of the Ten Martyrs," 6–9. Urbach, *The Sages,* 1:521–523; 2:920–921, ns. 43–47. Zeitlin's connection between the Book of Jubilees and the legend of the Ten Martyrs is farfetched, however.

51. Urbach, *The Sages,* 1:521–523; 2:920–921, ns. 43–47. I have already mentioned the exceptional remarks of R. Joshua in B. *Sanhedrin* 110b.

52. A more immediate example is *Midrash Mishle* (ca. 7th–10th centuries) 1, 13, ed. Buber, 45.

53. His *Seliha, Ezkerah elohim,* relates the story of the ten martyrs. Idelsohn, *Jewish Liturgy,* 246. *The Standard Jewish Encyclopedia* (Hebrew Edition) (Israel, 1969), 1:190; On the use of this motif, I. Elbogen, *Jewish Liturgy: A Comprehensive History,* ed. J. Heinmann et al. (Philadelphia, Jerusalem, New York, 1993), 182, 227. On Amittai's liturgy and mysticism, Scholem, *Major Trends,* 84; *Kabbalah,* 34–35, 311. According to Idelsohn, *Elleh Ezkerah* is a poem by Kallir, *Jewish Liturgy,* 320. Kallir's works had a profound influence on the liturgy of Byzantine Jewry. Idelsohn, *Jewish Liturgy,* 36–37.

54. Eusebius had already assigned martyrs the same role. "We write to you, brethren, the story of the martyrs and of the blessed Polycarp, who put an end to the persecution by his martyrdom as though adding the seal." Eusebius, *Ecclesistical History,* 4, 15, 3. *The Loeb Classical Library,* tr. K. Lake (London and New York, 1926).

55. On Shabbettai, see Starr, *The Jews in the Byzantine Empire,* 51–60; Sharf, *Jews and Other Minorities in Byzantium,* 160–177; A. Sharf, "Shabbettai Donnolo as a Byzantine-Jewish Figure," *Bulletin of the Institute of Jewish Studies* 3 (1975), 1–18; A. Sharf, *The Universe of Shabbetai Donnolo* (Watminster, 1976). On his mysticism, G. Scholem, *Kabbalah,* 28, 33–34, 40; E. R. Wolfson, "The Theosophy of Shabbetai Donnolo, with Special Emphasis on the Doctrine of *Sefirot* in his *Sefer Hakhmoni,*" *Jewish History* 6:1–2 (1992), 281–316.

56. The death of the ten rabbis was also noted by I. G. Marcus, "*Qiddush ha-Shem* in Ashkenaz and in the Story of Amnon of Mintz" (Hebrew), in *Sanctity of Life and Martyrdom,* 140 n. 32, 145.

57. R. Bonfil, "Can Medieval Storytelling Help Understanding Midrash? The Story of Paltiel: A Preliminary Study on History and Midrash," in *The Midrashic Imagination: Jews, Exegesis, Thought, and History,* ed. M. Fishbane (Albany, 1993), 250 n. 4.

58. S. Donnolo, introduction to *The Book of Creation, Sefer Hakhmoni,* ed. D. Casteli, *Il commento di Sabbetai Donnolo sul libro creazione* (Florence, 1880), 3–4; *The Chronicle of Ahimaatz,* 48. Starr, *The Jews in the Byzantine Empire,* 149, n. 87.

59. M. Amari, *Storia dei musulmani di Sicilia,* 2 vols. (1933–1935), 2:171–174; E. Ashtor, *The History of the Jews in Muslim Spain,* 2 vols. (Jerusalem, 1960), 1:130–131; C. Roth, *The History of the Jews of Italy* (Philadelphia, 1946), 53–58.

60. Thus, from Shabbettai's description it is not altogether clear if Rabbi Joel died during or before the attack.

61. *Sefer Hakhmoni,* 3–4.

62. Marcus also noticed this polemical element in the legend. "*Qiddush ha-Shem* in Ashkenaz, 137–138.

63. For instance, in Pseudo-Cyprian, *Adversus Judaeos*, in *Corpus Scriptorum Ecclesiasticorum Latinorum* (Vindobonae, 1868–1871), 3, 3, 135. On Judas as a generic term for Jews, Gaudentius, *Sermo* 13, *PL*, 20:933.

64. J. Parkes, *The Conflict of the Church and the Synagogue: A Study in the Origins of Antisemitism* (London, 1934), 130. J. Cohen, "The Jews as Killers of Christ in the Latin Tradition, from Augustine to the Friars," *Tradition* 39 (1983), 3–27.

65. Occisi quidem sunt, sunt et cremati, et captivorum more venditi, adeoque crevit illa venditio, donec pro uno argenteo triginta darentur captivi. *PL*, 157:571–572. On Peter, see C. Merchavia, *The Church Versus Talmudic and Midrashic Literature, 500–1248* (Jerusalem, 1970), especially, 112–113. A good discussion on the *Vindita Salvatoris* (The Savior's Vengeance) legend is provided by I. J. Yuval, "*Two Nations in Your Womb*": *Perceptions of Jews and Christians* (Tel Aviv, 200), 53–64.

66. *The Chronicle of Ahimaatz*, 70:20–22. The same notion appears in additional works. *The Poems of Amittay*, critical edition with introduction and commentary by Y. David (Jerusalem, 1975), 66:19.

67. H. Shirman, *Mivhar ha-Shirah ha-Ivrit be-Italyah* (Berlin, 1934), 12.

68. *The Poems of Solomon ha-Bavli*, 307, lines: 33–34, ed. E. Fleisher (Jerusalem, 1973); *Sefer Yosippon*, ed. D. Flusser, 2 vols. (Jerusalem, 1981), 1:251. For more information on Solomon's liturgy see, E. D. Goldschmidt, *On Jewish Liturgy: Essays on Prayer and Religious Poetry* (Hebrew) (Jerusalem, 1978), 341–348.

69. Solomon ha-Bavli, *Selihah*, in *A History of Hebrew Liturgical and Secular Poetry* (Hebrew), ed. A. M. Habermann, 2 vols. (Masada, 1972), 2:22. The idea of human sacrifice continued to be alluded to in the liturgy of Italian Jews. In the first half of the eleventh century, Rabbi Yehiel ben Abraham of Rome wrote in one of his *Selihot* that he "joyfully and cheerfully wishes to sanctify You," *A History of Hebrew Liturgical and Secular Poetry*, 2:26.

70. H. Schirmann, *A Selection of the Hebrew Poems of Italy*, 22.

71. *Av le-Rahem*, 252, lines 9, 14; *Orakh Zedakkah*, 260–261, lines 22–24; 268, lines 65–68, in *The Poems of Solomon ha-Bavli*.

72. *The Poems of Solomon ha-Bavli*, 259, lines 7–8, 46–48; 337, lines 15–16, 45.

73. *The Poems of Solomon ha-Bavli*, *Orakh Zedakkah*, 261, lines 25–28; 308, line 38.

74. *The Poems of Solomon ha-Bavli*, 342, lines 15–16.

75. Schirmann, *A Selection of the Hebrew Poems of Italy*, 31.

76. Schirmann, *A Selection of the Hebrew Poems of Italy*, 34–35.

77. *Sefer Yosippon*, vol. 2, introduction and Chapter 3; 2:105. The author provides us with a significant study of the book and with extremely useful comments. And see also, Y. Baer, "The Hebrew *Sefer Yosippon*" (Hebrew) in *Sefer Dinaburg* (Dinur) (Jerusalem, 1949), 178–205; *Sefer Yosippon*, 2: 86, 96; D. Flusser, "The Author of *Sefer Yosippon*, His Character and His Period" (Hebrew) *Zion* 18 (1953), 109–126. S. Bowman, "Sefer Yosippon: History and Midrash," *The Midrashic Imagination*, 280–294, especially 282.

78. *Sefer Yosippon*, 2:95, 98, 127–128, 132–140, 154–155, 164.

79. *Sefer Yosippon*, 1:50, [emphasis mine]. On the book see the following note.

80. This is another side to Bowman's valuable observations: "The author of Yosippon has given us then a midrash in form, style, and method. But his midrash is also a

history (much like Josephus), as defined by both his critical approach to the sources and by the narrative form in which the results of his investigations are presented to the reader," "Sefer Yosippon: History and Midrash," 284. But he continues, "it is insufficient to refer to Yosippon's scholarship as midrash without a qualifying definition of the term," 289.

81. *Sefer Yosippon*, 1:272–273.

82. The text is a bit confusing here. I adjusted my translation for clarification, without, I believe, changing Yosippon's meaning.

83. Flusser correctly observes that Philo's answer is absent in Josephus's *Antiquities*. An undelivered answer, however, is prepared by Philo in his *Embassy*. This description is different from the originals of *Jewish Antiquities* 18:271, *Jewish War* 2:196–197; or Philo's *Embassy* 192, *Embassy* 229–236.

84. See Baer, "The Hebrew *Sefer Yosippon*," 196–199; Flusser, *Sefer Yosippon*, 1:60–61.

85. *Sefer Yosippon*, 1:65.

86. "*Olot u-shlamim*," *Sefer Yosippon*, 1:212. Flusser indicates that the phrase *shillem nafsho* betokens a regular death, rather than martyrdom, although he is aware that in *Psalms Raabah*, verses 28 and 76, the term *shillem nafsho* does retain a martyrological meaning. *Yosippon*, 1:68–69, and see n. 27, also 2:166 n. 480. It is significant to note that Yosippon does not employ the ordinary term *leha-shlim nafsho*, which may have the meaning of a regular death. Rather, he uses the term *ve-shellem nafsho* to indicate peace offering (*qorban*). Another possibility is to read the term as a verb, that is, *shillem*, "sacrificed." A similar use can be found in Solomon ha-Bavli's poem, *Te'allat Tzari*. Solomon, a contemporary countryman of the author of *Sefer Yosippon*, used the term as a gerund (*shillum*), namely the act of sacrifice. *The Poems of Solomon ha-Bavli*, 340, line: 45. The term *shellem* appears in the Bible as "peace-offering" in the following places: Leviticus 7:11–36; 3:6; Deuteronomy 27:7 Judges 20:27; Amos 5:22. See also, *mishnah Zevahim*, 5:5. Although Yosippon does not make a direct connection between the word and an offering in the story of Eleazar, other chapters of the book demonstrate the author's awareness of the notion of human sacrifice. Two centuries after Yosippon, the phrase *shillem nafsho* appeared in the Hebrew compositions of the First Crusade in an obvious martyrological context. In 1140, Rabbi Solomon, mentioned in his description of the crusaders' attack on the Worms community that, as the Jewish martyrs of Worms "handed over their souls to their Creator, they cried out 'Hear O Israel! The Lord is our God, the Lord is one.'" *Sefer Gezerot Ashkenaz ve-Zarfat*, ed. A. Habermann (Jerusalem, 1945), 25. Another martyrologist of the twelfth century, Rabbi Eliezer ben Nathan, employed the phrase in his *Selihah*, published in Habermann's *A History of Hebrew Liturgical and Secular Poetry*, 2:186. These events are discussed in the next chapter. A connection, then, between the word *shallem* and sacrifice in *Sefer Yosippon* would not be inconceivable.

87. *Sefer Yosippon*, 1:72.

88. *Sefer Yosippon*, 1:73.

89. *Sefer Yosippon*, 1:75, 72.

90. *Sefer Yosippon*, 1:74.

91. *Sefer Yosippon*, 1:337–338. I translated "fornicator" (*noef*) to mean "enemy."

92. *Sefer Yosippon*, 1:158.

93. *Sefer Yosippon*, 1:394.

94. *Sefer Yosippon*, 1:396.

95. *Sefer Yosippon*, 1:429.

96. *Sefer Yosippon*, 1:430. Flusser there considers the possibilities that these two conclusions may be the addition of a later author.

97. *Sefer Yosippon*, 1:72. "Do not think [Antiochus] that God has forsaken us, for out of His love [to us] He brought about this honor upon us," does not exist in the original text of 2 Macc. 7.

98. *Sefer Yosippon*, 1:69.

99. *Sefer Yosippon*, 1:312. Note, *neheragim al Shemo* and not *al qiddush Shemo.*

100. An identical martyrological usage of this verse appears in B. *Sanhedrin* 74a, *Pesahim* 25a, and Y. Ber. 6:6–9; but note the obligatory, legal language, especially of B. *Sanhedrin* 74a, despite the reference to love.

101. Parkes, *The Conflict of the Church and the Synagogue*, 398; Starr, the *Jews in the Byzantine Empire*, 175.

102. Boyarin relies on the midrash on Exodus 15:2, the Mekhilta, to support a connection between love and Jewish martyrdom. In this the midrash stands almost alone. Boyarin makes an important observation that may explain why "Christian martyrology may very well have entered Jewish consciousness as early as the late second century . . . but this midrash probably found its form in the third century, a time of massive persecution of Christians and the development of Christian martyrology, the period of the persecution of Christians under Decius in 250–251 and under Valerian at the end of the decade." *Dying for God*, 113. As I argued in the previous chapter, the rabbis labored to prevent the infiltration of Christian martyrological ideas. See also the bibliography that Boyarin cites in his discussion, 108–114. On balancing fear and love as Jewish motivations, Urbach, *The Sages*, 1:400–419, especially, 406, 416–417, 2:871 n. 93. On 1:417 Urbach writes: "this mystical-martyrological conception of love could only be adopted by a few." Or on 1:418: "Even those Tannaim and Amoraim who appraised the love of God most highly, nevertheless regarded the fear of Heaven as an indispensable condition for attaining to love." See again Urbach's "Asceticism and Suffering in the Torah of the Sages."

103. *Sefer Yosippon*, 1:340. It is worth mentioning that in 2 Sam. 24:17 David compares his nation to an innocent lamb. Verse 25 there concludes with David sacrificing *olot u-shellemim* to stop the plague.

104. Repeated also in John 13.

105. *Sefer Yosippon*, 1:412.

106. *Sefer Yosippon*, 1:312–313.

107. Baer, "The Hebrew Sefer Yosippon," 193–194; Flusser, *Sefer Yosippon*, 1:312.

108. Already the eighth-century *Life of St. Andrew the Fool* gives a descriptive picture of heaven in the image of Constantinople. C. Mango, "The Life of St. Andrew the Fool Reconsidered," *Revista di Studi Bizantini e Slavi*, 11 (1982), 297–313; Whittow, *The Making of Byzantium*, 13, 127, 130, 392 n. 20 for additional bibliography.

109. S. Runciman, *A History of the Crusades*, 3 vols. (Cambridge, 1951–1954), 1:32, 84, 103. A. A. Vasiliev, *The History of the Byzantine Empire* (Madison, 1952), 336. The veneration of death is reflected also in the words of Theodore (759–826), abbot of the monastery of Studion in Constantinople. Theodore encouraged his sick mother while on her deathbed and expressed his joy, for she was about to assume death and glory.

110. The background in Whittow, *The Making of Byzantium*, 305–309.
111. Flusser already noticed the connection between the ninth-century Christian concept of martyrdom and celestial reward and the one presented in *Sefer Yosippon*, 2:96–98. On the popes' epistles and the issue of martyrdom, see Runciman, *A History of the Crusades*, 1:84, 103. For additional historical and political background, see D. C. de Iongh, *Byzantine Aspects of Italy* (New York, 1967), 75–117; R. Browning, *The Byzantine Empire* (New York, 1980), 80–81; A. A. Vasiliev, *Byzantium and Islam* (Madison, 1928), 309, 396–397.
112. *Patrologia cursus completus, series Latina* (below, *PL*), ed. J. P. Migne, 115: 656–657; 161:720; Pope Leo's letter can be found also in D. J. Mansi, *Sanctorum conciliorum nova et amplissima collectio*, 53 vols. in 60 (Austria, 1960), 14:888.
113. Migne, *PL*, 126:816. Mansi, *Sanctorum conciliorum nova*, 17:104; 17:3, 42, 47, for similar references by John to the glory of the Christian soldiers in their war against the Saracens.
114. *Sefer Yosippon*, 1:340, 312.
115. It is possible that Yosippon also had in mind Isaiah 9:1. But the contrast of light and darkness was a regular motif in early Christian depictions of heaven. Dryhthelm's vision is among the more famous examples. In his vision of hell and heaven, "a man of shining countenance and wearing bright robes" guided Dryhthelm through a very pleasant plain, clearer than the brightness of the daylight or the rays of the noontime sun. "In this meadow there were innumerable bands of men in white robes, and many companies of happy people sat around; as he led me through the midst of the troops of joyful inhabitants. . . . I saw in front of us a much more gracious light than before; and amidst it I heard the sweetest sound of people singing." *Bede's Ecclesiastical History of the English People*, eds. Bertram Colgrave and R. A. B. Mynor (Oxford, 1969), pp. 488–495. See also S. Shepkaru, "To Die for God: Martyrs' Heaven in Hebrew and Latin Crusade Narratives," *Speculum* 77:2 (2002), 313–314.
116. *Sefer Yosippon*, 1:424. He continues to elaborate on this issue throughout his speech, 1:425–427.
117. *Sefer Yosippon*, 1:382.
118. *Sefer Yosippon*, 1:79. Such inspirational use of the Maccabean rebels was made already by the seventh-century historian Elishe in his narration of the Vardan Mamikonean revolt against Persian attempts to force Zoroastriansim in the fifth century. Whittow, *The Making of Byzantium*, 207.
119. *Sefer Yosippon*, 1:381–382.
120. Mango, *Byzantium*, 152.
121. *Sefer Yosippon*, 1:8, especially n. 29.
122. Vasiliev, *The History of the Byzantine Empire*, 336. Background in Whittow, *The Making of Byzantium*, 293–298; Nikephoros's attempt, 351–352.
123. On the evolution of the idea of holy war, see H. E. J. Cowdrey, "The Genesis of the Crusades," *The Holy War*, ed. T. P. Murphy (Columbus, 1976), 9–32; J. A. Brundage, "Holy War and the Medieval Lawyers," *The Holy War*, 99–140, especially 104–105, 117.
124. Eleazar's test by God may imply, according to Flusser, the author's familiarity with the midrashic description in *Avot de-Rabbi Nathan*, 1, chapter 33. Already 1 *Maccabees* 2:52 writes: "Was not Abraham found faithful in time of trial . . . ?" It must be noted, Yosippon does not incorporate martyrdoms of rabbinic figures. More

likely, Yosippon relies here on the Maccabean version. He utilizes the phrase, "he who was tested in Antiochus's days and was killed for (*neherag al*) God his Lord," *Sefer Yosippon*, 1:65, to delineate Antiochus's persecution and Eleazar's martyrological response. Repeated in 1:35 94–95, and in the story of Raksius, 1:104. We have met the original Razis in 2 Maccabees 14:37–52. The variations of the name in Abel, *Les Livres des Maccabées*, 467.

125. *The Chronicle of Ahimaatz*, 41.

126. *The Chronicle of Ahimaatz*, 23–24.

127. *The Chronicle of Ahimaatz*, 24.

128. R. Bonfil, "Can Medieval Storytelling Help Understanding Midrash?," 232. On the historic figure behind Paltiel see, B. Lewis, "Paltiel, A Note," *Bulletin of the School of Oriental and African Studies* 30 (1967), 177–181.

129. *The Chronicle of Ahimaatz*, 15, 25.

130. *PL* 137; B. Blumenkranz, *Les auteurs chrétiens latins du moyen age sur les juifs et le judaisme* (Paris, 1963), 227–228.

131. Divine Justice instilled the fear of transgression in the hearts of the *Tannaim* and *Amoraim*, as well as in their predecessors. On fear as motivation, see also Urbach, *The Sages*, 355–359, 520–523.

132. *The Chronicle of Ahimaatz*, 29:3–5.

133. *The Chronicle of Ahimaatz*, 17:14.

134. *The Chronicle of Ahimaatz*, 12:18. See also I. G. Marcus, "History, Story and Collective Memory: Narrativity in Early Ashkenazic Culture," *The Midrashic Imagination*, 270. Marcus writes: "Like *Yosippon*, the Narrative of Ahimaaz also contains vignettes of people who are not powerful or remarkably learned but who are described as holy and righteous, descended from the saintly exiles of Jerusalem."

135. *Sefer Yosippon* makes extensive use of the term. In his speech in Jerusalem, Josephus calls his mother "my holy mother," 1:370; Queen Alexandra is the "holy Queen," 1:34. Already noticed by Flusser, 2:109–110.

136. *The Vision of Daniel* praises Emperor Leo VI (886–912) for not enforcing the anti-Jewish policy of his father, Basil. The anonymous author refers to the Jews who unwillingly accepted baptism in a language that later will describe martyrs. *Ginze Schechter*, 1:319; Starr, *The Jews in the Byzantine Empire*, 143–147 n. 83, n. 84; *The Vision of Daniel*, in *The Chronicle of Ahimaatz*, 46–47; Sharf, *Jews and other Minorities*, 202; Baron, *A Social and Religious History*, 3:181.

137. *The Chronicle of Ahimaatz*, 33:13.

138. The late tenth- or eleventh-century *Midrash Tehillim*, 16:4, speaks about the generation of the persecution and those who died to "sanctify Your Name."

139. P. Brown, *The Cult of the Saints: Its Rise and Function in Latin Christianity* (Chicago, 1981), 81.

140. Delehaye, *The Legends of the Saints*, 54.

141. *Sherira Gaon's Epistles* (Hebrew), ed. B. M. Levin (Jerusalem, 1972), 74–75.

142. R. Bonfil, "Between the Land of Israel and Babylon: A Study of the Jewish Culture in Southern Italy and in Christian Europe in the Early Middle Ages," *Shalem* 5 (1977), 1–30.

143. The epistle was reprinted by Mann, *Texts and Studies*, 1:24. N. Golb and O. Pritsak, *Khazarian Hebrew Documents of the Tenth Century* (Ithaca and London, 1982), 86, 90–91 n. 49. On Hasday, see Y. Baer, *A History of the Jews in Christian Spain*,

tr. L. Schoffman, 2 vols. (Philadelphia, Jerusalem, 1992), 1:16, 29, 46. For general background in Jewish–Christian relations in the precrusade period, see C. Roth, "European Jewry in the Dark Ages: A Revised Picture," *Hebrew Union College Annual* 23 (1950–1951), 151–169; Sharf, *Byzantine Jewry: From Justinian to the Fourth Crusade*, 170.

144. Because the epistle mentions the *Book of Yosippon* it is obvious that it was written after 952. The last known oppression in Italy under the Byzantine regime took place under Emperor Romanos, who was deposed in 944. Flusser suggests that the epistle depicts an event that took place during or after the crisis of 1096. *Sefer Yosippon*, 2:253. The stylistic contrast between the epistle and the Hebrew crusade chronicles seems to negate Flusser's suggestion. Thus, the epistle must have been written sometime before 1096. Mann, *Texts and Studies*, 1:12–16; U. Cassuto, "*Una lettera ebraica de secolo X*," in *Giornale della Societa Asiatica Italiana*, 29, 97–110; S. Krauss, "*Un document sur l'histoire de Juifs en Italie*," *Revue des études juives* 67 (1920), 40–43; A. Sharf, *Byzantine Jewry* (London, 1971), 179; Golb and Pritsak, *Khazarian Hebrew Documents of the Tenth Century*, 86–90.

145. Flusser, *Sefer Yosippon*, 2:63–64 n. 183.

146. Mann, *Texts and Studies*, 1:23–24.

147. Starr, *The Jews in the Byzantine Empire*, 154.

148. Mann, *Texts and Studies*, 1:24.

149. The metaphor had been used by the author of *Sefer Yosippon*, 1:312–313, and a century later, it was used again by Rabbi Ahimaatz. *The Chronicle of Ahimaatz*, 24:27.

150. Within Byzantine Jewry there circulated the idea that a lack of three elements causes calamities: prayer, repentance, and piety. Each sacrifice substituted in this story for each of these missing elements. The idea appears in Rabbi Amittai's *Selihot*, *The Chronicle of Ahimaatz*, 101:20–24.

151. Mann, *Texts and Studies*, 1:25.

152. *Sefer Yosippon*, 1:272–273.

153. Mann, *Texts and Studies*, 1:24–25.

154. *The Chronicle of Ahimaatz*, 33.

155. *The Chronicle of Ahimaatz*, 30, 33.

156. Baer, "The Hebrew *Sefer Yosippon*," 183. The influence of Italian Jewry on Ashkenazic martyrology was so vigorous, in Baer's mind, that he concluded his article with the assumption that the author of *Sefer Yosippon* was from Ashkenaz, "perhaps France or Italy," 205. Baer's identification of tenth-century Jewish Italian culture with twelfth-century Ashkenaz led him to this generalization.

157. A. Grossman, "The Roots of *Qiddush ha-Shem* in Early Ashkenaz" (Hebrew), in *Sanctity of Life and Martyrdom*, 99–130; idem, "The Cultural and Social Background of Jewish Martyrdom in 1096," in *Facing the Cross*, 55–73, supported by Bonfil's "Between the Land of Israel and Babylon." A. Grossman, *The Early Sages*, 48.

158. The mother's death in Gittin 57b does not indicate an act of martyrdom. "She, too, went up on the roof and fell (*nafellah*) and died." Perhaps this line alludes to a suicide, which it tries to dismiss. *Lamentaions Rabbah* 53 to 1:16 has, "Some days later that woman went mad and fell off a roof and died." See *Semahot* 2:2. A person who climbs to the top of a tree or "to the top of a roof and fell to his death" should not be considered a suicide if a public declaration of intent is not made. *Semahot*, ed. M. Higger (New York, 1932).

159. Razis indeed is said to have killed himself (2 Macc. 14:45–46), but he did not reach the status of Eleazar and the mother's seven sons. This is still the case in *Sefer Yosippon*.
160. For Spain, Joseph ha-Cohen, *Emeq ha-Bachah*, ed. M. Letteris (Cracow, 1895), 7; Baron, *A Social and Religious History*, 3:247 n. 49; Baer, *A History of the Jews in Christian Spain*, 1:11–14; Ashtor, *The History of the Jews in Muslim Spain*, 1: chapters 1 and 2; R. Dozy, *Spanish Islam* (London, 1972), 215–241; J. Parkes, *The Jew in the Medieval Community: A Study of His Political and Economic Stiutation* (London, 1938), 14–17; Bachrach, *Early Medieval Jewish Policy in Western Europe*, 3–26. For Merovingian France, Baron, *A Social and Religious History*, 3:47–54; Parkes, *The Jew in the Medieval Community*, 15; Bachrach, *Early Medieval Jewish Policy in Western Europe*, 55–57, 60–64.
161. The ninth-century life of Patriarch Methodios, who had reestablished icons, misrepresented him as a near martyr. His hagiography was not unique in doing this. Various authors advanced themselves as worthy martyrs. Regardless of the historical value of such opposing sacred propaganda, both iconoclasts and iconodules owed their victories to martyrs' immolations. Whittow, *The Making of Byzantium*, 147–159.
162. Whittow, *The Making of Byzantium*, 281.
163. Flusser, *Sefer Yosippon*, 2:63–64 n. 183. Grossman, "The Roots of *Qidush ha-Shem*," 110 n. 24.
164. K. B. Wolf, *Christian Martyrs in Muslim Spain* (Cambridge, 1988), 24–25; Ashtor, *The History of the Jews in Muslim Spain*, 1:56–58; Dozy, *Spanish Islam*, 268–307. On the social aspects of the phenomenon and the martyrs' identity crisis, J. A. Coope, *The Martyrs of Cordoba: Community and Family Conflict in an Age of Mass Conversion* (Lincoln, 1995).
165. Wolf, *Christian Martyrs in Muslim Spain*, 67, n. 21.
166. Dozy, *Spanish Islam*, 286; Ashtor, *The History of the Jews in Muslim Spain*, 1:60.
167. T. W. Arnold, *The Preaching of Islam* (New York, 1913), 141.
168. Wolf, *Christian Martyrs in Muslim Spain*, 29.
169. Wolf, *Christian Martyrs in Muslim Spain*, 70.
170. Wolf, *Christian Martyrs in Muslim Spain*, 30.
171. Wolf, *Christian Martyrs in Muslim Spain*, 33.
172. Wolf, *Christian Martyrs in Muslim Spain*, 35.
173. Wolf, *Christian Martyrs in Muslim Spain*, 34–35.
174. Wolf, *Christian Martyrs in Muslim Spain*, 126, n. 49. On her martyrologies, see E. Duchett, *Death and Life in the Tenth Century* (Michigan, 1967), 254–259. As Gonzalo de Berceo's Miracles of Our Lady demonstrates, Theophilus was still popular in thirteenth-century Christendom. Gonzalo de Berceo, *Miracles of Our Lady*, tr. by R. T. Mount and A. G. Cash (Lexington, 1997), 129–147; J. E. Keller, *Gonzalo De Berceo* (New York, 1972), 138.
175. Ashtor, *The History of the Jews in Muslim Spain*, 1:78; *The Chronicle of Ahimaatz*, 13:5.
176. On the connections between Muslim Spain and Byzantium in the middle of the tenth century, see Mann, *Texts and Studies*, 1:12–16; Ashtor, *The History of the Jews in Muslim Spain*, 1:114–116, 153.
177. Agus, *The Heroic Age of Franco-German Jewry* (New York, 1969), 38.
178. Mann, *Texts and Studies*, 1:10, 21–22. Baron, *A Social and Religious History*, 3:155–156.

179. Mann, *Texts and Studies*, 1:21.

180. Mann, *Texts and Studies*, 1:22 lines 17–18. Mann reads this line "the news of the king" and therefore, concludes that the "writer informs him [the Emperor] that his letter has reached Abd ar-Rahman," 10.

181. Mann, *Texts and Studies*, 1:22, line 19.

182. Hasday's activism on behalf of the Jews is also noticed by Jean, the abbot of St. Arnoul of Metz. *PL*, 137:301–302; *MGH*, S. 4:371–372, 4:371–372; Blumenkranz, *Les auteurs chrétiens*, 232–233.

183. Mann, *Texts and Studies*, 1:22, line 15. On Hasday's diplomatic efforts on behalf of Jews, see Golb and Pritsak, *Khazarian Hebrew Documents of the Tenth Century*, 75–86.

184. Mango, *Byzantium*, 100.

185. The Seljuks still witnessed various descending groups from these heretical movements. Sharf, *Jews and Other Minorities*, 110.

186. Eusebius, *Church History*, 5.16.13–14. See also Droge and Tabor, *A Noble Death*, 136–138.

187. *The Chronicle of Theophanes*, *Annus Mundi* 6214, 93.

188. Sharf, *Jews and Other Minorities*, 111. Sharf treats Theophanes' report with reservation.

189. Mango, *Byzantium*, 95.

190. Mango, *Byzantium*, 99.

191. Of significance is E. Peters's observation that "To a certain extent the heretical movements of Byzantium after the sixth century are not very different from the kinds of heresies that abounded in the fourth and fifth centuries. . . . In Byzantium old heresies had a great capacity for survival and new ones a great capacity for growth in a fertile religious culture. . . ." *Heresy and Authority in Medieval Europe: Documents in Translation*, ed. E. Peters (Philadelphia, 1980), 51.

192. Starr, *The Jews in the Byzantine Empire*, 92–93; *Mansi* 14:120; Baron, *A Social and Religious History*, 3:314 n. 3, agrees with Starr that the connection between the two groups results from Leo's confusion. Cf. Sharf, *Jews and Other Minorities*, 112.

193. "Ekkehardi chronicon universale sub anno 723," in *Monumenta Germaniae Historica (MGH*, below), 6:157. The martyrdom of the eleventh-century heretic, Basil, could have provided additional inspiration. M. Lambert, *Medieval Heresy: Popular Movements from Bogomil to Hus* (New York, 1976), 19.

194. A survey is provided by Lambert, *Medieval Heresy*, 7–23.

195. Ostrogorsky, *History of the Byzantine State*, 174–175.

196. Migne, *PL*, 142:635. English translations are available in R. Glaber, *Le cinq livres de ses histoires*, in *Collection de textes pour servir a l'etude et a l'enseignement de l'histoire*, I ed. M. Prou (Paris, 1866), 49–50; in Rodvlfi Glabri, *Historiarum Libri Quinque*, ed. and tr. by J. France (Oxford, 1989), 93. Translated segments are also available in W. L. Wakefield and A. P. Evans, *Heresies of the High Middle Ages* (New York, 1991), 73.

197. Glaber, 2, 12, 23; translation from France, *Historiarum*, 92. Wakefield and Evans, *Heresies of the High Middle Ages*, 73. It should be mentioned here that by 970 central and southern Italy inclined politically and culturally toward western Europe, breaking off the political ties with the declining Byzantine Empire. At the end of the tenth century, Italy was absorbed into the Holy Roman Empire; in 959 Pope John XII called on the German Emperor Otto I to rescue him from King Berengar and,

in return, crowned him as the Roman Emperor of the West – that is, Germany and Italy. In 967, Otto II was crowned as coemperor by Pope John XIII. Such political changes, of course, are not always immediately followed by cultural transitions.

198. Glaber, 2, 11, 22. Migne, *PL*, 142:635. R. Glaber, *Le cinq livres de ses histoires*, 49–50. Wakefield and Evans, *Heresies of the High Middle Ages* (New York, 1991), 72–73. France, *Historiarum*, 91.

199. See again, Starr, *The Jews in the Byzantine Empire*, 91, n. 11.

200. J. Starr, "Le mouvement messianique au début du VIII siècle," *Revue de études Juives*, 102 (1937), 81–92.

201. Starr, *The Byzantine Empire*, 177.

202. *Responsa of the Geonim, Gates of Righteousness* (in Hebrew) (Salonika, 1792), 24 n. 7, 10.

203. Sharf argues that the reference to Montanists is Leo's mistake. Thus the Jews and the Montanists here are one and the same. This does not change my hypothesis. If correct, Sharf's argument shows that Jews practiced self-sacrifice. *Jews and Other Minorities*, 115.

204. Glaber, *Historiarum Liber Quinque*, 4, 5, 2. France's translation [emphasis mine].

205. Parkes, *The Conflict of the Church and the Synagogue*, 126; Starr, *The Jews of the Byzantine Empire*, 92–93; Sharf, *Jews and Other Minorities*, 114.

206. *Sefer ha-Miqtsoot*, ed. S. Assaf (Jerusalem, 1947), introduction, 7.

207. Baron, *A Social and Religious History*, 6:367, n. 93.

208. B. *Shabbat* 130a.

209. B. *Sanhedrin* 74a.

210. B. *Sanhedrin* 74a–b.

211. *Tosefta Sotah* 13.

212. B. *Avodah Zarah* 18a.

213. B. *Berakhot* 61b.

214. *Sefer ha-Miqtsoot*, 17, 10. An English translation is also available in Baron, *A Social and Religious History*, 6:83.

215. Perhaps to distinguish between "martyrdom" and "suicide." See *Semahot*. 8:12.

CHAPTER 5: *ZARFAT*

1. *Sefer ha-Yashar*, ed. S. Rosenthal (Berlin, 1898), sec. 46, 90. On early respona of the scholars of Bari, I. A. Agus, "Rabbinic Scholarship in Northern Europe," in *The Dark Ages: Jews in Christian Europe, 711–1096*, ed. C. Roth (Rutgers, 1966), 192 n. 21. See also R. Bonfil, "Between Eretz Israel and Babylonia" (Hebrew), *Shalem* 5 (1987), 1–30.

2. In *Major Trends*, Scholem already pointed out their contribution to mysticism in the west. J. Dan, "The Beginnings of Jewish Mysticism in Europe," *The Dark Ages: Jews in Christian Europe*, 282–290.

3. A. Grabois has pointed out that there are considerable cultural and developmental differences between the communities of the Rhine valley and those of the French kingdom. "The Leadership of the *Parnasim* in the Northern French Communities in the Eleventh and Twelfth Centuries: the '*Boni Viri*' and the Elders of the Cities'" (Hebrew), in *Culture and Society in Medieval Jewish History*:

Studies Dedicated to the Memory of Haim Hillel Ben-Sasson, eds. M. Ben-Sasson, R. Bonfil, and J. R. Hacker (Jerusalem, 1989), 303–314. Yet, even the French kingdom was not homogeneous. Provence and northern France formed two different geopolitical and cultural unities. S. Schwarzfuchs, "France under the Early Capets," in *The Dark Ages: Jews in Christian Europe*, 157–160.

4. Discussion and bibliography on the First Crusade are provided in Chapter 6. The scholarly focus on 1096 is discussed by S. Schwarzfuchs, "The Place of the Crusades in Jewish History" (Hebrew), in *Culture and Society in Medieval Jewish History*, 251–255.

5. Well demonstrated by A. Grossman, "The Immigration of the Kalonymous Family from Italy to Germany" (Hebrew), *Zion* (1975), 154–185, especially, 168, 181, on the importance of Provence, 170; on Italy and France as the countries of origin, 182–183, on the thirteenth-century Ashkenazic myth, 184. For example, see Isaac ben Moses, *Or Zarua*, 4 vols. in 2, (Zhitomir, 1862–1890), 2:125 n. 275.

6. I. Elbogen, *The Prayers of Israel* (Hebrew) (Tel Aviv, 1972), 248–249. An English translation of the book is entitled *Jewish Liturgy: A Comprehensive History*, ed. J. Heinmann et al. (Philadelphia, Jerusalem, New York, 1993), 255.

7. A case in point is the midrashic heroine, Mattathias's daughter (in Solomon's poem, Yohanan's daughter), who sacrificed her modesty to incite the Maccabees to fight the Greeks. Habermann, *A History of Hebrew Liturgical and Secular Poetry*, 127–128. See also the *midrashim* for *Hanukah* in *Bet ha-Midrash*, 1:132–136.

8. Flusser, *Sefer Yosippon*, 2:64–66, especially 64.

9. Y. Baer, "Rashi and the Historical Reality of His Time" (Hebrew), *Tarbiz* 20 (1948), 320–332, especially 326, 330, 331. On Rashi's life, commentary, and influence, see I. Agus, "Rashi and His School," in *The Dark Ages: Jews in Christian Europe*, 210–248.

10. A. Grossman, *The Early Sages of France* (Hebrew) (Jerusalem, 1995), 388–389, especially 400, 582.

11. Grossman, *The Early Sages of France*, 147, 322.

12. Dinur, *Israel ba-Golah* (Tel Aviv, 1958–1972), 1:3, 259, sections 19, 20, and 255, section 1; Grossman, *The Early Sages*, 49 n. 77 and 51 n. 83; Fleisher, *The Poems of Solomon ha-Bavli*, 28–31.

13. Fleisher, *The Poems of Solomon ha-Bavli*, 30, ns. 87, 34.

14. R. Joseph Tov Ellem, *Teshuvot Geonim Kadmonim*, ed. D. Kassel (Berlin, 1848), 61; Dinur, *Israel ba-Golah*, vol. 1:3, 255, section 3.

15. *Bet ha-Midrash*, 6:137; Grossman, *The Early Sages*, 86–102, especially 86, 88, 92.

16. Habermann, *The Poems of Rabbi Shimon bar Isaac* (Hebrew) (Berlin & Jerusalem, 1938), 13; Fleisher, *The Poems of Solomon ha-Bavli*, 34, 69, n. 161. Transmissions from Italian to French rabbis are meticulously traced by A. Grossman, *The Early Sages of France: Their Lives, Leadership and Works* (Hebrew) (Jerusalem, 1995), 48.

17. Habermann, *The Poems of Rabbi Shimon bar Isaac*, 187.

18. Habermann, *The Poems of Rabbi Shimon bar Isaac*, 171.

19. Habermann, *The Poems of Rabbi Shimon bar Isaac*, 107–135.

20. Grossman, *The Early Sages*, 111.

21. Habermann, *A History of Hebrew Liturgical and Secular Poetry*, 181–182; Flusser, *Sefer Yosippon*, 2:66.

22. A. Grossman, *The Early Sages of France*, 40–42.

23. *Sefer Gezerot*, 11–15. A translation is available in R. Chazan, *Church, State and Jew in the Middle Ages* (West Orange, 1980), 295–300. For the identification of Le Mans, see

R. Chazan, "The Persecution of 992," *Revue des études juives*129 (1970), 218; Schwarz-fuchs, "France under the Early Capets" has Limoges, 146; followed by Grossman, *The Early Sages of France*, 19. On this incident, see also Chazan, *Medieval Jewry in Northern France* (Baltimore and London, 1973), 12–15, and *European Jewry and the First Crusade* (Los Angeles, London, 1987), 34–35; Baron, *A Social and Religious History*, 4:92; K. R. Stow believes the story to be a fiction. *Alienated Minority: The Jews of Medieval Latin Europe* (Cambridge, London, 1994), 96.

24. Chazan identifies him as Count Hugh III of Maine. *Church, State and Jew*, 295.

25. Mann, *Texts and Studies*, 1:16–21; 32–33. A. J. Zuckerman, "The Nasi of Frankland in the Ninth Century and Colaphus Judaeorum in Toulouse," *Proceedings of the American Academy for Jewish Research* 33 (1965), 51–82. Golb and Pritsak, *Khazarian Hebrew Documents of the Tenth Century*, 90–94. In 1018, Hugues, the chaplain of Viscount Aimeri de Rochechouart, struck hard enough to kill the Jew. S. Schwarzfuchs, "France and Germany under the Carolingians," in *The Dark Ages: Jews in Christian Europe*, 136.

26. *Sefer Gezerot*, 13, 15. On the practice at Béziers, Bouquet, *Recueil des Historiens des Gaules et de la France* (Paris, 1877) 12:436; Adémar of Chabannes' report, *MGH. S.*, 4:139. See also Schwarzfuchs, "France and Germany under the Carolingians," 136.

27. *Sefer Gezerot*, 13, in the language of The Book of Esther 3:13.

28. Schwarzfuchs, "France and Germany under the Carolingians," 136–142; B. Blumenkranz, "The Roman Church and the Jews," in *The Dark Ages: Jews in Christian Europe*, 74, 76, 78.

29. *Sefer Gezerot*, 14.

30. Schwarzfuchs, "France under the Early Capets," 154.

31. *Sefer Gezerot*, 14–15.

32. C. Roth already suggested a connection between Purim and the origins of anti-Jewish libels. "The Feast of Purim and the Origins of the Blood Accusation," *Speculum* 4 (1933), 520–526.

33. Above, Chapter 2.

34. *Sefer Yosippon*, 1:272. See also the late appendix, 1:440–441; Gudemann, *Sefer Ha-Torah veha-Hayim*, 1:83.

35. Again, *Sefer Yosippon*, 1:272–273.

36. Not an unusual ending for this genre, according to K. R. Stow, "A Tale of Uncertainties: Converts in the Roman Ghetto," *Festschrift Shelomo Simonsohn*, ed. D. Carpi (Tel Aviv, 1992).

37. Following R. Chazan's hypotheses, this letter could be dubbed a time-bound narrative. *God, Humanity and History: The Hebrew First Crusade Narrative* (Berkeley, Los Angeles, London, 2000), 2.

38. *Sefer Gezerot*, 11.

39. The practice recommended here did not deliver consistently. "Your congregation declared a convocation and proclaimed a holy fast day," lamented Rabbi Shimon ben Isaac. "But You did not see [us], we tormented our souls but You were not aware." Habermann, *The Poems of Rabbi Shimon ben Isaac*, 171–172, see also 140. In the case described the fast and self-inflicted torment also seem to be in vain. No specific events are linked to these days of public fasts.

40. Berliner, *Ozar Tov* (1878), 46; Habermann, *Gezerot*, 19–21. R. Chazan has dealt with this set of persecutions in "1007–1012: Initial Crisis for Northern European Jewry,"

Proceedings of the American Academy for Jewish Research 38–39 (1970–1971), 101–117, especially, 102–103; idem, *Medieval Jewry in Northern France* (Baltimore, 1973), pp. 12–15.

41. In *The "1007 Anonymous" and Papal Sovereignty: Jewish Perceptions of the Papacy and Papal Policy in the High Middle Ages,* in the Hebrew Union College Annual Supplements 4 (Cincinnati, 1984), K. R. Stow argues that the account was written in the thirteenth century. Stow based his arguments on anachronistic thirteenth-century terms. In my opinion, there are ample reasons to place the account in the early eleventh century. This is true especially in regard to the first section of the account, the stories of persecutions and voluntary death. The second section, about the activities of R. Jacob ben Yequtiel, may have been touched up later. If indeed the account were written in the thirteenth century, we would have seen the language and notions of the First Crusade Hebrew chronicle, which will be discussed in the next chapter. For instance, the notion of heavenly rewards, which dominates these chronicles, is completely absent in our account. See Shepkaru, "From After Death to Afterlife," idem, "To Die for God." To some extent, the same is true about the symbol of the *aqedah.* These notions dominated twelfth- and thirteenth-century Hebrew narratives of persecutions. As we shall see, eleventh-century Latin accounts corroborate the Hebrew report. See also Chazan's "Review of K. Stow, The '1007 Anonymous' and Papal Sovereignty," *Speculum* 62 (1987): 728–731, and Schwarzfuchs, "France under the Early Capets," 147–148. But see also Stow, *Alienated Minority,* 95.

42. Schwarzfuchs, "France under the Early Capets," 149.

43. "It became fully evident that this great crime [the demolition of the Holy Sepulcher] had been done by the wickedness of the Jews." Bouquet, *Recueil des historiens des Gaules et de la France,* 10:32; Migne, *PL,* 142:635; Blumenkranz, *Les auteurs chrétiens,* 256; *Historiarum Libri Quinque,* ed. J. France, 135. Mann, *The Jews in Egypt,* 1:26.

44. Raoul Glaber, 2, 7, 24. Bouquet, *Recueil des historiens des Gaules et de la France,* 10:34; Migne, *PL,* 142:657–659; Blumenkranz, *Les auteurs chrétiens,* 256–257. *Historiarum Libri Quinque,* ed. J. France, 135–137. A translation is also provided by G. G. Coulton, *Life in the Middle Ages* (New York, Cambridge, 1931), 4. For the problems of returning converts and how the Jewish leaders dealt with these problems, see Grossman, *The Early Sages,* 122–127.

45. Raoul Glaber, 2, 7, 25. Bouquet, *Recueil des historiens des Gaules et de la France,* 10:34; Migne, *PL,* 142:635; Blumenkranz, *Les auteurs chrétiens,* 256–257; *Historiarum Libri Quinque,* ed. J. France, 137.

46. Bouquet, *Recueil des historiens des Gaules et de la France,* 10:152; Migne, *PL,* 141:60; *MGH, S.* 4:136–137; Blumenkranz, *Les auteurs chrétiens,* 250–251. See also R. Landes, "The Massacres of 1010: On the Origins of Popular Anti-Jewish Violence in Western Europe," in *From Witness to Witchcraft: Jews and Judaism in Medieval Christian Thought,* ed. J. Cohen (Harrassowitz, 1996), 79–112.

47. I. A. Agus, "Democracy in the Communities of the Early Middle Ages," *Jewish Quarterly Review* 43 (1952–1953), 174; *Responsa of the Tosafists* (Hebrew), ed. I. A. Agus (New York, 1954), 39–42; idem, *Urban Civilization in Pre-Crusade Europe,* 2 vols. (New York, 1965), 1:176; H. Soloveitchik, *The Use of Responsa as a Historical Source* (Hebrew) (Jerusalem, 1990), 77–86; Grossman, *The Early Sages of France,* 20, and more generally on Tov Ellem, 46–81. Joseph's played an essential role in the life

of the community, especially of Limoges and Anjou. F. Rosenthal, ed. *Sefer ha-Yashar le-Rabenu Tam* (Berlin, 1898), 90.

48. J. Shatzmiller, "Desecrating the Cross: A Rare Medieval Accusation" (Hebrew) in *Studies in the History of the Jewish People and the Land of Israel* (1980), 5:159–173. E. Horowitz, "Medieval Jews Face the Cross" (Hebrew), *Facing the Cross: The Persecutions of 1096 in History and Historiography*, ed. Y. T. Assis et al. (Jerusalem, 2000), 123.

49. A. Berliner, *Sefer Rashi* (Frankfurt, 1905), 155; Baer, "Rashi," 324.

50. *Annales Quedinburgenses* in *MGH, Script*, 3:81; Blumenkranz, *Le auteurs chrétiens*, 250; Chazan, "1007–1012: Initial Crisis," 107, n. 18.

51. Grossman, *The Early Sages*, 111.

52. *Sefer Gezerot*, 16; Chazan, "1007–1012: Initial Crisis," 102.

53. *Sefer Gezerot*, 17; Habermann, *Selihot u-Pizmonim le-Rabbenu Gershom Me'or ha-Golah* (Jerusalem, 1944), 13; Chazan, "1007–1012: Initial Crisis," 108; Graetz associates the conversion of Wecelinus (1005), Duke Conrad's chaplain, with the reason for the expulsion. Graetz, *History of the Jews*, 3:245.

54. B. Blumenkranz, "The Roman Church and the Jews," 82 in *The Dark Ages: Jews in Christian Europe.*

55. For example, see his poem *Zekhor Brit Abraham*, H. Brody and M. Wiener, *Mivhar ha-Shirah ha-Ivrit* (1922, Lipzig), 72–74. For similar expressions in other poems, see *Piyyutei Rashi*, ed. A. Habermann, 9–10, 11–12, 15–16, 18–20, 23; Grossman, *The Early Sages*, 162–165.

56. Habermann, *The Poems of Rabbi Shimon ben Isaac*, 85, 160–161, 120–124, 40–41.

57. *The Memorial Book of the Worms Community*, 5; Graetz, *History of the Jews*, 3:247.

58. Bouquet, *Recueil des historiens des Gaules et de la France*, 10:162.

59. Again, the source refers to Robert the Pious (996–1031), who was crowned as his father Hugh's co-king. He abstained from wars and was considered a "mediocre king."

60. Esther 3:8 and Psalms 83:5.

61. Raoul Glaber, 3, 7, 24.

62. *Sefer Gezerot*, 19.

63. *Sefer Gezerot*, 19–20.

64. *Sefer Yosippon*, 1:272.

65. *Sefer Yosippon*, 1:272; *Sefer Gezerot*, 19.

66. *Sefer Yosippon*, 1:338.

67. Merchavia, *The Church Versus Talmudic and Midrashic Literature*, 89, 92. Migne, *PL*, 116:156. On Agobard's intensive disputations with Jews, Merchavia, 73, 75, 79. More generally, Blumenkranz, *Les auteurs chrétiens*, 152–168, especially, 165–167; idem, "The Roman Church and the Jews," 80; Schwarzfuchs, "France and Germany under the Carolingians," 136–142; Bachrach, *Early Medieval Jewish Policy in Western Europe*, 98–102, 109–111, 120–122; J. Cohen, *Living Letters of the Law: Ideas of the Jews in Medieval Christianity* (Berkeley, Los Angeles, London, 1999), 123–145.

68. Bouquet, *Recueil des historiens des Gaules et de la France*, 10:152. Blumenkranz, *Les auteurs chrétiens*, nos. 213, 232; idem, *Juifs et Chrétiens Dans Le Monde Occidental 430–1096* (Paris, 1960), 69, 73, 103.

69. A survey of female martyrs is provided by S. Noble, "The Jewish Woman in Medieval Martyrology," in *Studies in Jewish Bibliography History and Literature in Honor of I.*

Edward Kiev, ed. C. Berlin (New York, 1971), 347–355, especially 349. Reprinted in *The Fifth World Congress of Jewish Studies* (Jerusalem, 1972), 2:133–140. As will be shown in the next chapter, not enough attention is given in this survey to the importance of the women of 1007.

70. *Sefer Yosippon*, 1:316–317.

71. Habermann, *The Poems of Rabbi Shimon bar Isaac*, 187; 171 ;107–135.

72. Habermann, *The Poems of Rabbi Shimon bar Isaac*, 134.

73. Habermann, *The Poems of Rabbi Shimon bar Isaac*, 133–134; A. Habermann, *History of Hebrew Liturgical and Secular Poetry*, 180.

74. Habermann, *The Poems of Rabbi Shimon bar Isaac*, 187.

75. Habermann, *The Poems of Rabbi Shimon bar Isaac*, 40–41.

76. Habermann, *The Poems of Rabbi Shimon bar Isaac*, 147.

77. Raoul Glaber, *Histoires*, in Migne, *PL*, 142:635; Blumenkranz, *Les auteurs chrétiens*, 256. *Historiarum Libri Quinque*, ed. J. France, 135.

78. Bouquet, *Recueil des historiens des Gaules et de la France*, 10:152. There are two versions of Adémar's report. The other does not indicate Jewish self-killing. Blumenkranz raises the possibility that the version that mentions Jewish suicides is a later one and refers to the martyrs of the First Crusade. Blumenkranz, *Les auteurs chrétiens*, 251, n. 3. However, the other Hebrew and Latin sources of the period indicate a Jewish martyrological reaction.

79. Habermann, *Gezerot*, 20. For the identification of the city of Radom, see N. Golb, *History and Culture of the Jews of Rouen in the Middle Ages* (Tel Aviv, 1976), 1–5.

80. Blumenkranz, "The Roman Church and the Jews," 74. At this time the Church continued to display its traditional policy of protection and discrimination toward the Jews. About this policy, see Baron, *A Social and Religious History*, 4: 5–6.

81. For further details, see the analysis of Chazan, "1007–1012: Initial Crisis," 111–113. In line with a number of sources, both Latin and Hebrew, Chazan concludes that at the turn of the eleventh century, the Pope extended his governmental authority within the religious and secular realms. And see also R. Jacob bar Yequtiel's response to Duke Richard of Normandy: "You do not possess the authority over Israel to convert them from their creed nor can you affect them at all, unless the permission of the Pope of Rome is bestowed." Here we see again that R. Jacob represented all the Jews of northern Europe. *Sefer Gezerot*, 20.

82. On "foundation myth," see A. Brelich, "Symbol of a Symbol," *Myth and Symbols*, eds. J. M. Kitagawa and C. H. Long (Chicago and London, 1969), 196–198.

83. Weiner and Weiner, *The Martyr's Conviction*, 54.

84. *Sefer Gezerot*, 21.

85. *Sefer Gezerot*, 20. To assert Jacob's leadership and its legitimacy, he is eventually given the epitaph "*katzin*" (leader). The biblical meaning of the term *katzin* is "a leader." See Judges 11:11; Micah 3:1. Moreover, the author passed Rabbi Jacob's rulership to his sons Isaac and Judah, whom "the governor welcomed." This was not only a political recognition; the children of R. Jacob received a divine acknowledgment for their future leading role in the community because of Rabbi Jacob's deeds.

And the Holy One blessed be He annulled the persecution through this holy man [Rabbi Jacob bar Yequtiel]. And [for that] the Lord fondly remembered him and his offspring after him, to give them an everlasting hope and future.

86. This does not mean that the event did not take place and that Jews did not undergo martyrdom; "some myths . . . deal with people who really existed and with events that actually took place." H. Tudor, *Political Myth* (New York, Washington, London, 1972), 137–138. See also, M. Eliade, *Myth and Reality,* tr. by W. R. Trask (New York, 1968), 5.

87. *Sefer Gezerot,* 20, 21. More generally see, S. Schwarzfuchs, "L'opposition Tsarfat-Provence: la Formation du Judaisme du Nord de la France," in *Hommage à Georges Vajda: Études d'histoire et de pensée juives,* eds. G. Nahon and C. Touati (Louvain, 1980), 135–150.

88. See J. A. Arlow, "Ego Psychology and the Study of Mythology," *Journal of the American Psychoanalytic Association* 9 (1961), 371–393.

89. R. Girard, *Violence and the Sacred,* tr. by P. Gregory (Baltimore, 1977), 250–273. See also, Weiner, *The Martyr's Conviction,* 54.

90. Grossman, *The Early Sages of France,* 29–42.

91. Chazan, "1007–1012: Initial Crisis." According to Grossman, Jewish-Christian relations had got off to a bad start already in the tenth century. *The Early Sages of France,* 16–21. Stow questions the credibility of our two Hebrew sources but agrees that they do reflect the "mood of the late and early eleventh centuries." *Alienated Minority,* 94–95.

92. A partial list of these communities is given in the document itself. On early settlements, see Y. Baer, "The Origins of the Organization of the Jewish Community of the Middle Ages" (Hebrew), *Zion* 15 (1950), 1–41; S. Eidelberg, "The Community of Troyes before the Time of Rashi" (Hebrew), *Sura* 1 (1953–1954), 48–57; I. Agus, "Democracy in the Communities of the Early Middle Ages," 155–176; Chazan, *Medieval Jewry,* 10 n. 5.

93. Jacob is said to have settled with thirty Jews in Flanders. *Gezerot,* 21. At Châlons only two families are mentioned in Tov Ellem's responsum. Schwarzfuchs, "France under the Early Capets," 153; Agus, "Democracy in the Communities of the Early Middle Ages," 172.

94. Baer, "The Origins of the Organization of the Jewish Community of the Middle Ages," 1–41.

95. L. Finkelstein, *Jewish Self-Government in the Middle Ages* (New York, 1924), 149; Chazan, *Medieval Jewry in Northern France,* 16.

96. *Teshuvot Rashi,* ed. I. Elfenbein (New York, 1943), 287 n. 246 and 289 n. 247.

97. Agus, *Urban Civilization,* 1:174; "Democracy in the Communities of the Early Middle Ages," 173–176; Chazan, *Medieval Jewry in Northern France,* 20–21; Soloveitchik, *The Use of Responsa as a Historical Source,* 77, 80 ns. 75–78; Grossman, *The Early Sages of France,* 31.

98. B. *Baba Metzia* 62a.

99. Agus, "Democracy in the Communities of the Early Middle Ages," 172; S. Eidelberg, "The Community of Troyes Before the Time of Rashi," 48–57; I. Agus, *The Heroic Age of Franco-German Jewry* (New York, 1969), 185–276; Chazan, *Medieval Jewry in Northern France,* 18–24.

100. Agus, *Urban Civilization,* 2:448.

101. Agus, *Urban Civilization in Pre-Crusade Europe,* 2:789. Agus, *The Heroic Age of Franco-German Jewry,* 355.

102. Zedekiah b. Abraham, *Shibbolei ha-Leket*, 2 vols. ed. A. Y. Hasidah, (Jerusalem, 1987). Quoted from Agus, *The Heroic Age*, 355. On the importance of Joel ha-Levi's book for the study of early Ashkenazic Jews, see Grossman, *The Early Sages*, 24–25, 439. According to Grossman, Zedekiah b. Abraham relied extensively on early precrusading Ashkenazic material.

103. In a few lines, Y. Baer linked the Jewish martyrological behavior to the religious movement of the monastery of Cluny. Baer, however, focused on the persecutions of 1010, without explaining the actual Jewish behavior. Nevertheless, Baer's suggestion to look for external influences on the Jews is valuable. "The Religious and Social Tendency of *Sefer Hasidim*" (Hebrew), *Zion* 3 (1938), 1–50, especially 3–5; reprinted in *The Religious and Social Ideas of the Jewish Pietiests in Medieval Germany*, ed. I. G. Marcus (Jerusalem, 1986), 81–50, especially 83–85.

104. Jews should be "preached to without ceasing" but not forced to convert, Pope Leo VII reminded churchmen. Blumenkranz, *Le auteurs chrétiens*, 219–221; idem, "The Roman Church and the Jews," 81; C. Roth, "Italy," in *The Dark Ages: Jews in Christian Europe*, 116; Blumenkranz, "Germany," *The Dark Ages: Jews in Christian Europe*, 167; E. A. Synan, *The Popes and the Jews in the Middle Ages* (New York, London, 1967), 60.

105. On heretics in western Europe see, I. da Milano, "L'eresia popolare del secolo XI nell' Europa Occidentale," *Studi Gregoriani* 2 (1947), 43–89; R. Moore, *Origins of European Dissent* (Oxford, 1985), 35–36; J. B. Russell, *Dissent and Reform in the Early Middle Ages* (New York, 1965), 111–113.

106. Raoul Glaber, 3, 8, 26.

107. Wakefield and Evans. *Heresies of the High Middle Ages*, 82.

108. "King Robert commanded that they [the heretics] be first deposed from priestly rank, then cast out of the Church, and finally consumed by fire." Wakefield, *Heresies of the High Middle Ages*, 75.

109. Wakefield and Evans, *Heresies of the High Middle Ages*, 79, 81.

110. Interestingly, Raoul assigned the source of heresy to a woman from Italy who settled in Orléans.

111. Raoul Glaber, for example, "rursus coepit inuidus diabolus per assuetam sibi Iudaeorum gentem uere fidei cultribus uenenum sue nequitie propinare," 3, 7, 24 and 3, 8, 26 for the heretics.

112. Migne, *PL*, 142:635; Blumenkranz, *Les auteurs chrétiens*, 256–257. Raoul Glaber wrote, "We see clearer than daylight that as the Last Day progresses … perilous times were imminent for the souls of men." These feelings of the approach of the Day of Judgment were expressed also in a Church council at the beginning of the tenth century. The council declared the beginning of the last century of the world. *Cambridge Medieval History*, 3:199; H. Focillon, *The Year 1000* (New York, 1969), 39–72.

113. Parkes, *The Jew in the Medieval Community*, 39.

114. Adémar of Chabannes (988–1034) has 1020, *PL*, 141:64; *MGH. S* (Hanover, 1841), 4:139; Blumenkranz, *Les auteurs chrétiens*, 251; idem, "The Roman Church and the Jews," 76. A different text suggests 1017, *Annales Ecclesiastici*, 16 (Bari, 1849), 42. G. Tellenbach, *The Church in Western Europe from the Tenth to the Early Twelfth Century*, tr. T. Reuter (Cambridge, 1993), 74. R. Landes trusts Adémar, *Relics, Apocalypse,*

and the Deceits of History: Adémar of Chabannes, 989–1034 (Cambridge, 1995), chapter 14. C. Roth rejects the accusation against the Jews, *The History of the Jews in Italy* (Philadelphia, 1946), 72; Stow doubts the whole story, *Alienated Minority*, 95. Horowitz disagrees with them both, "Medieval Jews Face the Cross," 129–130. In his opinion, both the accusations and the punishment are authentic.

115. Blumenkranz, *Les auteurs chrétiens*, 251, 257.

116. M. Barkum, *Disasters and the Millennium* (London, 1974), 26–27, and see also 32–52. On millenarian movements, see N. Cohn, *The Pursuit of the Millennium* (New York, Oxford, 1970), 21–33.

117. Raoul Glaber, 2, 6, 11. Translation from *Historiarum Libri Quinque*, ed. J. France, 71.

118. An interesting comment in the letter about 992 is worth exploring. After his conversion, Sehoq decided to "travel in the vicinities of the cities and investigate the communities, each of the peoples and their gods. From there he went forth to the Jewish communities in the cities which he found." *Gezerot*, 11. The author here refers to the different provinces of Gaul, and the "peoples and their gods" must refer at this time to the heretics.

119. Adémar of Chabannes, *Chronique*, in *Collection de textes pour servir a l'etude et a l'enseignement de l'histoire, 20*, ed. J. Chavanon (Paris, 1897), 184–185. English quotation from Wakefield and Evans, *Heresies of the High Middle Ages*, 75.

120. Wakefield and Evans, *Heresies of the High Middle Ages*, 76. Adémar's report is supported by Raoul Glaber.

121. Wakefield and Evans, *Heresies of the High Middle Ages*, 81.

122. In the same year, the Byzantine emperor Basil II (976–1025) managed to defeat Lombard revolts and secure the imperial grip in Italy. F. Chalandon, *Histoire de la domination normande en Italie et en Sicile*, 2 vols. (New York, 1960), 1: 42–57.

123. Wakefield and Evans, *Heresies of the High Middle Ages*, 86.

124. Wakefield and Evans, *Heresies of the High Middle Ages*, 88–89. Raoul Glaber says that they were only "burnt to death" (*igne cremauere*). *Historiarum Libri Quinque*, ed. J. France, 178.

125. *Libri Historiarum*, 5, 11, in *MGH. SRM*, 1:1 (Hanover, 1951), 205–206; Blumenkranz, *Les auteurs chrétiens*, 70.

126. *Gesta Treverorum, MGH, S.* (Hanover, 1848), 182–183. J. Aronius, *Regesten zur Geschichte der Juden in fränkischen und deutschen Reiche* (Berlin, 1902), 76, n. 160. Blumenkranz, "The Roman Church and the Jews," 82.

127. Wakefield and Evans, *Heresies of the High Middle Ages*, 75.

128. Wakefield and Evans, *Heresies of the High Middle Ages*, 79.

129. There are other associations. For instance, Raoul Glaber, 3, 6, 8; "Raynard the Judaizer," 3, 6, 23.

130. Wakefield and Evans, *Heresies of the High Middle Ages*, 83.

131. Bouquet, *Recueil des historiens des Gaules et de la France*, 6:231, 7:224, 8:300; for the report of Helgald, 10:115; 241.

132. Adémar of Chabannes in Bouquet, *Recueil des historiens des Gaules et de la France*, 10:152.

133. Bouquet, 10:115.

134. Glaber, 2, 9, 18–19. France's translation, *Historiarum Libri Quinque*, 83–85.

135. C. Erdmann already pointed to the connection between the idea of holy wars as appearing in Pope Urban's speech at Clermont and Glaber's association of casualties in war with the Christian act of love. *The Origins of the Idea of the Crusade*, tr. by M. W. Baldwin and W. Goffart (Princeton, 1977), 15 n. 28 and 54 n. 79.

CHAPTER 6: *VE-ASHKENAZ*: TRADITIONAL MANIFESTATIONS

1. The three Hebrew sources were first published by A. Neubauer and M. Stern in *Hebraische Berichte über die Judenverfolgungen wahrend der Kreuzzuge* (Berlin, 1892). The sources were reprinted in Habermann's *Sefer Gezerot Ashkenaz ve-Zarfat*. English translations are available in S. Eidelberg's *The Jews and the First Crusade* (Madison, 1977). The anonymous's and R. Solomon bar Simson's narratives have been translated by R. Chazan. All the translations below are mine unless otherwise indicated. The interrelationship among the three narratives is discussed by I. Sonne, "Nouvel examen des trois rélations hebräiques sur les persécutions de 1096," *Revue des études juives* 96 (1933), 137–152; A. Sapir Abulafia, "The Interrelationship between the Hebrew Chronicles of the First Crusade," *Journal of Semitic Studies* 27 (1982), 221–239. E. Haverkamp's critical edition of the three Hebrew documents is about to appear. Regarding the different methodological approaches to these sources, see note 14.

2. In the *Mainz Anonymous*, Habermann, *Gezerot*, 93. Eidelberg, 99–100. Chazan, *European Jewry*, 225–226. See also *The Chronicle of Solomon bar Simson*. Peter the Hermit from Amiens and the Church-appointed preacher of Berri arrived with his army at the Rhineland in the spring of 1096.

> When he arrived there in Trier, he and his multitude of people, on his way to Jerusalem, he brought with him a letter from the Jews of France, [suggesting] that in all the places where... [he encounters] Jews, they would give him provision for his journey [so that] he would speak well for the sake of Israel, for he was a priest and his words were obeyed.

Sefer Gezerot, 53; Eidelberg, 62; Chazan, *European Jewry*, 287–288. According to Ekkehard of Aura, Peter's band treated the Jews of Regensburg differently and forced the Jews to undergo baptism. Ekkehard of Aura, "Chronicon universale," *MGH, Scrip.*, 6:208. Baer saw in Rashi's commentary to Isaiah 53:4, 9 references to the events in France. "Rashi and the Historical Reality of His Time" [Hebrew], 320–321.

3. Guibert of Nogent, *Histoire de sa vie*, ed. G. Bourgin (Paris, 1907), 118; *Self and Society in Medieval France*, tr. J. Benton (New York, 1970), 134–135.

4. Richard of Poitiers, "Chronicon," in Bouquet, 12:411–412. Also, Geoffrey of Breuil, "Chronica," in Bouquet, 12:428.

5. Hugh of Flavigny in Bouquet (1869), 12:623; Sigebert of Gembloux, "Chronica," in *MGH, Script.*, 6:367; *Historiae Regum Francorum* in Bouquet (1877), 12:218. See also N. Golb, *The Jews in Medieval Normandy: A Social and Intellectual History* (Cambridge, 1998), 117–127.

6. The document was first published by Mann, *Text and Studies*, 1:31–33. Discussions in N. Golb, "New Light on the Persecution of French Jews at the Time of the First Crusade," *Proceedings of the American Academy for Jewish Research* 34 (1966),

1–64; ibid, *The Jews in Medieval Normandy*, 127–130. Cf. Chazan, *Medieval Jewry in Northern France*, 26 n. 53 and *European Jewry*, 311 n. 24.

7. R. Chazan, "The Anti-Jewish Violence of 1096: Perpetrator and Dynamics," in *Religious Violence between Christians and Jews: Medieval Roots, Modern Perspectives*, ed. A. S. Abulafia (New York, 2002), 21–43.

8. D. Goitein, "Obadyah, a Norman Proselyte," in *The Journal of Jewish Studies* 4 (1953), 80–81; Golb, "New Light on the Persecution of French Jews at the Time of the First Crusade," 31–32; J. Prawer, "The Autobiography of Obadyah the Norman: A Convert to Judaism at the Time of the First Crusade," in *Studies in Medieval Jewish History and Literature*, ed. I. Twersky (Cambridge, 1979), 110–132; Golb, *The Jews in Medieval Normandy*, 121 n. 28; Marcus, "From 'Deus Vult' to the 'Will of the Creator,'" 95.

9. Only in 1170 was the canonization of saints and martyrs reserved solely to the Church. Guibert's and other Church officials' endeavors to correct the situation were in vain, for in many cases the emotional populace refused to yield to logic or to Church policy. Guibert of Nogent, *Treatise on Relics*, I, chapter I, col. 614. English translation by Coulton, *Life in the Middle Ages*, 15–21.

10. *Sefer Gezerot*, 78; Eidelberg, 88.

11. *Sefer Yosippon*, 1:430.

12. Again, Mann, *Texts and Studies*, 1:24.

13. *Sefer Gezerot*, 56; Eidelberg, 66–67; Chazan, *European Jewry*, 293.

14. Different methodological approaches to the three Hebrew narratives are discussed by I. Sonne, "Which Is the Earlier Account of the Persecutions of 1096?" (Hebrew), *Zion* 12 (1947–1948), 74–81. Sonne sensed that the Solomon bar Simson Chronicle contains "fruits of fabrication," but his observation was generally ignored until recently. Y. Baer, "The Persecution of 1096" (Hebrew), *Sefer Asaf*, ed. M. D. Cassuto et al. (Jerusalem, 1953), 126–140; R. Chazan, "The Hebrew First Crusade Chronicles," *Revue des études juives* 133 (1974), 235–254; idem, "The Hebrew Chronicles: Further Reflections," *Association for Jewish Studies Review* 3 (1978), 79–98; idem, *European Jewry and the First Crusade*, 40–49; "The Facticity of Medieval Narrative: A Case Study of the Hebrew First Crusade Narratives," *Association for Jewish Studies Review* 16 (1991), 31–56, and his *God, Humanity, and History*. G. D. Cohen, "The Hebrew Crusade Chronicles and the Ashkenazic Tradition," in *Minhah le-Nahum: Biblical and Other Studies in Honor of Nahum M. Sarna*, eds. M. Fishbane and M. Brettler (Sheffield, 1993), 36–53. E. Haverkamp affirms some important historical facts in her "'Persecutio' und 'Gezeroh' in Trier Während des Ersten Kreuzzüges," in *Juden und Christen zur Zeit Der Kreuzzüge*, ed. A. Haverkamp (Sigmaringen, 1999), 35–71. I. G. Marcus introduced a new approach to these documents. He views these documents as a production of "literary imagination" in response to the events. "From Politics to Martyrdom: Shifting Paradigms in the Hebrew Narratives of the 1096 Crusading Riots." *Prooftexts* 2 (1982), 40–52; see also his review of Chazan's European Jewry, in *Speculum* 64 (1989), 685–688, idem, "The Representation of Reality in the Sources of the 1096 Anti-Jewish First Crusade Riots," *Jewish History* 13:2 (Fall 1999), 37–48; idem, "History, Story and Collective Memory: Narrativity in Early Ashkenazic Culture," *Prooftexts*, 10 (1990), 365–388. Following Marcus's suggestion, J. Cohen holds the narratives to be mainly a reflection of the twelfth-century Ashkenazic culture of the survivors. "The Persecution of 1096: The Sociocultural Context of the Narratives

of Martyrdom" (Hebrew), *Zion* 59 (1994), 169–208; "The Hebrew Crusade Chronicles in Their Christian Cultural Context," in *Juden und Christen zur Zeit Der Kreuzzüge*, ed. A. Haverkamp (Sigmaringen, 1999), 17–34. Cf. I. J. Yuval, "The Language and Symbols of the Hebrew Chronicles of the Crusades," *Facing the Cross*, 101–117. For an excellent summary of these scholarly approaches, see J. Cohen. "From History to Historiography: The Study of the Persecutions and Constructions of their Meaning" (Hebrew) in *Facing the Cross*, 16–31. On medieval writings in general, see also G. Spiegel, "History, Historicism, and the Social Logic of the Text in the Middle Ages," *Speculum* 65 (1990), 59–86.

15. *Sefer Gezerot*, 32; Eidelberg, 33; Chazan, *European Jewry*, 256.

16. *Sefer Gezerot*, 46; Eidelberg, 52; Chazan, *European Jewry*, 277.

17. J. A. Prawer, *The History of the Jews in the Latin Kingdom of Jerusalem* (Oxford, 1988), 19–45.

18. More generally, H. Soloveitchik has shown that French Jewry did not tend to accept Ashkenazic customs. *Halakhah, Economy, and Self-Image* (Jerusalem, 1985), 84.

19. E. Zimmer, "The Persecutions of 1096 as Reflected in Medieval and Modern Minhag Books," in *Facing the Cross*, 157–170, especially 160–161, 170.

20. The four versions are by Guibert of Nogent, "Gesta Dei per Francos," *RHC Oc.*, 4:137–140; Fulcher of Chartres, *Historia Hierosolymitana*, ed. H. Hagenmeyer (Heidelberg, 1913), 132–138; Robert of Rheims, "Historia Hierosolimitana," *RHC Oc.*, 3:727–730; Baldric of Dol, "Historia Jerosolimitana," *RHC Oc.*, 4:12–16. In Baldric's version Urban did not use the term *martyrdom* when promising the crusaders a celestial reward, but Urban did use the term *martyr* when instructing how the crusade should be conducted and also when giving the examples of other early Christian heroes. See also, the anonymous *Gesta Francorum et aliorum Hierosolymytanorum*, ed. and tr. R. M. Hill (London, 1962), 1–2. See H. E. J. Cowdrey's important article, "Martyrdom and the First Crusade," in *Crusade and Settlement*, ed. P. W. Edbury (Cardiff, 1985), 46–56.

21. "Historia Hierosolimitana," *RHC Oc.*, 3:727–730. Translation from E. Peters, *The First Crusade: The Chronicle of Fulcher of Chartres and Other Source Material* (Philadelphia, 1998), 27.

22. Orderic Vitalis, *Historia aecclesiastica*, ed. M. Chibnall (Oxford, 1969), 3:216–217; emphasis mine.

23. Fulcher of Chartres, *Historia Hierosolymitana*, ed. H. Hagenmeyer, Prologue.

24. The nonmartyrological patterns included (1) Direct Jewish contact with the crusaders, suggesting to them large payments of goods and money. *Sefer Gezerot*, 26–27, 53, 94; Chazan, *European Jewry*, 85. (2) In numerous incidents, the Jews turned to their Christian neighbors to seek shelter and support. *Sefer Gezerot*, 87. (3) Others turned for help to the political authorities, both central (Emperor Henry IV) and local. *Sefer Gezerot*, 27, 51–52; Chazan, *European Jewry*, 88. (4) A number of Jews preferred to depend on the local religious authority and hid in their castles or churches. Bernold of St. Blasien, "Chronicon," *MGH, Scrip.*, 5: 465. Bishop Ruthard's attempt to save Jews is depicted in *MGH, Scrip.*, 6:729; *Sefer Gezerot*, 26, 40–41, 54–55, 94; Chazan, *European Jewry*, 95. (5) The Latin and the Hebrew sources mention Jewish conversions to Christianity either out of conviction or out of fear. The conversion of a Trier Jew named Micah seems to be a genuine one. See *MGH, Scrip.*, 8:190. The source indicates that Micah's conversion was an isolated incident. Chazan,

European Jewry, 102. As we shall see below in more detail, a large number of Jews converted to gain time to sacrifice their children or bury the dead. *Sefer Gezerot,* 95–96. In Regensburg, the entire community converted, *ibid.*, 56–57; in Moers, *ibid.*, 50–51; about Jews who returned to Judaism, *MGH, Scrip.*, 2:246. Ekkehard of Aura's chronicle indicates that most of the Jews "returned [to their creed] like dogs to their vomit after their baptism" because of Emperor Henry IV's permission to do so. *MGH, Scrip.*, 6:208. According to Guibert of Nogent, Jews were also baptized by force in Rouen. Guibert of Nogent, *De Vita Sua*, ed. E. R. Labande (Paris, 1981), 246–248, and in Bouquet, 7:240; Chazan, *European Jewry*, 99–105. (6) An unusual response was adopted by groups of Jews and individuals who decided to resist the crusaders in a military-like fashion. *Sefer Gezerot*, 57, 96, 99–100; Chazan, *European Jewry*, 97.

25. *The Memorial Book of the Worms Community* still praises Rabbi Shimon ben Isaac. "He served the communities and illuminated the eyes of the Diaspora by his poems." Quoted in Dinur, *Israel ba-Golah*, 1:1, 169.

26. *Piyute Rashi*, ed. A. Habermann (Jerusalem, 1941), 10, 13, 15–17, 18, 19, 24.

27. Some of Gershom's works also bear Byzantine influence.

28. In Gershom's *Zekhor Brit Abraham* ("Remember Abraham's Covenant"), H. Brody and M. Wiener, *Mivhar ha-Shirah ha-Ivrit* (1922, Lipzig), 62–64.

29. This dilemma is addressed by H. Soloveitchik, "Religious Law and Change: The Medieval Ashkenazic Example." In *Association for Jewish Studies Review* 8:2 (1987), 205–221, and by A. Gross, "Historical and Halakhic Aspects of the Mass Martyrdom in Mainz: An Integrative Approach," in *Facing the Cross*, 171–192. Gross relies on the martyrs' statements and especially on *Bereshit Rabbah* to understand how they justified taking one's life. *Bereshit Rabbah*, however, is not mentioned by our sources, and I doubt that the masses could apply the same erudite sophistication to their decision making that Gross shows. In my opinion, these *post factum* attempts were written later to justify the behavior of 1096. To understand this behavior, we need to understand not only the *Halakhah* but also the period.

30. *Sefer Gezerot*, 30; Eidelberg, 30; Chazan, *European Jewry*, 253.

31. *Sefer Gezerot*, 27; Eidelberg, 26, Chazan, *European Jewry*, 248–249.

32. The idea goes back to B. *Sanhedrin* 102a. Chazan, *God, Humanity, and History*, 58–59, 152–153, Cohen, "The Persecutions of 1096," 179.

33. The report is cited by A. David, "Historical Records of the Persecutions during the First Crusade in Hebrew Works and Hebrew Manuscripts" (Hebrew), in *Facing the Cross*, 202–203.

34. *Sefer Gezerot*, 27; Eidelberg, 26; Chazan, *European Jewry*, 248. "Satan also came," from Job 2:1. The existence of early rabbinic and mystical traditions in Ashkenaz was studied by Y. Baer, *Israel among the Nations* (Hebrew) (Jerusalem, 1955), 36–39; P. Schäfer, "The Ideal of Piety of the Ashkenazi Hasidim and Its Roots in Jewish Tradition," *Jewish History* 4 (1990), 199–211; Marcus, "History, Story, and Collective Memory," 275 n. 45; E. R. Wolfson, *Through a Speculum That Shines: Vision and Imagination in Medieval Jewish Mysticism* (Princeton, 1994), 80; idem, "Martyrdom, Eroticism, and Asceticism in Twelfth-Century Ashkenazi Piety," in *Jews and Christians in Twelfth-Century Europe*, ed. M. A. Signer and J. Van Engen (Indiana, 2001), 171–220.

35. *Sefer Gezerot*, 38; Eidelberg, 41–42; Chazan, *European Jewry*, 265.

36. Similarly to the claim that the Ashkenazic leadership vanished from the world a year prior to the crusade, the later Ashkenazic report erroneously claims that the great rabbi Shimon died three days before the eruption of violence. A woman visiting the synagogue heard a divine voice coming from among the Torah scrolls. She relayed the incident to R. Shimon, who understood that a decree had been issued from heaven. Because "it would be impossible to annul the decree, he prayed that he would die before its fulfilment." His death wish was granted only in this account, for as we know R. Shimon had passed away sometime in the first quarter of the eleventh century. David, "Historical Records of the Persecutions during the First Crusade in Hebrew Works and Hebrew Manuscripts," 202–203.

37. Evil Rome and Samael in *Hikhalot Rabbati*, *Bet ha-Midrash* 3:87; 6:31, 32; in *Solomon bar Simson Chronicle*, *Gezerot*, 27. *Hamishi be-Shabbat* in *Hikhalot Rabbati*, *Bet ha-Midrash* 3:86; 6:31; in the narratives of 1096, *Gezerot*, 25, 73. This additional information is omitted in the *Mainz Anonymous*. The ten martyrs studying the rules of Passover just before their executions, *Bet ha-Midrash*, 6:22, 32.

38. The medieval martyrs in *Sefer Gezerot*, 45; Eidelberg, 51; Chazan, *European Jewry*, 276–277. R. Shimon and R. Ishmael in *Bet ha-Midrash*, 2:65. It also echoes the rationale behind the decree imposed by the community of Troyes in the early eleventh century, as attested in R. Joseph Tov Ellem's responsum.

39. For one of many references to vengeance, punishment of the enemy, and the redemption of Israel, see *Gezerot*, 59. I. J. Yuval dealt with the Ashkenazic notion of reprisal in "Vengeance and Damnation, Blood and Defamation: From Jewish Martyrdom to Blood Libel Accusations" (Hebrew), *Zion* 58 (1993).

40. *Sefer Gezerot*, 27; Eidelberg, 25; Chazan, *European Jewry*, 247.

41. *Semahot* 8:8. Ed D. Zlotnick, (New Haven, 1966), 59.

42. *Sefer Gezerot*, 27; Eidelberg, 25; Chazan, *European Jewry*, 248.

43. Godfrey's statement in Habermann, *Gezerot*, 26–27; Eidelberg, 24–25; Chazan, *European Jewry*, 247. More general statements of revenge, *Gezerot*, 24, 28, 72, 103. On this old Christian motif, R. Chazan, *Medieval Stereotypes and Modern Antisemitism* (Berkeley, Los Angeles, London, 1997), 13.

44. Other Jews ascribed the sin of the Golden Calf and "In the day that I visit" to Christians. It shows the centrality of this argument in Jewish–Christian polemics. D. Berger, "On the Image and Destiny of Gentiles in Ashkenazic Polemical Literature" (Hebrew), in *Facing the Cross*, 74–91.

45. *Sefer Gezerot*, 73; Eidelberg, 80.

46. *Sefer Gezerot*, 39; Eidelberg, 43; Chazan, *European Jewry*, 267.

47. *Sefer Gezerot*, 98; Eidelberg, 106; Chazan, *European Jewry*, 233.

48. *Sefer Gezerot*, 48–49; Eidelberg, 56; Chazan, *European Jewry*, 281–282.

49. *Gezerot*, 49; Eidelberg, 57; Chazan, *European Jewry*, 282.

50. Marcus, "From Politics to Martyrdom;" idem, "Hierarchies, Religious Boundaries and Jewish Spirituality in Medieval Germany," *Jewish History* 1:2 (1986), 7–26. Chazan, *European Jewry and the First Crusade*, 126.

51. *Sefer Yosippon*, 1:394.

52. *Sefer Yosippon*, 1:396.

53. *Sefer Yosippon*, 1:430.

54. *Sefer Gezerot*, 25, 40, 44, 47, 53, 57, 93, 94, 99. See the incidents of 992 and 1007–1012 in the previous chapter.

55. *Sefer Gezerot*, 25; 37; 74; 96. Another phrase that is probably taken from *Sefer Yosippon* 15:6 is "a copper frying-pan," the instrument of torture used against the oldest brother in the story of the mother and her seven sons. *Sefer Gezerot*, 48, 31, 36, 49, 100, 104. *Sefer Yosippon*, 1:15, 1:67, 1:67, 1:83, 1:89. To be sure, this was not the first time *Sefer Yosippon* surfaced in Ashkenazic works. Already Rabbi Gershom of Mainz, the Light of the Exile, had employed the book in his study center. His liturgical *piyyut* for *Hanukkah* also bears the marks of *Sefer Yosippon*. Habermann, *A History of Hebrew Liturgical and Secular Poetry*, 181–182; Flusser, *Sefer Yosippon*, 2:66.

56. The *Gesta Francorum* mentions the arrival of the pontiff with his delegation, including the priests (*presbiteris*), 1, 2. "God wills it" became the crusaders' battle cry. At the battle of Antioch, for instance, "The Franks altogether shouted in a loud voice: 'God wills it, God wills it.' " ("tunc alta voce omnes simul Franci exclamaverunt: 'Deus hoc uult, Deus hoc uult.' " Fulcher, *Historia Hierosolymitana*, 1.17.5. *Gesta Francorum*, 7, "'*Deus uult, Deus uult, Deus uult!*' *una uoce conclamant.*"

57. *Sefer Gezerot*, 48–49; Eidelberg, 56; Chazan, *European Jewry*, 281–282.

58. S. Spiegel's classic study of the legend of Isaac's binding is, of course, essential. *The Last Trial* (New York, 1993).

59. Marcus, *Rituals of Childhood*, 7.

60. In other words, they recited the benediction of *tsiduk ha-din*, which is said at funerals.

61. *Sefer Gezerot*, 41; Eidelberg, 45; Chazan, *European Jewry*, 269.

62. *Sefer Gezerot*, 31–32; Eidelberg, 32; Chazan, *European Jewry*, 255.

63. *Sefer Gezerot*, 96; Eidelberg, 103–104; Chazan, *European Jewry*, 231.

64. *Sefer Gezerot*, 50, 52, 77, 81, 100, also, 43; Eidelberg, 49; Chazan, *European Jewry*, 273. And also, "May the merit and righteousness and reverence and their innocence and their bindings [of sacrifices] serve us as a champion of right and an advocate before the Almighty. May He deliver us from the wicked exile of Edom soon in our days. May our true messiah arrive, Amen, soon in our days." See also, *Sefer Gezerot*, 50, 52. Further discussion in Yuval, "*Two Nations in Your Womb*," 169–170.

65. Marcus, *Rituals of Childhood*, 6. See also his, "A Jewish–Christian Symbiosis: The Culture of Early Ashkenaz," 450–516, in *Cultures of the Jews*. It provides a good survey of the development of the Ashkenazic community in the context of Jewish–Christian relations.

66. *Sefer Gezerot*, 35; Eidelberg, 47; Chazan, *European Jewry*, 260.

67. *Sefer Yosippon*, 1:72.

68. *Sefer Gezerot*, 55; Eidelberg, 66; Chazan, *European Jewry*, 292.

69. *Sefer Gezerot*, 33, 101; Eidelberg, 34–35, 110; Chazan, *European Jewry*, 258, 238.

70. *Sefer Gezerot*, 33–34; Eidelberg, 35; Chazan, *European Jewry*, 258.

71. *Sefer Gezerot*, 38; Eidelberg, 42; Chazan, *European Jewry*, 265–266.

72. *Sefer Gezerot*, 39, 97; Eidelberg, 42, 105; Chazan, *European Jewry*, 266, 279.

73. *Sefer Gezerot*, 56; Eidelberg, 66–67; Chazan, *European Jewry*, 293.

74. *Sefer Gezerot*, 25; Eidelberg, 22; Chazan, *European Jewry*, 244.

75. *Sefer Gezerot*, 79; Eidelberg, 89.

76. *Sefer Gezerot*, 34, 101–102; Eidelberg, 35–36, 111–112; Chazan, *European Jewry*, 258–259, 238–239.

77. *Sefer Gezerot*, 102; Eidelberg, 112; Chazan, *European Jewry*, 239.

78. Other reports on events in 1096 continue to show the influence of *Yosippon's* version of the story. The question of the seventh son to his mother in *Yosippon* recalls Abraham bar Asher's challenge ("How long will you delay me?") to the crusaders. *Sefer Gezerot*, 42; Eidelberg, 46–47; Chazan, *European Jewry*, 271. "A copper frying-pan," *Sefer Yosippon* 1:70, in which the mother's oldest son was tortured also penetrated our texts. Finally, the martyrdom of the elder Samuel bar Mordechai was made reminiscent of the Hellenistic story of the elder Eleazar, who is missing in the rabbinic text. *Sefer Gezerot*, 42; Eidelberg, 46–47; Chazan, *European Jewry*, 271.

79. *Sefer Gezerot*, 32; Eidelberg, 33; Chazan, *European Jewry*, 256.

80. I. G. Marcus makes a similar observation about the portrayal of Jewish women and men as Priests and as Abraham. "Mothers, Martyrs, and Moneymakers: Some Jewish Women in Medieval Europe," *Conservative Judaism*, vol. 38:3 (Spring 1986), 38.

81. *Sefer Gezerot*, 79; Eidelberg, 89. The *Solomon bar Simson Chronicle* gives a similar description to that of R. Eliezer bar Nathan, but he does not mention the story of the besieged women. *Sefer Gezerot*, 50–51. Eidelberg, 58–59; Chazan, *European Jewry*, 284.

82. *Sefer Gezerot*, 75; Eidelberg, 83.

83. M. Breuer considered foreign influences, but his non-Jewish examples ignore the crusade. "Women in Jewish Martyrology" (Hebrew), in *Facing the Cross*, 141–149.

84. Albert of Aix, *RHC Oc.*, 4:272.

85. Albert, *RHC Oc.*, 4:293; emphasis mine.

86. H. Hagenmeyer, *Die Kreuzzugsbriefe aus den Jahren 1088–1100* (Innsbruck, 1901), 137–138.

87. *Gesta Francorum*, 41.

88. Peter Tudebodes, *Historia de Hierosolymitano Itinere*, publié par John Hugh Hill et Laurita Hill (Paris, 1977), 52, 76.

89. *Sefer Gezerot*, 24; Eidelberg, 21; Chazan, *European Jewry*, 243.

90. *Sefer Gezerot*, 28, 98; Eidelberg, 27, 106; Chazan, *European Jewry*, 249, 233. Albert of Aix also indicates that crusaders were led by a goose and a she-goat. *RHC Oc.*, 4:291–292.

91. *RHC, Oc.*, 4:293.

CHAPTER 7: *VE ASHKENAZ*: MANIFESTATIONS OF A MILIEU

1. Chazan calls the Jewish behavior a "countercrusade." He writes: "The Jews show much of the same religious frenzy that swept European society at the end of the eleventh century. . . . the Jews under attack responded with much the same militance and readiness for self-sacrifice out of which the crusading movement had been spawned." *European Jewry*, 132, and 133, 193.

2. Marcus's observation regarding the French Tosafists as an example for the Jewish Renaissance of the twelfth century sits well with the martyrological dynamics described below. Marcus writes: "Although the degree to which each of these is a revival of ancient lore or an innovation has been hotly debated, I think that they are both. That is, the dynamic of revival and transformation which is claimed for Latin Christian culture in the twelfth century is exhibited in these cases as well. The German-Jewish examples look and claim to be conservative in focus, and they are,

but they are also adaptations of older material in a new setting, within Christian Europe." "The Dynamics of Jewish Renaissance and Renewal in the Twelfth Century," in *Jews and Christians in Twelfth-Century Europe*, 35.

3. Again, *Bet ha-Midrash*, 2:64–72.
4. Version B in *Bet ha-Midrash*, 6:27. This description is missing in version C, *Bet ha-Midrash* 6:34.
5. *Sefer Gezerot*, 32; Eidelberg, 33; Chazan, *European Jewry*, 256. The *Anonymous, Sefer Gezerot*, 99; Eidelberg, 108; Chazan, *European Jewry*, 235. In other places in the chronicles the authors paraphrased the phrase. For example, *Sefer Gezerot*, 55; Eidelberg, 65; Chazan, *European Jewry*, 291.
6. *Sefer Gezerot*, 48; Eidelberg, 56; Chazan, *European Jewry*, 281. Recall that Song of Songs 1:3 was already used with a martyrological meaning in *Mekhilta de-Rabbi Ishmael, de-Shira* 3, (Horowitz-Rabin edition), 127. On the verse of Song of Songs 1:3 and its mystical and martyrological meaning, see Abraham ben Azriel, *Arugat ha-Bosem*, ed. E. E. Urbach (Jerusalem, 1939–1963), 4:49; M. Fishbane, *The Kiss of God: Spiritual and Mystical Death in Judaism* (Seattle and London, 1994), 14–18, 25–35, and especially 61–62 and n. 16. On the exegetical construction and mystical meaning of R. Solomon bar Simson's chronicle, see 71–74.
7. See Wolfson, "Martyrdom, Eroticism, and Asceticism in Twelfth-Century Ashkenazi Piety," 173.
8. *Sefer Gezerot*, 31; Eidelberg, 32; Chazan, *European Jewry*, 255. *Sefer Gezerot*, 75; Eidelberg, 82. *Sefer Gezerot*, 50; Eidelberg, 58; Chazan, *European Jewry*, 283. *Sefer Gezerot*, 52; Eidelberg, 60–61; Chazan, *European Jewry*, 286. *Sefer Gezerot*, 82; Eidelberg, 93.
9. *Sefer Gezerot*, 48; Eidelberg, 56; Chazan, *European Jewry*, 281.
10. Shemaryah, *Sefer Gezerot*, 51; Eidelberg, 60; Chazan, *European Jewry*, 285.
11. *Sefer Gezerot*, 37; Eidelberg, 40; Chazan, *European Jewry*, 264.
12. *Sefer Gezerot*, 47; Eidelberg, 54; Chazan, *European Jewry*, 279. For the geographic location of *Ilana* see, Eidelberg's and Chazan's notes.
13. *Sefer Gezerot*, 104; Eidelberg, 115; Chazan, *European Jewry*, 242.
14. In the spirit of John 3.2, "We shall see Him as He is," *City of God*, 22.30; *PL*, 41:802–804.
15. This statement is reminiscent of R. Akiva's martyrological statement (Ber. 61b), which will be echoed repeatedly in the Hebrew narratives of 1096. It is not necessary to assume that Anselm relied on Akiva's martyrological statement of divine love, for he could have been quoting from Matt. 22.37, Luke 10.27, or Mark 12.30. This is one more example that illustrates the difficult task of tracing cultural influences.
16. Peter Tudebode, *Historia*, 69. William was one of the four Frenchmen under the command of Emicho, who were involved in the massacres of the Ashkenazic Jews. Golb, *The Jews of Medieval Normandy*, 124.
17. Peter Tudebode, *Historia*, 79–81.
18. *Historia Hierosolymitana*, Prologue, 3.
19. Raymond of Aguilers, *Historia Francorum qui ceperunt Iherusalem* in *Le Liber De Raymond D'Aguiler*, publié par John Hugh Hill et Laurita Hill (Paris, 1969), 138.
20. Before the First Crusade, one of the strongest advocates of the message of self-sacrifice for God and Christians was Pope Gregory VII. Following his predecessors John VIII, Leo IV, and Leo IX, Gregory attempted to launch his own campaign against the enemies of Christendom. Like Urban after him, Gregory viewed death for Jesus and the country as noble. Additionally, he presented dying for others as a

divine command. It was "the example of our Redeemer and the bond of fraternal love which command that we ought to lay down our lives to deliver" the Christians of the East. Gregory found support in 1 John 3:16: "Because he [Christ] laid down his life for us we ought to lay down our lives for the brethren."

21. Baldric of Dol, *RHC Oc.*, 4:12–16.

22. Translation in Peters, *The First Crusade*, 46.

23. Hagenmeyer, *Die Kreuzzugsbriefe*, 137–138.

24. Translation in Peters, *The First Crusade*, 46.

25. *Sefer Gezerot*, 35; Eidelberg, 37; Chazan, *European Jewry*, 261.

26. *Sefer Gezerot*, 49–50; Eidelberg, 58; Chazan, *European Jewry*, 283. This phenomenon is reminiscent of the Christian martyrs' movement in ninth-century Muslim Cordova (see again Chapter 4). The first and most zealous martyrs were individuals of mixed marriages and Christians who had converted to Islam and wished to return to their original creed through martyrdom. They too felt compelled to confirm and demonstrate their Christian identity. This kind of voluntary death coincided with the Augustinian principle that even the unbaptized should be considered Christian when perishing by martyrdom for a Christian cause. E. Malone, *The Monk and the Martyr* (Washington, DC, 1950), 1. In the medieval Franco-German environment, the Augustinian principle that martyrdom substitutes for baptism was recalled in the eleventh century by Bonzino of Sutri in *Liber de vita christiana*. Cowdrey, "Martyrdom and the First Crusade," 54 n. 3.

27. Jacob's claim that he was not fully accepted by his community because he was a convert, and the question of the convert from Xanten, shed more light on the status of converts and their feelings in the Ashkenazic society.

28. *Sefer Gezerot*, 42; Eidelberg, 47; Chazan, *European Jewry*, 271; emphasis mine.

29. *Sefer Gezerot*, 45; Eidelberg, 51; Chazan, *European Jewry*, 276–267; emphasis mine.

30. *Gesta Francorum*, 64–65; emphasis mine. Also reported by Peter Tudebode, 106–107.

31. *Gesta Francorum*, 64 n. 1.

32. Quoted from M. Bishop, *The Middle Ages* (Boston, 1987), 77.

33. F. Gies, *The Knight in History* (New York, 1987), 21–46.

34. Baldric of Dol, *RHC Oc.*, 4:16. Translation in Peters, *The First Crusade*, 32; emphasis mine.

35. Peter Tudebodes, *Historia*, 68–69. See also 107 for similar references to betrayal.

36. Peter Tudebode, *Historia*, 67.

37. R. Somerville, *The Councils of Urban II, Vol. 1: Decreta Claromontensia* (Amsterdam, 1972), 74. L. and J. Riley-Smith, *The Crusades: Idea and Reality, 1095–1274* (London, 1981), 39–40. Also in Peters, *The First Crusade*, 44–45. Similarly, in Baldric of Dol's version, crusaders should offer themselves "to Him as a living sacrifice." *RHC Oc.* 4:12–16.

38. *Sefer Gezerot*, 29–30; Eidelberg, 28–30; Chazan, *European Jewry*, 251–252.

39. Ekkehard of Aura in *MGH, Scrip.*, 6:208; Annales Wirziburgenses in *MGH, Scrip.*, 2:246.

40. Again, not long before the attacks on the Jews, Pope Urban reminded the faithful that "it is better for you to die in battle than to behold the sorrows of your race and of your holy places." Baldric of Dol, *RHC Oc.*, 4:16. The ideal of fighting unto death preceded the First Crusade. See below Vitalis' description of the self-destruction of defeated soldiers.

41. *Sefer Gezerot*, 31, 75; Eidelberg, 31–32; Chazan, *European Jewry*, 254.

42. Male fighters: *Sefer Gezerot*, 30, Eidelberg, 30; Chazan, *European Jewry*, 252; Female fighters: *Gezerot*, 31, 75; Eidelberg, 32; Chazan, *European Jewry*, 254–255.

43. *Sefer Gezerot*, 29–30; Eidelberg, 29; Chazan, *European Jewry*, 252.

44. The same terminology is used in the parallel description of the anonymous author. *Sefer Gezerot*, 99–100; Eidelberg, 108; Chazan, *European Jewry*, 235.

45. *Sefer Gezerot*, 99–100; Eidelberg, 108; Chazan, *European Jewry*, 235–236. See also, R. Solomon bar Simson's similar description of the incident. *Sefer Gezerot*, 30; Eidelberg, 32; Chazan, *European Jewry*, 252–253.

46. G. Kisch has suggested that Jews were legally permitted to carry weapons in self-defense and that they in fact did. *The Jews in Medieval Germany* (Chicago, 1949), 111–113, 121. Not so according to Schwarzfuchs, "France Under the Early Capets," 154 n. 21. He maintains that protecting the Jews was the responsibility of the feudal lord.

47. *Sefer Gezerot*, 44; Eidelberg, 50; Chazan, *European Jewry*, 274. R. Eliezer bar Nathan narrates the same story and adds that in addition, a woman acted in the same fashion. *Sefer Gezerot*, 77; Chazan, *European Jewry*, 274.

48. *Sefer Gezerot*, 96–97; Eidelberg, 103–105; Chazan, *European Jewry*, 229–231.

49. *Sefer Gezerot*, 97; Eidelberg, 104; Chazan, *European Jewry*, 231.

50. *Church History*, 6.41.22.

51. For other similarities to Eusebius, see Shepkaru, "Death Twice Over."

52. For instance, "Then also appeared from the mountains a countless host of men on white horses, whose banners were all white. . . . this was the succour sent by Christ, and that the leaders were St. George, St. Mercurius, and St. Demetrius." *Gesta Francorum*, 69.

53. *Sefer Gezerot*, 74; Eidelberg, 82.

54. On the influence of the 1096 events on *Hasidei Ashkenaz*, Marcus, "Hierarchies, Religious Boundaries and Jewish Spirituality in Medieval Germany," *Jewish History* 1:2 (Fall 1986), 17. The connection between 1096 and the rise of *Hasidei Ashkenaz* is still being debated. J. Dan, *The Esoteric Theology of Ashkenazi Hasidism* (Hebrew) (Jerusalem, 1968), 32–33; idem, "The Problem of Sanctification of the Name in the Speculative Teaching of the German *Hasidim*," in *Milhemet Qodesh u-Martirologiah* (Jerusalem, 1968), 121–129; Chazan, *European Jewry*, 143–144.

55. *Sefer Hasidim*, ed. J. Wistinetzki (Frankfort, 1924), no. 359. On *Sefer Hasidim*, see Scholem, *Major Trends*, 83; Y. Baer, "The Religious and Social Tendency of *Sefer Hasidim*" (Hebrew), *Zion* 3 (1938), 1–50, reprinted in *Studies in the History of the Jewish People* (Jerusalem, 1985), 175–224; I. G. Marcus, *Sefer Hasidim: MS. Parma H 3280* (Hebrew) (Jerusalem, 1985), 9–31. The complexity of the book is demonstrated by Marcus, "*Hasidei Ashkenaz* Private Penitentials: An Introduction and Descriptive Catalogue of their Manuscripts and Early Editions," in *Studies in Jewish Mysticism*, ed. J. Dan and F. Talmage (Cambridge, 1982), 57–84; the dating of the book is discussed by H. Soloveitchik, "Concerning the Date of *Sefer-Hasidim*" (Hebrew), in *Culture and Society in Medieval Jewry*, 383–388.

56. *Sefer Hasidim* (Bologna, 1538), par. 7. Quoted in full and discussed by Marcus, "Hierarchies, Religious Boundaries, and Jewish Spirituality," 17–18.

57. Tosafot Sukkah, 45a, s.v. *Miyad*. Urbach, *The Tosaphists: Their History, Writings and Methods* (Hebrew), 2 vols. (Jerusalem, 1986), 2:676–677.

58. Shepkaru, "From After Death to Afterlife"; idem, "To Die for God."

59. Another reason that the source is pre-1096.
60. Robert of Rheims, *Historia Hierosolimitana, RHC Oc.*, 3:727–728.
61. Baldric of Dol, *RHC Oc.*, 4:12–16. In Guibert of Nogent's version of Urban's speech, the pope promised crusaders "the glorious reward of martyrdom." *Gesta Dei per Francos, RHC Oc.*, 4:137–140.
62. "Epistula II Alexii I Komneni ad Oderisim I de Marsis abbatem Casinensem," in Heinrich Hagenmeyer, *Die Kreuzzugsbriefe aus den Jahren 1088–1100* (Innsbruck, 1901), p. 153. This is not the first time Alexius makes use of martyrdom. Martyrs play a role also in his epistle to Robert I of Flanders, Hagenmeyer, *Die Kreuzzugsbriefe*, 134.
63. In Luke 16.22, Lazarus "died and was carried by the angels into Abraham's bosom." Lazarus, however, was not a martyr.
64. Peter Tudebode, 116.
65. Peter Tudebode, 79–81. Similarly to the discrepancies found in the three Hebrew narratives, the *Gesta Francorum* omits the dialogue between Rainald and the emir, 3–4.
66. Shepkaru, "To Die for God," 319–320.
67. In the spirit of John 3.2, "We shall see Him as He is," and again Augustine's *City of God*, "There we shall rest and see, see and love, love and praise [God]." 22.30; *PL*, 41:802–804.
68. "Letter of Daimbert of Pisa, Godfrey of Bouillon, and Raymond of Saint Gilles, from the Land of Israel to the Pope," in Hagenmeyer, *Die Kreuzzugsbriefe*, p. 173.
69. *Sefer Gezerot*, 62. *Redumim*, literally "the sleeping ones," indicating their interim situation between slaughter and return to life. This notion nicely concurs with the phrase "Abraham's bosom" in Adhémar's story. He "fell asleep in the Lord (*obdormivit in Domino*), that is in the bosom of Abraham."
70. *Sefer Gezerot*, 48–49; Eidelberg, 56–57; Chazan, *European Jewry*, 281–282.
71. *Sefer Gezerot*, 87.
72. Eliezer bar Nathan, *Sefer Gezerot*, 74; Eidelberg, 82.
73. *Sefer Gezerot*, 55; Eidelberg, p. 65; Chazan, *European Jewry*, 291.
74. *Sefer Gezerot*, 52; Eidelberg, p. 61; Chazan, *European Jewry*, 287.
75. *Sefer Gezerot*, 25; Eidelberg, 22; Chazan, *European Jewry*, 244.
76. *Sefer Gezerot*, 31; Eidelberg, 31; Chazan, *European Jewry*, 254.
77. *Sefer Gezerot*, 42; Eidelberg, 47; Chazan, *European Jewry*, 271.
78. *Sefer Gezerot*, 37–38; Eidelberg, 40–41; Chazan, *European Jewry*, 263.
79. *Sefer Gezerot*, 37–38; Eidelberg, 40–41; Chazan, *European Jewry*, 264.
80. *Sefer Gezerot*, 31; Eidelberg, 31; Chazan, *European Jewry*, 253–254.
81. *Sefer Gezerot*, 31, 39; Eidelberg, 31, 43; Chazan, *European Jewry*, 254.
82. *Sefer Gezerot*, 45; Eidelberg, 51; Chazan, *European Jewry*, 276.
83. *Sefer Gezerot*, 96; Eidelberg, 103–104; Chazan, *European Jewry*, 230.
84. *Sefer Gezerot*, 47, Eidelberg, 54; Chazan, *European Jewry*, 279. Albert of Aix reports the attack on Cologne in *RHC Occ.* 4:292. For the attacks at Cologne, see Chazan, "The Deeds of the Jewish Community of Cologne," *Journal of Jewish Studies* 35 (1984), 185–195; idem, *European Jewry*, 74–75, 93–94.
85. Antiphons for the Feast of the Assumption of the Blessed Virgin Mary (August 15), at Vespers: from the Roman Mass. J. Campbell, *The Hero with a Thousand Faces* (Princeton, 1973), 120. The celebration of the divine maternity dates back

to fifth-century Armenia. After the Council of Ephesus (431) had defined the divine maternity, the feast and its liturgical commemoration became popular. In the seventh century, the feast and its liturgy were accepted at Rome as the feast of the Assumption. C. Bouman, "The Immaculate Conception in the Liturgy," in *The Dogma of the Immaculate Conception: History and Significance*, ed. E. D. O'Connor (Notre Dame, 1958), 113–159.

86. J. Baschet, "Medieval Abraham: Between Fleshly Patriarch and Divine Father," *Modern Language Notes*, 108 (1993), 738–758; D. H. Weiss, "Biblical History and Medieval Historiography: Rationalizing Strategies in Crusader Art," *Modern Language Notes*, 108 (1993), 710–737.

87. *Sefer Gezerot*, 45; Eidelberg, 51; Chazan, *European Jewry*, 276–277.

88. *Bet ha-Midrash*, 3:89 Also, B. *Berakhot* 10a: "As the Holy One, blessed be He, sees but cannot be seen." Also Midrash to Ps. 103.1; 217a: "The Holy One, blessed be He, sees the works of His hands but they cannot see Him." This is, of course, one of the Talmudic opinions.

89. *Sefer Gezerot*, 52; Eidelberg, 61; Chazan, *European Jewry*, 286.

90. More details in Shepkaru, "To Die for God," 330–332.

91. *Sefer Gezerot*, 48–49; Eidelberg, 56–57; Chazan, *European Jewry*, 281–282.

92. *Sefer Gezerot*, 48–49; Eidelberg, 56–57; Chazan, *European Jewry*, 281–282. Staying close to the medieval text, I deliberately left Isa. 64.3 unchanged and unpunctuated.

93. Translation in E. A. Petroff, *Medieval Women's Visionary Literature* (New York, Oxford, 1986), 182.

94. For messianic expectation and revenge as the conclusion of the story, see especially, *Sefer Gezerot*, 50; Eidelberg, 58; Chazan, *European Jewry*, 283. The issue of messianic expectations in Ashkenaz received recently a great deal of attention thanks to Yuval's important studies, *"Two Nations in Your Womb"* and "Vengeance and Damnation, Blood and Defamation."

95. On the Jewish awareness of the role celestial Jerusalem had in crusade thinking, R. Chazan, "Jerusalem as Christian Symbol during the First Crusade: Jewish Awareness and Response," in *Jerusalem: Its Sanctity and Centrality to Judaism, Christianity, and Islam*, ed. L. I. Levin (New York, 1999), 382–392.

96. On language and polemics, A. S. Abulafia, "Invectives against Christianity in the Hebrew Chronicles of the First Crusade," in *Crusade and Settlement*, 66–72.

97. *Sefer Gezerot*, 103–104; Eidelberg, 114; Chazan, *European Jewry*, 241.

98. *Sefer Gezerot*, 38, 42; Eidelberg, 46; Chazan, *European Jewry*, 271, and *Sefer Gezerot*, 49; Eidelberg, 57; Chazan, *European Jewry*, 282, and also, *Sefer Gezerot*, 33, 100; Eidelberg, 109. In Worms, *Sefer Gezerot*, 74; Eidelberg, 81. In Speyer, *Sefer Gezerot*, 39; Eidelberg, 40; Chazan, *European Jewry*, 266.

99. Peter is quoted from Chazan, *Church, State, and Jew*, 246–247.

100. *Sefer Gezerot*, 51; Eidelberg, 60 and see there n. 184; Chazan, *European Jewry*, 285. Cohen finds other relevant Christological motifs that could be associated with Jesus' story. "The Hebrew Crusade Chronicles," pp. 26–27. "*Peger muvas*" is taken from Isaac 14:19. This is another example that demonstrates the use of Jewish and Christian motifs in their polemics.

101. *Sefer Gezerot*, 101; Eidelberg, 111; Chazan, *European Jewry*, 238.

102. *Sefer Gezerot*, 42; Eidelberg, 46–47; Chazan, *European Jewry*, 271.

103. *Sefer Gezerot*, 39; Eidelberg, 43; Chazan, *European Jewry*, 266–267.

104. *Sefer Gezerot*, 49; Eidelberg, 57–58; Chazan, *European Jewry*, 283.

105. Marcus, *Rituals of Childhood*, 12.
106. *Sefer Gezerot*, 45; Eidelberg, 51; Chazan, *European Jewry*, 275.
107. *Sefer Gezerot*, 77; Eidelberg, 86.
108. *Sefer Gezerot*, 45; Eidelberg, 52; Chazan, *European Jewry*, 276.
109. *Sefer Gezerot*, 45; Eidelberg, 52; Chazan, *European Jewry*, 276.
110. *Sefer Gezerot*, 46; Eidelberg, 53; Chazan, *European Jewry*, 277. The story is also narrated by Eliezer bar Nathan, who identifies the town as Wevelinghofen and adds to the list of those who died in the water the names of Rabbi Levi bar Samuel and all his family members, a woman named Rachel, and Rabbi Solomon the *Cohen*. As mentioned, Eliezer's version differs from Solomon bar Simson's version.
111. Orderic Vitalis, 4:205–207.
112. Fulcher of Chartres, *Historia Hierosolymitana*, 1.8.3. Raymond of Aguilers also reports a similar miracle of imprinted crosses, but not after drowning. *Historia*, 102.
113. *Sefer Gezerot*, 25; Eidelberg, 23, Chazan, *European Jewry*, 245.
114. *Sefer Gezerot*, 78 Eidelberg, 87.
115. As Marcus demonstrated, Ashkenazic children were taken to rivers during their schooling initiation rites. The immersion in water symbolized their immersion in Torah study. *Rituals of Childhood*, 81. See also the rest of Marcus's analysis, 7, 49, 71, and Chapter 5.
116. *Sefer Gezerot*, 52; Eidelberg, 61; Chazan, *European Jewry*, 286. The complete verse from Ps. 42:2 reads: "As the heart pants after the water brooks, so my soul pants after You, O God."
117. *Monumenta Germaniae Historica, Sc.* (Hanover, 1848), 8:190. See also Yuval, "Vengeance and Damnation, Blood and Defamation," 76 n. 149. We have seen another indication in Albert of Aix, *RHC Oc.* 4:293.
118. *Sefer Gezerot*, 56; Eidelberg, 67; Chazan, *European Jewry*, 293.
119. For the impact of these events on Jewish history and historiography, see Schwarzfuchs, "The Place of the Crusades in Jewish History" (Hebrew), 251–267; J. Cohen, "A 1096 Complex? Constructing the First Crusade in Jewish Historical Memory, Medieval and Modern," in *Jews and Christians in Twelfth-Century Europe*, 9–25.

CHAPTER 8: SINGING IN THE FIRE

1. For instance, see J. Katz, *Exclusiveness and Tolerance: Studies in Jewish–Gentile Relations in Medieval and Modern Times* (Oxford, 1961), 83–84.
2. As mentioned, a detailed discussion of the different Jewish reactions, including conversion, is provided by Chazan, *European Jewry*. Analyzing metaphors and symbols, J. Cohen and I have suggested recently that the problem of conversion runs deeper than the sources were ready to admit openly. "Between Martyrdom and Apostasy: Doubt and Self-Definition in Twelfth-Century Ashkenaz," *Journal of Medieval and Early Modern Studies* 29:3 (Fall 1999), 431–473; Shepkaru, "Death Twice Over."
3. I. J. Yuval, "Vengeance and Damnation, Blood and Defamation: From Jewish Martyrdom to Blood Libel Accusations"; idem, "*Two Nations in Your Womb*," to be further discussed below. To be clear, Yuval's important study focuses not only on the issue of libels. Although on this particular point Yuval and I do not see eye to eye, his extremely important research further stimulated mine.

4. J. Cohen believes "that the reclassification of the Jews, together with other enemies of the church, within a broader category of infidels or *heretics began during the twelfth century* [emphasis mine] to disempower the hermeneutically crafted Jew of patristic theology, depriving him of that singularity which distinguished him and underlay his worth. . . . The labeling of the Jews as heretics offers a good case in point." *Living Letters of the Law*, 159.

5. *Self and Society*, 211–213. Guibert's accusations against the Jews are discussed by J. M. Ziolkowski, "Put in No-Man's-Land: Guibert of Nogent's Accusations against a Judaizing and Jew-Supporting Christian," in *Jews and Christians in Twelfth-Century Europe*, 110–122.

6. *Self and Society*, 209–210. A Jew is also said to have offered his house for the count's adulterous affair with an old and ugly woman, which he pursued despite being married to a beautiful woman. Here again a Jew serves as a facilitator of evil and diabolism. *Self and Society*, 211.

7. *Sefer Gezerot*, 95; Eidelberg, 102; Chazan, 228. On the date of this event, see J. Hacker, "About the Persecutions during the First Crusade" (Hebrew), *Zion* 31 (1966), 227–229. Chazan is correct in rejecting H. Bresslau's suggestion that the story is of fourteenth-century provenance. *European Jewry*, 338 n. 38.

8. Yuval, "*Two Nations in Your Womb*," 195.

9. France, 82. Reports of cannibalism and inhuman savagery by starving crusaders surfaced also in their Latin accounts.

10. For example, the twelfth- or early thirteenth-century *Gesta Romanorum*, tale 13, describes a mother killing her daughter; tale 18 imparts Julian's killing of his parents; and tale 102 depicts the killing of a disloyal wife. *Gesta Romanorum: Entertaining Stories*, tr. by C. Swan (London, New York, 1925), 97–99; 114–116; 224–226.

11. According to Baldric of Dol, the pope compared the crusaders to the children of Israel who were led out of Egypt by divine force and "have taken that land [of Israel] by their arms, with Jesus as leader. They have driven out the Jebusites and other inhabitants and have themselves inhabited earthly Jerusalem, the image of celestial Jerusalem." *RHC Oc.*, 4:12–16.

12. *Gesta Francorum*, 2.

13. Similarly argued also by Marcus, "From 'Deus Vult' to the 'Will of the Creator'," 92–100.

14. Thomas Aquinas, *Selected Writings*, ed. and tr. with an introduction by R. McInerny (Penguin Classics, 1998), IX.

15. "*et ita denuo lotum atque aliis uestibus indutum transtulerunt illud in ecclesiam beati Stephani martyris.*" *Bede's Ecclesiastical History of the English People*, eds. B. Colgrave and R. A. B. Mynors (Oxford, 1969), 241.

16. M. H. King, *The Life of Christina of St-Trond by Thomas of Cantipré* (Saskatoon, 1986), 1–33.

17. Gregory of Tours, *Gloria Martyrium*, 100, followed by the thirteenth-century Jacobus de Voragine, *The Golden Legend: Readings on the Saints*, 2 vols., tr. by W. G. Ryan (Princeton, 1993), 2:87–88. Gregory of Tours, *Gloria Martyrium*, Book 1, Chapter 10. A translation by R. Van Dam is available. *Glory of the Martyrs* (Liverpool, 1988), 29–32.

18. Mentioned by M. Minty, "*Qiddush ha-Shem* in German Christian Eyes in the Middle Ages" (Hebrew), *Zion* 59 (1994), 209–266. Reference on 251 n. 161.

19. Baldric of Dol, *RHC Oc.*, 4:4, 23. On holy wars between Christians, see N. Housley, "Crusades Against Christians: Their Origins and Early Development, c. 1000–1216," *Crusade and Settlement*, 17–36.

20. A. S. Abulafia, "The Intellectual and Spiritual Quest for Christ and Central Medieval Persecution of Jews," in *Religious Violence between Christians and Jews*, 61–85. Abulafia writes: "it seems clear that by delving into the very heart of internal Christian thought and spirituality we have uncovered a rich reservoir of anti-Jewish thought that strongly implied that Jews, who had no intention of converting, had nothing positive to contribute to reforming Christian society," 80. As we shall see, this intellectual development will have devastating implications for the Jews. In her *Christians and Jews in the Twelfth-Century Renaissance* (London, New York, 1995), 73, 78, Abulafia argues that the exclusion of Jews started in the same century. Of course, there were also positive developments in the twelfth century. I. G. Marcus, "The Dynamics of the Jewish Renaissance and Renewal in the Twelfth Century," in *Jews and Christians in Twelfth-Century Europe*, 27–45.

21. See again, Shepkaru, "Death Twice Over;" Cohen, "The Hebrew Crusade Chronicles in Their Christian Cultural Context."

22. A. Haverkamp, "Baptised Jews in German Lands during the Twelfth Century," in *Jews and Christians in Twelfth-Century Europe*, 293 n. 47, and the reference there to E. Haverkamp's Ph.D. dissertation.

23. *MGH, Script.*, 2:246; 8:190–1.

24. Aronius, *Regesten*, n. 188; 202; 218.

25. Aronius, *Regesten*, n. 204, and see *MGH, Script.*, 6:208. As A. Haverkamp has argued, the church distinguished between different types of forced converts to decide who should be allowed to return to Judaism. "Baptised Jews in German Lands during the Twelfth Century," 255–310, especially 260–267.

26. *Sefer Gezerot*, 56. Ephraim of Bonn regarded the return of converts as a divine "miracle." *Sefer Gezerot*, 122; Eidelberg, 131.

27. According to Rabbi Isaac ben Moses of Vienna, Rabbi Gershom mourned over his son's death for fourteen days, although he had converted to Christianity. *Or Zarua*, 2:176 n. 428. Rashi, too, mentioned Rabbi Gershom's ruling on converts, affirming that Rabbi Gershom "prohibited to mention the disgrace (of temporary conversion) not only to the culprits themselves who eventually returned to Judaism, but even to their descendants." Agus, *Urban Civilization*, 2:501; idem, "Rabbinic Scholarship in Northern Europe," in *The Dark Ages*, 205. Rashi also relied on the Talmudic dictum: "Even though he Sinned, he remains a Jew." J. Katz, "Even Though He Sinned, He Remains A Jew," *Tarbitz* 27 (1958), 204–217; Blumenkranz, "The Roman Church and the Jews," in *The Dark Ages*, 83.

28. *Sefer Hasidim*, ed. J. Wistinetzki, second ed. (Frankfort, 1924), 84, no. 357; 465; no. 1922. Urbach, *The Tosaphists*, 1:82–83, 244–245, 407.

29. J. M. Elukin, "The Discovery of the Self: Jews and Conversion in the Twelfth Century," in *Jews and Christians in Twelfth-Century Europe*, 63–76.

30. Otto of Freising, *Gesta Friderici*, 58.

31. Ekkehard of Aura in *MGH, Scrip.*, 6:208; Aronius, *Regesten*, ns. 206, 214, 218.

32. R. Chazan, "From the First Crusade to the Second: Evolving Perceptions of the Christian–Jewish Conflict," in *Jews and Christians in Twelfth-Century Europe*, 46–62, especially 59: "For Christians, this meant a growing sense of the Jews as immediate

enemies, poised to strike at any moment; for the Jews, this meant a heightened sense of contemporary confrontation. . . . "

33. *Sefer Gezerot*, 115–116; Eidelberg, 122.

34. For the Second Crusade and later twelfth-century incidents, see R. Chazan, "R. Ephraim of Bonn's *Sefer Zechirah*," *Revue des études juives* 132 (1973), 119–126, and his "Ephraim ben Jacob's Compilation of Twelfth-Century Persecutions," *Jewish Quarterly Review* 84 (1993–1994), 397–416.

35. *Sefer Gezerot*, 115; Eidelberg, 121. The name of Ashdod, a city in southern Israel, is a play on the word *pillage*. See Eidelberg, 171 n. 4, and 172 n. 5 for other plays on words.

36. *Sefer Gezerot*, 115.

37. Otto of Freising, *Gesta Frideric I Imperatoris*, ed. B. De Simson (Hanover, 1912), 58.

38. Bouquet, 15:606.

39. *Sefer Gezerot*, 116; Eidelberg, 122.

40. Bouquet, 15:606; Chazan, *European Jewry*, 174–178, and see there, n. 21.

41. Bouquet, 15:641–642. Peter's poisonous allegations against the Jews find explicit expression in his *Tractatus adversus Judeorum investeratam duritiem*, in *L. P.*, 189:507, 602.

42. *Sefer Gezerot*, 115–116; Eidelberg, 122.

43. *Sefer Gezerot*, 117; Eidelberg, 124.

44. J. Riley-Smith, "Christian Violence and the Crusades," in *Religious Violence between Christians and Jews*, 3–20.

45. Otto of Freising, *Gesta Frideric*, 58.

46. *Sefer Gezerot*, 121; Eidelberg, 131. C. Roth, *History of the Jews in England* (Oxford, 1942), 10.

47. *Sefer Gezerot*, 118; Eidelberg, 127.

48. We have seen other plays on the words "Ashdod" and "Rudlfe," as is the case with the Israeli city Hadarah, which intended to convey fear *(haradah)*. *Sefer Gezerot*, 115; Eidelberg, 121.

49. *Sefer Gezerot*, 117; Eidelberg, 124.

50. *Sefer Gezerot*, 118; Eidelberg, 125.

51. *Sefer Gezerot*, 117; Eidelberg, 124.

52. *Sefer Gezerot*, 118.

53. *Annales Herbipolenses, MGH, Script.* (Hanover, 1859), 16:3.

54. *Sefer Gezerot*, 116; Eidelberg, 123.

55. *Sefer Gezerot*, 119; Eidelberg, 127.

56. *Sefer Gezerot*, 44. R. Eliezer bar Nathan narrated the same story about Isaac, but did not provides his father's name. *Sefer Gezerot*, 77; Chazan, *European Jewry*, 274.

57. The Latin *Annales Herbipolenses, MGH Script.*, 16:3 corroborates Ephraim's report.

58. *Sefer Gezerot*, 119; Eidelberg, 127–128.

59. *Sefer Gezerot*, 119; Eidelberg, 127.

60. *Sefer Gezerot*, 130–131.

61. *Sefer Gezerot*, 131.

62. *Sefer Gezerot*, 132.

63. *Sefer Gezerot*, 163. On imperial protection during the Third Crusade, see R. Chazan, "Emperor Frederick I, the Third Crusade, and the Jews," *Viator* 8 (1970), 83–93.

64. *Sefer Gezerot*, 164.

65. These places have not been convincingly identified yet. Ephraim's closing statement of the French section in his report – "As for the other French communities, we have not heard of any person being slain or forcibly converted at that time" – may indicate that the descriptions of the attacks on the three locales refer to events in France. But the previous description of events in Germany leaves the placement of these locales open. As mentioned, Otto of Freising confirms bloody anti-Jewish violence in Germany and France. Otto of Freising, *Gesta Friderici*, 58. Baron suggests that the names of the above-mentioned locales may have been misspelled and, therefore, can be read as Dreux, Saulieu, and Courson. *Social and Religious History*, 5:119–120, especially n. 39.

66. *Sefer Gezerot*, 120; Eidelberg, 128–129.

67. *Sefer Gezerot*, 120; Eidelberg, 129.

68. *Sefer Gezerot*, 123; Eidelberg, 132; [emphasis mine]. Eliezer Bar Nathan, *Sefer Gezerot*, 82; Eidelberg, 92.

69. Bouquet, 15:641. Other letters also exhibit the frequent use of the notion of martyrdom and the adoration of "the tombs of the precious martyrs." *The Letters of Peter the Venerable*, ed. G. Constable, 2 vols. (Cambridge, 1967), 1:23, 237, 300.

70. Bernard of Clairvaux, "To the English People," tr. B. S. James in *The Letters of St. Bernard of Clairvaux* (Chicago, 1953), 462. Also see Bernard's elaborate discussion on the Christian martyrs and the commemoration of the "martyrdom" of the Maccabees, 144–147.

71. *MGH, Script.*, 16:3.

72. B. *Sanhedrin* 49a, Deuteronomy 21:23. Ephraim refers here to the defeated crusaders of the disastrous Second Crusade.

73. *Sefer Gezerot*, 122; Eidelberg, 132. The reference here is to Ps. 44:23 and Midrash Sifre Deuteronomy, *Va'ethanan* 32. Ephraim's Spanish contemporary, R. Judah ha-Levi, also acknowledged in *The Kuzari* his awareness of martyrdom and the popularity of the concept among Christian and Muslims, who

fight with one another, each of them serving his God with pure intention ... committing murders, believing that this is a most pious work and brings them nearer to God. They fight with the belief that paradise and eternal bliss will be their reward.

Judah ha-Levi, The *Kuzari*, tr. by H. Hirschfeld (New York, 1964), part I, s. 2, 39.

74. Bernard of Clairvaux, *De Consideratione* 2, in Migne, *LP*, 182, 741. In this apologetic treatise, Bernard presents himself as a shield and a martyr, who protects God from the fire of the critics.

75. Musurillo, *The Acts of the Christian Martyrs*, 15. Jacques de Vitry uses the same image in *The Life of Marie d'Oignies*. After her death, her face had a "dove-like expression." Quoted in Petroff, *Medieval Women's Visionary Literature*, 183.

76. Petroff, *Medieval Women's Visionary Literature*, 182.

77. Petroff, *Medieval Women's Visionary Literature*, 119.

78. For other uses of the term *purpurin*, see Spiegel, *The Last Trial*, 26, Eidelberg, 179 n. 69. On the term's association with vengeance, Yuval, "*Two Nations in Your Womb*," 110–114. Yuval correctly points out that after 1096 the term assumed new meanings. For the Christian concept of divine vengeance and the punishment of the martyrs' offenders, see *Saints and their Cults: Studies in Religious Sociology, Folklore and History*, ed. S. Wilson (Cambridge, 1983), S. Wilson's introduction, 30–31.

79. A. Funkenstein, "Changes in the Patterns of Christian Anti-Jewish Polemics in the 12th Century" (Hebrew), *Zion* 33 (1968), 125–144; R. Chazan, *Daggers of Faith* (Berkeley, Los Angeles, London, 1989), 1, 12–13, 21–24.

80. The dead were buried outside the walls of the city.

81. *Sefer Gezerot*, 120–121; Eidelberg, 129–130. According to E. Urbach, R. Peter dwelled in Carinthia, Austria, and died in France. *The Tosaphists*, 1:223–224. R. Baruch of Worms counts R. Peter among the French Tosafists. *The Tosaphists*, 1:350. Baron, *Social and Religious History*, 5:300, n. 39.

82. Urbach, *The Tosaphists*, 1:223–225.

83. *Sefer Gezerot*, 121; Eidelberg, 130 [emphasis mine].

84. On the employment of the stigmata in Latin crusading accounts see, Shepkaru, "Martyrs' Heaven," 322.

85. Adding to this dilemma is G. Nahon's citation of R. Tam that " 'the children of Esau [that is, the Christians] respect Israel more than all the nations' (*Sefer ha-Yashar, Novellae* 196, 130)." "From the Rue aux Juifs to the Chemin du Roy: The Classical Age of French Jewry, 1180–1223," in *Jews and Christians in Twelfth-Century Europe*, 322.

86. *Sefer Gezerot*, 124–126; 142–146.

87. By that time similar accusations were already circulating in France. King Louis VII dismissed accusations of Jewish murder in Pontoise, Janville, and Epernay. Habermann, *Gezerot*, 145–146; Rigord, *Gesta Philippi Augusti*, in Bouquet, 17:5–6; Lamber Waterlos, *Chronica*, in Bouquet, 13:520; Gaufredi Vosiensis, *Chronicon*, in Bouquet, 12:438.

88. On her association with moneylenders, S. Einbinder, "Pucellina of Blois: Romantic Myths and Narrative Conventions," Jewish History 12.1 (1998), 29–46; idem, *Beautiful Death*, 47.

89. *Sefer Gezerot*, 144.

90. In a different version the number of dead amounted to thirty-two. For a fuller analysis of these developments, see S. Spiegel, "In Monte Dominus Videbitur: The Martyrs of Blois and the Renewal of the Accusations of Ritual Murder" (Hebrew), *The Mordecai M. Kaplan Jubilee* (Hebrew vol.), 267–287, especially 275–276; R. Chazan, "The Blois Incident of 1171: A Study in Jewish Intercommunal Organization," *Proceedings of the American for Jewish Research* 36 (1968), 13–31; idem, *Medieval Jewry in Northern France*, 32–61.

91. *Sefer Gezerot*, 125. The Jews consulted among themselves and with friendly neighbors as to the right sum of protection money. It was decided by all that this sum would satisfy the governor, Theobald, indicating that the amount offered was not a gross miscalculation on the part of the Jews. In other words, there is room to suggest that money or other forms of payment could not have saved the Jews of Blois in this particular conflict.

92. Only a small number of Jews was temporarily imprisoned or forced to convert. W. C. Jordan, *The French Monarchy and the Jews: From Philip Augustus to the Last Capetians* (Philadelphia, 1989), 18–19.

93. On the sources, see Chazan, "The Blois Incident," 18–21; on the poetry and its emphasis, see Einbinder, *Beautiful Death*, 27–30, 50–64; idem, "The Jewish Martyrs of Blois, 1171," in *Medieval Hagiography: A Sourcebook*, ed. T. Head (New York, London, 2000), 537–560.

94. *Sefer Gezerot*, 125.
95. "The fire cannot control us, why should not we come out [of the fire]." *Sefer Gezerot*, 125.
96. Hrotsvit of Gandersheim has her heroine, Karitas, thrown into a "glowing red-hot" furnace. "Playfully she walked among the flames-spewing vapors, quite unhurt,/ and sang hymns in praise of her God." *The Dramas of Hrotsvit of Gandersheim*, tr. and with an introduction by K. M. Wilson (Saskatoon, 1985), 128.
97. Musurillo, *The Acts of the Christian Martyrs*, 15.
98. *Vita SS. Rodulphi et Dominic Loricati, PL*, 144:1020. Translation in D. Robertson, *The Medieval Saints' Lives: Spiritual Renewal and Older French Literature* (Lexington, 1995), 19. I have slightly altered the translation.
99. Jacobus de Voragine, *The Golden Legend*, 1 :387. Bede reported that a bishop entered his burning church to stop the fire just by standing there. Because the fire would not consume his holy body, the church was saved from the fire. *Bede's Ecclesiastical History of the English People*, 158.
100. King, *The Life of Christina of St-Trond*, 1–33.
101. Robertson, *The Medieval Saints' Lives*, 18, 45, 55, 71.
102. *Sefer Gezerot*, 144; for 1096, see again *Sefer Gezerot*, 27; Eidelberg, 26; Chazan, 248. "Satan also came," Job 2:1.
103. *Sefer Gezerot*, 142.
104. *Sefer Gezerot*, 143.
105. *Sefer Gezerot*, 38; Eidelberg, 41.
106. I. Elbogen, *Jewish Liturgy: A Comprehensive History*, ed. by J. Heinemann, tr. by R. P. Scheindlin (Philadelphia, New York, Jerusalem, 1993), 71. To be further discussed in the next chapter.
107. *Saints and their Cults*, 29–30.
108. Yuval, "*Two Nations in Your Womb*," 212; idem, "The Language and Symbols of the Hebrew Chronicles of the Crusades," 111–115; see also, I. Ta-Shma, "The Source and Place of the Prayer '*aleinu le-shabeah*" (Hebrew), *Frank Talmage Memorial Volume*, ed. B. Walfish (Haifa, 1993), 1 :85–88 (Hebrew section).
109. *Sefer Gezerot*, 144.
110. Another indication is the emphasis on the word *qaddosh* (holy or saint) on tombstones and in the Hebrew literature of the period. Jordan, *The French Monarchy and the Jews*, 20–22.
111. Chazan, *Medieval Jewry*, 49; idem, "The Bray Incident of 1192: Realpolitik and Folk Slander," *Proceedings of the American for Jewish Research* 37 (1969), 1–18.
112. This incident is reported by Ephraim ben Jacob of Bonn, *Sefer Gezerot*, 128, and corroborated by the anonymous chronicler of Laon, in Bouquet, 18:707; by Rigord's *Gesta Philippi Augusti*, in Bouquet, 17:6. Chazan, "The Bray Incident of 1192," idem, *Medieval Jewry in Northern France*, 69–70, 93–94. Chazan has Bray-sur-Seine, but Jordan suggests Brie-Comte-Robert. Jordan, *The French Monarchy and the Jews*, 35–37, especially, 271 n. 80.
113. Philip Augustus, "the most Christian king" in the words of his biographer, Rigord, often showed his dislike in actions against the Jews. Bouquet, 17:6, 25.
114. According to the anonymous chronicler of Laon, the number of slain reached ninety-nine. Bouquet, 18:707. Jordan designates the man, "one of his [the king's] dependents." *The French Monarchy and the Jews*, 270 n. 77.

115. Perhaps for this reason, Ephraim does not indicate active martyrdom in these two cases. In Jordan's opinion, "Philip exacted vengeance." *The French Monarchy and the Jews*, 36.
116. For a fuller discussion of Philip's political struggle, Chazan, *Medieval Jewry*, 68–70.
117. *Sefer Gezerot*, 126.
118. *Sefer Gezerot*, 133–136. Hillel's poem, *Gezerot*, 137–141.
119. According to H. Soloveitchik, the book's *terminus ad quem* is no later than the first quarter of the thirteenth century. "Concerning the Date of *Sefer Hasidim*," in *Culture and Society in Medieval Jewry*, 383–388.
120. *Sefer Hasidim* (Wistinetzki, second ed.), 82 no. 247, 84 no. 257, 253 no. 1013, 254 no. 1017, 449 no. 1862. Maimonides discusses these issues in "The Epistle on Martyrdom." Maimonides, in his clear and direct style, urges the reader to distinguish between real persecutions and potential persecutions. Moreover, he advises that even in real persecutions one should try to escape the test rather than submit to death, which is always an undesirable and a "foreign act" in his mind. "The Epistle on Martyrdom" in A. Halkin and D. Hartman, *Epistles of Maimonides: Crisis And Leadership* (Philadelphia and Jerusalem, 1993), 14–34.
121. *Sefer Hasidim* (Wistinetzki, second ed.), 85 nos. 261, 262. See also *Sefer Hasidim*, ed. R. Margaliot (Jerusalem, 1957), 438 nos. 702–703.
122. *Sefer Hasidim* (Wistinetzki, second ed.), 85 no. 259; *Sefer Hasidim*, ed. Margaliot, 191 no. 200, 192 no. 201.
123. *Sefer Hasidim* (ed. Wistinetzki), 465, no. 1922. See also *Sefer Hasidim* (ed. Margaliot), 190, no. 197; 192, no. 202.
124. *Sefer Hasidim* (ed. Margaliot), 192 no. 202.
125. *Sefer Hasidim* (ed. Wistinetzki), 428 no. 1798.
126. *Sefer Hasidim* (ed. Wistinetzki), 85 no. 258.
127. *Sefer Hasidim* (ed.Wistinetzki), 449 no. 1862. Translation in Chazan, *European Jewry*, 143–144.
128. As noted by J. Dan, "The Problem of Sanctification of the Name in the Speculative Teaching of the German *Hasidim*" (Hebrew) in *Milhemet Kodesh u-Martyrologiah* (Jerusalem, 1967), 121–129; reprinted in *The Religious and Social Ideas of the Jewish Pietists in Medieval Germany*, 207–215. R. Chazan finds similar motifs in the 1096 sources and works of the German Hasidim. "The Early Developments of *Hasidut Ashkenaz*," *Jewish Quarterly Review* 75:3 (January 1985), 199–211.
129. *Sefer Hasidim* (ed. Margaliot), 161 no. 158.
130. *Sefer Hasidim* (ed. Margaliot), 436 n. 698. See the same example in *Bet ha-Midrash*, 6, in the story of the Ten Martyrs. See also the same advice for women, *Sefer Hasidim*, 436 n. 699.
131. *Sefer Hasidim* (ed. Margaliot), 437 n. 700. See the examples from B. *Sanhedrin* 74a, *Eruvin* 96a–b, and *Bereshit Rabba* 82:8 in Chapter 3.
132. *Sefer Hasidim* (ed. Margaliot), 191 n. 199 and again 191–192 nn. 200–201, 438 nn. 702–703.
133. Another example is the story of the Jewish woman who refused to let a Christian woman cure her son with a magical stone that had been taken from Jesus' grave. J. Shatzmiller, "Doctors and Medical Practice in Germany around the Year 1200: The Evidence of *Sefer Hasidim*," *Journal of Jewish Studies* 33 (1982), 583–593, especially

588, 593. The example resembles the Talmudic story about the dying Ben Dama (B. *Avodah Zarah* 27b). See again Chapter 3.

134. *Sefer Hasidim* (ed. Margaliot), 436 n. 697.

135. *Sefer Hasidim* (ed. Margaliot), 192–193 n. 203.

136. See the cases discussed in Jacob Tam's *Sefer ha-Yashar* (Berlin, 1898), 43–46. See also, Jacob Tam's statement in Isaac b. Moses's *Or Zarua*, 2:174–176 n. 428. Urbach, *The Tosaphists*, 1:82–83, 112.

137. See H. Soloveitchik, "Three Themes in *Sefer Hasidim*," *Association for Jewish Studies Review* 1 (1976), 325–339; Marcus, *Piety and Society*, 106–192; idem, "The Politics and Ethics of Pietism in Judaism: The Hasidim of Medieval Germany," *The Journal of Religious Ethics*, 8:2 (1980), 227–258; reprinted in Hebrew in *The Religious and Social Ideas of the Jewish Pietist in Medieval Germany*, 253–278, especially 261, where Marcus admonishes to treat *Sefer Hasidim* cautiously when reconstructing the social history of Ashkenazic Jews.

138. More generally on the dialectical differences between the Pietists and the Tosafists, E. Kanarfogel, *Jewish Education and Society in the High Middle Ages* (Detroit, 1993), 71–72.

139. According to Soloveitchik, "the striking formulation of the Tosafot (*A.Z.* 18a) ... might be suspected as being a later heightening of a more measured formulation by possibly the greatest talmudist of the time." "Religious Law and Change," 210 n. 8. Stow reminds us that "Even the *tosafot* of Jacob Tam and Isaac of Dampierre, both of whom are often cited by name, are in their present form reworked and revised versions of the originals." *Alienated Minority*, 148.

140. In Grossman's opinion, the Ashkenazic Jews relied on Aggadic material to support their decisions. "The Roots of *Qiddush ha-Shem*," followed by I. Ta-Shma, "The Attitude of Medieval German Halakhists to Aggadic Sources" (Hebrew), in *Facing the Cross*, 150–156. Cf. Soloveitchik, "Religious Law and Change."

141. *Avodah Zarah* 18a, s. v. *ve-al yehabel atzmo*; Urbach, *The Tosaphists*, 2:112; Chazan, *European Jewry*, 156. Surprisingly, Resh Lakish's view that "the words of Torah are firmly held by one who kills himself (*memit atzmo*) for it" (B. *Berakhot* 63b) was never understood as a justification for self-killing. See again Chapter 3 above.

142. *Daat Zekanim me-Rabbenu Baalei ha-Tosafot*, ed. I. J. Nunez-Vaez (Livorno, 1783), to Gen. 9:5, s.v. *ve-akh*. See also *Sefer ha-Yashar*, 42.

143. H. Soloveitchik, "Catastrophe and Halakhic Creativity: Ashkenaz – 1096, 1242, 1306 and 1298," *Jewish History* 12:1 (1998), 74; Urbach, *The Tosaphists*, 1:253.

144. *Tosafot al Massekhet Avodah Zarah le-Rabbenu Elhanan*, ed. D. Fränkel (Husatyn, 1901), to *Avodah Zarah*, 18a, s.v. *mutav sheyitlenu*.

145. *Yam shel Shlomoh, Bava Qama* 8:59. But see Soloveitchik's comment, "Religious Law and Change," 210 n. 8. On the Ri, Urbach, *The Tosaphists*, 1:227–253.

146. *Sefer Tosafot ha-Shalem: Commentary on the Bible*, ed. J. Gellis (Jerusalem, 1982), 1:262.

147. *Daat Zekenim*, to Gen. 9:5, s.v. *ve-akh*.

148. *Or Zarua*, 2:176 n. 428.

149. As Soloveitchik pointed out, the Ritva concluded that Jacob Tam permitted the killing of children. *Gilyonei Tosafot in Hidushei ha-Ritva al Avodah Zarah* (Jerusalem, 1978), 18a, s.v. *ha*. But the concluding remarks that would support Ritva's opinion

in *Gilyonei Tosafot* "would appear to be those of the *Gilyonei Tosafot*." Soloveitchik, "Religious Law and Change," 210 n. 8. See again, *Sefer Tosafot ha-Shalem*, 1:262–263.

150. On the Jewish perception of Christians in France, see Jordan's analysis of Dinah's exegesis. *The French Monarchy and the Jews*, 11–14. A. Grabois also noticed this deterioration. "Les juifs et leurs seigneurs dans la France Septentrionale aux Xie et XIIe siècles," in *Les Juifs Dans L'Histoire de France*, ed. M. Yardeni (Leiden, 1980), 11–23, especially, 23.

151. This conclusion coincides with the more general picture, which depicts the academies of French Jewry as the leading institutions of learning and spiritual guidance of all northern Europe in the late twelfth and early thirteenth centuries. On the Tosafists in England, see Urbach, *The Tosaphists*, 2:493–520. Chazan, *Medieval Jewry in Northern France*, 96. Ephraim of Bonn mentions in his report one more incident of martyrdom before entering into the description of events related to the Third Crusade. The report mentions only the death of Rabbi Judah b. Menahem.

152. *Sefer Gezerot*, 126.

153. D. Wachtel, "The Ritual and Liturgical Commemoration of Two Medieval Persecutions," Master's thesis (Columbia University, 1995), 9–14. The Chmielnitzki massacre is discussed in the conclusion below. E. Zimmer also expressed doubts with respect to Blois. "The Persecutions of 1096 as Reflected in Medieval and Modern Minhag Books," 161.

154. Jordan, *The French Monarchy and the Jews*, 20.

155. *Sefer Gezerot*, 121. Eidelberg, 132. Roth, *The History of the Jews in England*, 10.

156. The best-known sources that describe the events in England are in Latin, not Hebrew. Roger of Hoveden, *Chronica, in Rerum Britannicarum Medii Aevi Scriptores*, ed. W. Stubbs, (London and Oxford, 1870), 3:14; J. Jacobs, *The Jews of Angevin England* (London, 1983), 105–106; Richard of Devizis, *Chronicon Ricardi Divisensis de Regis Gestis Ricardi Primi*, ed. J. T. Appleby (London, Edinburgh et al., 1963), 3–4. English translation in Jacobs, *The Jews of Angevin England*, 133–134; Roth, A *History of the Jews of England*, 19–20.

157. Jacobs, *The Jews of Angevin England*, 106.

158. The most detailed source is of William of Newbury, *Historia Rerum Anglicarum*, ed. H. C. Hamilton, 2 vols. (London, 1856), 2:3. English translation by Jacobs, *The Jews of Angevin England*, 102. Robert of Gloucester describes these events in a poem translated by Jacobs, The *Jews of Angevin England*, 106–107.

159. Ephraim ben Jacob of Bonn, in *Sefer Gezerot*, 127. The events are mentioned also in Menahem bar Jacob's poem, *Alelai li* (Woe unto me), in *Sefer Gezerot*, 147, and in Joseph bar Asher of Chartres, *Eloh'im B'alunu*, *Sefer Gezerot*, 152; Roth, *A History of the Jews in England*, 19.

160. *Sefer Gezerot*, 127.

161. William of Newbury, *Historia Rerum Anglicarum*, 2:15–16; Jacobs, *The Jews of Angevin England*, 113–114.

162. Ralph of Diceto, *Imagines Historiarum, in Rerum Britannicarum Medii Eavi Scriptores*, ed. W. Stubbs, 2 vols. (London, 1876), 2:75–78; Jacobs, *The Jews of Angevin England*, 112.

163. Ralph of Diceto, *Imagines Historiarum*, 2:75–78; Jacobs, *The Jews of Angevin England*, 112.

164. William of Newbury, *Historia Rerum Anglicarum*, 2:17–18. Jacobs, *The Jews of Angevin England*, 115–116.
165. Ralph of Diceto, 2:78; Jacobs, *The Jews of Angevin England*, 112.
166. Ralph of Diceto, 2:78; Jacobs, *The Jews of Angevin England*, 113.
167. William of Newbury, *Historia Rerum Anglicarum*, 2:21–22; Jacobs, *The Jews of Angevin England*, 120. From this passage it is understood that some Jews escaped death by conversion. They accepted baptism only "as a matter of pretense" to return to Judaism. Rabbi Elijah and his followers, however, rejected even the tactic of temporary conversion. For R. Elijah, see Jacobs, 116, and the discussion below.
168. Jacobs, *The Jews of Angevin England*, 121.
169. Jacobs, *The Jews of Angevin England*, 121–122.
170. In 1120, St. Norbert has established the Premonstratensian order of Canons Regular at Premontre near Laon.
171. William of Newbury, *Historia Rerum Anglicarum*, 2:24–26; Jacobs, *The Jews of Angevin England*, 124.
172. William of Newbury, *Historia Rerum Anglicarum*, 2:25–26; Jacobs, *The Jews of Angevin England*, 125.
173. William of Newbury, *Historia Rerum Anglicarum*, 2:27; Jacobs, *The Jews of Angevin England*, 126.
174. But the great Aaron of York of the next century was Joce's son.
175. William of Newbury, *Historia Rerum Anglicarum*, 2:26; Jacobs, *The Jews of Angevin England*, 126–127.
176. Robert of Cricklade, the prior of Frideswide (ca. 1141–1180), purchased several Hebrew copies of *Sefer Yosippon* from the Jews of England in his search for the historical Jesus. C. Roth, *The Jews in Medieval Oxford* (Oxford, 1951), 121; Flusser, *Sefer Yosippon*, 2:58–59. Perhaps this mid-twelfth-century revelation of ancient Jews killing their own served as a catalyst in the spread of blood libels in England, which started to circulate around the same time. Surprisingly, the riots against English Jewry did not commence with libels, as was the case on the continent. If Jewish behavior indirectly contributed to these calumnies, it is astounding that in England, of all places, no libels were attached to the riots. We should recall that these libels are believed to have originated in England, where Jewish self-killing occurred more than in any other place in twelfth-century Europe.
177. William of Newbury, *Historia Rerum Anglicarum*, 2:27; Jacobs, *The Jews of Angevin England*, 127.
178. Jacobs, *The Jews of Angevin England*, 125
179. William of Newbury, *Historia Rerum Anglicarum*, 2:24–26; Jacobs, *The Jews of Angevin England*, 123, 124.
180. William of Newbury, *Historia Rerum Anglicarum*, 2:27; Jacobs, *The Jews of Angevin England*, 128.
181. William of Newbury, *Historia Rerum Anglicarum*, 2:25–26; Jacobs, *The Jews of Angevin England*, 128.
182. Jacobs, *The Jews of Angevin England*, 129.
183. J. Shatzmiller also sees greed and dislike of moneylenders as a motivation for collective violence. *Shylock Reconsidered: Jews, Moneylending, and Medieval Society* (Berkeley, Los Angeles, Oxford, 1990), 48–49.
184. *Sefer Gezerot*, 127.

185. Ralph of Diceto, 2:78; Jacobs, *The Jews of Angevin England*, 112.
186. *Sefer Gezerot*, 138–139.
187. H. Gross, *Gallia Judaica dictionnaire geographique de la France d'apres les sources rabbiniques* (Paris, 1897), 123; Chazan, *Medieval Jewry*, 93–94.
188. William of Newbury, *Historia Rerum Anglicarum*, 2:26; Jacobs, *The Jews of Angevin England*, 126.
189. *Sefer Gezerot*, 152–154.
190. *Sefer Gezerot*, 125; Urbach, *The Tosaphists*, 1:114, n. 1. As already mentioned, the martyr known as Rabbi Peter was also Jacob Tam's student; *Sefer Gezerot*, 120–121; Eidelberg, 129–130.
191. Urbach, *The Tosaphists*, 1:142–144.
192. Urbach, *The Tosaphists*, 1:144–146.
193. *Sefer Gezerot*, 145; Chazan, "The Blois Incident of 1171," 19.
194. I. Davidson, *Otzar ha-Shirah ve-ha-Piyyut* (New York, 1925–33), 4:398; Urbach, *The Tosaphists*, 1:146; Spiegel, "In Monte Dominus," 269.
195. William of Newbury, *Historia Rerum Anglicarum*, 2:26–27; Jacobs, *The Jews of Angevin England*, 127.
196. Another martyr of the school of Rabbi Jacob Tam is Rabbi Elijah of York, also known as "our holy Rabbi Elijah." Urbach, *The Tosaphists*, 2:496, 661.
197. William of Newbury, *Historia Rerum Anglicarum*, 2:25; Jacobs, *The Jews of Angevin England*, 124–125.

CHAPTER 9: FIRE FROM HEAVEN

1. S. Bernfeld, *Sefer ha-Demaot: Meoraot ha-Gezerot veha-Redifot ve-Hashmadot*, 3 vols. (1860–1940), 1:257.
2. *Sefer Gezerot*, 170, and 171 in R. Solomon bar Abraham's poem.
3. *Sefer Gezerot*, 171.
4. *Sefer ha-Demaot*, 1:265–266.
5. *Sefer Gezerot*, 168.
6. *Sefer Gezerot*, 172–175.
7. An observation made by G. Langmuir, *Toward a Definition of Antisemitism* (Berkeley and Los Angeles, 1990), 263–281. Blood libels are also reported in the Erfurter chronicle. *Annales Erphordenses*, in *MGH, Script.*, 16:31.
8. A. Darmesteter, "*L'Autodafé de Troyes* (24 avril 1288)," *Revue des études juives* 2 (1881), 199–247, especially 243–244; Chazan, *Medieval Jewry*, 181. According to G. Langmuir, until the Fulda libel, no ritual murder libels were reported in Germany. *Toward a Definition of Antisemitism*, 263–281. According to I. J. Yuval, "by 1187 there already existed suspicions in Germany that Jews did, in fact, commit ritual murder." " 'They Tell Lies: You Ate the Man': Jewish Reaction to Ritual Murder Accusations," in *Religious Violence between Christians and Jews*, 86–106, especially 89–90.
9. *Sefer Gezerot*, 173.
10. *Sefer Gezerot*, 172–175.
11. J. Shatzmiller has shown that the inquisition occasionally also acquitted Jews. But a very aggressive inquisition emerged in this period. "L' Inquisition et les juifs de Provence au XIIIe siècle," *Provence Historique* 23 (1973), 327–338, especially 331–332; Jordan, *The French Monarchy and the Jews*, 226.

12. *Sefer Gezerot,* 176–178.
13. Voluntary conversion was a growing problem. According to J. Shatzmiller, voluntary conversion reached its climax in the middle of the thirteenth century. "Jewish Converts to Christianity in Medieval Europe: 1200–1500," in *Cross-Cultural Convergences in the Crusader Period: Essay Presented to Aryeh Grabois on his Sixty-Fifth Birthday,* eds. M. Goodich, S. Menache, and S. Schein (New York, 1995), 297–318, especially 308, 316–317. As W. C. Jordan has suggested, voluntary conversion was a growing problem among young Jewish males. "Adolescence and Conversion in the Middle Ages: A Research Agenda," in *Jews and Christians in Twelfth-Century Europe,* 77–93. I. G. Marcus, "Jews and Christians Imagining the Other in Medieval Europe," *Prooftexts* 15 (1995), 222.
14. In 1236, Frederick II referred to the Jews as *servi camere.* The implications are discussed by G. I. Langmuir, "*Tanquam Servi*: The Change in Jewish Status in French Law about 1200," in *Les Juifs dans l'Histoire de France,* 25–54.
15. Translated by S. Grayzel, *The Church and the Jews in the XIIIth Century* (New York, 1965), 226–230; Runciman, *A History of the Crusades,* 3:195–217; Chazan, *Medieval Jewry,* 135–136. Similarly, see the epistle of Pope Innocent IV, in *MGH, Scrip.,* 409.
16. Solomon ibn Verga, *Shevet Yehudah,* ed. Azriel Shohet (Jerusalem, 1947), 147–148. Deadly riots against the Jews of Bretagne, Anjou, and Poitou in 1236 are also mentioned in the late *Chronicon Britannicum, REJ* 14, 85.
17. Isaac ben Moses, *Or Zarua,* ed. A. Lehrn, 4 vols. in 2 (Zhitomir, 1862), 2:40 n. 13. In general, Isaac believed that he was living in time of persecutions. 2:40 n.11. See also *Likut Rishonim for M. Erubin* (1992), 125. Also there: "If the Jews do not help [i.e., defend] themselves, they [the enemy] would kill them."
18. *Normanniae nova chronica,* ed. A. Cheruel (Caen, 1850), 23–24; Chazan, *Medieval Jewry,* 137.
19. As G. I. Langmuir has noted, around the same year, Jews became the targets of psychological rather than religious violence. By psychological violence, Langmuir means violence that was motivated by irrational fantasies of paranoid people. "At the Frontier of Faith," in *Religious Violence between Christians and Jews,* 153. A major contributor to these fantasies was the story of the young Hugh of Lincoln, which resulted in the execution of nineteen Jews by King Henry III. G. I. Langmuir, "The Knight's Tales of Young Hugh of Lincoln," *Speculum* 47 (1972), 459–482.
20. *Sefer Gezerot,* 186–190.
21. *Sefer Gezerot,* 191.
22. Darmesteter, "*L'Autodafé de Troyes*," 199–236. *Sefer Gezerot, 203–212;* Chazan, *Medieval Jewry, 179–81;* on the religious motifs, see idem, "*The Bray Incident of 1192,*" 9–14.
23. On these incidents, see J. Shatzmiller's excellent discussion in "The Albigensian Heresy as Reflected in the Eyes of Contemporary Jewry" (Hebrew), in *Culture and Society in Medieval Jewry,* 333–352. On Friar Pablo Christiani, J. Cohen, *The Friars and the Jews: The Evolution of Medieval Anti-Judaism* (Ithaca and London, 1982), 108–128; idem, *Living Letters of the Law,* 339–340. See also S. Shahar, "The Relationship between Kabbalism and Catharism in the South of France," in *Les Juifs dans l'Histoire de France,* 55–62.
24. A. Neubauer, "Literary Gleanings VIII," *Jewish Quarterly Review* (old series) 5 (1892–1893), 714. Quoted in Chazan, *Medieval Jewry,* 152, and see discussion there. Chazan

believes that the reference is to the Dominican Paul Christian. J. Shatzmiller cautiously argues that there are good chronological reasons to identify our Paul as Paul
Christian. "A Provencal Chronography in the Lost Account of Shem Tov Shantzulo"
(Hebrew), *Proceedings of the American Academy for Jewish Research* 52 (1985), 43–61,
especially 45–48; idem, "Paulus Christiani, un aspect de son activité anti-juive," *in*
Hommage à Georges Vajda, 203–217; *La Deuxième Controverse de Paris: Un Chapitre*
dans la polémique entre Chrétiens et Juifs au Moyen Âge, ed. J. Shatzmiller, Collection
de la *Revue des études juives* 15 (Paris, 1994), 15–22. See also R. Chazan, *Barcelona and*
Beyond: The Disputation of 1263 and Its Aftermath (Berkeley, Los Angeles, Oxford,
1992).

25. On the association of Judaism with heretics, see Cohen, *The Friars and the Jews*,
77–79, 91. Cf. Chazan, *Medieval Stereotypes*, 160–161.

26. Such attitudes would make the very participation in a polemical dispute a frightening
experience. D. Berger has noticed an elevated level of fear in the Jewish polemics
of the period. "Mission to the Jews and Jewish–Christian Contacts in the Polemical
Literature of the High Middle Ages," *American Historical Review* 91 (1986), 576–591.
On Jews as stubborn heretics, J. Cohen, "The Jews as the Killers of Christ in the Latin
Tradition, from Augustine to the Friars," *Traditio* 39 (1983), 1–27.

27. See again Shatzmiller, "Jewish Converts to Christianity in Medieval Europe: 1200–
1500," and Jordan, "Adolescence and Conversion in the Middle Ages: A Research
Agenda."

28. As demonstrated by the story of Yom Tov, the son of Moses of London. To make
martyrdom even more impressive, suicide is the form of death. See also, A. Kupfer,
"Toward a Geneology of the Family of R. Moses bar Yom Tov ("The Knight of the
World") of London" (in Hebrew), *Tarbiz* 40 (1971), 385–387.

29. *Sefer Gezerot*, 209. Einbinder discusses the five surviving laments for the Troyes
martyrs in *Beautiful Death*, 38–39, 126–148; idem, "The Troyes Elegies: Jewish Martyrology in Hebrew and Old French," *Viator* 30 (1999), 201–230.

30. For the dove motif, see R. Jacob bar Judah's poem, *Sefer Gezerot*, 205; R. Solomon
Simhah ha-Sofer, *Sefer Gezerot*, 207; R. Meir bar Eliav's poem, *Sefer Gezerot*, 211.
Overcoming fire, Jacob bar Judah, *Sefer Gezerot*, 203, 204; R. Solomon Simhah ha-
Sofer, *Sefer Gezerot*, 207, 208; R. Meir bar Eliav, *Sefer Gezerot*, 210.

31. Jordan, *The French Monarchy and the Jews*, 258; Stow, *Alienated Minority*, 301.

32. On his relations to Ashkenaz, see E. Kanarfogel, *Peering through the Lattices: Mystical,*
Magical, and Pietistic Dimensions in the Tosafist Period (Detroit, 2000), 239.

33. *La Deuxième Controverse de Paris*, 44–56; Cohen, *Living Letters of the Law*, 339.

34. Yuval stresses the importance of vengeance in commemoration prayers. "*Two Nations*
in Your Womb," 152–153.

35. Ta-Shma traces the early use of *aleinu le-shabeah* for optional individual prayers.
"The Source and Place of the Prayer *aleinu le-shabeah*"; Yuval, "*Two Nations in Your*
Womb," 206–207.

36. On *Mahzor Vitry*, Grossman, *The Early Sages of France*, 171–172; on the *Alenu*, A. Z.
Idelsohn, *Jewish Liturgy and Its Development* (New York, 1932), 116, 232.

37. M. Hallamish, *Kabbalah: In Liturgy, Halakhah and Customs* (Hebrew) (Jerusalem,
2000), 627–629.

38. Rabbi Abraham ben Azriel, *Sefer Arugat ha-Bosem*, ed. E. E. Urbach, 4 vols.
(Jerusalem, 1939–1963), 4:49.

39. S. Baer (ed.), *Seder Avodat Yisrael* (Redelheim, 1848), 233. Chazan, *European Jewry and the First Crusade*," 145.

40. *Or Zarua*, 2:21 n. 47; Here, the *Or Zarua* refers to *Sefer ha-Miqtsoot*. As seen in Chapter 4 above, *Sefer ha-Miqtsoot* dealt with the issue of *qiddish ha-Shem* and its place in the community. On the *Qaddish* in different communities, see Idelsohn, *Jewish Liturgy*, 85.

41. Shepkaru, "From After Death to Afterlife"; idem, "Martyrs' Heaven."

42. Idelsohn, *Jewish Liturgy*, 87.

43. Isaac ben Moses of Vienna, *Or Zarua*, 2:11; Elbogen, *Jewish Liturgy*, 82. See also Aaron ha-Cohen of Lunel, *Orhot hayyim*, ed. M. B. E. Shlezinger (Berlin, 1899), 1:212–214. His discussion includes the date in which, according to Aaron, R. Akiva and the rest of the Ten martyrs were executed.

44. For *Av ha-Rahamim*, see Idelsohn, *Jewish Liturgy*, 142; Elbogen, *Jewish Liturgy*, 162.

45. Elbogen, *Jewish Liturgy*, 82, 408 n. 11. More generally, Idelsohn, *Jewish Liturgy*, 88, 200. On the etymology of names for books of the martyrs, Marcus, "A Jewish-Christian Symbiosis: The Culture of Early Ashkenaz," 464.

46. *Or Zarua*, 2:125 n. 276. Idelsohn, *Jewish Liturgy*, 220; I. G. Marcus deals with this transition to the collective in his, "*Qiddush ha-Shem* in Ashkenaz and the Story of R. Amnon of Mainz" (Hebrew) in *Sanctity of Life and Martyrdom*, 131–147; idem, "Une Communauté pieuse et le doute: Mourir pour la Sanctification du Nom (*Qiddouch ha-Chem*) en Achkenaz (l'Europe du Nord) et l'histoire de rabbi Amnon de Mayence," *Annales: Histoire, Sciences Sociales* 5 (September–October 1994), 1031–1047.

47. As Yuval eloquently has shown in "*Two Nations in Your Womb*," and "Vengeance and Damnation, Blood and Defamation: From Jewish Martyrdom to Blood Libel Accusations."

48. Elbogen, *Jewish Liturgy*, 82.

49. *Saints and their Cults*, 27–28.

50. M. Goodich, "The Politics of Canonization in the Thirteenth Century: Lay and Mendicant Saints," in *Saints and their Cults*, 182.

51. *The Chronicle of Jocelin of Brakelond: A Picture of Monastic life in the Days of Abbot Samson*, ed. E. Clark (London, 1903), 79.

52. Already so in antiquity; P. Brown, *The Cult of the Saints: Its Rise and Function in Latin Christianity* (Chicago, 1981), 124.

53. F. S. Paxton, *Christianizing Death: The Creation of a Ritual Process in Early Medieval Europe* (Ithaca and London, 1990), 43, and see also 25–26.

54. C. Daniell, *Death and Burial in Medieval England*, 1066–1550 (London, New York, 1997), 2–8.

55. Magnus, count of Orkney, for instance, was considered a martyr, although he was murdered by a cousin in a family feud. Magnus is not alone in this category. D. Weinstein and R. M. Bell, *Saints and Society: The Two Worlds of Western Christendom, 1000–1700* (Chicago and London, 1982), 78, 160.

56. P. Delooz, "Towards a Sociological Study of Canonized Sainthood," in *Saints and Their Cults*, 206.

57. Isaac ben Joseph of Corbeil, *Sefer Mitsvot Qatan* (Satmor, 1935) [reprinted, Jerusalem, 1987], commandment 3, 2–3.

58. Based on this example, it seems that Isaac referred to the slain Saul of 2 Samuel 1. On the example of Saul and its different meanings in 1096, see Shmuel Shepkaru, "Death Twice Over," 244. On Saul and the *tosafists*, see E. Kanarfogel, "Halakhah and Mezi'ut (Realia) in Medieval Ashkenaz: Surveying the Parameters and Defining the Limits," *Jewish Law Annual* 14 (2003), sections 3 and 4.

59. Urbach, *The Tosaphists*, 2:573.

60. Einbinder, *Beautiful Death*, 132–133.

61. Among the martyrs of Koblenz the memorial books list R. Joseph who "slaughtered his two sisters" and the wife of R. Abraham bar Moses and his children who were slaughtered. *Sefer ha-Demaot*, 1:317.

62. Urbach, *The Tosaphists*, 2:522.

63. *Sefer Gezerot*, 179–185; R. Meir ben Baruch of Rothenburg, in *Teshuvot, Pesakim, u-Minhagim*, ed. I. Z. Cahana, 3 vols. (Jerusalem, 1957–1962), 2:54. See D. Berger's important article, "Jacob Katz on Jews and Christians in the Middle Ages," in *The Pride of Jacob: Essay on Jacob Katz and His Work*, ed. J. M. Harris (Cambridge and London, 2002), 41–63, especially 45–51.

64. See again the comments to Gen. 9:5 in *Sefer Tosafot Ha-Shalem*, ed. J. Gellis, 262–263.

65. *Sefer Gezerot*, 227.

66. *Sefer Gezerot*, 214–216.

67. *Sefer Gezerot*, 220.

68. *Die Königsaaler Geschichts-Quellen mit den Zusätzen und der Fortsetzung des Domherrn Franz Von Prag*, ed. J. Loserth, Fontes Rerum Austriacarum (Vienna, 1875), 137–138. M. Rubin also cites revenge as a reason for the violence. In her opinion, the allegations of host desecration served to incite and to help the Christian narrators to justify the violence. *Gentile Tales: The Narrative Assault on Late Medieval Jews* (New Haven and London, 1999), 48–57, especially 53.

69. *Sefer ha-Demaot*, 2:33. See also the poetry, 41–59.

70. Stow, *Alienated Minority*, 231.

71. *Sefer Gezerot*, 213–219.

72. *Sefer Gezerot*, 214.

73. *Sefer Gezerot*, 221. See also 223. R. Tamar bar Menahem also emphasizes the slaughtering of children and women, *Sefer Gezerot*, 227.

74. *Sefer Gezerot*, 202, 213, 214, 215.

75. *Sefer Gezerot*, 228.

76. *Sefer Gezerot*, 218. The motif of singing in the fire is repeated by R. Moses bar Elazar, *Sefer Gezerot*, 224, 225.

77. Peter the Venerable, *Sermones tres*, ed. G. Constable, *Revue Bénédictine*, 64 (1954), 232–254, quotation from 252. See also J. Cohen, "Christian Theology and Anti-Jewish Violence in the Middle Ages: Connections and Disjunctions," in *Religious Violence between Christian and Jews*, 44–60, especially 51. For a discussion on martyrological polemics, Shepkaru, "Martyrs' Heaven," 333–341.

78. This pressure is also reflected in the Jewish literature of the period; Chazan, *Daggers of Faith*, 25–48. Cohen goes further and claims that the aggressive actions of the midthirteenth century against the Jews emerged from a new Christian view of Judaism, which abrogated the permission for Jews to live as Jews within Christian society. *The Friars and the Jews*. See also R. Bonfils, "The Image of Judaism in

Raymond Martini's *Pugio Fidei*" (Hebrew), *Tarbiz* 40 (1971), 360–375; cf. Chazan, *Daggers of Faith*, 170–181.

79. A similar view was already echoed by *Sefer Hasidim*. See *Sefer Hasidim*, ed. R. Margaliot, 439, n. 704.

80. *Sefer Gezerot*, 227. Another reference to *Elleh Ezkerah* on p. 228 there.

81. *Teshubot, Pesaqim, u-Minhagim*, 2:sec. 59. Also cited in Shimshon ben Zadok's *Tashbetz* (Cremona, 1557), 40, par. 415; Urbach, *The Tosaphists*, 2:547; D. Tamar, "Chapters on the History of the Sages of the Land of Israel and Italy and their Literature" (in Hebrew), *Kiryat Sefer* 33 (1958), 376–380.

82. D. Tamar, "Chapters on the History of the Sages of the Land of Israel and Italy and their Literature," 376; idem, "More on the Opinion of Rabbi Meir of Rothenburg on the Issue of *Kiddush ha-Shem*," *Kiryat Sefer* 34 (1959), 376–377. On the relationship between the two scholars, see Urbach, *The Tosaphists*, 2:576–577. Fishbane, *The Kiss of God*, 140 n. 2. More generally on Ashkenaz and the Tosafists, see E. Kanarfogel, *Peering through the Lattices*, 239; I. Ta-Shma, "Sefer ha-Maskil: An Unknown French Jewish Composition from the End of the Thirteenth Century" (Hebrew), *Mehqerei-yerushalayyim be-mahshevet yisrael* 2.3 (1982–83), 416–438, especially, 435–436.

83. For Spain, Baer, *A History of the Jews in Christian Spain*, 2:15–16. On these events see, D. Nirenberg, *Communities of Violence: Persecution of Minorities in the Middle Ages* (Princeton, 1996).

84. *Shevet Yehudah* (Piatrakov edition), 31; *Sefer ha-Demaot*, 2:66, and 67–86 for additional material. On the leaders of the movement and the places that came under attack, Shatzmiller, "A Provencal Chronography in the Lost Account of Shem Tov Shantzulo," 52–53.

85. Jordan adds that the riots "were attacking not only a valuable royal commodity, they were defying the authority of the king himself." *The French Monarch and the Jews*, 244.

86. Guillaume de Nangis, *Chronique latine de Guillaume de Nangis de 1113 à 1300 avec les continuations de cette chronique de 1300 à 1368*, ed. H. Géraud (Paris, 1843), 2:31–35. Jordan, *The French Monarchy and the Jews*, 244.

87. Baer, *A History of the Jews in Christian Spain*, 2:20.

88. See again, Langmuir, "At the Frontier of Faith," in *Religious Violence between Christians and Jews*, 152–153.

89. P. Ziegler, *The Black Death* (New York, 1969), 102; J. Shatzmiller, "Les juifs de Provence pendant la pest noire," *Revue des études juives* 133.3–4 (July–December, 1974), 457–480.

90. Heinricus de Diessenhoven, in *Fontes rerum germanicarum*, ed. Boehmer (Stuttgart, 1868), 4:68.

91. *The Chronicle of Jean de Venette*, tr. J. Birdsall, ed. R. A. Newhall (New York, 1953), 50.

92. Quoted in J. R. Marcus, *The Jew in the Medieval World: A Sources Book: 315–1791* (New York, 1981), 47. On money as one of the main motivations for massacres during the Black Death, Shatzmiller, *Shylock Reconsidered*, 49. Shatzmiller quotes a local chronicler from Erfurt: "I think that the root of their [the Jews'] disaster were the huge, infinite sums of money which barons and knights, citizens and peasants owed them."

93. *Chronique de Jean le Bel*, ed. J. Viard and E. Déprez (Paris, 1904–1905), 1:225–226.

94. Quoted in J. R. Marcus, *The Jew in the Medieval World*, 44.

95. Wedding motifs abound in Christian martyrology. For example, see Petroff, *Medieval Women's Visionary Literature*, 17, 81–82, 183.

96. Marcus, *The Jew in the Medieval World*, 47.

97. Ziegler, *The Black Death*, 96. Clement acknowledged that looting Jewish property and destroying notarial records and other evidence of indebtedness were among the reasons for the massacres. Shatzmiller, *Shylock Reconsidered*, 49.

98. Parkes, *The Jews in the Mediaeval Community*, 118; Ziegler, *The Black Death*, 106–107.

99. Ziegler, *The Black Death*, 103.

100. Ziegler, *The Black Death*, 106.

101. Hinrici Rebdorfensis, *Annales Imperatorum*, in *Fontes rerum germanicarum*, ed. Boehmer (Stuttgart, 1868), 4:534.

102. Ziegler, *The Black Death*, 103.

103. Marcus, *The Jew in Medieval World*, 47. Ziegler, *The Black Death*, 103–106.

104. Urbach, *The Tosaphists*, 1:388; Abraham ben Azriel, *Sefer Arugat ha-Bosem*, 1:222 n. 11, and 4:207.

105. *Ha-Semak mi-Zurich*, ed. I. Rosenberg (Jerusalem, 1973), 1:57–58.

106. Reminiscent of R. Tam's disapproval of mourning for the death of infants who had been forcibly converted, and his suggestion to rejoice in the infant's death, as it had been saved from the possibility of becoming a non-Jewish adult. *Or Zarua*, 2:174 n. 428.

107. Marcus, *The Jew in the Medieval World*, 46–47.

108. R. S. Gottfried, *The Black Death: Natural and Human Disaster in Medieval Europe* (London, 1983), 49.

109. H. H. Mollaret and J. Borssolet, *La Peste, Source Méconnue d'Inspiration Artistique* (Paris, 1965), 60. Quoted from Ziegler, *The Black Death*, 275.

110. C. Ginzburg, *Ecstasies: Deciphering the Witches' Sabbath* (New York, 1991).

111. A. Foe, *The Jews of Europe after the Black Death* (Berkeley, Los Angeles, London, 2000), 17–18.

112. Jean de Venette, 49–50.

113. Jean de Venette, 49. Gottfried refers to additional saints, *The Black Death*, 87.

114. Henry Knighton, *Chronicon*, ed. J. R. Lumby (Series 92) (London, 1889), 61; Gottfried, *The Black Death*, 59.

115. M. Dols, *The Black Death in the Middle East* (Princeton, 1977), 113; Gottfried, *The Black Death*, 82.

116. Jacob ben Moses Halevi Möllin, *Sefer Maharil, Minhagim*, ed. S. J. Shpizer (Jerusalem, 1989), 167.

117. *Sefer ha-Demaot*, 2:87–106. The citation is from 106.

118. Lists of places can be found in *Das Martyrologium des Nürnberger Memorbuches*, ed. S. Salfeld (Berlin, 1898), 68–89.

119. Elbogen, *Jewish Liturgy*, 282.

120. *Das Martyrologium des Nürnberger Memorbuches*, 5–15, 61.

121. *Sefer Maharil, Minhagim*, 152–155, 158–159, 236–237, 414–415. *Das Martyrologium des Nürnberger Memorbuches*, 81.

122. The final expulsion from France was 1394. The number of the French Jews, however, was very small. Jordan, *The French Monarchy and the Jews*, 250. On the expulsion from England, R. Stacey, "Parliamentary Negotiation and the Expulsion of the Jews from England," *Thirteenth Century England*, vol. 6 (Woodbridge, 1997), 77–101.

123. *Das Martyrologium des Nürnberger Memorbuches*, 81; Ziegler, *The Black Death*, 108–109.

124. Baer, *A History of the Jews in Christian Spain*, 2:24–34.

125. The letter can be found in Piatrakov edition, 1904, of *Shevet Yehudah* (reprinted by the Bnei Issakhar Institute, Jerusalem, 1992), 174. Baer, *A History of the Jews in Christian Spain*, 2:96.

126. *Shevet Yehudah* (Piatrakov edition, 1904), 175.

127. Baer, *A History of the Jews in Christian Spain*, 2:107.

128. *Shevet Yehudah* (Piatrakov edition, 1904), 175; also, Baer, *A History of the Jews in Christian Spain*, 2:104–105.

129. M. Saperstein, "A Sermon on the Akeda from the Generation of the Expulsion and its Implication for 1391," in *Exile and Diaspora: Studies in the History of the Jewish People Presented to Professor Haim Beinart*, ed. A. Mirsky et al. (Jerusalem, 1991), 111–113.

130. Baer, *A History of the Jews in Christian Spain*, 2:165–166.

131. *Shevet Yehudah*, 118–119, 127.

132. Baer, *A History of the Jews in Christian Spain*, 2:162–163.

133. *Shevet Yehudah* (Piatrakov edition), 174–175.

134. R. Ben Shalom has made important comments on this subject in "*Qiddush ha-Shem* and Jewish Martyrdom in Aragon and Castille in 1391" (Hebrew), *Tarbits* 70:2 (2001), 227–282.

135. On Christianity, Maimonides to *Avodah Zarah*; on Islam, *Teshuvot ha-Rambam*, ed. J. Blau (Jerusalem, 1960), 2:726. A fuller discussion in A. Grossman, "*Qiddush ha-Shem* in the Eleventh and Twelfth Centuries: Between Ashkenaz and the Islamic Countries" (Hebrew), in *Peamim* 75 (1998), 27–46, especially 30–31; On Maimonides' views on Islam, A. Shlusberg, "Rambam's Approach to Islam," *Peamim* 42 (1990), 38–60. See also *Epistles of Maimonides: Crises and Leadership*, by A. Halkin and D. Hartman.

136. His Epistle on Martyrdom suggests that a certain distinguished rabbi disagreed with him. *Epistles of Maimonides*, 13, 15.

137. H. Z. Hirschberg, "The Almohade Persecutions and the India Trade: A Letter from the Year 1148, in *Yitzhak F. Baer Jubilee Volume*, 147; Grossman, "*Qiddush ha-Shem* in the Eleventh and Twelfth Centuries," 28.

138. As Baer has tried to explain the high numbers of *conversos*. *A History of the Jews in Christian Spain*, 1:96–98; H. Soloveitchik, "Religious Law and Change," 210 n. 10. Additional explanations are offered by H. Soloveitchik, "Between *Arav* and *Edom*" (Hebrew), in *Sanctity of Life and Martyrdom*, 149–152; M. Ben-Sasson, "The Prayers of the *Anusim*," in *Sanctity of Life and Martyrdom*, 153–166. See also B. Septimus, "Narboni and Shem Tov on Martyrdom," in *Studies in Medieval Jewish History and Literature*, ed. I. Twersky (Cambridge, London, 1984), 2:447–455. Ben Shalom "*Qiddush ha-Shem* and Jewish Martyrdom," 242–243.

139. See, for example, the introduction in Hasdai's *Sefer Or Adonai* (*Light of the Lord*), Ferrara edition, 1555, republished by Gregg International Publisher (Westmead, Farnborough, Hants., 1969); Baer, *A History of the Jews in Christian Spain*, 2: 85.
140. Baer, *A History of the Jews in Christian Spain*, 2:37. A. Grossman, "The Connections between Spanish Jewry and Ashkenazic Jewry in the Middle Ages" (Hebrew), in *Moreshet Sepharad: The Sephardi Legacy*, ed. H. Beinart (Jerusalem, 1992), 180; A. Gross, "The Ashkenazic Syndrom of Qiddush ha-Shem in Portugal in 1497," *Tarbitz* 64 (1995), 83–114.
141. On Aaron's familiarity with the *SMQ*, Urbach, *The Tosaphists*, 2:574.
142. *Orhot Hayyim*, ed. M. B. E. Shlezinger (Berlin, 1899), 2:26.
143. S. Goldin, *The Ways of Jewish Martyrdom* (Hebrew) (Lodd, 2002), 240, quotes only the debate over the sacrifice of children. He, therefore, argues that Aaron supported the act. The rest of the text, in my opinion, rejects not only such practices but even self-destruction.
144. *Orhot Hayyim*, 2:26–27.
145. Grossman, "The Connections between Spanish Jewry and Ashkenazic Jewry in the Middle Ages," 182; Baer, *A History of the Jews in Christian Spain*, 1:374; Urbach, *The Tosaphists*, 2:586.
146. Baer, *A History of the Jews in Christian Spain*, 1:316–317; Urbach, *The Tosaphists*, 2:590–591, 594, 596.
147. For example, Baer, *A History of the Jews in Christian Spain*, 1:320, 324; for Rabbenu Tam, see Urbach, *The Tosaphists*, 2:593, 595.
148. Urbach, *The Tosaphists*, 2:598.
149. H. Beinart, "Castilian Jewry," in *Moreshet Sepharad*, 22; Grossman, "The Connections between Spanish Jewry and Ashkenazic Jewry," in *Moreshet Sepharad*, 174–189. Jacob's *Turim* (Rows) contains guidelines regarding the use of liturgy.
150. Recall that R. Tam made the same reference, based on Isaiah 2:3, to the city of Bari. See again Chapter 5 above. Hasdai's letter, *Shevet Yehudah* (Piatrakov edition, 1904), 174. Baer, *A History of the Jews in Christian Spain*, 2:97.
151. In a previous violent incident in 1367, eight thousand Jews are reported to have died in the city of R. Asher. Beinart refers to the eight thousand casualties as "*dying for qiddush ha-Shem.*" "Castilian Jewry," 24. No such title is given to the victims by Baer, *A History of the Jews in Christian Spain*, 1:367. See also C. Roth, "A Hebrew Elegy on the Martyrs of Toledo, 1391" *Jewish Quarterly Review* 34 (1948), 127–129, 137–141.
152. Baer, *A History of the Jews in Christian Spain*, 2:151.
153. G. Scholem published the document in "New examinations of R. Abraham ben Eliezer ha-Levi" (Hebrew), *Kiryat Sefer* 7 (1931), 152–155; and also in *Chapters in the History of Kabbalistic Literature* (Hebrew) (Jerusalem, 1931), 125; see also his *Major Trends*, 146.
154. Scholem, *Kiryat Sefer*, 441–442; Fishbane, *The Kiss of God*, 52–54.
155. Urbach, *The Tosaphists*, 2:579.
156. Moses Galante, *Kehillat Yaacov, Safed 1578* (Jerusalem, 1977), 73a.
157. Solomon Luria, *Sefer Yam Shel Shlomoh: al Masekhet Bava Qama*, vol. 13 (Jerusalem, 1994).

CHAPTER 10: SHIFTING PARADIGMS

1. J. Hacker, "'If We Forgot Our Lord's Name and Opened Our Palms to a Foreign God': The Evolving of Interpretation Against the Background in Spain in the Middle Ages" (Hebrew), *Zion* 57 (1992), 271.

2. Scholem, "New examinations of R. Abraham ben Eliezer ha-Levi," 153–154. See also J. Hacker, "Was *Qiddush ha-Shem* Transferred to the Spiritual Discipline?" *Sanctity and Life*, 221–232, especially, 230.

3. Scholem, "New examinations of R. Abraham ben Eliezer ha-Levi," 153–154. Similar symbolism can be detected between the lines of the Hebrew sources of 1096. Shepkaru, "Death Twice Over."

4. As well demonstrated by Fishbane's *The Kiss of God*.

5. In *Sefer ha-Demaot* (Berlin, 1926), 3:116–117. Translation from *The Literature of Destruction: Jewish Responses to Catastrophe*, ed. D. G. Roskies (Philadelphia, New York, Jerusalem, 1988), 110–113.

6. *Sefer ha-Demaot*, 3:115 (my translation). In another case, the Jews are said to have preferred death by the sword than by starvation in hiding. See also 3:122. But others are said to have been killed without the mention of a choice at all (3:124).

7. *Sefer ha-Demaot*, 3:119. In this case, as in many others, the Cossacks also took hostages for financial profit.

8. J. Katz, *Exclusiveness and Tolerance: Studies in Jewish–Gentile Relations in Medieval and Modern Times* (Oxford, 1961), 143–168, especially, 151–155; idem, "Martyrdom in the Middle Ages and in 1648–9" (Hebrew), in *Sefer Yovel le-Yitzhak F. Baer*, ed. S. Ettinger et al. (Jerusalem, 1961), 318–337. See also *Sefer ha-Demaot*, 3:127, 130–131. See also the ransom attempts described by Y. Kaplan, "Jewish Refugees from Germany and Poland–Lithuania in Amsterdam during the Thirty Years War" (Hebrew), in *Culture and Society in Medieval Jewry*, 604–607.

9. "*The Epistle on the Ascendence of the Soul.*" Another unspecified libel ended with the death *al qiddush ha-Shem* of the accused. A. Rubinstein, *In Praise of the Baal Shem Tov [Shivhei ha-Besht]* (Hebrew) (Jerusalem, 1991), 255. Clearly, this was not a case of a massacre and an unclear case of martyrdom.

10. In a different tale, R. Akiva and "the martyrs whose names no one knows" revealed to the Besht that the massacre at Pavlysh, as in other cases, was decreed from heaven. Twenty-four Jews were accused of the murder of a four-year-old Christian. Twelve of them were tortured to death, whereas the rest survived because they converted. As in the legend of the Ten Martyrs, the heavenly demand for martyrs could not be reversed in Pavlysh, because the cancellation of the decree "could have caused great trouble." Rubinstein, *In Praise of the Baal Shem Tov*, 210–212; *Literature of Destruction*, 113–114.

11. *Sefer ha-Demaot*, 3:291–292 (my translation).

12. In Umam, the ransack and slaughter coincided. Even Jews who managed to bribe the attackers were killed thereafter. *Sefer ha-Demaot*, 3:293.

13. A. Mintz, "The Russian Pogroms in Hebrew Literature and the Subversion of the Martyrological Ideal," *Association for Jewish Studies Review* 7–8 (1982–1983), 265. See also, Cohen, *Under Crescent and Cross*, 177–179. And compare, for example, the death of the brothers R. Moses and R. Judah, the sons of R. Yekutiel (Poland, 1596), *Sefer ha-Demaot*, 3:101, to that of Rabbi Samuel bar Gedaliah, "the bridegroom," and Yehiel

bar Samuel in 1096, see Chapter 6. Similar remarks are applicable to descriptions of the Chmielntzky pogroms. C. Shmeruk, "Yiddish Literature and Collective Memory: The Case of the Chmielnitzky Massacres" (Hebrew), *Zion* 53 (1986), 371–389.

14. I found Smith's discussion on the Holocaust very useful. *Fools, Martyrs, Traitors*, 310–316.

15. R. Hillel Zeitlin relied on Maimonides to explain the application of *qiddush ha-shem* to the victims of the Holocaust. His reply is in M. Lensky, *The Life of the Jews in the Warsaw Ghetto* (Hebrew) (Jerusalem, 1983), 209. D. Schwartz, "The Bravery of Masada and the Martyrs of the Holocaust" (Hebrew), in *Ets Avot: Qiddush ha-Shem in the Holocaust in Thought, Halakhah, and Agadah*, ed. D. Schwartz and I. Hakel-man (Jerusalem, 1993), 201–217, especially 216; H. Kanfo, "Manifestations of Divine Providence in the Gloom of the Holocaust," in *I Will Be Sanctified: Religious Responses to the Holocaust*, ed. Y. Fogel, tr. E. Levin (Northvale, Jerusalem, 1998), 15–23, especially 15–17. For more religious interpretations, see there E. Melik, "'He Shall Live by Them': The Way of the Belzer Rebbe, Aaron Roke'ah, in the Holocaust," 183–210, especially 187; G. Naor, "A Difference of Opinion among *Poskim* Regarding the Parameters of Kiddush Hashem," 89–104, especially 102–104; and E. Alfasi, "Three Topics in the Laws of Martyrdom," 105–114. On Maimonides, see I. Taverski, "*Qiddush ha-Shem* and *Qiddush ha-Hayyim* – Aspects of Holiness in the Teaching of Maimonides" (Hebrew), in *Sanctity of Life and Martyrdom*, 167–190.

16. Otherwise, if they survived their attempt, they would be punished by twenty-five lashes and prolonged solitary confinement. That was the case in Dachau after 1933. B. Bettelheim, *The Informed Heart: Autonomy in a Mass Age* (Illinois, 1960), 151.

17. Even those who watched a suicide were immediately punished. Bettelheim, *The Informed Heart*, 155.

18. E. L. Fackenheim, *The Jewish Return into History: Reflection in the Age of Auschwitz and a New Jerusalem* (New York, 1978), 247.

19. Fackenheim, *The Jewish Return into History*, 246.

20. "A resisting life," is Fackenheim's phrase. M. L. Morgan, *Dilemmas in Modern Jewish Thought* (Bloomington, 1992), 106.

21. Schwartz, "The Bravery of Masada and the Martyrs of the Holocaust," 211.

22. Of course, cases of actual martyrdom still existed. R. Abraham-Mordekhai, for instance, chose death over setting his Torah scrolls on fire. Y. Aibeshits, *In Holiness and Bravery* (Hebrew) (Jerusalem, 1993), 11–14.

23. Quoted in Morgan, *Dilemmas in Modern Jewish Thought*, 87–88; For R. Oshry, 79, 89.

24. *I Believe: Testimonies on the Lives and Deaths of People of Faith during the Holocaust* (Hebrew), ed. M. Eliav (Jerusalem, 1965), 71.

25. L. Baeck, *The Essence of Judaism* (New York, 1948), 268.

26. P. Lewinska, *Twenty Months in Auschwitz* (New York, 1968), 41; in Fackenheim, *The Jewish Return into History*, 250, the line is italicized.

27. As penned by K. Zetnick, *The Clock Overhead* (Hebrew) (Jerusalem, 1960), 29.

28. R. Mintz, *Those Innocent of Sin*. Quoted in Schwartz, "The Bravery of Masada and the Martyrs of the Holocaust," 214. The translation is mine.

29. Fackenheim, *The Jewish Return into History*, 249, italics in original.

30. To be clear, I am not suggesting that Jewish behavior or martyrdom contributed in any form to the Holocaust.
31. Baeck, *The Essence of Judaism*, 216. Baeck focuses here on the Jewish concept of loving others, including your enemy. Thus he writes about Elazar, "He insisted even then that it is better to suffer wrong than to do it," 216.
32. E. Wiesel, *The Oath* (New York, 1973), 237.

Bibliography

PRIMARY SOURCES

Aaron ha-Cohen of Lunel. *Orhot hayyim.* Ed. M. B. E. Shlezinger. Berlin, 1899.

Abelard, Peter. *Dialogus inter Philosophum Judaem et Christianum.* In Ed. J. P. Migne, *Patrologia Latina,* Paris, 178.

Adémar of Chabannes. *Chronique.* In *Collection de textes pour servir a l'etude et a l'enseignement de l'histoire,* 20. Ed. J. Chavanon. Paris, 1897.

Agus, I. A., Ed. *Responsa of the Tosafists* (Hebrew). New York, 1954.

Albert of Aix. "Liber Christianae expeditionis." In *Recueil des historiens des croisades, historiens occidentaux,* 4.

Annales Ephordenses. In *Munumenta Germaniae Historica, Scriptorum,* 16.

Annales Herbipolenses. In *Munumenta Germaniae Historica, Scriptorum,* 16.

Annales Quedinburgenses. In *Munumenta Germaniae Historica, Scriptorum,* 3.

Annales Wirziburgenses. In *Munumenta Germaniae Historica, Scriptorum,* 2.

Anselm of Canterbury. *Cure Deus Homo?* Ed. and tr. J. Hopkins and H. Richardson. Toronto and New York, 1976.

Anselm of Canterbury. *Monologion.* Ed. J. Hopkins. *A New Interpretive Translation of St. Anselm's Monologion and Proslogion.* Minneapolis, 1986.

Appian of Alexandria. *Roman History.* In *The Loeb Classical History.* Tr. H. White. London, New York, 1912–1913.

Aquinas, Thomas. *Selected Writings.* Ed. and Tr. R. McInerny. Penguin Classics, 1998.

Asaf, S. *Sources for the History of Education in Israel* (Hebrew). 4 vols. Tel Aviv and Jerusalem, 1925–1943.

Assaf, S., Ed. *Sefer ha-Miqtsoot.* Jerusalem, 1947.

The Assumption of Moses: A Critical Edition with Commentary. Ed. J. Tromp. Leiden, 1993.

Augustine, Bishop of Hippo. *De civitate Dei.* In *The Loeb Classical Library.*

Avot de-Rabbi Nathan. Ed. S. Schechter. Vienna, 1887.

Baldric of Dol. "Historia Jerosolimitana." In *Recueil des historiens des croisades, historiens occidentaux,* 4.

Bede's Ecclesiastical History of the English People. Ed. B. Colgrave and R. A. B. Mynors. Oxford, 1969.

ben Abraham, Zedekiah. *Sefer Shibbolei ha-Leket.* Ed. A. Y. Hasidah. Jerusalem, 1987.

ben Azriel, Abraham. *Arugat ha-Bosem.* Ed. E. E. Urbach, 4 vols. Jerusalem, 1939–1963.

ben Joseph of Corbeil, Isaac. *Sefer Mitsvot Qatan.* Satmor, 1935 [reprinted, Jerusalem, 1987].

ben Meir Tam, Jacob. *Sefer ha-Yashar.* Ed. S. Rosenthal. Berlin, 1898.

ben Moses, Isaac. *Or Zarua.* Ed. Lehrn, A. 4 vols. in 2. Zhitomir, 1862–1890.

ben Moses Halevi Möllin, Jacob. *Sefer Maharil, Minhagim.* Ed. S. J. Shpizer. Jerusalem, 1989.

ben Zadok, Shimshon. *Tashbetz.* Cremona. 1557.

Berliner, A., ed. *The Memorial Book of the Worms Community* (Hebrew). 1887.

Berliner, A., ed. *Sefer Rashi.* Frankfort, 1905.

Bernard of Clairvaux. *To the English People.* Tr. S. James in *The Letters of St. Bernard of Clairvaux.* Chicago, 1953.

Bernold of St. Blasien, "Chronicon." *Monumenta Germaniae Historica, Scriptorum,* 5.

Blau, J., Ed. *Teshuvot ha-Rambam.* 4 vols. Jerusalem, 1960.

Bouquet, M., Ed. *Recueil des Histories des Gaules et de la France.* 24 vols. Paris, 1737–1904.

Brody, H., and Wiener, M., Eds. *Mivhar ha-Shirah ha-Ivrit.* Leipzig, 1922.

Buber, S., Ed. *Lamentations Rabbah* (Hebrew). Vilna, 1899.

Buber, S., Ed. *Midrash Mishle.* Jerusalem, 1964–1965.

Cassius Dio. *Roman History.* In *The Loeb Classical Library,* 9 vols. Ed. E. Cary. Cambridge, London, 1914–1927.

Charles, H. R., Ed. and Tr. *The Testaments of the Twelve Patriarchs.* London, 1908.

Charles, H. R., Ed. *The Book of Jubilees.* In *The Apocrypha and Pseudopigrapha of the Testament.* 2 vols. Oxford, 1913.

Charles, H. R., Ed. "The Testament of Moses," or "The Assumption of Moses." In *The Apocrypha and Pseudopigrapha of the Testament.* 2 vols. Oxford, 1913.

Charlesworth, J., Ed. *The Old Testament Pseudepigrapha.* 2 vols. Garden City, 1983–85.

Cheruel, A., Ed. *Normanniae nova chronica.* Caen, 1850.

Clark, E., Ed. *The Chronicle of Jocelin of Brakelond: A Picture of Monastic Life in the Days of Abbot Samson.* London, 1903.

Crispin, G. *Gislebert Crispini disputatio judei et christiani.* Ed. B. Blumenkranz. Utrecht, 1961.

Daat Zekanim me-Rabbenu Baalei ha-Tosafot. Ed. I. J. Nunez-Vaez. Livorno, 1783.

Daniel. Translation and commentary by H. Goldwurm, with an overview by Nosson Scherman. New York, 1979.

David, Y., Ed. *The Poems of Amittay* (Hebrew). Jerusalem, 1975.

Davidson, I., Ed. *Otzar ha-Shirah ve-ha-Piyyut.* New York, 1925–1933.

de Bruyne, D., and Sodar, B., Eds. *Les Anciennes Traductions Latines Des Machabées* [Anecdota Maredsolana, vol. 4]. Abbaye de Maredsous, 1932.

Donnolo, Shabbettai, *Sefer Hakhmoni.* Ed. D. Casteli, *Il commento di Sabbetai Donnolo sullibro creazione.* Florence, 1880.

Eidelberg, S. Tr. *The Jews and the Crusaders.* Hoboken, 1971.

Ekkehard of Aura. "Hierosolymita." In *Recueil des historiens des croisade, historiens occidentaux.* 5.

Ekkehard of Aura. "Chronicon universale." In *Monumenta Germaniae Historica, Scriptorum,* 6.

Elhanan ben Isaac. *Tosafot al Massekhet Avodah Zarah le-Rabbenu Elhanan.* Ed. D. Frankel. Husatyn, 1901.

Ephraim ben Jacob of Bonn. *Sefer Zechirah.* In *Sefer Gezerot Ashkenaz ve-Zarfat.* Ed. A. Habermann. Jerusalem, 1945.

Eusebius, *History of the Church From Christ to Constantine.* Tr. G. A. Williamson. New York, 1965.

Eusebius. *The Ecclesiastical History.* In *Loeb Classical Library.* 2 vols. London, New York, 1926–1932.

Eybeschuets, David Solomon. *Arvie Nahal.* Vol. II, Piotrkow, 1888.

The First Book of the Maccabees. Tr. S. Tedesche with the commentary of S. Zeitlin. New York, 1950.

Flavius, Josephus, *Jewish Antiquities.* In *The Loeb Classical Library.* 9 vols. Ed. A. Wikgren. Cambridge, 1926–1965.

Flavius, Josephus. *Jewish War.* In *The Loeb Classical Library,* 3 vols. Tr. H. St. J. Thackeray. Cambridge, 1926–1965.

Flavius, Josephus. *Against Apion.* In *The Loeb Classical Library.* Tr. H. St. J. Thackeray. Cambridge, 1926.

Fleisher, E., Ed. *The Poems of Solomon ha-Bavli.* Jerusalem, 1973.

Flusser, D., Ed. *Sefer Yosippon.* 2 vols. Jerusalem, 1981.

Friedmann, M., Ed. (Meir Ish-Shalom). *Seder Eliyahu Rabbah ve-Seder Eliyahu Zuta.* Vienna, 1904.

Fontes rerum germanicarum. Ed. J. F. Boehmer. Stuttgart, 1868.

Fulcher of Chartres. *Historia Hierosolymitana.* Ed. H. Hagenmeyer. Heidelberg, 1913.

Galant, Moses. *Kehillat Yaacov, Safed 1578.* Jerusalem, 1977.

Gaon, Natronai. *Gates of Righteousness, Responsa of the Geonim.* Salonika, 1972.

Gellis, J., Ed. *Sefer Tosafot ha-Shalem: Commentary on the Bible.* 5 vols. Jerusalem, 1982.

Gerhon of Reichersberg. *De Investigatione Antichristi.* In *Monumenta Germaniae Historica,* Scriptorum, 3.

Geoffrey of Breuil, "Chronica." In *Recueil des Histories des Gaules et de la France,* 12.

Gesta Francorum et aliorum Hierosolymytanorum. Ed. R. M. Hill. London, 1962.

Gesta Romanorum: Entertaining Stories. Tr. C. Swan. London, New York, 1925.

Gesta Treverorum. In *Monumenta Germaniae Historica, Scriptorum* (Hanover, 1848), 8.

Glaber, R. *Le cinq liver de ses histoires.* In *Collection de textes pour servir a l'etude et a l'enseignement de l'histore.* Vol. I. Ed. M. Prou. Paris, 1886.

Gonzalo de Berceo, *Miracles of Our Lady.* Tr. R. T. Mount and A. G. Cash. Lexington, 1997.

Gregory of Tours: Gloria Martyrium. Tr. R. Van Dam. Liverpool, 1988.

Gudemann, M. *Sefer Huke ha-Torah ha-Kadmonim* (The Book of the Early Laws of the Torah). Printed in *Sefer ha-Torah veha-Hayim be-Artsot ha-Maarav bi-Yeme ha-Benim (Geschichte des Erziehungswesens und der Cultur der abendländischen Juden, während des Mittelalters).* 3 vols. Jerusalem, 1971.

Gudemann, M. *Tanna de-rabbi Eliyahu.* In *Sefer Ha-Torah veha-Hayim.* 3 vols. Jerusalem, 1972.

Guibert of Nogent. *Histoire de sa vie.* Ed. G. Bourgin. Paris, 1907.

Guibert of Nogent. *De Vita Sua.* Ed. E. R. Labande. Paris, 1981.

Guibert of Nogent. *Treatise on Relics.* Tr. G. G. Coulton, *Life in the Middle Ages.* New York, Cambridge, 1931.

Guibert of Nogent. "Gesta Dei per Francos." In *Recueil des historiens des croisades, historiens occidentaux,* 4.

Guibert of Nogent. *Self and Society in Medieval France.* Tr. J. Benton. New York, 1970.

Guillaume de Nangis, *Chronique latine de Guillaume de Nangis de 1113 à 1300 avec les continuations de cette chronique de 1300 à 1368.* Ed. H. Géraud. Paris, 1843.

Habermann, A., Ed. *The Poems of Rabbi Shimon bar Isaac* (Hebrew). Berlin and Jerusalem, 1938.

Habermann, A. Ed. *Selihot u-Pizmonim le-Rabbenu Gershom Me'or ha-Golah.* Jerusalem, 1944.

Habermann, A. Ed. *Sefer Gezerot Ashkenaz ve-Zarfat.* Jerusalem, 1945.

ha-Bavli, Solomon. *Selihah.* Ed. A. Habermann, *A History of Heberw Liturgical and Secular Poetry.* 2 vols. Massada, 1972.

ha-Cohen, Joseph. *Emeq ha-Bachah.* Ed. M. Letteris. Cracow, 1895.

Hadas, M., Ed. and Tr. *The Third and Fourth Maccabees.* New York, 1953.

Hai ben Sherira Gaon. In *Teshuvoth ha-Geonim.* Ed. A. Harkavy, *Zikkaron la-rishonim we-gam la-ahronim.* Berlin, 1887.

ha-Levi, Judah. *The Kuzari.* Tr. H. Hirschfeld. New York, 1964.

Harkavy, A., Ed. *Teshuvoth ha-Geonim. Zikkaron la-Rishonim we-Gam la-Ahronim.* Berlin, 1887.

Hasdai Crescas, *Sefer Or Adonai.* Ferrara edition, 1555, republished by Gregg International Publisher. Westmead, Farnborough, Hants, 1969.

Ha-Semak mi-Zurich. Ed. I. Rosenberg. Jerusalem, 1973.

Heinricus de Diessenhoven. In *Fontes Rerum Germanicarum,* 4. Ed. Boehmer. Stuttgart, 1868.

Higger, M., Ed. *Semahot.* New York, 1932.

Historiatum Libri Ouingue, Ed. and Tr. J. France. Oxford, 1989.

Horovitz, S., and Finkelstein, L., Eds. *Sifre on Deuteronomy.* New York, 1969.

Horowitz, H. S., and Rabin, D. A., Eds. *Mekhilta de-Rabbi Ishmael.* Jerusalem, 1970.

Hidushei ha-Ritva al Avodah Zarah. Eds. M. Goldshtain and D. Metsger. Jerusalem, 1978.

Howlet, R., Ed. *Chronicles of the Reign of Stephen, Henry II, and Richard I.* 4 vols. London, 1884–1889.

Hugh of Flavigny, "Chronicon." In *Recueil des Histories des Gaules et de la France,* 12.

Ibn Daud, Abrahahm. *The Book of Tradition.* Ed. D. G. Cohen. Philadelphia, 1967.

ibn Verga, Solomon. *Shevet Yehudah.* Piatrakov edition, 1904.

ibn Verga, Solomon. *Shevet Yehudah.* Ed. Azriel Shohet. Jerusalem, 1947.

ibn Verga, Solomon. *Shevet Yehudah.* Reprinted by the Bnei Issakhar Institute. Jerusalem, 1992.

Jacobs, J., Ed. and Tr. *The Jews of Angevin England.* London, 1983.

Jacobus de Voragine. *The Golden Legend: Readings on the Saints.* 2 vols. Tr. W. G. Ryan. Princeton, 1993.

Jean de Venette, *The Chronicle of Jean de Venette.* Tr. J. Birdsall. Ed. R. A. Newhall. New York, 1953.

Jellinek, A., Ed. *Bet ha-Midrash.* 6 vols. in 2. 2d ed. Jerusalem, 1938.

Klar, B., Ed. *The Chronicle of Ahimaatz.* Jerusalem, 1974.

Knighton, Henry. *Chronicon.* 2 vols. (Series 92) Ed. J. R. Lumby. London, 1889.

Levin, B. M., Ed. *Sherira Gaon's Epistles* (Hebrew). Jerusalem, 1972.

Livy, with an English translation. In *The Loeb Classical Library.* London, New York, 1919–1959.

Luria, Solomon. *Sefer Yam Shel Shlomoh: al Masekhet Bava Qama.* Vol. 13. Jerusalem, 1994.

Maimonides, Moses. *Iggeret ha-Shemad.* In *Igrot ha-RMBM.* Ed. I. Shillat. Jerusalem, 1976.

Mann, J., Ed. *Texts and Studies in Jewish History and Literature.* 2 vols. Cincinnati, 1931.

Mansi, J. D. et al., Eds. *Sanctorum Conciliorum Collectio.* 53 vols. in 60. Graz and Verlagsanstalt, 1960–1961.

Margaliot, R., Ed. *Sefer Hasidim.* Jerusalem, 1957.

Martyr, Justin. *The Dialogue with Trypho,* tr. W. A. Lukyn. London, New York, 1930.

Migne, J. P., Ed. *Patrologiae cursus completus. Series Latina.* 221 vols. Paris, 1844–1864.

Migne, J. P., Ed. *Patrologiae cursus completus, Series Graeco-latina.* 28 vols. Paris, 1857–1887.

Monumenta Germaniae Historica, Scriptorum. 32 vols. Hanover, 1826–1934.

Muller, J., Ed. *The Responses of the Geonim of East and West* (Hebrew). Berlin, 1888.

Neubauer, A., and Stern M., Eds. *Hebraische Berichte uber die Judenverfolgungen wahrend der Kreuzzuge.* Berlin, 1892.

Orderic Vitalis. *Historia aecclesiastica.* Ed. M. Chibnall. Oxford, 1969.

Otto of Freising. *Gesta Frideric I Imperatoris.* Ed. B. De Simson. Hanover, 1912.

The Oxford Book of Medieval Latin Verse. Ed. F. J. E. Raby. Oxford, 1959.

Paul of St. Peter of Chartres, *Vetus Aganon. Ed Benjamin-Edme-Charles Guerard,* in *Cartulaire de l'abbaye de Saint-Peter de Chartres (Collection des cartulaires de France,* vol. 1 in *Collection de documents inedits sur l'histoire de France,* ser. 1 : *Historia Politique.),* 2 vols. Paris, 1840.

Peter the Venerable. *The Letters of Peter the Venerable.* Ed. G. Constable. 2 vols. Cambridge, 1967.

Peter of Zittau. *Die Königsaaler Geschichts-Quellen mit den Zusätzen und der Fortsetzung des Domherrn Franz Von Prag.* Ed. J. Loserth (Fontes Rerum Austriacarum). Vienna, 1875.

Philo of Alexandria. *The Embassy to Gaius.* In *The Loeb Classical Library.* Tr. F. H. Colson and G. H. Whitasker. Cambridge, London, New York, 1962.

Philo of Alexandria. *On Josephus.* In *The Loeb Classical Library.* Vol. 6. Tr. F. H. Colson and G. H. Whitasker. Cambridge, London, New York, 1962.

Philo of Alexandria. *Every Good Man is Free.* In *The Loeb Classical Library.* Vol. 9. Tr. F. H. Colson and G. H. Whitasker. Cambridge, London, New York, 1962.

Pliny the Elder, *Natural History.* In *The Loeb Classical History.* Tr. H. Rackham. Cambridge and London, 1967.

Plutarch. *Agis and Cleomenes.* In *The Loeb Classical Library.* Vol. 10. Tr. B. Perrin. London and New York, 1916.

Pseudo-Cyprian. *Adversus Judaeos.* In *Corpus Scriptorum Ecclesiasticorum Latinorum.* Vol. 3. Vindobonae, 1868–1871.

Ralph of Diceto. *Imagines Historiarum.* In *Rerum Britannicarum Medii Eavi Scriptores.* Ed. W. Stubbes. 2 vols. London, 1876.

Raymond of Aguilers. *Historia Francorum qui ceperunt Iherusalem* in *Le Liber De Raymond D'Aguiler,* pubilié par John Hugh Hill et Laurita Hill. Paris, 1969.

Recueil des Histories des Gaules et de la France. 24 vols. Paris, 1868–1904.

Reeg, G. *Die Geschichte von den Zehn Märtyren: Synoptische Edition mit Übersetzung und Einleitung.* Tübingen, 1985.

Richard of Devizis. *Chroncon Ricardi Divisensis de Regis Gestis Riccardi Primi.* Ed. J. T. Appleby. London et al., 1963.

Richard of Poitiers. "Chronicon." In *Recueil des Histories des Gaules et de la France,* 12.

Robert of Rheims. "Historia Hierosoylimitana." In *Recueil des historiens des croisades, historiens occidentaux,* 3.

Roger of Hoveden. *Chronica.* In *Rerum Britannicarum Medii Eavi Scriptores.* Ed. W. Stubbs. Vols. 1–4. London and Oxford, 1868–1871.

Salfeld, S., Ed. *Das Martyrologium des Nürnberger Memorbuches.* Berlin, 1898.

Schechter, S., Ginzberg, L., and Davidson, I., Eds. *The Vision of Daniel* (Hebrew). In *Ginze Schechter.* 3 vols. New York, 1927–1929.

Schirmann, H. *A. Selection of the Hebrew Poems of Italy* (Hebrew). Berlin, 1934.

Sefer ha-Demaot: Meoraot ha-Gezerot veha-Redifot ve-Hashmadot. Ed. S. Bernfeld. 3 vols. Berlin, 1923–1926.

Sefer ha-Yashar le-Rabenu Tam. Ed. F. Rosenthal. Berlin, 1989.

Sigebert of Gembloux, "Chronica." In *Monumenta Germaniae Historica, Scriptorum,* 6.

Simocatta, Theophylactus. *The History of Theophlyact Simocatta.* Tr. M. Whitby and M. Whitby. Oxford, 1986.

Solomon ben Isaac of Troyes (Rashi). *Piyute Rashi.* Ed. A. Habermann. Jerusalem, 1941.

Strabo. *Geography.* Tr. J. L. Horace. London, New York, 1917–1933.

Tacitus, C. *The History.* Tr. A. J. Church and W. S. Brodribb. Ed. Moses Hadas. New York, 1942.

Tedesche, S., Tr. and Zeltlin, S., Ed. *The Second Book of Maccabees.* New York, 1954.

Tertullian. *Ad Martyras.* In *The Writings of Tertullian* (Ante-Nicene Christian Library). 3 vols. Edinburgh, 1870.

Tertullian, *Antidote for the Scorpion's Sting.* In *The Writings of Tertullian* (Ante-Nicene Christian Library). 3 vols. Edinburgh, 1870.

Tertullian. *Ad Martyras.* "To Scapula," in *Apologetical Works.* In *The Fathers of the Church,* 19 vols. New York, 1950.

Teshuvot, Pesakim, u-Minhagim. Ed. I. Z. Cahana. 3 vols. Jerusalem, 1957–1962.

Teshuvot Rashi. Ed. I. Elfenbein. New York, 1943.

Theodor, J., and Albeck, C., Eds. *Midrash Bereshit Rabbah.* 3 vols. Jerusalem, 1965.

Theophanaes, *The Chronicle of Theophanes.* Tr. H. Turtledove. Philadelphia, 1982.

Tosafists. *Commentary on the Talmud.* Printed in all standard editions of Talmud.

Tosafotal Massekhet Avodah Zarah le-Rabbenu Elhanan. Ed. D. Fränkel. Husatyn, 1901.

Tov Ellem, Joseph. *Teshovot Geonim Kadmonim.* Ed. D. Kasle. Berlin, 1848.

Tudebodes, Peter. *Historia de Hierosolymitano Itinere,* publié par John Hugh Hill et Laurita Hill. Paris, 1977.

William of Tyre. In *Recueil des historiens des croisade, historiens occidentaux.* Vol I.

William of Newbury. *Historia rerum anglicarum.* 2 vols. Ed. H. C. Hamilton. London, 1856.

Winterbottom, M., Ed. *Three Lives of English Saints.* Toronto, 1972.

Wistinetzki, J., Ed. *Sefer Hasidim.* Frankfort, 1924.

Zlotnick, D., Ed. *Semahot.* New Haven, 1966.

Abel, F.-M. *Les Livres des Maccabées*. Paris, 1949.

Abel F.-M. and Starcky, J. *Les livres de Maccabées*. Paris, 1961.

Aberbach, M. *The Roman-Jewish War (66–70 A.D.): Its Origins and Consequences*. London, 1966.

Abrahams, I. *Jewish Life in the Middle Ages*. Philadelphia and Jerusalem, 1993.

Abulafia, A. S. "The Interrelationship between the Hebrew Chronicles of the First Crusade." *Journal of Semitic Studies* 27 (1982), 221–239.

Abulafia, A. S. "Invectives against Christianity in the Hebrew Chronicles of the First Crusade." *Crusade and Settelement*. Ed. P. W. Edbury, 66–72. Cardiff, 1985.

Abulafia, A. S. *Christians and Jews in the Twelfth-Century Renaissance*. London, New York, 1995.

Abulafia, A. S. "The Intellectual and Spiritual Quest for Christ and Central Medieval Persecution of Jews." In *Religious Violence between Christians and Jews: Medieval Roots, Modern Perspectives*. Ed. A. S. Abulafia, 61–85. New York, 2002.

Adinolfi, P. M. "Elogia di l'autore di I Macc. 6.43–46; il gesto di Eleazaro?," *Antonianum* 39 (1964), 177–186.

Agus, A. *The Binding of Isaac and Messiah*. Albany, 1988.

Agus, I. A. *Urban Civilization in Pre-Crusade Europe*. 2 vols. New York, 1965.

Agus, I. A. "Rabbinic Scholarship in Northern Europe." In *The Dark Ages: Jews in Christian Europe, 711–1096*. Ed. C. Roth, 189–209. Rutgers, 1966.

Agus, I. A. "Rashi and His School." In *The Dark Ages: Jews in Christian Europe, 711–1096*. Ed. C. Roth, 210–248. Rutgers, 1966.

Agus, I. A. *The Heroic Age of Franco-German Jewry*. New York, 1969.

Agus, I. A. "Democracy in the Communities of the Early Middle Ages." *Jewish Quarterly Review* 43 (1952–1953), 155–176.

Alexander, P. S. "'The Parting of the Ways' from the Perspective of Rabbinic Judaism." In *Jews and Christians: The Parting of the Ways A.D. 70 to 135*. Ed. J. D. G. Dunn, 1–25. Tübingen, 1993.

Aibeshits, Y. *In Holiness and Bravery* (Hebrew). Jerusalem, 1993.

Alfasi, E. "Three Topics in the Laws of Martyrdom." In *I Will Be Sanctified: Religious Responses to the Holocaust*. Ed. Y. Fogel and Tr. E. Levin, 105–114. Northvale, Jerusalem, 1998.

Allon, G. *The History of the Jews in the Land of Israel in the Time of the Mishnah and Talmud* (Hebrew). 2 vols. Tel Aviv, 1966.

Allon, G. *Studies in the History of Israel* (Hebrew). 2 vols. Ha-Kibutz Ha-Meuchad, 1967.

Alvarez, A. *The Savage God: A Study of Suicide*. New York, 1972.

Alvarez, A. "The Background." In *Suicide*. Ed. M. P. Battin and D. J. Mayo, 7–32. New York, 1980.

Amari, M. *Storia dei musulmani di Sicilia*. 2 vols. 1933–1935.

Amir, Y. "The Term *IOUDAISMOS*, A Study in Jewish-Hellenistic Self-Identification," *Immanuel* 14 (1982), 34–41.

Arlow, J. A. "Ego Psychology and the Study of Mythology." *Journal of the American Psychoanalytic Association* 9 (1961), 371–393.

Arnold, T. W. *The Preaching of Islam*. New York, 1913.

Aronius, J. *Regesten zur Geschichte der Juden in fränkischen und deutschen Reiche.* Berlin, 1902.

Ashtor, E. *The History of the Jews in Muslim Spain* (Hebrew). 2 vols. Jerusalem, 1960.

Atkinson, M. J. *Discovering Suicide.* Pittsburg, 1978.

Bachrach, B. S. *Early Medieval Jewish Policy in Western Europe.* Minneapolis, 1977.

Baeck, L. *The Essence of Judaism.* New York, 1948.

Baer, S., Ed. *Seder Avodat Yisrael.* Redelheim, 1848.

Baer, Y. A. "The Religious and Social Tendency of *Sefer Hasidim*" (Hebrew). *Zion* 3 (1938), 1–50.

Baer, Y. A. "Rashi and the Historical Reality of His Time" (Hebrew). *Tarbiz* 20 (1948), 320–332.

Baer, Y. A. "*The Hebrew Sefer Yosippon*" (Hebrew). In *Sefer Dinaburg.* Ed. Ben Z. Dinur and Y. Baer, 178–205. Jerusalem, 1949.

Baer, Y. A. "The Origins of the Organization of the Jewish Community of the Middle Ages" (Hebrew). *Zion* 15 (1950), 1–41.

Baer, Y. A. "The Persecution of 1096" (Hebrew). In *Sefer Asaf.* Ed. M. D. Cassuto et al., 126–140. Jerusalem, 1953.

Baer, Y. A. *Israel Among the Nations* (Hebrew). Jerusalem, 1955.

Baer, Y. A. "Israel, the Christian Church, and the Roman Empire from the Time of Septimius Severus to the Edict of Toleration of A.D. 313." In *Studies in History.* Ed. A. Fuks and I. Halpern. Scripta Hierosolymitana 7, 79–147. Jerusalem, 1961.

Baer, Y. A. "The Persecution of the Monotheistic Religion by Antiochus Epiphanes" (Hebrew). *Zion* 38 (1971), 32–47.

Baer, Y. A. *Galut* (Hebrew). Jerusalem, 1980.

Baer, Y. A. *Studies and Essays in the History of the Jewish People* (Hebrew). Jerusalem, 1985.

Baer, Y. A. *A History of the Jews in Christian Spain.* Tr. L. Schoffman, 2 vols. Philadelphia, Jerusalem, 1992.

Baras, Z. "The Testimonium and Martyrdom of James." In *Josephus, Judaism, and Christianity.* Ed. L. H. Feldman and G. Hata, 338–348. Detroit, 1987.

Bar-Kochva, B. *The Battels of the Hasmoneans: The Times of Judas Maccabaeus.* Jerusalem, 1980.

Bar-Kochva, B. *Judas Maccabaeus: The Jewish Struggle against the Seleucids.* Cambridge, New York, 1989.

Bar-Kochva, B. *Pseudo-Hecataeus on the Jews: Legitimizing the Jewish Diaspora.* Berkeley, Los Angeles, London, 1996.

Barclay, J. M. G. *Jews in the Mediterranean Diaspora: From Alexander to Trajan (323 B. C. E.–117 C. E.).* Edinburgh, 1996.

Barkum, M. *Disasters and the Millennium.* London, 1974.

Barnes, T. "Tertullian's *Scoriace.*" *Journal of Theological Studies* 20:1 (April, 1969), 105–132.

Baron, S. W. *The Jewish Community.* 3 vols. Philadelphia, 1948.

Baron, S. W. *A Social and Religious History of the Jews.* 18 vols. 2d ed. New York, 1952–1983.

Barrett, A. A. *Caligula: The Corruption of Power.* New Haven, London, 1989.

Bartlett, J. R. *The First and Second Books of the Maccabees.* Cambridge, 1973.

Bartlett, J. R. *Jews in the Hellenistic World: Josephus, Aristeas, The Sibylline Oracles, Eupolemus.* Cambridge, New York, 1985.

Baschet, J. "Medieval Abraham: Between Fleshly Patriarch and Divine Father." *Modern Language Notes* 108 (1993), 738–758.

Batnitzky, L. "On the Suffering of God's Chosen: Christian Views in Jewish Terms." In *Christianity in Jewish Terms*. Ed. T. Frymer-Kensky et al., 203–220. Colorado and Oxford, 2000.

Battin, P. M. *Ethical Issues in Suicide*. New Jersey, 1991.

Baumgarten, A. I. *The Flourishing of Jewish Sects in the Maccabean Era: An Interpretation*. Leiden, New York, Köln, 1997.

Baumgarten, A. I. "Invented Traditions of the Maccabean Era," *Geschichte–Tradition– Reflexion: Festschrift für Martin Hengel Zum 70. Geburtstag*. Ed. H. Cancik, H. Lichtenberger, and P. Schäfer, 1:197–210, Tüsbingen, 1996.

Beinart, H. "Castilian Jewry." In *Moreshet Sepharad: The Sephardi Legacy*. Ed. H. Beinart, 11–35. Jerusalem, 1992.

Ben-Haim, Trifon, D. "Some Aspects of Internal Politics Connected with the Bar Kochva Revolt" (Hebrew). In *The Bar-Kokhva Revolt*. Ed. A. Oppenheimer and U. Rappaport, 13–26. Jerusalem, 1984.

Ben-Sasson, M. "Italy and 'Ifriqua from the 9th to the 11th Century." In *Les Relations intercommunautaires juives en Méditerranée occidentale XIIIe-XXe siècles, ed. Miège, J. L.*, 34–50. Paris, 1984.

Ben-Sasson, M. "The Prayers of the *Anusim*" (Hebrew). In *Sanctity of Life and Martyrdom*. Ed. I. M. Gafni and A. Ravitzky, 153–166. Jerusalem, 1992.

Ben Shalom, I. "Events and Ideology of the Yavneh Period As Indirect Causes of the Bar Kochva Revolt" (Hebrew). In *The Bar-Kokhva Revolt*. Ed. A. Oppenheimer and U. Rappaport, 1–12. Jerusalem, 1984.

Ben Shalom, R. "*Qiddush ha-Shem* and Jewish Martyrdom in Aragon and Castille in 1391" (Hebrew). *Tarbits* 70:2 (2001), 227–282.

Ben Zevi, I. *The Exiled and the Redeemed*. Tr. I. Abbady. Philadelphia, 1957.

Beachler, J. *Suicide*. New York, 1979.

Bell, A. A., Jr., "Josephus and Pseudo-Hegesippus." In *Josephus, Judaism, and Christianity*. Ed. L. H. Feldman and G. Hata, 349–361. Detroit, 1987.

Bendict, B. Z. *The Torah Center in Provanse*. Jerusalem, 1985.

Bentzen, A. "Daniel 6: Ein Versuch zur Vorgeschichte der Märtyrerlegende." In *Festschrift A. Bertholet*. Ed. W. Baumgartner, O. Eissfeldt, K. Elliger, and L. Rust, 58–64. Tübingen, 1950.

Berger, D. "Mission to the Jews and Jewish–Christian Contacts in the Polemical Literature of the High Middle Ages." *American Historical Review* 91 (1986), 576–591.

Berger, D. "From Crusade to Blood Libels to Expulsions: Some New Approaches to Medieval Antisemitism." *Second Annual Lecture of the V.J. Selmanowitz Chair of Jewish History*, Touro College, Graduate School of Jewish Studies. New York, 1997.

Berger, D. "On the Image and Destiny of Gentiles in Ashkenazic Polemical Literature" (Hebrew). In *Facing the Cross: The Persecutions of 1096 in History and Historiography*. Ed. Y. T. Assis et al., 74–91, Jerusalem, 2000.

Berger, D. "Jacob Katz on Jews and Christians in the Middle Ages." In *The Pride of Jacob: Essay on Jacob Katz and His Work*. Ed. J. M. Harris, 41–63. Cambridge and London, 200.

Bettelheim, B. *The Informed Heart: Autonomy in a Mass Age*. Illinois, 1960.

Bevan, E. R. *The House of Seleucus*. 2 vols. London, 1902.

Bickerman, E. "The Date of Fourth Maccabees." In *Louis Ginzberg Jubilee Volume,* 115–112. New York, 1945. Reprinted in *Studies in Jewish and Christian History,* 1:276–281. Leiden, 1976.

Bickerman, E. *The God of the Maccabees.* Tr. H. R. Moehring. Leiden, 1979.

Bilde, P. "The Roman Emperor Gaius Caligula's Attempt to Erect His Statue in the Temple in Jerusalem." *Studia Theologica* 32 (1978), 67–93.

Bishop, M. *The Middle Ages.* Boston, 1987.

Blanchetière, F. "The Threefold Christian anti-Judaism" In *Tolerance and Intolerance in Early Judaism and Christianity.* Ed. G. N. Stanton and G. G. Strounsa, 185–210. Cambridge, 1998.

Blank, S. H. "The Death of Zechariah in Rabbinic Literature." *Hebrew Union College Annual* 12-13 (1937–1938), 327–346.

Bloch, P. "Rom und die Mystiker der Merkaba." In *Festschrift zum siebzigsten Geburtstage Jakob Guttmanns.* Ed. M. Philippson, 113–124. Leipzig, 1915.

Blumenkranz, B. *Juifs et Chrétiens Dans Le Monde Occidental 430–1096.* Paris, 1960.

Blumenkranz, B. *Les auteurs chrétiens latins du moyen age sur les juifs et le judaisme.* Paris, 1963.

Blumenkranz, B. "The Roman Church and the Jews." In *The Dark Ages: Jews in Christian Europe, 711–1096.* Ed. C. Roth, 69–99. Rutgers, 1966.

Blumenthal, "*Tselem*: Toward an Anthropopathic Theology of Image." In *Christianity in Jewish Terms.* Ed. T. Frymer-Kensky et al., 337–347. Colorado and Oxford, 2000.

Bond, H. K. *Pontius Pilate in History and Interpretation.* Cambridge, 1998.

Bonfil, R. "The Image of Judaism in Raymond Martini's *Pugio Fidei*" (Hebrew). *Tarbiz* 40 (1971), 360–375.

Bonfil, R. "Tra due mondi, Prospettive di ricerca sulla storia culturale degli Ebrei dell 'Italia meridionale nell 'alto Medioevo," *Italia Judaica. Atti del I Convegno internazionale, Bari 18-22 maggio 1981* (Rome, 1983), 135–158.

Bonfil, R. "Between the Land of Israel and Babylon: A Study of the Jewish Culture in Southern Italy and in Christian Europe in the Early Middle Ages." *Shalem* 5 (1987), 1–30.

Bonfil, R. "Myth, Rhetoric, History? A Study in the Chronicle of Ahima'az" (Hebrew). In *Culture and Society in Medieval Jewry: Studies Dedicated to the Memory of Haim Hillel Ben-Sasson.* Ed. M. Ben-Sasson, R. Bonfil, and J. R. Hacker, 99–135. Jerusalem, 1989.

Bonfil, R. "Can Medieval Storytelling Help Understanding Midrash? The Story of Paltiel: A Preliminary Study on History and Midrash." In *The Midrashic Imagination: Jews, Exegesis, Thought, and History.* Ed. M. Fishbane, 228–254. Albany, 1993.

Borgen, R. "Emperor Worship and Persecution in Philo's *In Flaccum* and *De Legatione ad Gaium* and the Revelation of John." In *Geschichte–Tradition–Reflexion: Festschrift für Martin Hengel Zum 70. Geburtstag.* Ed. H. Cancik, H. Lichtenberger, and P. Schäfer, 3:493–509. Tübingen, 1996.

Boswell, J. *Life of Johnson.* Ed. G. B. Hill. 6 vols. Oxford, 1887.

Bouman, C. "The Immaculate Conception in the Liturgy." In *The Dogma of the Immaculate Conception: History and Significance.* Ed. E. D. O'Connor, 113–159. Notre Dame, 1958.

Bowersock, W. G. *Martyrdom and Rome.* Cambridge, 1995.

Bowman, S. *The Jews of Byzantium 1204-1453.* Alabama Press, 1985.

Bowman, S. "Sefer Yosippon: History and Midrash. In *The Midrashic Imagination: Jews, Exegesis, Thought, and History*. Ed. M. Fishbane, 280–294. Albany, 199.

Bowman, S. "'Yosippon' and Jewish Nationalism." *Proceedings of the American Academy for Jewish Research* 61 (1995), 23–51.

Boyarin, D. *Intertextuality and the Reading of Midrash*. Bloomington and Indianapolis, 1990.

Boyarin, D. *Dying For God: Martyrdom and the Making of Christianity and Judaism*. Stanford, 1999.

Brandon, S. G. F. *Jesus and the Zealots: A Study of the Political Factor in Primitive Christianity*. Manchester, 1967.

Brelich, A. "Symbol of a Symbol." In *Myth and Symbols*. Ed. J. M. Kitagawa and C. H. Long, 195–208. Chicago and London, 1969.

Breuer, M. "Women in Jewish Martyrology" (Hebrew). In *Facing the Cross: The Persecutions of 1096 in History and Historiography*. Ed. Y. T. Assis et al., 141–149. Jerusalem, 2000.

Bronwnlee, W. H. "Maccabees, Books of," *Anchor Bible Dictionary*. Ed. D. N. Freedman, 3:201–215, New York, London, 1992.

Brown, P. *The Cult of the Saints: Its Rise and Function in Latin Christianity*. Chicago, 1981.

Browning, R. *The Byzantine Empire*. New York, 1980.

Brundage, J. A. "Holy War and the Medieval Lawyers." In *The Holy War*. Ed. T. P. Murphy, 99–140. Columbus, 1976.

Bruce, F. F. "The Book of Daniel and the Qumran Community." In *Neotestamentica et Semitica: Studies in Honor of Matthew Black*. Ed. E. E. Ellis and M. Wilcox, 221–235. Edinburg, 1969.

Brundage, A. "Holy War and the Medieval Lawyers." *The Holy War*. Ed. T. P. Murphy, 9–32. Columbus, 1976.

Brunt, P. A. "Charges of Provincial Maladministration under the Principate." In *Ha-Mered Ha-Gadol: ha-Sibot veha-Nesibot li-Feritsato*. Ed. A. Kasher, 103–141. Jerusalem, 1983.

Butler, A. H., Thurston, S. J., and Attwater, D., Eds. *Butler's Lives of the Saints*, 4 vols. New York, 1968.

Campbell, J. *The Hero with a Thousand Faces*. Princeton, 1973.

Cassuto, U. "*Una lettera ebraica de secolo X*." In *Giornale della Societa Asiatica Italiana*, 29, 97–110.

Chadwick, H. *Oxford History of Christianity*. Ed. J. McManner. Oxford, 1990.

Chalandon, F. *Histoire de la domination normande en Italie et en Sicile*. 2 vols. New York, 1960.

Charles, R. H. *The Apocrypha and Pseudepigrapha of the Old Testament*. Vol. 2. Oxford, 1913.

Charles, R. H. *A Critical and Exegetical Commentary on the Book of Daniel*. Oxford, 1929.

Charles, R. H. *Eschatology: The Doctrine of a Future Life in Israel, Judaism and Christianity*. New York, 1970.

Charlesworth, J. El. *The Old Testament Pseudepigrapha*. 2 vols. Garden City, 1983–1985.

Chavasse, A. *Le Sacramentaire Gelasie*. Strasborg, 1958.

Chazan, R. "The Blois Incident of 1171: A Study in Jewish Intercommunal Organization." *Proceedings of the American for Jewish Research* 36 (1968), 13–31.

Chazan, R. "The Bray Incident of 1192: Realpolitik and Folk Slander." *Proceedings of the American for Jewish Research* 37 (1969), 1–18.

Chazan, R. "The Persecution of 992." *Revue des études juives* 129 (1970), 217–221.

Chazan, R. "Emperor Frederick I, the Third Crusade, and the Jews." *Viator* 8 (1970), 83–93.

Chazan, R. "1007–1012: Initial Crisis For Northern European Jewry." *Proceedings of the American for Jewish Research* 38–39 (1970–1971), 101–117.

Chazan, R. *Medieval Jewry in Northern France.* Baltimore and London, 1973.

Chazan, R. "R. Ephraim of Bonn's Sefer Zechirah." *Revue des études juives* 132.1–2 (1973), 119–126.

Chazan, R. "The Hebrew First Crusade Chronicles." *Revue des études juives* 133 (1974), 235–254.

Chazan, R. "The Hebrew Chronicles: Frurther Reflections." *Association for Jewish Studies Review* 3 (1978), 79–98.

Chazan, R. *Church, State, and Jew in the Middle Ages.* New York, 1980.

Chazan, R. "The Deeds of the Jewish Community of Cologne." *Journal of Jewish Studies* 35 (1984), 185–195.

Chazan, R. "The Early Developments of *Hasidut Ashkenaz.*" *Jewish Quarterly Review* 75:3 (1985), 199–211.

Chazan, R. "Review of K. Stow, The '1007 Anonymous' and Papal Sovereignty." *Speculum* 62 (1987), 728–731.

Chazan, R. *European Jewry and the First Crusacde.* Los Angeles, London, 1987.

Chazan, R. *Daggers of Faith.* Berkeley, Los Angeles, London, 1989.

Chazan, R. "The Facticity of Medieval Narrative: A Case Study of the Hebrew First Crusade Narratives." *Association for Jewish Studies Review* 16 (1991), 31–56.

Chazan, R. *Barcelona and Beyond: The Disputation of 1263 and Its Aftermath.* Berkeley, Los Angeles, Oxford, 1992.

Chazan, R. "Ephraim ben Jacob's Compilation of Twelfth-Century Persecutions." *Jewish Quarterly Review* 84 (1993–1994), 397–416.

Chazan, R. *Medieval Stereotypes and Modern Antisemitism.* Berkeley, 1997.

Chazan, R. "Jerusalem as Christian Symbol during the First Crusade: Jewish Awareness and Response." In *Jerusalem: Its Sanctity and Centrality to Judaism, Christianity, and Islam.* Ed. L. I. Levine, 382–392. New York, 1999.

Chazan, R. *God, Humanity and History: The Hebrew First Crusade Narratives.* Berkeley, Los Angeles, London, 2000.

Chazan, R. "From the First Crusade to the Second: Evolving Perceptions of the Christian–Jewish Conflict." In *Jews and Christians in Twelfth-Century Europe.* Ed. M. A. Signer and J. Van Engen, 46–62. Indiana, 2001.

Chazan, R. "The Anti-Jewish Violence of 1096: Perpetrator and Dynamics." In *Religious Violence between Christians and Jews: Medieval Roots, Modern Perspectives.* Ed. A. S. Abulafia, 21–43. New York, 2002.

Chilton, B., and Neusner, J. *Comparing Spiritualities: Formative Christianity and Judaism on Finding Life and Meeting Death.* Harrisburg, 2000.

Choron, J. *Suicide.* New York, 1972.

Coggins, A. J. *Samaritans and Jews.* Oxford, 1975.

Cohen, G. D. "The Story of Hannah and Her Seven Sons in Hebrew Literature" (Hebrew). In *Mordecai M. Kaplan Jubilee Volume.* Ed. M. Davis, 109–122. New York, 1953.

Cohen, G. D. "Esau as Symbol in Early Medieval Thought." In *Jewish Medieval and Renaissance Studies*. Ed. A. Altmann, 19–48. Cambridge, 1967.

Cohen, G. D. "Messianic Postures of Ashkenazim and Sepharadim." In *Studies of the Leo Baeck Institute*. Ed. M. Kreutzberger, 117–156. New York, 1967.

Cohen, G. D. "The Hebrew Crusade Chronicles and the Ashkenazic Tradition." *Minhah le-Nahum: Biblical and Other Studies in Honor of Nahum M. Sarna*. Ed. M. Fishban and M. Brettler, 36–53. Sheffield, 1993.

Cohen, H. H. "Suicide in Jewish Law." In *Encyclopaedia Judaica* Vol. 15, 1972.

Cohen, J. "Roman Imperial Policy toward the Jews from Constantine until the End of the Palestinian Patriarchate (ca. 429)." *Byzantine Studies* 3 (1976), 1–29.

Cohen, J. *The Friars and the Jews: The Evolution of Medieval Anti-Judaism*. Ithaca, 1982.

Cohen, J. "The Jews as the Killers of Christ in the Latin Tradition, from Augustine to the Friars." *Tradition* 39 (1983), 3–27.

Cohen, J. "Recent Historiography on the Medieval Church and the Decline of European Jewry." In *Pope Teachers and Canon Law in the Middle Ages*. Ed. J. B. Sweeney and S. Chodorow, 251–262. Ithaca and London, 1989.

Cohen, J. "The Persecution of 1096: The Sociocultural Context of the Narratives of Martyrdom" (Hebrew). *Zion* 59 (1994), 169–208.

Cohen, J. *Living Letters of the Law: Ideas of the Jews in Medieval Christianity*. Berkeley, Los Angeles, London, 1999.

Cohen, J. "The Hebrew Crusade Chronicles in Their Christian Cultural Context." In *Juden und Christen zur Zeit Der Kreuzzüge*. Ed. A. Haverkamp, 17–34. Sigmaringen, 1999.

Cohen, J. "Between Martyrdom and Apostasy: Doubt and Self-Definition in Twelfth-Century Ashkenaz." *Journal of Medieval and Early Modern Studies* 29:3 (Fall 1999), 431–473.

Cohen, J. "From History to Historiography: The Study of the Persecutions and Constructions of their Meaning" (Hebrew). In *Facing the Cross: The Persecutions of 1096 in History and Historiography*. Ed. Y. T. Assis et al., 16–31. Jerusalem, 2000.

Cohen, J. "A 1096 Complex? Constructing the First Crusade in Jewish Historical Memory, Medieval and Modern." In *Jews and Christians in Twelfth-Century Europe*. Ed. M. A. Michael and A. Signer and John Van Engen, 9–25. Notre Dame, 2001.

Cohen, J. "Christian Theology and Anti-Jewish Violence in the Middle Ages: Connections and Disjunctions." In *Religious Violence between Christians and Jews: Medieval Roots, Modern Perspectives*. Ed. A. S. Abulafia, 44–60. New York, 2002.

Cohen, J. D. S. *Josephus in Galilee and Rome*. Leiden, 1979.

Cohen, J. D. S. "Ioudaios: 'Judaean' and 'Jews' in Susanna, First Maccabees, and Second Maccabees." In *Geschichte–Tradition–Reflexion: Festschrift für Martin Hengel Zum 70. Geburtstag*. Ed. H. Cancik, H. Lichtenberger, P. Schäfer, 1:211–219. Tüsbingen, 1996.

Cohen, J. D. S. *The Beginnings of Jewishness: Boundaries, Varieties, Uncertainties*. Berkeley, Los Angeles, London, 1999.

Cohen, R. M. *Under Crescent and Cross*. Princeton, 1994.

Cohn, N. *The Pursuit of the Millennium*. New York, Oxford, 1970.

Coles, R. A. *Reports of Proceedings in Papyri*. Bruxelles, 1966.

Collins, J. J. "Apocalyptic Eschatology as the Transcendence of Death." *Catholic Biblical Quarterly* 36 (1974), 21–43.

Collins, J. J. "The Court-Tales of Daniel and the Development of Apocalyptic." *Journal of Biblical Commentary* 94 (1975), 218–234.

Collins, J. J. *The Apocalyptic Vision of the Book of Daniel.* Atlanta, 1977.

Collins, J. J. *Daniel, First Maccabees, Second Maccabees: Old Testament Message.* Vol. 15. Wilmington, 1981.

Collins, J. J. *Daniel.* Minneapolis, 1993.

Coope, J. A. *The Martyrs of Cordoba: Community and Family Conflict in an Age of Mass Conversion.* Lincoln, 1995.

Corbishley, T. "The Cronology of the Reign of Herod the Great." *Journal of Theological Studies* 36 (1935), 22–32.

Coulton, G. G. *Life in the Middle Ages.* 4 vols. in 1. New York, Cambridge, 1931.

Cowdrey, H. E. J. *The Epistolae Vagantes of Pope Gregory VII.* Oxford, 1972.

Cowdrey, H. E. J. "The Genesis of the Crusades." In *The Holy War.* Ed. T. P. Murphy, 9–32. Columbus, 1976.

Cowdrey, H. E. J. "Martyrdom and the First Crusade." In *Crusade and Settlement.* Ed. W. P. Edbury, 46–56. Cardiff, 1985.

Cross, F. N., Jr. *The Library of Ancient Qumran.* Garden City, 1961.

Daly, R. J. "The Soteriological Significance of the Sacrifice of Isaac," *Catholic Biblical Quarterly* 39 (1977), 45–75.

Daly, R. J. *Christian Sacrifice: The Judaeo Christian Background before Origin.* Washington, 1978.

Da Milano, I. "L'eresia popolare del secolo XI nell' Europa Occidentale." *Studi Gregoriani* 2 (1947), 43–89.

Dan, J. "The Beginnings of Jewish Mysticism in Europe." In *The Dark Ages: Jews in Christian Europe, 711–1096.* Ed. C. Roth, 282–290. Rutgers, 1966.

Dan, J. *Esoteric Theology of Ashkenazi Hasidism* (Hebrew). Jerusalem, 1968.

Dan, J. "The Problem of Sanctification of the Name in the Speculative Teaching of the German *Hasidim*" (Hebrew). In *Milhemet Qodesh u-Martirologiah*, 121–129. Jerusalem, 1967.

Dan, J. "The Importance and Meaning of the Story of the Ten Martyrs" (Hebrew). *Studies in Literature Presented to Simon Halkin.* Ed. E. Fleischer, 15–22. Jerusalem, 1973.

Dan, J. *The Hebrew Story in the Middle Ages* (Hebrew). Jerusalem, 1974.

Dan, J. "*Pirqe Hekhalot u-Ma'aseh Aseret Haruge Malkhut.*" *Eshel Be'er Sheva* 2 (1980), 63–80.

Dan, J. *The Ancient Jewish Mysticism.* Tel Aviv, 1993.

Dan, J. *Jewish Mysticism*, 4 vols. Northvale and Jerusalem, 1998.

Dancy, J. C. *A commentary on I Maccabees.* Oxford, 1954.

Daniell, C. *Death and Burial in Medieval England, 1066–1550.* London, New York, 1997.

Darmesteter, L. "*L'Autodafe de Troyes* (24 avril 1288)." *Revue des études juives* 2 (1881), 199–247.

Daube, D. "The Linguistics of Suicide." *Philosophy and Public Affairs* 1, no. 4 (1972), 437–487.

David, A. "Stories on the Persecutions in Germany in the Middle Ages" (Hebrew). In *A. M. Habermann Jubilee Volume: Studies in Medieval Hebrew Literature.* Ed. Z. Malachi, 69–83. Jerusalem, 1977.

David, A. "Historical Records of the Persecutions during the First Crusade in Hebrew Works and Hebrew Manuscripts" (Hebrew). In *Facing the Cross: The*

Persecutions of 1096 in History and Historiography. Ed. Y. T. Assis et al., 193–205. Jerusalem, 2000.

Davies, P. "Hasidim in the Maccabean Period." *Journal of Jewish Studies,* 28–29 (1977), 127–140.

Davies, W. D. "A Note on Josephus, Antiquities 15:136." *Harvard Theological Review* 47/3 (1954), 135–140.

De Boer, M. C. "The Nazoreans: Living at the Boundary of Judaism and Christianity." In *Tolerance and Intolerance in Early Judaism and Christianity.* Ed. G. N. Stanton and G. G. Strounsa, 239–262. Cambridge, 1998.

De Iongh, D. C. *Byzantine Aspects of Italy.* New York, 1967.

De Jonge, M. "Jesus' death for others and the death of the Maccabean martyrs." In *Text and Testimony: Essays on New Testament and Apocryphal Literature in Honour of A. F. J. Klijn.* Ed. T. Baarda, A. Hilhorst, G. P. Luttikhuizen, and A. S. van der Woude, 142–151. Kampen, 1988.

De Jonge, M. "Test. Benjamin 3:8 and the Picture of Joseph as 'A Good and Holy Man'." In *Die Entstehung Der Jüdishen Martyrologie.* Ed. J. W. Van Henten, 204–214, Leiden, New York, Köln, 1989.

De Jonge, M. "Jesus' Role in the Final Breakthrough of God's Kingdom." In *Geschichte–Tradition–Reflexion: Festchrift für Martin Hengel Zum 70. Geburtstag.* Ed. H. Cancik, H. Lichtenberger, and P. Schäfer, 3:265–286, Tübingen, 1996.

Delcor, *Le Livre de Daniel.* Paris, 1971.

Delehaye, H. "Passio sanctorum sexaginta martyrum," *Analecta Bollandiana* 28 (1904), 289–307.

Delehaye, H. *The Legends of the Saints,* tr. by D. Attwater. New York, 1962.

Delooz, P. "Towards a Sociological Study of Canonized Sainthood." In *Saints and their Cults: Studies in Religious Sociology, Folklore and History.* Ed. S. Wilson, 189–216. Cambridge, 1983.

Derfler, S. L. *The Hasmonean Revolt: Rebellion or Revolution.* Lewiston, Lampeter, Queenston, 1990.

De Ste Croix, "Aspects of the 'Great' Persecutions." *Harvard Theological Review* 47 (1954), 75–113.

De Ste Croix. "Why Were the Early Christians Persecuted?" In *Studies in Ancient Society: Past and Present Series.* Ed. M. I. Finley, 210–249. London and Boston, 1974.

De Ste Croix. "Why Were the Early Christians Persecuted? A Rejoinder." In *Studies in Ancient Society: Past and Present Series.* Ed. M. I. Finley, 256–262. London and Boston, 1974.

Dihle, A. "C. Judaism: I. Hellenistic Judaism." In *Theological Dictionary of the New Testament.* Ed. G. Kittel and G. Fridrich, 9:632–635. Eerdmans, 1974.

Dinur, B. Z. Ed. *Israel ba-Golah.* 2 vols. in 8. 2d ed. Tel Aviv, 1958–1972.

Dols, M. *The Black Death in the Middle East.* Princeton, 1977.

Doran, R. "2 Maccabees and 'Tragic History,'" *Hebrew Union College Annual* 50 (1979), 110–114.

Doran, R. "The Martyrs: A Synoptic View of the Mother and her Seven Sons." In *Ideal Figures in Ancient Judaism: Profiles and Paradigms.* Ed. G. W. E. Nickelsburg and J. J. Collins. *Society of Biblical Literature Septuagint and Cognate Studies* 12 (1980), 189–221.

Doran, R. *Temple Propaganda: The Purpose and Character of 2 Maccabees.* Catholic Biblical Association of America. Washington, DC, 1981.

Dorff, E. N. "Another Jewish View of Ethics, Christian and Jewish." In *Christianity in Jewish Terms*. Ed. T. Frymer-Kensky et al., 127–134. Colorado and Oxford, 2000.

Douglas, J. *The Social Meanings of Suicide*. Princeton, 1967.

Dozy, R. *Spanish Islam*. London, 1972.

Droge A. J., and Tabor, J. D. *A Noble Death: Suicide and Martyrdom among Christians and Jews in Antiquity*. San Francisco, 1992.

Dublin, I. L. *Suicide. A Sociological and Statistical Study*. New York, 1963.

Dublin, I. L. *To Be or Not To Be: A Study of Suicide*. New York, 1933.

Dubois, D. "La mort de Zacharie: mémoire juive et mémoire chrétienne." *Revue des études Augustinennes* 40 (1994), 23–38.

Duchett, E. *Death and Life in the Tenth Century*. Michigan, 1967.

Dunn, J. D. G. "Two Covenants or One? The Interdependence of Jewish and Christian Identity," *Geschichte–Tradition–Reflexion: Festschrift für Martin Hengel Zum 70. Geburtstag*. Ed. H. Cancik, H. Lichtenberger, and P. Schäfer, 3:107–113, Tübingen, 1996.

DuPont-Sommer, A. *Le Quatrième Livre des Machabées: Introd., traduction et notes*. Paris, 1939.

Durkheim, E. *Suicide: A Study in Sociology*. 6th ed. New York, 1966.

Edwards, P. "The Meaning and Value of Life" *Encyclopedia of Philosophy*. Ed. P, Edwards. New York, 1967.

Efron, J. "Holy War and Redemption in the Period of the Hasmoneans" (Hebrew). In *Milhemet Kodesh u-Martirologiah*, 7–34. Jerusalem, 1967.

Efron, J. "Bar Kochva in the Light of the Palestinian and the Babylonian talmudic Tradition." In *The Bar Kochva Revolt*. Ed. A. Oppenheimer and U. Rappaport, 47–105. Jerusalem, 1984.

Efron, J. *Studies on the Hasmonean Period*. Leiden, New York, 1987.

Eidelberg, S. "The Community of Troyes before the Time of Rashi" (Hebrew). *Sura* 1 (1953–1954), 48–57.

Eidelberg, S. *The Jews and the First Crusade*. Madison, 1977.

Einbinder, L. S. "Pucellina of Blois: Romantic Myths and Narrative Conventions." *Jewish History* 12.1 (1998), 29–46.

Einbinder, L. S. "The Troyes Elegies: Jewish Martyrology in Hebrew and Old French." *Viator* 30 (1999), 201–230.

Einbinder, L. S. "The Jewish Martyrs of Blois, 1171." In *Medieval Hagiography: A Sourcebook*. Ed. T. Head, 537–560. New York, London, 2000.

Einbinder, L. S. *Beautiful Death: Jewish Poetry and Martyrdom in Medieval France*. Princeton and Oxford, 2002.

Elbogen, I. *Jewish Liturgy: A Comprehensive History*. Ed. J. Heinmann et al. Philadelphia, Jerusalem, New York, 1993.

Eliade, M. *Myth and Reality*. Tr. W. R. Trask. New York, 1968.

Eliade, M. *Images and Symbols*. Tr. P. Mairet. New York, 1969.

Eliav, M. (ed.) *I Believe: Testimonies on the Lives and Deaths of People of Faith during the Holocaust* (Hebrew). Jerusalem, 1965.

Elukin, J. M. "The Discovery of the Self: Jews and Conversion in the Twelfth Century." In *Jews and Christians in Twelfth-Century Europe*. Ed. M. A. Michael A. Signer and John Van Engen, 63–76. Notre Dame, 2001.

Epstein, J. N. *Introduction to Tannaitic Literature: Babylonian Talmud and Yerushalmi* (Hebrew). Jerusalem, 1957.

Erdmann, C. *The Origin of the Idea of the Crusade.* Tr. M. W. Baldwin and W. Goffart. Princeton, 1977.

Fackenheim, E. L. *The Jewish Return into History: Reflection in the Age of Auschwitz and a New Jerusalem.* New York, 1978.

Farberow, L. N., and Shneidman, E. S., Eds. *The Cry for Help.* New York, 1961.

Farmer, W. R. *Maccabees, Zealots, and Josephus: An Inquiry into Jewish Nationalism in the Greco-Roman Period.* New York, 1956.

Feldman, L. H. "Masada: A Critique of Recent Scholarship." *Christianity Judaism and other Greco-Roman Cults Studies for Morton Smith Sixty, Part Three:Judaism berofr 70,* 218–248. Leiden, 1975.

Feldman, L. H. *Josephus and Modern Scholarship (1937–1980).* Berlin, 1984.

Feldman, L. H. "Josephus' *Jewish Antiquities* and Pseudo-Philo's Biblical Antiquities." In *Josephus, the Bible, and History.* Ed. L. H. Feldman and G. Hata, 59–80. Detroit, 1989.

Ferorelli, N. *Gli Ebrei Nell'Italia Meridionale.* Bologna, 1966.

Finkelstein, L. *Jewish Self-Government in the Middle Ages.* New York, 1924.

Finkelstein, L. "The Ten Martyrs." In *Essays and Studies in Memory of Linda R. Miller.* Ed. I. Davidson, 29–55. New York, 1938.

Finkelstein, L. *Mavo le-Masekhtot Avot ve-Avot de-Rabbi Natan.* New York, 1950.

Finkelstein, L. *The Pharisees: The Sociological Background of their Faith.* 2 vols. Philadelphia, 1962.

Finkelstein, L. *Akiva: Scholar, Saint and Martyr.* London, 1990.

Fischel, H. A. "Martyrs and Prophets." *Jewish Quarterly Review* 37 (1946–1947), 265–280.

Fishbane, M. *The Kiss of God: Spiritual and Mystical Death in Judaism.* Seattle and London, 1994.

Fletcher, J. *"Euthanasis: Our Right to Die."* Morals and Medicine. 1954.

Flusser, D. "Jewish Origin of Christianity" (Hebrew). In *Y. Baer Jubilee Volume,* 75–98. Jerusalem, 1960.

Flusser, D. "Jewish Sources of Christian Martyrdom and Their Influence on Its Fundamental Concepts" (Hebrew). In *Milhemet Kodesh u-Martirologiah,* 61–71. Jerusalem, 1967.

Flusser, D. "The Author of Sefer Yosippon, His Character and His Period" (Hebrew). *Zion* 18 (1953), 109–126.

Flusser, D. "He Has Planted It [i.e., the Law] as Eternal Life in Our Midst" (Hebrew). *Tarbiz* 58 (1988–9), 147–53.

Focillon, H. *The Year 1000.* New York, 1969.

Foe, A. *The Jews of Europe after the Black Death.* Berkeley, Los Angeles, London, 2000.

Fox, L. R. *Pagans and Christians.* New York, 1986.

Frend, W. H. C. *Martyrdom and Persecution in the Early Church: A Study of a Conflict from the Maccabees to Donatus.* Garden City, 1967.

Frend, W. H. C. "The Failure of the Persecutions in the Roman Empire." In *Studies in Ancient Society.* Ed. M. I. Finley, Past and Present Series, 263–287. London and Boston, 1974.

Frey, R. G. "Did Socrates Commit Suicide?" In *Suicide.* Ed. M. P. Battin and D. J. Mayo. New York, 1980.

Fulimer, W. E. "The Chronology of the Reign of Herod the Great." *Jewish Theological Seminary* 17 (1966), 283–298.

Funkenstein, A. "Changes in the Patterns of Christian Anti-Jewish Polemics in the 12th Century" (Hebrew). *Zion* 33 (1968), 125–144.

Gafni, I. M. "Josephus and I Maccabees." In *Josephus, the Bible, and History*. Ed. L. H. Feldman and G. Hata. Detroit, 1989.

Gafni, I. M. "Babylonian Rabbinic Culture." In *Cultures of the Jews: A New History*. Ed. D. Biale, 238–239. New York, 2002.

Gaston, L. *Paul and the Torah*. Vancouver, 1987.

Gay, J. *L'Italie meridionale et l'empire byzantin, 867–1071*. Paris, 1904.

Geiger, J. "The History of Judas Maccabaeus: One Aspect of Hellenistic Historiography" (Hebrew). *Zion* 49 (1984), 1–8.

Gero, S. "Byzantine Imperial Prosopgraphy in a Medieval Hebrew Text." *Byzantion* 47 (1977), 157–162.

Gibbs, P. J. Ed., *Suicide*. New York, Evanston, London, 1968.

Gibbs, R. "Suspicions of Suffering." In *Christianity in Jewish Terms*. Ed. T. Frymer-Kensky et al., 221–229, Colorado and Oxford, 2000.

Gies, F. *The Knight in History*. New York, 1987.

Gilat, Y. D. *R. Eliezer Ben Hyrcanus: A Scholar Outcast*. Ramat Gan, 1984.

Gilchrist, J. "The Erdmann Thesis and the Canon Law." *Crusade and Settlemen*. Ed. W. P. Edbury, 35–45. Cardiff Press, 1985.

Ginzburg, C. *Ecstasies Deciphering the Witches' Sabbath*. New York, 1991.

Girard, R. *Violence and the Sacred*. Tr. P. Gregory. Baltimore, 1977.

Goitein, D. "Obadyah, a Norman Proselyte." *The Journal of Jewish Studies* 4 (1953), 80–81.

Golb, N. "New Light on the Persecution of French Jews at the Time of the First Crusade." *Proceedings of the American Academy for Jewish Research* 34 (1966), 1–64.

Golb, N. *History and Culture of the Jews of Rouen in the Middle Ages*. Tel Aviv, 1976.

Golb, N. *The Jews in Medieval Normandy: A Social and Intellectual History*. Cambridge, 1998.

Golb, N., and Pritsak, O. *Khazarian Hebrew Documents of the Tenth Century*. Ithaca and London, 1982.

Goldenberg, R. "The Jewish Sabbath in the Roman World up to the Time of Constantine the Great." In *Aufstieg und Niedergang der römischen Welt*, II, vol. 19.1 (Berlin, 1979), 414–447.

Goldenberg, R. "Talmud." In *Judaism: A People and Its History. Religion, History, and Culture: Selections from the Encyclopaedia of Religion*. Ed. R. M. Seltzer, 102. New York, London, 1989.

Goldin, J. *The Fathers According to Rabbi Nathan*. New Haven, 1995.

Goldin, S. "The Socialisation for Kiddush ha-Shem among Medieval Jews." *Journal of Medieval History*, vol. 23, no. 2 (1997), 117–138.

Goldin, S. *The Ways of Jewish Martyrdom* (Hebrew). Lodd, 2002.

Goldschmidt, D. E. *On Jewish Liturgy: Essays on Prayer and Religious Poetry* (Hebrew). Jerusalem, 1978.

Goldstein, J. A. *1 Maccabees: A New Translation with Introduction and Commentary*. AB 41. Garden City, 1976.

Goldstein, J. A. *2 Maccabees: A New Translation with Introduction and Commentary.* AB 41a. Garden City, 1983.

Goldstein, S. *Suicide in Rabbinic Literature.* New Jersey, 1989.

Goodich, M. "The Politics of Canonization in the Thirteenth Century: Lay and Mendicant Saints." In *Saints and Their Cults: Studies in Religious Sociology, Folklore and History.* Ed. S. Wilson, 169–187. Cambridge, 1983.

Gottfried, R. S. *The Black Death: Natural and Human Disaster in Medieval Europe.* London, 1983.

Grabar, A. *Martyrium: Recherches sur le culte de reliques et l'art chrétien antique.* 2 vols. London, 1972.

Grabbe, L. L. *Judaism from Cyrus to Hadrian.* 2 vols. [with continuing pagination]. Minneapolis, 1992.

Grabbe, L. L. "Sadducees and Pharisees." In *Judaism in Late Antiquity: Part 3. Where We Stand: Issues and Debates in Ancient Judaism.* Ed. A. J. Avery-Peck and J. Neusner, 1:35–62. Leiden and Brill, 1999.

Grabbe, L. L. *Judaic Religion in the Second Temple Period.* London and New York, 2000.

Grabbe, L. L. "Eschatology in Philo and Josephus." In *Judaism in Late Antiquity: Part 4, Death, Life-after-Death, Resurrection and the World-to-Come in the Judaism of Antiquity.* Ed. A. J. Avery-Peck and J. Neusner, 163–185. Leiden and Brill, 2000.

Grabois, A. "Les juifs et leurs seigneurs dans la France Septentrionale aux XIe et XIIe siècles." In *Les Juifs Dans L'Histoire de France.* Ed. M. Yardeni, 11–23. Leiden, 1980.

Grabois, A. "The Leadership of the *Parnasim* in the Northern French Communities in the Eleventh and Twelfth Centuries: the '*Boni Viri*' and the Elders of the Cities'" (Hebrew). In *Culture and Society in Medieval Jewish History: Studies Dedicated to the Memory of Haim Hillel Ben-Sasson.* Ed. M. Ben-Sasson, R. Bonfil, and J. R. Hacker, 303–314. Jerusalem, 1989.

Graetz, H. *History of the Jews.* 6 vols. Philadelphia, 1891–1898.

Grayzel, S. *The Church and the Jews in the XIIIth Century.* 2d ed. New York, 1965.

Grisé, Y. *Le Suicide Dans La Rome Antique.* Paris, 1982.

Gross, A. "The Ashkenazic Syndrom of Qiddush ha-Shem in Portugal in 1497." *Tarbitz* 64 (1995), 83–114.

Gross, A. "Historical and Halakhic Aspects of the Mass Martyrdom in Mainz: An Integrative Approach." In *Facing the Cross: The Persecutions of 1096 in History and Historiography.* Ed. Y. T. Assis et al., 171–192. Jerusalem, 2000.

Gross, H. *Gallia Judaica dictionnaire geographique de la France dáprès les sources rabbiniques.* Paris, 1897.

Grossman, A. "The Immigration of the Kalonymide Family from Italy to Germany" (Hebrew). *Zion* 40 (1975), 154–185.

Grossman, A. *The Early Sages of Ashkenaz* (Hebrew). Jerusalem, 1988.

Grossman, A. "The Roots of *Qiddush ha-Shem* in Early Ashkenaz" (Hebrew). In *The Sanctity of Life and Martyrdom.* Ed. I. M. Gafni and A. Ravitzky, 99–130. Jerusalem, 1992.

Grossman, A. "The Connections between Spanish Jewry and Ashkenazic Jewry in the Middle Ages" (Hebrew). In *Moreshet Sepharad: The Sephardi Legacy.* Ed. H. Beinart, 174–189. Jerusalem, 1992.

Grossman, A. *The Early Sages of France: Their Lives, Leadership and Works* (Hebrew). Jerusalem, 1995.

Grossman, A. "*Qiddush ha-Shem* in the Eleventh and Twelfth Centuries: Between Ashkenaz and the Islamic Countries" (Hebrew). *Peamim* 75 (1998), 27–46.

Grossman, A. "The Cultural and Social Background of Jewish Martyrdom in 1096" (Hebrew). In *Facing the Cross: The Persecutions of 1096 in History and Historiography.* Ed. Y. T. Assis et al., 55–73. Jerusalem, 2000.

Gruen, E. S. *Heritage and Hellenism: The Reinvention of Jewish Tradition.* Berkeley, Los Angeles, London, 1998.

Gruenwald, I. "*Qiddush ha-Shem*: An Examination of a Term" (Hebrew). *Molad* 1 (1968), 476–484.

Gruenwald, I. "Intolerance and Martyrdom: From Socrates to Rabbi Aqiva." In *Tolerance and Intolerance in Early Judaism and Christianity.* Ed. G. N. Stanton and G. G. Strounsa, 7–29. Cambridge, 1998.

Gutman, J. "The Mother and Her Seven Sons in the Aggadah and the Second and Fourth Books of the Hasmoneans" (Hebrew). In *Commentationes Iudaico-Hellenisticae in memoriam Iohannis Lewy.* Ed. M. Schwabe and J. Gutman, 25–37. Jerusalem, 1949.

Guttmann, A. "The Significance of Miracles for Talmudic Judaism." *Hebrew Union College Annual* 20 (1974), 364–406.

Guttmann, A. *Rabbinic Judaism in the Making: A Chapter in the History of the Halakha from Ezra to Judah I.* Detroit, 1979.

Habermann, A. M. *A History of Hebrew Liturgical and Secular Poetry* (Hebrew). 2 vols. Rmat-Gan, 1972.

Habermann, A. M. *Rabbenu Gershom the Light of the Exile.* Jerusalem, 1944.

Habicht, C. 2 *Makkabäerbuch*," Jüdische Schriften aus hellenistisch-röischer Zeit. Vol. 1 *Historische und legendarische Erzählugen.* Gütersloh, 1976b.

Hacker, J. "About the Persecutions during the First Crusade" (Hebrew). *Zion* 31 (1966), 225–231.

Hacker, J. "Was *Qiddush ha-Shem* Transferred to the Spiritual Discipline?" (Hebrew). In *Sanctity of Life and Martyrdom.* Ed. I. M. Gafni and A. Ravitzky, 221–232. Jerusalem, 1992.

Hacker, J. "'If We Forgot Our Lord's Name and Opened Our Palms to a Foreign God': The Evolving of Interpretation against the Background in Spain in the Middle Ages" (Hebrew). *Zion* 57 (1992), 247–274.

Hadas, M. *Hellenistic Culture: Fusion and Diffusion.* New York, 1959.

Hagenmeyer, H. *Die Kreuzzugsbriefe aus den Jahren 1088–1100.* Innsbruck, 1901.

Halbertal, M. "Coexisting with the Enemy: Jews and Pagans in the Mishnah." In *Tolerance and Intolerance in Early Judaism and Christianity.* Ed. G. N. Stanton and G. G. Strounsa, 159–172. Cambridge, 1998.

Halbwachs, M. *The Causes of Suicide.* Tr. H. Goldblatt. New York, 1978.

Halkin, A., and Hartman, D. *Epistles of Maimonides: Crisis and Leadership.* Philadelphia and Jerusalem, 1993.

Hallamish, M. *Kabbalah: In Liturgy, Halakhah and Customs* (Hebrew). Jerusalem, 2000.

Hanhart, R. "Zun Text des 2. und 3. Makkabäerbuches: Probleme der Überlieferung, der Auslegung und der Ausgabe," *Nachrichten von der Akademie der Wissenschaften in Göttingen; Philologisch-Historische Klasse*, 427–478. Göttingen, 1961.

Hankoff, D. L. "Judaic Origins of the Suicide Prohibition." In *Suicide: Theory and Clinical Aspects.* Ed. D. L. Hankoff and B. Einsidler. Litteleton, 1979.

Harrington, D. J. *The Maccabean Revolt: Anatomy of a Biblical Revolution.* Wilmington, 1971.

Hartman, F. L., and DiLella, A. A. *The Book of Daniel.* Doubleday, 1978.

Hasan-Rokem, G. *Web of Life: Folklore and Midrash in Rabbinic Literature.* Tr. B. Stein. Stanford, 2000.

Hauerwas, S. "Christian Ethics in Jewish Terms: A Response to David Novak." In *Christianity in Jewish Terms.* Ed. T. Frymer-Kensky et al., 135–140. Colorado and Oxford, 2000.

Haverkamp, A. "Baptised Jews in German Lands during the Twelfth Century." In *Jews and Christians in Twelfth-Century Europe.* Ed. M. A. Michael, A. Signer, and John Van Engen, 255–310. Notre Dame, 2001.

Haverkamp, E. " 'Persecutio' und 'Gezerah' in Trier während des Ersten Kreuzzuges." In *Juden und Christen zur Zeit der Kreuzzüge.* Ed. A. Haverkamp, 35–71. Sigmaringen, 1999.

Heaton, E. W. *The Book of Daniel.* London, 1956.

Hengel, M. *Judaism and Hellenism: Studies in their Encounter in Palestine during the Early Hellenistic Period.* 2 vols. Tr. J. Bowden. Philadelphia, 1974.

Hengel, M. *Jews, Greeks and Barbarian: Aspects of the Hellenization of Judaism in the Pre-Christian Period.* Philadelphia, 1980.

Herford, R. T. *Christianity in Talmud and Midrash.* New York, 1978.

Herr, M. D. "Persecutions and Martyrdom in Hadrian's Days." In *Milhemet Kodesh u-Martirologiah,* 76–83. Jerusalem, 1967.

Herr, M. D. "The Question of Halakhot of War on Sabbath" (Hebrew). *Tarbitz* 30 (1971), 242–56; 341–356.

Herr, M. D. "Persecutions and Martyrdom in Hadrian's Days." *Studies and History.* Ed. D. Asheri and I. Shatzman. *Scripta Hierosolymitana,* 23, 85–125. Jerusalem, 1972.

Hirschberg, H. Z. "The Almohade Persecutions and the India Trade: A Letter from the Year 1148." In *Yitzhak F. Baer Jubilee Volume.* Ed. S. Ettinger et al. 134–153. Jerusalem, 1960.

Hirschler M. "Midrash *Asarah Harugei Malkhut*" (Hebrew), *Sinai* 71 (1974), 218–228.

Hoener, H. W. *Herod Antipas.* Cambridge, 1972.

Hoenig, S. "Maccabbees, Zealots, and Josephus – Second Commonwealth Parallelism," *Jewish Quarterly Review* 49 (1958/1959), 75–80.

Hoenig, S. "The Sicarii in Masada-Glory or Infamy?" *Tradition* 11 (1970), 5–30.

Holtz, A. "Kiddush and Hillal Hashm." In *Faith and Reason: Essays in Judaism.* Ed. R. Gordis and R. B. Waxman, 79–86. New York, 1973.

Horowitz, E. "Medieval Jews Face the Cross" (Hebrew). In *Facing the Cross: The Persecutions of 1096 in History and Historiography.* Ed. Y. T. Assis et al., 118–140. Jerusalem, 2000.

Housley, H. "Crusades against Christians: Their Origins and Early Development, c. 1000–1216." *Crusade and Settlement.* Ed. W. P. Edbury, 17–36. Cardiff Press, 1985.

Hyman, A. *The History of the Tannaim and the Amoraim*(Hebrew). 3 vols. Jerusalem, 1964.

Idel, M. *Kabbalah: New Perspectives.* New Haven and London, 1988.

Idel, M. "In the Light of Life: A Study in Kabbalistic Eschatology" (Hebrew). In *Sanctity of Life and Martyrdom.* Ed. I. M. Gafni and A. Ravitzky, 191–211. Jerusalem, 1992.

Idelsohn, A. Z. *Jewish Liturgy and Its Development.* New York, 1932.

Isaac, B. "Judea after A.D. 70." *Journal of Jewish Studies*, 34–35 (1984), 44–50.

Isaac, B. "The Revolt of Bar Kokhva as Described by Cassius Dio and Other Revolts against the Romans in Greek and Latin Literature." In *The Bar-Kokhva Revolt.* Ed. A. Oppenheimer and U. Rappaport, 106–112. Jerusalem, 1984.

Jacobs, L. "How Much of the Babylonian Talmud is Pseudepigraphic?" *Journal of Jewish Studies*, 28–29 (1977), 46–59.

Jacoby, S. *Wild Justice: The Evolution of Revenge.* New York, 1983.

Jellinek, A., Ed. *Bet ha-Midrah.* 6 vols. in 2. Jerusalem, 1967.

Jenkins, R. *Byzantium: The Imperial Centuries A.D. 610–1071.* New York, 1966.

Jordan, W. C. *The French Monarchy and the Jews: From Philip Augustus to the Last Capetians.* Philadelphia, 1989.

Jordan, W. C. "Adolescence and Conversion in the Middle Ages: A Research Agenda." In *Jews and Christians in Twelfth-Century Europe.* Ed. M. A. Michael, A. Signer, and John Van Engen, 77–93. Notre Dame, 2001.

Kaegi, W. *Byzantium and the Early Islamic Conquests.* Cambridge, 1992.

Kahanah, A. *Ha-Sepharim Ha-Hitzoniim* (Hebrew). 2 vols. Tel Aviv, 1956.

Kalmin, R. "Christians and Heretics in Rabbinic Literature of Late Antiquity." *Harvard Theological Review* 87:2 (April 1994), 155–169.

Kampen, J. *The Hasideans and the Origin of Pharisaism.* Atlanta, 1988.

Kanarfogel, E. *Jewish Education and Society in the High Middle Ages.* Detroit, 1993.

Kanarfogel, E. *Peering through the Lattices: Mystical, Magical, and Pietistic Dimensions in the Tosafist Period.* Detroit, 2000.

Kanarfogel, E. "Halakhah and Mezi'ut (Realia) in Medieval Ashkenaz: Surveying the Parameters and Defining the Limits." *Jewish Law Annual* 14 (2003), 193–224.

Kanfo, H. "Manifestations of Divine Providence in the Gloom of the Holocaust." In *I Will Be Sanctified: Religious Responses to the Holocaust.* Ed. Y. Fogel, and Tr. E. Levin, 15–23. Northvale, Jerusalem, 1998.

Kaplan, Y. "Jewish Refugees from Germany and Poland–Lithuania in Amsterdam during the Thirty Years War" (Hebrew). In *Culture and Society in Medieval Jewry: Studies Dedicated to the Memory of Haim Hillel Ben-Sasson.* Ed. M. Ben-Sasson, R. Bonfil, and J. R. Hacker, 587–622. Jerusalem, 1989.

Kasher, A. "The Causes and the Circumstantial Background of the Jewish War Against Rome." In *Ha-Mered Ha-Gadol: ha-Sibot veha-Nesibot li-Feritsato.* Ed. A. Kasher, 9–92. Jerusalem, 1983.

Kasher, A. *Edom, Arabia, and Isreal* (Hebrew). Jerusalem, 1988.

Katz, J. "Even Though He Sinned, He Remains a Jew." *Tarbitz* 27 (1958), 204–217.

Katz, J. "Martyrdom in the Middle Ages and in 1648–9" (Hebrew). In *Sefer Yovel le-Yitzhak F. Baer.* Ed. S. Ettinger et al., 318–337. Jerusalem, 1960.

Katz, J. *Exclusiveness and Tolerance: Studies in Jewish–Gentile Relations in Medieval and Modern Times.* Oxford, 1961.

Katz. P. "The Text of 2 Maccabees Reconsidered," *Zeitschrift für die neutestamentliche Wissenschaft,* 51 (1960), 10–30.

Katz. P. "Eleazar's Martyrdom in 2 Maccabees: The Latin Evidence for a Point of the Story." *Studia Patristica* 4.2. Ed. F. L. Cross, 118–124. Berlin, 1961.

Kaufman, D. "*Liste de rabbins dressee par Azriel Trabotto.*" *Revue des études Juives,* 24 (1882), 208–225.

Keller, J. E. *Gonzalo De Berceo.* New York, 1972.

Kellermann, U. *Auferstanden in den Himmel: 2 Makkabäer 7 und die Auferstehung der Märtyrer* (SBS 95). Stuttgart, 1979.

Kellermann, U. "Das Danielbuch und die Märtyretheologie der Auferstehung." In *Die Enstehung der Jüdischen Martyrologie*. Ed. J. W. Van Henten, 51–75. Leiden, 1989.

Kennard, J. S. "Judas of Galilee and his Clan." *Jewish Quarterly Review* 36 (1945/1946), 281–286.

Kimelman, R. "Birkat Ha-Minim and the Lack of Evidence for an Anti-Christian Jewish Prayer in Late Antiquity." In *Jewish and Christian Self-Definition*. Ed. E. P. Sanders et al., 2:226–244; 391–403. Philadelphia, 1980.

King, M. H. *The Life of Christina of St-Trond by Thomas of Cantipré*. Saskatoon, 1986.

Kisch, G. *The Jews in Medieval Germany*. Chicago, 1949.

Klauck, H.-J. "Brotherly Love in Plutarch and 4 Maccabees." In *Greeks, Romans, and Christians: Essays in Honor of A. J. Malherbe*. Ed. D. L. Balch, E. Ferguson and W. A. Meeks, 144–156. Minneapolis, 1990.

Klausner, J. *The History of the Second Temple* (Heberw). 2d ed., 5 vols. Jerusalem, 1950.

Kloner, A. "Hideout-Complexes from the Period of Bar Kochva in the Judean Plain." In *The Bar-Kokhva Revolt*. Ed. A. Oppenheimer and U. Rappaport, 153–171. Jerusalem, 1984.

Krauss, S. "Ten Martyrs" (Hebrew). In *ha-Shilloach* 44 (1925), 10–22, 106–117, 221–223.

Krauss, S. "*Un nouveau texte pour l'histoire judeo-byzantin*." *Revue des études juives* 87 (1929), 1–7.

Krauss, S. "*Un document sur l'histoire de Juifs en Italie*." *Revue des études juives* 67 (1920), 40–43.

Krey, C. A., Ed. and Tr. *The First Crusade*. Gloucester, 1985.

Kupfer, A. "Toward a Geneology of the Family of R. Moses bar Yom Tov ("The Knight of the World") of London" (in Hebrew). *Tarbiz* 40 (1971), 385–387.

Lacocque, A. *The Book of Daniel*. Atlanta, 1979.

Ladouceur, D. J. "Josephus and Masada." In *Josephus, Judaism, and Christianity*. Ed. L. H. Feldman and G. Hata, 95–113. Detroit, 1987.

Lambert, M. *Medieval Heresy: Popular Movements from Bogomil to Hus*. New York, 1976.

Landes, R. *Relics, Apocalypse and the Deceits of History: Adémar of Chabannes, 989–1034*. Cambridge, 1995.

Landes, R. "The Massacres of 1010: On the Origins of Popular Anti-Jewish Violence in Western Europe." In *From Witness to Witchcraft: Jews and Judaism in Medieval Christian Thought*. Ed. J. Cohen, 79–112. Harrassowitz, 1996.

Langmuir, I. G. "The Knight's Tales of Young Hugh of Lincoln." *Speculum* 47 (1972), 459–482.

Langmuir, I. G. "*Tanquam Servi*: The Change in Jewish Status in French Law about 1200." In *Les Juifs dans l'Histoire de France*. Ed. M. Yardeni, 25–54. Leiden, 1980.

Langmuir, I. G. *Toward a Definition of Antisemitism*. Berkeley and Los Angeles, 1990.

Langmuir, I. G. "At the Frontiers of Faith." In *Religious Violence between Christians and Jews: Medieval Roots, Modern Perspectives*. Ed. A. S. Abulafia, 138–156. New York, 2002.

Larson, M. A. *The Essene Heritage*. New York, 1967.

Laupot, E. "Tacitus' Fragment 2: The Anti-Roman Movement of the *Christiani* and the Nazoreans." *Vigiliae Christianae* 54:3 (2000), 233–247.

Le Blant, E. *Le Persecuteurs et les martyrs aux premiers siecles de notre ere*. Paris, 1893.

Lensky, M. *The Life of the Jews in the Warsaw Ghetto* (Hebrew). Jerusalem, 1983.

Leon, J. *The Jews of Ancient Rome.* Philadelphia, 1960.

Lester, Gene, and Lester, David. *Suicide: The Gamble with Death.* New Jersey, 1971.

Levenson, D. J. *The Death and the Resurrection of the Beloved Son.* New Haven and London, 1993.

Levi, I. "*Le Martyre des Sept Macchabees dans La Pesikta Rabbati.*" *Revue de études Juives* 54 (1907), 138–141.

Levi, I. "L'Apocalypse de Zerubabel." *Revue de études Juives* 68 (1914), 131–150.

Levien, L. I. "The Jewish–Greek Conflict in First Century Caesarea." *Journal of Jewish Studies,* 24–25, (1974) 381–397.

Levinger, J. "Daniel in the Lions' Den: A Model of National Literature of Struggle." *Beth Mikra* 70 (1977), 329–333; 394–395.

Lewinska, P. *Twenty Months in Auschwitz.* New York, 1968.

Lewis, B. "Paltiel, A Note." *Bulletin of the School of Oriental and African Studies* 30 (1967), 177–181.

Licht, J. "Taxo or the Apocalyptic Doctrine of Vengeance." *Journal of Jewish Studies* 12, 3 and 4, (1961), 95–105.

Lieberman, S. "The Martyrs of Caesarea." *Anuaire de L'Institut de Philologie et d'Historie Orientales et Slaves* 7 (1939–1944), 395–446.

Lieberman, S. "Palestine in the Third and Fourth Centuries." *Jewish Quarterly Review* 36 (1945–1946), 329–370 and 37 (1946–1947), 239–253.

Lieberman, S. "The Publication of the Mishnah." *Hellenism in Jewish Palestine: Studies in the Literary Transmission, Belief, and Manners of Palestine in the I Century C.E,* 83–99. New York, 1950.

Lieberman, S. "On Persecution of the Jewish Religion" (Hebrew). In *Salo W. Baron Jubilee Volume.* Ed. S. Liberman, Heb. vol., 213–245. 3 vols. New York, 1974.

Lieberman, S. *Tosefta Ki-Fshutah: A Comprehensive Commentary on the Tosefta* (in Hebrew). 10 vols. New York, 1955–1988.

Lieu, J. M. "Accusations of Jewish Persecution in Early Christian Sources, with Particular Reference to Justin Martyr and the Martyrdom of Polycarp." In *Tolerance and Intolerance in Early Judaism and Christianity.* Ed. G. N. Stanton and G. G. Strounsa, 279–295. Cambridge, 1998.

Linder, A. *Roman Imperial Legislation of the Jews.* Jerusalem, 1983.

Loftus, F. "The martyrdom of the Galilean Troglodytes." *Jewish Quarterly Review,* 66 (1976), 213–223.

Loftus, F. "The Anti-Roman Revolts of the Jews and the Galileans," *JQR,* 68 (1977), 78–98.

Luz, M. "Eleazar's Second Speech on Masada and Its Literary Precedents," *Rheinisches Museum für Philologie* NF 126 (1983), 25–43.

Maccoby, H. *The Mythmaker: Paul and the Invention of Christianity.* San Francisco, 1987.

Malinowski, B. *Crime and Custom in Savage Society.* New York, 1926.

Malkin, A., and Hartman, D. *Epistles of Maimonides: Crisis and Leadership.* Philadelphia and Jerusalem, 1993.

Malone, E. *The Monk and the Martyr.* Washington, DC, 1950.

Mamigliano, A. D. *Giudea Romana – Richerche sull' organizazione della Giudea sotto il dominio romano (63 A.C.–70 D.C.).* Amsterdam 1967 (Bologna 1973).

Mango, C. *Byzantium: The Empire of New Rome.* New York, 1980.

Mango, C. "The Life of St. Andrew the Fool Reconsidered." *Revista di Studi Bizantini e Slavi* 11 (1982), 297–313.

Mango, C. "Constantinople, ville sainte." *Critique* 48 (1992), 625–633.

Mann, J. "Changes in the Divine Service of the Synagogue due to Religious Persecutions." *Hebrew Union College Annual* 4 (1927), 252–259.

Mann, J. *The Jews in Egypt and in Palestine under the Fatimid Caliphs.* 2 Vols. New York, 1970.

Mantel, D. H. "*Ha-Menne'em le-Merd Bar-Kokhva.*" In *Milhemet Qodesh u-Martirologiah*, 35–57. Jerusalem, 1967.

Mantel, D. H. *The Men of the Great Synagogue* (Hebrew). Tel Aviv, 1983.

Marcus, I. G. "The Politics and Ethics of Pietism in Judaism: The *Hasidim* of Medieval Germany." *The Journal of Religious Ethics* 8:2 (1980), 227–258.

Marcus, I. G. *Piety and Society: The Jewish Pietiests of Medieval Germany.* Leiden, 1981.

Marcus, I. G. "From Politics to Martyrdom: Shifting Paradigms in the Hebrew Narratives of the 1096 Crusading Riots." *Prooftexts* 2 (1982), 40–52.

Marcus, I. G. "*Hasidei Ashkenaz* Private Penitentials: An Introduction and Descriptive Catalogue of their Manuscripts and Early Editions." In *Studies in Jewish Mysticism.* Ed. J. Dan and F. Talmage, 57–84. Cambridge, 1982.

Marcus, I. G. *Sefer Hasidim: MS. Parma H 3280* (Hebrew). Jerusalem, 1985.

Marcus, I. G. "Hierarchies, Religious Boundaries and Jewish Spirituality in Medieval Germany." *Jewish History* 1:2 (Fall 1986), 7–26.

Marcus, I. G. "Mothers, Martyrs, and Moneymakers: Some Jewish Women in Medieval Europe." *Conservative Judaism*, 38:3 (Spring 1986), 34–45.

Marcus, I. G. Review of *European Jewry and the First Crusade* by R. Chazan. *Speculum* 64 (1989), 685–688.

Marcus, I. G. "History, Story and Collective Memory: Narrativity in Early Ashkenazic Culture." *Prooftexts* 10:3 (Fall 1990), 365–388.

Marcus, I. G. "*Qiddush ha-Shem* in Ashkenaz and in the Story of R. Amnon of Mainz" (Hebrew). In *Sanctity of Life and Martyrdom.* Ed. I. M. Gafni and A. Ravitzky, 131–147. Jerusalem, 1992.

Marcus, I. G. "Une communauté pieuse et le doute: Qiddush ha-Chem (mourir pour la sanctification du nom) chez les juifs d'Europe du Nord et l'histoire de rabbi Amnone de Mayence." *Annales: Histoire, Sciences Sociales* 5 (September–October 1994), 1031–1047.

Marcus, I. G. "Jews and Christians Imagining the Other in Medieval Europe." *Prooftexts* 15 (September 1995), 209–226.

Marcus, I. G. *Rituals of Childhood: Jewish Acculturation in Medieval Europe.* New Haven and London, 1996.

Marcus, I. G. "The Representation of Reality in the Sources of the 1096 Anti-Jewish First Crusade Riots." *Jewish History* 13:2 (Fall 1999), 37–48.

Marcus, I. G. "From 'Deus Vult' to the 'Will of the Creator'": Extremist Religious Ideologies and Historical Reality in 1096 and Hasidei Ashkenaz" (Hebrew). In *Facing the Cross: The Persecutions of 1096 in History and Historiography.* Ed. Y. T. Assis et al., 92–100. Jerusalem, 2000.

Marcus, I. G. "The Dynamics of Jewish Renaissance and Renewal in the Twelfth Century." In *Jews and Christians in Twelfth-Century Europe.* Ed. M. A. Signer and J. Van Engen, 27–45. Indiana, 2001.

Marcus, I. G. "A Jewish-Christian Symbiosis: The Culture of Early Ashkenaz." In *Cultures of the Jews: A New History*. Ed. D. Biale, 449–516. New York, 2002.

Marcus, J. R. *The Jew in the Medieval World: A Sources Book: 315–1791*. New York, 1981.

Martin, M. R. "Suicide and Self-Sacrifice." In *Suicide*. Ed. M. P. Battin and D. Mayo, 1980.

Mason. A. J. *The Historic Martyrs of The Primitive Church*. Longmans, 1905.

Mayer, E. H. *The Crusades*. Tr. J. Gillingham. Oxford, 1988.

Melik, E. "'He Shall Live by Them': The Way of the Belzer Rebbe, Aaron Roke'ah, in the Holocaust." In *I Will Be Sanctified: Religious Responses to the Holocaust*. Ed. Y. Fogel and Tr. E. Levin, 183–210. Northvale, Jerusalem, 1998.

Menninger, A. K. *Man Against Himself*. New York, 1938.

Merchavia, Ch. *The Church Versus Talmudic and Midrashic Literature [500–1248]*. Jerusalem, 1970.

Milano, A. *Storia degli Ebrei in Italia*. Roma, 1963.

Milano, A. *Il Ghetto di Roma*. Roma, 1988,

Milik, J. T. *Ten Years of Discovery on the Wilderness of Judean*. London, 1957.

Miller, F. "The Background to the Maccabean Revolution: Reflections on Martin Hengel's 'Judaism and Hellenism.'" *Journal of Jewish Studies* 29 (1978), 1–21.

Minty, M. "*Qiddush ha-Shem* in German Christian Eyes in the Middle Ages" (Hebrew). *Zion* 59 (1994), 209–266.

Mintz, A. "The Russian Pogroms in Hebrew Literature and the Subversion of the Martyrological Ideal." In *Association for Jewish Studies Review* 7–8 (1982–1983), 263–300.

Mirsky, A. *Ha'piyut*. Jerusalem, 1990.

Mizugaki, W. "Origen and Josephus." In *Josephus, Judaism, and Christianity*. Ed. L. H. Feldman and G. Hata, 325–337. Detroit, 1987.

Mollaret H. H. and Borssolet, J. *La Peste, Source Méconnue d'Inspiration Artistique*. Paris, 1965.

Momigliano, A. *Richerche sull' organizazione della Giudea sotto il dominio romano* (63 A.C.–70 D.C.). (Reprint of the edition Bologna 1934). Amsterdam, 1967.

Momigliano, A. *Prime linee di storia della tradizione Maccabaica* (Turino, 1931), 2d ed. Amsterdam, 1968.

Moore, G. F. *Judaism in The First Centuries of the Christian Era: The Age of the Tannaim*. 3 vols. Cambridge, 1927–1930.

Moore, R. *Origins of European Dissent*. Oxford, 1985.

Mor, M. *The Bar-Kochba Revolt: Its Extent and Effect* (Hebrew). Jerusalem, 1991.

Morgan, M. L. *Dilemmas in Modern Jewish Thought*. Bloomington, 1992.

Musurillo, H. *The Acts of the Pagan Martyrs: Acta Alexandrinorum*. Oxford, 2000.

Nahon, G. "From the Rue aux Juifs to the Chemin du Roy: The Classical Age of French Jewry, 1108–1223." In *Jews and Christians in Twelfth-Century Europe*. Ed. M. A. Signer and J Van Engen, 311–339. Notre Dame, 2001.

Najman, H. "The Writings and Reception of Philo of Alexandria." In *Christianity in Jewish Terms*. Ed. T. Frymer-Kensky et al. Colorado and Oxford, 2000.

Naor, G. "A Difference of Opinion among *Poskim* Regarding the Parameters of Kiddush Hashem." In *I Will Be Sanctified: Religious Responses to the Holocaust*. Ed. Y. Fogel and Tr. E. Levin, 89–104. Northvale, Jerusalem, 1998.

Neubauer, A. "Literary Gleanings VIII." *Jewish Quarterly Review* (old series) 5 (1892–1893), 713–714.

Neusner, J. "The Rabbinic Traditions about the Pharisees before A.D. 70: The Problem of Oral Transmission." *Journal of Jewish Studies* 21–23 (1971), 1–18.

Neusner, J. "From Exegesis to Fable in Rabbinic Traditions about the Pharisees." *Journal of Jewish Studies* 24–25 (1974), 263–269.

Neusner, J. *From Politics to Piety: The Emergence of Pharisaic Judaism.* New York, 1979.

Neusner, J. *Ancient Israel after Catastrophe.* Charlottesville, 1983.

Neusner, J. *Israel after Calamity: The Book of Lamentation* (Valley Forge, 1995).

Neusner, J. "Josephus' Pharisees: A Complete Repertoire," *Josephus, Judaism, and Christianity.* Ed. L. H. Feldman and G. Hata, 274–292. Detroit, 1987.

Neusner, J. *The Incarnation of God: The Character of Divinity in Formative Judaism.* Philadelphia, 1988.

Nickelsburg, G. W. E. *Resurrection, Immortality, and Eternal Life in Intertestamental Judaism.* Cambridge, 1972.

Nickelsburg, G. W. E. *Studies on the Testament of Moses.* Cambridge, 1973.

Nickelsburg, G. W. E. *Jewish Literature between the Bible and the Mishnah.* Philadelphia, 1981.

Nickelsburg, G. W. E., and Stone, M. E. *Faith and Piety in Early Judaism.* Philadelphia, 1983.

Nikiprowetzky, V. "La mort d'Eleazar fils de Jaïre et les courants apologétiques dans le *De bello judaico*de Flavius Josèphe." In *Hommages à André Dupont-Sommer.* Ed. A. Caquot and M. Philonenko, 461–490. Paris, 1971.

Nikiprowetzky, V. "Josephus and the Revolutionary Parties." In *Josephus the bible, and history.* Ed. L. H. Feldman and G. Hata. Detroit, 1989.

Nirenberg, D. *Communities of Violence: Persecution of Minorities in the Middle Ages.* Princeton, 1996.

Noble, S. "The Jewish Woman in Medieval Martyrology." In *Studies in Jewish Bibliography History and Literature in Honor of I. Edward Kiev.* Ed. C. Berlin, 347–355. New York, 1971.

Novak, D. "*Mitsvah.*" In *Christianity in Jewish Terms.* Ed. T. Frymer-Kensky et al., 115–126. Colorado and Oxford, 2000.

Oesterley W. O. E., and Box, G. H. "I Maccabees, Sirach." In *The Apocrypha and Pseudepigrapha of the Old Testament.* Ed. R. H. Charles, 1:59–124. Oxford, 1913.

O'Hagan, A. "The Martyr in the Fourth Book of Maccabees." *Studii Biblici Franciscani Liber Annuus* 24 (1974), 94–120.

Oppenheimer, A. "Oral Law in the Books of Maccabees." *Immanuel* 6 (1976), 34–42.

Oppenheimer, A. "The Sanctity of Life and Martyrdom in the Wake of Bar Kokhba's Rebellion" (Hebrew). In *Sanctity of Life and Martyrdom.* Ed. I. M. Gafni and A. Ravitzky, 85–97. Jerusalem, 1992.

Oron, M. "Parallel Versions of the Story of the Ten Martyrs and of the Book of Hekhalot Rabbti" (Hebrew). *Eshel be'er Sheva* 2 (1980), 81–95.

Ostrogorsky, G. *History of the Byzantine Sate.* Tr. J. M. Hussey. New Brunswick, 1969.

Parkes, J. *The Conflict of the Church and the Synagogue: A Study in the Origins of Antisemitism.* London, 1934.

Parkes, J. *The Jew in the Medieval Community: A Study of His Political and Economic Stiutation.* London, 1938.

Paxton, F. S. *Christianizing Death: The Creation of a Ritual Process in Early Medieval Europe*. Ithaca and London, 1990.

Peers, A. E. *Ramon Lull, A Biography*. London, 1929.

Perowne, S. *The Life and Times of of Herod's the Great*. London, 1956.

Perowne, S. *The Later Herods*. London, 1958.

Peters, E. *Christian Society and the Crusades*. Philadelphia, 1971.

Peters, E., Ed. *Heresy and Authority in Medieval Europe: Documents in Translation*. Philadelphia, 1980.

Peters, E., Ed. and Tr. *The First Crusade: The Chronicle of Fulcher of Chartres and other Source Materials*. Philadelphia, 1998.

Petroff, E. A. *Medieval Women's Visionary Literature*. New York, Oxford, 1986.

Pfeifer, R. H. *History of New Testament Times with an Introduction to the Apocrypha*. New York, 1941.

Porteous, N. W. *Daniel: A Commentary*. Philadelphia, 1965.

Prawer, A. J. "The Autobiography of Obadyah the Norman: A Convert to Judaism at the Time of the First Crusade." In *Studies in Medieval Jewish History and Literature*. Ed. I. Twersky, 110–132. Cambridge, 1979.

Prawer, A. J. *The History of the Jews in the Latin Kingdom of Jerusalem*. Oxford, 1988.

Pritz, R. A. *Nazarene Jewish Christianity: From the End of the New Testament Period until Its Disappearance in the Fourth Century*. Jerusalem, 1992.

Rabello, A. M. "The Edicts on Circumcision as a Factor in the Bar Kochva Revolt." In *The Bar-Kokhva Revolt*. Ed. A. Oppenheimer and U. Rappaport, 27–46. Jerusalem, 1984.

Rabinowitz, M. Z. *Ginzei Midrash* (Hebrew). Tel Aviv, 1976.

Rajak, T. *The Jewish Dialogue with Greek and Rome: Studies in Cultural and Social Interaction*. Leiden, Boston, Köln, 2001.

Rajak, T. "Greeks and Barbarians in Josephus." In *Hellenism in the Land of Israel*. Ed. J. J. Collins and G. E. Sterling, 246–262. Indiana, 2001.

Rappaport, U. "Relationships between Jews and Non-Jews in the Land of Israel and the Great Revolt Against Rome." *Tarbiz* 47 (1978), 1–14.

Rappaport, U. "Comments on the Period of Antiochus' Decrees with Relation to the Book of Daniel" (Hebrew). In *The Seleucid Period in the Land of Israel*. Ed. B. Bar Kochva, 65–83. Tel Aviv, 1980.

Rauch, J. "Apocalypse in the Bible." In *Journal of Jewish Lore and Philosophy*. Ed. D. Neumark. 1919.

Rhoads, D. M. *Israel in Revolution: 6–74 C.E. A Political History Based on the Writings of Josephus*. Philadelphia, 1976.

Riddle, D. *The Martyrs: A Study in Social Control*. Chicago, 1931.

Riley-Smith, J. "Crusading as an Act of Love." *History* vol. 65 (n. 214) (June 1980), 177–192.

Riley-Smith, J. "An Approach to Crusading Ethics." *Reading Medieval Studies* 6 (1980), 3–19.

Riley-Smith, J. *The First Crusade and the Idea of Crusading*. Philadelphia, 1986.

Riley-Smith, J. "Christian Violence and the Crusades." In *Religious Violence between Christians and Jews: Medieval Roots, Modern Perspectives*. Ed. A. S. Abulafia, 3–20. New York, 2002.

Riley-Smith, L., and Riley-Smith, J. S. C. *The Crusades: Idea and Reality, 1095–1274*. London, 1981.

Rives, J. B. *Religion and Authority in Roman Carthage from Augustus to Constantine.* Oxford, 1995.

Robert, L. "Epigrammes d'Aphrodisias." *Hellenica* 4 (1984), 127–135.

Robert, L. *Le Martyre de Pionios, Prêtre de Smyrne.* Ed. G. W. Bowersock and C. P. Jones, 105–111, Washington, DC, 1994.

Robertson, D. *The Medieval Saints' Lives: Spiritual Renewal and Older French Literature.* Lexington, 1995.

Roos, L. " 'God Wants It!': The Ideology of Martyrdom of the Hebrew Crusade Chronicles and Its Jewish and Christian Background." Ph.D. dissertation. Uppsala, 2003.

Rophe A. *The Prophetical Stories* (Hebrew). Jerusalem, 1982.

Rose, J. H. "Suicide." In *Encyclopaedia of Religion and Ethics.* Ed. J. Hastings, 12:21–24. New York, 1925.

Roskies, D. G. *The Literature of Destruction: Jewish Responses to Catastrophe.* Philadelphia, New York, Jerusalem, 1988.

Rosner, F. "Suicide in Biblical, Talmudic, and Rabbinic Writings." *Tradition: A Jurnal of Ortodox Thought,* 11:3, 1970–1971.

Ross, S. A. "Embodiment and Incarnation: A Response to Elliot Wolfson." In *Christianity in Jewish Terms.* Ed. T. Frymer-Kensky et al., 262–268. Colorado and Oxford, 2000.

Rost, L. *Judaism Outside the Hebrew Canon: An Introduction to the Documents.* Tr. D. E. Green. Nashville, 1976.

Roth, C. "The Feast of Purim and the Origins of the Blood Accusation." *Speculum* 4 (1933), 520–526.

Roth, C. *History of the Jews in England.* Oxford, 1942.

Roth, C. "A Hebrew Elegy on the Martyrs of Toledo, 1391." *Jewish Quarterly Review* 34 (1948), 127–129, 137–141.

Roth, C. "European Jewry in the Dark Ages: A Revised Picture." *Hebrew Union College Annual* 23 (1950–1951), 151–169.

Roth, C. *The Jews in Medieval Oxford.* Oxford, 1951.

Roth, C. *The History of the Jews of Italy.* Philadelphia, 1964.

Rowland, C. *Radical Christianity: A Reading of Recovery.* New York. 1988.

Rsahkover, R. "The Christian Doctrine of the Incarnation." In *Christianity in Jewish Terms.* Ed. T. Frymer-Kensky et al., 254–261. Colorado and Oxford, 2000.

Rubin, M. *Gentile Tales: The Narrative Assault on Late Medieval Jews.* New Haven and London, 1999.

Rubinstein, A. *In Praise of the Baal Shem Tov [Shivhei ha-Besht]* (Hebrew). Jerusalem, 1991.

Runciman, S. *A History of the Crusades.* 3 vols. Cambridge, 1951–1954.

Rushing, A. W. "Individual Behavior and Suicide." In *Suicide.* Ed. J. P. Gibbs, 96–112. London, 1968.

Russell, J. B. *Dissent and Reform in the Early Middle Ages.* New York, 1965.

Safrai, S. "The Pharisees and the Hasidim." *Sidic* 10 (1977), 12–16.

Safrai, S. "*Qiddush ha-Shem* in the Teachings of the Tannaim" (Hebrew). *Zion* 44 (1979), 28–42.

Safrai, S. *Be Shilhe ha-Bayit ha-Sheni uvi-Tekufat ha-Mishnah.* Jerusalem, 1983.

Safrai, S. "The Hasidim and the Men of Deeds" (Hebrew). *Zion* 50 (1985), 133–154.

Salzman, M. *The Chronicle of Ahimaatz.* Columbia, 1942.

Sandmel, S. *Judaism and Christian Beginnings*. New York, 1978.

Sanders, E. P. *Paul, the Law, and the Jewish People*. Philadelphia, 1983.

Sanders, E. P. *Judaism: Practice and Belief 63 BCE–66 CE*. London and Philadelphia, 1992.

Saperstein, M. "A Sermon on the Akeda from the Generation of the Expulsion and its Implication for 1391." In *Exile and Diaspora: Studies in the History of the Jewish People Presented to Professor Haim Beinart*. Ed. A. Mirsky et al., 103–124. Jerusalem, 1991.

Septimus, B. "Narboni and Shem Tov on Martyrdom." In *Studies in Medieval Jewish History and Literature*. Vol. 2. Ed. I. Twersky, 447–455. Cambridge and London, 1984.

Schäfer, P. "The Causes of the Bar Kokhba Revolt." In *Studies in Aggadah, Targum and Jewish Liturgy in Memory of Joseph Hinemann*. Ed. J. J. Petuchowski and E. Fleischer, 74–94. Jerusalem, 1981.

Schäfer, P. "The Ideal of Piety of the Ashkenazi Hasidim and Its Roots in Jewish Tradition." *Jewish History* 4 (1990), 199–211.

Schäfer, P. *The History of the Jews in Antiquity: The Jews of Palestine from Alexander the Great to the Arab Conquest*. Luxembourg, 1995.

Schatkin, M. "The Maccabean Martyrs." *Vigilae Christianae* 28 (1974), 97–113.

Scheiber, A. "The Epistle of Meshullam ben Kalonymus ben Moses the Elder to Constantinople Regarding the Karaties." *Sefer ha-Yovel le -R. Mahler*, 19–23. Tel Aviv, 1974.

Schiffman, L. H. "At the Crossroads: Tannaitic Perspectives on the Jewish–Christian Schism." In *Jewish and Christian Self-definition*. Ed. E. P. Sanders, A. I. Baumgaten, and A. Mendelson, 2:115–156. Philadelphia, 1980.

Schiffman, L. H. "Jewish Sectarianism in Second Temple Times." In *Great Schisms in Jewish History*. Ed. R. Jospe and S. M. Wagner, 1–46. New York, 1981.

Schiffman, L. H. *Who Was a Jew? Rabbinic and Halakhic Perspectives on the Jewish–Christian Schism*. New Jersey, 1985.

Schiffman, L. H. "The Conversion of the Royal House of Adiabene in Josephus and Rabbinic Sources." In *Josephus, Judaism, and Christianity*. Ed. L. H. Feldman and G. Hata, 293–312. Detroit, 1987.

Schiffman, L. H. *The Eschatological Community of the Dead Sea Scrolls*. Atlanta, 1989.

Schiffman, L. H. *Law, Custom, and Messianism in the Dead Sead Sect* (Hebrew). Jerusalem, 1993.

Scholem, G. "New Examinations of R. Abraham ben Eliezer ha-Levi" (Hebrew). *Kiryat Sefer* 7 (1931), 152–155.

Scholem, G. *The Origins of Kabbalah*. 1948.

Scholem, G. *Jewish Gnosticisim, Merkabah Mysticism and Talmudic Tradition*. New York, 1960.

Scholem, G. *Major Trends in Jewish Mysticism*. New York, 1961.

Scholem, G. *Kabbalah*. New York, 1974.

Schreckenberg, H. "The Works of Josephus and the Early Christian Church." In *Josephus, Judaism, and Christianity*. Ed. L. H. Feldman and G. Hata, 315–324. Detroit, 1987.

Schubert, K. *The Dead Sea Community: Its Origin and Teachings*. New York, 1959.

Schürer, E. *The History of the Jewish People in the Age of Jesus Christ* (175 B.C.–A.D. 135), 3 vols. Ed. G. Vermes and F. Millar. Edinburgh, 1979.

Schwartz, D. "What Should He Answer? And He Should Live by Them" (Hebrew). In *Sanctity of Life and Martyrdom*. Ed. I. M. Gafni and A. Ravitzky, 69–83. Jerusalem, 1992.

Schwartz, D. "The Bravery of Masada and the Martyrs of the Holocaust" (Hebrew). In *Ets Avot: Qiddush ha-Shem in the Holocaust in Thought, Halakhah, and Agadah*. Ed. D. Schwartz, and I. Hakelman, 201–217. Jerusalem, 1993.

Schwartz, J. "Judea in the Wake of The Bar Kochva Revolt." *The Bar Kochva Revolt*. Ed. A. Oppenheimer and U. Rappaport, 215–223. Jerusalem, 1984.

Schwartz, S. *Imperialism And Jewish Society, 200 B.C.E. to 640 C.E.* Princeton and Oxford, 2001.

Schwarzfuchs, S. "France under the Early Capets." In *The Dark Ages: Jews in Christian Europe, 711–1096*. Ed. C. Roth, 157–160. Rutgers, 1966.

Schwarzfuchs, S. "France and Germany under the Carolingians." In *The Dark Ages: Jews in Christian Europe, 711–1096*. Ed. C. Roth, 122–142. Rutgers, 1966.

Schwarzfuchs, S. "L'opposition Tsarfat-Provence: la Formation du Judaisme du Nord de la France." In *Hommage à Georges Vajda: Études d'histoire et de pensée juives*. Ed. G. Nahon and C. Touati, 135–150. Louvain, 1980.

Schwarzfuchs, S. "The Place of the Crusades in Jewish History" (Hebrew). In *Culture and Society in Medieval Jewish History: Studies Dedicated to the Memory of Haim Hillel Ben-Sasson*. Ed. M. Ben-Sasson, R. Bonfil, and J. R. Hacker, 251–268. Jerusalem, 1989.

Seeley, D. *The Noble Death: Graeco-Roman Martyrology and Paul's Concept of Salvation* [Journal for the Study of the New Testament, Supplement Series 28]. Sheffield, 1990.

Setton, K. A. *History of the Crusades*. 5 vols. Madison, 1969–1984.

Shahar, S. "The Relationship between Kabbalism and Catharism in the South of France." In *Les Juifs dans l'Histoire de France*. Ed. M. Yardeni, 55–62. Leiden, 1980.

Shallit, A. *Herods The King – The Man and his Deeds* (Hebrew). Jerusalem, 1960.

Sharf, A. "Heraclius and Mahomet." *Past & Present* 9 (1956), 1–16.

Sharf, A. *Byzantine Jewry: From Justinian to the Fourth Crusade*. New York, 1971.

Sharf, A. "Shabbettai Donnolo as a Byzantine-Jewish Figure." *Bulletin of the Institute of Jewish Studies* 3 (1975), 1–18.

Sharf, A. *The Universe of Shabbetai Donnolo*. Watminster, 1976.

Sharf, A. *Jews and Other Minorities in Byzantium*. Jerusalem, 1995.

Shatzmiller, J. "L' Inquisition et les juifs de Provence au XIIIe siècle." *Provence Historique* 23 (1973), 327–338.

Shatzmiller, J. "Les juifs de Provence pendant la pest noire." *Revue des études juives* 133.3–4 (July–December, 1974), 457–480.

Shatzmiller, J. "Jews 'Separated from the Communion of the Faithful in Christ' in the Middle Ages." *Studies in Medieval Jewish History and Literature*. Ed. I. Twersky, 307–314. Cambridge and London, 1979.

Shatzmiller, J. "Desecrating the Cross: A Rare Medieval Accusation" (Hebrew). In *Studies in the History of the Jewish People and the Land of Israel* (1980), 5:159–173.

Shatzmiller, J. "Paulus Christiani, un aspect de son activité anti-juive." In *Hommage à Georges Vajda: Études d'histoire et de pensée juives*. Ed. G. Nahon and C. Touati, 203–217. Louvain, 1980.

Shatzmiller, J. "Doctors and Medical Practice in Germany around the Year 1200: The Evidence of *Sefer Hasidim*." *Journal of Jewish Studies* 33 (1982), 583–593.

Shatzmiller, J. "A Provencal Chronography in the Lost Account of Shem Tov Shantzulo" (Hebrew). *Proceedings of the American Academy for Jewish Research* 52 (1985), 43–61.

Shatzmiller, J. "The Albigensian Heresy as Reflected in the Eyes of Contemporary Jewry" (Hebrew). In *Culture and Society in Medieval Jewry: Studies Dedicated to the Memory of Haim Hillel Ben-Sasson.* Ed. M. Ben-Sasson, R. Bonfil, and J. R. Hacker, 333–352, Jerusalem, 1989.

Shatzmiller, J. *Shylock Reconsidered: Jews, Moneylending, and Medieval Society.* Berkeley, Los Angeles, Oxford, 1990.

Shatzmiller, J. *La Deuxième Controverse de Paris: Un Chapitre dans la polémique entre Chrétiens et Juifs au Moyen Âge.* Ed. J. Shtzmiller, 15–22, Collection de la *Revue des études juives.* Paris, 1994.

Shatzmiller, J. "Jewish Converts to Christianity in Medieval Europe: 1200–1500." In *Cross-Cultural Convergences in the Crusader Period: Essay Presented to Aryeh Grabois on his Sixty-fifth Birthday.* Ed. M. Goodich, S. Menache, and S. Schein, 297–318. New York, 1995.

Shepkaru, S. "From after Death to Afterlife: Martyrdom and Its Recompence." *Association for Jewish Studies Review* 24.1 (1999), 1–44.

Shepkaru, S. "To Die for God: Parallel Images of Martyrs' Afterlife in Hebrew and Latin Crusading Accounts." *Speculum* 77:2 (2002), 311–341.

Shepkaru, S. "Death Twice Over: Dualism of Metaphor and Realia in 12th-Century Hebrew Crusading Accounts." *Jewish Quarterly Review* 93.1–2 (July–October 2002), 217–256.

Sherwin-Whit, N. "Why Were the Early Christians Persecuted? An Amendment." *Studies in Ancient Society.* Ed. M. I. Finley, Past and Present Series, 250–255. London and Boston, 1974.

Shillat, I. *"Targum Bilti Yaduah Shel Iggert ha-Shemad la-RMBM."* *Sinai* 95, 154–164.

Shirman, H. *Mivhar ha-Shirah ha-Ivrit be-Italyah.* Berlin, 1934.

Shlusberg, A. "Rambam's Approach to Islam." *Peamim* 42 (1990), 38–60.

Shmeruk, C. "Yiddish Literature and Collective Memory: The Case of the Chmielnitzky Massacres" (Hebrew). *Zion* 53 (1986), 371–389.

Shneidman, S. E. *Definition of Suicide.* New York, Chichester, Brisbane, Toronto, Singapore, 1985.

Shneidman, S. E. "Preventing Suicide." *American Journal of Nursing* 65: 5 (1965), 10–15.

Sievers, J. "The Role of Women in the Hasmonean Dynasty." In *Josephus, the Bible, and History.* Ed. L. H. Feldman and G. Hata, 132–146. Detroit, 1989.

Sievers, J. *The Hasmoneans and Their Supporters: From Mattathias to the Death of John Hyrcanus I.* Atlanta, 1990.

Silving, H. "Suicide and the Law." *Clues to Suicide.* Ed. S. Shneidman and L. N. Farberow, 79–94. New York, 1957.

Simon, M. *Recherche d'Histoire Judéo-Chrétienne.* Paris, 1962.

Simon, M. *Versu Israel: A Study of the Relations between Christians and Jews in the Roman Empire (135–425).* Tr. H. McKeating. Oxford, 1986.

Smallwood, E. M. "Some Comments on Tacitus Annales XII." *Latomus* 18 (1959), 560–567.

Smallwood, E. M. *The Jews under Roman Rule: From Pompey to Diocletian.* Leiden, 1976.

Smallwood, E. M. "High Priest and Politics in Roman Palestine." *Ha-Mered Ha-Gadol: ha-Sibot veha-Nesibot li-Feritsato.* Ed. A. Kasher, 231–253. Jerusalem, 1983.

Smallwood, E. M. "Philo and Josephus as Historians of the Same Events." In *Josephus, Judaism, and Christianity.* Ed. L. H. Feldman and G. Hata, 114–129. Detroit, 1987.

Smith, M. "Palestinian Judaism in the First Century." In *Israel: Its Role in Civilization.* Ed. M. Davis, 75–81. New York, 1956.

Smith, M. *Palestinian Parties and Politics That Shaped the Old Testament.* New York and London, 1971.

Soloveitchik, H. "Three Themes in Sefer Hasidim." *Association for Jewish Studies Review* 1 (1976), 325–339.

Soloveitchik, H. *Halakhah, Economy, and Self-Image.* Jerusalem, 1985.

Soloveitchik, H. "Religious Law and Change: The Medieval Ashkenazic Example." In *Association for Jewish Studies Review* 8:2 (1987), 205–221.

Soloveitchik, H. "Concerning the Date of *Sefer-Hasidim*" (Hebrew). In *Culture and Society in Medieval Jewry: Studies Dedicated to the Memory of Haim Hillel Ben-Sasson.* Ed. M. Ben-Sasson, R. Bonfil, and J. R. Hacker, 383–388, Jerusalem, 1989.

Soloveitchik, H. *The Use of Responsa as a Historical Source* (Hebrew). Jerusalem, 1990.

Soloveitchik, H. "Between *Arav* and *Edom*" (Hebrew). In *Sanctity of Life and Martyrdom.* Ed. I. M. Gafni and A. Ravitzky, 149–152. Jerusalem, 1992.

Soloveitchik, H. "Catastrophe and Halakhic Creativity: Ashkenaz – 1096, 1242, 1306 and 1298." *Jewish History* 12:1 (1998), 171–185.

Somerville, R. *The Councils of Urban II, Vol. 1: Decreta Claromontensia.* Amsterdam, 1972.

Sonne, "Nouvel examen des trois rélations hebräiques sur les persécutions de 1096." *Revue des études juives* 96 (1933), 137–152.

Sonne. "Which Is the Earlier Account of the Persecutions of 1096?" (Hebrew). *Zion* 12 (1947–1948), 74–81.

Southern, W. R. *Saint Anselm and His Biographer.* Cambridge, 1963.

Spero, S. "In Defense of the Defenders of Masada," *Tradition* 11 (1970), 31–43.

Spiegel, G. "History, Historicism, and the Social Logic of the Text in the Middle Ages." *Speculum* 65 (1990), 59–86.

Spiegel, S. "From the Legends of the *Aqedah*" (Hebrew). *Sefer ha-Yovel le A. Marx.* Ed. S. Lieberman, 471–537. New York, 1950.

Spiegel, S. "In Monte Dominus Videbitur: The Martyrs of Blois and the Renewal of the Accusations of Ritual Murder" (Hebrew). In *The Mordecai M. Kaplan Jubilee* (Hebrew vol.), 267–287. New York, 1953.

Spiegel, S. *The Last Trial: On the Legends and Lore of the Command to Abraham to Offer Isaac as a Sacrific: The Akedah.* Tr. J. Goldin. New York, 1993.

Stacey, R. "Parliamentary Negotiation and the Expulsion of the Jews from England." *Thirteenth Century England,* vol. 6 (Woodbridge, 1997), 77–101.

Stanton, G. N. "Justin Martyr's Dialogue with Trypho: Group Boundaries, 'Proselytes' and 'God-Fearers.'" In *Tolerance and Intolerance in Early Judaism and Christianity.* Ed. G. N. Stanton and G. G. Strounsa, 263–278. Cambridge, 1998.

Starr, J. "Le mouvement messianique au début du VIII siècle." *Revue de études Juives* 102 (1937), 81–92.

Starr, J. *The Jews in the Byzantine Empire.* New York, 1939.

Stemberger, G. "The Maccabees in Rabbinic Traditions." In *The Scriptures and The Scrolls: Studies in Honour of A. S. Van Der Woude on the Occasion of His 65 th Birthday.* Ed. F. G. Martinez, A. Hilhorst, and C. J. Labuschagne, 193–203. Leiden, New York, Köln, 1992.

Stern, M. "The Books of the Maccabees" (Hebrew). In *Biblical Encyclopaedia.* Vol. 5, 286–303, Jerusalem, 1958.

Stern, M. "The Reign of Herod." *The Herodian Period, World History of the Jewish People.* Ed. M. Avi-Yonah, 7. Jerusalem, 1975.

Stern, M. "Herod's Policy and the Jewish Society in the End of the Second Temple."
    Tarbiz 35 (1976), 235–253.

Stern, M. "The Suicide of Eleazar Ben Yaer and His Men in Masada" (Hebrew). *Zion* 47
    (1982), 367–398.

Stern, M. "The Status of the Province of Judaea and Its Principates during the Juliu-
    Claudian Empire." In *Ha-Mered Ha-Gadol: ha-Sibot veha-Nesibot li-Feritsato.* Ed. A.
    Kasher, 93–101. Jerusalem, 1983.

Stern, M. "Josephus and the Roman Empire as Reflected in The Jewish War." In
    Josephus, Judaism, and Christianity. Ed. L. H. Feldman and G. Hata, 71–80. Detroit,
    1987.

Stow, R. K, *The "1007 Anonymous" and Papal Sovereignty: Jewish Perceptions of the
    Papacy and Papal Policy in the High Middle Ages.* In *The Hebrew Union College Annual
    Supplements* 4. Cincinnati, 1984.

Stow, R. K. "A Tale of Uncertainties: Converts in the Roman Ghetto." In *Festschrift
    Shelomo Simonsohn.* Ed. D. Carpi. Tel Aviv, 1992.

Stow, R. K. *Alienated Minority: The Jews of Medieval Latin Europe.* Cambridge, London,
    1994.

Stroumsa, G. G. "Tertullian and the Limits of Tolerance." In *Tolerance and Intolerance
    in Early Judaism and Christianity.* Ed. G. N. Stanton and G. G. Strounsa, 173–184.
    Cambridge, 1998.

Synan, E. A. *The Popes and the Jews in the Middle Ages.* New York, London, 1967.

Tamar, D. "Chapters on the History of the Sages of the Land of Israel and Italy and their
    Literature" (Hebrew). In *Kiryat Sefer* 33 (1958), 376–380.

Tamar, D. "More on the Opinion of Rabbi Meir of Rothenburg on the Issue of *Kiddush
    ha-Shem.*" *Kiryat Sefer* 34 (1959), 376–377.

Tamarin, A. H. *Revolt in Judea: The Road to Masada.* New York, 1968.

Ta-Shma, I. "Sefer ha-Maskil: An Unknown French Jewish Composition from the
    End of the Thirteenth Century" (Hebrew). *Mehqerei-yerushalayyim be-mahshevet
    yisrael* 2.3 (1982–1983), 416–438.

Ta-Shma, I. "The Source and Place of the Prayer '*aleinu le-shabeah*" (Hebrew). In
    Frank Talmage Memorial Volume. Ed. B. Walfish, 1:85–88 (Hebrew section). Haifa,
    1993.

Ta-Shma, I. "The Attitude of Medieval German Halakhists to Aggadic Sources" (Hebrew).
    In *Facing the Cross: The Persecutions of 1096 in History and Historiography.* Ed. Y. T.
    Assis et al., 150–156. Jerusalem, 2000.

Taverski, I. "*Qiddush ha-Shem* and *Qiddush ha-Hayyim* – Aspects of Holiness in the
    Teaching of Maimonides" (Hebrew). In *Sanctity of Life and Martyrdom.* Ed. I. M.
    Gafni and A. Ravitzky, 167–190. Jerusalem, 1992.

Tcherikover, V. "Antiochia in Jerusalem" (Hebrew). *Tarbiz,* 20 (1949), 61–67.

Tcherikover, V. "Antiochus' Decrees and Their Problems" (Hebrew). *Eshcholot,* 1 (1954),
    86–109.

Tcherikover, V. "The Decline of the Jewish Diaspora in Egypt in the Roman Period."
    Journal of Jewish Studies 13–15 (1963), 1–37.

Tcherikover, V. *Hellenistic Civilization and the Jews.* Fifth Printing. Tr. S. Applebaum.
    New York, 1979.

Teixdor, J. *The Pagan God.* Princeton, 1977.

Tellenbach. G. *Church State and Christian Society at the Time of the Investiture Contest.*
    Tr. R. F. Bennett. Oxford, 1970.

Tellenbach. G. *The Church in Western Europe from the Tenth to the Early Twelfth Century.* Tr. T. Reuter. Cambridge, 1993.

The Standard Jewish Encyclopedia. 2 vols. (Hebrew Edition). Jerusalem, 1969.

Thielman, F. *From Plight to Solution: A Jewish Framework for Understanding Paul's View of the Law in Galatians and Romans.* Leiden, 1989.

Tudor, H. *Political Myth.* New York, Washington, London, 1972.

Urbach, E. E. "Ascesis and Suffering in Talmudic and Midrashic Sources." *Yitzhak F. Baer Jubilee Volume.* Ed. S. Ettinger, et al., 48–68. Jerusalem, 1960.

Urbach, E. E. "The Tradition of Mysticism in the Period of the Tanni'm" (Hebrew). In *Studies in Mysticism and Religion Presented to Gershom G. Scholem on His Seventieth Birthday.* Ed. R. J. Z. Werblowsky et al., 1–28. Jerusalem, 1967.

Urbach, E. E. *The Sages, Their Concepts and Beliefs.* 2 vols. Tr. I. Abrahams. Jerusalem, 1975.

Urbach, E. E. *The Tosaphists: Their History, Writings and Methods* (Hebrew). 2 vols. Jerusalem, 1986.

Van Der Horst, P. W. *Ancient Jewish Epitaphs: An Introductory Survey of a Millenium of Jewish Funerary Epigraphy (300 BCE–700 CE).* Kampen, 1991.

Van Henten, J. W. *The Maccabean Martyrs as Saviours of the Jewish People: A Study of 2 and 4 Maccabees.* Leiden, New York, Köln, 1997.

Van Henten, J. W. "Antiochus IV as a Typhonic Figure in Daniel 7." In *The Book of Daniel in the Light of New Findings.* Ed. A. S. Van Der Woude, 223–243, Leuven, 1993.

Van Hooff, A. J. L. *From Autothanasia to Suicide: Self-Killing in Classical Antiquity.* London and New York, 1990.

Vasiliev, A. A. *Byzantium and Islam.* Madison, 1928.

Vasiliev, A. A. *The History of the Byzantine Empire.* Madison, 1952.

Vermes, G. *Scripture and Tradition in Judaism: Haggadic Studies.* Leiden, 1983.

Versnel, H. S. "Two Types of Roman Devotio." *Mnemosyne* 29 (1976), 365–410.

Versnel, H. S. "Self-Sacrifice, Compensation and the Anonymous Gods." In *Le sacrifice dans l'antiquité.* Ed. O. Reverdin and B. Grange, 135–194. Genève, 1981.

Wakefield, L. W., and Evans, A. P. *Heresies of the High Middle Ages.* New York, 1991.

Wachtel, D. "The Ritual and Liturgical Commemoration of Two Medieval Persecutions." Master's thesis. Columbia University, 1995.

Weiner, E., and Weiner, A. *The Martyr's Conviction: A Sociological Analysis.* Atlanta, 1990.

Weinstein, D., and Bell, R. M. *Saints and Society: The Two Worlds of Western Christendom, 1000–1700.* Chicago and London, 1982.

Weiss, D. H. "Biblical History and Medieval Historiography: Rationalizing Strategies in Crusader Art." *Modern Language Notes* 108 (1993), 710–737.

Wesselius, J. W. "Language and Style in Biblical Aramaic: Observations on the Unity of Daniel II-VI." *Vetus Testamentum* 38 (1988), 194–208.

Whittow, M. *The Making of Byzantium, 600–1025.* Los Angeles, 1996.

Wiesel, E. *The Oath.* New York, 1973.

Williams, D. S. *The Structure of 1 Maccabees.* Washington, 1999.

Williams, G. *The Sanctity of Life and the Criminal Law.* New York, 1974.

Williams, J. *The Will to Believe. "Is Life Worth Living?"* New York, 1927.

Wills, L. M. *The Jew in the Court of the Foreign King: Ancient Jewish Court Legends* (Harvard Dissertations in Religion 26; Minneapolis, 1990).

Wilson, E. *On Human Nature.* Cambridge and London, 1975.

Wilson, K. M. *The Dramas of Hrotsvit of Gandersheim.* Saskatoon, 1985.

Wilson, S., Ed. *Saints and Their Cults: Studies in Religious Sociology, Folklore and History.* Cambridge, 1983.

Wolf, K. B. *Christian Martyrs in Muslim Spain.* Cambridge, 1988.

Wolfson, R. E. "The Theosophy of Shabbetai Donnolo, with Special Emphasis on the Doctrine of *Sefirot* in His *Sefer Hakhmoni. Jewish History* 6:1–2 (1992), 281–316.

Wolfson, R. E. *Through a Speculum That Shines: Vision and Imagination in Medieval Jewish Mysticism.* Princeton, 1994.

Wolfson, R. E. "Judaism and Incarnation: The Imaginal Body of God." In *Christianity in Jewish Terms.* Ed. T. Frymer-Kensky et al., 239–254. Colorado and Oxford, 2000.

Wolfson, R. E. "Martyrdom, Eroticism, and Asceticism in Twelfth-Century Ashkenazi Piety." In *Jews and Christians in Twelfth-Century Europe.* Ed. M. A. Signer and J. Van Engen, 171–220. Indiana, 2001.

Yadin, Y. *Masada.* Tel Aviv, 1966.

Yassif, E. "Folktales in Megillat Ahimaatz" (Hebrew). *Mekharim Yerushalayyim be-sifruth ivrit* 4 (1984), 18–42.

Yassif, E. "The Hebrew Narrative Anthology in the Middle Ages." *Prooftexts* 17 (1997), 153–175.

Yerushalmi, Y. H. *Zakhor: Jewish History and Jewish Memory.* Seattle and London, 1982.

Young, R. D. "The 'Woman with the Soul of Abraham': Traditions about the Mother of the Maccabean Martyrs." In *'Women Like This': New Perspectives on Jewish Women in the Greco-Roman World.* Ed. A.-J. Levine, 67–81. Atlanta, 1991.

Yuval, I. J. "Vengeance and Damnation, Blood and Defamation: From Jewish Martyrdom to Blood Libel Accusations" (Hebrew). *Zion* 58 (1993), 33–90.

Yuval, I. J. "The Language and Symbols of the Hebrew Chronicles of the Crusades" (Hebrew). In *Facing the Cross: The Persecutions of 1096 in History and Historiography.* Ed. Y. T. Assis et al., 101–117. Jerusalem, 2000.

Yuval, I. J. *"Two Nations in Your Womb": Perceptions of Jews and Christians* (Hebrew). Tel Aviv, 2000.

Yuval, I. J. "'They Tell Lies: You Ate the Man': Jewish Reaction to Ritual Murder Accusations." In *Religious Violence between Christians and Jews: Medieval Roots, Modern Perspectives.* Ed. A. S. Abulafia, 86–106. New York, 2002.

Zambelli, M. "La composizione del secondo libro di Maccabei e la nuova cronologia di Antioco IV Epifane," *Miscellanea greca e romana* (Studi pubblicati dall'Istituto italiano per la storia antica 16, Rome, 1965), 195–299.

Zeitlin, S. *Josephus on Jesus: With Particular Reference to the Slavonic Josephus and the Hebrew Josippon.* Philadelphia, 1931.

Zeitlin, S. *The Book of Jubilees, Its Character and Its Significance.* Philadelphia, 1939.

Zeitlin, S. "The Legend of the Ten Martyrs and Its Apocalyptic Origins." *Jewish Quarterly Review* 36 (1945–1946), 1–16.

Zeitlin, S. "The Names Hebrew, Jew and Israel: A Historical Study," *Jewish Quarterly Review* 43 (1952–1953), 369–379.

Zeitlin, S. "Masada and the Sicarii: The Occupants of Masada." *Jewish Quarterly Review* 55 (1965), 314–317.

Zetnick, K. *The Clock Overhead* (Hebrew). Jerusalem, 1960.

Ziegler, P. *The Black Death.* New York, 1969.

Ziesler, A. J. "Luke and the Pharisees." In J. Nusner, *From Politics to Piety: The Emergence of Pharisaic Judaism*, 161–172. New York, 1979.

Zimmer, E. "The Persecutions of 1096 as Reflected in Medieval and Modern Minhag Books." In *Facing the Cross: The Persecutions of 1096 in History and Historiography*. Ed. Y. T. Assis et al., 157–170. Jerusalem, 2000.

Zimmerman, F. "The Aramaic Origin of Daniel 8–12." *Journal of Biblical Literature 57* (1938), 255–272.

Ziolkowski, J. M. "Put in No-Man's-Land: Guibert of Nogent's Accusations against a Judaizing and Jew-Supporting Christian." In *Jews and Christians in Twelfth-Century Europe*. Ed. M. A. Signer and J. Van Engen, 110–122. Indiana, 2001.

Zuckerman, A. J. "The Nasi of Frankland in the Ninth Century and Colaphus Judaeorum in Toulouse." *Proceedings of the American Academy for Jewish Research 33* (1965), 51–82.

Index